Publications of the
CENTRE FOR REFORMATION AND RENAISSANCE STUDIES

Essays and Studies, 3

Series Editor   Konrad Eisenbichler

Victoria University
in the
University of Toronto

A Renaissance of Conflicts

Visions and Revisions of
Law and Society in Italy and Spain

Edited by John A. Marino & Thomas Kuehn

Toronto
Centre for Reformation and Renaissance Studies
2004

CRRS Publications
Centre for Reformation and Renaissance Studies
Victoria University in the University of Toronto
Toronto, Ontario M5S 1K7
Canada

© 2004 by the Centre for Reformation and Renaissance Studies
All rights reserved
Printed in Canada

National Library of Canada Cataloguing in Publication

A Renaissance of conflicts : visions and revisions of law and society in Italy and Spain / edited by John A. Marino and Thomas Kuehn.

(Essays and studies ; 3)
Includes bibliographical references and index.
ISBN 0-7727-2022-3

1. Justice, Administration of—Italy—History. 2. Justice, Administration of—Spain—History—16th century. I. Marino, John A. II. Kuehn, Thomas, 1950– III. Victoria University (Toronto, Ont.). Centre for Reformation and Renaissance Studies IV. Series: Essays and studies (Victoria University (Toronto, Ont.). Centre for Reformation and Renaissance Studies) ; 3.

KJC630.R46 2004   340'.115'0945   C2004-900953-2

No part of this book may be translated or reproduced in any form, by print, photoprint, microfilm, or any other means, without written permission from the publisher.

Cover design: Paragraphics

Typesetting and printing: Becker Associates

Contents

Illustrations	vii
List of Contributors	ix
Acknowledgments	xi
Foreword: Eric Cochrane and Julius Kirshner at the University of Chicago *Anthony Grafton*	1
Introduction *John A. Marino and Thomas Kuehn*	17

Part I: Law, Commentary, and Consulting

1. River of Law: Bartolus's *Tiberiadis* (*De alluvione*) *Osvaldo Cavallar* — 31

    Appendix 1: Bartolus, *Tiberiadis (De alluvione)*, edited by Osvaldo Cavallar — 83

    Appendix 2: Bartolus, *Tiberiadis (De alluvione)*, figures — 117

2. Public Responsibility for Failure to Prosecute Crime? An Inquiry into an Umbrian Case by Bartolo da Sassoferrato *Susanne Lepsius* — 131

    Appendix: Bartolus, *Isti nostri Nucerini*, edited by Susanne Lepsius — 161

Part II: Usury

3. Usury, Conscience, and Public Debt: Angelo Corbinelli's Testament of 1419 *Lawrin Armstrong* — 173

    Appendix 1: Angelo Corbinelli, Testament, edited by Lawrin Armstrong — 215

    Appendix 2: Extracts from Florentine Testaments, edited by Lawrin Armstrong — 238

4. Law, Religion, and Economics: Jewish Moneylenders in Christian Cortona
   Daniel Bornstein   241

Part III: Citizenship and Inheritance

5. Piero Amadi Imitates His Betters: 'Original Citizenship' in Venice
   James Grubb   259

6. Literature Meets Law: A Consilium of Antonio Strozzi for Lodovico Ariosto
   Thomas Kuehn   279

Part IV: Religion and Society

7. How to Harass an Inquisitor-General: The Polyphonic Law of Friar Francisco Ortíz
   Lu Ann Homza   299

8. A Bridge Between Renaissance and Counter-Reformation: Some Sources of Theatine Spirituality
   William V. Hudon   337

Part V: Politics, History, and Prophecy

9. An Anti-Campanellan Vision on the Spanish Monarchy and the Crisis of 1595
   John A. Marino   367

10. The Morandi Affair and Seventeenth-Century Rome
    Brendan Dooley   395

Epilogue: Contexts
   Lauro Martines   421

Index   433

Illustrations

Cover Illustration: 'Sileat figura iudicii loquatur iustitia,' in *Statuta Hospitalis Hierusalem*. Rome: n.p., 1586. (Newberry Library, Chicago, Illinois)

Plate 1: Eric Cochrane circa 1984. (Courtesy of Lydia Cochrane)

Plate 2: Julius Kirshner at Villa I Tatti, 1996. (Courtesy of Jessica Kirshner)

Plate 3: Biblioteca Apostolica Vaticana (BAV), Barb. lat. 1398, fol. 165v with Figures 9 and 10. (© BAV).

Plate 4: 'Porta citatione,' p. 68 in Annibale Carracci. *Diverse Figure*. Rome: Lodouico Grignani, 1646. (University of Chicago Library, Special Collections Research Center)

Plate 5: 'Administrent non contrahant fratres,' in *Statuta Hospitalis Hierusalem*. Rome: n.p., 1586. (Newberry Library, Chicago, Illinois)

Plate 6: 'Vende quadri,' p. 19 in Annibale Carracci. *Diverse Figure*. Rome: Lodouico Grignani, 1646. (University of Chicago Library, Special Collections Research Center)

Plate 7: 'Tanquam omnia possidentes, et nihil habentes,' in *Statuta Hospitalis Hierusalem*. Rome: n.p., 1586. (Newberry Library, Chicago, Illinois)

Figures 1–22. Biblioteca Apostolica Vaticana (BAV), Barb. lat. 1398, fol. 162v–170r. (© BAV).

List of Contributors

Lawrin Armstrong (Centre for Medieval Studies, University of Toronto) is the author of *Usury and Public Debt in Early Renaissance Florence: Lorenzo Ridolfi on the 'Monte commune'* (2002).

Daniel Bornstein (Texas A&M University) is the author of *The Bianchi of 1399: Popular Devotion and Orthodoxy in Late Medieval Italy* (1985), a co-editor of *Women and Religion in Medieval and Renaissance Italy* (1996), and the editor and translator of *Dino Compagni's Chronicle of Florence* (1986) and *Life and Death in a Venetian Convent: The Chronicle and Necrology of Corpus Domini, 1395–1436* (2000).

Osvaldo Cavallar (Nanzan University) is the author of *Francesco Guicciardini, giurista: i ricordi degli onorari* (1991) and a co-editor of *A Grammar of Signs: Bartolo da Sassoferrato's Tract On Insignia and Coats of Arms* (1994).

Brendan Dooley (International University, Bremen) has published *Science, Politics, and Society in Eighteenth-Century Italy: The Giornale de' Letterati d'Italia and Its World* (1991), *The Social History of Skepticism: Experience and Doubt in Early Modern Culture* (1999), *Science and the Marketplace in Early Modern Italy* (2001), *Morandi's Last Prophecy and the End of Renaissance Politics* (2002), and has edited and translated, *Italy and the Baroque: Selected Readings* (1995). He has taught at Harvard University and worked on the Medici papers in Florence.

Anthony Grafton (Princeton University) is the author of *Joseph Scaliger: A Study in the History of Classical Scholarship*, 2 vols. (1983–1993), and has published *Forgers and Critics: Creativity and Duplicity in Western Scholarship* (1990); *Defenders of the Text: The Traditions of Scholarship in an Age of Science, 1450– 1800* (1991); *Commerce with the Classics: Ancient Books and Renaissance Readers* (1997); *The Footnote: A Curious History* (1997); *Cardano's Cosmos: The Worlds and Works of a Renaissance Astrologer* (1999); *Leon Battista Alberti: Master Builder of the Italian Renaissance* (2000); *Bring Out Your Dead: The Past as Revelation* (2001).

James Grubb (University of Maryland, Baltimore County) is the author of *Firstborn of Venice: Vicenza in the Early Renaissance State* (1988) and *Provincial Families of the Renaissance: Private and Public Life in the Veneto* (1996).

Lu Ann Homza (College of William and Mary) has written *Religious Authority in the Spanish Renaissance* (2000).

William V. Hudon (Bloomsburg University) has edited *Theatine Spirituality: Selected Writings* (1996), and contributed to the rethinking of Catholic Reform in 'Religion and Society in Early Modern Italy: Old Questions, New Insights,' *American Historical Review* 101 (1996): 783–804.

Thomas Kuehn (Clemson University) is the author of *Emancipation in Late Medieval Florence* (1982), *Law, Family & Women: Toward a Legal Anthropology of Renaissance Italy* (1991), *Illegitimacy in Renaissance Florence* (2002), and a co-editor of *Time, Space, and Women's Lives in Early Modern Europe* (2001).

Susanne Lepsius (University of Frankfurt) is a co-editor of *A Grammar of Signs : Bartolo da Sassoferrato's Tract On Insignia and Coats of Arms* (1994) and is publishing a two-volume study of Bartolo da Sassoferrato's treatise on witnesses and proof: *Der Richter und die Zeugen* (2002) and *Von Zweifeln zur Überzeug* (2003).

John A. Marino (University of California, San Diego) is the author of *Pastoral Economics in the Kingdom of Naples* (1988), has edited *Early Modern Italy, 1550–1796* (2002) and *Early Modern History and the Social Sciences: Testing the Limits of Braudel's Mediterranean* (2002), and has co-edited and co-translated, *Good Government in Spanish Naples* (1990).

Lauro Martines (University of California, Los Angeles-emeritus) lives and works in London. He published two path-breaking books early in his career that remain classics: *The Social World of the Florentine Humanists, 1390–1460* (1963) and *Lawyers and Statecraft in Renaissance Florence* (1968). His most recent books include *Strong Words: Writing and Social Strain in the Italian Renaissance* (2001) and *April Blood: Florence and the Plot against the Medici* (2003).

Acknowledgments

The authors of the essays are former students of Eric Cochrane and Julius Kirshner. We all remember and are indebted to them for their characteristic comments, challenging conversations, and incisive criticism. Eric and Jules shared an infectious engagement and energy, and they practiced in their publications the same kind of critical judgment and love for debate and disputation that they preached in the classroom. We are very pleased that one of their fellow Florentine historians, Lauro Martines, has joined us to write an epilogue remembering the kind of historiographical tradition that Eric and Jules instilled in us during their Chicago collaboration between 1970 and 1985. Their lessons live with us, and we try to repay our debt to them everyday with our students and in our own research and writing.

We miss those animated intellectual exchanges with Eric and regret that we could not have shared with him our growth into maturity. Jules has continued to provide inspiration through his path-breaking work in legal history and to offer constant and unwavering support in carrying on their joint legacy. Lydia Cochrane, who has entered our guild as the premier translator of French and Italian historical works, has adopted all of us, continues to welcome us as part of her family, and assists us whenever we visit Chicago.

We would like to thank another member of our Chicago cohort, Paul Gehl, Custodian of the John M. Wing Foundation on the History of Printing, The Newberry Library, for assistance with illustrations, and the Newberry Library for publication permission. Lydia Cochrane helped find illustrations at Regenstein Library, and our thanks to Alice Schreyer, Director Special Collections Research Center, University of Chicago Library, for publication permission. The Biblioteca Apostolica Vaticana and its Prefetto, Monsignor Farina, graciously granted permission for publication of the Bartolus images. Thanks to Lydia Cochrane for providing the photograph of Eric Cochrane and to Jessica Kirshner for that of Julius Kirshner.

Special thanks to Konrad Eisenbichler and Nicholas Terpstra, Centre for Reformation and Renaissance Studies, Victoria University in the University of Toronto, for their assistance and encouragement in seeing the manuscript through the press. Publication subvention funds have been provided by Richard Attiyeh (Vice Chancellor of Research and

Dean of Graduate Studies, University of California San Diego) and Patrick Schloss (Provost and Vice President for Academic Affairs, Bloomsburg University).

Thanks to Amy Matthews for her assistance in proofreading and preparing the index.

Foreword

Eric Cochrane and Julius Kirshner at the University of Chicago

Anthony Grafton

In 1973 an article by Julius Kirshner appeared in *Speculum*.[1] Graduate and undergraduate students passed the word, and one after another we trooped into the section of the third floor in the Regenstein Library that housed the new numbers of history periodicals. The trip proved worthwhile. Kirshner's article was stunning, in many ways, from the force and eloquence of its style to the depth and density of its footnotes. Its last few pages offered a new text, based on a terrifying range of published and unpublished sources, of a consilium or legal opinion on citizenship by the fourteenth-century jurist Bartolus of Sassoferrato. This seemed a piece of the deepest imaginable scholarship. Yet what really took the reader's breath away was less the young author's obvious erudition than the self-assurance with which he made clear that he regarded his editorial handiwork as provisional, since so little was yet known about Bartolus's writings and the manuscripts that contained them.

The article was more than a philological tour de force. Kirshner showed, with great clarity and elegance, how Bartolus had developed a concept of citizenship that could preserve the rights of both old and new inhabitants of an Italian city. An erudite and pragmatic lawyer, Bartolus had drawn as he worked on both hints in the corpus of Roman law and his own experience of political life. And Kirshner not only teased out the ways in which legal principles and the textures of daily experience intersected in this one short text, but used the tightly focused case study to argue a broad methodological thesis. Students of later medieval law could not just descend into the labyrinths of medieval legal commentary and hope to find their way out again with their prey intact. In order to

---

[1] Kirshner, '*Civitas sibi faciat civem*,' pp. 694–713; for the later development of Kirshner's research in this field see his '*Consilia* as Authority in Late Medieval Italy,' pp. 107–140, and for a similar argument in a rather different area of law, see his 'Wives' Claims,' pp. 256–303.

interpret the development of legal reasoning and statute law historically, they must also follow the lawyers back into communal and notarial archives, and through them into the crowded, noisy streets and squares of Renaissance cities. Only by doing so could they identify the social, political and economic conditions that had confronted the lawyers—and thus situate technical legal theories, as Kirshner did, in local historical circumstances.

Most strikingly of all, though implicitly, Kirshner challenged a very fashionable distinction. In the late 1960s many scholars, often following Erwin Panofsky's lead, argued that Renaissance humanists, whose keen historical sense detected the distance between ancient laws and modern social realities, had little or no common ground with medieval jurists and theologians, who had no sense of anachronism and accordingly believed that they could apply classical texts to modern circumstances without worrying about such novelties as Christianity. Bartolus, in Kirshner's account, understood quite clearly that Roman law offered no clear basis for his concept of *civilitas contracta*. Yet he preferred it to the alternatives and based his consilium not on authority but on reason. Evidently one could have a sharp historical sense without being or wanting to become a humanist. Kirshner was a young scholar, who had arrived at Chicago three years before, after studying at Columbia and in Rome and a brief stint teaching at Bard College. His article, accordingly, made a powerful impression—especially on the community of history students at Chicago, obsessed as we were with the semiotics of scholarly publication. From its prominent location to its massive scholarly apparatus, Kirshner's article bore all the signs of novelty and erudition. These identified the author as someone to watch, and students crowded into his courses, from Western Civ sections to graduate seminars, to do exactly that.

This little story is typical, in many ways, of historical studies at Chicago. Then, as now, undergraduates and graduate students took the same courses; worked in the same libraries; and took pride in their ability to parachute into scholarly controversies, working through dense and demanding journal articles and primary sources. Then, as now, undergraduate and graduate students took a deep interest in their professors—not so much in their appearance and personal lives, which normally, and rightly, provoke only derision, as in their scholarship and teaching, which we followed with a rapt attention reminiscent of the interest provoked by Nasdaq in the later 1990s. Then as now, finally, gifted new members of the department of history found themselves not so much surrounded as besieged soon after their arrival by throngs of young and critical students who already regarded themselves as colleagues and who wanted nothing more than to add new tools to those in their toolboxes or to sharpen the ones they already possessed. Publish an exciting article and you ran the risk—as became clear in the event—of disappearing in a cloud of disciples.

Kirshner's impressive debut in Italian history—for such it seemed to those who had not read his earlier technical publications in Italian and English—was accompanied, in the same year, by a second and even more striking Italianist venture of a very different kind, also the work of a Chicago professor: Eric Cochrane's *Florence in the Forgotten Centuries*.[2] Kirshner, a new assistant professor, belonged to a menaced breed that would become even rarer as the financial crisis of the seventies took hold. Cochrane, a full professor who had taught at Chicago since 1957, belonged to the university's ruling class. But he did not live by the norms of a group of professors once memorably described, in a visiting committee's report, as Barsetshire canons. He had long since established himself as an iconoclastic, energetic teacher (until he reached his fifties, he challenged all comers to play handball with him, offering an A to anyone who won). He had also won wider recognition as the leading American expert on eighteenth-century Italy—a field which he had studied not only at Yale, where he did his PhD, but also at Florence, where he had worked with the great Italian scholar Delio Cantimori.[3] Remarkably, Cochrane had turned himself into a major Renaissance scholar as well, since the local authorities at Chicago assumed that anyone who worked on pre-modern Italy could also teach and write about the more glorious earlier period, and invited him forcefully to do so.[4] More remarkable still, he had started to study the Counter-Reformation in and outside Italy—a field cultivated in the United States, in those distant days, by very few scholars except his life-long friends John Tedeschi and Natalie Zemon Davis, and members of the more erudite religious orders.[5] In 1970 he had brought out a learned and lively anthology of articles on *The Later Italian Renaissance, 1525–1630*. His own contributions to this still indispensable book, like his courses, made clear that he hoped to fill the historiographical abyss that opened, in English, with the fall of the late Florentine Republic in 1530, and did not really close again until Garibaldi marched on Rome.[6]

---

[2] Cochrane, *Florence in the Forgotten Centuries, 1527–1800*.

[3] Cochrane, *Tradition and Enlightenment in the Tuscan Academies, 1690–1800*; see also his 'The Settecento Medievalists,' pp. 35–61. On Cantimori see Cochrane and Tedeschi, 'Delio Cantimori, Historian,' pp. 438–445.

[4] See esp. Cochrane, 'Machiavelli, 1940–1960,' pp. 113–136, an important review article that Cochrane always described as a command performance.

[5] See for example Cochrane, 'New Light on Post-Tridentine Italy,' pp. 291–319.

[6] Cochrane, *The Later Italian Renaissance, 1525–1630*; see esp. Cochrane, 'The End of the Renaissance in Florence,' pp. 7–29, reprinted in *The Later Italian Renaissance, 1525–1630*, pp. 43–73, and Cochrane's 'Introduction,' ibid., pp. 7–20.

4   A Renaissance of Conflicts

Florence in the Forgotten Centuries, however, astonished even students who had taken Cochrane's innovative courses. Written with great brio and produced with unusual elegance, the book offered not a sober, social-science based history of institutions, families, and rulers, but a pyrotechnical series of essays on individuals. It started from Cosimo I de' Medici, the founder of the grand duchy and the creator of a particular and very influential urban culture (Cochrane always emphasized that the modern tourist's Florence was far more the work of Cosimo and his successors than of the fifteenth-century Cosimo and his brilliant grandson Lorenzo). But Cochrane devoted a number of his 'medallions,' as he called them, to intellectuals and artists—some of whom, like Scipione Ammirato, were not household names even in learned households. He paid as much attention to architecture and literary style as to economic and political change. And though he had laid a solid scholarly foundation for the work, grubbing for years in Italian archives and libraries—as his fifty-page bibliographical appendix clearly showed—he made clear that he intended his book not for his professional colleagues, but for the educated general reader. A pioneering essay in the cultural history of cities, as striking in presentation as in argument, the book elicited wrinkled foreheads and cries of warning from some of Cochrane's professional colleagues. But it also identified him as an individual in a profession of conformists, someone whose work followed no trend, took no account of fashion, and marked out new paths that it would take a generation of younger scholars to level and pave. Chicago students, as well as readers around the country, took note.

The young medievalist, passionately committed to the most arcane practices of European *Rechtsgeschichte*, and the middle-aged early modernist, as passionately dedicated to the provocative historical essay, seemed an odd couple at the time. Yet they soon joined in a remarkable series of collaborative ventures—ventures in scholarship and, as the studies collected in this volume and the vast number of undergraduate and graduate papers and theses written for them attest, in teaching. Together, they did a great deal to transform the local world of historical practice. History at Chicago, in the 1960s, stood out chiefly for its cosmopolitanism. William McNeill had attracted a group of historians that practiced world history—as McNeill himself taught it—long before the term became fashionable. The Chicago history department boasted, in its publications, of its unique range and depth in fields outside American and European history. Master scholars traced the history of Chinese populations, reconstructed the economy and society of pre-modern Russia and Latin America, followed European soldiers and travelers to the Middle East, Africa, and Asia and then teased out the intellectual consequences of the stories and images they brought home. Its best-known member was McNeill himself, and its best-known recent product his best-selling, National Book Award-winning *The Rise of the West* (1963) and *Venice, the Hinge of Europe* (1963)—Eurocentric but thrillingly broad-gauged studies cast on a continental scale. American history, in the Chicago scale of things, took a rather modest back seat—though the coming of John Hope Franklin, Arthur Mann, Neil Harris, Stanley Katz, Barry Karl and many others gradually transformed the department into a major center of innovation in that field as well. Europe, by contrast, occupied a more central position. All undergraduates still had to take a year long, document-based course on western civilization, mostly taught by the department's junior faculty—and, in the nature of things, chiefly by its Europeanists. And advanced undergraduates and graduate students continued to flood into monographic courses and graduate seminars on European topics from antiquity to the twentieth century.

Many of the department's most charismatic young teachers, after all—Keith Baker, Emile Karafiol, Lester Little, William McGrath, Peter Novick, William Sewell, Peter Stearns, Noel Swerdlow—were Europeanists—even if they tended to concentrate on aspects of the western past that fell outside the traditional boundaries of Western Civ. Though senior, Cochrane—like Hanna Gray and Jock Weintraub—also continued to devote himself to undergraduate teaching. He offered as intensive, demanding and personal a version of Western Civ as any of his colleagues. So did Kirshner. Both made a natural fit for that sector of the department that still saw teaching as a vocation. The question was whether they could also show that what we now call 'old Europe' still mattered to American historiography—that Europeanists could produce the original forms of scholarship that Chicago really existed to foster. Kirshner's article and Cochrane's book proved that it did, and by doing so made clear that even the most radically innovative history department must leave space for the study of the heartland of European culture. Both would continue to show the central importance of their work to major fields of European history—in Cochrane's case, above all to historiography, to which he dedicated his magisterial *Historians and Historiography in the Italian Renaissance*, and in Kirshner's above all to the social, economic and legal history of fifteenth-century Florence, which he enriched with studies of the Monte delle Doti, a number of them undertaken in collaboration with Anthony Molho.[7]

Cochrane and Kirshner, moreover, understood and embodied other traits that made Chicago distinctive. Nothing made either of them happier than a good fight—especially one provoked by a student who thought

---

[7] Cochrane, *Historians and Historiography in the Italian Renaissance*; Kirshner, *Pursuing Honor While Avoiding Sin*; Kirshner, "'Ubi est ille?'" pp. 556–584; Kirshner and Molho, 'The Dowry Fund,' pp. 403–438.

that one of them had made a significant mistake or omission. In 1968, Cochrane happily turned one session of his summer Western Civ course over to an irate senior from the math department who had read Neugebauer's *The Exact Sciences in Antiquity* and felt bound to point out that a course that omitted the ancient Near East falsified the historical record. Both Cochrane and Kirshner throve through the years on dealing with Chicago's competitive, critical and cranky students. Both remained dedicated to teaching undergraduates, long after many of their senior colleagues had abandoned both the required Western Civ course and the larger enterprise of general education. Kirshner played a central role, and Cochrane an important one, in the transformation of the old anthologies known as Topics into the new series that the University of Chicago Press would publish, with no small splendor, in the 1980s.

Both, moreover, took the intellectual combativeness that made their classrooms live into the public sphere, as editors of and writers for the *Journal of Modern History*. This always solid and respectable periodical became, in the hands of Kirshner and Keith Baker along with John Boyer, and Cochrane as contributor and discussion partner, something more: the stage on which they could mount what Lucien Febvre called *combats pour l'histoire*. More than one attractive and apparently shipshape historical vessel was wrecked on the sharp critical reefs that they cultivated in the *Journal*. This special, agonistic quality of both men's worth fit the local context and built on it—even as it sometimes provoked horror outside Chicago from readers less used to the local culture of confrontation. No celebration of Cochrane's life and work could have been more appropriate than the one staged by the Newberry Library, entitled *Debates in Memory of Eric Cochrane*, at which his sharpest critics and the victims of his own sharpest critiques met and argued with his friends and admirers.

For all the elective affinity that bound Cochrane and Kirshner to the University of Chicago, both men also played some special roles there—roles less easy to accommodate to the local norms. Both of them, in the first place, regularly contradicted one of Chicago's founding myths. Every public figure at Chicago seemed, at least in the sixties and seventies, to repeat at every possible opportunity that the university was the finest of its kind in the world. Often, nauseatingly often, they quoted Robert Maynard Hutchins's remark that Chicago was not a good university, just the best one in existence. This rhetoric never reached more inflated heights than at those times of crisis, like the 1968–1969 sit-in, which made clear how serious the university's structural problems were, and how inhumanly it often dealt with its junior members. Cochrane did not, to my knowledge, directly criticize the traditional Chicago rhetoric. He felt a deep and permanent loyalty to the institution. Long after he achieved international eminence, he remained grateful to the university that had given him a position in the academic dog years of the 1950s, and refused all calls to go elsewhere for a higher salary and a lower teaching load. But he maintained a clear pose of skepticism towards claims on behalf of any institution, and he never accepted the university's self-adulation at face value. Cochrane's Yankee independence manifested itself on many occasions and in many ways. He was by far the most senior member of the faculty to plead, in public, for lenience towards the students expelled and suspended for participating in the sit-in. Then and later, moreover, Cochrane took a special pleasure in subverting Chicago occasions that seemed dedicated to self-praise. Nothing tickled his sense of humor more than reading aloud, at the ceremony where the University of Chicago Press declared *Florence in the Forgotten Centuries* the best book by a faculty member that the Press had published that year, all of the most negative reviews that the book had received. Cochrane showed that one could love a university—as he loved the city of Chicago—in full knowledge of its faults.

Kirshner, for his part, mercilessly lacerated the pretensions of what he saw, and came to love, as a naive domestic institution. He regularly portrayed Columbia, his graduate alma mater, as superior in every way. Butler Library's stacks groaned under more and more outré books than Regenstein's; Columbia's graduate programs were more rigorous and demanding than Chicago's; Columbia students worked harder, received less encouragement, and produced more original and lasting scholarship than their counterparts on the Midway. Above all, Columbia stood for a particular scholarly style: European archival scholarship, based on Herculean excavations among unknown sources, as practiced by Paul Oskar Kristeller, John Mundy, Eugene Rice and others. Kirshner's riffs on these themes exposed the fallacies of provincial self-adulation with an edged wit that educated its objects. No one could work with him—or Cochrane—for more than a month or two without seeing Chicago as it really was: a great university, with a number of distinctive traits, but not the one and only treasure-house that preserved the riches of western erudition from the depredations of a savage time.

Cochrane and Kirshner agreed, moreover, on another un-Chicagoan principle—one that shaped their approach to graduate teaching. Students who wanted to study Europe seriously, they insisted, must not only master all the documents connected with their subjects, but also learn the confoundingly alien language and mores of their chosen country's scholarly community. The European orientation that Cochrane and Kirshner practiced, and that they offered as a model to their students, had little to do with the ritual invocations of the *Annales* and *Past and Present* that resounded from classroom lecterns across North America. For both of them, in the first place, Europe meant Italy. And Italy, in their view, meant not only archives waiting to be plundered by North Americans, but also scholarly traditions going back hundreds of years, which anyone who hoped to shed light on the institutions of a commune or the writings of a historian must master. Italy meant great scholars—a few of them, like Delio Cantimori, Arnaldo Momigliano, Franco Venturi, Eugenio Garin, and Hans Baron already known in the English-speaking world, but many more of them unknown, even if, like Giorgio Spini, they had done as masterly work on Puritan America as on Counter-Reformation Italy. Italy meant disciplines little known in the United States— like the scholarship of the Italian civil and canon lawyers whose magnificently learned, massively unreadable books and articles bulked immense on Kirshner's bookshelves. Italy meant an apprenticeship that would take years—an apprenticeship that required extensive reading in a secondary literature that stretched back through the Risorgimento into the Baroque era, and before that into the Renaissance, as well as a year or two of work in the archives. And, in the end, Italy meant France and Germany, since no one could hope to master the history of Italy without working through the untranslated studies of such masters as Jean Delumeau and Peter Herde.

Both men loved living in Italy, and both were fluent speakers and writers of Italian. Cochrane achieved so powerful a sense of identity with his beloved Florence that the purity of his Tuscan accent and usage astonished visitors. But neither Cochrane nor Kirshner expected most of their students to attain a second identity as a European scholar and writer. In a profound way, in fact, neither of them believed or hoped that most American scholars could ever achieve this. Even after writing *Florence in the Forgotten Centuries*, Cochrane still defined his chief task as surveying and summarizing the work of the Italians in an accessible, cogent way for American students. Kirshner, for his part, plunged into the sort of document-based, gloss-laden scholarship that preoccupied Italian jurists. But he recognized that to work responsibly on this level, American historians would always have to be miniaturists, to confine themselves to the level of minute and technical detail. Both Cochrane and Kirshner had enjoyed unusual opportunities to spend time in Italy—opportunities that few of their students could hope to share. Both sent those students for whom funding was available to work in the settings—from Italy to England—where they could find sources and pursue their interests in some depth. But deep convictions about the limits of what any American scholar could hope to achieve in Europe guided their practice as teachers and set clear limits to the projects they felt they could responsibly encourage.

Cochrane and Kirshner rejected the notion of a second identity in another, larger sense as well. Seeing themselves as American scholars, working at a necessary distance from Italy, they also regarded each variety of Italian scholarship as one school among many—as a necessary, but not sufficient, source for those large-scale mosaic portraits of a European society that American professors of history must assemble for the students in their courses and the readers of their books. As Americans, both thought themselves obliged to elude the disciplinary frontier guards that preserved each local community and each technical discipline in Italy from corruption at the hands of outsiders. A tradition of intense specialization made it very difficult for Italian specialists in the Middle Ages to work across chronological boundaries into the Renaissance. Strong lines of ideological and scholarly barbed wire made it as good as impossible for Marxist historians from Florence to find anything of interest in the Counter-Reformation in the same city. And a rooted conviction, somehow connected with the Resistance to Fascism, that God—or truth—lies only in the archive and the document inspired a crippling guilt in any Italian who hoped to work on the history of more than one city, to say nothing of the Peninsula as a whole, or to make any sort of general point. Deeply though Cochrane and Kirshner admired the Italians who had created local traditions of deep and specialized erudition, they both insisted on their right to cross the boundaries of time, space, and political and disciplinary communities. Their willingness to do so enabled them to offer their students a kind of instruction that had, at the time, and probably has even now no parallels for range and breadth—a brand of history that discovered creative energies in both republics and principalities, in both institutional and cultural history, and in both the independent cities of the Italian middle ages and in the curia and new religious orders of the Counter-Reformation. The same intellectual range and freedom underpinned the extraordinary survey of Italian history in the century after the Sack of Rome that Kirshner edited and completed after Cochrane's premature death.[8]

The brand of history that Cochrane and Kirshner practiced was richly interdisciplinary. Both encouraged students to learn enough about the art and architecture, music and literature of pre-modern Europe to include them in their courses. But neither ever followed fashion. Around the globe, in the 1970s and 1980s, new methods and methodologies were blossoming like a hundred weeds. Votaries sprang up like mushrooms in new fields, like the history of the family, proclaiming that their work would roll back the heavens and make new revelations appear, so long as they received the research grants, graduate fellowships and library subscriptions that their innovative work required. Those who—like the present writer—proposed to work on traditional specialties like intellectual history were kindly informed by their contemporaries, over and over again, that such subjects had become obsolete in the brave new worlds of history from the bottom up, historical demography, and Foucauldian

---

[8]Cochrane, *Italy 1530–1630*.

épistémés (all of which were quite familiar to Chicago students by the late 1960s). Cochrane and Kirshner steadfastly insisted that every new method must meet the same tests of clarity, coherence, and truth to the original sources that the great practitioners of traditional historiography had fashioned in the nineteenth century.[9] Their seminars, and the *Journal of Modern History* in the period when Kirshner was a co-editor and Cochrane a close associate, became schools of criticism in an age when criticism was out of fashion.

In a university that treated graduate students as superior to undergraduates and scholarly research as more important than any form of teaching, Cochrane and Kirshner stood out for the passion with which they taught everyone from the sophomores in Western Civ to the graduate students trying to sneak their finished theses past the scrutiny of the university's rightly feared dissertation office. As teachers, moreover, they had a number of things in common. The first was their insistence on the absolute need to use primary sources—ideally in their original languages, but when necessary in translation. And not just to use them, but also to squeeze them, until they had yielded every drop of historical juice they contained. Both Cochrane and Kirshner knew how to interrogate a text until it gave up information of many different kinds. Many students will remember how Cochrane drew from one letter by Machiavelli a Chicago-school account of street-corner society in early sixteenth-century Florence, or how Kirshner insisted, long before microhistories made the point common knowledge, that a rich legal case somehow preserved in its documents the entire society that it had torn apart, just as the lava of Vesuvius preserved the society of Herculaneum and Pompeii. Their choices of texts to read with students were innovative and daring—at every level from Western Civ, for which they produced an original and wide-ranging volume of sources, to graduate work on Latin legal texts. Kirshner, in particular, enjoyed making the editing of complex texts into a rich form of collaboration with younger scholars.[10] In their hands, the teaching of European history became a voyage with no set destination, one that students could share and in the course of which they might study lands and beings that their teachers had failed even to glimpse.[11]

Their second principle was to tell the story that the documents revealed in sharp, plain and lively English. Cochrane and Kirshner began their careers in a scholarly world dominated by patriarchs. Some of these authority figures believed and taught that long, Latinate words and

---

[9] For an amusing case in point see Cochrane, 'The Profession of the Historian in the Italian Renaissance,' pp. 51–71.
[10] See for example Cavallar, Degenring and Kirshner, *A Grammar of Signs*.
[11] See further Martines's epilogue to this volume, 'Contexts,' pp. 421–431.

frequent use of the passive voice proved the seriousness of what they did. By the mid-1980s, the youthful revisionists who helped to begin the culture wars were wielding a new jargon of their own to challenge what they saw as a repressive establishment. Outside the academy, in the America of the New Left and the Italy of the Years of Lead, language itself degenerated in a mad carnival that rather resembled the revolution in Corcyra, as analyzed by Thucydides. Through it all, both remained faithful, first to last, to a shared ideal of clean, American prose, and both demanded that their students learn how to produce it.

The effort that both men put into criticizing and polishing their students' work seems even more astonishing in retrospect than it did at the time. Other Chicago professors who took teaching seriously normally decorated one's papers with marginalia in red, inscribed a careful paragraph of balanced praise and criticism on the last page, and recommended, to those who needed it, the purchase of a copy of Strunk and White. Cochrane, by contrast, often emulated the scholars of the period he studied, and produced irate and eloquent commentaries longer then his students' original texts. Receiving one of these was an event in its own right. Breathless and sweaty, one opened the thick envelope, fumbling with the firmly glued flap. A thick typescript, messier then now thanks to applications of Liquid Paper, emerged. Rows of numbers ran down the margins of the familiar sheets. Underneath them appeared a second, unfamiliar stack of onionskin pages, typed by Cochrane with such force that the keys had sometimes torn the paper. Doubtless all those who benefited from these commentaries have plenty of Cochranisms branded upon their memories (my favorite specimen, 'What's wrong? This is a good paragraph,' indicates the tenor of the other comments that he addressed to me). Kirshner, for his part, wielded a marker and traced a filigree of red or black across the text. But he showed just as little charity as Cochrane for obscurity, jargon and the other sins to which student historians who take themselves seriously are liable. It is not yet clear whether, as Lawrence Stone argued some years ago, a revival of historical narrative has taken place. But it is clear that no one did more than Cochrane and Kirshner to convince young historians, at a formative moment in their lives, that style mattered—mattered as much as any other tool in the historian's kit.

Cochrane and Kirshner could both seem harsh. They saw it as their duty to judge their colleagues—and their students—by the highest possible standards. When they set out to shape young scholars, they took as their model not the potter, who molds soft clay with gentle hands, but the sculptor, who uses sharp steel to cut marble. It could be painful to serve as the block of stone within which one of them thought he had discovered a historian, still unformed. In the Chicago context, however, both stood out for their humanity, and both brought into the grim graduate courses of the seventies and eighties something of the warmth, openness and humor that characterized good undergraduate teaching in the same period.

Their age is over now, and the string of students who benefitted from their teaching has been broken. Cochrane died, suddenly, on a train in his beloved Italy, depriving friends and students of a discussion partner so vigorous and alive that his sudden disappearance seemed impossible. A few years later, Kirshner's career at Chicago was brusquely interrupted by an unhappy episode. By the early 1990s, the tradition established almost twenty years before had come to an end. The teaching of early modern European history goes on at Chicago, and at a very high level. But it has taken new directions that must be described and evaluated in their turn by a new generation of students and scholars. Meantime, we can look back, with a measure of clarity and a measure of charity, and recognize something of what this unique and durable collaboration meant for historical scholarship and historical teaching at a great university.

Princeton University
Princeton, NJ

Works Cited

Cavallar, Osvaldo, Susanne Degenring, and Julius Kirshner, *A Grammar of Signs: Bartolo da Sassoferrato's Tract on Insignia and Coats of Arms*. Berkeley: Robbins Collection, 1994.

Cochrane, Eric W. 'The Settecento Medievalists.' *Journal of the History of Ideas* 19,1 (1958): 35–61.

Cochrane, Eric W. 'Machiavelli: 1940–1960.' *The Journal of Modern History* 33,2 (1961): 113–136.

Cochrane, Eric W. *Tradition and Enlightenment in the Tuscan Academies, 1690–1800*. Chicago: University of Chicago Press, 1961.

Cochrane, Eric W. 'The End of the Renaissance in Florence,' *Bibliothèque d'Humanisme et Renaissance* 27 (1965): 7–29, reprinted in *The Later Italian Renaissance, 1525–1630*, pp. 43–73.

Cochrane, Eric W. 'New Light on Post-Tridentine Italy: A Note on Recent Counter-Reformation Scholarship,' *Catholic Historical Review* 56 (1970): 291–319.

Cochrane, Eric W, ed. *The Late Italian Renaissance, 1525–1630*. New York: Harper & Row, 1970.

Cochrane, Eric W. *Florence in the Forgotten Centuries, 1527–1800: A History of Florence and the Florentines in the Age of the Grand Dukes*. Chicago: University of Chicago Press, 1973.

Cochrane, Eric W. *Historians and Historiography in the Italian Renaissance*. Chicago: University of Chicago Press, 1981.

Cochrane, Eric W. 'The Profession of the Historian in the Italian Renaissance,' *Journal of Social History* 15 (1981): 51–71.

Cochrane, Eric W. *Italy 1530–1630*, ed. Julius Kirshner. London and New York: Longman, 1988.

Cochrane, Eric and John Tedeschi. 'Delio Cantimori, Historian,' *Journal of Modern History*, 39 (1967): 438–445.

Kirshner, Julius. '*Civitas sibi faciat civem*: Bartolus of Sassoferrato's Doctrine on the Making of a Citizen,' *Speculum* 48 (1973): 694–713.

Kirshner, Julius. *Pursuing Honor While Avoiding Sin: The Monte delle Doti of Florence*. Quaderni di 'Studi senesi', 41. Milan: Giuffrè, 1978.

Kirshner, Julius. '"*Ubi est ille?*": Franco Sacchetti on the *Monte Comune* of Florence.' *Speculum* 59 (1984): 556–584.

Kirshner, Julius. 'Wives' Claims Against Insolvent Husbands in Late Medieval Italy' pp. 256–303 in *Women of the Medieval World: Essays in Honor of John H. Mundy*. ed. Julius Kirshner and Suzanne F. Wemple. Oxford and New York: Blackwell, 1985.

Kirshner, Julius. '*Consilia* as Authority in Late Medieval Italy: The Case of Florence.' pp. 107– 140 in *Legal Consulting in the Civil Law Tradition*, ed. M. Ascheri, I. Baumgärtner, and J. Kirshner. Berkeley: The Robbins Collection, 1999.

Kirshner, Julius and Anthony Molho. 'The Dowry Fund and the Marriage Market in Early Quattrocento Florence.' *Journal of Modern History* 50 (1978): 403–438.

Martines, Lauro. 'Epilogue: Contexts' pp. 421–431 in *A Renaissance of Conflicts: Visions and Revisions of Law and Society in Italy and Spain*, ed. John A. Marino and Thomas Kuehn. Toronto: Centre for Reformation and Renaissance Studies, 2004.

Plate 1: Eric Cochrane circa 1984 (Courtesy of Lydia Cochrane).

Plate 2: Julius Kirshner at Villa I Tatti, 1996 (Courtesy of Jessica Kirshner).

Introduction

John A. Marino and Thomas Kuehn

Machiavelli's classic formulation of the priorities for the establishment and maintenance of the state, 'good arms and good laws,' gives overriding importance to military affairs because it was written in the midst of the determinative crisis of Renaissance Italy during the long Italian Wars after the 1494 French Invasions. Still, not all conflicts were military, and to civic disputes Machiavelli assigned a role for an ethic of civic justice. In contrast to the expediencies of the art of war, which are always open to the uncertainties of the battlefield, the day-to-day exercise of the art of justice is institutionalized in legislation and courts and routinized in the practices of judges, lawyers, and litigants. The legal system in its daily dramas and hum-drum disputes of civil and criminal cases created the same kind of enduring and cohesive community consciousness that Machiavelli assigned to familial religion. The law—in its defense of elite prerogatives, the articulation of societal norms, and the defusing of personal vengeance—promoted solidarity by rationalizing conflict in legalistically controlled settings. The practice of daily life in Renaissance Italy was far from the humanistic paeans on human dignity, the tortured dilemma over *fortuna* and *virtù* (what's due to chance or one's own ability), or the recovery of ancient forms in art, literature, and thought. The Renaissance in the streets was filled with work and leisure, the sacred and profane, cooperation and competition, cohesion and contestation—all mediated by the control of property, the ambiguities of the exchange of goods and ideas, and the rule of law.

Families and individuals, church and state in the late medieval and early modern period relied upon the law to establish and maintain their power and authority. For fractious societies in the pre-modern Italian states and Spain, the law along with religion and language forged common bonds among citizens and institutions as it linked them to a shared, universal Roman tradition and helped create the modern state. In disputes over property, enforcement of order, assertion of rights and privileges, and confirmation of authority, legal processes put in play contending parties. The goal of this ritualized combat was to adjudicate disputes and to resolve the divergence between norms and practices without physical violence. In the process of controversy, litigants, at least temporarily, surrendered their individual claims to the arbitration of the law as they subordinated themselves to the collective judgment of the court. The moderating force of the law extended beyond the time and space of any one particular case to create continuities across parties and polities. Law institutionalized conflict as a social norm. Its conservative effect was both to maintain the status quo and to provide the avenue for gradual, orderly change within the context of tradition. Thus, the study of the law and legal cases reveals the long-term current of society, both its stability and continuity as well as its nodes of crisis and transformation. Law, of course, was not the only mode for the expression and transaction of conflict. Some conflicts were not suited for courts or appropriately displayed in legal terms or texts. And any single dispute might meander in and out of the precincts of law. The relationships of the ideals and norms in question could beg for a variety of treatments.

The essays in this collection all gravitate around conflicts in varying degrees. In most instances these were legal conflicts. The different essays, taken as a whole, display similarities of approaches across the spectrum of political and jurisdictional traditions from Umbria, Tuscany, Venice, Rome, and Naples to Italy's sixteenth-century rulers in Castile and point to a shared tradition of dispute and resolution. In both ecclesiastical/spiritual and state/secular matters, whether of private conscience or public policy, a characteristic mode of legal reasoning and legal rulings structured debates and decisions. Another theme here, explicit in some essays and implicit across the whole of them, is continuity (of ideals, of problems, of modes of resolution) running from the late Middle Ages to the Enlightenment. Sharp breaks in legal, political, or religious ideals and behavior were not as frequent and not as sharp as many historians have supposed. These continuities emerge, in turn, from a common methodological approach. The authors of these essays all engage in close, careful reading of key texts and their polyvalent terms. Whether those were the terms of civil or canon law, spirituality or astrology, each author has had to grapple with their multiple possibilities, contexts, custom, and practice, which reveal the shifts and continuities in their possible meanings.

The two essays in Part One present aspects of the law in an abstracted form, as jurisprudential science, though with a very practical bent. They concentrate on singular texts of Bartolus of Sassoferrato (1314–1357) which treat the subjects of water management and prosecution of crime and both raise issues of communal liability *and* power, as well as the role of law in elaborating them. Osvaldo Cavallar examines the problem of determining boundaries of real property given the meandering nature of rivers, and uses the metaphor of the river to demonstrate how legal questions flow from similar sources and are connected together. Using an autograph manuscript from the Vatican Library, Cavallar lays out the peculiar geometry Bartolus used in considering the problems of ownership and use of riverine deposits. The text itself and the fascinating drawings Bartolus added to illustrate his resolutions are reproduced in an appendix. Bartolus's entire corpus is summarized in the river metaphor and his place in the history of jurisprudence defined within the context of our contemporary interest in the history of ecology and the management of natural resources. In the second essay, Susanne Lepsius presents a consilium of Bartolus on a town's obligation to prosecute crime, and offers a significant contribution to debates over the origins of public criminal law and its relation to late medieval state formation. The case raises the question of the responsibility of a city or collective entity in pursuing criminals or harboring fugitives through inaction. Both essays explain how Bartolus's ideas reflect theory and practice and how law works at a fundamental level in articulating a society's conscious ideals and unconscious mental habits.

The two essays in Part Two examine the relationship between norms and practices of law on the more intimate level of private debts and credits with regard to the usury prohibition. Lawrin Armstrong's careful study of the 1419 testament of the Florentine wool merchant Angelo Corbinelli examines this will to understand the interests and concerns of the merchant near his hour of death. The problem of scruples of conscience about having attained some wealth illicitly, including through investments in Florence's funded public debt, reveals the importance of the usury prohibition on economic life. Among the causes fueling Corbinelli's hesitations, Armstrong finds, were disputations he had witnessed which held up to the light credit practices of the funded public debt. Armstrong asks if the opinions of lawyers and theologians about usury actually influenced creditors. Daniel Bornstein examines the case of Jewish moneylenders in Christian Cortona. Complaints that these Jews exceeded their license led in 1428 to intervention by the College of Doctors of Law of Florence as arbitrators. Cortona's dissatisfaction with that settlement led to a broader appeal for juristic support, and a number of Perugian, Bolognese, and other jurists offered consilia holding that the Jews could lend only at pawn, not against real property. Later in the century the deteriorating position of the Jewish moneylenders in Cortona followed a path similar to that followed elsewhere, when the opening of a *monte di pietà* would allow poor Christians to borrow small sums without the taint of usury. Whether in the acts of a single Florentine contemplating the fate of his soul for engaging in speculation on shares of the funded public debt or in the machinations of the civic fathers of Cortona to insulate citizens from the usury of Jewish moneylenders, we see the power of ecclesiastical and secular rules up against the contrary pull of political and economic needs.

Among the important types of texts used in evidence in these essays, particularly revealing about the linkage between law and life are the *consilia* ('opinions'). These dense Latin texts were the sites in which jurists grappled with anomalies thrown up by social practice and competing interests, and by local customs and laws, in comparison to the norms of learned civil and canon law. While litigants were concerned with immediate gains and losses, lawyers and judges remained aware of the law and the potential effects of practices to expose problems in the law or, in extreme cases, to render the learned law ineffective on a local level. As professionals, moreover, they operated within a heritage of pedagogy and argument.

In Part Three the two essays take off from case situations to expose anomalies of legal status—in one, the *cittadini originari* in Venice; in the other, the bastard sons of a prominent noble. James Grubb shows that, even in the special case of 'the most Serene Republic' of Venice, conflicts between norms and practices arose and needed resolution. Fifteenth- and sixteenth-century family memoirs provide evidence on how Venetian 'original citizens,' a class of state functionaries, developed a corporate identity and attempted to imitate the style of Venetian nobles. A notable example was Piero Amadi, who deserted his lower class wife with expressions of social superiority and distinction. Thomas Kuehn analyzes a *consilium* written by the Florentine lawyer Antonio Strozzi for the poet Lodovico Ariosto concerning an inheritance dispute with two illegitimate nephews. Kuehn uses this incident in two different ways. On the one hand, it shows how an attorney and 'client' interacted and communicated. On the other, it demonstrates that law gave definition to illegitimate status in terms of marital status at the time of conception, while social practice looked to habitation, education, and other circumstances and contingencies. Elite attitudes between fathers and sons, among brothers, and towards bastards broaden our understanding of the family, with its complementary and conflictual relations. The sorts of arguments advanced and the competing interests at stake are reminders that status was very much negotiable and contested, not settled, and subject to legal dispute and definition.

That same contestation could arise as well in regard to religion and spirituality, then and now. In Part Four Lu Ann Homza examines the Spanish inquisition's pursuit of a defiant cleric and the inquisitors' memory of that pursuit in a parallel case a few years later. The case concerns a Spanish Franciscan tried by the Inquisition for his enthusiastic support of a *beata*, a popularly acclaimed female 'living saint,' and shows how the accused attempted to turn the tables by becoming the accuser. Friar Francisco Ortiz's lengthy defense is grounded in technical legalities and sets out a multiplicity of unjust and illegal practices in an accusation against his prosecutor, the Inquisitor General. William Hudon's essay on

Theatine spirituality turns to one of the orders most important devotional writers, Lorenzo Scrupoli, and his connection with the ideas of the Franciscan nun Camilla Battista da Varano. Hudon argues against those who see a sharp break in 'Counter-Reformation' attitudes towards female spirituality and devotional practice in a revisionist reading of the continuing influence of late medieval piety. He contests prevailing notions of confessionalization in Reformation history with an analysis of the 'human' dimensions of Theatine spirituality, which has otherwise been taken as paradigmatic of repressive papal autocracy.

The concluding pair of essays in Part Five both deal with the political implications of bold religious positions—the role of apocalyptic prophecy and astrological ideas on late sixteenth- and seventeenth-century politics. John Marino examines the apocalyptic prophecies of a Spanish jurist, office-seeker, resident in Rome, who interpreted the Book of Daniel in terms of the 1595 threat from the French, Turks, and Protestants, as a gloss on the history of the Spanish monarchy, in order to argue that Tommaso Campanella and Giordano Bruno were only two of many who employed late Renaissance apocalyptic prophecy to interpret contemporary politics. The final article by Brendan Dooley employs the audacious astrological predictions of the death of Urban VIII by Orazio Morandi to explore their implications for papal treatment of Galileo. Because of Galileo's association with well-known astrologers such as Morandi, Dooley argues that Urban's sharp hostility to Galileo's *Dialogue* resulted from the pope's condemnation of astrology. All of the essays in Parts Four and Five thus explore the rationale behind institutional identities and practices.

This collection of essays vitally reflects the remarkable collaboration between Eric Cochrane (1928–1985) and Julius Kirshner, two leading scholars and teachers at the University of Chicago between 1970 and 1985, a collaboration cut short with Cochrane's sudden passing while on research leave in Italy. It fell to Kirshner both to continue their work with graduate students and to bring Cochrane's final works to print.[1] Both men, as scholars and teachers, handed to their students certain methodological and theoretical commitments, which continue to inform work in the field. All ten authors and Anthony Grafton, whose foreword remembers those

---

[1] Cochrane, *Italy 1530–1630*. Undergraduate teaching in the Western Civilization course at Chicago was another point of collaboration, with Cochrane contributing an important teaching essay in a separate pamphlet to the nine-volume collection of readings, Cochrane, *Western Civilization at the University of Chicago*. In addition to working with John Boyer as general editor, Kirshner co-edited vol. 4 with Karl Morrison (*Medieval Europe*); Cochrane and Kirshner co-edited vol. 5 (*The Renaissance*); and Cochrane, Charles Gray, and Mark Kishlansky co-edited vol. 6 (*Early Modern Europe*).

Chicago years and reflects upon the meaning and practice of historical scholarship and teaching at a great research university, were students of one or both of these scholars. Lauro Martines, their colleague and friend, examines the challenges and consequences of this emphasis on 'contexts' in his incisive thoughts on historiographical practices in his Epilogue.

Cochrane, a 'militant revisionist' (Kirshner's words), turned his considerable energies into a lifelong argument that the Renaissance in Italy in general and Florence in particular did not succumb to decadence after 1530.[2] Rather, Cochrane saw continuity and consolidation of the achievements and principles developed by humanists and artists in the fifteenth century, and he taught his students to see those continuities in all sorts of sources and situations through close reading and critical interpretation of evidence both known and neglected. He argued that only with a series of destabilizing events in the first third of the seventeenth century did a period of relative decline, or just complacence, commence. Yet Cochrane never submitted his self-conscious periodization as a new orthodoxy; it was meant to stir debate and critical assessment of historical work, with his crowning achievement, the magisterial *Historians and Historiography in the Italian Renaissance*.[3]

Kirshner's contribution to a revised sense of the Renaissance and early modern history has not been a matter of periodization but a more methodological insertion of the hermeneutics of civil and canon law into historical research. In investigating citizenship,[4] usury and public debt

---

[2]Cochrane, 'The Settecento Medievalists' and 'French Literature and the Italian Tradition' are related to his first book, Cochrane, *Tradition and Enlightenment in the Tuscan Academies*. His commitment to studying the 'end' of the Renaissance and rethinking the relationship between Renaissance and Enlightenment has made the phrase, 'Italy in the Forgotten Centuries,' a commonplace of modern Italian studies; see, Cochrane, 'The End of the Renaissance in Florence'; *The Late Italian Renaissance;* and *Florence in the Forgotten Centuries*. For his essays leading up to his Longman series survey, Cochrane, *Italy 1530–1630*, see, Cochrane, 'Science and Humanism in the Italian Renaissance,' 'The Transition from Renaissance to Baroque,' 'Disaster and Recovery: 1527–1750,' and 'The Renaissance academies in their Italian and European setting.'

[3]Cochrane, *Historians and Historiography in the Italian Renaissance* is a tour-de-force of bibliography, a genre Cochrane had practiced from early articles such as Cochrane, 'Machiavelli: 1940–1960' and 'New light on post-Tridentine Italy: A Note on Recent Counter-Reformation Scholarship' to his posthumous, 'Southern Italy in the Age of the Spanish Viceroys.'

[4]Kirshner, 'Paolo di Castro on *Cives ex Privilegio*,' 'Messer Francesco di Bici degli Albergotti,' '*Civitas sibi faciat civem*,' '"Ars Imitatur Naturam,"' 'A Consilium of Rosello dei Roselli,' 'Between Nature and Culture,' 'Citizen Cain of Florence,' and Kirshner and Mayali *Privileges and Rights of Citizenship*.

funds,[5] women and dowry,[6] he has employed an array of legal sources (commentaries and glosses, statutes, notarial texts) alongside other sources (council debates and deliberations, diaries and memoirs, and literary texts), which give expression to cultural meanings or to economic and social activity in order to recover conflicts of meaning and interest and ranges of potential for dealing with them. Privileged among these sources, and carefully examined with students as well, have been consilia.[7] Brought to bear on them have been not only painstaking familiarity with late medieval legal exegetical and dialectical methods but an informed, critical use of insights borrowed from anthropology, sociology, critical theory, and more. Here too the goal was to excite debate and further research.

The best historical work we as students learned from both of our teachers was that which provoked in others a desire to pursue research, engage in criticism, challenge received wisdom, and keep reading well after other books and articles had begun to gather dust. Cochrane summed up what he had learned (and taught!) 'after some eight or nine years...invested in studying the historians of the Italian Renaissance.'

> I must admit that I myself have benefitted—and that I hope others will also benefit—from the chief lesson they have taught me: that history can be both aesthetically pleasing and politically *engagée* without ceasing to be scientifically accurate. . . . It was they who first insisted that knowledge about the past had to be discovered, not merely transmitted, and that it could be organized into compartments that correspond both to historical reality and to the conceptual framework of the human mind. Above all, it was they who first proclaimed, at least in modern times, that the effort required to obtain that knowledge was both rewarding to others and satisfying to themselves.[8]

---

[5]Kirshner, 'From Usury to Public Finance.' Numerous articles have presented and developed Kirshner's original thesis: Kirshner, 'Papa Eugenio IV e il monte comune,' 'The Moral Theology of Public Finance,' 'Raymond de Roover on Scholastic Economic Thought,' 'Conscience and Public Finance,' 'The Moral Problem of Discounting Genoese *Paghe*,' 'Reading Bernardino's Sermon on the Public Debt,' 'Storm over the *Monte Comune*,' '"*Ubi est ille?*"' 'A Question of Trust,' and 'Encumbering Private Claims to Public Debt.'

[6]Kirshner, *Pursuing Honor While Avoiding Sin*; 'Wives' Claims against Insolvent Husbands'; '*Maritus Lucretur Dotem Uxoris*'; 'Materials for a Gilded Cage'; 'Donne maritate altrove'; Kirshner and Molho, 'The Dowry Fund and the Marriage Market'; Kirshner and Pluss, 'Two Fourteenth-Century Opinions'; Kirshner and Lo Prete, 'Peter John Olivi's Treatises'; and Kirshner and Klerman 'The Seven Percent Fund of Renaissance Florence.'

[7]Kirshner, 'Some Problems in the Interpretation of Legal Texts *re* the Italian City-States'; '*Consilia* as Authority in Late Medieval Italy'; 'Baldus de Ubaldis on Disinheritance'; and 'Custom, Customary Law and *Ius Commune* in Francesco Guicciardini.'

[8]Cochrane, *Historians and Historiography in the Italian Renaissance*, p. xix.

It is supremely appropriate that a volume dedicated to these two outstanding scholars, mentors, and friends begins with Bartolus and ends with Galileo. It is our hope and intention that these essays are of such quality to contribute to that tradition.

University of California, San Diego   *Clemson University*
La Jolla, CA   *Clemson, SC*

Works Cited

Cochrane, Eric W. 'The Settecento Medievalists.' *Journal of the History of Ideas* 19 (1958): 35–61.

Cochrane, Eric W. 'Machiavelli: 1940–1960.' *The Journal of Modern History* 33 (1961): 113–136.

Cochrane, Eric W. *Tradition and Enlightenment in the Tuscan Academies, 1690–1800*. Chicago: University of Chicago Press, 1961.

Cochrane, Eric W. 'French Literature and the Italian Tradition in Eighteenth-Century Tuscany.' *Journal of the History of Ideas* 23 (1962): 61–76.

Cochrane, Eric W. 'The End of the Renaissance in Florence.' *Bibliothèque d'Humanisme et Renaissance* 27 (1965): 7–29, reprinted in *The Later Italian Renaissance, 1525–1630*, pp. 43–73.

Cochrane, Eric W., ed. *The Late Italian Renaissance, 1525–1630*. New York: Harper & Row, 1970.

Cochrane, Eric W. *Florence in the Forgotten Centuries, 1527–1800: A History of Florence and the Florentines in the Age of the Grand Dukes*. Chicago: University of Chicago Press, 1973.

Cochrane, Eric W. 'Science and Humanism in the Italian Renaissance.' *American Historical Review* 81 (1976): 1039–1057.

Cochrane, Eric W. 'The Transition from Renaissance to Baroque: The Case of Italian Historiography.' *History and Theory* 19 (1980): 21–38.

Cochrane, Eric W. 'The Profession of the Historian in the Italian Renaissance.' *Journal of Social History* 15 (1981): 51–71.

Cochrane, Eric W. *Historians and Historiography in the Italian Renaissance*. Chicago: University of Chicago Press, 1981.

Cochrane, Eric W. 'Disaster and Recovery: 1527–1750' pp. 165–186 in *The Italians: History, Art, and the Genius of a People*, ed. John Julius Norwich. London and New York, 1983.

Cochrane, Eric W. 'The Renaissance Academies in their Italian and European Setting' pp. 21–39 in *The Fairest Flower: The Emergence of Linguistic National Consciousness in Renaissance Europe*. Florence: Presso l'Accademia della Crusca, 1985.

Cochrane, Eric W. "Southern Italy in the Age of the Spanish Viceroys: Some Recent Titles." *Journal of Modern History* 58 (1986): 194-217.

See also, Cochrane, 'The Profession of the Historian in the Italian Renaissance.'

Cochrane, Eric. *Western Civilization at the University of Chicago. An Introduction for Teachers*. University of Chicago Readings in Western Civilization. Gen. eds. John W. Boyer and Julius Kirshner. Chicago: University of Chicago Press, 1986.

Cochrane, Eric. *Italy 1530-1630*. Ed. Julius Kirshner. London and New York: Longman, 1988.

Cochrane, Eric, Charles M. Gray, and Mark A. Kishlansky, eds. *Early Modern Europe: Crisis of Authority*, vol. 6. University of Chicago Readings in Western Civilization. Gen. eds. John W. Boyer and Julius Kirshner. Chicago: University of Chicago Press, 1987.

Cochrane, Eric and Julius Kirshner, eds. *The Renaissance*, vol. 5. University of Chicago Readings in Western Civilization. Gen. eds. John W. Boyer and Julius Kirshner. Chicago: University of Chicago Press, 1986.

Kirshner, Julius. "Papa Eugenio IV e il monte comune: documenti su investimento e speculazione nel debito pubblico di Firenze." *Archivio Storico Italiano* 127 (1969): 339-82.

Kirshner, Julius. "From Usury to Public Finance: The Ecclesiastical Controversy over the Public Debts of Florence, Genoa and Venice (1300-1500)." PhD dissertation, Columbia University, 1970.

Kirshner, Julius. "The Moral Theology of Public Finance: A Study and Edition of Nicholas de Anglia's *Quaestio disputata* on the Public Debt of Venice." *Archivum Fratrum Praedicatorum* 40 (1970): 47-72.

Kirshner, Julius. "Paolo di Castro on *Cives ex Privilegio:* A Controversy over the Legal Qualifications for Public Office in Early Fifteenth-Century Florence" pp. 229-64 in *Renaissance Studies in Honor of Hans Baron*, ed. Anthony Molho and John A. Tedeschi. Dekalb, IL: Northern Illinois University Press, 1971.

Kirshner, Julius. "Messer Francesco di Bici degli Albergotti d'Arezzo, Citizen of Florence (1350–1376).' *Bulletin of Medieval Canon Law*, n.s. 2 (1972): 84–90.

Kirshner, Julius. '*Civitas sibi faciat civem*: Bartolus of Sassoferrato's Doctrine on the Making of a Citizen.' *Speculum* 48 (1973): 694–713.

Kirshner, Julius. '"Ars Imitatur Naturam": A Consilium of Baldus on Naturalization in Florence.' *Viator* 5 (1974): 289–331.

Kirshner, Julius. 'Raymond de Roover on Scholastic Economic Thought' pp. 15–36 in *Business, Banking and Economic Thought in Late Medieval and Early Modern Europe: Selected Studies of Raymond de Roover*, ed. Julius Kirshner. Chicago and London, University of Chicago Press, 1974.

Kirshner, Julius. 'Some Problems in the Interpretation of Legal Texts *re* the Italian City-States.' *Archiv für Begriffsgeschichte* 19 (1975): 16–27.

Kirshner, Julius. 'Conscience and Public Finance: A *Questio disputata* of John of Legnano on the Public Debt of Genoa' pp. 434–453 in *Philosophy and Humanism: Renaissance Essays in Honor of Paul Oskar Kristeller*, ed. Edward P. Mahoney. Leiden: Brill, 1976.

Kirshner, Julius. 'A Consilium of Rosello dei Roselli on the Meaning of "Florentinus," "de Florentia," and "de populo."' *Bulletin of Medieval Canon Law*, n.s. 6 (1976): 87–91.

Kirshner, Julius. 'The Moral Problem of Discounting Genoese *Paghe*, 1450–1550.' *Archivum Fratrum Praedicatorum* 47 (1977): 109–167.

Kirshner, Julius. *Pursuing Honor While Avoiding Sin : the Monte delle Doti of Florence*. Quaderni di 'Studi senesi', 41. Milan: Giuffrè, 1978.

Kirshner, Julius. 'Between Nature and Culture: An Opinion of Baldus of Perugia on Venetian Citizenship as Second Nature.' *Journal of Medieval and Renaissance Studies* 9 (1979): 179–208.

Kirshner, Julius. 'Reading Bernardino's Sermon on the Public Debt' pp. 547–622 in *Atti del simposio internazionale cateriniano-bernardiniano: Siena, 17–20 aprile 1980*, ed. Domenico Maffei and Paolo Nardi. Siena: Accademia Senese degli Intronati, 1982.

Kirshner, Julius. 'Storm over the *Monte Comune*: Genesis of the Moral Controversy over the Public Debt of Florence.' *Archivum Fratrum Praedicatorum* 53 (1983): 219–276.

Kirshner, Julius. '"*Ubi est ille?*": Franco Sacchetti on the *monte comune* of Florence.' *Speculum* 59 (1984): 556–584.

Kirshner, Julius. 'A Question of Trust: Suretyship in "Trecento" Florence' pp. 129–145 in *Renaissance Studies in Honor of Craig Hugh Smyth*. Florence: Giunti Barbera, 1985.

Kirshner, Julius. 'Wives' Claims against Insolvent Husbands in Late Medieval Italy' pp. 256–303 in *Women of the Medieval World: Essays in Honor of John H. Mundy*, ed. Julius Kirshner and Suzanne F. Wemple. Oxford and New York: Blackwell, 1985.

Kirshner, Julius. '*Maritus Lucretur Dotem Uxoris Sue Premortue* in Late Medieval Florence.' *Zeitschrift der Savigny-Stiftung für Rechtsgeschichte* 108 (1991): 111–155.

Kirshner, Julius. 'Materials for a Gilded Cage: Non-Dotal Assets in Florence, 1300–1500' pp. 184–207 in *The Family in Italy from Antiquity to the Present*, ed. David I. Kertzer and Richard P. Saller. New Haven and London: Yale University Press, 1991.

Kirshner, Julius. 'Encumbering Private Claims to Public Debt in Renaissance Florence' pp. 19–75 in *The Growth of the Bank as Institution and the Development of Money-Business Law*, ed. Vito Piergiovanni. Berlin: Duncker & Humblot, 1993.

Kirshner, Julius. 'Citizen Cain of Florence' pp. 175–189 in *La Toscane et les Toscans autour de la Renaissance: Cadres de vie, société, croyances, Mélanges offerts a Charles-M. de La Roncière*. Aix-en-Provence: Université de Provence, 1999.

Kirshner, Julius. '*Consilia* as Authority in Late Medieval Italy: The Case of Florence' pp. 107–140 in *Legal Consulting in the Civil Law Tradition*, ed. M. Ascheri, I. Baumgärtner, and J. Kirshner. Berkeley: The Robbins Collection, 1999.

Kirshner, Julius. 'Donne maritate altrove. Genere e cittadinanza in Italia' pp. 377–429 in *Tempi e spazi di vita femminile tra medioevo ed età moderna*, ed. S. Seidel Menchi, A. Jacobson Schutte, T. Kuehn. Bologna: Il Mulino, 1999.

Kirshner, Julius. 'Baldus de Ubaldis on Disinheritance: Contexts, Controversies, *Consilia*.' *Ius Commune: Zeitschrift für europäische Rectsgeschichte* 27 (2000): 119–214.

Kirshner, Julius. 'Custom, Customary Law and *Ius Commune* in Francesco Guicciardini' pp. 151–179 in *Bologna nell'età di Carlo V e Guicciardini*, ed. Emilio Pasquini and Paolo Prodi. Bologna: Il Mulino, 2002.

Kirshner, Julius and Jacob Klerman. 'The Seven Percent Fund of Renaissance Florence' pp. 367–398 in *Banchi pubblici, banchi privati e monti di pietà nell'Europa preindustriale*. Genoa: Società Ligure di Storia Patria, 1991.

Kirshner, Julius and Laurent Mayali, eds. *Privileges and Rights of Citizenship: Law and the Juridical Construction of Civil Society*. Berkeley: The Robbins Collection, 2002.

Kirshner, Julius and Kimberly Lo Prete. 'Peter John Olivi's Treatises on Contracts of Sale, Usury and Restitution: Minorite Economics or Minor Works?' *Quaderni fiorentini per la storia del pensiero giuridico moderno* 13 (1984): 233–286.

Kirshner, Julius and Anthony Molho. 'The Dowry Fund and the Marriage Market in Early Quattrocento Florence.' *Journal of Modern History* 50 (1978): 403–438.

Kirshner, Julius and Karl F. Morrison, eds. *Medieval Europe*, vol. 4. *University of Chicago Readings in Western Civilization*, Gen. eds. John W. Boyer and Julius Kirshner. Chicago: University of Chicago Press, 1986.

Kirshner, Julius and Jacques Pluss. 'Two Fourteenth-Century Opinions on Dowries, Paraphernalia and Non-dotal Goods.' *Bulletin of Medieval Canon Law*, n.s. 9 (1978): 65–77.

Part I

Law, Commentary, and Consulting

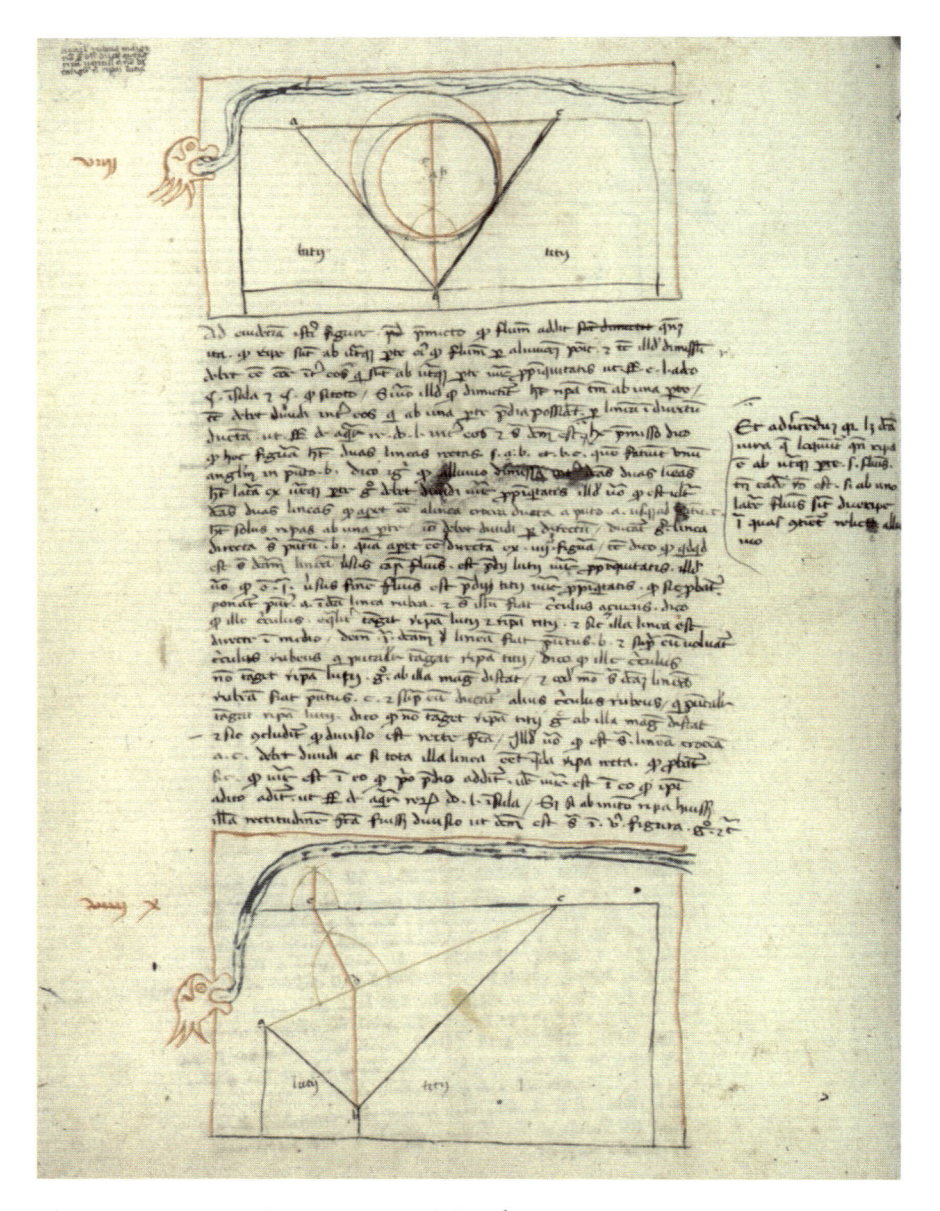

Plate 3: BAV, Barb. Lat. 1398, fol. 165v with Figures 9 and 10. (© BAV).

River of Law: Bartolus's *Tiberiadis* (*De alluvione*)*

Osvaldo Cavallar

In the late summer of 1355, shortly after returning to Perugia from an important embassy to Charles IV in Pisa, where the emperor had stopped on the way to Germany from his coronation in Rome, Bartolus de Saxoferrato composed his tract *Tiberiadis*— also known as *De fluminibus* (*On Rivers*).[1] Though known to historians of European continental law, this tract has been neither closely studied nor critically edited. Yet it treats a relevant and compelling topic: the legal status of rivers and the alterations to the landscape caused by rivers.[2] In this sense, it can be

---

*References to the first section of *Tiberiadis* (*De alluvione*), which appears in Appendix 1, are given by line number(s); the original figures drawn by Bartolus are reproduced in Appendix 2. For Bartolus's works I have used the Venetian edition of 1521 (repr. Rome, 1996); and, for the printed version of *Tiberiadis*, the Bolognese edition of 1576 (repr. Turin, 1964). The references to the *Corpus iuris civilis*, *Corpus iuris canonici*, and Accursius's *Glossa*, are given in abbreviated form. The abbreviation BAV stands for Biblioteca Apostolica Vaticana, and KBA for Koninklijke Bibliotheek Albert I of Bruxelles. This research was made possible by a grant (Pache I-A) from Nanzan University, Nagoya-Seto (Japan). A special thanks to the librarians of the Kojima-Toshokan, Hamajima Mayu and Sato Yuko, for the kindness with which they have responded to my bibliographical requests.

[1]On this embassy and its political and juridical implications, see Segoloni, 'Bartolo da Sassoferrato e la *civitas Perusina*,' 515–671. As a renowned university professor, Bartolus had obtained the privilege to legitimate any of his students who had not been born within a lawful marriage, as well as two honorific titles: that of 'imperial counselor' (*consiliarius*) and that of 'table companion' (*familiaris domesticus commensalis*). For the documents attesting the grant of the titles, see Lancellotto, *Vita Bartoli*, 30–35. He had also, allegedly, received a coat of arms depicting a rampant lion with two tails. The evidence for whether this coat of arms was actually granted has been examined by Cavallar, Degenring, and Kirshner, *A Grammar of Signs*, 8–26. With no supporting evidence, Mario Cignoni rejects the idea that such a grant did not occur in his edition and translation of *De insigniis et armis*. For a critique of his edition and Italian translation of *De insigniis et armis*, see Cavallar and Kirshner, 'Ne ultra scarpas,' 297–311.

[2]For the prominent role of rivers in the legislation on the environment of the early modern period, see Pratilli and Zangheri, *La legislazione medicea*.

regarded as the first tract devoted to legal geography or, broadly speaking, one of the first discussions of environmental issues produced by one of the major medieval jurists. In Bartolus's own intellectual production, it occupies a salient position for it is the cornerstone on which he built his three most famous political and legal tracts—*De Guelphis et Gebellinis* (*On Guelphs and Ghibellines*), *De regimine civitatis* (*On the Government of the City*), and *De tyranno* (*On Tyranny*). As jusgenerativity is concerned, for well over two centuries after its publication it constituted the point of departure for any jurist, geometrician, and land surveyor who addressed questions related to the division of an alluvial deposit, an island born in the middle of a river, and an abandoned riverbed. In the conservative realm of medieval jurisprudence, it presents a striking example of an interdisciplinary approach to phenomena caused by the mutating life of rivers by bringing geometry into the sacred precincts of legal discourse.

Though the strategy required by the introduction to the edition of a medieval text calls for a philological approach—such as, describing the manuscripts transmitting the text and their relationship, analyzing the variant readings, and the like—, I have decided to take a more free approach. And, at least at this stage, there is a reason to side the strict requirements of philology: the present edition is based on Bartolus's holograph. Thus, my approach will focus on some of the problems posed by this intriguing tract—such as, when and where it was written, its organization, and its relationship with the other tracts Bartolus wrote between his return from the embassy to the emperor and his death in 1357. Without pretending to be exhaustive, my main concerns are with the author's ideas, how they reflect theory and statutory practice, and how law articulates a society's conscious ideals and unconscious mental habits. In one instance, fiction—such as letting Lorenzo Valla take the stage and criticize Bartolus's Latin—enters into the text. The purpose of this unhistorical musing is simple: spare the readers from a lengthy analysis of Bartolus's language to show how close it was to the language spoken in the city market; in short, how an academically trained jurist appropriated the language and the daily problems of ordinary citizens. Last but not least, it is my little tribute to Eric Cochrane who in his workshops sanctioned the legitimacy of such a device, provided that the content conforms to the humanistic standards of truthfulness.

Having posted a few guideposts, we can now begin to follow the meandering course of Bartolus's *Tiberiadis*.[3] As Bartolus wrote in the

---

[3] For medieval legal texts, especially Accursius's Glossa, as a sort of hypertext, see Speciale, '*Apparatus*,' 47–59. The same can also be said of the commentaries

preface to *Tiberiadis*, when the short summer vacation came,[4] 'in order to relax' he left the city to stay at 'a certain villa overlooking the Tiber situated near Perugia.'[5] Although several locations have been proposed for this 'villa,' the place where Bartolus spent his vacation remains uncertain and, after all, its precise location is immaterial.[6] One should not think, moreover, that it was from that villa that he contemplated the river. The text uses the verb *accedo* (to go, come, or approach); thus, it was while going to that villa that Bartolus had the leisure to observe the river. The structure of the sentence—both the verbs *vacarem* and *accederem* are ruled by the same *cum*—indicates that it was not 'from' the villa but rather while 'going' to the villa that he observed the Tiber.

Whether he could view the river from the villa, as has been traditionally thought, or simply saw it along the way, it was the sight of the meandering

---

and tracts produced after the Glossa.

[4] For the calendar of medieval universities, see Bellomo, *Saggio sull'università*, 200–201; and Ermini, *Storia della Università*, 84–86. Typically, classes began on October 18 and lasted until the middle of August or early September.

[5] *Tiberiadis* lines 13–15. The term 'villa' should not be understood as corresponding to the modern Italian or English 'villa.' For the meaning of this term, see Bartolus *ad Const. Qui sint rebelles*, in *Opera*, vol. 9, fol. 100ra: 'nos autem dicimus villas, edificia sine muris vel fossis, que ville seu vici nullam habent iurisdictionem de iure communi sed subsunt alicui civitati.' For the absence of jurisdiction, Id. *ad legem Cum res* (D. 39.2.1), vol. 5, fol. 28r, no. 3: 'Est tertia universitas minima, ut castrum, villa et similia. Et ista si quidem subsunt alicui civitati vel alteri castro magno nullam iurisdictionem habent, sed civitas cui subsunt habet iurisdictionem in eis.' And Bartolus, *Opera*, vol. 9, fol. 139r: '[villa] secundum propriam significationem dicitur a vallo, hoc est civitas que [ed. non] cingitur muro, scilicet vallo, secundum Huguicium. Sed in uso nostro villa appellatur quedam vicinia plurium habitantium sine aliquo municipio, que, proprie loquendo, dicitur vicus.'

[6] Though a Perugian tradition places the 'villa' in Deruta, this identification is problematic, for Deruta is described as a *castello di poggio*, and therefore as a *castrum* (a fortified place), and from 1321 it had a *podestà*. For Deruta as a *castello di poggio*, see Grohmann, *Città e territorio*, 1:933–934, where the walls of the castle (1296) and the town (1428) are mentioned several times. For a concise institutional history of Deruta, with bibliography, see Nico Ottaviani, *Lo statuto di Deruta*, VII–L. As an alternative to Deruta, San Cipriano de Boneggio has been proposed, for it appears in Bartolus's will as the possession he bequeathed to his wife. This possession was explicitly mentioned for the simple reason that Bartolus bequeathed it to his wife, Pellina. This does not mean that it was the jurist's sole possession; the rest of his possessions, which were unspecified, were left to his sons, Francesco and Aloisio, *iure hereditatis*. For the *catasto* declaration of Francesco Alfani (Bartolus's nephew) and the list of his immovable properties, which might include goods already possessed or acquired by Bartolus, see Grohmann, *Città e territorio*, 1:246–252, and 412–416. It has also been suggested that the villa was located between Val Vitiano and Ponte San Giovanni. For this suggestion, see Walther, 'Wasser in Stadt und Contado,' 890, note no. 21.

34   A Renaissance of Conflicts

Tiber that may have prompted Bartolus to ponder some factual questions related to the nature of rivers, just as the embassy to Pisa may have prompted him to draft the first part of his tract *On Insignia and Coats of Arms*.[7] Some questions—for instance, how to divide alluvial deposits, an island born in the middle of a river, and an abandoned riverbed—were probably dictated by the sight of the river itself, others just concocted in his mind. From a previous period of sickness, he had learned a valuable lesson: the strength of the body could not be recovered unless one's mental disposition was cheerful. That state of mind could be attained only by returning to speculation and the pleasure this activity had always given him, for 'a sad mind dries up the bones.' For Bartolus, speculation was never a self-contained activity. Its ultimate purpose was to provide his students with something useful, something they would appreciate and that would be new to him and them.[8] But putting into writing the problems and the solutions he had intuited would have spoiled his vacation. The circumstances leading to the composition of *Tiberiadis* (discussed below) are narrated in the charming and oft-quoted preface to this tract.[9]

Tiberiadis comprises three sections: the first, known to historians of European law as *De alluvione* (*On Alluvial Deposits*), explains how to divide equitably the alluvial deposits a river made available; the second, *De insula* (*On Island*), how to divide an island born in the middle of a river among the landowners on both sides of the river; and the third, *De alveo* (*On Riverbed*), discusses issues related to an abandoned riverbed. According to its form, *Tiberiadis* may be considered a word-for-word commentary on a fragment of Roman law, *lex Adeo* (D. 41.1.7.1–6), corresponding to Inst. 2.1.20–24.[10] Although deeply rooted in the medieval

---

[7] It is perhaps nothing more than a coincidence, but two years after the completion of this tract a controversy on an island born in the middle of the Rhine occurred in Germany. For the details of the case, see Trusen, '*Insula in flumine nata*,' 294–338. If one cannot expect that at such an early time the canonists involved in this case would cite Bartolus's tract, nonetheless this legal battle hints that Bartolus's tract was not mere ruminations.

[8] Bartolus *ad prooem*. Cod., vers. *Omnes gaudentes*, vol. 9, fol. 2ra. Bartolus's biblical citation is taken from Proverbs 17:22. The label 'multum inherens practice' Baldus de Ubaldis attached to Bartolus—that is, a jurist who was 'deeply rooted in judicial practice' or 'had a keen eye to practical questions'—has often been mentioned. In contrast, Bartolus's interest in pedagogy has not yet received appropriate attention. On the meaning of *practica* and cognates, see Segoloni, '*Practica, practicus, practicare*,' 52–103.

[9] *Tiberiadis* lines 13–52.

[10] *De alluvione* corresponds to §§ 1–2 of *lex Adeo*, *De insula* to §§ 3–4, and *De alveo* to §§ 5–6. This fragment by Gaius establishes basic rules for solving issues on ownership caused by three typical phenomena occurring in rivers: alluvial

exegetical tradition of the commentary,[11] this tract displays an unprecedented feature: a mixing of disciplines—that is, law and Euclidean geometry. The first two sections of the commentary on *lex Adeo* are followed by a series of geometrical figures and diagrams meant to illustrate both principles of Euclidean geometry and models for dividing alluvial deposits or an island born in the middle of a river. Each figure receives an appropriate explanation, so that, at least for *De alluvione*, the amount of text devoted to the commentary on *lex Adeo* balances that of the figures. For *De insula* the ratio between the text taken up by the commentary and that devoted to the explanation of the figures is 3:2, yet the figures number only seventeen, instead of the twenty-two of the preceding section. In contrast, the third section, *De alveo*, contains no figures, for the division of an abandoned riverbed can be performed according to the schemes presented in the two previous sections.[12]

Though not so popular as Bartolus's tract *On Insignia and Coats of Arms*, a tract transmitted by more than one hundred and seventeen manuscripts, there are thirty manuscripts containing a copy of *Tiberiadis* that I have been able to identify.[13] Printed in the *editio princeps* (Venice, 1472) of his works, it has seen separate editions, such as the one prepared by Ercole Bottrigari, published in Bologna in 1576 and then reprinted in 1964 with an essay by Guido Astuti.[14] Not unexpectedly, it found a

---

deposits, an island born in midst of the stream, and the abandonment of the original bed. On the legal construction of alluvial deposits in Roman law, see Maddalena, *Gli incrementi fluviali*, 4–119.

[11] On this literary genre, see the various essays in *Der Kommentar in Antike und Mittelalter*.

[12] That the division of an abandoned riverbed should be performed according to the criteria set forth in the first and second section is stated explicitly by Bartolus himself in *De alveo*. See Bartolus, *Opera*, vol. 9, fols. 140vb: 'Tunc inter eos, qui ab una parte predia possident, fit divisio pro modo latitutidinis cuiusque predii, que latitudo prope ripam sit ... et ideo eodem modo quo supra in alluvione ostendimus. Si vero alveus ita derelinqueretur, quod ab utraque parte essent predia, tunc inter eos, qui possident predia ab utraque parte, fiet divisio iure vicinitatis et propinquitatis, et sic per medium, ut dictum est de insula.'

[13] For a partial listing of the manuscripts, see Dolezalek, *Verzeichnis*, s.v. 'Bartolus, *Tractatus Tiberiadis*.' For the manuscripts housed in German libraries, see Casamassima, *Codices operum Bartoli*, 248; for the manuscripts in Spanish libraries, see García y García, *Codices operum Bartoli*, 173. A description of some of the manuscripts housed in the BAV is given in *A Catalogue of Canon and Roman Law Manuscripts in the Vatican Library*, 1:318 (Vat. lat. 2289); 2:191 (Vat. lat. 2625); 216 (Vat. lat. 2641); 246 (Vat. lat. 2660). For the number of the extant manuscripts of *De insigniis*, see Cavallar and Kirshner, 'Ne ultra scarpas,' 297, 300–302.

[14] Bartolus de Saxoferrato, *Tractatus de fluminibus*; and Bartolus, *Commentaria*, vol. 9, fols. 128ra–142ra. For other printed editions of this tract, see Kamp, *Bartolus*

receptive audience among jurists. For before civil engineering became an established academic discipline, society relied on the theoretical knowledge of jurists and the practical skill of land surveyors to settle problems caused by wandering rivers.[15] The Veronese jurist Bartolomeo Cipolla, for instance, incorporated whole sections of *Tiberiadis* in his tract devoted to agrarian law.[16] The Florentine painter and architect Sigismondo Coccapani went further. He translated Bartolus's *prooemium* into Italian and, without bothering to substitute Bartolus's name with his own, used it as a preface to his tract '*Del modo di ridurre il fiume di Arno in canale*'—a borrowing that went undetected by the modern editor of Coccapani's tract.[17] Recent scholarship has also paid attention to Bartolus's intriguing tract, as well as to the broader problem of water management and supply in the Middle Ages, showing a special interest in municipal legislation.[18] Historians of geometry, cartography and art have also discussed the figures of this tract, perhaps more than historians of law.[19] The art historian Michael Baxandall has used the figures of an early printed edition to illustrate how two representational conventions were brought to coexist within the same frame: the conceptualized and schematic view of geometry that looks at rivers, fields, and borders from above and the 'natural' way of seeing things represented by the landscape, the contours of trees, animals, sirens, and buildings inserted in the figures.[20] Needless to say, Bartolus's original drawings do not lend any support to this natural way of seeing.

If *lex Adeo* was a staple of the architectonic commentaries on the *Corpus iuris civilis*, the sixteenth and seventeenth centuries witnessed an increased attention to issues like the juridical status of rivers and waters. Battista Aimo, Egidio Bossi, Cornelio Benincasa and Antonio Gobbi, to mention just a few names, figure among prominent jurists who addressed this set of legal issues.[21] Undoubtedly the popularity of such tracts cannot

---

de Sassoferrato, 86–87.

[15] For the tasks and knowledge of geometry of land surveyors, see Toneatto, *Codices artis mensoriae*; Toneatto, 'L'*ars mensoria*,' 308–326; and, for the edition of a tract on *ars mensoria*, see Johannes de Muris, *De arte mensurandi*.

[16] Caepolla, *De servitutibus*, vol. 6, t. 2, fols. 211v–243v.

[17] On this, see Cavallar, 'Il Tevere sfoccia nell'Arno,' 223–231.

[18] Nico Ottaviani, 'Alcuni aspetti della problematica sulle acque,' 58–63; Walther, 'Wasser in Stadt und Contado,' 888–897; and Frova, 'Le traité *De fluminibus*,' 81–89, but this entire issue of *Mediévales* is very relevant to the topic of rivers. For the technological aspects of water management, see *Working with Water in Medieval Europe*; and, for an earlier period, Squattriti, *Water and Society*.

[19] Maanen, 'Over het verdelen van aangeslibd land,' 161–168; Dainville, 'Cartes et contestations,' 99–121, especially 117–120.

[20] Baxandall, *Painting and Experience*, 32–33.

be separated from the interest the early modern state took in the management of rivers and the development of their resources.[22] From the sixteenth century on, moreover, developments in the field of geometry enabled jurists and civil engineers to refine their methods for dividing alluvial deposits.[23]

A glance at the index of the doctoral dissertations, pamphlets, and other legal works printed in Germany between 1600 and 1800 indicates that the triptych Bartolus had depicted never lost its appeal.[24] The principle for dividing alluvial deposits posited by the jurist Azo and Accursius in the thirteenth century and amply illustrated by Bartolus did not go unchallenged, as the lively dispute that engaged Carlo Carazzi and an anonymous 'dottore Parmeggiano' illustrates.[25] According to Carazzi, the method exposed by this anonymous jurist was irrational, for it produced a division of alluvial deposits that looked like an impracticable chessboard. Thus, Bartolus's authority had to be somehow reinstated; the practical wisdom of land surveyors who had measured and distributed land for centuries could not have been entirely wrong. Despite Carazzi's claim to have developed a method different from that of Bartolus for allotting alluvial deposits, the structure of his work remained indebted to Bartolus: a series of geometrical principles, subdivided into definitions and propositions, followed by instances of application.[26] The geometrical

---

[21] Aimo, *Tractatus de fluviorum alluvionibus*; Bossi, *Tractatus de aquis et fluminibus*, 596–600; Benincasa, *Compendiolum de alluvione*, in his comprehensive commentary *Ad tit. De constitutionibus*; Gobbi, *Tractatus varii in quibus universa aquarum materia*. For a later period and the persistent interest jurists took in issues related to rivers, see Ghiringhelli, 'Dottrina e cultura civile,' 207–221, and Dezza, 'Giacomo Giovanetti,' 223–234.

[22] For Perugia and the interest papal administration took in rivers, especially the Tiber, see Cutini Zazzerini, 'La normativa sulle acque,' 64–71.

[23] See, for instance, Baratteri, *Architettura d'acque*; Baratteri, *Degl'incrementi fluviali*; Castelli, *Distributione vniuersale dell'architettura de' fiumi*; and Guglielmini, *Della natura de fiumi*. For a dispute on alluvial soil, in which the Perugian monastery of San Pietro had been involved, the commission of maps by experts, and their use, see Migliorati, 'La committenza,' 97–98. For Florence and the recurring problems related to the river Arno, see Coccapani, *Trattato del modo di ridurre il fiume di Arno*, 13–108.

[24] Tsuno, *Katalog juristischer Dissertationen*, 33, Iacobus von Aschen, *De iure alluvionis*; 60, Valentinus Bart, *De alluvionibus*; 126, Nicolaus Beselin, *De insulis*; 398, Henricus von Einsiedel, *De fluminibus*; 458, Lotharius Feind, *De iuribus fluminum*; 900, Herman C. Kegel, *De iure riparum*.

[25] Carazzi, *Modo del dividere l'alluvioni*; and his *Dubitationi d'autore incerto*.

[26] For the figures illustrating the three different methods of dividing successive alluvial deposits, see Carazzi, *Dubitationi d'autore incerto*, 6–7, and 13–16. The diagrams Carrazzi proposed may appear to be a Byzantine construction (four

schemes devised by Bartolus to divide alluvial deposits and an island born in the middle of a river were also challenged by Jean Borrel, a French monk, Battista Aimo, and Claudio Tebalducci.[27] Lastly, *Tiberiadis* has also seen a translation into German, as well as a partial one into English.[28]

Archeology of knowledge aside, Bartolus's triptych continues to generate interest even in our times. In the hands of a mathematician *Tiberiadis* became a tool to lead eleven-year-old Dutch students toward the integration of Latin and geometry, to teach them the importance of mathematics for society, and to introduce them to the collective elaboration of simple solutions to juridical problems.[29] Before encountering the legal criterion of a division based on proximity (*ius proximitatis*, or *ius propinquitatis*)[30] and Bartolus's diagrams on how to apply it, the pupils based the division on their own sense of justice, proposing, for instance, to divide the alluvial deposit among the families who did not yet have any property.[31]

Were the Dutch students aware that the manuscript their teacher put in front of them (BAV, Barb. lat. 1398) was the autograph of the first section of *Tiberiadis*, one of the few extant texts wholly in the handwriting of Bartolus?[32] Since the codex containing the autograph of *De alluvione*

---

triangularly shaped alluvial deposits added to each other), but it is precisely this kind of construction that exploits the limitations of the different methods of dividing alluvial soil.

[27] Borrel, *Opera geometrica*, 97–133; tellingly, the relevant section is titled: *De fluviaticis insulis secundum ius civile dividendis, ubi confutatur Tyberias Bartoli*. Borrel's work comprises a series of tracts mostly focused on geometry and ancient history: *De arca Noe, cuius formae, capacitatisque fuerit. De Sublicio ponte Caesaris. Confutatio quadraturae circuli ab Orontio Finaeo factae. Ad locum Quintiliani geometricum explanatio. Ad problema cubi duplicandi. De fluentis aquae mensura. Emendatio figurationis organia Columella descripti. De libra & statera. De pretio margaritarum. De divisione fructus arboribus in confinio natae. Geometriae cognitionem iureconsulto necessariam*. More veiled is the refutation brought by Tebalducci in his *La Tiberiade di Bartole da Sasferrato*. Dismissing these works as the product of a «tardo imitatore e contradittore»—as, for instance, Astuti did—underplays the jusgenerativity of *Tiberiadis* and obscures the inherent limitations of the method and schemes Bartolus advanced for dividing alluvial deposits.

[28] For the translations, see Astuti's preface to *De fluminibus seu Tyberiadis*, p. V. An English translation of *De alluvione*, based on Bottrigari's edition, has been prepared by Paul de Plussy as a requirement for his master of arts. I wish to express my gratitude to him for sending me a copy of his translation.

[29] Maanen, 'Teaching Geometry,' 37–45.

[30] *Tiberiadis* lines 858–859, 896–898, 1014–1015 for *ius proximitatis*; and lines 791–793, 805–807, 853–854, 873, 888–889, 894–895, 967–968 for *ius propinquitatis*. The two expressions are interchangeable.

[31] I wish to express my gratitude to Prof. Jan van Maanen for his clarifications on the criteria his pupils used when discussing the distribution of land.

[32] For the identification of another specimen of Bartolus's handwriting, see

has been described in an exemplary fashion by Vincenzo Colli, here it suffices to say that it belonged to Baldus de Ubaldis, Bartolus's prize pupil and intellectual heir.[33] It comprises a series of works on civil law by authors ranging from Franciscus de Aptis to Guido da Suzaria, from Philippus de Cassolis to Tancredus de Corneto, as well as material Baldus excerpted from canonists like Guido de Basio (Archidiaconus) and Bernardus de Parma.[34] The identification of the script as Bartolus's own handwriting has been made by Colli.[35] The drawing of geometrical figures and diagrams, too, can be safely attributed to Bartolus. A comparison of the script of the tract and that of the geometrical figures (the letters of the alphabet used to indicate geometrical points and lines; the stereotypical names of Lutius, Titius, Caius, and Sempronius used to denote the owners of pieces of land adjacent to the river; and a few other words used in the figures) dispels possible doubts on the identity of the author. Colli's minute analysis of the material composition of this codex has also explained the mishap that occurred at the beginning of the tract, where one folio (fol. 159rv) was left blank: the first two folios have been spoiled and then rewritten.[36] How this section of the tract came into the hands of Baldus's family and whether it was the copy the author retained for himself or, more unlikely, part of the fair copy given to the authorities of the University of Perugia are questions to which no precise answer can be given.[37] A respectful note, praying for Bartolus's eternal rest, appended at the end of the text shows that Bartolus was already dead when the holograph came into Baldus's possession or, more likely, when the whole codex was assembled.[38]

Ascheri, 'The Formation of the *Consilia* Collections,' 188–201; and Colli, 'Collezioni d'autore,' 336–337, especially note 45, for another specimen of Bartolus's handwriting.

[33]Colli, 'Collezioni d'autore,' 323–346.

[34]Ibid., pp. 341–345, for the complete list of the works contained in this manuscript.

[35]Ibid., p. 333: 'l'identità della mano che li ha scritti ... è così evidente che in questo caso le immagini possono parlare da sole.' My own comparison of ms. BAV Barb. lat. 1398 and the text of the two autograph *consilia* contained in ms. Ravenna, Biblioteca Classense, 448, no. 9, and no. 11 fully endorses Colli's position.

[36]Ibid., pp. 333–335. A note, 'nichil deficit' [nothing is missing], on top of fol. 159r alerts the reader that no text is missing.

[37]For the vicissitudes of Baldus's library, see Colli, 'Il Cod. 351 della Biblioteca Capitolare,' 255–282; Colli, '*Consilia* dei giuristi,' 173–225; Colli, 'L'esemplare di dedica,' 69–117; Colli and Monacchia, 'Un elenco di libri,' 185–215. And also Colli, 'Collezioni d'autore,' 336–338, for a note on the dispersion of Bartolus's library.

[38]The note says: 'Explicit tractatus de fluminibus per dominum Bar[tolum] de Saxoferrato, anima cuius requieschat in pace.' Colli has not identified the author of this note; see Colli, 'Collezioni d'autore,' 340–341. According to Colli, this codex

After Bottrigari published his revised edition of *Tiberiadis* there was no attempt to produce a critical edition.[39] The discovery of the holograph containing the original drawings by Bartolus calls for a new edition, which I have undertaken (see Appendix 1). I am well aware that a partial edition is not an optimal solution,[40] but it is unlikely that the entire holograph will be discovered.[41] Yet there is another reason for a new edition, even of only one section: the original drawings by Bartolus himself (see Appendix 2). The geometrical figures and diagrams were drawn in color—a simple but effective tool that enabled the jurist to convey information without redundancy. A careful choice and consistent use of colors enabled him to differentiate between 'nature' and 'culture,' so that the artificial construct of Euclidean geometry never mixes with the 'natural' lines of rivers and fields: geometry is simply superimposed. The colors of the figures, much more than the oft-quoted dream narrated in the introduction, speak of Bartolus's consciousness of both the limits and potentialities of a cognitive tool like geometry. In contrast to the holograph, the printed editions cluttered the figures with redundant elements, such as buildings, castles, trees, animals, and sirens, and, as a consequence, the geometrical figures grew smaller and became almost illegible.[42] The absence of color compelled the early printers to use other

---

was among Baldus's books that were brought back to Perugia from Pavia, after his death in 1400. If he took along Bartolus's holograph when he went to Pavia, we may presume that Baldus cherished it as one of his prized possessions.

[39]Already the title page of his edition advertised the revision of the text: 'nunc denum restitutus.' The preface lists other errors Bottrigari sought to emend: in the figures, the letters indicating geometrical points and lines that had been inverted, transposed, and duplicated; and, in the text, the allegations of Roman law that had been altered or added.

[40]I eventually plan to publish the critical edition of the whole tract.

[41]The manuscript tradition also shows that this tract was not always transmitted in its entirety. See, for instance, Barcelona, Archivo de la Corona de Aragón, ms. Ripoll 67, fols. 34v–42v; Barcelona, Biblioteca del Cabildo, ms. 85, fols. 231ra–300vb; Seo de Urgel, Biblioteca del Cabildo, ms. 2109, fols. 337ra–347vb; Toledo, Biblioteca del Cabildo, ms. 28-16, fols. 164ra–172va; Trier, Stadtbibliothek, ms. 975/923 4°, fols. 129r-139, containing only *De alluvione*. For another abridged version, leaving out entirely the two sections on geometry and rearranging the sections relevant for a jurist, see BAV, Vat. lat. 2625, fols. 135r-146v. For manuscripts omitting the introduction and the two sections on geometry, see KBR, II/3592, fols. 182r–196v; BAV, Vat. lat. 2641, fols. 54rb–63rb; and BAV, Vat. lat. 2660, fols. 171r–192v. And, for a manuscript that has preserved only the two sections on geometry, see Firenze, Biblioteca Riccardiana, ms. 1030, fols. 180r–206r.

[42]Clumsiness in drawing the figures, when they were copied, is also evident in the manuscript tradition. For manuscripts that left a blank space for the figures, see Cues, Bernkastel, ms. 257, fols. 124ra–144va; and BAV, Vat. lat. 2289, fols. 47vb–69ra; and also Seo de Urgel, Biblioteca del Cabildo, ms. 2109, fol. 347rv,

devices such as the insertion of additional letters and lines in the figures and forced them to transpose those letters into the text itself.[43] In Bottrigari's edition, a new figure has been inserted to illustrate the case of the two mills and the proper placement of the ducts of water of one of the mills.[44] Another change introduced in the printed editions was the suppression of the heads of animals Bartolus drew to indicate the origin and the direction of the flow of the river.[45] Restoring those heads to the figures will give us an additional facet of Bartolus's personality, his freehanded pictures of fanciful animals, to be placed next to 'a person of short stature' [*homo parve stature*] who 'eat with moderation' [*comedebat ... ad pondus*], to have his mind always sharp and unaltered by food or wine.[46]

For a moment, let us imagine that the Roman humanist and arch anti–Bartolist Lorenzo Valla, while teaching at the University of Pavia, had read the first part of Bartolus's tract *Tiberiadis* instead of *On Insignia and Coats of Arms*, which he attacked with ferocity. How would he have reacted?

The handwriting—not the cluttered, spiky, eye-straining Gothic detested by Petrarch, but a quite elegant Gothic cursive on the verge of becoming a *semigotica*—would not discourage reading.[47] Yet, the human-

---

where the last two figures were omitted and a blank space left. In ms. Firenze, Biblioteca Riccardiana, 1030, fols. 184r–206r, ingenuity supplied the absence of colors: the scribe wrote the names of the colors beside the relevant black lines of the figures.

[43] When he rendered the geometrical figures in black and white, Bottrigari recognized the difficulty posed by the colors ('Que quidem difficultas maxima erat'). His task became even more difficult because he could not easily find manuscripts with the original colors.

[44] *De fluminibus seu Tyberiadis*, 48, where both mills are on the same side of the river. The figure was drawn erroneously, for the *quaestio* presupposes that one of the mills is on the other side of the river. This illustration was set aside from the others and no consecutive number was given to it. A figure representing the two mills appears also in BAV, Ross. lat. 1061, fol. 7v; for a clumsier drawing, see, KBR, II, 1442, fol. 231r. The Venetian edition of 1521 does not reproduce the figure of the two mills; see Bartolus, *Opera*, vol. 9, fol. 133v. For the *quaestio* on the two mills, see *Tiberiadis* lines 1049–1070.

[45] For an elaborate rendering of the heads of animals, see BAV, Ross. lat. 1061, fols. 3ra–14vb.

[46] For the first of these two personal characteristics, see Condorelli, 357–364. For the second, see the 'Vita Bartoli' of Diplovatazio, *Liber de claris iuris consultis*, 274–287, citation on p. 286. For the effects of food and wine on the mind of a student, see Francesco Zabarella, *De modo docendi et studendi*. This text has been edited and translated into English by Julius Kirshner and myself for a forthcoming anthology of medieval legal texts in English translation.

[47] For the paleographical description of Bartolus's handwriting, see Colli, 'Collezioni d'autore,' 333.

ist would point out the inconsistent spelling of words like *alluvio*, at times written with a double *l*, but more often with only one, and that some adjectives demand an *x* at the end—and 'felis Perusina civitas' sounds like a Latin spoken by a farmer. Similarly, he would sharply reprove the insertion of another *n* before a *gn*, as in 'mangnus theologus'; and, on the same line, censor the change of *m* into an *n* before a palatal consonant, as in 'senper' instead of *semper*, and 'anplius' instead of *amplius*.[48] Supposing that the humanist could digest all of the abbreviations so often used by medieval legal writers, it would not escape his attention that Bartolus frequently omits, even at the end of a word, the sign indicating the abbreviation—'huis' stands for *huius*, 'rpa' for *ripa*, 'constituta' for *constitutam*, and 'ad circumferentia' for *ad circumferentiam*.[49] From a grammatical point of view, Valla would not let go unpunished errors like the wrong agreement between a noun and its corresponding relative pronoun, for instance, 'de lapillis ... que' (properly: 'de lapillis ... qui', for *lapillus* is a masculine noun), or between an adjective and its corresponding noun, for instance, 'colles ... culta' (properly: 'colles ... culti', for *collis*, too, is masculine), or such impossible combinations as 'figuras... per que,' in which grammar requires 'figuras ... per quas.'[50]

Yet such errors could be considered mere distractions, permissible in a text that stood between the first draft and the polished copy submitted to the University of Perugia.[51] A more serious flaw would be the series of etymologies to which Bartolus resorted in his explanation of the law: the Tiber did not derive its name from the Roman emperor Tiberius but from the king of Alba, Tiberinus.[52] Undoubtedly, riding the hobbyhorse

---

[48] *Tiberiadis* line 9 for *felis Perusina civitas*; line 43 for *mangnus teologus*; lines 110, 283, 393 for *senper*; lines 76, 534 for *anplius*; line 579 for *ingnorantur*. For the way in which Valla worked with the texts of classical authors, see Regoliosi, *Nel cantiere del Valla*, 1–35, 63–115.

[49] *Tiberiadis* line 14 for *constituta[m]*; line 32 for *hui[u]s*; line 117 for *r[i]pa*; line 90 for *intellige[n]dum*; line 179 for *altitud[in]is*; line 187 for *pla[n]ities*; and line 643 for *ad circumferentia[m]*. In the edition, the missing material has been supplied in square brackets.

[50] *Tiberiadis* line 68 for *lapillis ... que*; line 177 for *colles ... culta*; and line 578 for *figuras ... per que*.

[51] Three additional instances of Bartolus's proverbial 'distraction' can be given. Beginning with figure 5, he misnumbered all the figures up to figure 20. When he drew figure 9, he made another small error: the big red circle should have touched only the field of Lutius, not both that of Lutius and Titius. And, in the cross-references to the figures, he twice miscited the number of the figure: figure 14 for figure 15, and figure 10 for figure 11.

[52] *Tiberiadis* lines 6–8. Significantly, Papias, cited by Bartolus on other etymologies, has the 'right' explanation. See Papias, *Vocabulista*, s.v. *Tyberis*, 351.

of Renaissance rhetoric, Valla would have had plenty of opportunities to amuse his readers by making fun of the derivation of the noun *mons* from the verb *movere* (immovable mountains are not 'turned around' by cultivation).[53] The naïve attempt to derive the meaning of *planus* (flatland) from the Greek *platos* would have had Valla, the author of the *Collatio Novi testamenti*, smiling, to say the least.[54] There is no need to insist on the point that he would demolish Bartolus's attempt to derive the meaning of the word *ager* (field) from the verb *agere* (to do, perform)—that is, to cultivate and plow a piece of land with oxen.[55] For Valla, asses, not oxen, would be undoubtedly more fitted for plowing those pieces of land. Yet since Bartolus did not invent those etymologies but borrowed them from Huguccius and Papias and, more remotely, from Isidore of Seville and Varro, he was only partly at fault: his crime would be that of 'uncritical borrowing.'

Since Valla trashed the fancy theory of colors that Nicola Alessandri, Bartolus's son-in-law and the author of the second part of *On Insignia and Coats of Arms*, had advanced, pointing out that in nature many more colors exist than those Alessandri had listed and capriciously ranked, he would not have spared the use of words like *açurus* (blue) and *ialnus* (yellow)—two terms Bartolus used to describe the colors he would resort to when drawing the geometrical figures.[56] Especially a term like *açurus* would indicate that Bartolus was 'accustomed to converse more with women than men' and adopted an effeminate and barbarous way of speaking.[57] Similarly, in obedience to the canons of Renaissance esthetics,

---

[53] *Tiberiadis* lines 161–163. For the negative construction of the meaning of words used by jurists when interpreting the law, see Sbriccoli, *L'interpretazione dello statuto*, 344–356; and for the argument grounded on the etymology of a word, ibid., pp. 191–200. For another etymology of the term *mons*, see Petrus Helias, *Summa super Priscianum*, 1:112: 'Dicunt tamen plures quod 'mons' dicitur a 'munio munis,' eo, scilicet, quod locum cui montes astant muniuntur.'

[54] *Tiberiadis* lines 186–188.

[55] Ibid., lines 130–132.

[56] Ibid., lines 717–723. Bottrigari, too, could not conceal his uneasiness about the names of the colors Bartolus used; see his preface to *De fluminibus seu Tyberiadis*, s.p.: 'nunc rubeum, nunc flavum (eius verba recensebo) aut zaldum, vel croceum, modo azureum, sive ceruleum, modo nigrum vocati.'

[57] This criticism appears in Valla's letter to Piercandido Decembrio; for the English translation of this letter, see Cavallar, Degenring, and Kirshner, *A Grammar of Signs*, 179–200, especially p. 194; see Guerra Medici, *L'aria di città*, 11, for the misogynistic attitudes of the humanists. For the basic colors available in the late Middle Ages (blue, red, yellow, brown, and black), especially in relation to dresses, see Muzzarelli, *Gli inganni delle apparenze*, 46–50. If terms like *açurus* and *ialnus* can be criticized from Valla's point of view, one should not neglect that the adoption of these vernacular terms, instead of their literary and cultured equiva-

he would not have let go undisputed the insertion of heads of animals to indicate the *caput fluminis* (the origin of the river) and the direction of the flow of the stream.[58] For those little monsters were unnatural as the words *açurus* and *ialnus*. As the printers of *Tiberiadis* have done, the heads of the animals had to be suppressed and the geometrical figures cluttered with more or less classicizing buildings or naturalistic landscapes letting the auxiliary value of geometry subside in favor of a colorless aesthetic.

But let us leave Valla. The best-known part of *Tiberiadis* is certainly the introduction (*prooemium*). In an engaging manner it describes the time, circumstances, and difficulties related to the composition of this work. As in the tract *On Insignia and Coats of Arms*, it has provided historians of continental medieval law with details to enrich Bartolus's chronically meager biography.[59] In the late summer of 1355, while vacationing in that 'villa' near Perugia, Bartolus began to consider factual questions related to the changes caused by a river. Yet, to avoid spoiling his vacation, he set aside his thoughts. On the next morning, in a dream a gentle and mysterious figure appeared to him bringing a reed pen, a ruler, and a compass.[60] The message was clear: the thoughts of the previous day must be preserved in writing. A mild attempt to decline the invitation caused the nocturnal visitor to remind Bartolus that it runs counter to the moral virtue called fortitude to desist from a worthy

---

lents, indicates how much Bartolus, the jurist, was attuned to the life of the city.

[58] *Tiberiadis* lines 718–719.

[59] For instance, that he learned geometry, and perhaps Hebrew, from the Franciscan theologian and mathematician Guido de Perusio. The identification of the anonymous person who taught Bartolus Hebrew as Jehudá da Perugia was posited by Roth, *The Jews in the Renaissance*, 138; but rejected by Toaff, *Gli Ebrei a Perugia*, 22, who identifies that Hebrew teacher as Guido de Perusio. A careful distinction between these persons was maintained by Sheedy, *Bartolus on Social Conditions in the Fourteenth Century*, 112–113, 162, 185; and by Segoloni, 'Bartolo e la *civitas Perusina*,' 550–551. On Bartolus's alleged knowledge of Hebrew, see also Cavallar, Degenring, and Kirshner, *A Grammar of Signs*, 26–29. Colli has pointed out that ms. Barb. lat. 1398 contains one specimen of Hebrew handwriting and a Hebrew numeration also running through fols. 157r–170v (Bartolus's holograph); see Colli, 'Collezioni d'autore,' 345–346. Since the Hebrew note refers to the number of quaternions comprised in this codex and contains the transliteration of the name of Amedeo di Zenobio degli Ubaldi (Baldus's nephew), we can rest assured that Bartolus had no part in it.

[60] *Tiberiadis* lines 18–23. For the role of dreams in juridical literature, see Quaglioni, 'Giovanni da Legnano e il *Somnium Viridari*,' 145–167; and in general, see the volume edited by Paravicini Bagliani, *Träume im Mittelalter, Ikonologische Studien*; and, for the meaning of early morning dreams, Manselli, 'Il sogno come premonizione,' 219–244.

enterprise on grounds of the fear of being scorned—the saints and Christ himself did not behave in a cowardly way. In the next two days Bartolus completed the figures and the accompanying explanation comprised in the first part of the tract—that is, the section called *De alluvione*.[61] On the third day, he ran into unexpected obstacles related to the geometrical demonstrations or the drawing of the diagrams.[62] Fortunately, it happened that Guido de Perusio, a Franciscan friar[63] 'well learned in every field' [*universalis in omnibus*], passed by. Providentially, a heavy rain prevented Guido from continuing his journey and kept him there for one full day—'unum diem integrum naturalem,' Bartolus noted with legal precision.[64] That fortuitous event not only gave him plenty of time to solve the geometrical problems, but also reassured Bartolus that God was behind the plan of the tract and approved the unorthodox marriage between law and geometry. On the third and fourth day he drew all the figures found in the second section of the tract and wrote the accompanying explanation—that is, *De insula*. The third and last part, *De alveo*, was completed after he reverted to Perugia. Later that year he intended to submit the revised text to the authorities of Perugia's university—deferentially referred to as 'Your University' [*universitati vestre*].[65]

The unique ending of one manuscript copy of Bartolus's tract *On Guelphs and Ghibellines* seems to indicate even the precise day in which *Tiberiadis* was finished: July 10.[66] Quaglioni in his critical edition of *De*

---

[61] For the topic of malevolent criticism as addressed in the introduction to narrative texts, see Bourgain, 'Les prologues des textes narratifs,' 252–253.

[62] An attempt to figure out the nature of those difficulties and the kind of help Bartolus received from Guido de Perusio will be made when the whole critical edition of *Tiberiadis* is presented.

[63] That Guido de Perusio belonged to the Franciscan order (O.F.M.), is also indicated by ms. BAV, Regin. lat. 1891, fol. 2r: 'Me visitavit quidam frater minor, Guido de Perusio de ordine fratrum minorum, magnus theologus universalis in omnibus'; and by ms. Seville, Biblioteca Colombina, 83-8-13, fol. 159rb, giving the same information.

[64] Not much is known about this Franciscan friar. In 1357, with two other friars he was sent to Dalmatia. On this occasion he was called 'lector' and received a travel allowance of five florins, while his two companions received four; see Cenci, *Documentazione di vita assisana,* 1:123; and Piana, *Chartularium studii bononiensis,* 25. For the records of unusual meteorological phenomena, such as heavy snowfalls and violent thunderstorms during the summer, see Grohmann, *Città e territorio,* 1:86–87.

[65] *Tiberiadis* lines 13–52. For the regulations concerning the presentation of the text of lectures, *quaestiones* and *repetitiones* to the authorities of the university and for the dispositions attempting to limit absenteeism of professors, see Ermini, *Storia della Università di Perugia,* 91–94, and 85.

[66] Lübeck, Bibliothek der Hansestadt Lübeck, ms. jur. gr. 2° 23, fol. 46rb. For a

Guelphis et Gebellinis has rightly excluded the possibility that the suspension of academic activities due to an interdict might coincide with the summer vacations Bartolus mentioned in the introduction to *Tiberiadis*. If an interdict suspended academic activities, that suspension would be hard to qualify as a summer vacation. Furthermore, there is no evidence that the killing of an intruding student and the imposition of an interdict by ecclesiastical authorities occurred in 1355. Since the same manuscript contains a copy of both *De Guelphis and Gebellinis* and *Tiberiadis*, it is likely that the date refers to the time when the copyist finished his transcription, not to the time when Bartolus completed the two tracts. As Quaglioni has rightly suggested, this manuscript, transcribed at Erfurt, was based on an earlier copy made in Perugia.[67] Finally, if the ambassadors returned from their mission on July 8, it is impossible that just two days later Bartolus would have finished writing *Tiberiadis* and *De Guelphis et Gebellinis*.

Though in the holograph of *Tiberiadis* Bartolus asserts that the tract was submitted to the authorities of the University of Perugia in 1355, one may reasonably doubt whether the presentation actually occurred. In the holograph, as well as the entire manuscript tradition and printed editions, the date is obviously incomplete. The full date, and often even the *indictio*, is a very common feature, if not an indispensable one, of all the *quaestiones disputatae* and *repetitiones* submitted to the academic authorities, as it is attested for other works Bartolus presented to the University of Pisa and Perugia.[68] The full date, *indictio* included, was given by Nicola Alessandri when he published *On Insignia and Coats of Arms*.[69] One manuscript, Florence, Biblioteca Nazionale II, IV, 108, indicates that Alessandri appended it to *On Tyranny* when this text was submitted to the university on November 11, 1357.[70] Thus I suspect that

---

brief history of this manuscript, see Casamassima, *Codices operum Bartoli*, no. 81, 104–105. For this unique colophon, see Quaglioni, *Politica e diritto nel Trecento italiano*, 91: 'Et finitus est eodem die quo tractatus tyberiadis videlicet .x. mensis Julii et quia studium fuit interdictum propter quondam scolarem occisum in domo cuiusdam perusini qui habuit quendam famulam in domo propter <quam> predictus scolaris domum prefati civis ingressus est.'

[67] Ibid., 96.

[68] Casamassima, *Codices operum Bartoli*, 32–33 no. III, 36 no. IX, 48 no. III, 71–72 no. II, 93–94 no. II, 101 no. III, 117 no. III, 118 no. VIII, 119 no. II, 120 no. IX, 121 no. XI, 163 no. IX, 175 no. VI, 185; and for the tracts, notably *De represaliis*, p. 5 no. IV, p. 12 no. II, p. 37 no. II, 101 no. II, 104 no. II, 122 no. V., 134 no. II, 163 no. VII, 176 no. II, 181 no. I, 196 no. I, 204 no. I, 213 no. IV.

[69] Cavallar, Degenring, and Kirshner, *A Grammar of Signs*, 144 for some examples of explicits containing the full date (January 20, 1357).

[70] For this unique *explicit*, see Quaglioni, *Politica e diritto*, 109. Bartolus 'non publicavit morte perventus. Sed publicavit post eius mortem d. Nicolaus Alessandri

the omission of the full date in the prologue of *Tiberiadis* was done on purpose, and Bartolus would have duly inserted the month and the day just before, or at the moment of, the presentation. As in the case of his *On Insignia and Coats of Arms*, it is very likely that the manuscript of *Tiberiadis* remained in his drawer, presumably because it was not completely finished or polished, and started to circulate after Bartolus's death.[71] Significantly, no manuscript copy of *On Guelphs and Ghibellines*, *On the Government of the City*, and *On Tyranny* has the official date of the presentation.

The oneiric aura attending this well-crafted *prooemium* may blur the fact that, though original, Bartolus is following the stylistic canons of medieval writing and, while capturing the attention of the readers, gives all the elements required by the introduction to an academic text. The manuscript of *Tiberiadis* owned by the Národní Muzeum (Prague), and now on display in the office of the president of the Czech Republic, makes this clear. Marginal rubrics call the attention to the reason for the composition the tract (*causa moventis*), the name of the author (*nomen auctoris*), the title of the work (*intitulatio tractatus*), and the division of the entire tract into three parts (*divisio huius operis*).[72]

Traditionally, *Tiberiadis* has been reckoned among Bartolus's tracts.[73] Yet to call it a tract (*tractatus*) may be misleading, for, in a marginal note on the first folio of the holograph, Bartolus wrote 'proemium ad librum Tiberis'—that is, introduction to the 'book' on the Tiber—perhaps an indication that he had a broader plan in his mind than a mere tract.[74] To this view some support is given by ms. Cambridge, Mass., Harvard Law

---

de Perusio legum doctor, eius gener, sub anno domini M° CCC° LVII, die XI° mensis novembris, et dicitur quod ideo ipsum non publicavit quia non perfecerat ipsum.'

[71] Showing that, especially the second and third part of *Tiberiadis*, were not polished up requires a lengthly excursus. For the moment, one single example should suffice. While in the holograph Barolus deleted all the 'inquit' and 'ait' after he transcribed the Roman fragments on which he was about to comment, the manuscripts transmitting the second and third part of *Tiberiadis* still show the presence of those pleonastic 'inquit' and 'ait.'

[72] Prague, Národní Muzeum, ms. a. 5, fol. 11rab. For the prologues to academic books, see Minnis, *Medieval Theory of Authorship*, 9–39.

[73] As used here, the term 'tract' (*tractatus*), is just a convenient way to refer to a genre of juridical literature—a genre that, thanks to Bartolus, became firmly established. For the issues related to such a classification, see Cortese, *Il Rinascimento giuridico*, 66–70, with bibliography. For a broad construction of the term *tractatus*, see Weimar, 'Die legistische Literatur,' 43–83.

[74] In the cross-references to the other two sections of *Tiberiadis*, moreover, Bartolus constantly used the term *liber*. See, for instance, *Tiberiadis* lines 320–323: 'De rivis vero ... in sequenti libro, ubi de insula tractabimus, dicetur'; and lines 295–296: 'et quod dicam in secundo et tertio libro huius.'

School Library, 75, containing the text of *Tiberiadis*, *De Guelphis et Gebellinis*, *De regimine civitatis*, and *De tyranno*. Significantly, in the explicit of *De tyranno* the scribe stated: 'Explicit tractatus de tiranno et sic tota materia Tiberiadis, per famosissimum ll. doc. Bartolum. Deo gracias. Anno 1475 in Camerino.'[75] Admittedly, this manuscript is a late witness. Nonetheless, the sequence of the four tracts and the explicit lend some plausibility to the view that if not the author himself at least one scribe thought that the four tracts constituted an unbreakable unity. Thus it cannot be excluded that the 'liber' to which Bartolus referred might comprise something more than one single tract— that is, *Tiberiadis*.

The order in which this interlocked work had been composed needs clarification, and one must distinguish between three stages: the two sections on the geometrical figures, the commentary on *lex Adeo*, and the revision of the entire work and the drafting of the introduction. As I said above, *Tiberiadis* comprises three sections: *De alluvione*, *De insula*, and *De alveo*. While the structure of the first two is symmetrical, the third is not. *De alluvione* opens with a substantive commentary on paragraphs 1 and 2 of *lex Adeo*, running from the bottom of folio 157r to the top of folio 162v. The commentary is followed by a section comprising twenty-two figures meant to illustrate both principles of Euclidean geometry and schemes for allotting alluvial deposits. Similarly, *De insula* opens with a sustained commentary on paragraphs 3 and 4 of *lex Adeo*, and it is followed by a series of seventeen figures illustrating how to divide equitably an island born between the two banks of a river among the landowners on both sides of the river.[76] The third section, *De alveo*, contains no figures and it is the continuation of the commentary on paragraphs 5 and 6 of *lex Adeo*. If we consider only *De alluvione* (but the same can be said of *De insula*), there are no cross-references between the commentary on *lex Adeo* and the explanation of the figures. On the contrary, there are cross-references within the three sections devoted to the commentary on the Roman fragment.[77] These two parts, the commen-

---

[75]Fol. 80r. For another indication of the date of transcription, see fol. 166r (Perugia 1475). For a brief description of this manuscript, see Izbicki, 'Texts Attributed to Bartolus de Saxoferrato,' 383–384.

[76]For the sake of precision, it should be noted that the last two figures of *De alluvione* and the last three figures of *De insula* illustrate instances of application of geometry to situations that have no relation to changes affecting rivers.

[77]For instance, explaining the word *flumen* (river), Bartolus refers the reader to the third section, for it was there that the legislator made clear he meant public rivers; and, explaining the term *rivus* (a small river), he sends the reader to the second section, for it was there that the text of the law used this term. Similarly, when discussing sudden changes affecting the course of a river—for instance an earthquake or a landslide—he sends the reader to the third section, for only alluvial

tary and the explanation of the figures, had been composed on two separate occasions and then combined when the running commentary had been completely finished. Needless to say, the introduction was the last part to be written.

What Bartolus wrote in the first four days of his sojourn at the villa overlooking the Tiber were the two parts devoted to the exposition of geometrical figures and diagrams. The wording of the introduction confirms this—'in the first two days I drew the figures of the first book and wrote the accompanying explanation' [*in duobus diebus primi libri figuras conposui et exposui*]. Similarly, the third and fourth day were taken up by the drawing and explanation of the figures of the second section.[78] Earlier, in the introduction, Bartolus stated that the sight of the river prompted him to ponder factual problems (*quaestiones de facto*)— an expression that aptly describes the kind of issues addressed in the second section of *De alluvione* and *De insula*.[79] The section running from the top of folio 162v to the top of 170v seems a reasonable amount of work for two days. Indeed, it is difficult to conceive that a person could have written some sixteen folios in just two days. Even a copyist, to say nothing of a writer, could not produce so much in two days.[80]

The interlocked composition of *Tiberiadis* poses several questions. When was the plan of the whole work conceived? Was the commentary planned already from the outset or was it an idea that came to the author latter, perhaps because the sections on geometry seemed naked without juridical dress? Since *De alveo* was written after Bartolus returned to Perugia, when did he compose the remaining commentary to *lex Adeo*? Was it after the section on the figures? And, if so, did he elaborate on, or expand, some previous material—for instance, his lectures on the first part of the *Digestum novum*? I have no precise answers to such questions, only one marginal observation. In his classroom commentary on *lex Adeo*, the six paragraphs on which he commented here—that is, in *Tiberiadis*—are left out, and his commentary begins with paragraph *Cum quis*, that is paragraph 7.[81] Even if he did incorporate material from his previous

---

deposits occurring slowly and imperceptibly over a long period properly belong to the first section of the tract. For these cross-references, see *Tiberiadis* lines 272–273, 295–296, 320–323.

[78] Ibid., lines 40–41.

[79] Ibid., lines 15–17. For the difference between a *quaestio facti* and a *quaestio iuris*, see Bellomo, '*Factum e ius*.' 63–89; and Prosdocimi, '*Ex facto oritur ius*,' 802–813.

[80] For the medieval construction of the differences between the work of an author, a compiler, and copyist, see Minnis, *Medieval Theory of Authorship*, 73–117; and, for the terminology used by the jurists, Cavallar, Degenring, and Kirshner, *A Grammar of Signs*, 36–39.

lectures, the scope of the commentary on *lex Adeo* of *Tiberiadis* goes well beyond what one could possibly present in a classroom. The completion of the commentary also presupposes that Bartolus had his library at hand, and, even though he was an absorbed scholar, it seems unlikely that while going on vacation he took along Papias, Huguccius, Azo, Roffredus, the whole *Glossa* of Accursius, and Euclid.

The title, a plain *Tiberiadis* without the usual *De* followed by an ablative, is also curious. Walther, quoting from the printed edition, puts a question mark after *Tiberiadis*, calling attention to what he believes must be either a scribal misprint or an error committed by Bartolus himself.[82] That title might well be the product of the absorbed mind of a jurist who ruminated on nothing but law; but the holograph has 'and I entitled the whole work 'Tiberiadis'' [*et totum opus apellavi Tiberiadis*],[83] and, in a marginal rubric at the top of the same page, Bartolus wrote 'Incipit proemium ad librum Tiberis'—plausibly a sign of hesitation over the precise title of the work. For sure, it should be written with an *i*, not a *y*. The title *De fluminibus*, common in printed editions, is also attested by the manuscript tradition and the posthumous explicit appended at the end of the holograph.[84] A creative and forward-moving tension between *Book on the Tiber* and *Tiberiadis* pervades the work. If the intended title is *On the Tiber*, then recasting it as *De fluminibus* is not totally unwarranted, for its focus is on legal issues related to a river and its course. If it is *Tiberiadis*, the perspective is wider: the focus is no longer fixed on a specific river but on the legal issues of a whole region, including those

---

[81] Bartolus *ad legem Adeo*, vol. 5, fol. 81rb. In the case of *lex Quominus* (D. 43 12.2), where Bartolus inserted his *repetitio* on the same fragment in his commentary, he alerted the readers that they would find no specific commentary and they should instead consult the *repetitio*; see ibid., fol. 154vb. In the case of *lex Adeo*, however, there is no such cross-reference.

[82] Walther, 'Wasser in Stadt und Contado,' 891, note 23.

[83] *Tiberiadis* line 35.

[84] For the explicit, see above, note 38. For manuscripts bearing *De fluminibus* as title, see BAV, Vat. lat. 2289, fol. 47v: 'De fluminibus et abluv[ionibus]' (the whole tract); in the index, s.f., the same title; BAV, Vat. lat. 2641, fol. 54rb, on the margin: 'Tractatus de aluvione' (only the commentary on *lex Adeo*); in the index, s.f.: 'De fluminibus seu Tyberiadis'; Prague, ms. a. 5, fol. 11r: 'Tractatus de alveis et alluvionibus Bar[toli]' (the whole tract); Seo de Urgel, Biblioteca del Cabildo, ms. 2109, fol. 337ra: 'Incipit tractatus super materia alluvionis compositus per dominum Bartolum de Saxo Ferrato legum excellentissimum professorem' (only *De alluvione*); Firenze, Biblioteca Riccardiana, ms. 1030, fol. 184r: 'Incipit tractatus de fluminibus seu Tyberiadis dom[ini] Bar[toli] de Saxoferrato' (only the two sections on geometry); Munich, Bayerische Staatsbibliothek, Cod. Lat. 5462, fol. 25ra: 'Tractatus d[omini] Bar[toli] de aluvionibus' (the whole tract); and Cod. Lat. 26669, fol. 241ra: 'De aluvionibus trac[tatus] Bar[toli]' (the whole tract).

related to its main river. The best manuscript tradition, joined with a reading of the whole tract and a consideration of Bartolus's subsequent tracts, leads me to endorse the second option.[85]

The term *Tiberiadis*, as used by Bartolus, does not appear in any of the medieval, or classical, Latin dictionaries that I have been able to consult, and it could well be a term Bartolus himself devised, perhaps out of *mala grammatica* [bad grammar].[86] According to his explanation, it is the name of the region surrounding the Tiber, and, theoretically, it extends from the south side of the Emilian Apennine to Rome, including cities such as Perugia and Todi. The element that gives unity to the region is the river, the Tiber, which keeps its name unaltered form Mount Fumaiolo, its origin, to its estuary near Ostia.[87]

With a different meaning, the term *Tiberiadis* occurs in Papias; it refers to the region of Palestine surrounding the Sea of Galilee. Here, this lake is described as 'the most salubrious lake of the whole Judaea' [*omnibus lacis Iudeae salubrior*].[88] Although Papias was a desktop reference work,[89]

---

[85] For manuscripts bearing *Tiberiadis* as main title, see BAV, Regin. lat. 1891, fol. 2r: 'Tractatus Tiberiadis' (the whole tract); BAV, Vat. lat. 2625, fol. 136r: 'Tyberiadis. Incipit quidam tractatus editus per dominum Bartholum de Saxoferrato distinctus per tres libros' (only the commentary on *lex Adeo*); BAV, Ross. lat. 1061, fol. 3ra: 'In Dei nomine amen ... Incipit liber Tiberiadis editus et compositus a me Bartolo de Sassoferrato in augusta civitate Perusii' (the whole tract, but mutile at the and); KBR, II, 1442, fol. 224ra: 'Incipit liber quod dicitur Tiberiadis domini Bartoli de Saxo Ferrato' (the whole tract); Lübeck, Bibliothek der Hansestadt Lübeck ms. jur. gr. 2° 23 , fol. 149ra: 'Incipit tractatus Tyberiadis editus per excellentissimum legum doctorem dominum Bartholum de Saxoferrato civem Perusi[num]' (the whole tract); and Toledo, Biblioteca del Cabildo, ms. 28–16, fol. 164r, with a title supplied by a later hand: 'Bartholi de Saxoferrato Tyberiadis, sive de fluminibus tractatus, in tres partes divisus, scilicet de alluvione, de insula in flumine nata, de alveo fluminis' (only *De alluvione*). Trier, Stadtbibliothek ms. 975/923 (only *De alluvione*) has no title, but reads on fol. 139r: 'Explicit tractatus de alluvione. Incipit tractatus de insula'; KBR, ms. II, 3592, has no title, omits the introduction and reproduces only the commentary on *lex Adeo*. Barcelona, Archivo de la Corona de Aragón, ms. Ripoll 67, fol. 30v; Cues, Bernkastel, ms. 257, fol. 124ra; Munich, Bayerische Staatsbibliothek, Cod. Lat. 6636, fol. 241ra; and Melk, Stiftungbibliothek, ms. 1882, fol. 1ra (all transmitting the whole tract), have no title.

[86] Bartolus hesitated when declining the word *Tiberis*. In the first line of the holograph the form *Tiberis* is a correction. The earlier form, which is now hard to read, might have been *Tiberim*. It is likely that Barolus inserted the word 'flumen' after 'iuxta' and, as a consequence, 'Tiberim' had to be changed to 'Tiberis'.

[87] *Tiberiadis* lines 3–12.

[88] Papias, *Vocabulista*, 351. In *De insula* Bartolus made a brief reference to the way Scripture refers to the Sea of Galilee (*mare Galilee*) and noted that properly speaking it is a lake, not a sea; see *De fluminibus seu Tyberiadis*, 54.

[89] Bartolus cited Papias, usually together with Huguccius, on all the etymologies

it is difficult to say whether Bartolus had Papias's entry in mind. Nonetheless, note that the first section of *Tiberiadis* contains a reference to the *lacus Perusinus* (now Lake Trasimeno) and the fishing rights Perugia had on it, and that Bartolus extolled the salubrity of the territory around Perugia in the opening lines of this tract.[90] Very likely, it is the lexicon of the New Testament that, because of assonance, makes its way into Bartolus's geography of Central Italy. The New Testament, a text Barolus knew very well, refers to the Sea of Galilee as *mare Galileae quod est Tiberiadis* (Jh.6:1) and *mare Tiberiadis* (Jh.21:1).

If geography, not the microcosm of political entities, gives unity to a region, it is perhaps misleading to consider *Tiberiadis* a self-standing tract. The last two years of Bartolus's life saw an astonishing output of tracts. His monumental commentary on the *Digest* and *Code* was finished, and his juridical gaze could turn to problems that could not be adequately addressed in his lectures or *repetitiones*. In the late summer of 1355, after his return from Pisa, he produced the tracts *On Insignia and Coats of Arms* and *Tiberiadis*, immediately followed by *On Guelphs and Ghibellines*, *On the Government of the City*, *On Tyranny*, and *On Witnesses*. In addition, he wrote several *consilia*, two substantive *repetitiones*, and an extensive commentary on two imperial constitutions promulgated by Henry VII (*Ad reprimendum* and *Qui sint rebelles*).[91] Especially the tracts pose a question: are they monadic entities or are they linked by something more than the happenstance of chronology? In charting the terrain beyond chronology one may fall into the fatal error of attributing to the author a plan that exists only as an invention of retrospective consistency. With this caveat in mind, it is nonetheless possible to suggest how a series of tracts are related by more than recurring themes. The thematic connections between these seemingly disparate tracts are in fact many. For our purpose, two examples linking *Tiberiadis* to *Tractatus testimoniorum* (*On Witnesses*), which is examined in its own right by Susanne Lepsius in the next essay, should suffice.

Alluviums occur by infinitesimal increments that cannot be perceived by the eye—just like the growth of a gourd, to use the example given by the *Glossa*, so that no matter how intently one looks at that plant, one cannot see it growing.[92] For the jurist, then, the question becomes how a person can testify that an increment was alluvial, if that infinitesimal increment cannot be perceived. Leaving aside Bartolus's solution (he

---

that are found in *Tiberiadis*. See *Tiberiadis* lines 161–163 for *mons*; 186–188 for *planities*; 255–256 for *platea*; and *De fluminibus seu Tyberidis*, 99 for *alveus*.

[90] *Tiberiadis* lines 8–12, 3–8.
[91] Calasso, 'Bartolo da Sassoferrato,' 643.
[92] Glossa *Momento temporis* ad D. 41.1.7.1.

recognized the validity of such testimony, for only the river itself could have produced an alluvial deposit), we can see that this question led him to consider two cases where the key to their solution comes, so to speak, by the exclusion of other possible causes: in the absence of factual evidence or sensorial perception presumptive knowledge may serve as proof.[93] If the subject of the secret meeting of a city council is revealed, and during the meeting only one person has left the city hall, one may presume that this person made the disclosure.[94] In a more elaborate way the problem of how to assess a witness's testimony or a proof that is not based on sensorial perception was amply discussed in his unfinished tract *On Witnesses*.[95]

Similarly, the mysterious figure who appeared to Bartolus in a dream, in an attempt to overcome the dreamer's initial reluctance, evokes the specter of lack of 'fortitude.'[96] After this brief but resolutive appearance, as one of the four cardinal virtues fortitude reappears in the tract *On Witnesses*. Its role is of paramount importance, for, as Bartolus said, 'sometimes there is a desire to do what one knows is good, but for simple fear or fear of toil one desists from pursuing it.' Hence the necessity of fortitude.[97] Of the four virtues he announced he would illustrate (*De qualibet ergo singulariter videamus*), he succeeded in discussing only one, prudence; death prevented him from illustrating the remaining three.

---

[93] Presumptive knowledge plays an important role in the tract *On Guelphs and Ghibellines*. If belonging to the Guelph or Ghibelline party is an *affectio* or *partialitas*, to use Bartolus's terminology, how can a 'passion' or a movement of the soul be proved? Should one who says he has changed his mind and crossed over to the other party be believed? In these cases, an intervening external cause may give a clue to an internal change. For the relevant text of this criterion (*superveniente causa*), see Bartolus de Saxoferrato, *De Guelphis et Gebellinis*, lines 291–322, ed. by Quaglioni, *Politica e diritto*, 145–146.

[94] *Tiberiadis* lines 477–495 for the whole argumentation and the other analogous example of the guardian placed next to a sealed door for a while. If thereafter the seals are found broken and there is evidence that no other person has entered or exited the house, the rupture of the seals may be imputed to the guardian.

[95] The edition of this tract, accompanied by an extensive discussion of the dogmatic aspects of Bartolus's doctrine on witnesses, has been made by Lepsius, *Der Richter und die Zeugen*, 233–328, for the edition. On this tract, see also Quaglioni, *Civilis sapientia*, 107–125.

[96] *Tiberiadis* lines 25–31.

[97] Bartolus de Saxoferrato, *Tractatus testimoniorum*, ed. by Lepsius, 280, s.v. *Virtutum*: 'Quandoque est aliquis appetitus, per quem quis ab eo, quod bonum cognoscit, desistit propter timorem vel laborem et ad hunc appetitum nostrum refrenandum alia virtus necessaria est, scilicet fortitudo: hec vera sunt et legibus comprobantur. De qualibet ergo singulariter videamus.'

In contrast, the links between *Tiberiadis*, on one side, and *On Guelphs and Ghibellines* and *On the Government of the City*, on the other, are more visible. In their opening sections, these last two tracts look back at *Tiberiadis* and can be regarded as stages in an imaginary trip through the region Bartolus called *Tiberiadis*, or along the Tiber from Perugia to Rome. *Tiberiadis*, in this sense, provides the imaginary setting for the following two tracts. The first stage is the tract *On Guelphs and Ghibellines*, and its geopolitical center is the city of Todi, about forty kilometers downstream from Perugia. There is no need to suppose, as Marongiu does, that Bartolus took an actual trip to Todi to gather materials for *Tiberiadis*, or for *On Guelphs and Ghibellines*.[98] In *Tiberiadis* there is neither a reference to an actual trip to Todi nor a hint that particular problems related to that city had been included. On the contrary, the opening lines of *On Guelphs and Ghibellines* show that the third section of *Tiberiadis*, *De alveo*, had just been finished.[99]

Yet Bartolus was familiar with the political situation in Todi, for he served there as an assistant judge (*adsessor*) of the *podestà* before beginning his academic activity.[100] As his *consilia* show, moreover, he was up-to-date on what was happening in Todi.[101] The expression 'I found myself near the city of Todi' [*repperi me ... prope civitatem Tudertinam*] does not refer to his body but to his 'mind' [*animus*]—as the two words (*meus animus*) immediately preceding the expression *repperi* imply. The final stage of this mental voyage was the city of Rome, the *caput mundi*—a theme already echoed in the preface to *Tiberiadis*.[102] Just as Bartolus did not travel to Todi before writing *On Guelphs and Ghibellines*, so he did not travel to Rome to collect data for his *On the Government of the City*. The flow of the Tiber brought him back to the place from which the river of law originated.[103] The circle was closed.

---

[98] Marongiu, 'Il regime bipartitico,' 2:335.

[99] Bartolus de Saxoferrato, *De Guelphis et Gebellinis*, lines 2–7, ed. by Quaglioni, *Politica e diritto*, 131: 'Ista cum circa litteralem expositionem scripsissem et super hanc tertiam partem Tyberiadis meus animus ferretur, repperi me infra centesimum lapidem ab urbe Romana prope civitatem Tudertinam, ibique vidi quod ea que litteraliter scripta sunt de flumine et eius alveo allegorice et moraliter dici possunt de hiis, que in civitate Tudertina precipue frequentantur.'

[100] Calasso, 'Bartolo da Sassoferrato,' 641. Baldus *ad legem Prius est* (C. 9.1.1), s.f.: 'Quarta est opinio Bartoli, qui fuit homo multum inherens practice, et fuit adsessor primo Tuderti, postea Pisis.'

[101] Bartolus, *Commentaria*, vol. 9, fol. 4v, cons. no. 7; fols. 5v–6r, cons. no. 10; fol. 26v, cons. no. 85; fol. 32rv, cons. no. 101; fols. 47v–48r, cons. no. 155; fol. 52r, cons. no. 169, fols. 52v–53r, cons. no. 172; fol. 60v, cons. no. 199; and fol. 69v, cons. no. 249.

[102] *Tiberiadis* lines 4–5.

[103] Ibid., lines 37–39.

The opening lines of the tract *On Guelphs and Ghibellines* show that it was written immediately after the third section of *Tiberiadis* was finished. The adjective *ista* refers to what was said in *De alveo* and, in its awkwardness, indicates that the ink of *Tiberiadis* had not yet dried.[104] The changes occurring in a riverbed prompted Bartolus to consider the legal implications of switching political affiliations, which occurred repeatedly in Todi. Medieval doctrine of textual interpretation ensured a smooth transition between such diverse tracts: from the literal exposition of a fragment of Roman law, he shifted to its allegorical interpretation.[105] The materiality of a river, flowing water, became a metaphor of human life: just as a river abandons its old bed and takes up a new one, so the men of Todi change their political affiliations. From now on, the discourse becomes political and it will remain on that level until the completion of the tract *On Tyranny*. The final stage of his voyage along the river was Rome. The opening section of *On the Government of the City* makes clear that, though not so elaborately as in the preceding tract, the idea of undertaking the same voyage is still present. The first sentence is clear but grammatically awkward: Bartolus has reached the last part of the Tiber.[106] Once he reached Rome, he could change his focus and encompass a wider territory, 'the whole Italy' full of tyrants—the ending of *On the Government of the City* introduces the next topic: tyranny.[107]

The introduction to the tract *On Tyranny* suggests that the previous series of works did constitute a unity: 'most pleasing subjects' [*dulcissimas materias*] satisfying both body and mind.[108] Though this flashback may

---

[104] Bartolus de Saxoferrato, *De Guelphis et Gebellinis*, lines 2–7, ed. by Quaglioni, *Politica e diritto*, 131. For the full text, see above note 99.

[105] Ibid., lines 5–9: 'vidi quod ea que litteraliter scripta sunt de flumine et eius alveo allegorice et moraliter dici possunt de his, que in civitate Tudertina precipue frequentantur. Nam tota nostra vita flumen seu aqua fluminis est, iuxta illud: 'Omnes morimur et quasi aque dilabimur in terram, que non revertuntur."

[106] Bartolus de Saxoferrato, *De regimine civitatis*, lines 2–3, ed. by Quaglioni, *Politica e diritto*, 149: 'Quia hec ultima pars Tyberis † et sic in urbe Romana, que caput est mundi.' Following ms. Cambridge, Mass., Harvard Law School Library, 75, fol. 72v, this last sentence may be read as: 'Quia hec est ultima pars Tyberis, et sic in urbe Romana, que caput est mundi.'

[107] Ibid., lines 480–483, p. 170: 'Et quia hodie Ytalia est tota plena tyrannis, ideo de tyranno aliqua ad iuristas spectantia videamus.'

[108] Bartolus de Saxoferrato, *De tyranno*, lines 2–4, ed. by Quaglioni, *Politica e diritto*, 175: 'Quia iam dudum in multis tractatibus laboravi dulcissimas materias pertractando, que corpus, cor et animam reddiderunt totaliter saporosam, sum adeo mellifluo sapore repletus.' Note that the authenticity of the introductory section of *De tyranno* is questionable and some manuscripts omit it. See, for instance, ms. Milan, Biblioteca Ambrosiana, I 249 inf., fols. 515v; and ms. Harvard Law School Library, 75, fol. 69v, which were unknown to Quaglioni when he prepared his path

well be vague, alluvial deposits and veiled or concealed tyranny share a common trait: both are phenomena difficult to prove; for, according to medieval standards regulating judicial proof, it is required that the depositions of a witness should be based on sensorial perception. But the human eye cannot perceive the infinitesimal increments by which alluvial deposits occur. Similarly, that one is an occult tyrant (*velatus tyrannus*) cannot be proved easily, for he neither acts openly nor goes frequently to the communal palace, rather he makes known his wishes and gives his orders by letters or messengers.[109] In *Tiberiadis* Bartolus established on solid juridical grounds the depositions of peasants attesting that the deposited soil was an alluvial increment and thus caused by nothing else but the river itself.[110] In *De tyranno*, building on the solution he had advanced in *Tiberiadis*, he addressed the issue of proving or damasking concealed tyranny. Canon law had considered the case of proving that a person belongs to the so-called *potentes* and, when summoned to court together with another party, that party may have cause to fear the adversary's power. According to canon lawyers the summoned party, under oath, may adduce fear (*perhorrescentia*) and be excused from appearing.[111] As Bartolus aptly observed, that oath has a limited effect: it proves only the psychological status[112] (*animus*) of the summoned party and does not incriminate the *potens* in any way.[113] Consequently, another form of proof had to be sought. Recalling the first section of *Tiberiadis*, Bartolus granted that there are deeds that cannot be proved directly (*per se probari non potest*). The infinitesimal increments of fluvial deposits cannot be seen, yet there is no doubt the river caused the deposit. Similarly, the paternity of a child (*filii generatio*) may be doubted. Yet if a child is born to cohabiting husband and wife the law presumes that the child is theirs and, for the jurists, this constitutes a full

---

breaking edition. For the remaining manuscripts omitting the introductory section, see Quaglioni, *Politica e diritto*, 108–113. If one considers the problems Bartolus discussed in *On Guelphs and Ghibellines* and *On the Government of the City* with attention, it is very difficult to see how the subject matter of these two tracts can be qualified as 'most pleasing subjects.'

[109] Ibid., lines 702–704, p. 210: 'Sed qualiter poterit hoc probari, cum talis sic velatus tyrannus per se non facit, in palatio raro intrat, sed suis scriptis et nunciis regimina obediunt?'

[110] *Tiberiadis* lines 477–495.

[111] On this, see *c. Statutum* (VI. 1.3.11.1).

[112] On the sufficiency of the oath to establish the psychological status (*animus*) of a person, see Philippus Probus *Additiones* ad Johannes Monacus, *Glossa aurea*, fol. 38v, n. 33.

[113] Bartolus de Saxoferrato, *De tyranno*, lines 704–705, ed. by Quaglioni, *Politica e diritto*, 210: 'Ei autem contra quem iuratur nullum aliud preiudicium generatur.'

proof (*plena probatio*). Accordingly, if there is proof that a city is divided (and by chance that one party has been expelled), that enormous crimes are committed but are not punished, that the citizens are severely oppressed and that the person having the lawful title to rule is the most powerful person in that city—all this constitutes a sufficient proof of tyranny. For such deeds cannot have been performed by anybody else in the city but the tyrant himself.[114] Both alluvial increments accrued to fields and the existence of a veiled tyrant is proved in the same manner—that is, indirectly and by the exclusion of any other possible cause.

Each stage of the voyage presents a peculiar set of problems: Todi and *On Guelphs and Ghibellines*, that of a government based on two warring factions concomitantly ruling the city; Rome and *On the Government of the City*, that of baronial factionalism; and *On Tyranny*, to include it among the others, that of a whole region plagued by tyrants. *Tiberiadis* is no less concerned with the political life of the city than the three later tracts, though tradition has conferred on it the title *De fluminibus* (a tract on 'environmental problems,' to use modern terminology).[115] The sight of the Tiber gave Bartolus the idea of a tract on rivers. As he was completing the tract, he commenced his imaginary trip along the Tiber and through the region he called *Tiberiadis*. With the lapse of time, the factual questions with which he began his inquiry had mushroomed into a tract of over one hundred pages. When he wrote the preface, he realized that he had gone well beyond the discussion of issues related to rivers and, at the last moment, adjusted his focus accordingly: '[I intend] to discuss not only the Tiber but also the many problems occurring in the region of the Tiber.'[116] By adjusting the focus and entitling the work *Tiberiadis*, he widened the horizon.

The running commentary on *lex Adeo* touches upon a wide spectrum of issues ranging from jurisdiction to witnesses; and from customs to matters of criminal law, including questions on how to interpret municipal statutes. The juridical life of the city and questions arising from urban and rural situations, notarial practices, and a considerable number of definitions (e.g., flatland, hill, mountain, valley, river, and torrent) are as important as

---

[114] Ibid., lines 711–730, pp. 210–211.

[115] Just as Todi and Rome were the geopolitical centres of *On Guelphs and Ghibellines* and *On the Government of the City*, Perugia may be regarded as the center of *Tiberiadis*, which, indeed contains several references to Perugia. See, for instance, *Tiberiadis* lines 8–12, and 446–448, for the 'lacus Perusinus' (Lake Trasimeno); and also, for the section *De insula*, see *De fluminibus seu Tyberiadis*, 90–92, for a case prompted by the statutes of Perugia.

[116] *Tiberiadis* lines 36–37. Note that this sentence is a marginal addition and, very likely, was not in the first draft of the introduction.

the allocation of alluvial deposits.[117] The literary genre of the commentary gave Bartolus endless possibilities to explore and address such issues. Indeed, he had more freedom than in his lectures, as he was unconstrained by space or time or by Gaius's seminal text. Do alluvial increments add or detract[118] from the territorial jurisdiction of a city, diocese, or barony? What are the different meanings of the term 'jurisdiction'? How should one construe its relational nature?[119] Does that term pertain to 'public law' [*ius publicum*] and, if so, how? As something that can be used by everybody (*publicus usus*) or as something that a city possesses as private entity and can be used only by those who have the permission to do so from the city? The jurist's distinction between *ius publicum* and *publicus usus* requires a brief explanation. That any person, including foreigners, can petition a magistrate for justice, exemplifies the *publicus usus* of jurisdiction—that is, what we would call 'right' to justice. Fines and the revenues of the confiscation of the goods of the rebels exemplify the 'private' [*ea que civitas possidet ut privatus*] or municipal dimension of jurisdiction.[120]

Beyond jurisdiction, the commentary touches upon other issues. Does the law on alluvial deposits apply to the soil a river added to a religious

---

[117] *Tiberiadis* lines 157–205 for the definitions. Legally relevant, these definitions have attracted the attention of owners and users of manuscripts; see, for instance, KBR, II, 3592, fol. 183r; and Seville, Biblioteca Colombina, ms. 83-8-13, fol. 160rb, where all the definitions are marked on the margins. All the definitions Bartolus gave were taken over entirely by Cipolla in his tract *De servitutibus rusticorum praediorum*, fol. 236ra, no. 1, for *mons*; fol. 237ra, no. 1–2, for *collis*; fol. 237rab, no. 1–4, for *vallis*; fol. 242rab, no. 1–3, for *torrens*. The discussion of terms like 'mountain' (*mons*) and 'hill' (*collis*) is related to changes in agricultural practices and the consequent alterations of the landscape. On how agriculture affected the landscape from the Middle Ages to the Renaissance, see Sereni, *Storia del paesaggio agrario*, 132–142, and 198–226 for the degradation of the territory caused by deforestation.

[118] On the whole issue of borders and their legal construction by the jurists of the *ius commune*, see Marchetti, '*De iure finium*,' especially pp. 187–199 for Bartolus's *Tiberiadis*.

[119] *Tiberiadis* lines 410–457. On the concept of jurisdiction, see Costa, '*Iurisdictio*,' 119–120, and 161–164, for Bartolus. For the father's jurisdiction within his family, see Quaglioni, '*Quilibet in domo sua dicitur rex*,' 344–358. Note that in *Tiberiadis* Bartolus stressed the relational nature of the father's jurisdiction and pointed out that sons (and daughters) have the 'right' to ask for 'support' (*alimenta*). Reciprocity is also fundamental in the public sphere: the subjects have the right to ask for justice and, if their demands go unanswered, their superior may be punished by an higher authority.

[120] For the *iura civilia*, the protection to which a citizen was entitled, see *Tiberiadis* lines 371–373. Another example of something Perugia possessed 'ut privatus' was the authority to grant the license to fish in Lake Trasimeno. On the revenues of the lake, see Regni, 'La *comunantia fructus aque lacus*,' 157–217.

or public place, like a cemetery or square?[121] How should a judge assess the testimony of a farmer on alluvium,[122] when this natural phenomenon cannot be perceived by sight? And, by extension, how much weight should be given to a statement on an event that is not apprehended by a sensorial perception but is the result of an inference of the mind? Questions of criminal law are also discussed, often in connection with the formulations adopted by municipal statutes. For instance, suppose that the statutes punish crimes that occurred in the plains of the Tiber. What if a crime is committed on its banks or an alluvial deposit? Does it fall under the statute? In contrast to a litigation on ownership, Bartolus construed his interpretation of the wording of the statutes so as to allow the prosecution of the crime.[123] There is also an autobiographical reference to the time Bartolus spent in Pisa, first as a judge, then as a professor, and to what he saw of the local marble quarries.[124]

Let us consider briefly the part containing the figures. Introducing geometry into a field like law, a remarkable novelty, and illustrating it with concrete examples, constitute the core of the second part of *De alluvione*. Yet Bartolus, in an attempt to show how geometry can be useful in other situations, leaves the banks of a river and reverts to the city, presenting a question that could fall under the literary genre of *quaestiones statutorum*.[125]

Suppose that the statutes establish the penalty of capital punishment for any damage done to property valued more than ten florins.[126] Now

---

[121] *Tiberiadis* lines 259–271.

[122] Ibid., lines 477–488.

[123] Ibid., lines 211–235.

[124] Ibid., lines 324–327; and the glossa *Flumina* ad Inst. 2.1.2.

[125] Such 'practical' questions were the main concern of the scribe who copied the text transmitted by ms. BAV, Vat. lat. 2625, fols. 136r–146v. He omitted entirely the second part of *De alluvione* and *De insula* containing the geometrical figures. Yet he transcribed Bartolus's discussion concerning the instruments of division of property and summarized the case of the barrel of wine (fols. 140v–141r) found at the end of *De alluvione*. Then he inserted (fol. 141rv) Bartolus's discussion of the term *caput* (the head, beginning, origin), which is found in *De insula*, before transcribing the second section of the tract. Moreover, after transcribing *De alveo*, he inserted (fol. 146v) Bartolus's discussion of the term *civitas* (city), which is found in *De insula*. Finally, he appended half of Bartolus's *repetitio ad legem Quominus* (D. 43.12.2). On the literary genre of the *quaestiones*, see Fransen, *Les questions disputées*, 225–277; Kantorowicz, 'The *Quaestiones disputatae*,' 1–65; and Bellomo, *I fatti e il diritto*.

[126] *Tiberiadis* lines 1103–1134; and also lines 1049–1070, for the case of the pact between the two owners of two mills and the proper placement of the water ducts. Bartolus presented this case as a 'questionem ocurrentem de facto.' A similar issue is discussed in his *repetito ad legem Quominus* (D. 43.12.2), see *Commentaria*, vol.

one breaks into a house and destroys a barrel of wine of which only one stave remains. Given that on the quality of the wine there are no doubts, the only question is that of determining the capacity of the barrel and thus whether the damage exceeds the amount established by the statute. Resorting to two geometrical demonstrations, Bartolus shows how to calculate the circumference of the broken barrel starting from the remaining stave. Once the circumference is determined, the calculation of the capacity of the barrel can be performed by any of the city's land surveyors, including the small adjustments required by its convexity.[127] Besides, there is a relevant discussion on how to interpret the wording of instruments of division of property, a problem Bartolus had seen occurring—for instance, when the expression 'right ahead' [*per directum*] had been employed.[128] Although staying in a villa in the countryside, he was occupied with the dispositions of municipal statutes.[129]

The application of geometry to daily problems, for instance, drawing a straight line across a piece of land up to the river, leads to a discussion of the customary practices of peasants and their ways of marking the borders between fields, accompanied by a criticism of the way in which notaries drafted their instruments of division of landed property and recorded the boundaries.[130] Attention is also paid to the way in which locals named places, mountains or hills, and an acceptance of those local practices.[131] In view of the role the *rustici* played in *Tiberiadis*, it seems possible to say that from a legal point of view there is a 'reevaluation' of this social group deeply distrusted by the inhabitants of the city.[132]

Beyond *De alluvione*, in the last three figures of *De insula* Bartolus abandons once more the river and returns to a set of 'factual problems emerging almost daily' [*questiones quotidianas et de facto emergentes*],

---

5, fols. 155rb–157ra.

[127] On the mathematical rules used by the city surveyors to calculate the capacity of a barrel, see Simi, 'Regole per la determinazione della capacità delle botti,' 391–414, with an ample bibliography on the mathematical and empirical rules for determining the capacity of a barrel; and Baxandall, *Painting and Experience*, 86–93.

[128] *Tiberiadis* lines 1071–1100.

[129] Tellingly, ms. BAV, Vat. lat. 2625, where the scribe entirely omitted the two sections on geometry of *De alluvione* and *De insula*, has preserved the *quaestio* on the broken barrel of wine, for the reason that it was meaningful to a jurist, see fol. 141r. Similarly, this manuscript has also preserved (fol. 140v) the discussion on the proper drafting of instruments concerning the division of property that Bartolus inserted in the second part of *De alluvione*.

[130] *Tiberiadis* lines 1071–1100. For the 'description of boundaries' as a semiotic system, see Lagazzi, 'I segni sulla terra,' 13–29; and Lagazzi, *Segni sulla terra*.

[131] *Tiberiadis* lines 180–181, 193–194, 204–205.

[132] On this distrust and the cunning of peasants, which was even a literary topos, see Mazzi and Raveggi, *Gli uomini e le cose*, 15–34.

prompted by Perugia's statutes requiring that any parcel of land not belonging to a town or village (*castrum vel villa*) be assigned to the nearest town or village.[133] If there is only one inhabited center, the implementation of the statute presents no obstacles; the situation becomes more complex when there are several centers near the unclaimed land. Geometry offers a way to divide that land equitably among the neighboring centers. Moreover, the commentary on *lex Adeo* of *De insula* contains substantive discussions prompted by words of the Roman fragment and with no immediate relation to the changes occurring in a river. The term *nullius* (belonging to nobody) leads into a discussion of newly occupied lands, legislation and jurisdiction; the term *media pars* (the middle), into an analysis of how the term *capud* is used with reference to persons, institutions, time, and place; and the term *latus* (the side), into a discussion of the vocabulary used to denote directions, such as 'above' and 'below,' 'left' and 'right.'[134] Similarly, in *De alveo* the term *incipit* (begins) leads into a discussion of the different ways in which expressions such as 'to begin' and 'to end' are used; and the term *stricta ratione* (strictly speaking) leads into a philosophically flavored discussion of the relationship between form and substance.[135] For Bartolus, the analysis of the meaning of words was no mere exercise in lexicography or display of erudition; it impinged on the interpretation of statutes and legal instruments drafted by notaries. The flexibility of the commentary is certainly the main reason for this series of excursuses. But considering them digressions would prevent us from seeing the flow of Bartolus's thoughts and understanding *Tiberiadis* as an exercise in legal geography.

If Bartolus fixed his juridical gaze upon the Tiber Valley, it was not to impose law on the surrounding world. He wished instead to derive from social practices and customs legal norms or elements that could be useful to lawyers and judges to settle legal problems. As Paolo Grossi has pointed out, medieval jurisprudence shifted its focus from the sovereign owner to the thing itself; from the rights of the owner to the economical relationship between person and thing—a relationship shaped by time and work.[136] Tellingly, while the 'owners' of Tiberiadis never go beyond

---

[133] *De fluminibus seu Tyberiadis*, 90–96. The purpose of assigning a piece of unclaimed land to a specific community was to make that land available and ready for cultivation; on this practice, see *Statuto del Comune di Perugia*, 1:312–315, chapters 329–331.

[134] *De fluminibus seu Tyberiadis*, 55–60, 62–65, and 69–75.

[135] Ibid., pp. 102–106, and 109–115. On this philosophical excursus, see Walther, 'Wasser in Stadt und Contado,' 893–896.

[136] On this, which is working with what Paolo Grossi has aptly called 'le situazioni reali,' see his *Le situazioni reali*, 67–128, and 153–159 for Bartolus's construction of ownership.

the stereotypical names of Lutius, Tititus, Caius, and Sempronius, the land acquires a material consistency that can be manipulated by geometry. The agrarian world—in particular the reality of a not-yet-owned alluvial deposit, an island born in the middle of a stream, or an abandoned riverbed— was a challenging situation for the jurist. How could he construe a relationship, if the thing did not exist before? Acquisition does not necessarily take the form of ownership, but follows a preexisting order or relationship with the surrounding world—that is, the already possessed field on the banks of the river. If an alluvial deposit accrues to a religious or consecrated place, for instance, a cemetery, it becomes the property of the first occupant, for the cemetery as *locus sacer* (sacred place) belongs to nobody.[137] If it accrues to a piece of land, one has to look at how the relationship between person and thing was construed. If the relationship was of ownership (*iure dominii*), the alluvial deposit takes the same status; if of *quasi-dominium*, it becomes *quasi-dominium*; if it is held as real security (*iure pignoris*), it is held under the same legal title; and, if it is just a hope of a future commodity, the new land takes the same legal configuration.[138]

Bartolus treated Gaius's seminal fragment with the same freedom with which he treated Euclid. For him, geometry was a way to rationalize the surrounding space. As a jurist, he preferred a space shaped by geometry to a discontinuous and open one, for an uninterrupted borderline, or delimitation, makes that space available to agriculture. In short, delimiting and assigning the alluvial deposit is a way to make it productive.

The paucity of details on Bartolus's life is endemic to medieval legal scholarship. His writings (commentaries, tracts, *consilia*, *repetitiones*, and *quaestiones*) are professional and rarely allow the reader to see beyond the jurist at work. Consequently, historians have seized upon each and every piece of information and assembled them to create a figure who could withstand the sharp criticism of the humanists. Knowledge of Hebrew would make him into a forerunner of scholars like Giannozzo Manetti and Giovanni Pico della Mirandola. A solid grasp of geometry would attest to his wide-ranging intellectual interests. Does *Tiberiadis*

---

[137] *Tiberiadis* lines 259–271. Similarly, a public place like a square was treated as a *res nullius*. If an alluvial deposit accrued to a square, the first occupant became the owner. By law, the *agri limitati*—that is, land, the boundaries of which were settled by land-surveyors—could not be extended on grounds of *ius alluvionis*. Typically, the newly conquered lands that the emperors distributed among soldiers as a reward belonged to this category. Since they were a token of the benevolence of the prince (*beneficium principis*), their size could not be altered. On the *agri limitati*, see *Tiberiadis* lines 384–409.

[138] Ibid., lines 236–271.

bespeak Bartolus's command of geometry? In contrast to Hebrew, the answer, for once, is positive.

Any discussion of the role of geometry in *Tiberiadis* involves a threefold set of issues: first, in chronological order, Bartolus's acquisition of that knowledge; second, how he actually used it; and, last, how it relates to law.

Despite Segoloni's careful research, Bartolus's early formation remains a mystery.[139] By his own declaration, we know that at the age of fourteen he started to attend Cynus's lectures at Perugia's university and evidently had the intellectual preparation to do so.[140] His first tutor (*magister*) was Patrus de Assisio, who imparted him 'basic instruction' [*primas literas docuit*], and it was owing to this Franciscan friar that he was able to attend the university.[141] That Petrus was instrumental in Bartolus's early formation and made a profound impression on his pupil cannot be doubted. But how much geometry, if any at all,[142] Bartolus might have learned from this remarkable friar is a matter open to conjecture. Experience of this world (*vir... expertus*)—after all, Petrus directed his pupil to the university, not to a Franciscan convent—moral integrity (*nullius hypocrisis*), and saintly life (*mire sanctitatis*) were the traits that impressed Bartolus. Erudition (*doctrina*), the aspect with which we are concerned, should not be construed too broadly, but rather as *in sacris erudiri*.[143] Even for

---

[139] Segoloni, 'Aspetti del pensiero giuridico e politico,' 640.

[140] Bartolus *ad legem Quidam cum filium* (D. 45.1.132), vol. 6, fol. 55ra, no. 8. The expression Bartolus used here to refer to his early training, 'habui unum magistrum,' does not preclude that he might have had other teachers.

[141] For the figure of Pietro of Assisi, the Franciscan friar whose memory Bartolus recalled with deep emotion when commenting on *lex Quidam cum filium* (D. 45.1.132), see Fortini, 'Frate Piero da Assisi,' 2:253–260; Ranzato, 'Cenni e documenti su Fr. Pietro d'Assisi,' 3–11. Transforming Bartolus's *primas litteras* into *artes liberales*, as Walther, for instance, does, distorts the meaning of the text; Walther, 'Wasser in Stadt und Contado,' 888.

[142] The index of the literary works compiled for Cenci's survey of two hundred and thirty years of life in Assisi may give an indication of the cultural interest of the members of the Umbrian province. The compiler lists no books on geometry and twice mentions a text on mathematics, a 'liber de abbaco', see Cenci, *Documentazione di vita assisiana*, 3:17*–22*. For a later period, the early sixteenth century, there is some evidence that such practical skills as the art of land surveying were taught: a certain 'Mag. Baldassarri geometro,' was invited to Assisi to teach his art (*agrimensuratio*); ibid., pp. 1213–1214. For the Franciscan *studium* of Perugia, which was flourishing in the early thirteenth century, and the dispositions of the Umbrian province concerning studying, see Cenci, 'Ordinazioni dei capitoli provinciali,' 5–31, especially 11. While the dispositions carefully regulate the study of theology, not much attention is given to other disciplines.

[143] For the debate on poverty and the role of the 'intellectuals' inside the

Franciscan historians, the main source of information on Petrus's activity in Perugia is Bartolus.[144] Similarly, neither Bartolus's age nor the requirements for admission to the University of Perugia should be over stressed. The age of fourteen was common for medieval students beginning their higher education, and under canon law, a boy fourteen years old could take the oath required by the process of matriculation. Moreover, except for the payment of the matriculation fee, there were no strict or specific academic requirements for admission to a medieval corporation like a *universitas* or a *studium generale*.[145]

By the beginning of the fifteenth century the situation had changed. In the age of humanism, the canonist Francesco Zabarella outlined the kind of preparation one could expect from a law student. The curriculum he delineated comprises first 'grammar school,' followed by a period of two years, or at the most three, devoted to logic and philosophy.[146] The disciplines that could be profitably studied by a would-be-lawyer in this period were logic, rhetoric, and natural and moral philosophy. Looking back at his own experience, Zabarella stated that for two years and part of the third, he studied logic and philosophy. Furthermore, he discouraged the study of other disciplines together with law, banning even books of poetry from the rooms of the students. He did not exclude that, after completing the doctoral course, the jurist could turn his attention to other fields, but the purpose was 'to appear in front of the students more learned' not to go into what we would now call an 'interdisciplinary field.' In short, the purpose of this expansion of academic interests is ostentation: 'to appear more learned,' not to be such.[147] In this system, geometry has no place. It is also very unlikely that it might have been taught during grammar school, since at this stage reading and writing were associated with mathematics or the abacus.[148]

No matter how and when Bartolus learned geometry, he realized that sciences such as geometry and medicine could be very useful to jurists

---

Franciscan order, see Jemolo, 'Il *Liber minoritarum* di Bartolo,' 29–74.

[144] Ranzato, 'Cenni e documenti,' 3–4.

[145] On the requirements for admission to a medieval university and the process of matriculation, see Schwinges, 'Admission,' 171–194. For the students of the University of Perugia, see Ermini, *Storia della Università*, 63–76.

[146] For methods and content of this grammar school, see Gehl, *A Moral Art*, 20–81. Significantly, there is no mention of studying geometry in grammar schools of the Trecento. For a more detailed description of the educational curriculum in medieval and Renaissance Italy, see Black, *Humanism and Education*, 34–172.

[147] For Zabarella's *De modo studendi*, see note 46.

[148] For instance, Francesco Guicciardini, who studied law in Florence, Pavia, and Padua, reports that before going to law school he studied some Greek, soon forgotten, the 'abacus,' which he mastered quite well, and some logic. See, Guicciardini, *Ricordanze*, 54–57.

and judges to settle *quaestiones de facto*. Following Cynus, he stated that in Roman law there were an almost infinite number of texts allowing judges to consult an expert. Physicians could be asked to settle questions on wounds and scars; doctors, that is, university professors, to attest the preparation of one of their students; masons and architects to appraise the construction of buildings; and goldsmiths to assay the quality of coins.[149] Yet, it was one thing to consult an expert and leave the final decision to the judge, and quite another to combine geometry with law to illustrate a series of principles posited by Roman law. As the oft-quoted dream shows, Bartolus knew that law ought not to be profaned; if philosophical jargon had little appeal for the jurist, that of geometry had even less.[150] He was also aware that jurists practiced a 'conservative' discipline; their attacks could be vicious and escalate from derision to verbal abuse.[151] Therefore, he resorted to geometry with a precise purpose in mind: 'to demonstrate only those things that cannot be grasped immediately'—as he stated at the beginning of the section on the geometrical figures.[152] That he used geometry with that purpose in mind is clear from his exposition of Figure 7, where he refers to the *rustici* (peasants, but also those who do not know law or geometry) and their erroneous way of dividing property. While peasants would simply prolong the borderline of two fields until it met the river, the correct line dividing the alluvial deposit should be perpendicular to the old bank of the river, that is, making two right angles.[153] In a simpler way, he illustrated a similar misconception in Figure 2, where the two angles formed by the intersection of line *lk* and line *nm* are two right angles. The figure in question should be considered in itself, not in relation to the frame of the paper on which it was drawn: the orientation of the figure does not change the nature of the two right angles.[154]

---

[149]Bartolus *ad const. Omnem* (D. prooem.), vol. 1, fol. 3r, no. 8–9. For another substantial discussion of the role of experts, especially physicians, see his *Consilia*, cons. no. 37, vol. 9, fol. 188rv. But already Diplovatazio doubted, with good reasons, Bartolus's authorship of this piece.

[150]Referring to the political philosophy of Aristotle and Egidius Romanus, Bartolus noted that, though he would use their arguments, he would not adopt their terminology: 'verbis autem suis vel Aristotelis non utar: illa enim iuriste, quibus loquor, non saperent.' For the entire passage, see Quaglioni, *Politica e diritto*, 153. In the following century, Zabarella, thinking perhaps of Baldus, expressed similar concerns: borrowing terminology from another field would confuse the students and obscure the meaning of law; see note 46.

[151]*Tiberiadis* lines 23–25.

[152]Ibid., lines 578–579: 'ideo figuras ad oculum demostrantes inserui, per quas illa sola docere intendo, que communiter ingnorantur.'

[153]Ibid., lines 756–765.

[154]Ibid., lines 625–629.

By consistently using a set of colors for the geometrical figures and alerting readers that he would give an explanation whenever he would introduce any new element or color in the figures,[155] Bartolus stressed the cognitive value of geometry. The colors differentiated between 'nature' and 'culture,' between the river and the borderlines of the fields, on one side, and the superimposed structure of geometry, on the other; and between legal reality of property and a cognitive tool. By its power to generate presumptions about reality, like the unshaped alluvial deposit, geometry becomes a cognitive tool and produces knowledge useful to a judge asked to decide a case and to a jurist asked to render an opinion. The possibilities of geometry did not prevent Bartolus from lucidly grasping its limitations, especially when faced with a complex and irregular borderline. Knowing that the border's actual configuration never conformed to the abstract patterns of geometry and that alluvial increments could take place at different times and in diverse locations, he advised jurists to reduce as much as possible the actual configuration of the borderline to a geometrical figure or a combination of figures.[156]

If his introduction of geometry was cautious, Bartolus's actual use of the Euclidean definitions and propositions shows another side of his personality: his didactic ability. Though not word-for-word, his demonstrations and definitions are very close to those found in medieval Latin translations of Euclid.[157] Not satisfied with one demonstration, he often presents alternatives: a shorter or a different way to demonstrate the same proposition.[158] The most emblematic example is that of the determination of the circumference of the broken barrel of wine (Figures 21 and 22). When explaining Figure 3 (how to divide a given line into two equal segments using a ruler or a compass), he first gives one corollary that would become handy when dividing alluvial deposits on grounds of proximity (*iure proximitatis*), and then shows how to employ the compass to make a right angle on any given line.[159] On one occasion, didactics caused him to abandon the rigorous language of geometry for an unorthodox but effective explanation: if a thread uniting two points is stretched to infinity, that would show that the entire line is straight.[160]

---

[155] Ibid., lines 717–723.
[156] Ibid., lines 1039–1048. Maddalena, *Gli incrementi fluviali*, 120–128, where resort to geometry is indicated as a criterion alien to Roman law.
[157] For the Latin translation of Euclid's *Elements*, I have used Busard, *The First Latin Translation of Euclid's Elements*; and *Robert of Chester's (?) Redaction of Euclid's Elements*.
[158] *Tiberiadis* lines 1103–1134.
[159] Ibid., lines 631–660.
[160] Ibid., lines 596–597.

If the way in which Bartolus integrated law and geometry, the extent to which he knew geometry, and the way in which he actually used it can be studied using any of the printed editions or a manuscript, there are some features that remain undisclosed unless one turns to the holograph. Over printed editions, copies, and copies of copies, the holograph has two obvious advantages. It permits us, first, to establish a better edition of the text and, second, particularly in this case, to observe how the author worked and revised his text. Two examples of the readings of the original manuscript will suffice. As a term of comparison, I cite the edition prepared by Bottrigari who, by his own declaration, restored the text as well as possible. The first example is as follows. The gentle and mysterious figure who appeared to Bartolus in a dream speaks in this way: 'Ecce aportavi tibi calamum quo scribas, circinum quo mensures et figuras fatias circulares et lineam qua lineas ducas figurasque formes' [Look, I brought you a reed pen for writing, a compass for measuring and drawing circular figures, and a ruler for drawing straight lines and making the figures].[161] The printed edition, as well as some manuscripts, owing to homoeoteleuton, reads instead: 'Ecce apportavi tibi calamum quo mensuras et figuras facies circulares, et regulam qua lineas ducas figurasque formes.'[162] Leaving aside the *linea* turned into *regula*, unless one is a Giotto, it is quite difficult to draw a circular figure freehand. The second example is this. The same person, in an attempt to persuade a reluctant Bartolus to start writing, says: 'qui benefatientes non curaverunt contumelias, derisiones et verbera' [the saints and Christ himself] did not mind verbal abuse, mockery, and flogging].[163] In the printed edition the word *verbera* becomes a pleonastic *verba iniuriosa* and Bartolus's crescendo—from verbal abuse (*contumelia*), to mockery (*derisio*), to being flogged or beaten—disappears, leaving us just a river of words.

Was Bartolus, as a tradition going back to Diplovatazio has it, a jurist focused on problems and oblivious to precise and pertinent citations of Roman law? I think not, for in *De alluvione* I have found only two *leges* misquoted. While citing almost literally *lex Adeo*, § *Insula*,[164] he gave as a reference *lex Inter eos* (D. 41. 1.29). The cited text is from the Roman

---

[161] Ibid., lines 21–23.

[162] Prague, ms. a. 5, fol. 11rab: 'ecce apportavi calamum tibi quo mensures et figuras facies et lineam qua duces figuras et formas'; KBR, II, 1442, fol. 224rb: 'ecce apportavi tibi calamum quo [me. *del.*] mensures et figuras facias circulares et lineam quia linea ducas figuras que formas'; Cues, ms. 257, fol. 124ra: 'Ecce apportavi tibi calamum quo mensures et figuras facias circulares et lineam qua linea ducas figurasque formes.'

[163] *Tiberiadis* line 28.

[164] D. 41.1.7.3: 'pro modo latitudinis cuiusque praedii, que latitudo prope ripam sit.' Bartolus, citing by memory, omits 'cuiusque praedii'; *Tiberiadis* lines 740–741.

jurist Gaius and states the criteria for dividing an island born in the middle of a river: if it lies in the midstream, it belongs to those who have holdings on the banks to the extent that their holdings follow the bank. The reference is to Paulus and addresses the same issue: each of the owners will hold to the extent that each held the bank, as if a straight line were drawn through the island. In view of Bartolus's argument, both texts are pertinent; for in Figure 6 the criterion for the division is the extent to which each owner holds the bank. Since both texts considered the extent to which the owners held the bank, the confusion between the two texts is somewhat understandable. Another miscited allegation of Roman law is *lex Si ego*, § *Quod tamen* (D. 6. 2.11.7). Instead of this fragment Bartolus quoted the following one, *lex Si sponsus* (D. 6.2.12);[165] nonetheless, the reference to the paragraph (*Quod tamen*) is correct. If one other citation got scrambled, that is, § 1 of the title *De iure personarum* (Inst. 1.3.1) and *lex Libertas* of the title *De statu hominum* (D. 1.5.4), the reason was that the wording of the two fragments is the same.[166] Since these three miscited passages appear in all manuscripts and printed editions, it is certain that the text saw no further revisions. Whether three miscitations are many or few is a matter of opinion; but one should avoid applying modern standards of accuracy to the composition of texts that largely relied on memory.[167] The slur that Bartolus had a feeble memory and was oblivious to precise citation, and that he regularly concocted a problem and its solution, but then had to rely on his colleague, Francesco Tigrini, for the exact citations or supporting laws, does not find support in the holograph of *Tiberiadis*.

At the risk of establishing a new myth, the overall impression one has from studying the holograph (especially the small corrections and erased words) is that his hand could not keep up with the speed of his mind. Before completing a sentence, he tends to begin the next one. Then, he has to turn back, delete the new sentence and finish the old one. Among several instances of this 'running forward' to the next sentence or concept, one should be pointed out. When explaining Figure 13, Bartolus stated that there are two ways to draw a line from the circumference of a circle

---

[165] *Tiberiadis* line 239.

[166] Both fragments, D. 1.5.4 and Inst. 1.3.1, have: 'nisi si quid vi aut iure prohibetur.' To indicate the supporting Roman fragment Bartolus used the expression 'ut supra.' It is likely therefore that the reference should be to the *Digest* rather than the *Institutes*. See *Tiberiadis* line 504.

[167] Especially in the case of the so-called direct citation, one should be aware of the distinction between the simple reciting, which is the word-for-word repetition of a text, and retaining and speaking, or *sententialiter recitare*, which is citing a text according to its meaning. On the role of memory in medieval culture, see Carruthers, *The Book of Memory*, especially pp. 189–220, for memory and authority.

right to its center or, in other words, two ways to determine the location of the unknown center of a circle. When explaining Figure 16, in what seems to be a blatant contradiction, he stated that there are three ways to perform the same operation. A note on the margin, 'immo duplex' [on the contrary, a twofold way], points out the blunder. Yet the next sentence explains why such an error occurred: given that there are four owners involved, three perpendicular lines should be drawn to the circular line representing the old bank of the river, that is, to the black borderline between the field of Lutius and Titius, Titius and Gaius, and Gaius and Seius.[168] Precision in language is a salient feature of his writing. After the expression 'questions arising from,' he added 'de facto'. Indeed, all the questions related to the allocation of alluvial deposits are questions de facto, not de jure.[169] Guido de Perusio stopped at Bartolus's villa not for a day, but for twenty-four hours (*unum diem integrum nauralem*).[170] Pleonastic expressions, for instance, *inquid* or *dum ait* (the text says, where the text says) inserted after the citation of the Roman law fragments he was about to explain, were all deleted.[171] After defining a mountain as an 'elevated place' [*locus altus*], he added in the margin 'de magna altitudine': the elevation must be great to distinguish mountains from hills.[172] A long-winded expression as 'tale quod totum potest quodammodo dici' [such that in some ways it could be called] was deleted and the three adjectives linked with a simple conjunction (*vel*).[173] Precision also extends to citations of Roman law: a (wrong) reference to the title *De acquirendo rerum domino* (D. 40.1) was deleted and replaced with the right one, *De damno infecto* (D. 39.2).[174] Citations of Roman law and references to the *Glossa* are also pertinent and to the point. After discussing the wording of a statute punishing crimes perpetrated in the plains adjacent to the Tiber, Bartolus took up the question of a crime committed on the banks of the river. Then he inserted a reference to *lex Recte dicimus*—pertinent, at least in an analogical way, for it establishes that polluting the water of a well makes one liable, just as if the fresh water of a field had been polluted or tampered with.[175] The misnumbered figures were, in the end, corrected; and the wrongly drawn figure, too, was corrected not by redrawing it, but in an elegant marginal note calling

---

[168] *Tiberiadis* lines 972–974.
[169] Ibid., line 16.
[170] Ibid., line 46.
[171] Ibid., line 81 note 20; line 236 note 67; line 272 note 77, line 353 note 102; line 371 note 106; line 374 notes 107 and 108.
[172] Ibid., line 161.
[173] Ibid., line 143 note 38.
[174] Ibid., line 76.
[175] Ibid., lines 228–230 note 66.

attention to the error.[176] Lastly, the wrong cross-references to the figures were corrected and the corresponding number given in a marginal note.[177]

Substantial additions, running for several lines in the margins, are always relevant, allowing us to see how his thoughts developed. A discussion of the legal status of the ditches and slopes adjacent to a road concluded with the unsatisfactory expression 'for the same reason' [*eadem ratione*].[178] Properly, the slope between a ditch and the adjacent road belongs neither to the road, for it is untransitable, nor to the owner of the adjacent field, for he already owns the slope adjacent to his field. Therefore, Bartolus inserted a passage explaining why, in his opinion, that piece of land should be treated and considered as if it were in the public domain.

All the marginal additions and corrections found in the holograph appear as an integral part of the text in the whole manuscript tradition. Conversely, except for scribal errors, homoeoteleutons, and the decision of the copyist to suppress parts of the tract, or to cut and paste the material, the manuscript tradition shows that Bartolus made no further changes to the text of *De alluvione*.[179] The holograph is the definitive version of *De alluvione*.

Conclusions

As with any of Bartolus's tracts, there are issues that cannot be discussed here and have to be set aside momentarily, for they impinge more on the subject matter of the tract rather than the place *Tiberiadis* occupies in Bartolus's work. Particularly in a politically fragmented region like fourteenth-century Umbria, the legal construction of rivers is fraught with problems. Can they be construed as belonging to the fisc and are they included in the so-called *regalia*? Medieval conceptualization of alluvial deposits abandoned some of the concepts elaborated by Roman jurists, replacing, for instance, the Roman distinction between phenomena of accretion to the field and the birth of a thing distinct from the field with

---

[176] See the tables in Appendix 2.

[177] *Tiberiadis* line 1005 note 253; and line 1109 note 283.

[178] Ibid., lines 117–123.

[179] A proof that Bartolus did not make further additions or changes requires a collation of all the extant manuscripts, which I have undertaken for the critical edition of the whole tract. For brevity's sake, two negative proofs should be sufficient. First, the wrongly drawn figure (figure 9) appears in the correct way in the manuscripts; see BAV, Regin. lat. 1891, fol. 9r; BAV, Chigi E. VII. 212, fol. 86v; Firenze, Biblioteca Riccardiana, ms. 1030, fol. 199v. Second, the miscited fragment of Roman law, *lex Inter eos* (D. 41.1.29), appears unaltered in the manuscript tradition, see, for instance, Lübeck, ms. jur. gr. 2° 23, fol. 155ra; Trier, ms. 975/923, fol. 136v; Cues, ms. 257, fol. 128vb; Toledo, ms. 28–16, fol. 169rb; and Munich, Cod. Lat. 5462, fol. 29ra, and Cod. Lat. 6636, fol. 244va, which had been transcribed by the same person.

the distinction between proper and improper alluvium. Consequently, *alluvio* became a concept capable of including two things—accretion and dereliction—and the field could be considered the main thing (*principale*) and the accrued or relinquished land an adjunct (*accessorium*). If medieval jurists adopted different legal constructs, as historians of Roman law indicate,[180] what caused them to change? In short, what are the distinguishing traits of medieval jurisprudence with regard to rivers and the changes affecting a river? Geometry, too, present a series of yet unanswered questions. Is the use of a geometrical model consistent with the tenets of Roman jurisprudence? Geometry was surely a very helpful tool, but is usefulness or practicality the sole possible explanation for its introduction into law? How does the medieval conceptualization of alluvial deposits relate to the introduction of geometry? The reception and the jusgenerativity of Bartolus's *Tiberiadis* are two other unexplored fields. What were the long-term consequences of the introduction of geometry into a legal work for solving factual questions? How did the professionalization of medieval society affect law? And, conversely, how did law react to this professionalization?[181] Lastly, it is not possible to address here the substantial question of why and on what grounds Bartolus's schemes for dividing alluvial soil and the like had been contested, modified and rejected by several authors, including jurists.[182]

Up to the time of Napoleonic codifications, the authoritative voice of Bartolus reverberated through European continental jurisprudence and beyond. While his writings became a point of reference for students, jurists, and lawyers, his prestige attracted into his *Opera* spurious works.[183] Universities established courses (*lectura Bartoli*) to familiarize prospective lawyers and jurists with his work. Trivial as it is, the motto 'no one can be

---

[180]For some of the changes introduced by Azo, Accursius, and Bartolus, see Maddalena, *Gli incrementi fluviali*, 120–128.

[181]On this professionalization, see *Medieval Callings*; and Verger, *Men of Learning in Europe*.

[182]See, for instance, Aimo, *Tractatus de fluviorum alluvionibus*, 202–206 for an alternative method of allotting alluvial soil. And also Borrel, *Opera geometrica*, 113–133, as well as Tebalducci, *La Tiberiade*, 42–138, for the figures comprised in *De alluvione*.

[183]The first attempt to separate authentic from spurious works goes back to Diplovatazio in his 'Vita Bartoli'. For single works distracted from Bartolus's *Opera*, see Era, 'Due trattati attribuiti a Bartolo,' 219–225; Campitelli, 'Il tractatus *De cicatricibus* di Francesco Albergotti,' 269–88; Valentini, 'Il *Tractatus de tabellionibus* di Baldo degli Ubaldi,' 3–167; Maffei, 'Il *Tractatus percussionum*,' 7–18; Ascheri, 'Streghe e 'devianti',' 81–99; Ascheri, 'Bartolo da Sassoferrato: il 'suo' *tractatus consiliare*,' 212–223; Kirshner, 'A *Quaestio de usuris*,' 256–261; Cavallar, Degenring, and Kirshner, *A Grammar of Signs*, 29–87; Cavallar, 'Agli albori della medicina legale,' 27–89; and G. Colli, '*Attribuuntur Bartolo tamen non sunt Bartoli*,' 145–191.

a good jurist without being a Bartolist' [*nemo iurista nisi bartolista*] captures his position in European legal culture.[184] With the advent of codifications, while his voice faded into history, his works became an invaluable mine for late medieval and Renaissance historians looking for insights into social practices ranging from citizenship to dowry, into perennial issues spanning everything from the conflict of laws to fiscal policy, as well as political thought.[185] His library, of barely fifty-four volumes between law and theology, was dispersed, though fragments of his holographs have been discovered.[186] Owing to his stature, his voice came down to us filtered through texts copied over and over and, in the editions printed in the late sixteenth and early seventeenth century, duly accommodated to the humanistically trained ears of the readers. On the few occasions in which some of his works have been critically edited, the absence of holographs has compelled the editors to render his voice in an aseptic and standardized medieval Latin.[187] The holograph gives us back his 'voice,' not only the *ipsissima verba Bartoli* but also his precise and clear drawings—a mirror of the clarity of his thinking.

As the manuscript tradition shows, jurisprudence has received *Tiberiadis* with mixed feelings; in general, while the commentary on *lex Adeo* was sympathetically received, the two sections on geometry could be set aside. For the jurists who addressed issues such as the division of an alluvial deposit, an island born in the middle of river, and an abandoned riverbed, Bartolus's tract shows that it was a seminal work. In short, it shows its jusgenerativity. Yet it is the unsubstantiated addition (*De fluminibus*) to the title that indicates how this tract was received: isolated from the series of tracts produced from 1355 to 1357, it became an essay on fluviatic matters, instead of a tract on legal geography providing the scenario for the successive works.

Recurring themes link the tracts from *Tiberiadis* to *On Tyranny*. The flashbacks at the beginning of *On Guelphs and Ghibellines*, *On the*

---

[184] On these well-known aspects of Bartolus's authoritative position, see Cortese, *Il diritto nella storia medievale*, 2:425–436, especially, 427–428; and 459, note 8, for the Iberian Peninsula where to Accursius's and Bartolus's opinion it was granted by royal decree the value of subsidiary norm.

[185] Kirshner, '*Civitas sibi faciat civem*,' 694–713; Kirshner, 'Donne maritate altrove,' 377–429; Vismara, 'I patti successori nella dottrina di Bartolo,' 2:755–783; now in *Scritti di storia giuridica*, 6:275–301; Berliri, *L'ordinamento tributario*; Smith, 'Bartolo on the Conflict of Laws,' 157–275; Beale, *Bartolus on the Conflict of Laws*; and, for political thought, see Woolf, *Bartolus of Sassoferrato*; Skinner, *The Foundations of Modern Political Thought*, 1:9–12, 49–65.

[186] For the consistency of his library, see Diplovatazio, *Liber de claris iuris consultis*, 286. For the location of some of Bartolus's autographs, see above n. 32.

[187] The difficulties and the unavoidable choices facing the editors of Bartolus's works have been lucidly presented by Quaglioni, *Diritto e politica*, 126, note 23.

Government of the City, and *On Tyranny* indicate that even for the author these tracts were not monadic entities. If the imaginary voyage of the author does not link Perugia, Todi, and Rome, the Tiber does. Aside from the Tiber, there is another river flowing through the region called *Tiberiadis*: the river of law. It has its origin in Rome and flows, so to speak, in the opposite direction of the Tiber—from the center to the periphery.[188] Could this river of law 'unify' a politically fragmented territory into a region called Tiberiadis?

In contrast to Florence, Milan, and Venice, Perugia never developed into a territorial city-state. At the time of Bartolus's embassy to the emperor, Perugia's municipal liberty was in a precarious situation and, after 1370, was lost. Its distant protector, the German emperor, retreated from Italy and,[189] in 1368, transferred to the pope his rights on all the lands that comprised his previous donations, including Perugia, Spoleto, and Città di Castello. For Perugia there was no reason not to accept the new lord. Both Segoloni and Quaglioni have pointed out how Bartolus's writings reflect the political situation and the problems of that period.[190] The spectacle in Pisa—an emperor profitably selling titles, dignities, and insignias—may have left Bartolus disillusioned not so much with the sacred institution of the empire but with its present titleholder—which may be one of the reasons he could never bring himself to finish his tract *On Insignia and Coats of Arms*. Other problems were more pressing. If legal thought could not alter Perugia's precarious position, it could freely envisage a criterion for bringing stability to the region: the rule of law. A Tiberiadis—that is, a region, not a state—under the rule of law was the other 'dream' Bartolus had during his summer vacation.[191] A dream he told in *Tiberiadis*, *On Guelphs and Ghibellines*, and *On the Government of the City*. A dream that turned into a nightmare in *On Tyranny*, for the river of law had ceased to flow.

Nanzan University
Nagoya-Seto, Japan

---

[188] *Tiberiadis* lines 37–39.

[189] See Petrarch's meeting with the emperor earlier that year in Milan, 25 February 1355, Petrarch, *Letters on familiar matters*, Book XIX, 3, 'To his Lelius, that one must not seek false glory, just as one must not scorn true glory,' 77–82.

[190] For the political situation of that period, as well as Bartolus's views on the statutus of Perugia, see Segoloni, 'Bartolo e la *civitas Perusina*,' 565–567; for the policy pursued by the cardinal legate, Egidius de Albornoz (a threat to Perugia's municipal liberty), especially in relation to the tract *De tyranno*, see Quaglioni, *Diritto e politica*, 15–38, 57–71.

[191] For a 'passionate' attack on the 'liberal state' and its heritage, see Grossi, *L'ordine giuridico medievale*.

Works Cited

Manuscript Sources

Barcelona, Archivo de la Corona de Aragon
    Ripoll 67, fols. 34v–42v
Barcelona, Biblioteca del Cabildo
    MS. 85, fols. 231ra–300vb
Bruxelles, Koninklijke Biblioteek Albert I
    II/3592, fols. 182–196v
    II/1442, fols. 224ra–242r
Cues, Bernkastel
    MS. 257, fols. 124ra–144va
Florence, Biblioteca Riccardiana
    MS. 1030, fols. 184r–206r
Lübeck, Bibliothek der Hansestadt Lübeck
    MS. jur. gr. 2° 23, fols. 149ra–173rb
Melk, Stiftungbibliothek
    MS. 1882, fols. 1–28v
Munich, Bayerische Staatsbibliothek
    Cod. Lat. 5462, fols. 25ra–40vb
    Cod. Lat. 6636, fols. 241ra–254vb
    Cod. Lat. 26669, fols. 127–161
Prague, Národni Muzeum
    MS. a. 5, fols. 11ra–37va
Seo de Urgel, Biblioteca del Cabildo
    MS. 2109, fols. 337ra–347vb
Seville, Biblioteca Colombina
    MS. 83-8-13, fols. 159ra–183va
Toledo, Biblioteca del Cabildo
    MS. 28-16, fols. 164ra–172va
Trier, Stadtbibliothek
    MS. 975/923 4°, fols. 129–139
Vatican City, Biblioteca Apostolica Vaticana
    Barb. lat. 1398, fols. 157–170v
    Chigi E.VII.212, fols. 79–113ra
    Regin. lat. 1891, fols. 2–27v
    Ross. lat. 1061, fols. 3ra–14vb
    Vat. lat. 2289, fols. 47vb–96ra
    Vat. lat. 2625, fols. 135–146v
    Vat. lat. 2641, fols. 54rb–63rb
    Vat. lat. 2660, fols. 171–192v

Published Sources

Accursius, Franciscus. *Glossa*. Lyon, 1627. Reprint, Osnabrück: Otto Zeller, 1965.
Aimo, Battista. *Tractatus de fluviorum alluvionibus*. Venice, 1581.
Antico Gallina, Mariavittoria, ed. *Aque interne: Uso e gestione di una risorsa*. Milan: Edizioni ET, 1996.
Ascheri, Mario. 'The Formation of the *Consilia* Collection of Bartolus of Saxoferrato and Some of His Autographs' pp. 188–201 in *The Two Laws. Studies in Medieval Legal History Dedicated to Stephan Kuttner*, ed. Laurent Mayali and Stephanie A. J. Tibbetts. Washington, D.C.: The Catholic University of America, 1990.
Ascheri, Mario. 'Bartolo da Sassoferrato: il 'suo' *tractatus* consiliare e i suoi *consilia*' pp. 212–223 in *Diritto medievale e moderno. Problemi del processo, della cultura e delle fonti giuridiche*. Rimini: Maggioli, 1991.
Ascheri, Mario. 'Streghe e 'devianti': alcuni *consilia* apocrifi di Bartolo da Sassoferrato?' pp. 81–99 in *Diritto medievale e moderno. Problemi del processo, della cultura e delle fonti giuridiche*. Rimini, Maggioli, 1991.
Baratteri, Giovanni Battista. *Architettura d'acque di Gio. Battista Baratteri ... divisa in otto libri ...Opera d'utile, e necessaria, non solo a quelli, che vogliono attendere alla medesima architettura; ma etiandio a quei dottori, e procuratori, che haueranno cause dipendenti dalle cose in essi contenute*. Piacenza, 1656.
Baratteri, Giovanni Battista. *Degl'incrementi fluviali ossia il secondo il terzo ed il quarto libro della prima parte di Gio. Batt. Barattieri illustrati con note ... da Baldassarre Orsini*. Perugia, 1791.
Bartolo da Sassoferrato. Studi e documenti per il VI centenario. 2 vols. Milan: Giuffrè. 1962.
Bartolo da Sassoferrato. *Commentaria*, 9 vols. Venice, 1526; reprint, Rome: Il Cigno Galileo Galilei, 1996.
Bartolo da Sassoferrato. *Tractatus de fluminibus seu Tyberiadis*. Bologna, 1576; reprint, Turin: Bottega d'Erasmo, 1964.
Baxandall, Michael. *Painting and Experience in Fifteenth Century Italy*, Oxford and New York: Oxford University Press. 1972.
Bazàn, Bernardo C., John Wipple, Gérard Fransen, and Danielle Jacquart, ed. *Les questions disputeés et les questions quodlibétiques dans les facultés de théologie, de droit et de médicine*. Turnhout: Brepols, 1985.
Beale, J. Henry. *Bartolus on the Conflict of Laws*. Cambridge: Cambridge University Press, 1914.
Bellomo, Manlio. *Saggio sull'università nell'età del diritto comune*. Catania: Giannotta, 1988.
Bellomo, Manlio. '*Factum* e *ius*. Itinerari di ricerca fra le certezze e i dubbi del pensiero giuridico medievale' pp. 63–89 in *Medioevo edito e inedito. II. Scienza del diritto e società medievale*. Rome: Il Cigno Galileo Galilei, 1997.
Bellomo, Manlio. *I fatti e il diritto. Tra le certezze e i dubbi dei giuristi medievali (secoli XIII–XIV)*. Rome: Il Cigno Galileo Galilei, 2000.

Benincasa, Cornelio. *Compendiolum de alluvione*, in *Ad tit. De constitutionibus. In quo omnia ibi disceptari solita erudite disseruntur*. Perugia, 1572.
Berliri, Antonio. *L'ordinamento tributario della prima metà del sec. XIV nell'opera di Bartolo da Sassoferrato*. Milan: Giuffrè, 1997.
Black, Robert. *Humanism and Education in Medieval and Renaissance Italy*. Cambridge: Cambridge University Press, 2001.
Borrel, Jean (Iohannes Buteonis). *Opera geometrica*. Lyon, 1554.
Bossi, Egidio. *Tractatus de aquis et fluminibus*, in *Practica et tractatus varii seu quaestiones*. Basel, 1578.
Bourgain, Pascale. 'Les prologues des textes narratifs' pp. 245–273 in *Les prologues médiévaux*, ed. J. Hamesse. Turnhout: Brepols, 2000.
Busard, Hubertus L. L. and Menso Folkerts, ed. *Robert of Chester's (?) Redaction of Euclid's Elements, the So-Called Adelard II Version*. 2 vols. Basel and Boston: Birkhäuser, 1992.
Busard, Hubertus L. L. *The First Latin Translation of Euclid's Elements Commonly Ascribed to Adelard of Bath*. Toronto: Pontifical Institute of Medieval Studies, 1982.
Caepolla, Bartholomaeus. *De servitutibus rusticorum praediorum* fols. 209v–243v in *Tractatus universi iuris*, vol. 6/2. Venice, 1584.
Calasso, Francesco. 'Bartolo da Sassoferrato' pp. 640–669 in *Dizionario Biografico Italiano*, vol. 6. Rome: Istituto per l'Enciclopedia italiana, 1962.
Campitelli, Adriana. 'Il tractatus *De cicatricibus* di Francesco Albergotti attribuito a Bartolo da Sassoferrato.' *Annali di storia del diritto* 8 (1964): 269–288.
Caprioli, Severino, ed. *Statuto del Comune di Perugia*, 2 vols. Perugia: Deputazione di storia patria per l'Umbria, 1996.
Carazzi, Carlo. *Dubitationi d'autore incerto contra il modo del dividere l'alluvioni trovato da Carlo Carazzi: ... et risposte fatte da lui, con un discorso contra il modo accettato da un dottore parmeggiano*. Bologna, 1580.
Carazzi, Carlo. *Modo del dividere l'alluvioni, da quello di Bartolo et de gli agrimensori diverso: Mostrato con ragioni matematiche et con pratica*. Bologna, 1579.
Carruthers, Mary. *The Book of Memory. A Study of Memory in Medieval Culture*. Cambridge: Cambridge University Press, 1990.
Casamassima, Emanuele. *Codices operum Bartoli a Saxoferrato recensiti. Iter Germanicum*. Florence: Olschki, 1971.
Cascio Pratilli, Giovanni and Luigi Zangheri, ed. *La legislazione medicea sull'ambiente*. 4 vols. Florence: Olschki, 1994.
Castelli, Onofrio. *Distributione universale dell'architettura de' fiumi, & delle altre acque, del sig. conte Onofrio Castelli vmbro*. Milan, 1631.
Cavallar, Osvaldo, Susanne Degenring, and Julius Kirshner. *A Grammar of Signs. Bartolo da Sassoferrato's Tract On Insignia and Coats of Arms*. Berkeley: The Robbins Collection, 1994.
Cavallar, Osvaldo. 'Agli albori della medicina legale: I trattati *De percussionibus* e *De vulneribus*.' *Ius Commune* 26 (1999): 27–89.

Cavallar, Osvaldo and Julius Kirshner. '*Ne ultra scarpas*. Un cultore d'araldica fuorilegge.' *Ius Commune* 28 (2001): 297–311.
Cavallar, Osvaldo. 'Il Tevere sfoccia nell'Arno: Sigismondo Coccapani e il proemio al trattato *Tiberiadis* di Bartolo da Sassoferrato.' *Rechtsgeschichte* 3 (2003): 223–231.
Cenci, Cesare. *Documentazione di vita assisana, 1300–1530*. 3 vols. Grottaferrata: Ad Claras Aquas, 1974–1976.
Cenci, Cesare. 'Ordinazioni dei capitoli provinciali umbri dal 1300 al 1305.' *Collectanea Franciscana* 55 (1985): 5–31.
Cignoni, Mario, ed. *Bartolo da Sassoferrato: 'De insigniis et armis.'* Florence: Giampiero Pagnini, 1999.
Coccapani, Sigismondo. *'Trattato del modo di ridurre il fiume di Arno in canale' e altri scritti di architettura e di idraulica*, ed. Elisa Acanfora. Florence: Olschki, 2002.
Colli, Gaetano. '*Attribuuntur Bartolo et tamen non sunt Bartoli*. Prolegomeni ad una bibliografia analitica dei trattati fiuridici pubblicati nel XVI secolo.' *Il bibliotecario* (1996): 145–191.
Colli, Vincenzo. 'Il Cod. 351 della Biblioteca Capitolare 'Feliniana' di Lucca: editori quattrocenteschi e *Libri consiliorum* di Baldo degli Ubaldi (1327–1400)' pp. 255–282 in *Scritti di storia del diritto offerti dagli allievi a Domenico Maffei*, ed. Mario Ascheri. Padua: Antenore, 1991.
Colli, Vincenzo. 'Collezioni d'autore di Baldo degli Ubaldi nel MS Biblioteca Apostolica Vaticana, Barb. lat. 1398.' *Ius Commune* 25 (1998): 323–346.
Colli, Vincenzo. '*Consilia* dei giuristi medievali e produzione letteraria' pp. 173–225 in *Legal Consulting in the Civil Law Tradition*, ed. Mario Ascheri, Ingrid Baugärtner, and Julius Kirshner. Berkeley: The Robbins Collection, 1999.
Colli, Vincenzo. 'L'esemplare di dedica e la tradizione del testo della *Lectura super usibus feudorum* di Baldo degli Ubaldi.' *Ius Commune* 27 (2000): 69–117.
Colli, Vincenzo and Paola Monacchia. 'Un elenco di libri di Francesco di Baldo degli Ubaldi (1426?/1432)' pp. 185–215 in *Annali della Facoltà di Lettere e Filosofia. 2. Studi Storico-antropologici*, vol. XXXVI, n.s. XXII, 1998/1999. Perugia: Università degli Studi di Perugia, 2001.
Condorelli, Orazio. '*Homo parve stature et coloris turgidi et gibbosus*... Bartolo da Sassoferrato nell'anonima descrizione del ms. Napoli, Biblioteca Nazionale, VII.D.77.' *Rivista internazionale di diritto comune* 6 (1995): 357–364.
Cortese, Ennio. *Il Rinascimento giuridico medievale*. Rome: Bulzoni, 1992.
Cortese, Ennio. *Il diritto nella storia medievale*. 2 vols. Rome: Il Cigno Galileo Galilei, 1995.
Costa, Pietro. *'Iurisdictio': Semantica del potere politico nella pubblicistica medievale (1100–1433)*. 2 vols. Milan: Giuffrè, 1969.
Cutini Zazzerini, Clara. 'La normativa sulle acque: Controllo e salvaguardia dei territori (secoli XIII–XIX)' pp. 64–71 in *L'Umbria e le sue acque* ed. A. Grohmann. Perugia: Electa, 1990.
Dainville, Francois de. 'Cartes et contestations au XVe siècle (Maps and Litigations in the 15th Century).' *Imago Mundi* 24 (1970): 99–121.

Dezza, Ettore. 'Giacomo Giovanetti e la riforma del regime giuridico delle acque nel Codice Albertino' pp. 223–234 in *Acque interne*, ed. M. Antico Gallina. Milan: Edizioni ET, 1996.
Diplovatazio, Tommaso. *Liber de claris iuris consultis*, ed. Fritz Schulz, Hermann Kantorowicz, and Giuseppe Rabotti. *Studia Gratiana* 10 (1968).
Dolezalek, Gero. *Verzeichnis der Handschriften zum Römischen Recht bis 1600*. 4 vols. Frankfurt am Main: Max-Planck Institut, 1972.
Era, Antonio. 'Due trattati attribuiti a Bartolo: *De tabellionibus* e *Contrarietates iuris civilis Romanorum et iuris Longobardorum*' pp. 217–225 in *Bartolo da Sassoferrato. Studi e documenti*, vol. 2. Milan: Giuffrè, 1962.
Ermini, Giuseppe. *Storia della Università di Perugia*. Bologna: Zanichelli, 1947.
Fortini, Arnaldo. 'Frate Piero da Assisi primo maestro di Bartolo da Sassoferrato' pp. 251–260 in *Bartolo da Sassoferrato. Studi e documenti*, vol. 2. Milan: Giuffrè, 1962.
Fransen, Gérard. 'Les questions disputées dans les Facultés de droit' pp. 225–277 in *Les questions disputeés et les questions quodlibétiques dans les facultés de théologie, de droit et de médicine*, ed. Bernardo C. Bazàn, John Wipple, Gérard Fransen, and Danielle Jacquart. Turnhout: Brepols, 1985.
Frova, Carla. 'Le traité *De fluminibus* de Bartolo da Sassoferrato (1355).' *Médiévalés* 36 (1999): 81–89.
García y García, Antonio. *Codices operum Bartoli a Saxoferrato recensiti. Iter Hispanicum*. Florence: Olschki, 1973.
Geerlings, W. and Ch. Schulze, ed. *Der Kommentar in Antike und Mittelalter. Beiträge zu seiner Erforschung*, Leiden: Brill, 2002.
Gehl, Paul F. *A Moral Art. Grammar, Society, and Culture in Trecento Florence*. Ithaca and London: Cornell University Press, 1993.
Ghiringhelli, Robertino. 'Dottrina e cultura civile delle acque nella Lombardia della restaurazione: Il pensiero di Gian Domenico Romagnosi' pp. 207–221 in *Acque interne*, ed. M. Antico Gallina. Milan: Edizioni ET, 1996.
Gobbi, Antonio. *Tractatus varii in quibus universa aquarum materia*. Bologna, 1673.
Grohmann, Alberto. *Città e territorio tra medioevo ed età moderna (Perugia, secc. XII–XVI)*. 2 vols. Perugia: Editrice Perugia, 1981.
Grohmann, Alberto, ed. *L'Umbria e le sue acque. Fiumi e torrenti di una regione italiana*. Perugia: Electa, 1990.
Grossi, Paolo. *Le situazioni reali nell'esperienza giuridica medievale*. Padua: CEDAM, 1968.
Grossi, Paolo. *L'ordine giuridico medievale*. Rome and Bari: Laterza, 1995.
Guerra Medici, Maria Teresa. *L'aria di città. Donne e diritti nel comune medievale*. Naples: Edizioni Scientifiche Italiane, 1996.
Guglielmini, Domenico. *Della natura de fiumi: trattato fisico-matematico del dott. Domenico Guglielmini ... in cui si manifestano le principali proprietà de fiumi se n' indicano molte sin' hora non conosciute e si dimostrano d'una maniera facile le cause delle medesime*. Bologna, 1697.
Guicciardini, Francesco. *Ricordanze*, in *Scritti autobiografici e rari*, ed. Roberto Palmarocchi. Bari: Laterza 1993.

Izbicki, Thomas M. 'Texts Attributed to Bartolus de Saxoferrato in North American Manuscripts Collections' pp. 381–390 in *Friars and Jurists. Selected Studies*. Goldback: Keip, 1997.

Jemolo, Arturo C. 'Il *Liber minoritarum* di Bartolo e la povertà minoritica nei giuristi del XIII e XIV secolo' pp. 29–74, in *Scritti vari di Storia religiosa e civile*, ed. Francesco Margiotta Broglio. Milan: Giuffrè, 1965.

Johannes Monacus. *Glossa aurea*. Paris, 1535; reprint, Aalen: Scientia, 1968.

Johannes de Muris. *De arte mensurandi: A Geometrical Handbook of the Fourteenth Century*, ed. Hubertus L. L. Busard. Stuttgart: F. Steiner, 1998.

Kamp, Josephus. L. J. van De. *Bartolus de Saxoferrato, 1313–1357. Leven – werken – invloed – beteekenis*. Amsterdam: H. J. Paris, 1936.

Kantorowicz, Hermann. 'The *Quaestiones disputatae* of the Glossators.' *Tijdschrift voor Rechtsgeshiedenis* 16 (1939): 1–65.

Kirshner, Julius. 'A *Quaestio de usuris* Falsely Attributed to Bartolus of Sassoferrato.' *Renaissance Quarterly* 22 (1969): 256–261.

Kirshner, Julius. '*Civitas sibi faciat civem*: Bartolus of Sassoferrato's Doctrine on the Making of a Citizen.' *Speculum* 48 (1973): 694–713.

Kirshner, Julius. 'Donne maritate altrove. Genere e cittadinanza in Italia' pp. 377–429 in *Tempi e spazi di vita femminile tra medioevo ed età moderna*, ed. Silvia Seidel Menchi, A. Jacobson Schutte, and Thomas Kuehn. Bologna: Il Mulino, 1999.

Kuttner, Stephan and Reinhard Elze, ed. *A Catalogue of Canon and Roman Law Manuscripts in the Vatican Library*. 2 vols. Vatican City: Biblioteca Apostolica Vaticana, 1986–1987.

Lagazzi, Luciano. *Segni sulla terra: determinazione dei confini e percezione dello spazio nell'alto Medioevo*. Bologna: Clueb, 1991.

Lagazzi, Luciano. 'I segni sulla terra. Sistemi di confinazione e misurazione dei boschi nell'alto Medioevo' pp. 13–29 in *Il bosco nel Medioevo*, ed. Bruno Andreolli and Massimo Montanari. Bologna: Clueb, 1995.

Lancellotto, Giovanni Paolo. *Vita Bartoli iureconsulti*. Perugia, 1576.

Le Goff, Jacques, ed. *Medieval Callings*, trans. Lydia G. Cochrane. Chicago and London: University of Chicago Press, 1990.

Lepsius, Susanne. *Der Richter und die Zeugen. Eine Untersuchung anhand des Tractatus testimoniorum des Bartolus von Sassoferrato mit Edition*. Frankfurt am Main: Klostermann, 2003.

Maanen, Jan van. 'Teaching Geometry to 11 year old 'medieval lawyers.'' *Mathematical Gazette* 76, no. 475 (1992): 37–45.

Maanen, Jean van. 'Over het verdelen van aangeslibd land: Een brugklas project.' *Euclides* 60 (1984–1985): 161–168.

Maddalena, Paolo. *Gli incrementi fluviali nella visione giurisprudenziale classica*. Naples: Jovene, 1970.

Maffei, Domenico. 'Il *Tractatus percussionum* pseudo-bartoliano e la sua dipendenza da Odofredo.' *Studi senesi* 78 (1966): 7–18.

Manselli, Raoul. 'Il sogno come premonizione, consiglio e predizione nella tradizione medievale' pp. 219–244 in *I sogni nel medioevo. Seminario internazionale. Roma 2–4 ottobre 1983*, ed. Tullio Gregory (Lessico intellettuale europeo, 35). Rome: Edizioni dell'Ateneo,1985.

Marchetti, Paolo. *'De iure finium.' Diritto e confini tra tardo medievo ed età moderna*. Milan: Giuffrè, 2001.
Marongiu, Antonio. 'Il regime bipartitico nel trattato sui guelfi e i ghibellini' pp. 333–343 in *Bartolo da Sassoferrato. Studi e documenti*, vol. 2. Milan: Giuffrè, 1962.
Mayali, Laurent and Stephanie A. J. Tibbetts, ed. *The Two Laws. Studies in Medieval Legal History Dedicated to Stephan Kuttner*. Washington, D.C.: The Catholic University of America, 1990.
Mazzi, Maria Serena and Sergio Raveggi. *Gli uomini e le cose nelle campagne fiorentine del Quattrocento*. Florence: Olschki, 1983.
Migliorati, Carla. 'La committenza e la problematica originaria della cartografia sulle acque' pp. 87–98 in *L'Umbria e le sue acque*, ed. A. Grohmann. Perugia: Electa, 1990.
Minnis, Alastair J. *Medieval Theory of Authorship: Scholastic Literary Attitudes in the Later Middle Ages*. Philadelphia: University of Pennsylvania Press, 1984.
Muzzarelli, Maria Giuseppina. *Gli inganni delle apparenze. Disciplina di vesti e di ornamenti alla fine del medioevo*. Turin: Scriptorium, 1996.
Nico Ottaviani, Maria Grazia. 'Alcuni aspetti della problematica sulle acque nella legislazione statutaria umbra dei secoli XIII–XVI' pp. 58–63 in *L'Umbria e le sue acque*, ed. A. Grohmann. Perugia: Electa, 1990.
Nico Ottaviani, Maria Grazia, ed. *Lo statuto di Deruta in volgare dell'anno 1465*. Spoleto: Centro italiano di studi sull'alto medioevo, 1991.
Papias. *Vocabulista*. Venice, 1496; reprint, Turin: Bottega d'Erasmo, 1966.
Paravicini Bagliani, Agostino and Giorgio Stabile eds. *Träume im Mittelalter: Ikonologische Studien*. Stuttgart: Belser, 1989.
Petrarch, Francis. *Letters on Familiar Matters: Rerum familiarium libri, XVII–XXIV*, trans. Aldo S. Bernardo. Baltimore: Johns Hopkins University Press, 1985.
Petrus Helias. *Summa super Priscianum*, ed. Leo A. Reilly. Toronto: Pontifical Institute of Medieval Studies, 1993.
Piana, Cesare. *Chartularium Studii Bononiensis S. Francisci (saec. XIII–XVI)*. Analecta Franciscana, XI. Grottaferrata: Ad Claras Aquas, 1970.
Prosdocimi, Luigi. '*Ex facto oritur ius*. Breve nota di diritto medievale' pp. 802–813 in *Studi Senesi in memoria di Ottorino Vannini*. Milan: Giuffrè, 1957.
Quaglioni, Diego. '*Quilibet in domo sua dicitur rex*. (In margine ad alcune pagine di Francesco Calasso).' *Studi senesi* 89 (1977): 344–358.
Quaglioni, Diego. *Politica e diritto nel Trecento Italiano. Il 'De tyranno' di Bartolo da Sassoferrato (1314–1357). Con l'edizione critica dei trattati 'De Guelphis et Gebellinis', 'De regimine civitatis' e 'De tyranno.'* Florence: Olschki, 1983.
Quaglioni, Diego. 'Giovanni da Legnano e il *Somnium Viridari*: Il sogno del giurista tra scisma e concilio' pp. 145–167 in *'Civilis sapientia': Dottrine giuridiche e dottrine politiche fra medioevo ed età moderna*. Rimini: Maggioli, 1989.

Ranzato, Leone. 'Cenni e documenti su Fr. Pietro d'Assisi, O.F.M. (Fr. Pietruzzo della Pietà) 1300–1349.' *Archivum Franciscanum Historicum* 8 (1915): 3–11.

Regni, Claudio. 'La *comunantia fructus aque lacus* nella prima metà del secolo XV: Appalti e appaltatori.' *Bollettino della deputazione di storia patria per l'Umbria* 85 (1988): 157–217.

Regoliosi, Mariangela. *Nel cantiere del Valla. Elaborazione e montaggio delle 'Elegantiae.'* Rome: Bulzoni, 1993.

Roth, Cecil. *The Jews in the Renaissance.* New York: Harper & Row, 1965.

Sbriccoli, Mario. *L'interpretazione dello statuto. Contributo allo studio della funzione dei giuristi nell'età comunale.* Milan: Giuffrè, 1969.

Schwinges, Reiner C. 'Admission' pp. 171–194 in *A History of the Universities in Europe,* vol. 1, ed. Walter Rüegg, *Universities of the Middle Ages,* ed. H. De Ridder-Symones. Cambridge: Cambridge University Press, 1992.

Sconocchia, Sergio and Lucio Toneatto ed. *Lingue tecniche del greco e del latino. Atti del I Seminario internazionale sulla letteratura scientifica e tecnica greca e latina,* Trieste: Università degli Studi di Trieste, 1993.

Segoloni, Danilo. 'Bartolo da Sassoferrato e la *civitas Perusina*' pp. 513–671 in *Bartolo da Sassoferrato. Studi e documenti,* vol. 2. Milan: Giuffrè, 1962.

Segoloni, Danilo. '*Practica, practicus, practicare* in Bartolo e in Baldo' pp. 52–103 in *L'educazione giuridica. II. Profili storici.* Rimini, Maggioli, 1979.

Segoloni, Danilo. 'Aspetti del pensiero giuridico e politico di Bartolo da Sassoferrato' pp. 353–415 in *Il diritto comune e la tradizione giuridica europea,* Atti del convegno internazionale di studi in onore di Giuseppe Ermini, ed. D. Segoloni. Perugia: 1980.

Sereni, Emilio. *Storia del paesaggio agrario italiano.* Rome and Bari: Laterza. 1982.

Sheedy, Anna T. *Bartolus on Social Conditions in the Fourteenth Century.* New York: Columbia University Press, 1942.

Simi, Annalisa. 'Regole per la determinazione della capacità delle botti e il calcolo degli scemi in manoscritti italiani dei secc. XIV. XV e XVI.' *Physis* 30 (1993): 391–414.

Skinner, Quentin. *The Foundations of Modern Political Thought.* 2 vols. Cambridge: Cambridge University Press, 1978.

Smith, Clarence J. A. 'Bartolo on the Conflict of Laws.' *American Journal of Legal History* 14 (1970): 157–275.

Speciale, Giuseppe. '*Apparatus*: iper-testo vivo e aperto.' *Ius Commune* 28 (2001): 47–59.

Squattriti, Paolo. *Water and Society in Early Medieval Italy, AD 400–1000.* Cambridge: Cambridge University Press, 1998.

Squattriti, Paolo, ed. *Working with Water in Medieval Europe. Technology and Resource-Use.* Leiden: Brill, 2000.

Tebalducci, Claudio. *La Tiberiade di Bartole da Sasferrato: del modo di dividere l'alluvioni, l'isole, e gl'alvei: Con l'annotationi et espositioni di Claudio Tobaldutii da Montalboddo.* Rome, 1587.

Toaff, Ariel. *Gli Ebrei a Perugia.* Perugia: Deputazione di Storia patria per l'Umbria, 1975.

Toneatto, Lucio. 'L'*ars mensoria* fra Tardo Antico e Alto Medioevo' pp. 308–326 in *Lingue tecniche del greco e del latino. Atti del I Seminario internazionale sulla letteratura scientifica e tecnica greca e latina*, ed. Sergio Sconocchia and Lucio Toneatto. Trieste, Università degli Studi di Trieste,1993.

Toneatto, Lucio. *Codices artis mensoriae. I manoscritti degli antichi opuscoli latini d'agrimensura, V–XIX sec.* 3 vols. Spoleto: Centro italiano di studi sull'alto medioevo, 1994–1995.

Trusen, Winfried. '*Insula in flunine nata*. Ein kanonistischer Zivilprozess aus den Jahren 1357–1363/1364 um eine Insel im Mittelrhein.' *Zeitschrift der Savigny-Stiftung für Rechtsge-schichte, Kan. Abt.* 68 (1982): 294–338.

Tsuno, Ryuichi. *Katalog juristischer Dissertationen, Disputationen, Programme und anderer Hochschulschriften im Zeitraum von 1600 bis 1800 aus den Beständen der Universität Rostock*. Tokyo: Chuo University Library, 1982.

Ubaldis, Baldus de. *Lectura in VI–IX libros Codicis*, Lyon, 1498.

Valentini, Vittorio. 'Il *Tractatus de tabellionibus* di Baldo degli Ubaldi attribuito anche a Bartolo da Sassoferrato nonché a Gozzadino de' Gozzadini.' Studi Urbinati 34 (1965–1966): 3–167.

Verger, Jacques. *Men of Learning in Europe at the End of the Middle Ages*, trans. Lisa Neal and Steven Rendall. Notre Dame: University of Notre Dame Press, 2000.

Vismara, Giulio. 'I patti successori nella dottrina di Bartolo' pp. 275–301 in *Scritti di storia giuridica*, vol. 6. Milan: Giuffrè, 1988. (First published in *Bartolo da Sassoferrato. Studi e documenti*, vol. 2, pp. 755–783. Milan: Giuffrè, 1962).

Walther, Helmut G. 'Wasser in Stadt und Contado. Perugias Sorge um Wasser und der Flusstraktat *Tyberiadis* des Perusiner Juristen Bartolus von Sassoferrato' pp. 882–897 in *Mensch und Natur im Mittelalter* (Miscellanea Mediaevalia, 21/2), ed. Albert Zimmermann and Aandreas Speer, Berlin: Gruyter,1992.

Weimar, Peter. 'Die legistische Literatur und die Methode des Rechtsunterrichts der Glossatorenzeit.' *Ius Commune* 2 (1969): 43–83.

Woolf, C. N. Sidney. *Bartolus of Sassoferrato. His Position in the History of Medieval Political Thought*. Cambridge: Cambridge University Press, 1913.

Working with Water in Medieval Europe. Technology and Resource-Use, ed. Paolo Squattriti. Leiden: Brill, 2000.

Appendix 1
Bartolus, *Tiberiadis* (*De Alluvione*)
Edited by Osvaldo Cavallar

Criteria for the Edition

1) Proper names have been capitalized, including those referring to the divinity.
2) The letters indicating geometrical points and lines have been italicized.
3) The words or phrases of Gaius's fragment (D. 41.1.7.1-2) on which Bartolus commented upon, underlain in the holograph, have been rendered in italics.
4) Punctuation has been revised; and double quotation marks have been used for the conversation in the prologue.
5) The letters *u* and *v* have been distinguished, e.g., *aluuio* has been rendered as *aluvio*. The combination *ij* has been rendered as *ii*, e.g., *filij* as *filii*, and *edifitijs* as *edifitiis*. Similarly, in the figures, the Roman numerals have been given in the standard form, e.g., *ij* as *ii*, *iiij* as *iv*, and *viiij* as *ix*.
6) Inconsistent spellings, e.g., *aluvio* and *alluvio*; *trat*, *trait* and *trahit*; *apellatio* and *apelatio*; *mensurantur* and *mesurantur*; *iuxta* and *iusta*; and *nil* and *nichil*, have been maintained.
7) Words such as *caput*, *sicut*, and *mihi*, when abbreviated, have been rendered in their standard form.
8) Forms like *senper*, *anplius*, *enptio*, *sinpliciter*, and *inpossibile*, recur time after time in the holograph. Accordingly, when abbreviations occur, an *n* has been used before a palatal consonant like *p*; e.g., *inperator*, *tenpus*, *conplevi*, and *contenplari*.
9) In the case of more unusual spellings, the standard form has been used, e.g., *publicanis* for *plubicanis*, and *profluens* for *plofluens*. The notes, however, indicate the readings of the holograph.
10) Material missing owing to the absence of the sign of abbreviation has been supplied in square brackets, e.g., 'r[i]pa', 'hui[u]s', 'pu[n]tus', and 'linea[m]'.
11) Citations taken from Roman law, Accursius's *Glossa*, *Catonis disticha*, Euclids's *Elementa*, and Scripture, have not been placed between quotation marks. The notes and Bartolus's text indicate the provenance of the cited passage. Yet singled out words, e.g., *dictio'a'*, *verbum 'nostro'*, and *ponitur 'vires' pro effectu*, for clarity's sake, have been placed between single quotation marks.
12) In the allegations of Roman law, medieval peculiarities have been maintained, e.g., *ad vell.* for *Ad senatus consultum Velleianim* (D. 16.1).

13) Whenever the edition departs from the holograph, the notes reproduce the reading of the holograph.

14) In preparing the edition I have kept in mind the recommendations on editorial practice presented by Stephan Kuttner, 'Notes on the Presentation of Text and Apparatus in Editing the Works of Decretists and Decretalists,' *Traditio* 15 (1959), pp. 452-462.

Tiberiadis

In nomine Patris et Filii et Spiritus Sancti, amen.[1]

Tiberiadis est regio iuxta flumen Tiberis[2] constituta. Est autem Tiber flumen[3] notabile in Italie partibus. Transit enim per urbem Romanam, que cuntarum civitatum caput est et magistra, et in eiusdem urbis teritorio mare ingreditur, et ibi navigabile est, et usque ad mare retinet nomen suum. Dicitur autem Tiber a Tiberio, Romanorum inperatore, a quo aliquas leges latas habemus, et sub hoc nomine flumen hoc in nostris legibus pluries nominatur. Hoc etiam flumen montem illum laudabilem circuit, in quo est felis Perusina civitas situata, et per eius teritorium longo spatio transiens planities et colles et cetera loca ipsi flumini circunsta[n]tia habet bene habitata, edifitiis multis et pulcris ornata, fructifera, valde delectabilia viridaria enim esse videntur.

Cum igitur a lectura vacarem, et recreationis causa in quandam villam prope Perusium supra Tiberim costituta[m] accederem, incepi Tiberis circuitus, aluviones, insulas in flumine natas mutationesque alvei contenplari. Et circa multa dubia que[4] de facto ocurerant, et alia que ego ipse ex aspectu fluminis excitabam, quid iuris esset, cepi aliqualiter intueri, non tamen credens ultra procedere, ne recreationem propter quam acceseram inpedirem. Cumque nocte illa dormirem prope diem visum est mihi quod ad me quidam homo ve[n]iret, cuius aspectus mihi placidus erat, dixitque: 'Hec que cogitare cepisti scribe et, quia oculorum inspectione indiget, per figuras singna. Ecce aportavi tibi calamum quo scribas, circinum quo mensures et figuras fatias circulares, et lineam qua lineas ducas figurasque formes.' Cui dixi: 'Absit quod ea, que ad iura pertinent, per figuras singnem. Si enim facerem, longe plures essent derisores quam laudatores.' Tunc ille me turbato vultu aspitiens ait: 'Bartole, congnosco quod modicum Dei habes. Times enim de benefacto derideri? Quod vite Christi et sanctorum omnium contradicit, qui benefatientes non curaverunt contumelias, derisiones et verbera. Modicum etiam boni moralis habes. Timor enim hic, per quem a bono retraeis, illi virtuti morali oponitur, que fortitudo nuncupatur. In te enim est bene agere, tui vero arbitrii non est

---

[1] *in marg. dextr.* Incipit proemium ad librum Tiberis.
[2] Tiberis *corr. ex* Tiberim.
[3] *ms. add.* est *post* flumen.
[4] ocurerant *post* que *del.*

que quisque loqueretur.' Cui verecundus dixi: 'Tibi adsentio. Sed primo motu ductus sic respondi.' Qui ait: 'Incipias igitur secure, quia in hui[u]s operis prosecutione Dominus tecum erit et multa tibi aperiet, que tibi incongnita sunt.' Surgens igitur confisus in gratia eius, quem in prosecutione mecum
35 fucturum policitus erat, istud opus incipi, et totum opus apellavi Tiberiadis, ut[5] non solum de ipso Tibere, sed etiam de multis que in regione Tiberis ocurrunt, in ipso tractetur.[6] Putans congruum ut, sicut ab urbe Romana iura omnibus proceserunt, ita, quod de Tibere flumine Romano dicetur, a flumina cunta trahatur. Et eum in tres libros divisi: in primo tractaturus de aluvione;
40 in secundo de insula in flumine nata; in tertio de alveo. Et tunc in[7] duobus diebus primi libri figuras conposui et exposui; tertia vero die secundi libri figuras incepi et, cum aliqua mihi dubia ocurrissent et circa ea veementius cogitarem, me visitavit quidam frater Guido de Perusio, mangnus teologus, universalis in omnibus, qui meus fuerat, et erat in geometria magister, non
45 proposito remanendi. Sed tunc insurexit[8] pluvia ita mangna, quod mecum pernoctare choactus est et morari per diem integram naturalem. Tunc dixi: 'Vere congnosco quod in prosecutione operis Deus est.' Cum ipso predicta contuli et figuras secundi libri secum formare conplevi, et multa spiritualia gaudia ex collationibus spiritualibus secum habui. Quod autem in tertio libro
50 dicturus eram in mente servavi, et cum omnibus istis Perusium sum reversus et ea revidi et sub forma infrascripta libellum conposui. Et universitati vestre tradidi sub an[n]o Domini MCCCLV.

Gaius: Quod per aluvionem agro nostro flumen adiecerit, iure gentium adquiritur nobis. Per aluvionem autem id videtur adici, quod ita paulatim
55 adicitur, ut intelligere non possimus quantum quoquo momento tenporis additiatur. Quod si vis fluminis partem aliquam ex tuo predio detraxerit et meo predio appulerit, palam est tuam eam per[m]anere, plane si longiore tenpore fundo meo heserit arboresque quas secum trasserat in meum fundum / 157v/ radices egerint, ex eo tenpore videtur meo fundo aquisita
60 esse. Hec scripta sunt ff. de aquire. re. do., l. adeo, § preterea (D. 41.1.7.1-2).

Quod.[9] Optimum fuit hoc, quod de iure gentium erat, in scriptis redigere, cum ex hoc contenptiones varie oriantur. Verba itaque legis discutiamus. Ait lex 'quod'. Neutraliter acipe, id est quamcumque rem, ut ff. nau. ca., l. i, § ait pretor (D. 4.9.1.6). Sive igitur terram[10] puram sive lapides terre comistos
65 adiecerit fundo nostro, nostrum eficitur; etiam si fuerint gemme vel lapides pretiosi. Nec obstat Ist. de rerum divi., § item lapilli (Inst. 2.1.18), quia ibi loquitur de lapillis in litore maris inventis, qui[11] in nullius bonis sunt, hic de lapillis qui[12] predio nostro aditiuntur. Idem, si lingna vel aurum, vel

---

[5] tiberis *post* ut *del.*
[6] non solum-tractetur *add. in marg.*
[7] du[o]b. *post* in *del.*
[8] insurexit *add. in marg.*
[9] hec scripta-quod *suprascr.*
[10] sive *post* terram *del.*
[11] *ms.* que in *post* que *del.*

argentum vel pecuniam, predio nostro flumen adiecerit, nostrum erit. De quacumque enim re lex loquitur, dum tamen ita additiatur[13] quod terre choereat, ut patet ex verbo 'adiecerit', quod infra exponetur.[14] Nec hoc fieret inventoris pro parte, ut de tesauro dicitur, Ist. de re. di., § tesauros (Inst. 2.1.39), et ff. de aquir. re. do., l. nunquam, § tesaurus (D. 41.1.31.1). Non[15] enim erat hec pecunia[16] ab antiquo deposita, que tesaurus in dictis legibus dicitur, sed pecunia per vim aquarum ab incongnito loco transducta et predio nostro adiecta. Nec enim obstat ff.[17] de dan. infec., l. hoc anplius, § i, et ii (D. 39.2.9.1-2), et de incen.[18] rui. nau., l. ne quid (D. 47.9.7), quia hoc intelligo, quod cuius sint dicte res a[d]iecte ingnoratur, alias dominii nostri non eficerentur, ut ibi, et inferius declarabitur.[19]

Per aluvionem. Hoc ab ipsa lege exponitur et infra patebit.

Agro.[20] Ager locus in rure sine edifitio apellatur, ut ff. de ver. sy., l. fundi (D. 50.16.211). Quid ergo si, cum domum iusta flumen haberem, ibidem per alluvionem flumen adiecit? Certe meum erit. Idcirco enim hic legis lator agri nomine usus est, ut ostendat alluvionem respectu soli fieri, non edifitii superinpositi. Ad hoc etiam ostendendum in inferiori parte legis, quam supra[21] retulimus, predii et fundi nomine fecit mentionem, quorum apellatio generalis est, etiam ad edifitia, ut ff. de ver. sy., l. locus, et l. questio, et l. fundi (D. 50.16.60, 115, 211). Sed cum agri tres partes sint, scilicet[22] ipsius agri planities. Item, loca que ripe cedunt, scilicet ex quo primum a plano vergere incipit usque ad aquam, quod intellige[n]dum est de hiis que incipiunt vergere propter atrationem aque, ut ff. de fluminibus, l. penultima (D. 43.12.3), et ibi notatur.[23] Item, est ripa, hoc est id, quod flumen continet naturalem rigorem cursus sui retinens, ut ff. de fluminibus, l. i, § ripa (D. 43.12.1.5). Quomodo agro dicatur adici, posset queri. Sed respondeo: cuicumque dictarum partium aditiatur, satis est quod aparet, quia si via media esset ius aluvionis non inpediret, ut ff. de aquir. re. do., l.[24] Martius (D. 41.1.38), et ideo glossa Ist. e., super verbo 'adiecit' exponit: ponendo iusta predium.[25]

---

[12] *ms.* que; in *post* que *del.*
[13] *ms.* additiantur.
[14] dum tamen-exponetur *add. in marg.*
[15] erit *post* non *del.*
[16] loco *post* pecunia *del.*
[17] aqui. [rer. pos.?] *post* ff. *del.*
[18] dan. infec.-de incen. *add. in marg.*
[19] dum ait *post* declarabitur *del.*
[20] inquid *post* agro *del.*
[21] rel. *post* supra *del.*
[22] ipse ager *post* scilicet *del.*
[23] Glossa *Casus* ad D. 43.12.3.
[24] planit. *post* l. *del.*
[25] et ideo-predium *add. in marg.* Glossa *Adiicit* ad Inst. 2.1.20.

Queritur, cum ager venditur, an ripe et loca que ripe cedunt veniant mensuranda? Quod non videtur, ut ff. de contraen. enpt., l. litora (D. 18.1.51). In contrarium facit quod supra dixi, et videtur casus ff. de fun. instruc., l. predia, § ita legatum (D. 33.7.27.4), et ibi notatur.[26] Pro quo facit, quia dicta lex litora loquitur in litoribus maris, que comunia sunt, ripe autem fluminis sunt eorum qui prope predia possident, ut ff. de rerum di., l. riparum (D. 1.8.5). Respondeo: quod predicta non veniunt mensuranda nisi sit dictum,[27] sicut dicimus in limitibus fundi, qui choerent viis publicis, ut ff. de peri. et co. rei, l. id quod, § i (D. 18.6.7.1). Ratio autem est quia predicta non venduntur sed magis rei vendite acedunt, quod aparet quia per se vendi non posset. Cum enim riparum usus sit comunis de iure gentium, aparet quod propietas sola per se esset inutilis, cum senper duret usus alterius, ut ff. de usuf., l. iii, § ne tamen (D. 7.1.3.2). Ideo per se non censetur, sed alteri cedit. Et hoc vult dicere testus in dicta l. id quod, § i, de peri. et co. rei vendi., quod nota. Ex illo etiam collige quod, sicut se habent ripe, quia earum[28] usus est comunis, ita etiam se habent limites prediorum, qui viis publicis choerent, ut ar. dicte l. id quod, § i, et quod supra dictum est. Idem intelligo de fossis, que sunt inter viam et fundum, eadem ratione. Ille enim fosse sunt[29] eorum quorum prediis adherent, quod patet quia r[i]pa vie est ipsorum, ut l. Martius, de aquir. re. do. (D. 41.1.38), et not. Ist. de re. di., § riparum[30] (Inst. 2.1.4). Ergo fovea, que est inter illam ripam et fundum, non est nostra, ut ff. de aqua plu. ar., l. ii, § preterea (D. 39.3.2.2), et ibi notatur.[31] Via autem non potest dici, quia per ea[m] non itur nec comeatur, ergo non est via, ut l. ii, § ait pretor, ne quid in loco publico (D. 43.8.2.20). Puto tamen quod usus sit publicus sicut viarum.[32] Nec predictis obstat dicta l. predia, § ita legatum, de fun. instruc. (D. 33.7.27.4), quia ibi loquitur in ageribus et fossis, que sunt intra ipsum fundum, et sic sunt iure propietatis et usus domini ipsius fundi. Unde, cum vendantur, veniunt in mensura.

Sed dubitatur qualiter iste fosse, que sunt in fundo,[33] mensurentur, videlicet an mensurentur superfities que sunt a latere fovee et que est in fundo fovee;[34] an vero mensurentur cum toto agro, sicut si fovee plene essent? Respondeo: ager dicitur ab agendo, secundum Uguit[i]onem, et sic ab actu,[35] quia per eum possunt boves et alia animalia duci, quod inportat nomen actus. Si igitur fovea esset ita anpla et eius latera ita lata quod laborarentur, vel laborari possent cum bobus, dico eam mensurandam. Si

---

[26] Glossa *Aggeres* ad D. 33.7.27.4.
[27] ratio quia predicta *post* dictum *del.*
[28] *ms.* eorum.
[29] eius cuius *post* sunt *del.*
[30] Glossa *Adherent* ad Inst. 2.1.4.
[31] et ibi notatur *suprascr.* Glossa *Confinio* ad D. 39.3.2.2.
[32] enim fosse sunt-publicus sicut viarum *add. in marg.*
[33] dividantur *post* fundo *del.*
[34] fovee *suprascr.*
[35] secundum-actu *add. in marg.*

vero, ut sepe accidit, ripe fovearum sunt erecte, ita quod /f. 158r/ per eas
135 iri et agi non possit, tunc fovee mensurantur cum fundo ac si plene essent, et ita observatur.

Idem dico de ripis, que in fundo essent, ut siquidem cum bobus coli possent, earum superfities veniat mensuranda. Secus si ita erecte essent quod sic coli non possent, tunc enim mesuratur solum quod dicta ripa[36] continet,
140 sicut si in fundo aliquis murus esset, eadem ratione. Predicta [vera,] nisi aliter actum sit[37] expresse vel tacite, ut dicta l. id quod, § i, de periculo et co. rei vendi. (D. 18.6.7.1). Dico autem tacite, puta si ad mensuram quoddam predium venderetur montuosum, saxosum vel,[38] plagiosum seu[39] riposum, licet enim hoc propie ager non dicatur, quia per eum agi non potest, tamen
145 mensurabitur, sic enim actum videtur. De concavitate vero sulcorum, qui fiunt gratia anualis culture vel aque derivande, ut ff. de aqua plu. arcen., l. i, § de eo opere (D. 39.3.1.3), dico in mensura rationem non habendam, quoniam illa non est forma agri perpetua sed culture causa factam. Fovee vero et ageres ad perpetuam rei utilitatem fieri dicuntur, ut ff. de inpen. in
150 re. do. fac., l. inpense (D. 25.1.14). Ei autem quod dixi, predium quod totum est riposum seu plagiosum esse mensu[r]andum, contradicere videtur quod supra dixi: ripam et loca que ripe cedunt per se non posse vendi. Sed respondeo: omnia loca que a plano incipiunt vergere usque ad aquam, intelligendum est propter atractionem aque. Si enim intra duos montes
155 vadat[40] flumen non omnes penditie montis dicentur ripe, quoniam naturaliter vergunt versus aquam, ut notatur in dicta l. penultima, de fluminibus[41] (D. 43.12.3).

Huius gratia,[42] quid sit planus, investigandum est. Ad quod sciendum habenda est notitia eorum que plano oponuntur, ut mons, collis, vallis et
160 similia. Mons locus altus est, ut l. si edes, ff. de servi. ur. predi. (D. 8.2.38), quod intelligo de mangna altitudine, ut infra dicam.[43] Dicitur autem mons, secundum Uguitionem et Papiam,[44] a movendo per contrarium, quia non movetur. Quod intelligo non de ea immobilitate, que universe terre congruit,[45] sed quia non movetur, scilicet per culturam, id est non colitur.
165 Terra enim, que colitur, movetur. Durat igitur mons usque ad locum quo coli incipit. Penditie ergo montium culte, montis apellatione non con-

---

[36] *ms.* dictam ripam.
[37] tacite vel *post* sit *del.*
[38] tale quod totum posset quodammodo dici *post* vel *del.*
[39] plagiosum seu *add. in marg.*
[40] aqua *post* vadat *del.*
[41] Glossa *Publica* ad D. 43.12.3.
[42] quero *post* gratia *del.*
[43] quod intelligo-dicam *add in marg.*
[44] Papias, *Vocabulista* (Venetiis, 1496; repr. Turin, 1966), p. 210, s.v. *Mons*; Huguccius, *Magne derivationes,* s.v. *mons,* Paris, BN, ms. lat. 7622a, fol. 135va.
[45] q. *post* congruit *del.*

tinetur,[46] quia ibi terminatur mons, et ita utimur, nisi certi[47] loci usus aliter se haberet. Si tamen inter montem essent aliqua loca culta, montis apellatione continetur, sicut pars apelatione totius, ut ff. de rei ven., l. in rem, § item quecumque (D. 6.1.23.5).

Collis autem ab altitutdine mons dici potest.[48] Propie autem collis dicitur a colendo, quasi mediocres montes, qui coluntur; ita exponit glossa scripture divine super illo verbo psalmi: montes exultaverunt ut arietes et colles vellut agni ovium.[49] Sunt enim montes mangne altitudinis et comuniter sunt inculti; colles vero mediocris altitudinis et comuniter sunt culti. Intelligo autem colles habentes altitudinem propiam non continuatam cum maiorum montium altitudine. Si enim continuarentur, tunc si essent culti[50] dicerentur penditie montium, ut dictum. Horum causa in nonnullis partibus locus magne altitud[in]is, licet cultus, dicitur mons, et locus parve altitudinis, licet incultus, dicitur collis. Distinguitur ergo mons a colle altitudine vel cultura, vel exti[m]atione circumcolentium, simile ff. de fluminibus, l. i, § i (D. 43.12.1.1).

Vallis vero dicitur locus montibus vel collibus circumdatus, a vallo vallas, quod idem est quod circundare. Et est locus planus parve seu mediocris mangnitudinis.

Planus dicitur a 'platos' grece, quod idem est quod latum seu latitudo, secundum Uguitionem; dicitur etiam pla[n]ities, idem quod equalitas, secundum Papiam.[51] Duo igitur requiruntur: ut sit latus, et sint eius partes equales, id est equaliter plane,[52] ita quod una aliam non superexcedat.[53] Distinguitur ergo vallis a plano circundatione. Potest enim planus esse non circumdatus montibus[54] vel alia altitudine, ut iusta mare. Vallis autem non dicitur nisi aliqua altitudine circundetur. Item, difert[55] latitudine, quia etiam locus montibus circundatus, si mangne latitudinis est, planus dicitur. Hoc autem opinione circumcolentium exsti[m]atur. Difert enim ab equalitate, quia vallis dicitur etiam si habet concavitatem,[56] planus autem[57] equalitatem requirit. Equalitas autem plani qualis /f. 158v/ esse debeat dubitari potest.

---

[46]non continetur *add. in marg.*

[47]usu *post* loci *del.*

[48]et ideo glo. ff. de aqua plu. ar., l. ii, § item martius, ibi agerem, quod in fundo erat exponit agerem id est montem cum tam parva [latitu. *del.*] altitudo essent *post* potest *del.*

[49]Ps 113:6. Glossa *Colles* ad Ps 113:6.

[50] *ms.* culta.

[51]Papias, *Vocabulista*, p. 253, s.v. *Planus*; Huguccius, *Magne derivationes*, s.v. *Planus*, fol. 171vb.

[52]id est equaliter plane *suprascr.*

[53]dicitur enim-superexcedat *add. in marg.*

[54]si iusta mare *post* montibus *del.*

[55]a *post* difert *del.*

[56]qua *post* concavitatem *del.*

[57]con. *post* autem *del.*

Puto autem non omnimodam equalitatem requiri, sed suficit quod notabiliter in unam partem non vergat, vix[58] enim reperitur locus qui aliqualiter[59] in aliquam partem non pergat, saltim tamen quod perfluens[60] aqua decurrat. Ideo dixi suficere quod notabiliter non pergat, simile ff. de edili. edic., l. cui dens (D. 21.1.11). Notabiliter autem in unam partem pergere probabiliter potest dici quando inde aqua perfluens[61] multum de terra aufert, ita quod usum et culturam eius fatiat deteriorem, ar. ff. de aqua plu. ar., l. i, § finali (D. 39.3.1.23), et ar. de edili. edic., l. i, § sciendum (D. 21.1.1.7). In hiis autem multum circumcolentium opinio facit.

Fosse autem et agrorum et viarum ripe ipsius plani sunt; loquor autem de plano totali, ut si de plano Tiberis loquatur. Sicut enim fosse que sunt in fundo fundi sunt, ita que sunt in totali plano plani sunt, ut l. predia, § ita legatum, de fun. instruc. (D. 33.7.27.4). Et sic statuta que loquuntur de hiis, que in plano Tiberis commictuntur, locum haberent etiam in hiis que in dictis foveis et ripis comicti contingeret. Quid ergo si comicteretur in eo loco quo propter atracionem aque versus flumen vergit, an in plano Tiberis dicatur esse comissum? Quod non, videtur dicere enim dicta l. penultima, de[62] flu. (D. 43.12.3), ex quo a plano vergere incipit; sed dictio 'a' separationem denotat, ut ff. de act. en[p]ti, l. ratio, § finali (D. 19.1.3.4). Ergo ille locus sic vergens est separatus et distintus a plano. Respondeo: si queratur an talis locus apellatione agri mei contineatur, dicendum est quod non per rationem predictam. Si vero an totalis plani Tiberis apellatione contineatur, advertendum est, siquidem flumen per[63] planum vadit, ita quod ab utraque parte fluminis planum Tiberis nominetur, quod in dicto loco fieret, in plano factum esse dicetur. Quin imo etiam quod in ipso flumine fieret, in tali plano sub totali apellatione nominato factum esse diceretur. Cum enim in ipsum flumen aditus et exitus ab utraque parte aliter quam per[64] ipsum planum non habeat, merito ipsius plani apellatione continetur, ut in simili in multis casibus iura dicunt cui congruit, quia cum totum quod est ab utraque parte unius [fluminis] plani apellatione conti[n]eatur, ergo et ipsum flumen, alias flumen medium divideret, nec esset unus planus sed plures plani, ar. ff. de verbo. si., l. recte dicimus (D. 50.16.25). Facit et est quasi casus quia quod fit in aqua putei, in ipsa re factum esse videtur, ut ff. quod vi aut clam,[65] l. is qui in puteum (D. 43.24.11), in principio.[66] Quod si ab alia parte fluminis essent montes vel colles? Tunc ille locus propter

---

[58]vix *corr. ex* vis.
[59]non *post* aliqualiter *del.*
[60]perfluens *corr. ex* plefluens.
[61]*ms.* plofluens.
[62]p. *post* de *del.*
[63]flumen *post* per *del.*
[64]per *suprascr.*
[65]*ms.* de aqua cot.
[66]Facit et-principo *add. in marg.*

aque atractionem vergens plani apellatione non contineretur, sed ibi planus desinit et locus ille ripe fluminis cedit, ut dicta l. penultima, de fluminibus, nec etiam ipsum flumen aliunde enim habet aditum, ar. ff. uti poss., l. si duo, § [sed] si supra edes (D. 43.17.3.7), cum symilibus.

Nostro.[67] Noster quidem quantum ad presens spectat ager dicitur, sive ad nos pertineat iure dominii vel quasi, vel iure pingnoris vel ususfructus, vel quovis alio. Si enim ager ad nos spectat iure dominii, eodem iure aluvio perti[n]ebit,[68] ut hic. Idem si quasi dominii, ut ff. de public., l. si ego,[69] § quod tamen per aluvionem (D. 6.2.11.7); idem si pingnoris, ut ff. de pin. act., l. si convenerit, § si[70] nuda (D. 13.7.18.1), de pin., l. si fundus (D. 20.1.16), in principio; idem si iure ususfructus, ut ff. de usufr., l. item si fundi, § i (D. 7.1.9.1). Plus est, quia si fundus ad nos spe quadam spectaret, illo iure ad nos spectabit aluvio, ut ff. de le. i, l. quod in rerum, § i[i] (D. 30.1.24.2), eodem enim iure, quo fundus, censetur. Item, licet hic dicat 'agro nostro', Ist. e., § preterea (Inst. 2.1.20), dicit 'agro tuo'. Intelligo autem quod sit alicuius, id est ad aliquem iure privato pertineat. Si enim esset iuris publici via et vie aderet, iuris publici non eficeretur sed eorum qui prope viam predia possident, ut ff. de aquir. re. do., l. Martius (D. 41.1.38), et quod notatur Ist. de rerum divisione, § riparum[71] (Inst. 2.1.4). Que autem predia sunt civitatis, non tamen in usu publico, set per civitatem coluntur sicut per privatum, ea ius alluvionis habent, sunt enim tanquam privata, ut ff. de contrahen. en[p]t., l. sed Celsus (D. 18.1.6 pr.), in principio. Quid[72] dices si alicui canpo, in quo fiat forum, vel forte platee per alluvionem flumen addiderit? Respondeo: isti canpi platee sunt. Platea autem secundum Uguitionem et Papiam[73] idem est quod via anpla[74] /f. 160r/ seu via lata. Via ergo[75] est. Sed quod vie cedit, iuris publici non eficitur, ut dicta l. Martius.

Quid autem si alicui loco sacro vel religioso flumen adixerit, ut alicui cimiterio, vel loco aliter consecrato? Respondeo: ei non aquiritur. Non enim est ager noster, sed in nullius bonis est, ut ff. de re. di., l. i (D. 1.8.1). Nec potest dici quod queratur ei qui ab alia parte loci sacri predia possidet. Locus enim sacer medius inpedit aquisitionem, licet via non inpediret, ut ff. de aqua plu. ar., l. si prius, § sacro (D. 39.3.17.3 in c.), et de servit., l. servitutes, § finali (D. 8.1.14.2). Non enim potest dici quod locus sacer ita

---

[67] inquid *post* nostro *del.*

[68] id *post* pertinebit *del.*

[69] *ms.* de plubic. l. si sponsus.

[70] pingnori *post* si *del.*

[71] Glossa *Adherent* ad Inst. 2.1.4.

[72] autem *post* quid *del.*

[73] Papias, *Vocabulista*, p. 253, s.v. *Platea*; Huguccius, *Magne derivationes*, s.v. *Platea*, fol. 171vb.

[74] *fol. 159r alia manu in parte super. scripsit* Nichil deficit; *fol. 159v in parte infer. scripsit* Seu via lata.

[75] sed *post* ergo *del.*

dicatur predii sicut dicitur de via, in dicta l. Martius. Via enim destructa supletur a predio vicino, ut l. si locus, § finali, ff. quemad. ser. amic. (D. 8.6.14.1), quod de loco sacro non reperitur.[76] Puto autem quod talis alu[v]io in nullius bonis sit, sed ocupanti concedatur, sicut in alluvione, que agris
270 limitatis acedit, ut ff. de fluminibus, l. i, § si insula, et § sequenti (D. 43.12.1.6-7).

Flumen.[77] De flumine publico loquitur, ut patet in ea parte legis, quam in tertio libro declarabimus, quia exprimitur quod loquitur de flumine quod est iuris publici. Flumina publica sunt, que perennia et perpetua sunt, ut ff.
275 de flu., l. i, § ii (D. 43.12.1.2). Et ideo glossa Ist. de rerum di., § flumina (Inst. 2.1.2), super testu, qui dicit quod flumina omnia publica sunt, exponit: omnia, scilicet perpetua, ut Padus, Renus.[78] Quedam vero sunt privata, ut fossata in agris posita, que quandoque currunt, quandoque non.[79] Ista sunt verba glosse. Idem Rofredus, in libellis super interdicto Ne quid in flumine
280 publico, dicit quod flumina, que in yeme currunt in exstate non, sunt privata,[80] et bene dicit.[81] Ista enim vocantur torrentia, ut ff. de flu., l. i, § torrens (D. 43.12.1.2 in c.). Si igitur privata sunt, per aluvionem nemini potest tribuere. Si enim cursum mutat, senper solum remanet eius cuius primo erat. Quod autem dixi, non posse per aluvionem addicere, intelligas aponendo
285 ita quod predium exstendatur. Superponendo vero potest addicere, sicut enim pinguedo agri superioris additur agro inferiori, ut l. i, § finali, ff. de aqua plu. ar. (D. 39.3.1.23). Et si queratur cuius privati sint ista fossata seu torrentia, dico hoc facti esse. Potest enim probari quod per alicuius predium aqua prorupit et fosatum fecit vel inter predia plurium, tunc secundum
290 terminos antiquos inter predia divisa erant talia fossata, vel si potest probari qualiter sunt ab antiquo possessa, quod si, ut sepe accidit, nullum istorum vel aliud sufitiens possit probari, tunc puto illorum esse, qui prope ab utraque parte predia possident, cuiuslibet usque ad medium, ar. eius quod dicitur de insula et de alveo dimisso, ff. de aquir. re. do., l. adeo, § insula,
295 et § quod si toto (D. 41.1.7.3, 5), et quod dicam in secundo et tertio libro huius. Et est expressum ff. de aqua plu. arcen., l. ii, § preterea (D. 39.3.2.2), ubi testus dicit: si in confinio fossa posita sit. Et glossa exponit: in confinio, scilicet duorum prediorum, et sic erat comunis fovea.[82] Et sic infert quod, eo ipso quod est in confinio prediorum, [est] comunis. Quod etiam expres-
300 sius declarat ibi testus dum dicit: eam partem, que tibi accedit. Et sic expresse

---

[76]quod de-reperitur *add. in marg.*
[77]inquid *post* flumen *del.*
[78]fo. *post* Renus *del.*
[79]Glossa *Flumia* ad Inst. 2.1.2.
[80]ista enim v. *post* privata *del.*
[81]Rofredus ad tit. *Ne quid in flumine publico* (D. 43.13), Roffredi Beneventani, *Libelli iuris civilis,* in *Corpus Glossatorum Juris Civilis* (Lugduni, 1500; repr. Augustae Taurinorum 1968), vol. VI, p. 51.
[82]Glossa *Confinio* ad D. 39.3.2.2.

innuit quod eis, qui ab utraque parte predia posside[n]t, acedit. Quod intelligo, nisi ea fossata essent in usu publico, tunc enim dicerentur publica, ut ff. ne quid in loco publico, l. ii, § hoc interdictum (D. 43.8.2.2); et est expressum ff. ut in flumine publico non liceat, l. i, § fossa[83] (D. 43.14.1.5-6).

305 Sed quid si reperiuntur istrumenta antiqua in quibus[84] possesores prediorum a latere emerunt predium et pro fine fuit appositum fossatum? Videtur ad eos non pertinere. Ipsam enim rem emimus, non eius fines; pro quo facit quia fundi nichil est nisi quod intra se continet, ut ff. de ac. en., l. fundi (D. 19.1.17), in principio. Credo quod similiter intelligatur esse
310 eorum qui a latere predia possident, ut supra probatum est. Nec obstat quod fines non emuntur, quia fateor, sed tamen possibile est quod rei vendite acedunt, sicut si venderem fundum et poneremus pro fine ripam fluminis, sicut etiam si ponerem pro fine viam que, quo ad quid, fundo cedit, ut ff. de aquir. re. do., l. Martius (D. 41.1.38). Nec obstat dicta lex fundi (D.
315 19.1.17), quia illa regula, quod fundi nil est nisi quod intra se continet, patitur exceptionem per alias leges, ut in aque ductu, qui est extra predium, ut ff. de contraen. en[p]t., l. si aque ductus (D. 18.1.47), et in limitibus[85] prediorum et in[86] viis, ut supra dictum est, et in tali fossa sive fossato, ut dicta l. ii, § preterea, de aqua plu. arcen. (D. 39.3.2.2).

320 De rivis vero[87] et aliis nominibus fluminorum seu aliorum, que aquarum cursus singnificant, quid iuris sit et an[88] in eis aluvionis ius sit, in sequenti libro ubi de insula tractabimus dicetur, quoniam testus legis ibi de rivo facit mentionem.

Sed quero, quid si ripa[89] predii versus flumen naturaliter se exstendit,
325 quia forte erat ibi lapidicina crescens, de qua dicitur ff. soluto ma., l. divortio, § si vir in fundo (D. 24.3.7.13), et evidenter videtur Pisis apud montem Pisanum in lapidicinis marmoreis, vel forte terremotu in flumine ripa erecta coruit et ipsa iunta predio remanens fluminis alveum[90] per eum locum cessare fecit? Respondeo: puto /f. 160v/ totum illum locum domino predii
330 accedere, sicut per aluvionem. Omnes enim iste acessiones, que divina natura operante obveniunt nullo facto humano interveniente, eiusdem nature sunt, ut ff. de usufr., l. item si fundi, § i,[91] (D. 7.1.9.1), et hoc videtur sentire Acço in summa[92] Ist. de rerum di. Sive enim flumen predio meo addat et propter hoc ab eo recedat, sive recedat sinpliciter nil addendo,
335 nobis acesserit,[93] ut l. Martius, ibi: et hoc autem nil addendo recedit, sed

---

[83]Et est expressum-§ fossa *add. in marg.*
[84]quidam *post* quibus *del.*
[85]*ms.* limimitibus.
[86]vii. *post* in *del.*
[87]videamus *post* vero *del.*
[88]an *suprascr.*
[89]fluminis versus f. *post* ripa *del.*
[90]*[non bene legitur]* ... pro parte *post* alveum *del.*
[91]pro hoc facit quod *post* § i *del.*
[92]de *post* summa *del.*

ab eo naturali inpulsu. Istud autem incrementum,[94] quando ripa naturaliter excrescente contingit,[95] dici potest aluvio, quia latens incrementum est. Quando vero ruina vel terremotu hoc contingit, potest dici incrementum alvei recedentis,[96] de quo dicemus in tertio huius. Cum enim repente fiat, aluvio non est.

De lacu vero et[97] stangno dicendum quod quidam lacus et stangna sunt privata. Tunc non est dubium quod per aluvionem neque uni detrait neque alii addit. Sed locus ille, qui inundatur aqua laci vel stangni, etiam ita inundatus remanet eius cuius erat primo, ut ff. de aquir. re. do., l. lacus (D. 41.1.12), de aqua plu. ar., l. vicinus, § finali (D. 39.3.24.3). Quedam lacus et stangna sunt publica, et hoc duobus modis. Quandoque enim sunt publica, id est rei publice, ut ibi nullus pischetur, nisi cui res publica conmiserit, ut in laco Perusino, et tunc[98] idem quod si essent privata,[99] ut ff. de contraen. en., l. si Celsus (D. 18.1.6). Quedam sunt publica et in usu publico,[100] cum enim quilibet transit et in eo quilibet piscatur ad placitum, tunc addit et detrait per aluvionem sicut flumina publica, ut ff. de ver. sy., l. litus (D. 50.16.112), et ff. ut in flumine publico na. li., l. i[101] (D. 43.14.1).

Adiecerit.[102] Adiecta dicuntur ea que ita additiuntur ut uniantur, ut ff. de rei ven., l. in rem, § item quecumque (D. 6.1.23.5). Uniri autem dicuntur quando patres invicem choerent. Apparet enim evidenter id, quod per aluvionem aditur, alteri predio choerere. Si quid autem[103] sit quod aditiaur ita quod choereat, sive[104] terra, sive lingnum, sive es, nostrum erit. Illud autem quod per flumem ita in nostrum proicitur quod non cho[e]ret, licet nullius sit, tamen nostrum non est, sed ocupanti conceditur, ut patet in apibus et favo mellis ab apibus facto, ut ff. de aquir. re. do., l. naturalem, § apium (D. 41.1.5.2), Ist. de rerum di., § apium (Inst. 2.1.14). Hoc etiam aparet quia fundi non est nisi quod intra se continet, ita quod sit affissum, ut ff. de act. en[p]ti, l. fundi (D. 19.1.17 pr.), in principio. Facit de aquir. posse., l. iii, § Neratius[105] (D. 41.2.3.3).

Quid autem dicemus de arena, cuius partes invicem non choerent, an nostra efficiatur? Respondeo: cum hec materia terrea sit, nec cuius sit aparet,

---

[93]nobis acesserit *suprascr. corr. ex* aluvione.
[94]magis alveo naturali dicitur adquiri *post* incrementum *del.*
[95]dicitur aluvio quia latens direptam *post* contingit *del.*
[96]quoniam *post* recedentis *del.*
[97]et *suprascr. corr. ex* est.
[98]ut in-et tunc *add. in marg.*
[99]privata *corr. ex* privatus.
[100]per *post* publico *del.*
[101]et ff.-l. i *add. in marg.*
[102]inquid *post* adiecerit *del.*
[103]per flumen *post* autem *del.*
[104]ling. *post* sive *del.*
[105]Facit de-Neratius *add. in marg.*

cum ipso fundo confundi dicitur, sicut dicimus de pecunia mista cum pecunia, ut ff. de solut., l. si alieni (D. 46.3.78). Hoc etiam aparet quia comuniter omnia incrementa fluminis, que fiunt per aluvionem, sunt
370 aditamenta arenosa. De isto igitur iuris consultus sensit.
Iure gentium.[106] Hoc est ius quo omnes gentes utuntur, ut ff. de iusti. et iure, l. i, § finali (D. 1.1.1.4). Conpeteret ergo istud ius deportatis et ceteris qui iura civilia perdiderunt, ut ff. de penis, l. quidam sunt (D. 48.19.17).
Aquiritur[107] *nobis.*[108] Aquiri nobis intelligo eo iure quo ager primus ad
375 nos perti[n]ebat, ut supra dictum est, cum exposuimus verbum 'nostro'. Et fit hec aquisitio ipso iure gentium, absque alicuius hominis facto. An autem sic aquiri dicatur ut possideamus, quod per aluvionem aditur, dubitari potest. Sed, cum hoc quod aditur pars primi agri sit non novus ager, puto id, quod[109] a[d]iectum est, sicut primus ager possideretur, ar. ff. de aquir.
380 poss., l. iii (D. 41.2.3 pr.), in principio. In ea enim opinione quis videtur esse, ut velit totum fundum possidere, ut ff. de le. i, l. si ex toto (D. 30.1.8 pr.), in principio, et l. quod in rerum, § penultimo[110] (D. 30.1.24.3). Predicta autem non habent locum in agris limitatis, ut ff. de aquire. re. do., l. in agris (D. 41.1.16). Qui autem sint agri limitati, ibidem iuris consultus explanat.
385 Hoc est, agri capti ab hostibus et divisi /f. 161r/ inter milites, ut scieretur quid cuique datum esset, quid venisset, et quid in publico relictum erit,[111] ut dicta l. in agris, in fine. Si ergo princeps unum integrum territorium uni adsingnaret, non esset ager limitatus, quod patet quia non est divisus. Et hoc vult testus in dicta l. in agris, dum dicit quod si ager totus apud rem
390 publicam retinetur non est ager limitatus. Sed si unum territorium princeps inter plures dividit, tunc agri limitati sunt, nec ius aluvionis habet, ut dicta l. in agris, et de flu., l. i, § si insula (D. 43.12.1.6). Ratio huius potest esse quia postqaum princeps limitate dedit, vult quod senper limitate possideatur, ut senper sciatur quantum habuit benefitio principis, nec possit dici
395 quod habuerit benefitio fortune. Vel dic quod ratio est, quia flumina loco censitorum habentur, hoc est, illorum offitialium qui propter censum accipiunt de iure unius et dant alteri. Sed sicut dicti offitiales non possunt mutare concessionem factam per principem, ita nec flumen, ar. ff. de aquir. re. do., l. ergo, § penultimo (D. 41.1.30.3). Sed huic rationi contradicit
400 expositio Azonis, quam facit in Summa Ist. de rerum divi.,[112] ubi dicit flumina habentur loco censitorum, id est iudicum et principum, vel iurisconsultorum, ideo non habent ius alluvionis, quia propter illis prediis non tenetur solvere inpositiones,[113] ideo in alio graventur, ut C. de fund. li., l.

---

[106]inquid *post* gentium *del.*
[107]inquid *post* aquiritur *del.*
[108]inquid *post* nobis *del.*
[109]quod *repet. et del.*
[110]quero quid si territoria civitatum vel dioceses vel parochie *post* penultimo *del.*
[111]*[non bene legitur]* ... si *post* esset *del.*
[112]Azo ad tit. *De rerum divisione* (Inst. 2.1), in *Corpus Glossatorum Juris Civilis* (Papie 1506; repr. Augustae Taurinorum, 1966), vol. II, p. 354.

finali (C. 11.60[59].3), li. xi.[114] Vel dicas non esse querendam rationem, postquam habemus determinationem. In agris ergo limitatis non habet locum ius aluvionis. Sed quid si plura territoria capiantur et quodlibet territorium per se integrum diversis militibus adsingnetur? Respondeo: non esse agros limitatos, sicut si unum integrum uni adsingnaret, ut dictum est, ar. ff. de ver. ob., l. scire debemus (D. 45.1.29), ii responso.

Quero:[115] quid si territoria et iur[is]dictiones civitatum et episcopatum sunt divisa et terminata per cursum alicuius fluminis, an sicut flumen acipit de iure unius et dat alteri iure dominii, ita fatiat in iure iur[is]dictionis? Et videtur quod iurisdictiones non mutentur. Sunt enim limitate a principe, ergo videntur agri limitati, ut dicta l. in agris[116] (D. 41.1.16). Et si dicis quod hoc non aparet,[117] dicam iste limitationes sunt antique et a tenpore cuius memoria non existit, ergo habentur iure constituti per principem, ut ff. de aqua coti., l. hoc iure, § ductus aque (D. 43.20.3.4). Sic videntur limitati. Sed hec ratio non est sufitiens. Pone enim quod princeps non divisit territoria, vel sicut divisa invenit, ita divisa servavit, tunc agri limitati non dicentur, ut dictum est. Vel dicamus quod iurisdictio non mutatur, quia aluvio ea que sunt publica in alium non transfert, ut l. Martius, de aquir. re. do. (D. 41.1.38). Sed huic obstat quod supra dictum est, super verbo 'nostro', quia ea que publica sunt, hoc est civitatis, non in usu publico ius aluvionis habent. Cuius gratia videndum est an[118] iursditiones sint iuris publici. Et constat quod sic, ut ff. de iusti. et iure, l. i, § publicum ius (D. 1.1.1.2 in c.), ibi: magistratibus. Secundo, videndum est qualiter sint iuris publici, an tanquam ea que sunt in usu publico, an tanquam ea que civitas ut privatus possidet. Ad quod sciendum est quod sicut pater et filius,[119] dominus et servus, sunt corelativa, ita iurisdictio est quedam relatio domini in subditos. Et sicud pater[120] habet ius in filium, ita filius contra patrem habet quedam iura petendi alimenta et similia, ita in iursditione subditi habent quoddam ius petendi iustitiam a superiori, et[121] si ille denegat, delinquid et punitur, ut in aut. ut diferen. iu. (N. 86=A. 9.10.1), in principio, et ff. et C. de magistra. conven. (D. 27.8; C. 5.75), cum symilibus. Et istud ius est iuris publici, tanquam ea que sunt in usu publico. Quilibet enim potest a magistratu petere iustitiam, ut dicta l. i, § publicum ius, de iusti. et iure[122] (D. 1.1.1.2 in c.). Alio modo consideratur iursditio, prout est in ipso magistratu, civitate, comite vel barone. Et isto

---

[113]inpositiones *corr. ex* factiones(?).
[114]vel iurium-li. xi *add. in marg.*
[115]*in marg.* Quando territoria sunt divisa et terminata per cursum fluminum.
[116]§(?) *post* agris *del.*
[117]respondeo *post* aparet *del.*
[118]an *suprascr. corr. ex* qualiter.
[119]sunt *post* filius *del.*
[120]conpetit ius conta *post* pater *del.*
[121]et *repet. et del.*
[122]et isto modo iursditio *post* iure *del.*

modo iurisditio est iuris publici, eo modo quo sunt ea que civitas possidet ut privatus, /f. 161v/ quod patet quia non quilibet de civitate utitur, sed
440 solum cui res publica permiserit. Et ea que inde percipiuntur, ut multe, pene, banna et similia, ipsius civitatis vel domini sunt tanquam privata, ut ff. ne quid in loco publico, l. ii, § hoc interdictum[123] (D. 43.8.2.4).

Item, videndum est utrum iurisdictio conpetat cuilibet civitati vel domino etiam in ipso flumine usque ad medium ipsius fluminis terminantis. Et
445 respondeo: sic. Quia omnia, que sunt in confinio, sunt comunia eorum, qui ab utraque parte possident, ut l. arbor, comuni divi. (D. 10.3.19), de aqua plu. arc., l. ii, § preterea (D. 39.3.2.2), et de aquir. re. do., l. adeo, § finali (D. 41.1.7.13), et si[c,] de omni eo quod conmicteretur in ipso flumine, quilibet habet iurisditionem usque ad medium fluminis. Hiis premissis, in
450 questione proposita, cum in ipso flumine et solo ipsius civitati vel alteri domino vel episcopo conpetat ius iurisditionis tanquam privatum, et sic quo ad hoc flumen est privati iuris, dicendum est indubitanter quod per aluvionem, hoc est additionem vel detractionem, que fiat a flumine, non aditur vel detraitur iurisditioni, sicut supra dictum est de lacu, ut ff. de
455 contraen. en[p]t., l. Rutilia (D. 18.1.69), de aqua plu. arcen., l. vicinus, § finali (D. 39.3.24.3), de aquir. re. do., l. lacus (D. 41.1.12). Ar. contra predicta, ff. de aqua co. et ex., l. hoc iure, § si aquam (D. 43.20.3.2). Sed facilis est solutio si bene inspitiatur.[124]

Per aluvionem autem id videtur addici quod ita paulatim additur, ut
460 *intelligere non possimus quantum quoquo momento tenporis adicitur.* Ista verba legis sunt. Super illo autem verbo 'momento tenporis' glossa ait sic: Nam si tota die figas intuitum, inbecillitas visus tam subtilia incrementa perpendere non potest, ut in cucurbita ostendi potest. Unde dicitur latens incrementum, ut Ist., e., § preterea.[125] Ista sunt verba glosse, sunta ex Summa
465 Azonis, Ist. de rerum di.[126] Et advertendum quod id, quod testus dicit intelligere, glossa[127] intelligit: hoc est, per visum conprendere, et merito. Ut enim naturales dicunt, una est virtus intellectiva, que intelligit, et hec eadem in homine[128] mediante organo oculorum videt et per aurem audit, et sic de similibus. Hec autem expositio, licet[129] in verbis legis latoris
470 congrua sit, in dicto alicuius testis congrua non esset, qui de eo debet deponere, quod sinpliciter sensu corporis percipit, ut ff. de testa., l. qui testamento, § finali (D. 28.1.20.10), et C. de testi., l. testium (C. 4.20.18), et notatur per Inocentium, de testi., c. cum causam[130] (X. 2.20.37). Si igitur diceret testis aliquid esse, quia sic fieri intellexit, non probaret;[131] nec

---

[123]ut ff.-interdictum *add. in marg.*
[124]ar. contra-inspiciatur *add. in marg.*
[125]Glossa *Momento temporis* ad D. 41.1.7.1.
[126]Azo ad tit. *De rerum divisione* (Inst. 2.1), p. 354.
[127]exponit *post* glo. *del.*
[128]in homine *add. in marg.*
[129]per verba *post* licet *del.*
[130]Innocentius IV ad c. *Cum casuam* (Francofurti ad M., 1570), fols. 262r-263v.

475 exponeretur intellexit, id est vidit, quia potuit per alium modum ad hanc intellectionem pervenire, de quo non interrogatur.

Sed hic merito ocurrit dubitatio. Si enim hec[132] alluvio non potest per sensum corporis conprendi, ergo quid sit aluvio non poterit per testes probari. Dico tamen quod bene potest videri quod flumen addit, sed non 480 quantum quoquo momento, sicut in puero excrescente videmus. Dico etiam quod ex visione loci post incrementum adlatum potest videri et per visum conprendi, quod per aluvionem est[133] factum. Ex conpositione enim facta de terra addita hoc ma[n]ifeste per omnes conprenditur quod mi[n]utatim factum est, et quod a flumine factum, quoniam per alium fieri inpossibile 485 esset. Unde puto, testem probare, qui diceret quod ipse vidit incrementum adlatum, et vidit quod est alluvio addita a flumine minutatim. Idem puto in quacumque materia contingeret, ut si aparet aliquid factum, quod nisi ab uno fieri non potuit, quod aperta sit probatio illum fecisse. Quid enim si per certam oram unus ad domis custodiam sit dimissus constatque nullum alium 490 ingressum esse, et co[n]fines, qui clausi dimissi erant,[134] fracti reperiantur? Procul dubio ille, qui remansit, fecit. Et quid si plures erant in consilio super arduis et secretis, constat neminem exivisse vel cum alio loquutum esse, uno excepto, et reperitur negotium publicatum? Procul dubio ab illo factum est, cum ab alio factum esse[135] inpossibile sit, sicut hic inpossibile est ab alio 495 additum, quam a flumine.[136]

Quod si vis fluminis, et cet. Hic tractare incipit de incremento non per aluvionem, hoc est non paulatim et latenter, sed manifeste et palam. Ait ergo 'vis fluminis', id est, potentia fluminis. Multas enim singnificationes hec dictio [habet]: quandoque pro potentia, ut hic. Et in vulgari dicimus talis homo 500 habet mangnam vim, hoc est mangnam potentiam, quod non intelligitur de corporali, sed de ea que contingit ex multitudine amicorum, subditorum, vel divitiarum.[137] Quandoque pro violentia, ut supra quod metus causa, l. ii, et l. exstat (D. 4.2.2, 13), cum symilibus. Quandoque pro necessitate, ut supra de statu hominum,[138] l. libertas (D. 1.5.4), ibi: nisi quod vi, et cet. Dicimus 505 enim in vul- /f. 162r/ gari, ego fatio hoc vi, id est necessitate cogente facit, C. de resi. ven., l. non idcirco (C. 4.44.12). Item, acipitur pro potestate, ut[139] supra de tutelis, l. i (D. 26.1.1 pr.), in principio, et § i (D. 26.1.1.1), et Ist. de tutelis (Inst. 1.13.2), in principio. Et istis casibus declinatur in singulari[140]

---

[131] quia *post* probaret *del.*
[132] non potest per sen. *post* hec *del.*
[133] est *repet. et del.*
[134] cla. *post* erant *del.*
[135] fieri *post* esse *del.*
[136] deinde in verbis legis sequitur *post* flumine *del.*
[137] et in vulgari-vel divitiarum *add. in marg.*
[138] *ms.* de iure personarum (Inst. 1.3.1 = D. 1.5.4).
[139] ut *repet. et del.*
[140] t[a]n[tum] *post* singulari *del.*

tantum per omnes casus, plurali vero non utitmur. Reperitur tamen 'vires'
510 in plurali et ille non habent singularem. Et interdum ponitur 'vires' pro
effectu seu eficatia, ut ista stipulatio[141] habet vires, ut ff. de verbo. ob., l.
stipulatio ista, § hii qui (D. 45.1.38.6). Ponitur etiam 'vires', id est, virtutes,
ut ait Cato:[142] herbarum vires, et cet. Ponitur etiam pro pote[n]tia corporis,
ut talis homo habet mangnas vires.[143] Reperitur etiam 'vix' averbium, cuius
515 singnificatio ponitur ff. de iuditiis, l. vix (D. 5.1.53), et ad Vel., l. tutor (D.
16.1.19), cum symilibus.

Partem aliquam ex tuo predio detraxerit, et cet. Ut igitur hec legis pars
locum habeat, oportet constare quod pars illa, quam flumen predio meo
aplicuit ex tuo predio fuerit. Si vero cuius fuerit ingnoretur, tunc statim quod
520 terre mee aplicaretur, meum esset, ut supra in principio dictum est, et etiam
super verbo 'adiecerit'.

Et predio meo aplicuit, et cet. Sed Istit. de rerum divi., § quod si vis (Inst.
2.1.21), ubi est idem testus, dicitur 'aplicaverit', quod exponit glossa: id est
super posuerit, ut subicit, puta crustam terre vineate et arborate.[144] Ita dicit
525 glossa. Secundum hoc difert hec pars a precedenti, quia supra adiecit a
latere, hic super posuit. Licet autem hoc in se verum sit, tamen non puto
curandum; sive enim a latere, sive super fundo talem crusta[m] posuerit,
idem iuris est. Difert ergo quia in precedenti parte adiecit invisibiliter, hic
vero visibiliter et palam. Quid autem sit hoc, quod dicit: apulerit seu
530 aplicaverit, advertendum est. Potest autem hoc esse etiam sine unione rei
que aplicatur. Dicimus enim navem ad portum aplicasse vel apulisse, non
tamen unitur portui. Et si hoc modo crusta agri tui predio meo apulit, sine
dubio tua manet, ut hic, et a te poterit vendicari, ut supra de dapno infec.,
l. hoc anplius, § i (D. 39.2.9.1). Quandoque crusta agri tui meo[145] predio
535 aplicatur aliqua levi unione, ita quod potest de facili separari,[146] et tunc
idem. Ideo dicit testus: palam est, tuam eam permanere,[147] ut hic. Raro enim
terra potest apponi super terram, quin aliqualis aplicatio et unio fiat. Et ideo
hec lex notabiliter requirit, quod arbores radices emiserint, ut infra videbimus. Quandoque crusta agri tui meo predio aplicatur ita quod unitur, tunc
540 predii mei eficitur, ut infra dicetur.

Plane si longiori tenpore, et cet. Eandem materiam prosequitur, quando
ab initio crusta in meum fundum translata est sine unione. Si enim ab ipso
initio fuerit unita, ut quia multum cum terra agri mei involuta, ita quod nec
discerni nec separari posset, mea esset, ut dicta l. hoc anplius, § i, de danpno
545 infecto (D. 39.2.9.1). Sed quando ab initio sic unita non est, tunc ex post facto

---

[141] non *post* stipulatio *del*.

[142] er. *post* Cato *del*. *Disticha Catonis*, lib. II, praef.: 'quod si mage nosse laboras / Herbarum vires, Macer tibi carmina dicit.'

[143] partem aliquam ex tuo predio detraxerit *post* vires *del*.

[144] Glossa *Attulerit* ad Inst. 2.1.21.

[145] *ms.* medio.

[146] idem *post* separari *del*.

[147] et tunc-permanere *add. in marg*.

uniri potest, quod si fiat, ex tunc mea efficitur. Hoc autem qualiter fiat, unum exenplum hic ponitur, scilicet si longiori tenpore fundo meo heserit. Quod, ut glossa dicit, quidam exponebant x. vel xx. a[n]nis,[148] quod glossa reprendit. Suficit enim quod tanto tenpore stet, quod coaluerit arbor in terra, vel si forte crusta non habet arbores, suficit si tanto tenpore steterit quod, si ibi arbores essent, coaluissent. Ex cursu enim tanti tenporis presumitur facta unio terre. Et hec est mens huius litere. Puto etiam quod si infra modicum tenpus illa crusta propter pluviam sit dirupta et cum terra agri mei unita, quod statim sit effecta mea, ar. ff. de gla. lege., l. i, (D. 43.28.1), et dicta l. hoc anplius, § i (D. 39.2.9.1). Ex eo enim tenpore quo cum terra unitur fundo meo dicitur aquisita. Et advertendum, quia supra in aquisitione, que fit per aluvionem, dictum est quod aquiritur nobis, hic vero dicitur quod aquiritur fundo, quod verum est, prout glossa intelligit, quod hic loquitur de eo quod superponitur ipsi enim fundo aquiritur. Illud vero quod fundo aditur per exstensum potest domini destinationem possideri ut fundus separatus a primo, et sic magis persone quam fundo dicitur aquiri. Sed intelligendo quod hic etiam per exstenssum additur non est vis, quia sive aquiratur nobis, sive fundo nostro, idem est, ab initio /f. 162v/ enim fundo aquiritur, licet possimus postea separatim possidere destinatione nostra. Licet autem arbor choaluerit, an vendicari possit, glossa hic tenet quod possit peti actione in factum. Et hoc de arbore. Ipsa autem terra, postquam unita est, peti non potest, ut d. l. hoc anplius, § ita demum, de dapno infec. (D. 39.2.9.2 in c.).

Ante autem quam choaluerit, ipse dominus potest vendicare, dum tamen de danpno infecto caveat, ut dicta l. hoc anplius, § finali (D. 39.2.9.5). Ego autem, in cuius predium delata est crusta, possum agere contra dominum ut ipsam tollat vel pro derelicto habeat, ut l. pretor ait, § finali (D. 39.2.7.2), de dapno infec. Postquam vero unita est, hoc facere non possem, ut d. l. hoc anplius, § ii[149] (D. 39.2.9.2 in c.), vers. set nec ego. Ad figuras igitur veniamus.

Fig. prima.

Quia circa divisiones eius quod per aluvionem additur questiones plures vidi, quarum doctrinam dare inpossibile arbitror nisi res inspectioni oculorum subitiatur, ideo figuras ad oculum demostrantes inserui, per quas[150] illa sola docere intendo, que comuniter ingnorantur. Et in hoc utar aliquibus conclusionibus geometricis; nec hoc arbitretur incongruum, quoniam omnis alia scientia ancillatur huic. Est enim hec architetonica de aliis cuntis disponens, ut dicit Aristoteles in primo Etichorum.[151] Sciendum est igitur quod inter eos, qui ex una parte fluminis predia possident, id quod per alluvionem additur, vel quocumque modo, scilicet dimictendo insulam vel alveum,[152] comune est pro diviso pro modo latitudinis, que latitudo prope ripam sit, ut in l. adeo, § insula[153]

---

[148]Glossa *Longiore tempore* ad D. 41.1.7.2.
[149] *ms.* § i.
[150] *ms.* que.
[151]Aristoteles, *Etica Nicomachea*, VI, 4, 1140a.
[152]vel quocumque-vel alveum *add. in marg.*

(D. 41.1.7.3). Hoc autem fit ducendo lineam per directum per illam partem que adiecta est alluvione, seu per insulam, vel dimictendo alveum.

Ad ostendendum igitur que sit linea recta, seu per directum ducta, facta est ista figura. Sed an linea sit recta, quero tribus modis. Primo, an linea sit recta secundum se, et de hoc in hac figura. Secundo, an sit recta respectu alterius[154] linee supra quam cadit. Tertio, an linea sit recta respectu unius punti, qui est in angulo duarum linearum, hoc est an recte secet angulum per medium. De quolibet videamus. De primo, dico quod linea recta secundum se est ab uno punto ad alium exstensio, ut patet in prima linea supra posita. Sint duo punti a b, exstendatur linea ab uno punto ad alium, illa linea erit recta. Et si unus filus tangens illos duos punctos exstenderetur in infinitum, tota linea erit recta, ut patet ad sensum et figura demostrat. Item sciendum est, quod si fieret alia linea super duos punctos eque distantes a primis, ut c d, eque erit linea recta, et si in infinitum ille due linee exstenderentur, nunquam iungentur, ut ex figura patet ad sensum. Sed si fierent duo punti non eque distantes a primis, sed unus esset magis propinquus prime linee alius magis remotus,[155] ut e f, tunc protraendo lineam [linea] est directa secundum se,[156] ut precedens. Nam puntus e est magis remotus a linea cd quam puntus f. Tamen protraendo illas duas lineas necesse est eas simul iungi. Si vero secundus puntus esset remotus, ut g h, constat enim quod puntus g est magis propinquus precedenti linee, et puntus h est magis remotus, tunc quanto magis iste due linee exstenduntur, magis elongantur, ut patet ad sensum. Et predicta sunt multum nota in geometria, ut patet primo Euclidis.[157] /f. 163r/

Fig. ii.

Hec figura facta est ad ostendendum quomodo posita una linea recta super aliquo punto ipsius linee alia linea recta perpendiculariter et recte[158] cadit, quod congnoscitur quia quando supra unam lineam rectam alia recte et perpendiculariter cadit, tunc uterque angulus rectus erit. Sed si non caderet recte et perpendiculariter, tunc unus angulus erit acutus, alius erit latus et apertus, quem obtusum vocant. Exenplum primi dicti. Sit linea posita ab et puntus in ea positus d, super illo ducatur linea perpe[n]diculariter cd, tunc uterque angulus rectus erit et equalis ab utraque parte. Exenplum secundi dicti. Sit linea posita ef et puntus in ea positus g, super illa ducatur linea non recte sed perpendiculariter, ut si flectatur versus puntum f, et sit linea hg,[159] tunc angulus est acutus in illa parte versus quam flectitur, ab alia parte erit obtusus. Sed dubitatur: ponatur linea ik et in ea puntus m, et super

---

[153] *ms.* § adeo et § insula.
[154] figure super quam *post* alterius *del.*
[155] vel econtra prim. *post* remotus *del.*
[156] se *suprascr.*
[157] Euclides, *Elementa* I, def. 4, def. 24.
[158] fa.(?) *post* recte *del.*
[159] et sit linea hg *add. in marg.*

illum ducatur linea nm, que in nullam partem flectatur, et tunc in aspectu non videtur linea recta. Respondeo: vere est linea recta prima, scilicet *ik*, et alia super eam recte cadit, si consideretur secundum se, non si consideretur respectu[160] quadrature istius carte super qua describitur. Sed ad istud nullus est habendus respectus, sed solum ad lineam positam et ad illam que supra eam ducitur. Et hoc est utile scire[161] ad multa que infra dicentur.

Fig. iii.

Quia in divisione de qua tractaturi[162] sumus sepe[163] expedit divisio[n]es fieri per medium, ideo ad hoc docendum et demostrandum facta est ista figura. Ponatur[164] ergo[165] linea recta ab, quam volumus dividere per medium, ita quod in ipso libro possit cuique demostrari. Primo, ponam pedem circini in puncto *a* et exstendam circinum ultra /f. 163v/ medium linee, ut ostendit circulus rubeus, deinde ponam pedem circini in puncto *b*, et supra eum fatiam circulum equalem primo, ut ostendit circulus açurus, qui duo circuli se presindunt in duobus locis, ut aparet. Ducam igitur lineam recta[m] ab uno duorum puntorum, ubi circuli se presindunt, usque ad alium, ut ostendit linea cd. Dico quod hec linea dividit lineam datam per medium, ut aparet, et probatur sic: si ab equalibus equalia adimas, ea que remanent sunt equalia, ut dicit Euclides.[166] Sed equalis distantia est a puncto a usque ad circumferentia[m] circuli rubei, qualis est a puncto b ad circunferentiam circuli açuri, et per lineam cd equaliter adimitur ab utraque distantia. Ergo patet quod illud quod remanet de linea ab ab utraque parte est equale. Et sic linea cd eam secat per medium.

Item, ex predicta figura aparet alia demostratio, videlicet quod si inter *a* et *b* non esset linea ducta, sed esset spatium, quod inter dicta duo punta deberet dividi iure proximitatis, quod dicta linea *cd* dividit dictum spatium directo per medium, ita quod quidquid est supra est magis propinquum *a*, et quidquid est infra est magis propinquum *b*, etiam[167] si dicta linea *cd* exstenderetur in infinitum.

Aparet etiam ex dicta figura alia demostratio, videlicet quod si supra unam basim rectam due linee circulorum equalium se presindunt, et a puncto ubi se presindunt ducatur linea ad puntum qui est in medio dicte basis, illa linea perpendiculariter cadit et angulum facit rectum ab utraque parte, ut patet ad oculum et probatur ex precedentibus. Quia, si dicta linea dividit spatium per medium, aparet quod non flectitur versus aliquam partium et sic facit

---

[160] *ms.* respectus.
[161] m. *post* scire *del.*
[162] tractaturi *corr. ex* tractari.
[163] sepe *corr. ex* sepex.
[164] Ponatur *corr. ex* ponantur.
[165] duo punti a b et ducatur ab uno ad alium *post* ergo *del.*
[166] Euclides, *Elementa* I, Scientia universaliter communis 3; cfr. *Elementa* I, 10.
[167] etiam *repet. et del.*

angulum rectum ab utraque parte. Et ista sunt multum necessaria ad congnitionem
660 sequentium.

Fig. iv.

Figura ista facta est ad ostendendum qualiter posita una linea recta et punto in ea posito supra illum puntum alia linea recte et perpendiculariter ducatur,
665 ut ex hiis que posita sunt de necessitate concludatur. Sit igitur linea posita *ab*, et in ea puntus positus *c*, supra quem volo aliam lineam rectam perpendiculariter ducere. Fatiam igitur ab utraque parte illius punti positi duos puntos eque distantes, ut *d e*, deinde adsuma[m] duas[168] equales lineas cum duabus virgulis vel cordulis, et unam ponam super punto *d* aliam super punto *e*, et
670 anbas coniungam /f. 164r/ per modum trianguli in punto *f*. Postea ducam lineam a punto *c* posito usque ad puntum *f*. Dico igitur quod illa linea recte et perpendiculariter cadit supra lineam datam in punto dato. Hoc oculus ostendit, quia facit angulum rectum ab utraque parte.[169] Et probatur[170] in xi., primi Euclidis.[171] Vel brevius: sit data linea *gh*, et in ea ponatur puntus *i*, supra
675 quem volo perpendiculariter et recte lineam ducere. Fatiam duos puntos eque distantes ad puntum datum, ut *k m*, deinde ponam pedem circini in punto *k* et extendam circinum usque ad puntum *m*, et volvam supra versus illam partem versus quam volo lineam ducere. Deinde ponam pedem circini in punto *m*, et extendam usque ad puntum *k* et simili modo volvam. Sequitur quod ille due
680 linee circulares se invicem secabunt in punto *n*. Dico igitur quod si a punto *i* dato ducatur linea[172] ad puntum *n*, illa perpendiculariter et recte cadit supra datum puntum, eadem ratione qua supra. Et probatum est in precedenti figura, quoniam supra unam basim rectam due linee circulorum equalium se presindunt et a punto ubi se presindunt ducitur linea ad puntum qui est in medio dicte
685 basis.[173] Et si super illos duos puntos lineam in infinitum producas senper recte cadit, ut patet es hiis que dixi supra in prima figura. Hoc etiam patet ex his que dicta sunt,[174] quia dicta linea cadens ex utraque parte facit angulum rectum.

Fig. v.[175]

690 Figura ista est facta ad desingnandum tertium, quod in prima fuit quesitum, scilicet si ponatur unus puntus in angulo duarum linearum, et supra illum volo ducere lineam rectam seu perpendicularem, qualiter fiet, quod docet hec figura.[176] Ponantur ergo due linee, scilicet *ab* et *bc*, que conveniunt in uno punto *b* et ibi fatiunt angulum, cuiuscumque conditionis sit ille angulus, et

---

[168]virgulas *post* duas *del*.
[169]quia-parte *add. in marg*.
[170]primi Euclidis xi *post* probatur *del*.
[171]Euclides, *Elementa* I, 11.
[172]d. *post* linea *del*.
[173]et probatum-dicte basis *add. in marg*.
[174]in precedenti figura *post* sunt *del*.
[175]v[a] *corr. ex* iiij[a].
[176]f. *post* figura *del*.

supra illum puntum volo ducere lineam rectam. Fatiam igitur ab utraque parte anguli in illis lineis puntum eque distantem *d e*, et super illos duos pu[n]tos ponam duas lineas equales, que coniungantur in puncto *f*. Dico ergo quod si ducatur linea recta a puncto *f* usque ad puntum *b*, illa linea recte et perpendiculariter cadit supra *b*; quod patet quia si ducatur alia linea recta a puncto *d e*, illa secatur per medium. Et ibi erunt quatuor anguli recti, ut probatur per ix., primi Euclidis.[177] Preterea, in ipso angulo *b* fiunt duo anguli equales. Vel si vis aliter[178] probare et operari, ponas duas lineas *gh* et *hi*, que conveniant in puncto *h*, supra quem vis ducere lineam rectam. Faciam ab utraque parte in illis lineis puntum eque distantem *k m*. Deinde ponam pedem circini in puncto [*k*], quem protendam usque ad *m*, et volvam supra versus illam partem supra quam volo ducere[179] lineam. Deinde ponam pedem circini in puncto *m*, et exstendam usque ad puntum *k*, et volvam simili modo. Tunc ille due linee circulares se presindu[n]t in puncto *n*. Ducatur ergo linea recta a puncto *h* usque ad puntum *n*. Dico quod illa recte et perpendiculariter cadit supra puntum *h*, eadem ratione qua precedens. Et si ducatur alia linea recta a puncto *k* usque ad puntum *m*, illa secatur per medium per lineam *nh*, et erunt ibi quatuor anguli recti. Et in puncto *h* similiter fiunt duo anguli equales. Hiis premissis[180] ad evidentiam, nunc ad propositum veniamus ponendo predia, ripas et alluviones. /f. 164v/

Fig. vi.

Ad evidentiam omnium dicendorum premicto quod flumen senper desingnabitur per colorem açurum. Caput fluminis erit ab illa parte a qua erit caput alicuius animalis et versus aliam partem fluat.[181] Prediorum ripe per colorem nigrum; illud quod est medium inter predia et flumen intelligatur alluvio. Item, per aluvionem linee rubee facte sunt ille, que vere dividunt aluvionem; linee ialne seu croce[e] sunt facte causa demostrat[i]o[n]is vel disputationis. Et si quandoque fieret aliqua linea açura in ipsa figura declarabitur ad quem finem fiat.

Nunc ad presentem figuram veniamus. Et advertendum quod linea que est ripa omnium prediorum est recta omni rectitudine. Item duo predia paria habent confinia directa, adeo quod linea dividens predia directo cadit in lineam ripe, quod patet quia ab utraque parte facit angulum rectum. In istis ergo duobus prediis divisio est clara, quia protratur linea directo per aluvionem usque ad flumen, ut ostendit linea rubea. Et illa linea est directa respectu ripe, et directo coniungitur cum ripa dividente predia. Videndum restat de ripa que est inter predia Titii et predia Sei, et inter predia Sei et predia Mevii. In illis est dubium. Nam linee confinium dividentium predia,[182] licet sint directe in se, non tamen

---

[177] *ms.* per x primi Euclidis; Euclides, *Elementa* I, 9.
[178] aliter *suprascr.*
[179] circinum *post* ducere *del.*
[180] nunc *post* premissis *del.*
[181] caput fluminis-fluat *add. in marg.*
[182] non *post* predia *del.*

cadunt directe in illam lineam, que est ripa, quod apparet quia ab una parte fatiunt angulum acutum, ab alia obtusum. Si igitur per aluvionem ducerem lineam secundum rectitudinem linee confinium, ille due linee non irent usque ad flumen, sed iungerentur in puncto *a*, ut ostendunt line jalne. Et sic predium Sei, quod est maioris latitudinis iusta ripam, haberet minus de alluvione, nec protenderetur usque ad flumen. Dicendum est ergo, quod linea confinium dividens predia nullatenus atendenda est, quoniam in dicta l. adeo, § insula,[183] ff. de aquir. rerum do. (D. 41.1.7.3), dicitur: pro modo latitudinis, que latitudo prope ripam sit. Sic ergo fiat divisio: consideretur linea que est ripa, et consideretur ubi cadit linea dividens confinia, et ibi adsumatur unus puntus indivisibilis, ut ostendunt linee nigre, et ab utraque parte illius punti fia[n]t duo punti eque distantes[184] *b c*. Et ponatur pes circini in puncto *b*, et exstendatur ad puntum *c*, et volvatur versus alluvionem, et postea ponatur in puncto *c*, et exstendatur ad puntum *b*, et simili modo volvatur versus alluvionem, que due linee revolute se presindent in puncto *d*. Deinde ducatur linea recta a pu[n]to[185] adsunto usque ad puntum *d*, et protraatur usque ad flumen,[186] ut ostendit linea rubea. Dico igitur quod illa recte cadit super lineam que est ripa, ut probatum est supra in tertia figura. Et si est recta a puncto *d* usque ad lineam adsuntam, quantumcumque ultra protrahatur, recta erit, ut dictum est supra in prima figura. Et similis divisio inter Seium et Mevium, ut linee ducte ostendunt. /f. 165r/

Fig. vii.[187]

Hec figura habet lineam ripe uniformem. Et cum tractetur de divisione alluvionis omnes rustici protraherent lineam, secundum quod ostendit linea ialna ducta secundum rectitudinem[188] linee dividentis predia. Sed hanc rusticorum divisionem non esse bonam aparet quia linea debet duci recta secundum rectitudinem linee ripe,[189] ut ex precede[n]tibus liquet. Sed secundum illam non est recta, quod aparet quia linea ialna ducta versus caput fluminis facit angulum obtusum, versus pedem facit angulum acutum. Et e converso linea dividens predia versus caput fluminis facit angulum acutum, versus finem facit angulum obtusum, quod repungnat linee que ducitur recta. Fienda est ergo divisio aluvionis prout ostendit linea rubea ducta supra lineam ripe, que ab utraque parte facit angulum rectum, et sic ipsa recte cadit et perpendic[u]lariter, ut supra demostratum est. Et si dicatur quod ripe linea non est recta, respondeo: immo est recta secundum se, quod conside[r]andum est, non autem vadit secundum rectitudi[n]em linee prediorum, que est ab alia parte, quod in hoc advertendum non est.

---

[183] *ms.* l. inter eos (D. 41.1.29).
[184] a *post* distantes *del.*
[185] d. *post* adsunto *del.*
[186] dico quod *post* flumen *del.*
[187] vij[a] *corr. ex* vi[a].
[188] *ms.* rectitidiem.
[189] ripe *corr. ex* ripee.

Fig. viii.
Figura ista difert a precedentibus. Nam precedentes habent lineam rectam, hec vero habet duas lineas et in uno puncto fatiunt triangulum[190] obtusum, scilicet in illo puncto ubi sunt fines inter Lutium et Titium. Dico igitur quod ad dividendum alluvionem inter dicta duo predia debet duci linea, ut ostendit linea rubea ducta usque ad lineam açuram. Et quod illa linea cadat recte probatur quia factis duobus puntis eque distantibus et duabus lineis circularibus ductis supra eis,[191] ut ostendunt linee crocee,[192] ab illo puncto ubi se interseca[n]t usque ad punctum datum, linea cadit perpendiculariter, ut demostratum est supra in tertia figura. Hoc etiam probatur ratione propinquitatis, ut dicetur in sequenti figura. Illud vero quod est supra li[n]eam açuram, debet dividi hac si ripa esset recta, ut illa linea açura ostendit. Nam quod iuris est in eo, quod predio primo additur, idem iuris est in eo quod ipsi addito additur, ut ff. de aquir. re. do., l. insula (D. 41.1.56). Sed si ab initio ripa habuisset illam rectitudinem illo modo fuisset facta divisio, ut supra in via figura,[193] ergo et cet. Hoc in sequenti figura rectius et clarius demostrabitur. /f. 165v/

Fig. ix.[194]
Ad evidentiam istius figre premicto quod flumen addit[195] quandoque ita quod ripe sunt ab utraque parte eius quod flumen per aluvionem ponit, et tunc illud dimissum debet esse comune inter eos qui sunt ab utraque parte iure propinquitatis, ut ff. e., l. adeo, § insula, et § quod si toto (D. 41.1.7.3, 5). Si vero illud quod dimictitur habet ripam tantum ab una parte, tunc debet dividi inter eos qui ab una parte predia possident per lineam in directum ductam, ut ff. de aquir. re. do., l. inter eos (D. 41.1.29), et supra dictum est. Et advertendum quia, licet dicta iura que loquuntur quando ripa est ab utraque parte, scilicet fluminis, tamen eadem ratio est si ab uno latere fluminis sint due ripe infra quas continetur relicta alluvio.[196] Hoc premisso dico quod hec figura habet duas lineas rectas, scilicet *ab* et *bc*, que[197] fatiunt unum angulum in puncto *b*. Dico igitur quod alluvio dimissa inter dictas duas lineas habet latera ex utraque parte, ergo debet dividi iure propinquitatis. Illud vero quod est ultra dictas duas lineas, quod aparet esse a linea crocea ducta a puncto a usque ad punctum *c* habet solus ripas ab una parte, ideo debet dividi per directum. Ducatur ergo linea directa supra punctum *b*, quam aparet esse directam ex iii^a figura.[198] Tunc dico quod

---

[190] ob. *corr. ex* op. *et del. post* triangulum.
[191] ab illis *post* eis *del.*
[192] ut-crocee *add. in marg.*
[193] *ms.* v figura.
[194] viiij *corr. ex* viij. *In marg. sinistro:* circulus rubeus maior non est bene ductus, quia tangit ripam utriusque, quod non debet tangere nisi ripam Lutii.
[195] seu dimictit *post* addit *del.*
[196] et advertendum-relicta alluvio *add. in marg.*
[197] *ms.* quem.
[198] *ms.* iiij figura.

quidquid est supra dictam lineam versus caput fluminis, est predii Lutii iure propinquitatis. Illud vero quod est infra versus finem fluminis, est predii[199] Titii iure propinquitatis. Quod sic probatur: ponatur puntus *a* in dicta linea rubea, et supra illum fiat circulus açurus. Dico quod ille circulus equaliter
810 tangit ripam Lutii et ripam Titii, et sic illa linea est directe in medio. Deinde infra dictam lineam[200] fiat puntus *b*, et supra eum volvatur circulus rubeus, qui pu[n]taliter tangat ripam Titii. Dico quod ille circulus non tanget ripam Lutii, ergo ab illa magis distat. Et eodem modo supra dictam lineam rubeam fiat puntus *c*, et supra eum ducatur alius circulus rubeus, qui puntaliter tangat
815 ripam Lutii. Dico quod non tanget ripam Titii, ergo ab illa magis distat. Et sic concluditur quod divisio est recte facta. Illud vero quod est supra lineam croceam *ac* debet dividi ac si tota illa linea esset quedam ripa recta. Quod probatur sic: quod iuris est in eo quod primo predio additur, idem iuris est in eo quod ipsi adito aditur, ut ff. de aquir. rerum do., l. insula (D. 41.1.56).
820 Sed si ab initio ripa habuisset illam rectitudinem, facta fuisset divisio ut dictum est supra in vi^a figura,[201] ergo, et cet. /f. 166r/

Fig. x.[202]

In hac figura sunt due linee recte, scilicet *ab* et *bc*, que[203] in pu[n]to *b* fatiunt
825 angulum; verumtamen linea *ab* est minor quam linea *bc*, et in hoc difert a precedenti. Dico igitur ducendam esse lineam recta[m] a puncto *a* usque ad puntum *c*,[204] ut ostendit linea crocea. Et quidquid est infra dictas lineas procul dubio[205] habet ripas ab utraque parte. Et ideo debet dividi iure proximitatis, ut patet ex precedenti. Et ideo ducatur linea rubea[206] per
830 medium dividens a puncto *b* usque ad lineam croceam in puncto *d*. Illud vero quod est a linea crocea supra, habet ripam tantum ab uno latere per illam rettitudinem quam ostendit linea crocea *ac*. Et ideo debet dividi ducendo lineam rectam rubeam a puncto *d* usque ad lineam açuram in puncto[207] *e*. Illud vero quod est a dicta linea açura supra, debet dividi ducendo lineam
835 recta[m] supra illam lineam açuram, sicut si illa esset ripa. Et hoc per illam rationem, quia additum adito[208] est dividendum sicut aditum antiquo predio, ut dictum est in precedentibus. Et predicta vera[209] si proponatur questio sic sinpliciter, et per quem modum alluvio aceserit sit incertum. Si

---

[199] predii *corr. ex* prediii.
[200] d. *post* lineam *del.*
[201] *ms.* v figura.
[202] x *corr. ex* viiij.
[203] terminantur *post* que *del.*
[204] et *post* c *del.*
[205] a. *post* dubio *del.*
[206] rubea *suprascr.*
[207] d *post* puncto *del.*
[208] et cet. *post* adito *del.*
[209] et p. *post* vera *del.*

vero constaret quod primo alluvio addiderit certam partem, postea aliam, tunc declarabitur in sequenti figura.

Fig. xi.
Ista figura facta est ad decla[ra]ndum illud quod dictum est in precedenti. Si enim ponertur sinpliciter totam aluvionem esse dimissam, qualiter fienda esset divisio aparet ex dictis in tribus precedentibus figuris. Sed pone flumen primo per alluvionem dimisisse illam partem que continetur infra lineam rubeam ductam supra predia Lutii et Titii, dico quod primo tota illa aluvio erit Lutii et Titii, quorum prediis aderet, et Gaius nichil habebit ibi facere. Secunda vero aluvio dividetur ponendo aluvionem primam pro ripa, ut sic inter ipsam et predia Gaii et Seii[210] ducatur linea per medium secans ex doctrina data in precedentibus. Set oponitur quod de aluvione prima debeatur predio Gaii, nam inter predia Lutii Ti[ti]i et Gaii Seii su[n]t due linee que fatiunt angulum in puncto [*a*,] et sic pars aluvionis habet duo latera, ut ostendit linea crocea *bc*. Ergo illa debet dividi iure propinquitatis, ut dictum est. Sed pars illius aluvio[n]is est magis propinqua predio Gai. Quod patet, quia si super punto linee aluvionis prime posito ubi linea rubea secatur per lineam croceam in puncto *d*[211] fiat circulus, qui tangat puntaliter predium Titii, tamen occupabit partem de predio Gaii, ut ostendit circulus açurus. Respondeo: hoc quod alicui acrescat iure proximitatis habet locum quando illud, de quo aquirendo agitur, neutrius fundo choeret, ut insula, vel choeret uterque, ut alveus derelictus. Et ita loquuntur precedentia. Sed quando uni choeret et alii non, senper illi cedit cui choeret, nec atenditur proximitas alterius, ut ff. de aquir. re. do., l. insula (D. 41.1.56 pr.), in principio. /f. 166v/

Fig. xii.[212]
Figura ista facta est ut ostendatur quod quedam predia possunt esse quibus de alluvione non debetur usque ad flumen sed ante intermoritur, ut si ripa contineatur infra duas lineas, scilicet *ab* et *bc* et fatiant angulum in puncto *b*, qui angulus cadit quasi in puncto predii Titii. Primo ergo fiat linea rubea dividens per medium, ut linea *bd*, ut probatum est supra in viiij^a figura,[213] ex qua patet quod quidquid est a dicta linea supra versus caput fluminis cedit illi ripe *ab*, quidquid est ab illa linea infra versus finem fluminis cedit illi ripe *bc*. Et hoc ratione propinquitatis, ut dictum est. Nec predium Titii habet dividere cum vicino superiori et inferiori. Et si bene respicis puntus dividens predia cadit in lineis rectis secundum se. Ergo debet dividi ducendo supra eam lineam rectam, ut ostensum est supra in vij^a figura,[214] ut ostendit linea *ef* et linea *gf*. Et sic in puncto *f* portio contingens agrum Titii finitur et intermoritur. Si enim transiret ultra vel linea torqueretur nec iret recta, ut si volveres lineam *ef*

---

[210] *ms.* Seia.
[211] posito in-punto d *add. in marg.*
[212] xij *corr. ex* xj.
[213] *ms.* viij figura.
[214] ut ostensum est supra in vj figura *add. in marg.*

versus caput fluminis, vel si transieret ultra lineam *bd*, dares prime ripe plus
880 quam debet iure proximitatis, quod iura proibent.[215] Et si ponatur aluvionem sic sinpliciter acrevisse. Sed si poneres quod primo replevisset totu[m] angulum predii Titii usque ad lineam croceam *eg*, tunc deberet fieri divisio ut in sequenti figura.

885 *Fig. xiii.*[216]
Hec figura difert ab omnibus precedentibus. Nam hic ripa continetur tribus lineis, scilicet *ab* et *bc* et *cd*, et habet duos angulos, scilicet in puncto *b* et in puncto *c*. Tota igitur hec aluvio debet dividi iure propinquitatis, quia tota continetur infra plura latera. Primo igitur ducatur linea[217] /f. 167r/ rubea
890 per medium supra angulum *b*, et sit linea *be*. Deinde ducatur linea per medium dividens supra angulum *c*, et erit linea *cf*, que due linee secabunt se in puncto *g*.[218] Dico ergo quod portio alluvionis pertinens ad agrum Titii in dicto puncto *g* finietur, quia [si] fiat circulus açurus supra puncto *g* utramque lineam puntaliter tanget. Ergo ille est pu[n]tus in quo utriusque propinquitas
895 terminatur. Si vero excederes et velles facere circulum super puntum[219] *f*, vel puntum *e*, tunc uni partium accederet et ab alia elongaretur. Quidquid autem est infra illum triangulum *bgc* pertinet ad predium Titii iure propinquitatis, quod patet quia [si] infra illum triangulum ponatur centrum unius circuli in puncto *h*, qui tangat pu[n]taliter ripam Titii, nullam aliam ripam
900 tanget et sic illi est propinquor. Illud vero quod est supra puntum *g* debet dividi inter Lutium et Gaium per lineam directo ductam usque ad flumen. Et hec sufitiant de ripa que habet lineam vel lineas rectas. Restat videre de ripa que habet lineam circularem.

905 *Fig. xiv.*[220]
Ad evidentiam eorum que dictura sunt de figura circulari, sciendum est quod circulus est figura plana una quidem linea contenta, que circumfere[n]tia nominatur, in cuius medio puntus est a quo omnes linee ad circumferentiam exeuntes sibi invicem sunt equales, ut dicit Euclides in
910 primo.[221] Et [in] hac figura nam centrum est in puncto *a*, et omnes quatuor linee inde exeu[n]tes sunt sibi invicem equales, et si plures ducerentur idem esset. Item, aparet quod omnes linee predicte,[222] que in circu[m]ferentia sunt distantes, in centro fatiunt angulum. Item, premicto quod totum illud quod est in circulo infra aliquas duas lineas est magis propinquum illi parti
915 circumfere[n]tie[223] que in puntis dictarum duarum linearum terminatur, ut

---

[215] S[ed] *post* proibent *del.*
[216] xiij *corr. ex* xij.
[217] per medium *post* linea *del.*
[218] dig. *post* g *del.*
[219] est *post* puntum *del.*
[220] xiiij *corr. ex* xiij.
[221] Euclides, *Elementa* I, def. 15.
[222] *ms.* predicta

verbigratia adsummas partem circumferentie *bc* et a quolibet duc lineam rectam ad centrum, et sic fatiet triangulum *bac*. Dico quod quidquid est infra illum triangulum est magis propinquum illi parti circumferentie *bc* quam alicui alii, quod patet ad sensum. Et potes probare: ponatur centrum[224] *f* in aliqua parte infra dictum triangulm, et supra illum ducatur circulus açurus, qui tangat[225] puntaliter[226] illam partem *bc*. Dico quod nullam aliam partem circumferentie tanget. Ergo illi magis est propinqua. Et idem dicendum[227] est de eo quod continetur infra illum triangulum *bad*, et infra illum triangulum *dae*, et infra illum triangulum *cae*, ut evidenter aparet. /f. 167v/

Fig. xv.[228]

Quia in precedenti dictum est quod linee sunt ducende a centro ad circumferentiam, et quandoque ignoratur ubi sit centrum, et ideo expedit quod ducatur linea a circumferentia versus centrum, vel quod centrum inveniatur, ideo facta est hec figura, que duos habet circulos, et sic hoc fieri docet duobus modis. Primo sic: sit centrum quod non videtur *a*, ponatur in circumferentia unus puntus *b*, et ab utraque parte eiusdem punti duo alii eque distantes *c d*. Deinde ducatur linea recta *cd*, et istius linee inve[n]iatur medium in puncto *e*. Deinde ducatur linea recta *be*. Dico quod ista de necessitate vadit supra centrum, scilicet puntum *a*, ut probatur in primo tertii[229] libri Euclidis.[230] Hoc etiam patet quia fiat idem in alia parte circumferentie. Ponatur puntus *f* et ab utraque parte duo punti eque distantes *g h*. Deinde inve[n]iatur medium dicte linee ducte in punto *i*, deinde ducatur linea recta *fi*. Dico quod ista de[231] necessitate vadit versus centrum, et si ultra protendatur linea *be* et linea *fi* secabunt se in punto *a*, ubi est centrum. Concluditur ergo quod ibi, ubi dicte linee se secant, de necessitate est centrum. Hoc etiam fieri alio modo ad idem tendenti docet secundus circulus. Ponatur enim quod sit centrum, quod[232] non videtur, in puncto *a*, ponatur in circumferentia puntus *b* et ab utraque parte eiusdem punti duo alii eque distantes *c d*. Deinde ponatur pes circini in puncto *c*, et extendatur usque ad puntum *d* et volvatur supra et infra circulum, et eodem modo ponatur pes circini in punto *d* et exstendatur usque ad puntum *c*, et sic ille due linee circulares ducte se secabunt extra circulum in puncto *e*, et intra in punto *f*. Ducatur igitur linea recta *ef*, dico quod illa de necessitate vadit versus centrum.[233] Et eodem

---

[223]quam *post* circumferentie *del.*
[224]*ms.* centrtrum
[225]qui tangat *post* tangat *del.*
[226]in *post* puntaliter *del.*
[227]*ms.* diccendum.
[228]xv *corr. ex* xiiij.
[229]*ms.* secundi.
[230]Euclides, *Elementa* III, 1.
[231]neg. *post* de *del.*
[232]ms. centrus qui.
[233]*ms.* centrus.

modo si in alia parte circuli idem fiat, ut ponatur in circumferentia puntus *g*
950 et ab utraque parte duo punti eque distantes *h i*, deinde volvatur circinum
supra *h* et supra *i*, ut in precedenti dictum est, et sic dicte linee se secabunt
in punto *k* et in punto *m*. Ducatur linea *km* recta et illa ducit ad centrum, et
sic in illo punto ubi secabunt se linea *ef* et linea *km*, ibi erit centrum.

Hiis premissis ad evidentiam dico[234] quod ripa prediorum, que habet
955 lineam circularem, quandoque habet se ut continens, quia infra circulum
dimissa est aluvio; quandoque habet se ut contentum, quia aluvio continet
circularem ripam. Si primo modo, tunc aut ripa continens lineam circularem
continet minus[235] semicirculo, aut semicirculum, aut plus semicirculo. Totum
autem circulum continere non potest, quia sic flumen non haberet exitum.
960 Et hoc in figuris proximis declarabitur. /f. 168r/

Fig. xvi.

Si hec figura inspitiatur, tota continetur una linea, que est minus [semi]circulo, et ab ipsa ripa aluvio est contenta, et omne contentum est minus
965 contine[n]te, unde de alluvione non potest dari tantum quantum est ipsa
ripa. Item, licet sit una linea, tamen quia est rotunda habet duo latera se
respitientia. Ideo id quod continetur infra ipsam debet dividi iure propinquitatis, ut in precedentibus demostratum est. In quolibet ergo punto, ubi
fines predii terminantur, opereris ut inducas lineam que respitiat centrum,
970 secundum precedentem figuram. Quo facto, certum est quod illud quod
infra illas duas lineas continetur illi parti propinquior[236] est, ut probatum
est supra in xiii[a] figura.[237] Et quia triplex[238] modus est operandi ad
ducendum lineam[239] versus centrum, ut supra proxima figura dixi, ideo hic
in tribus ripis tripliciter opereris ducendo lineam rubeam usque ad flumen.
975 Et ad hoc ut redaris certus, quod ille linee respitiunt directo centrum, illum
centrum reperiet ultra flumen in puncto *a*, ut linee crocee ducte[240] ultra
rubeas ostendunt.

Fig. xvii.[241]
980 Figura hec difert a precedenti quia ibi aluvio non excessit continentiam ripe
rotunde, hic vero excessit. Unde id, quod continetur infra ipsam ripam,
debet dividi eo modo quo dictum est in precedenti. Id vero, quod est
supra[242] lineam açuram ductam a puncto *a* usque ad puntum *b*, debet dividi

---

[234] dico *suprascr.*
[235] circulo *post* minus *del.*
[236] et *post* propinquior *del.*
[237] ms. xiij.
[238] *in marg.* immo duplex.
[239] supra *post* lineam *del.*
[240] ostendunt *post* ducte *del.*
[241] xvij *corr. ex* xvj.
[242] supra *corr. ex* ultra.

ac[243] si ibi fuit ripa recta, ut linee ducte ostendunt, et in precedentibus pluries est probatum. / f. 168v/

Fig. xviii.[244]

Figura ista continet semicirculum, quod aparet quia linea recta transiens super diametrum aplicat extremitates suas ad utranque partem circumferentie, ut patet ex linea açura supra centrum *a*.[245] Et definitur sic: se[m]icirculus est figura plana diametro circuli et medietate circumferentie contenta, ut habetur in primo Euclidis.[246] In hac igitur figura dico quod omnia predia media,[247] que continentur infra ipsum se[m]icirculum habebunt de alluvione pro rata usque ad centrum,[248] supra illud nil possunt habere. Ratio: quia in illo[249] centro portio eorum terminatur in punto, qui punctus nullius latitudinis est. Nam punctus est cuius pars non est. Sed cum supra illum punctum linea quedam remaneat directa, ut ostendit linea açura, debet supra illam fieri divisio pro modo latitudinis cuiusque predii, ut dicit testus in l. inter eos[250] (D. 41.1.29). Sed latitudo nulla est supra illum punctum, que pertineat ad predia media, scilicet Titii et Gaii, ut dictum est, ergo et cet. Quidquid igitur est supra illud centrum pertinet[251] ad predia que sunt in extremitatibus, scilicet ad predia Lutii et Seii. Et dividetur inter eos linea perpendiculariter ducta supra illum centrum, ut ostendit linea rubea. Et predicta vera, si sic sinpliciter proponatur lineam ripe esse circularem, et alluvionem sic sinpliciter acrevisse. Inmaginandum est enim quod sic circulariter acreverit, ut ostendunt due[252] linee crocee sic circulariter ducte supra idem centrum, que due linee sunt posite extra eam. Et eodem modo intelligo acrevisse usque ad centrum. Sin autem poneres quod primo in una parte alluvio apulerit, postea in alia, tunc qualiter esset fienda divisio, patet ex dictis supra in xj^a figura.[253] /f. 169r/

Fig. xix.[254]

Figura ista est plus semicirculo, quod patet quia, si ducatur linea ab una parte circumferentie ad alia[m], centrum, quod est in puncto *a*, remanet infra

---

[243]ac *corr. ex* hac.
[244]xviij *corr. ex* xvij.
[245]ut *post* a *del.*
[246]Euclides, *Elementa* I, def. 18.
[247]media *add. in marg.*
[248]*ms.* centrus.
[249]pu[n]to *post* illo *del.*
[250]Ut dicit-inter eos *add. in marg.* Lex inter eos: *recte* l. adeo, § insula (D. 41.1.7.3): communis est eorum, qui ab utraque parte fluminis prope ripam predia possident, pro modo latitudinis cuiusque predii.
[251]q. *post* pertinet *del.*
[252]due *add. in marg.*
[253]*ms.* x figura; *in marg.* immo xj.
[254]xviiij *corr. ex* xviij.

illam[255] lineam. Dicendum est igitur quod omnia predia media, scilicet Titii,
1015 Gaii, Seii, debent habere pro rata iure proximitatis usque ad centrum, ut
dictum est in precedenti. A centro vero supra debet esse eorum prediorum,
que sunt ab utraque parte extremitatis, scilicet ad predia Lutii et Mevii, ut
linee rubee ducte ostendunt. Quod autem linea[256] rubea, que est supra centrum,
vadat per medium inter Lutium et Mevium potest de facili inveniri. Tamen, ut
1020 in hac figura probetur, facte sunt ibi linee crocee, que hoc ostendunt sic:
ponatur pes circini in puncto *b*, et exstendatur visibiliter ultra medium, et
ducatur circulariter. Deinde ponatur pes circini[257] supra punctum *c*, et
similiter exstendatur et ducatur, et consideretur ubi ille due linee se
presindunt, et ab illis puntis ducatur linea recta. Illa de necessitate secat per
1025 medium.

Fig. xx.[258]

Hec figura difert ab omnibus precedentibus. Nam illarum alique continentur
una linea recta, alique pluribus lineis rectis, alique linea una circulari. Ista
1030 vero continetur tribus lineis, quarum due sunt circulares, ut *ab*,[259] que est
prima, et *cd*, que est ultima, alia vero est recta ut media[260] *bc*. Dico ergo[261]
quod primo ducatur una linea recta crocea *ab*, et illud totum infra illam
lineam et antiquam ripam contentum est predii Lutii, et de illo ad Titium nil
pertinet, nec iure propinquitatis nec iure aderentie, ut patet ad sensum.
1035 Et eodem modo ducatur alia linea crocea recta *cd*, et illud totum pertinebit
ad Gaium, ad Titium vero nichil, eadem[262] ratione. Quo facto, remanet figura
tribus lineis rectis contenta, et sic qualiter divisio debeat fieri aparet ex xij^a
figura supra posita. Et hoc[263] hostendunt linee ducte rubee.

Illud etiam notandum est universaliter, quod concavitates que sunt in
1040 ripa unius predii, si sunt ita inregulares, quod in predictas figuras non
cadunt, debent reduci ad regularitatem et rectitudinem, ut in hac figura
factum est. Nam portus qui sunt in[264] insula, ipsius insule esse dicuntur, ut
ff. de publicanis,[265] l. Cesar (D. 39.4.15). Portus autem est quidam locus
conclusus seu quedam concavitas, que est[266] in ripa, ut ff. de ver. si., l.
1045 portus (D. 50.16.59). Ita concavitates, que sunt in ripa predii, debent esse ipsius
predii. Hec de figuris inregularibus dicta sunt,[267] ut si quando reperiuntur ad[268]

---

[255] illam *corr. ex* illas.
[256] que est su. *post* linea *del.*
[257] similiter *post* circini *del.*
[258] xx *corr. ex* xviiij.
[259] et cd *post* ab *del.*
[260] s[cilicet?] *post* media *del.*
[261] dico ergo *repet. et del.*
[262] eadem *corr. ex* eandem.
[263] *ms.* hic.
[264] ip[sius] *post* in *del.*
[265] *ms.* plubicanis.
[266] concavitas que est *corr. ex* concavitates que sunt.

regularitatem reducantur, quod figure inregulares sunt infinite. Nec de hiis potest dari doctrina, nisi reducantur ad figuras regulares. /f. 169v/

Predicta, que dicta sunt de linea recta, declarant questionem ocurentem
1050 de facto. Inter dominos molendi[n]orum superiorum et dominos molendinorum inferiorum erant pacta, quod clusa molendini inferioris non posset elevari altius, nisi usque ad certum clavum inmissum in quadam colunpna ad latus fluminis infissa; ab alia vero parte fluminis nulla colunpna reperiebatur. Querebatur: quantum ab alia parte fluminis clusam licebat altius elevare? Dubium erat quia,
1055 cum tantum unus puntus detur a quo linea debeat duci, scilicet ille clavus qui est in colunpna, ab alia vero parte non sit puntus. Videtur quod ab illa parte possit duci in quamcumque partem velit. Preterea, cum ab illa parte non sit positivum, scilicet quantum dicatur altum, non potest ibi dari conparativum, scilicet quod sit altius, ar. l. in testamento, de condi. et demostra. (D. 35.1.27).
1060 Sed respondetur quod illa verba, que dicunt quod clusa[269] non possit elevari altius illo clavo, debent intelligi[270] de tota clusa, ar. de servi. ur. predi., l. si servitus (D. 8.2.23). Et sic debet intelligi prout ille clavus respicit per totam longitudinem et latitudinem cluse per directum linea transducta, ar. C. de edifi. priva., l. i (C. 8.10.1), et sdicta l. inter eos, de aquir. re. domi.[271] (D. 41.1.29).
1065 Qualiter autem linea directo transducatur, aparebit si ab illo clavo exstendatur cordula versus aliam partem ripe. Deinde supra illam cordam plunbum seu perpe[n]diculum ponatur, et siquid corda plumbi cum[272] illa corda ducta a clavo facit angulos omnes rectos ad modum recte crucis[273] linea est recte ducta. Si vero anguli essent aliqui acuti, aliqui octusi, tunc linea vel esset nimis erecta,
1070 vel nimis depressa, ut patet ex hiis que dicta sunt supra in secunda figura.

Item,[274] fatiunt in ar. ad illud, quod sepe occurrit, maxime in istrumentis divisionum, ubi sepe apponitur quod unus habeat a tali loco usque ad talem, prout trait per directum, de quorum verborum singnificatione quandoque vidi dubitari. Dico igitur quod quandoque in istrumento apponitur totus locus
1075 per quem debet fieri dicta exstensio latitudinis; quandoque ponuntur extremitates limitate; quandoque aponitur una extremitas limitata alia vero obscura. Primo casu exenplum. Dicit istrumentum quod, quidquid est a tali via vel a tali flumine citra, prout trat per directum, sit primi; quod vero est ultra sit secundi. Hic dico quod per directum debet intelligi prout via vel flumen vadit,
1080 et licet non vadat recte, tamen recta apellatur, secundum quod cursus est directus, ut ff. de excusat. tu., l. non solum, § i[ii] (D. 27.1.10.3), ibi: via recta

---

[267] quoniam de hiis doctina alia dari non potest *post* sunt *del.*

[268] ut-ad *add. in marg.*

[269] quod *post* clusa *del.*

[270] prout ille clavus respicit per totam longitudinem et latitudinem cluse *post* intelligi *del.*

[271] quod autem *post* domi. *del.*

[272] cum *repet.*

[273] ad-crucis *add. in marg.*

[274] E[t] *ante* item *del.*

dirigens, et cet. Secundo casu exenplum. Si dicatur a tali termino usque ad talem, prout trait per directum, tunc certum est quod rectitudo est ab uno punto ad alium exstensio, ut dictum est in prima figura. Tertio casu exenplum. Quod
1085 primus habeat a tali termino, prout trahit per directum, usque ad flumen. Nam, licet terminus ipse sit certus et pu[n]talis quodammodo, tamen flumen est multum exstensum et ad multas partes fluminis potest duci linea recta ab illo termino. Ad hoc dico quod lapides, que ponuntur pro termino, consueverunt poni[275] taliter quod in certam partem videntur respicere, ut si
1090 lapis est longus non enim dicitur respicere a lateribus, sed per directum a parte anteriori acuta. Et ita vidi rusticos antiquos dicentes, quibus est standum in istis, ar. de le. iii, l. si corus (D. 32.1.79). A qualitate ergo termini hoc perpenditur, vel si[276] qualitas termini hoc non induceret, hic esset advertendum quod si terminus ille esset prope aliquam sepem[277] vel[278]
1095 limites, quod ab illis limitibus ducatur linea recta, hoc est, quod angulum rectum dimictat[279] in ripa, quod qualiter fiat, in superioribus clare declaratum est. Consulo tamen quod, qui talia istrumenta conponunt, curent clarius exprimere. Et hec de linea recta. Ea vero que dicta sunt de linea rotunda fatiunt argumentum, immo determinant questionem notabilem de facto
1100 emergentem, prout in sequenti figura declarabitur. /f. 170r/

Fig. xxi.
Figura ista dirimit questionem mangnam occurrentem de facto. Statuto cavebatur quod, qui per vim[280] dapnificaret alium de re valoris x.
1105 florenorum, deberet morte puniri. Contingit quod quidam ad domum alterius acessit et[281] vegetem vino plenam per vim efudit et vegetem destruxit, sola una doga remansit. Et de bonitate vini erat certum, sed de quantitate erat dubium, hoc est, quante capacitatis erat veges. Dico quod ex hiis que dicta sunt supra in xv^a figura[282] hoc poterit clare haberi hoc
1110 modo. Singnetur illa rotunditas illius doge in terra vel in tabula, ut ostendit linea nigra[283] *ab*. Constat enim quod illa est pars rotunditatis totius vegetis. Supra illam partem fiant singna ad inveniendum centrum, ut in illa xv^a figura[284] dictum est, et ducantur due linee,[285] et ubi ille due linee se presindunt constat quod ibi est centrum, ut in puncto *c*. Deinde pone pedem
1115 circini inmobilem[286] in puncto *c*, et exstende usque ad lineam *ab*, et perfitias

---

[275]poni *corr. ex* ponit.
[276]ad *post* si *del.*
[277]*ms.* aliquod sepe.
[278]ripam *post* vel *del.*
[279]dimictat *rept.*
[280]per vim *add. in marg.*
[281]domum *post* et *del.*
[282]*ms.* xiiij figura; *in marg.* immo in xv.
[283]b *post* nigra *del.*
[284]*ms.* xiiij figura.
[285]et ubi ille due *post* linee *del.*

circulum,[287] ut ostendit circulus rubeus ductus.[288] Dico quod de necessitate illa erat rotunditas vegetis. Si igitur habes longitudinem ex[289] doga remanente et rutunditatem ex circulo, quilibet comunis geometra sciet dicere capacitatem. Et si veges in medio esset largior, de facili ad equalitatem reducitur per messores comunes. Vel demostra idem brevius, ut in sequenti figura.

Fig. xxii.
Ista figura facta est ad demostrandum idem quod precedens, sed brevius. Constat enim quod doga vegetis habet duas lineas circulares, scilicet exteriorem et /f. 170v/ interiorem; et interior est minor; et quelibet respicit unum centrum. Item, doga vegetis habet duas lineas rectas, scilicet ab extremitate exteriori usque ad extremitatem interiorem. Sed duo punti[290] exteriores illarum linearum magis distant ad invicem, quam duo interiores, et ideo si dicte due linee protrahentur necesse est iungi, ut dictum est in prima figura.[291] Sit ergo grosities unius doghe vel duarum, prout ostendunt linee *abc* ab exteriori circulo usque ad interiorem. Deinde ducantur linee dogle recte ab utraque parte, et iungent se in puncto *d*. Ibi erit centrum circuli interioris et exterioris. Volvas ergo circulariter et habebis grositiem vegetis.[292]

---

[286]usque *post* inmobilem *del.*
[287]dico *post* circulum *del.*
[288]ex hoc *post* ductus *del.*
[289]l[ongitudine?] *post* ex *del.*
[290]duarum *post* punti *del.*
[291]Sit ergo rotunditas interior et exterior ut ostendit *post* figura *del.*
[292]*Post* vegetis *alia manu add.* Explicit tractatus de fluminibus per dominum Bar[tolum] de Saxoferrato, anima cuius requieschat in pace.

River of Law   117

Appendix 2
Bartolus, *Tiberiadis* (*De alluvione*), Figures

Figure 1:   Parallel and non-parallel lines (© BAV, Barb. Lat. 1398, fol. 162v).

Figure 2:   Types of angles: right, obtuse, and acute (© BAV, Barb. Lat. 1398, fol. 163r).

Figure 3:   Bisecting a given line *ab* (© BAV, Barb. Lat. 1398, fol. 163r).

Figure 4:   Two ways of drawing a perpendicular line (© BAV, Barb. Lat. 1398, fol. 163v).

Figure 5:   Two ways of bisecting an angle (© BAV, Barb. Lat. 1398, fol. 164r).

Figure 6:   Scheme for dividing an alluvial deposit when the borderline of the fields is a straight line (© BAV, Barb. Lat. 1398, fol. 164v).

Figure 7:   Scheme for dividing an alluvial deposit when the borderline of the fields is an oblique line (© BAV, Barb. Lat. 1398, fol. 165r).

Figure 8:   Scheme for dividing an alluvial deposit when the borderline of the fields is a segmented line (© BAV, Barb. Lat. 1398, fol. 165r).

Figure 9:   Scheme for dividing an alluvial deposit when the borderline of the fields is segmented. (© BAV, Barb. Lat. 1398, fol. 165v).

Figure 10: Scheme for dividing an alluvial deposit when the borderline of the fields is segmented (© BAV, Barb. Lat. 1398, fol. 165v).

Figure 11: Scheme for dividing two alluvial deposits (*aluvio primo relicta* = first alluvial deposit; *aluvio secundo relicta* = second alluvial deposit) (© BAV, Barb. Lat. 1398, fol. 166r).

Figure 12: Scheme for dividing an alluvial deposit when the borderline of the fields is segmented (© BAV, Barb. Lat. 1398, fol. 166v).

Figure 13: Scheme of dividing an alluvial deposit when the borderline of the fields is segmented (© BAV, Barb. Lat. 1398, fol. 166v).

Figure 14: The geometrical properties of the circle (© BAV, Barb. Lat. 1398, fol. 167r).

Figure 15: Two ways of finding the center of the circle (© BAV, Barb. Lat. 1398, fol. 167v).

Figure 16: Scheme for dividing an alluvial deposit when the borderline of the fields is less than a semicircle (© BAV, Barb. Lat. 1398, fol. 168r).

Figure 17: Scheme for dividing an alluvial deposit when the borderline is less than a semicircle (© BAV, Barb. Lat. 1398, fol. 168r).

Figure 18: Scheme for dividing an alluvial deposit when the borderline is a semicircle (© BAV, Barb. Lat. 1398, fol. 168v).

Figure 19: Scheme for dividing an alluvial deposit when the borderline is more than a semicircle (© BAV, Barb. Lat. 1398, fol. 168v).

Figure 20: Scheme for dividing an alluvial deposit when the borderline of the fields has a mixed configuration (© BAV, Barb. Lat. 1398, fol. 169r).

Figure 21: One-way of determining the circumference of a barrel (© BAV, Barb. Lat. 1398, fol. 170r).

Figure 22: An alternative way of determining the circumference of a barrel (© BAV, Barb. Lat. 1398, fol. 170r).

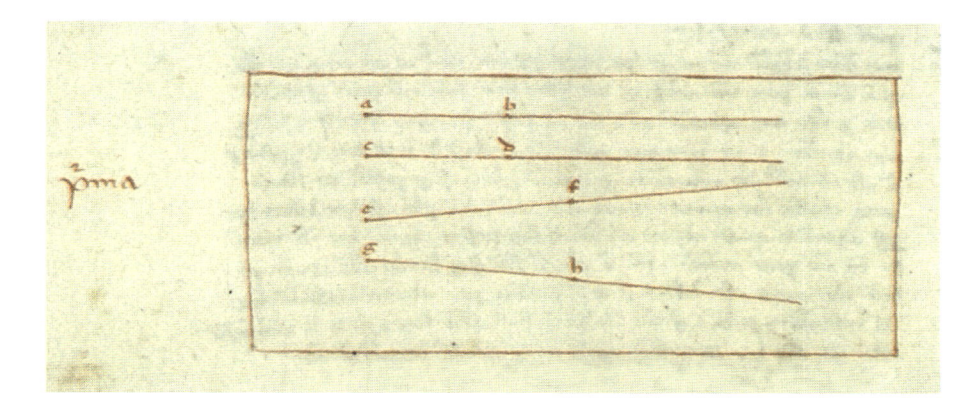

Figure 1: Parallel and non-parallel lines (© BAV, Barb. Lat. 1398, fol. 162v).

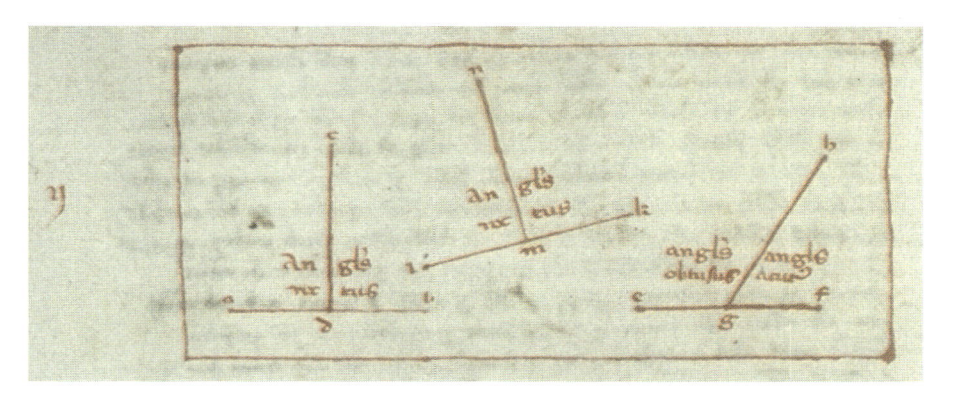

Figure 2: Types of angles: right, obtuse, and acute (© BAV, Barb. Lat. 1398, fol. 163r).

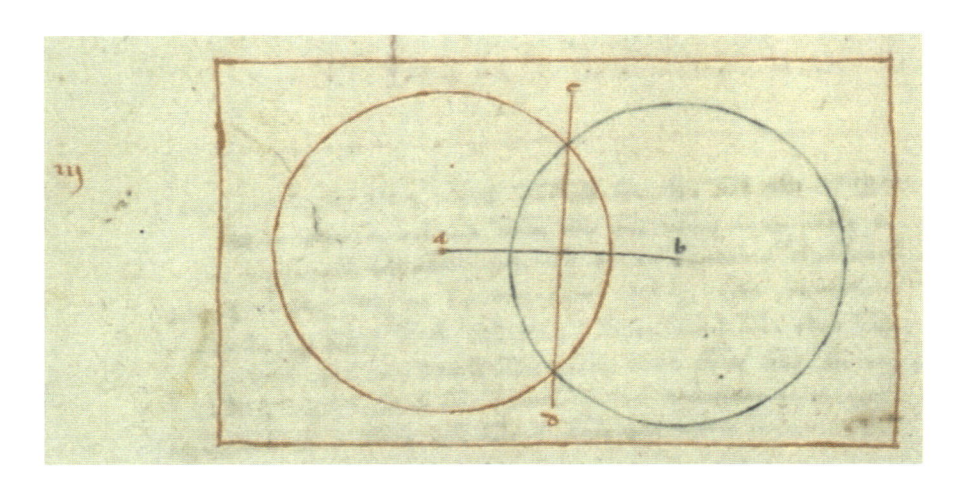

Figure 3: Bisecting a given line *ab* (© BAV, Barb. Lat. 1398, fol. 163r).

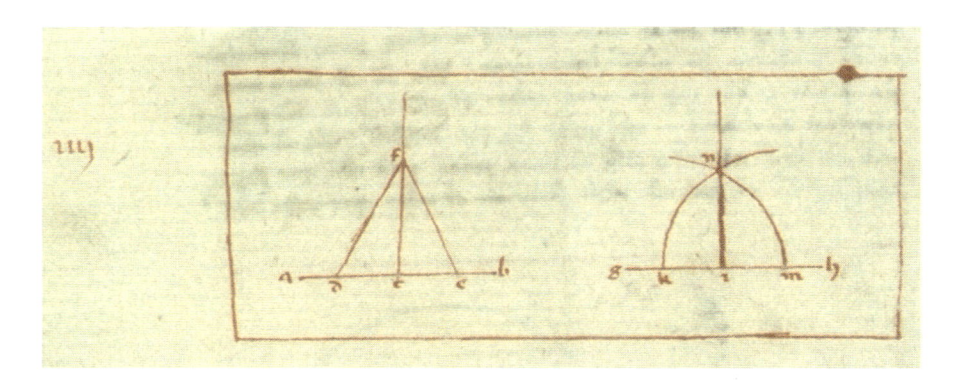

Figure 4: Two ways of drawing a perpendicular line (© BAV, Barb. Lat. 1398, fol. 163v).

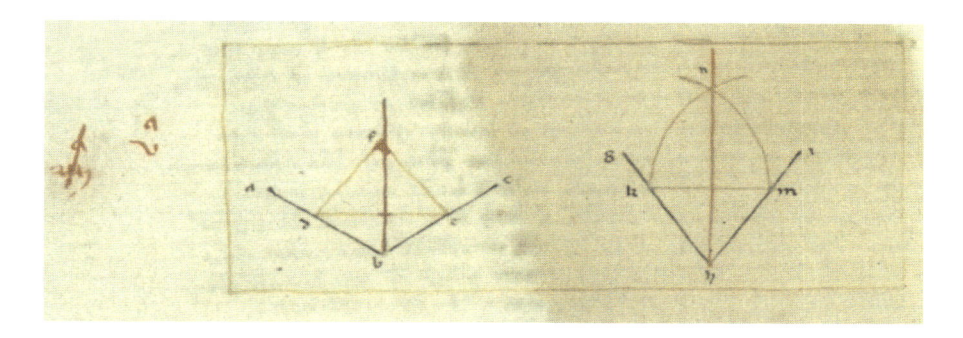

Figure 5: Two ways of bisecting an angle (© BAV, Barb. Lat. 1398, fol. 164r).

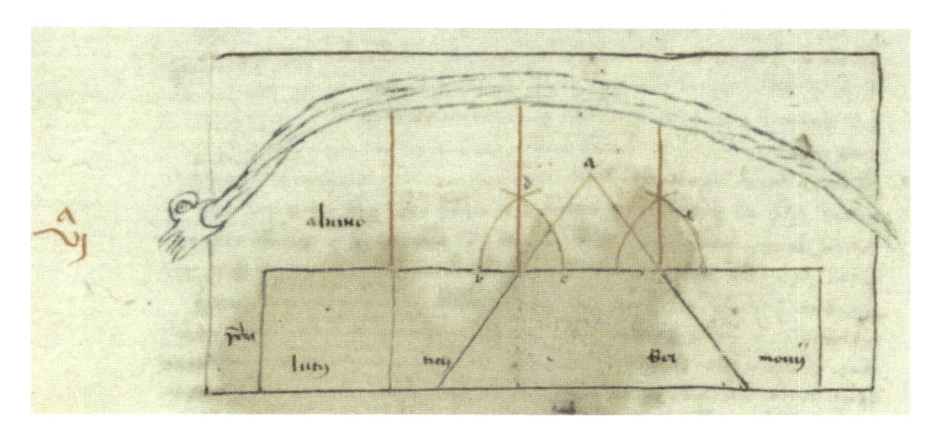

Figure 6: Scheme for dividing an alluvial deposit when the borderline of the fields is a straight line (© BAV, Barb. Lat. 1398, fol. 164v).

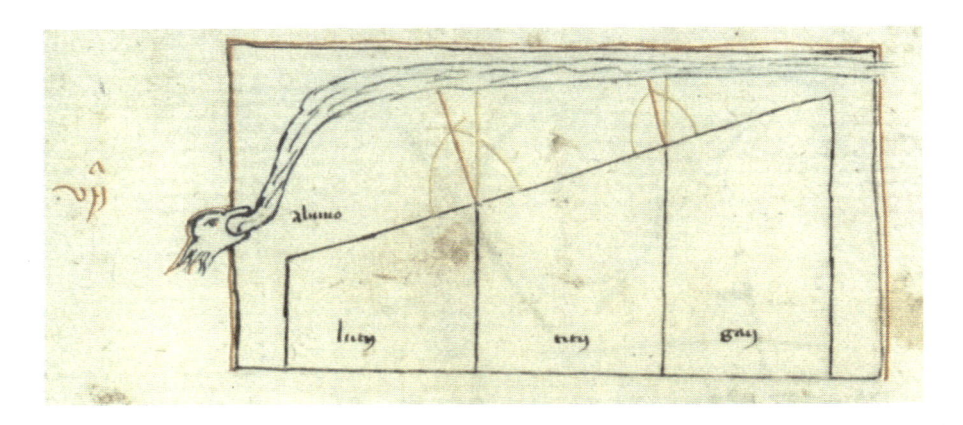

Figure 7: Scheme for dividing an alluvial deposit when the borderline of the fields is an oblique line (© BAV, Barb. Lat. 1398, fol. 165r).

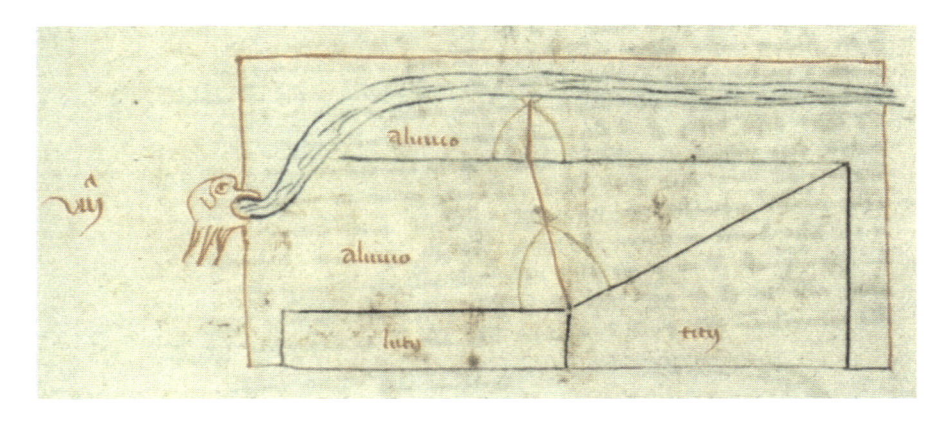

Figure 8: Scheme for dividing an alluvial deposit when the borderline of the fields is a segmented line (© BAV, Barb. Lat. 1398, fol. 165r).

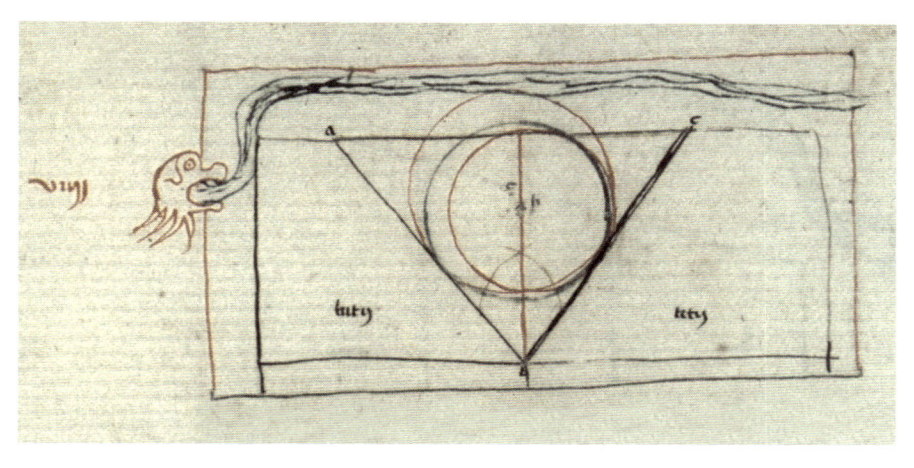

Figure 9: Scheme for dividing an alluvial deposit when the borderline of the fields is segmented. (© BAV, Barb. Lat. 1398, fol. 165v).

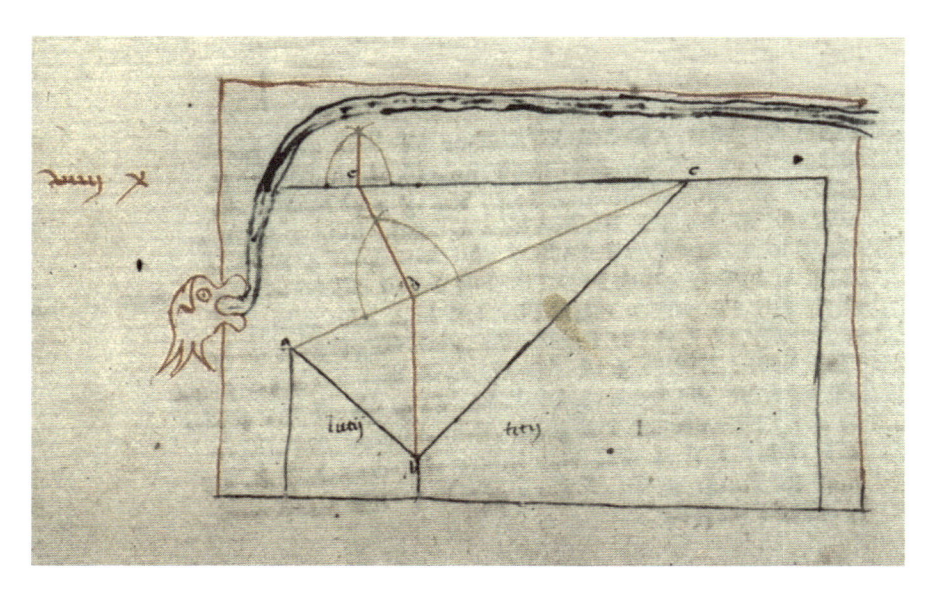

Figure 10: Scheme for dividing an alluvial deposit when the borderline of the fields is segmented (© BAV, Barb. Lat. 1398, fol. 165v).

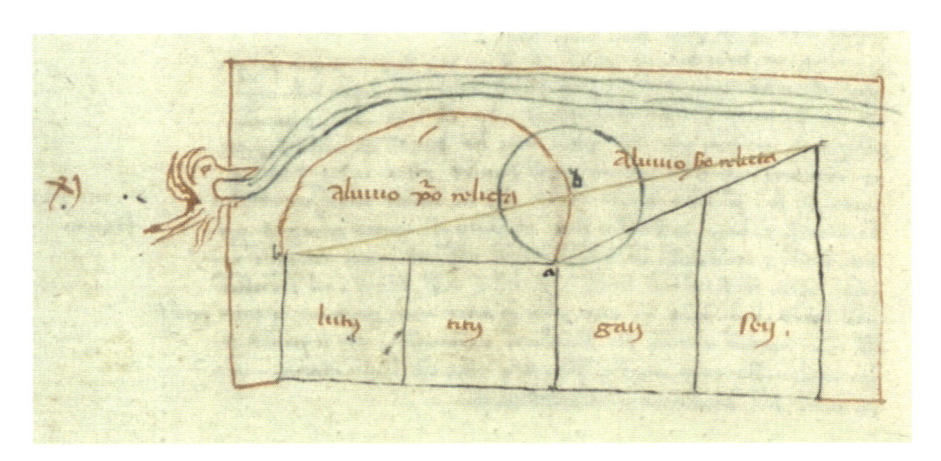

Figure 11: Scheme for dividing two alluvial deposits (*aluvio primo relicta* = first alluvial deposit; *aluvio secundo relicta* = seond alluvial deposit) (© BAV, Barb. Lat. 1398, fol. 166r).

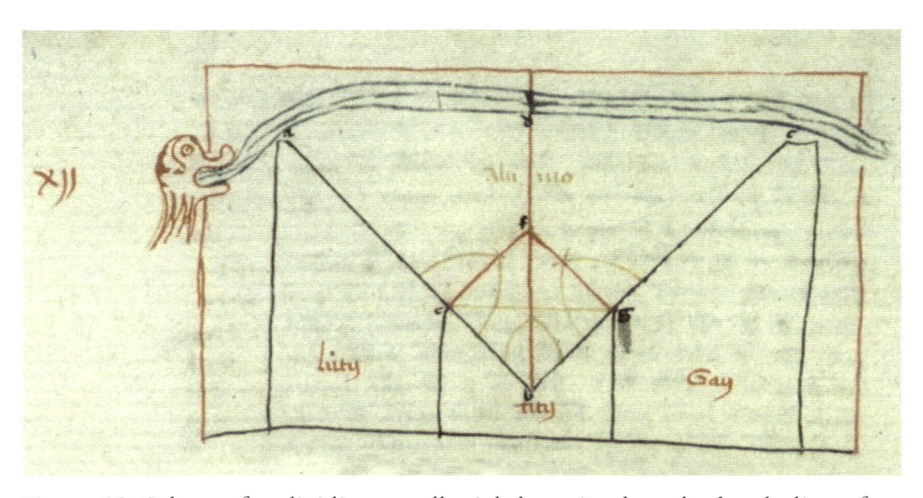

Figure 12: Scheme for dividing an alluvial deposit when the borderline of the fields is segmented (© BAV, Barb. Lat. 1398, fol. 166v).

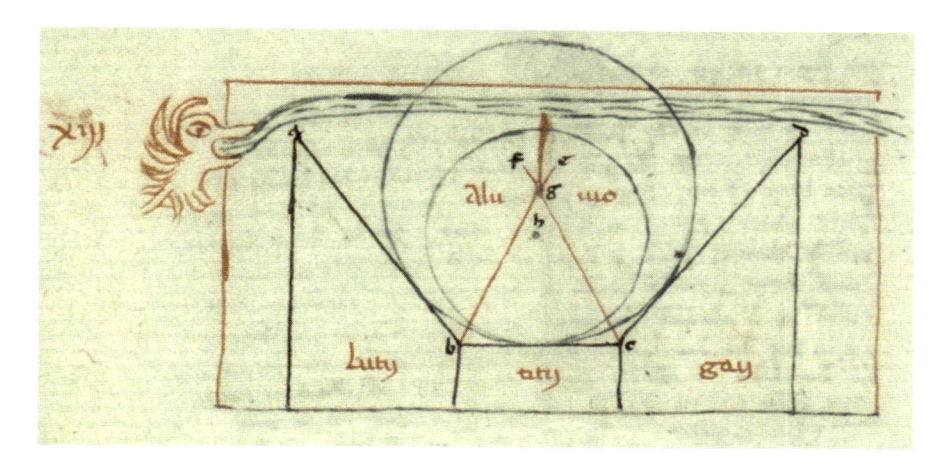

Figure 13: Scheme of dividing an alluvial deposit when the borderline of the fields is segmented (© BAV, Barb. Lat. 1398, fol. 166v).

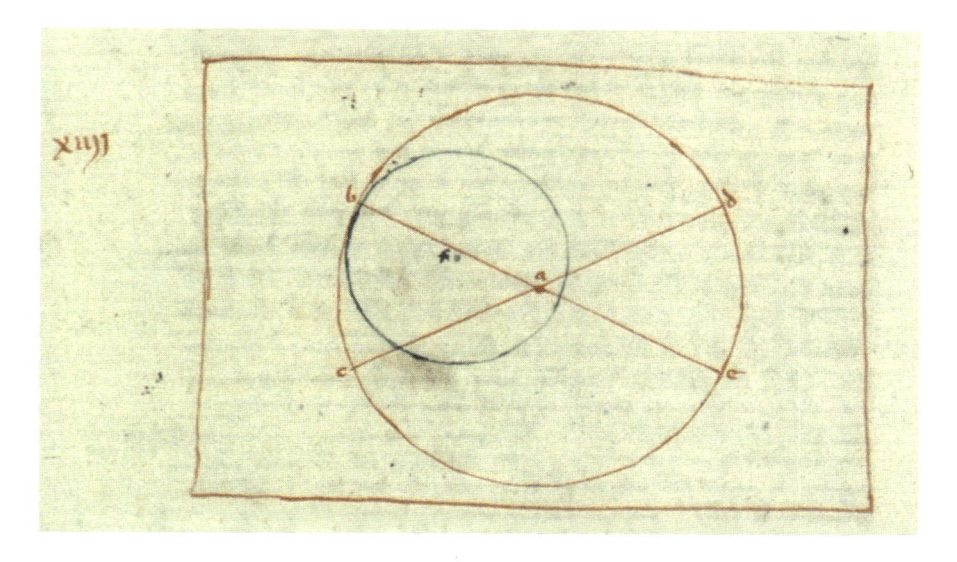

Figure 14: The geometrical properties of the circle (© BAV, Barb. Lat. 1398, fol. 167r).

126   A Renaissance of Conflicts

Figure 15: Two ways of finding the center of the circle (© BAV, Barb. Lat. 1398, fol. 167v).

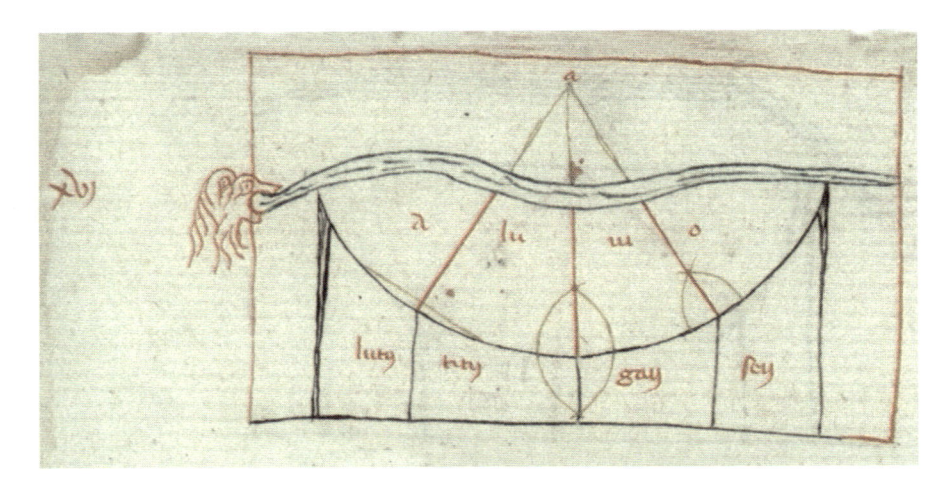

Figure 16: Scheme for dividing an alluvial deposit when the borderline of the fields is less than a semicircle (© BAV, Barb. Lat. 1398, fol. 168r).

River of Law   127

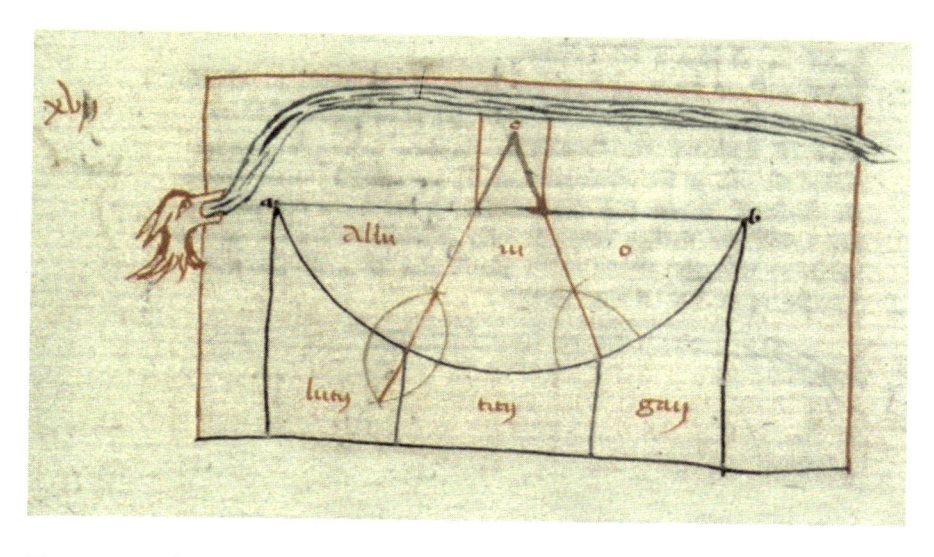

Figure 17: Scheme for dividing an alluvial deposit when the borderline is less than a semicircle (© BAV, Barb. Lat. 1398, fol. 168r).

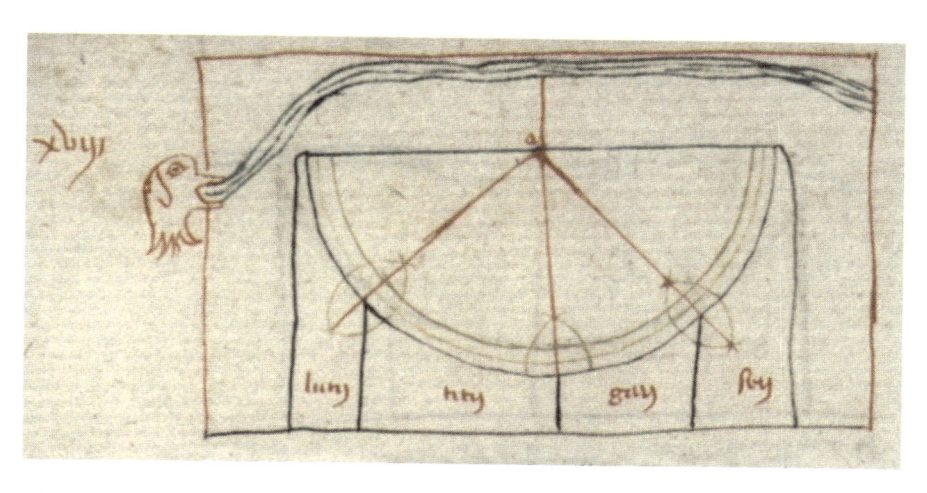

Figure 18: Scheme for dividing an alluvial deposit when the borderline is a semicircle (© BAV, Barb. Lat. 1398, fol. 168v).

128   A Renaissance of Conflicts

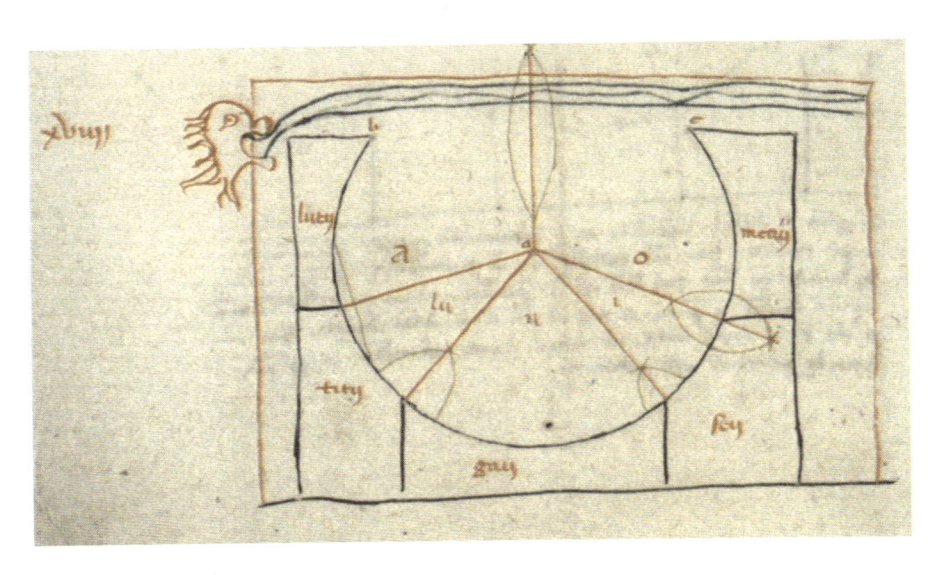

Figure 19: Scheme for dividing an alluvial deposit when the borderline is more than a semicircle (© BAV, Barb. Lat. 1398, fol. 168v).

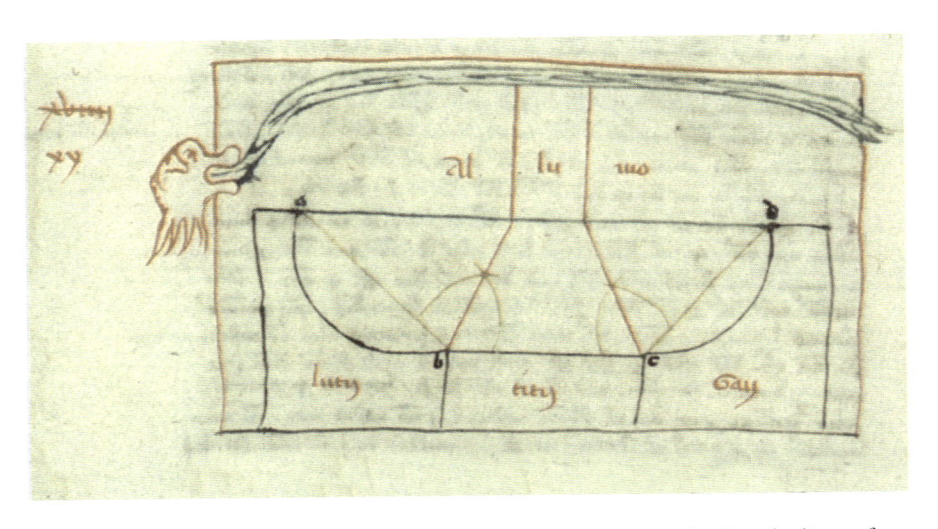

Figure 20: Scheme for dividing an alluvial deposit when the borderline of the fields has a mixed configuration (© BAV, Barb. Lat. 1398, fol. 169r).

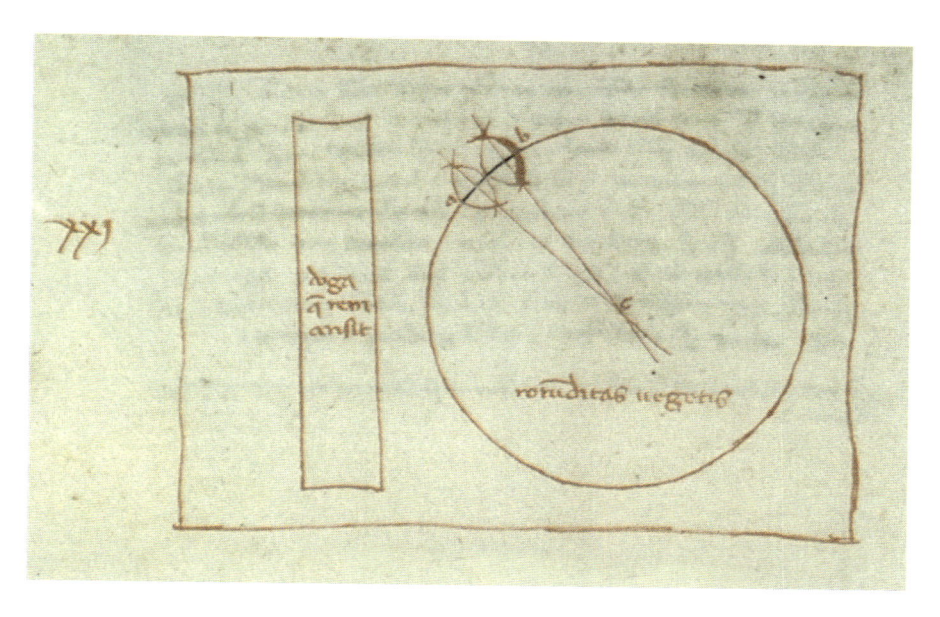

Figure 21: One-way of determining the circumference of a barrel (© BAV, Barb. Lat. 1398, fol. 170r).

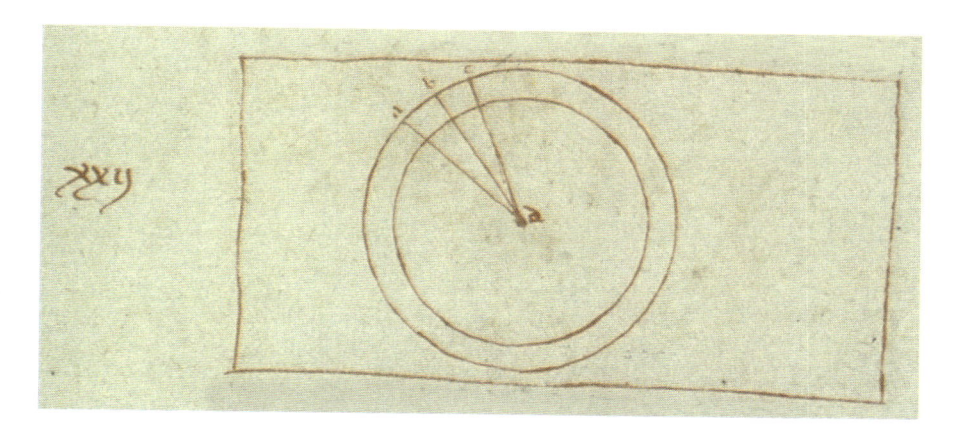

Figure 22: An alternative way of determining the circumference of a barrel (© BAV, Barb. Lat. 1398, fol. 170r).

Public Responsibility for Failure to Prosecute Crime? An Inquiry into an Umbrian Case by Bartolo da Sassoferrato

Susanne Lepsius[*]

A homicide occurred in Nocera in the middle of the fourteenth century. When no action was taken to bring the murderer to justice, the city as a whole was blamed for not having prosecuted the case. In the course of the city's defense, the famous jurist Bartolo da Sassoferrato (1314–1357) was asked for advice. He delivered a consilium on the question of whether the city could be considered negligent in not prosecuting the crime.

Bartolus's *consilium* will interest legal historians for its bearing on two questions: was there a concept of the public prosecution of crime in the Middle Ages, and could a collective entity be made responsible for a crime? Legal historical research has not given an adequate answer to either question. In this article I shall argue that in the Papal States the public responsibility of an entire community was generally accepted and that Bartolus mitigated this responsibility by introducing standards of individual diligence into the concept of public responsibility. His solutions were highly original, in particular when we consider how legal history research has conceived of these problems to date.

Historiography

According to a commonly held view, a demand for the public prosecution and punishment of crime developed in the course of the High Middle Ages. A recent German research project led by several renowned legal

---

[*] For helpful comments and suggestions in various stages of this article I would like to thank Prof. Lawrin Armstrong, Julius Kirshner, Thomas Kuehn, and Oliver Lepsius, as well as Eric Carlson for copy-editing the text. A shorter version of this article was presented on the panel 'Extraordinary legal mechanisms' at the 49th annual meeting of the Renaissance Society of America, Toronto, 27 March 2003, where I also received helpful remarks and comments.

historians has again inquired into the origins of public criminal law.[1] The first publications to emerge from this project stress several historical bases for this new understanding of the public prosecution and punishment of crime, but do not consider cases like the one I discuss here. Nevertheless, the project so far helps us to understand how the authorities' claim that the prosecution of crime should be public took shape.

Four factors are singled out. First, the rise, on the one hand, of a concept of a public peace order[2] inspired by the king's peace movement ('Landfriedensbewegung'),[3] and, on the other hand, of city statutes of the twelfth and thirteenth centuries that postulated peace as the highest communal good.[4] Secondly, city statutes defined as criminally sanctionable delicts such acts that bore a high risk of leading to violent eruptions, such as the carrying of arms and the uttering of abusive language. [5] Indeed, the more the city was defined as a *publica persona* possessing the right to prosecute crime—because every crime injured not only the offended party but also the city as a commune—the more new criminal delicts were constituted as public criminal offences, such as obstruction of public authority and breach of the peace.[6] An additional consequence of conceiving of the public authorities as injured by a criminal offence was that private settlements between the victim and the offender were no longer respected by the authorities, which would also prosecute the crime in their own right. [7] Thirdly, the older concept of liability simply

---

[1] Willoweit, 'Zum Begriff des Öffentlichen im späten Mittelalter,' p. 337.

[2] Willoweit, 'Die Entstehung des öffentlichen Strafrechts,' p. 2; Willoweit, 'Gewalt und Verbrechen, Strafe und Sühne im alten Würzburg,' p. 227.

[3] Stübinger, *Schuld, Strafrecht und Geschichte*, p. 315ff. The imposition of a payment of a *bot* to the king for breaching his peace is discussed as one important aspect of the progress toward an understanding of public criminal law by Groot, 'Proto-juries and Public Criminal Law in England,' pp. 24–26; and by Sharpe, 'Criminal Law as an Instrument of Conflict Control in Late Medieval and Early Modern England,' pp. 123f.

[4] Frenz, 'Frieden, Gemeinwohl und Gerechtigkeit,' pp. 111–145. For the statutes of the Italian cities in the late thirteenth century, of which Perugia and Bologna were the forerunners, see Sbriccoli, '"Vidi communiter observari,"' p. 236. On the other hand, Zorzi describes the same development as an increasing ideological mobilization toward the terms *pax* and *iustitia* by the new social strata of merchants and lawyers; see Zorzi, 'Negoziazione penale, legittimazione giuridica e poteri urbani nell'Italia comunale,' pp. 19f.

[5] Frenz, 'Frieden, Gemeinwohl,' pp. 129–134.

[6] Sbriccoli, '"Vidi communiter observari,"' p. 263.

[7] In the case of thirteenth-century England Klerman argues that private prosecution declined because royal officials as well as presenting juries no longer respected private settlements as preemptive for a public prosecution. According to him this change in official policy might have been influenced by contemporary

Public Responsibility for Failure to Prosecute Crime? 133

for the result of one's acts (*Erfolgshaftung*) gave way to the view that individual guilt on the part of the perpetrator (*Verschuldenshaftung*) must be established.[8] This new understanding was due mainly to the influence of the church, in particular through the practice of confession, which was particularly significant in canon law. Inquiry into the guilt of a perpetrator led to a more active legal system. It required, for instance, a judge who looked for the truth of a case by means of the new inquisitorial process that slowly came to replace the old accusatorial procedure between the victim or the victim's family and the offender.[9] Finally, alongside sanctions that had traditionally consisted solely of compensation of the victim by the offender, the law now imposed pecuniary fines for a breach of the peace payable to the court, the ruler, or to the public authorities.[10] In another step, pecuniary punishments were superseded by afflictive punishments that could not be relieved by merely paying a fee. This system of punishments presupposed a homogenous group of subjects whom the public authorities treated equally.[11] Likewise, in the fourteenth century certain crimes were defined that could not be pardoned by the public authorities.[12]

---

canon law; see Klerman, 'Settlement and the Decline of Private Prosecution in Thirteenth-Century England.' Similarly, it has been observed of the Italian city-states that private settlements (*pax privata*) would not have hindered city officials from prosecuting perpetrators; see Sbriccoli, '"Vidi communiter observari,"' pp. 259–262.

[8] A good survey of the historiographical developments behind the guilt concept is presented by Stübinger, *Schuld, Strafrecht und Geschichte*, pp. 312–401.

[9] Cohen, 'Inquiring Once More after the Inquisitorial Process.' Cohen, as well as Willoweit, 'Gewalt und Verbrechen,' stresses how long different types of procedures were used alongside each other, until well into the seventeenth century. Rousseaux, 'From Case to Crime: Homicide Regulation in Medieval and Modern Europe,' notices since about 1300 an intensified intervention of rulers to regulate homicide (146) and a desire to end or limit private feuds (151). The central role of the judge, upon whom a broad discretion (*arbitrium*) in prosecuting crime was conferred by the new inquisitorial forms of *ius commune* procedure, is underlined by Gouron, 'L'apport des juristes français à l'essor du droit pénal savant,' pp. 369–371, and by Sbriccoli, '"Vidi communiter observari,"' pp. 247–254.

[10] Groot, 'Proto-juries,' p. 24. Sbriccoli, '"Vidi communiter observari,"' p. 267 stresses how the pecuniary fine for breaching public peace was increasingly considered in the first place before compensating the victim's damage.

[11] Willoweit, 'Begriff des Öffentlichen'; Willoweit, 'Entstehung des öffentlichen Strafrechts,' p. 6f.

[12] Gauvard puts emphasis on an additional aspect, that of grace. Guaranteeing peace and pardoning crime are according to her both church-developed concepts which the French kings, but also dukes and counts, used in defining their public function. According to Gauvard a widespread pardoning practice of the French kings likewise demonstrates a concept of publicly prosecuting crime: pardoning

A recent German-Italian conference on criminality in the late Middle Ages and the early modern period has highlighted the tendency of the Italian historiography to emphasize the role of public criminal prosecution as an instrument of state formation. German research, by contrast, appears to stress the continuing potential of the public law as a resource by which individual victims could achieve personal satisfaction and remedies.[13] This research concludes that both private and public forms of criminal prosecution coexisted for a long time, and which of the two forms is stressed by any particular study depends largely on the sources used by the investigator. Studies of archival and court records accentuate the efforts of plaintiffs to prosecute defendants and highlight the continuation of private forms of criminal prosecution, although they do not document extrajudicial settlements or grace conferred by public authorities. The study of normative sources, on the other hand, often leads to the conclusion that slowly emerging official institutions engaged in forms of public prosecution from a very early stage.[14]

According to all of these studies, the public claim to the right to prosecute and punish crime finally led to a state monopoly on punishment

---

thus was the logical counterpart to the state claim of the authority to prosecute crime. Gauvard, '*De grace especial*', vol. 2, pp. 940–949; Gauvard, 'De la difficulté d'appliquer les principes théoriques du droit pénal,' pp.106–108, 117–119.

[13] Rousseaux, 'Construction et stratégies,' p. 328.

[14] Examples of more archive-based studies that consequently find 'messier' results of ongoing forms of private settlements after criminal offences, but also of private appealers' making a much more active use of the new instruments of public criminal law and its new procedural forms (for example, the inquisitorial process) as well as of the new institutions, are Sharpe, 'Criminal Law as an Instrument,' p. 122; and Klerman, 'Settlement and the Decline of Private Prosecution.' Klerman undertakes an extensive statistical analysis of the English eyre records and the edited rolls of King's Bench cases and concludes that during the thirteenth century private prosecution ('appeals' in English terminology) declined, because private settlements were no longer respected by public officials. Klerman does not go so far as to speak of the beginnings of a 'public prosecution of crime.' For Italy in the late thirteenth century, see Zorzi, 'Negoziazione penale,' pp. 17, 23–26. A norm-based approach, on the other hand, is presented by Groot, 'Proto-juries,' pp. 26–32, who sees the first important steps of a concept of public criminal law and prosecution as early as 1166 (Assizes of Clarendon), 1187 (afflictive punishments with Glanvill), and 1215 (introduction of the criminal jury trial). Sbriccoli sees the type of source upon which the research is based as crucial for the kind of results one can find. He stresses how much various forms of negotiated criminal justice are likely to be found using archival material, whereas the perception of a hegemonic prosecution apparatus and public prosecution of crime typically is due to a normative approach. See Sbriccoli, 'Giustizia negoziata, giustizia egemonica,' pp. 347f., 352–355. A similar point is made by Rousseaux, 'Construction et stratégies,' p. 340.

('Durchsetzung des staatlichen Strafanspruchs') and was crucial in state formation. However, these studies rarely reflect the problem under consideration here: whether the public claim to the right to prosecute and punish crime was paralleled by the public obligation to do so.[15] An investigation of public liability for failure to prosecute crime, as will be undertaken here in connection with a *consilium* of Bartolo da Sassoferrato, will shed additional light on the conceptual models and juristic argumentation that led to the monopolization of the criminal law by the public sphere. Bartolus' *consilium*, moreover, draws our attention to a region that has not been significantly studied by the ongoing German research project, despite its 'European' scope.

An examination of 'public responsibility' will illuminate another important theme of legal historical research, namely, the problem of collective guilt in the Middle Ages, which is usually treated as a problem of canon law. Although the need to make collective entities liable for the criminal acts of their members was apparently intensely felt in the Middle Ages, canon law hesitated to do so from fear of injuring innocent members of the collective entity along with the truly guilty. Thus, for example, excommunication, the strictest church sanction, could not be imposed on a collective subject: an interdict or pecuniary fine was the only allowable sanction.[16] The origins of the concept of collective responsibility are said either to lie in a German notion of *Gesamthaftung* or to be an original invention of church law,[17] although recently very early civilian contributions to the concept, notably by Johannes Bassianus in the late twelfth

---

[15] Analyzing the public obligation to prosecute crime is a fourth aspect of the research of Frenz, pp. 134–144. Frenz, who is one of the few scholars who discuss this question, traces this concept back to theological and canonical reflections on how to legitimize rulership in general. But in the German cities of the Middle Ages whose statutes she scrutinizes, there apparently did not exist any mechanism of legally enforcing this public obligation to prosecute crime. Apparently, the only remedy against city authorities continuously abstaining from criminal prosecution and thus themselves breaching law and peace in the city would have been a revolt of the citizens. On civil revolts in late medieval German cities that claimed to be restoring peace and law against treacherous city authorities, see, in general, Kannowski, *Bürgerkämpfe und Friedebriefe*.

[16] Gillet, *La personnalité juridique en droit ecclésiastique*, pp. 98f, 121–126; Clarke, 'A Question of Collective Guilt,' p. 113; Michaud-Quantin, *Universitas*, pp. 327–339.

[17] The 'Germanic' roots of the institute are stressed by Dahm, *Das Strafrecht Italiens im ausgehenden Mittelalter*, pp. 151–179, 151. Still fundamental is the study by Gierke, *Das deutsche Genossenschaftsrecht*, vol. 3: *Die Staats- und* Korporationslehre, pp. 231–236 (glossators), in particular p. 236, where he stresses the importance of a 'germanischer Genossenschaftsbegriff'—a Germanic idea of co-operative—pp. 338–350 (canon law), and pp. 402–410 (commentators).

century, have also been pointed out.[18] But even in the Middle Ages the idea of collective guilt came into conflict with the canonical concept of individual guilt. Medieval jurists are generally said to have helped to undermine a strict concept of public liability by introducing elements of individual guilt into any offences a community might commit.[19] Most often, the offences that might be imputed to a community in medieval doctrine represented delicts of failure to observe a legal obligation.[20]

The Nocera Case
and the Qualification of the *Consilium*

The example of legal expertise Bartolo da Sassoferrato gave to Bishop Alexander of Nocera falls somewhere between these two poles of historiographical interpretation. The case in which Bartolus was asked for advice was played out in Nocera, a city in western Umbria which was mentioned as early as 761 as the sea of a Lombard *castaldato*.[21] A bishop's see from an early period and part of the duchy of Spoleto, by the fourteenth century Nocera was directly subject to the pope as a result of the papal policy of recovering the Papal States, the so-called recuperation policy. Throughout the lifetime of Bartolo da Sassoferrato, the incumbent of the see of Nocera was Alexander, a Franciscan and Apostolic Penitentiary who was later beatified.[22] Bartolus's home town of Sassoferrato belonged to the diocese of Nocera.[23] Bishop Alexander thus followed a common pattern in seeking legal advice from a jurist with Umbrian associations, both by birth

---

[18]Based on very thorough source and manuscript studies, Chiodi has shown how decretists were the first to deal with the questions of delictal criminal responsibility of communities, which then were quickly taken over by the glossators, who turned out to be less reluctant to accept the general concept. See Chiodi, "'Delinquere ut universi,'" pp. 104–110 (on a *consilium* of Iohannes Bassianus), 135 (for the intersecting contributions made by the decretists and the glossators). Quaglioni has recently stressed that, particularly in later *ius comune* doctrine, corporate entities could also be held responsible for active commission of a misdeed and therefore that Chiodi's distinction between responsibility for the commission or omission of a crime should not be overemphasized. Quaglioni, "'Universi consentire non possunt,'" pp. 411–417.

[19]Dahm, *Das Strafrecht* Italiens, vol. 3, p. 179.
[20]Gillet, *La personnalité juridique*, p. 99.
[21]Fatteschi, *Memorie istorico-diplomatiche*, p. 169.
[22]Bishop Alexander (Vincioli) of Nocera (17 November 1327–1363); cf. Eubel, *Hierarchia catholica Medii*, p. 373; Gams, *Series episcoporum ecclesie Catholicae*, p. 710.
[23]Gams, *Series episcoporum ecclesie Catholicae*, p. 710.

and professional activity, since Bartolus was teaching law at the University of Perugia between 1343 and his death in 1357.[24]

Because of Alexander's long episcopacy, it is unfortunately impossible to determine precisely when Bartolus drafted his *consilium*. All of the manuscripts consulted and presented in the edition below are typical of *consilia* contained in manuscript collections that probably derived from a secondary copy remaining with the author.[25] For purposes of the present study, it has not been possible to locate the original *consilium* of Bartolus himself. Such an original *consilium* would usually have contained a red seal of authentication, a precise date, and possibly the opinions of other jurists as well. Most likely, it would have been preserved in the records of the diocese of Nocera or in those of the court of the rector of the duchy of Spoleto, which appears to have been the court before which the case was debated.

Bishop Alexander asked Bartolus for advice on behalf of the city of Nocera. Nocera's citizens had been accused of negligence in prosecuting a homicide that had been committed in their territory. An action had been brought by way of inquisition in the court of the rector of the duchy (*rector ducatus et eius curia*). Unfortunately, from the facts of the case as they can be reconstructed from the *consilium*, it is impossible to determine who brought the case to the notice of the rector's court and therefore who instigated further judicial proceedings by means of the inquisitorial procedure. A first court session had already taken place, during which witnesses who attested to the negligence of the city had been heard. Now Bishop Alexander wanted to know whether the simple statement of a witness about negligence, without giving further reasons for this testimony, was sufficient. On a more general level, he also wanted to know how the city could defend itself against the accusation of negligence and how, if this should become necessary in the course of the trial, it could instead even prove its diligence.

Apart from the case itself, the *consilium* displays some interesting peculiarities and on several points departs from the usual typology of *consilia*.[26] To begin with, it is clearly not a *consilium sapientis* written at

---

[24] On the custom of asking legal advice from local jurists in the late Middle Ages, see Kirshner, '*Consilia* as Authority in Late Medieval Italy,' pp. 109–111. On Bartolus's life and career, see Calasso, 'Bartolo da Sassoferrato,' p. 642 (which describes his tenure in Perugia after 1343).

[25] On the different manuscript traditions of medieval *consilia* (originals with a seal and copies already with the author), see Colli, 'Consilia dei giuristi medievali,' pp. 173–176.

[26] Five types of *consilia* in civil cases are distinguished by Ascheri, 'Le fonti e la flessibilità del diritto comune,' pp. 15–17.

138   A Renaissance of Conflicts

the request of the court but rather a *consilium pro parte* composed on behalf of the city of Nocera. In asking for advice, the bishop was apparently acting as the city's *procurator*, representing it against a charge of collective guilt lodged against it in the court of the duchy.[27] Language typical of a procurator is the reference to 'isti nostri Nucerini.' Our text, however, is also atypical insofar as it is never described as a *consilium*, certainly not a *consilium pro veritate*, as a *consilium* on behalf of one party to a process was often called.[28] Indeed, in his response, Bartolus did not even use the standard verb *consului*. Instead, Bishop Alexander had asked him for general advice, using the verb *rescribere*, a term usually reserved for the rescripts of the ancient Roman emperors and the popes in their decretals in response to individual cases.[29] Nor does our text contain the reference to divine authority that usually appeared at the beginning of a jurist's response or a reservation clause in which the jurist stated that he would give his opinion subject to the superior knowledge of other jurists.[30] As a *consilium*, it belongs more to the genre of archival sources and real court proceedings than to that of normative determinations.

Neither the peculiarities of the wording nor the content of the text suggest a *consilium* in the usual procedural sense. On the one hand, our text was clearly 'motivated,' that is, partial, containing extensive references to the Digest and the Justinianic Code, which was typical of a *consilium pro parte* in contrast to the shorter, legally binding and usually 'unmotivated' or impartial *consilium sapientis*.[31] On the other hand, apart from

---

[27] Canon law doctrine accepted procurators on behalf of an incriminated community if the procedure took place in the 'irregular' forms of inquisition and only if the crime was not capital; see Chiodi, '"Delinquere ut universi,"' pp. 175–194. That Bishop Alexander might have acted as a kind of procurator is thus another aspect of the rather frequent political representation of a city through its bishop in contrast to an antagonistic view juxtaposing the creation of the city-state as political entity and *coniuratio* to the political power of the bishop. On the political representation of the cities (in his study: Tuscan cities) through their bishops, see Tabacco, 'Vescovi e comuni in Italia,' pp. 253, 265.

[28] Ascheri, 'Le fonti,' p. 17.

[29] Apart from the specific terminology for *consilia* in the learned law of the Middle Ages as an entire genre of legal literature, the verb *rescribere* is used apparently in a narrower sense as asking advice in a specific legal matter from the Roman emperor or a jurist, whereas *consulere* implies the solution of an entire case with factual and legal problems. See Heumann-Seckel, *Handlexikon zu den Quellen des römischen Rechts,* and *Oxford Latin Dictionary,* s.v. 'consulere' and 'rescribere.'

[30] A *consilium sapientis* e.g., is usually introduced with the words *In Christi/ dei nomine amen* (Kirshner, '*Consilia* as authority,' pp. 120–123) and is most likely to end in the later Middle Ages with the clause *salvo saniori consilio* (Ascheri, 'Le fonti,' p. 41).

[31] Kuehn, '*Consilia* as Juristic Literature in Private Law,' p. 230f.

the introductory statements, which probably repeat the wording of Bishop Alexander's request, there is no additional description of the factual circumstances that might give a clearer impression of the actual case. Finally, the piece was clearly written at a stage in the process long beyond the preparatory phase, when a well-drafted *consilium* might, by a wealth of legal arguments and an impressive list of authorities bolstering the party's own legal position, convince a judge. Instead, it is clear that the witnesses had been heard and, apparently, their testimony had already been opened,[32] so that Bishop Alexander's request came in the eighth or ninth phase of the *ordo iudiciorum*, a process that usually involved ten steps. Even if we trust Bartolus's statement that he was working against time to reply to Alexander's request and was replying, despite his great workload, in a very short time,[33] it is hard to imagine how his advice could have made a difference in an inquisitorial process that was already at the stage of discussing the witness protocols.

These peculiarities, however, may be explained if we assume that Bishop Alexander was already considering an appeal against an anticipated unfavorable sentence in the provincial *rector*'s court or that he wanted to be generally informed on the legal possibilities of proving negligence in similar cases in the future. After all, according to Alexander, such cases were common and hence necessitated preparation against future actions for negligence.[34]

Interestingly, neither Bishop Alexander's request nor Bartolus's reply addressed the legal problem of whether there was an any juridical

---

[32]It says in the text that *testes* were *inquisiti* and that they had said, without further explanations of their knowledge, that the inhabitants of Nocera had been negligent in prosecuting crime in their town: 'nec reddunt causam sui dicti nec de causa fuerunt interrogati.' According to Roman canonical procedure the witnesses are always questioned in a separate room by the judge and his notaries in accordance with *interrogatoria* presented by the defendant party trying to impugn the trustworthiness of the witnesses. In the eighth period, then, the protocolled testimonies would be read to the parties and their procurators, who would then have the opportunity to discuss the testimonies and plead their cases. In the ninth step the judge left the courtroom to find the sentence according to the facts presented by applying the law. Finally, the tenth step of procedure would be that the judge would give his sentence. On the whole procedure in Roman-canon law and the questioning of witnesses in particular, see Lepsius, *Von Zweifeln zur Überzeugung*, pp. 24–30.

[33]'Ego vero sum modo in principio studii multis lectionibus occupatus. Unde ex eo, quod videre potui in illo modico tempore, quod ad illam investigacionem adhibui, rescribo que sencio' (Bartolus cons. I, 102, lines 14–17); and at the end of his consilium: 'Ista breviter modo comprehendi. Bartholus,' (line 154s).

[34]'Quia ista cottidiana sunt tam pro presenti quam pro futuro, rogamus quod plenius rescribere placeat' (line 10s).

foundation for trying a community—in this case an entire city—for not effectively prosecuting crime. Both focused immediately on the question of how to prove either negligence or diligence and thus on how to exculpate a *universitas*. By doing so, they indicated that they accepted the premise of the legally binding and enforceable obligation of a city to punish crimes such as homicide.

Normative Foundations for a Collective Responsibility

Among the several factors that might have governed such a case, Bartolus could have appealed to at least two: the provincial statutes referred to by Bishop Alexander and the Digest of Roman Law. Interestingly, he never referred to Dig. 48.19.16.10 § *Nonnumquam*, upon which he had commented so extensively as a *sedes materie,* developing a very subtle system of distinctions and explaining in which cases a community could be held to bear corporate liability.[35]

Bartolus would not have had to establish a delictal responsibility from general Roman law principles in the case of the Nucerini. In the first place, Alexander had asked him only about the question of proof. In the second place, there already existed a specific written norm defining the consequences for cities that failed to prosecute crime. Alexander himself had already referred to the *constitutiones provinciales* which allowed fines to be imposed on cities that were negligent or sluggish in prosecuting criminals.[36]

Considering that the entire case took place within the Papal States, it is notable that a chapter in the Egidian Constitutions formulated by the cardinal legate Albornoz for all the Papal States in 1357–1363[37] prescribed a pecuniary fine for any city that failed to prosecute serious crimes publicly. The pecuniary punishment had to be equivalent to the damage

---

[35] On the important improvements made by Bartolo da Sassoferrato in the question of corporate liability, see Ullmann, 'The Delictal Responsibility of Medieval Corporations.' For a recent treatment, but without reference to Ullmann's results, see d'Urso, 'Persona giuridica e responsabilità penale.'

[36] '... quia ipsi fuerunt negligentes et remissi in capiendo quosdam homicidas, ex quo crimine certa pena imposita est civitati secundum formam constitutionum provincialium' (Bartolus, consilium I, 102, c. 1, lines 2–4).

[37] Weber, *Die Constitutiones Sanctae Matris Ecclesiae des Kardinals Aegidius Albornoz*, pp. 37–52, 66f, sees the main motivation for the statutes given by Albornoz to the territories of the Papal States in the need to reestablish order and peace after the long period of neglect the Papal States had to endure during the Avignonese period of papal reign.

suffered by the victim's family, which also had to be compensated by the perpetrator. This rule came into play

> when, having diligently considered the place and time and other circumstances, it shall be established that men in whose territory the crime was committed were negligent or remiss in safeguarding the location of the crime, in capturing the malefactors, or in having them guarded or captured.
>
> [quando homines, in cuius territorio fuerit maleficium commissum, in custodiendo locum maleficii, in capiendo malefactores vel custodiri vel capi facere fuisse negligentes constiterit vel remissi, consideratis loco et tempore et aliis circumstantiis diligenter].

Such public responsibility was incumbent on any territorial entity, no matter how large it was, and it was bolstered by the requirement that the communes carefully supervise their territories. If a commune itself had jurisdiction for more serious crimes such as homicide, rape, and public disorder, it had to prosecute them within thirty days of the commission of the crime; if the commune did not possess jurisdiction for causae maiores, it had to denounce the crime and the perpetrator to the curia rectoris within eight days, where the crime would then be prosecuted.[38]

But we must look further than the rather late Egidian Constitutions as a normative foundation for the criminal responsibility of cities. The Egidian Constitutions were published during the session of the general parliament in Fano in late April and early May of 1357,[39] and Bartolus probably died soon after, in July 1357.[40] Similar regulations are most likely to have been already contained in earlier normative codifications, such as the constitutions of the papal legate Déaulx, specifically for the duchy

---

[38]'Quelibet universitas, civitas, castrum, comes, baro seu dominus alicuius castri vel rocche terras et loca, territorium et districtum suum diligenter custodiat et faciat custodiri, ita quod in eis rapinas, disrobationes, homicidia aliaque gravia maleficia minime committantur et, si fiant ibidem, si quidem de illis puniendum iurisdictionem ab ecclesia habent, infra triginta dies postquam commissa fuerint, secundum iusticiam, studeant penitus iudicare et dampna passis facere emendari. Et si dictam iurisdictionem non habent, malefactores rectori provinciae vel suo iudici maleficiorum cum effectu presentent infra VIII dies proximos a die maleficii perpetrati; . . .' (*Costituzioni Egidiane dell'anno MCCCLVII*, l. 4 c. 49, p. 189, lines 22–31, p. 190 lines 19–22 (the direct quote in our text). The sanction is to be found p. 190, lines 1–6: 'quod si non fecerint . . . dampna passis de bonis comunitatum seu dominorum, in quorum territorio exitterit facinus perpetratum, cum effectu restituant et emendent et in tantumdem solvendum per eos camere puniantur.'

[39]Weber, *Die Constitutiones Sanctae Matris Ecclesiae des Kardinals Aegidius Albornoz* p. 48.

[40]Calasso, 'Bartolus de Sassoferrato,' p. 643.

of Spoleto, of 1336.[41] More recent research has disclosed that the Egidian Constitutions drew heavily upon earlier written constitutions for Spoleto as well as those for the Mark of Ancona that were introduced regularly by the different provincial rectors, such as those of 1333 by Pierre de Castanet for Spoleto.[42] Indeed, in the modern edition of the latter statutes we find that communities were under a public legal obligation to prosecute crime, an obligation bolstered by criminal sanctions. Communities that failed to comply with their obligations in this respect were fined in accordance with their size: cities were subject to a *pena pecuniaria* of a thousand Cortonese pounds, fortified castles a fine of 500 pounds, and villages to a fine of 200 pounds.[43]

One important aim of the statutes for the papal territories was to enhance the effectiveness of public administration by introducing the principle of syndication, whereby public officials were reviewed at the end of their term of office, and by creating offices such as the *baiulus*, who was in charge of investigating crime.[44] Earlier regulations in the duchy of Spoleto, reminiscent of chapter 49 in the fourth book of the Egidian Constitutions, demanded that cities and communes keep the streets and territories free of dangerous criminals.[45] In the statutes of the cardinal legate Déaulx of 1336 there is a norm placing communes that

---

[41] On the activity of Déaulx, see Deviziani, *Fonti delle costituzioni Egidiane*, pp. VI, XXVIII.

[42] Schmidt, 'La recente scoperta degli Statuti del ducato di Spoleto del 1333,' underlines (p. 981) that the originality of Albornoz is not as great as has been supposed, since he drew more than one-fourth of his regulations from those Castanet had published during the provincial parliament in Spello in 1333.

[43] *Constitutiones Spoletani Ducatus a Petro de Castaneto edite (a. 1333)*, c. XXV (rubr.: 'Quod comunitates teneantur capere malefactores et de pena non capientium', pp. 122f.). According to these statutes, the serious crimes that had to be prosecuted by medieval communities within the papal states were homicide, kidnaping and robbery.

[44] For a description of the introduction of the syndication process (rather late) in the early fourteenth century, in comparison to Tuscany, where the institution of making public officials responsible for failing to meet their official duties was known since the thirteenth century, see Deviziani, *Fonti delle costituzioni Egidiane*, pp. XIV, XXVI (describing the introduction of the *baiulus* as 'unum legalem hominem et ydoneum'). See the edition of the statutes, c. 16, Deviziani, p. 47f. On the syndication process in general, see Engelmann, *Die Wiedergeburt der Rechtskultur in Italien durch die wissenschaftliche Lehre*, pp. 514–585, who does not mention the papal legislation in this field but focuses on the northern Italian regulations.

[45] Sella, 'Costituzioni dello Stato della Chiesa.' The constitutions of the duchy of Spoleto of 1333, on the other hand, do not establish such a responsibility, but only require communities to maintain the streets so that they can be securely used by voyagers, *Constitutiones Spoletani Ducatus*, c. LXX, p. 161.

hindered private individuals from pursuing their claims in courts, such as the provincial court, under the sanction of interdict, whereas individual persons, even if they were preeminent bishops, were to be sanctioned by excommunication.[46] This might also have been a way to enforce the public responsibility of communes to prosecute crime by giving individuals—that is, the family of a murdered person—the legal possibility to bring a commune's failure to prosecute crime to the knowledge of a higher court. An even earlier example of such a normative obligation to prosecute crime is the statutes of the city of Perugia of 1279. Here every smaller city or village in the Perugian territory was obliged at the risk of heavy fines to report any homicide on their territories to the Perugian officials so that the homicide, which before this would have been subject to accusatory forms of trial, could be prosecuted by way of inquisition.[47] Moreover, in the 1333 statutes of the duchy of Spoleto, the extraordinary mechanism of inquisitorial procedure, which could not ordinarily be used in criminal cases because of the risk of abuse, was reintroduced in cases where entire communities failed to comply with their public duty to prosecute crime.[48] With the provincial constitutions for the Papal States this responsibility was transferred to a higher level: even independent cities

---

[46] '... quod quicunque de Ducato de Spoleto per viam appellationis vel aliter in curia ducali agere vel iustitiam suam prosequi voluerit, vel iudicialiter contra universitates vel singulares personas civiliter vel criminaliter litigare, libere et impune hoc sibi facere permictatur;... Alioquin si per universitatem... in prosecutione huiusmodi iustitie directe vel indirecte fuerit impeditus... singulares personas... etiam si episcopali prefulgeant dignitate, excommunicationis incurrant sententiam ipso facto. Civitas autem et castrum seu quevis alia communitas ecclesiastico subiaceant interdicto' (Deviziani, *Fonti delle costituzioni Egidiani*, c. 21, p. 49s). In c. 16, p. 47s, of the same constitutions *baiuli* who failed to denounce a crime of which they had knowledge through *fama* within two days to the court of the province were punished by loss of their office, the payment of compensation to the victim, and an additional 'pena pro iudicis arbitrio.' Similarly, in the *Constitutiones Spoletani Ducatus*, c. 20 (rubr. 'De pena comunitatum impedientium appellantes vel causantes in ducali curia'), pp. 115–117.'

[47] On the statutes of Perugia of 1279, the public duty to prosecute crime and an individual case of the late thirteenth century, see Sbriccoli, '"Vidi communiter observari,"' pp. 255–266. More examples from statutary sources are indicated by Chiodi, '"Delinquere ut universi,"' p. 96. Only a few of them introduced real pecuniary punishments.

[48] *Constitutiones Spoletani Ducatus*, c. XXX (rubr. 'De inquisitionibus privatis non recipiendis et in quibus casibus possunt recipi'), pp. 129–131, 129 : 'Item ut periculum, quod ex privatis inquisitionibus solet evenire ... firmamus quod nulla inquisitio secreta recipiatur (130, l. 14–16)... nisi fieret contra civitates et loca, que non custodirent stratas et loca, ut non fierent robbarie et maleficia, et que exbanditos non caperent... .'

such as Nocera could be prosecuted in a higher court outside their own jurisdiction for having failed to fulfill their public duty of prosecuting crime.

As far as institutions were concerned, a papal administration for the duchy of Spoleto consisting mainly of the court of the rector, an exchequer (*thesaurarius*), a marshal, and several notaries had been established before 1357.[49] The provincial court as well as the rector moved between the cities of Foligno, Montefalco, Spella, and Bevagna but never resided in Nocera.[50] This explains why Bishop Alexander, as the legal representative of his subjects the Nucerini, apparently asked for advice against the encroachments of an outside court. Perhaps he intended to make an appeal on behalf of the Nucerini from the *curia rectoris* directly to the papal legate, as often happened in the course of the 1340s, a practice that led the rector of the province to protest officially that rebellious bishops were trying to circumvent his jurisdiction.[51] Another factor that may have guided Bishop Alexander was a privilege granted the inhabitants of Nocera by Pope Boniface VIII according to which they were not bound to appear before the court of the *rector ducatus*. Although the privilege was later revoked by Pope Benedict XI,[52] a sense of civic pride focused on Nocera's autonomous jurisdiction perhaps persisted until the time of Alexander.

Asking a famous jurist for advice was an obvious choice for Bishop Alexander, because the rector and the three judges of the provincial court of the duchy of Spoleto, one of whom was competent for criminal matters, were usually learned jurists. In the years 1306–1350 most of them held doctorates in civil law, some in canon law, and a few in both laws. These provincial court judges used to address professors of the nearby Umbrian University of Perugia for advice on difficult cases. In 1318, for example, Bartolus's teacher, Iacopo di Belviso, was asked for a *consilium sapientis*.[53]

---

[49] Reydellet-Guttinger, *L'Administration Pontificale*, pp. 23–32.

[50] Reydellet-Guttinger, *L'Administration Pontificale*, p. 31f. Waley, 'Il ducato di Spoleto dagli Svevi all'Albornoz,' pp. 194–197, assesses the overall personnel of the provincial administration of Spoleto in papal times, i.e. at the beginning of the fourteenth century, at about twenty-five persons, including the military.

[51] Reydellet-Guttinger, *L'Administration Pontificale*, p. 106.

[52] *Codex diplomaticus dominii temporalis S. Sedis I*, p. 398b: 'concessit (sc. Boniface VIII, S.L.) enim usque ad idem beneplacitum Nucerinis, ne in Curia Comitis, quem Rector ducatus predicti in comitatu Civitatis eorum ponit pro tempore, teneantur ullatenus respondere, nec Comes contra Civitatem eandem eiusque districtum et habitatores eorum possit iurisdictionem et officium suum quomodolibet exercere... Nos (sc. Benedict XI, S.L.) autem... de fratrum nostrorum consilio revocamus et in eis beneplacitum dicte sedis volumus esse finitum.'

[53] On the personnel of the provincial court in the duchy of Spoleto during the first half of the fourteenth century, see Reydellet-Guttinger, *L'Administration Pontificale*, pp. 99–105.

It seems rather unlikely, as one hypothesis has it,[55] that Bartolus himself had been a judge on this court for a short period in early 1340, since he never referred either in his commentaries or in the present *consilium* to practical experience, which was his custom in other contexts when he had such experience. It is, however, certain that he was an advocate general of the parallel provincial court of the Mark of Ancona in 1338[56] and thus certainly had some practical experience with jurisdiction according to the diverse provincial constitutions of the Papal States.

Let us suppose Bishop Alexander and Bartolus had either c. 25 of the 1333 statutes of the duchy of Spoleto or book 4, chapter 49, of the Egidian Constitutions in mind for the present case. It is then understandable why both were more interested in the arguments concerning this type of procedural problem than in the normative foundation of a communal responsibility for prosecuting crime. Both statutory provisions penalized all kinds of *universitates* for failure to fulfill a public duty. The delictal responsibility of a commune in cases of omission had always been less disputed in canon law doctrine, and Bartolus himself had accepted it for such constellations of omissions.[57] The new point in these statutes was the imposition of a pecuniary fine on the *universitas*. The fine was payable to the rector's court in addition to the pecuniary compensation that the community had to make to the family of the victim. Thus, we are dealing here with the case of noncapital crime (*crimen non capitale*). In contrast, canon law doctrine had usually only discussed the sanctions of excommunication (against

---

[55]Reydellet-Guttinger, *L'Administration Pontificale*, p. 103, n. 30. The close connection between jurisdiction in the *curia provinciae,* later on the *curia generalis* of the Papal States, is demonstrated by the fact that Angelo degli Ubaldis (1328–1400), also teaching at Perugia, commented on the Egidian Constitutions; see Colliva, 'Angelo degli Ubaldi e le "Constitutiones Aegidianae".'

[56]Calasso, 'Bartolo da Sassoferrato,' p. 643.

[57]Criminal responsibility of corporations for failure to act despite their official duties had been accepted by canon law doctrine since Huguccio; see Gillet, *Personnalité giuridique*, p. 99; Michaud-Quantin, *Universitas*, p. 328; Gierke, *Genossenschaftsrecht,* vol. 3, p. 345. Bartolus himself in his commentary on Dig. 48.19.16.10 had postulated a communal responsibility as unproblematic in cases of omissions and in cases where the *universitas* had actively committed public crimes, such as legislating bad statutes, oppressive taxation, and making inappropriate use of their jurisdictional powers. Ullmann, 'Criminal responsibility,' pp. 85–87; Dahm, *Strafrecht Italiens*, pp. 155–157; Gierke, *Genossenschaftsrecht*, vol. 3, pp. 403–407. Weber, *Constitutiones Matris Ecclesiae*, p. 120f, extrapolates the peculiarity of medieval Italian law, especially statutory law, in its punishment of 'echte Unterlassungsdelikte,' i.e., that not fulfilling a duty to act is sanctioned as harshly by criminal law as if one had actively committed the crime.

persons only) and interdicts (against communes) for criminal acts of communities.[58] But the juristic argument was not even about the adequacy of the concrete fine. Instead, it was about proof. Apparently, this was due to a formulation in the Egidian norms which evidently drew on a similar formulation in the 1333 provisions: the judge had to make a diligent effort to determine whether the people of a community were negligent and dilatory according to the specificities of the place and to the circumstances under which the crime had been committed (*consideratis loco et tempore et circumstantiis diligenter*).[59]

Requirements of Proof

In the first section of his answer to Bishop Alexander, Bartolus developed categories for proving a person's negligence in general (c. 1). In the second part, he discussed whether the witnesses in the actual case had sufficiently proved the charge that the entire city with its inhabitants had been negligent in the prosecution and punishment of the homicide (c. 2–5).

As for the proof of negligence in general, Bartolus distinguished whether the question was of the negligence of a person in a specific, single act that could be determined according to time and space. If a person had not performed a specific required act, the negligence was immediately proved by the fact that this act had not been performed. The only excuse for the person charged with negligence would be an external obstacle for which this person could not be blamed (c. 1, lines 20–23). The burden of proof for this kind of exculpatory obstacle apparently would fall on the person accused of negligence.

The facts of Bartolus's case, however, were different. A community's responsibility for prosecuting crime was a continuing public obligation that could not be confined to a specific time or to a distinct place ('Quandoque quis tenetur ad aliquid faciendum in genere ut in casu

---

[58] Clarke, 'Question of collective guilt,' pp. 104–114; Michaud-Quantin, *Universitas*, 329–339; Gillet, *Personnalité juridique*, pp. 124–126. Even as far as mere pecuniary punishments were concerned, there was some disagreement in learned doctrine on whether the money had to be paid exclusively from the property of the commune or, if the money were lacking, the community could extract it from its individual inhabitants, even those not personally responsible for the act of the community as a whole .

[59] *Costituzioni Aegidianae*, l. 4 c. 49, p. 190, line 20; *Constitutiones Spoletani Ducatus*, c. XXV, no. 4, p. 122 line 29 – p. 123 line 2: '... et similiter ad penam non teneatur, et si operam dederint ad malefactores predictos capiendos et per eos non steterint et (123) capere non potuerint, super quibus opere et *diligentia* (S.L.) nostre et nostrorum iudicum declarationi stare decernimus.'

proposito: tenetur enim commune ad capiendum malefactores' (lines 24–26). Three facts had to be proved in an accusation against a city. It had to be shown that the community had not prosecuted a crime in a specific case. Moreover, it was necessary to prove the community's knowledge of the actual crime (c. 1, lines 27–29). Furthermore, it must have been possible for the inhabitants of the city to apprehend the killer.[60] In place of the last requirement, the community must at least have had easy opportunity to delegate the action to somebody else if it had chosen to do so (c. 1 lines 46–48). If these cumulative requirements were met, the accusation of negligence against a community would hold, unless the accused community proved its diligence in attempting to accomplish everything possible to prosecute the crime. In such a case, the burden of proof would revert to the accuser, who would have to show additional reasons why the accused community should still be considered culpable. In all these cases, proof offered by witnesses would be successful when the witnesses declared themselves to have been present at the place of the homicide, so that the necessary pursuit of the perpetrator could not have taken place without their seeing it (c. 1 lines 48–57).

In the principal part of his inquiry, Bartolus applied these general considerations to the specific testimony the witnesses had already given at the inquisition by the judges of the Spoletan rector's court. In the first subdivision of this second part, he first showed how the testimony on the side of the accusation was not sufficient to prove the negligence of the commune of Nocera (c. 2 and 3, beginning of c. 4, line 79s). In a second section, he discussed how the city could also prove exceptions to the charge of negligence (c. 4, lines 87–131). Finally, Bartolus demonstrated how a commune might prove more generally that it had always been diligent in fulfilling its public responsibility for prosecuting crime (c. 5). With this last point, Bartolus followed the scheme of rule and exception he had developed earlier in his general reflections: in general, the negligence of the accused community had to be proved, although there were certain exceptional circumstances in which a city could not be held responsible. Only exceptionally would the city be able to counterprove its diligence.[61] Bartolus fulfilled the requirements of Bishop Alexander. He

---

[60] One example of a case in which the inhabitants had a good chance of apprehending the criminal was if the location of the crime was close enough to the city for people to come and raise a cry of alarm, the so-called 'hue and cry' ('... quod locus, in quo maleficium fuit commissum, erat ita prope civitatem... quod si homines sollicite traxissent et rumorem fecissent et alia, que circa hoc requiruntur secundum facti accidentiam, quod dictos malefactores capere potuissent.' [Bartolus cons. I. 102, c. 1, lines 34–37]).

[61] 'Et hoc probato, nisi ex alia parte probetur diligencia, negligencia est probata' (c. 1 lines 52s).

also furnished general rules on testimony in such cases. His *consilium* thus complied with Alexander's request for future guidance, since similar cases appear to have been frequent.[62]

In resolving the case itself, Bartolus concluded that the witnesses' testimony did not prove the negligence of which Nocera had been accused. Since the whole process against the Nucerini took the form of an inquisitorial procedure,[63] the accused community would not necessarily have an opportunity to question the foundations of the testimonies in the form of *interrogatoria*. Instead, the judge would have to verify by his own conviction whether the testimony was convincing, and especially whether the reasons for the statements given by the witnesses for their knowledge of the facts sufficed.[64]

In the case presented, the grounds for the testimony which the witnesses had given apparently were not sufficient. In general, Romano-canonical procedure required a witness to base his testimony on his own knowledge (*scientia*), which had to be derived from one of the five senses, usually vision (*visus*). But, as Bartolus pointed out, negligence was never a fact, but rather the absence of the due diligence, that is, a negative fact.[65] The proof of negative facts was assumed in procedural doctrine to be the devil's proof,[66] although Bartolus in this inquiry did not expressly refer to this hellish metaphor. Nevertheless, he drew the same conclusion from this dilemma as procedural doctrine had done; thus, he required the witness to base his or her testimony on facts that were restricted to a specific time and place. Apparently the witnesses had not met this requirement in the initial case referred to him by Bishop Alexander. Besides, witnesses testifying to negative facts were not allowed to draw their own conclusions from the facts they had seen, because drawing conclusions was not their procedural duty, but rather the judge's.[67]

---

[62]'et quid commune habeat facere ad suam defensionem probandam? Quia ista cottidiana sunt tam pro presenti quam pro futuro, rogamus quod plenius rescribere placeat...' (line 9–11).

[63]'inquisiti sunt' (line 1); 'Super qua inquisicione quidam testes examinati' (line 4–5); 'Dico inquisicionem non esse probatam...' (c. 2, line 61s).

[64]On the function of the judge in hearing witnesses in the inquisitorial procedure, see Lepsius, *Von Zweifeln zur Überzeugung*, pp. 9–12.

[65]'quia dicere aliquem esse negligentem est quid mere negativum seu privativum, quia negligencia nihil aliud est quam privacio diligencie; et privacio et negacio idem sunt,... ubi ista verba dolum malum abesse dicuntur negativa... .' (c. 2, lines 62–66).

[66]See for example, Martinus de Fano, *Ordo Iudiciorum*, p. 10f.; *Ordo Iudiciarius Aegidii Fuscararii*, III.1, c. 53, p. 103; *Summa de ordine iudiciario Magistri Damasi*, IV.4, c. 53f., p. 38f. Only indirect proof of a negative fact is possible, according to Tancred, 'Ordo iudiciarii,', p. 3 t. 5 § 2, p. 218f.

[67]'Preterea illi, qui dicunt de negligencia tantum nec reddunt rationem per

With these distinctions between positive and negative facts, as well as between subjective perception of facts through one of the five senses and conclusions based on facts, Bartolus was laying the foundation for the more profound analysis of the function of witnesses he developed later in his tract on testimony by witnesses.[68]

Although he might have concluded his reflections with the argument that the foundation of the testimony had not been sufficient to prove the negligence of the city of Nocera, Bartolus continued with some general considerations concerning the reasons for which the commune might be exculpated even though it had knowledge of a homicide committed in its territory and had failed to act.[69] From his contention that the answers would depend on the circumstances of every individual case,[70] we can conclude that from this point on – that is, for the entire second half of the inquiry – he was responding to the second part of Bishop Alexander's brief and trying to develop general rules for future cases.

According to Bartolus, factors that might exculpate a city from its public duty to prosecute a crime were (c. 4) the fact that the crime had been committed in a hidden place or secretly so that the commune did not have the opportunity of knowing about it, or that the crime had been committed in a place from which it was easy for the perpetrator to run away to another city's territory or to a fortified place, where it was impossible for the commune to pursue him. An exception, though, had to be made in cases in which the perpetrator fled to a fortress which pertained to the jurisdiction of the city in which the crime had been committed. In such cases Bartolus suggested as a precaution that the city should order its subject *castello* to extradite the perpetrator.[71] We can see here how much the question of an obligation to publicly prosecute crime was connected to the question of the territorial jurisdiction of a community.[72]

---

aliquem sensum corporis, magis iudicant per intellectum quam testificentur de facto ad quod adhibiti sunt' (c. 3, lines 80–82).

[68] Bartolo da Sassoferrato, Tractatus testimoniorum cc. 112–115. An edition of the entire tract is presented by Lepsius, *Der Richter und die Zeugen*, vol. 2, pp. 233–238, 319–322.

[69] 'Et omnia ista si bene advertantur, sunt ad probandum, quod communi non potest imputari negligencia.' (c. 4, lines 130s).

[70] 'Ad ultimum vero quid queritis, quid habeat probare commune ad sui defensionem, dico quod multa possunt occurrere secundum diversas facti accidencias...' (c. 4, lines 88–90).

[71] 'Si tamen illi, qui locum illum tenent, sunt de eorum iurisdictione, scilicet communis, consilium est quod eis faciat preceptum, quod restituant malefactores.' (Bartolus cons. I. 102, c. 4, lines 123–126).

[72] Marchetti has shown how the concept of a public criminal law required in particular for the Italian city-states a more precise definition of their territory and

Bartolus's references to wrongdoers fleeing to other territories or hiding in castles reflected an actual development in the fourteenth-century Papal States, in which dozens of new, heavily fortified castles (*rocche*) had been constructed, some of them by the popes themselves in the course of their recovery of the Papal States. Thus, a new papal *rocca* had been erected in San Fortunato, close to Montefalco (also duchy of Spoleto), in 1324.[73]

Besides these objective reasons for not prosecuting a killer although the city had knowledge of him, there might also be subjective reasons why it would be unreasonable to require a community to fulfill its legal responsibility. Without clearly distinguishing cases of objective or subjective impossibility to prosecute crime, Bartolus mentioned as an illustration of the subjective impossibility the case in which there were simply too many malefactors who could only be prosecuted through a large military action, possibly even civil war. Another reason might be that the city gates were closed, so that the perpetrator could not be followed. Finally, the city should be exculpated if the perpetrator fled into a church or a monastery, where he could not be followed, because the city had to respect the immunity of these places (c. 4, lines 127–129).

In the final section of his inquiry, Bartolus established criteria by which a city might prove its diligence in efficiently prosecuting a crime (c. 5). All of the examples required the active engagement of the city's officials or of the entire population. The city could, for instance, act through its officials by sending them after a fleeing wrongdoer, or in posting guards on the frontiers of its territory, whose responsibility it was to prevent the malefactor from fleeing (lines 136–138). The example of putting guards on the frontiers of the city's territory to prevent criminals from fleeing directly reflected a requirement which we can also find in the Egidian Constitutions[74] and which corresponded to a provision in the earlier constitutions of the duchy of Spoleto according to which no *universitas* or community should allow malefactors to cross its territory, but must instead attempt to apprehend the perpetrator of a crime and bring him to justice.[75]

The entire population could be called upon to catch the wrongdoer by raising the hue and cry or ringing the church bells (lines 138–143). In

---

the boundaries of jurisdiction; see Marchetti, 'I limiti della giurisdizione penale,' pp. 86–88, 91–94.

[73] Waley, 'Il ducato di Spoleto dagli Svevi all'Albornoz,' p. 194. Reydellet-Guttinger, *L'Administration Pontificale*, p. 18, mentions several *rocche* that were taken over by the papal legates from rebels who had established themselves there in 1330.

[74] l. 4 c. 49, p. 189: 'quelibet universitas, civitas... territorium et districtum suum diligenter custodiat et faciat custodiri.' The rubric of the entire chapter reads, 'Quod unaqueque terra teneat suas stratas et loca secura' (Constitutiones Aegidianae).

[75] *Constitutiones Spoletani Ducatus*, c. LXIII no. 10, p. 157.

the example of ringing the church bells Bartolus was apparently applying a topos of the canon law doctrine of collective responsibility. There it was argued that it was an indication that the deed of a community was truly collective if the entire population of a community had done something after the church bells had been rung. In such cases doctrine accepted a collective responsibility for any misdeed that had been actively committed by the multitude, because it was then presumed to act as a fictive legal entity.[76] In one of the many neat shifts by which he overturned pieces of learned law, Bartolus here used the argument to prove the community's diligence!

The final two ways by which a city might prove its diligence in the public prosecution of crime apparently referred to cases in which it was not possible to follow a criminal immediately after the deed, perhaps implying that the deed was not immediately discovered or that the criminal managed to escape. In such cases Bartolus required the entire population to carefully search all places in which the criminal might have hidden and to put out a public call (*preconium*) for the wanted criminal, also offering a reward for anybody who caught him (c. 5, lines 145–150). But, as Bartolus warned in his conclusion, the city would be able to plead due diligence in criminal prosecution only if these acts were done with true intent and not merely fictively.[77]

Bartolus almost exclusively invoked principles of Roman law throughout his discussion. Most of the passages he referred to describe cases of negligent behavior of individuals. But as we have seen, there was no need for him to explain why a community should be held responsible as an entity for not prosecuting a crime, because this had been normatively prescribed by the constitutions of the duchy of Spoleto. Some principles had already induced him in his commentaries to reflect on public responsibility for negligent failure to prosecute crime, the central Roman

---

[76] Gierke, *Genossenschaftsrecht*, p. 344, gives the citation 'pulsata campana et consilio congregato' (p. 404) (the definition by Iohannes Bassianus of a corporative act of a community: 'ad sonum campane vel tubae vel cornu vel ad tabulam pulsatam'); Michaud-Quantin, *Universitas*, p. 329f, underlines the distinction drawn by Odofredus that if people did not act in a collective form, such as after a council or the ringing of the bells, their act was considered only to have been done by a multitude of individuals and could not be imputed to the collective entity.

[77] 'si enim de hac fictione posset constare, nichil prodesset' (c. 5, lines 153–155). Also in commenting on Dig. 29.5.1.17 § *Occisorum*, f. 179va, Bartolus had insisted on the fact that the city must really try to catch the wrongdoer and not ring the bells just to exculpate itself, without truly prosecuting the criminal: 'Nota bene hunc casum contra homines villarum, castrorum vel civitatum qui erigunt rumorem et pulsant campanas et fingunt se velle capere malefactores et non posse, quod eis hoc non prosit.'

law passage for him being Dig. 29.5.1, *l. Cum aliter*. That passage of the Digest had decided that in the case of a head of a household who had been killed, all members of his family, including the slaves, were to be subjected to a public inquiry into whether one of them might have been the killer. Their responsibility derived from the fact they lived under the same roof. In the Roman law text the responsibility of all slaves who had not brought help to their lord when he was violently attacked and killed by a third person had also been established.

Bartolus had commented on this passage in discussing the question of public responsibility for prosecuting crime. Apparently he drew an analogy between the victim and the head of the household under Roman law and between the city's inhabitants and the slaves who, under Roman law, had an obligation to help the victim who was attacked. Already in his commentary Bartolus had pointed out some potentially exculpating considerations in the case of a city unable to capture a criminal, stressing, for example, the impossibility of prosecuting a criminal who had invaded the city with such a large group of followers that the entire city could not resist him, and proposing a case in which the city gates had been closed so that none of the inhabitants could pursue the wrongdoer on the spot.[78] Other references to commentaries by Bartolus in which he had already discussed similar problems of negligence are provided in the footnotes to the edition of the *consilium* presented below.

In the *consilium* considered here, Bartolus developed different standards by which the city's officials and the entire population had to act if the city as an entity wanted to exculpate itself from the charge of negligently failing to prosecute a crime or even to prove its diligence. Effortlessly, he reintroduced the categories of guilt that legal doctrine had already established for individuals in criminal cases. Introducing the categories of individual negligence into the concept of collective responsibility probably did not represent an 'erosion' of the Germanic principle of *Gesamthaftung*[79] but rather the assimilation of the concept of collective criminal responsibility to that of individual responsibility.

---

[78]'Quid enim si aliquis in villa venit cum tanta gente et commisit maleficium quod non posset tota villa resistere? Certe non tenetur...' (Bartolus ad Dig. 29.5.1.17 § *Occisorum*, f. 179ra no. 2); 'Argumentum pro castris comitatus, ut non puniantur, si de nocte non exiverunt ad capiendum committentes maleficium extra castrum, cum esset clausum castrum et claves non tenebantur per eos, alias secus' (Bartolus ad Dig. 29.5.3.6 § *Subvenitur*, f. 180ra).

[79]Dahm, *Strafrecht Italiens*, p. 179, who has a highly *Germanistic* outlook on Italian city statutes seems to regret that only a small fraction of the original principle of the Germanic principle of *Gesamthaftung* – that did not ask for individual guilt – survived the mitigating interpretations of this principle through learned doctrine. Thus he spoke of an 'erosion' of the former principle of *Gesamthaftung*.

Conclusion

Bartolus went far beyond the immediate questions arising from the specific normative question of collective guilt posited in the new constitutions in the Papal States to offer a general scheme of the procedural issues at hand. Although the genre of *consilia* is often thought to provide a direct reflection of social conditions in the Middle Ages, Bartolus followed the wishes of his client, Bishop Alexander, and formulated a more abstract piece of advice for prospective future cases of public responsibility. Nor did the ecclesiastical context of the affair prevent Bartolus—a professor of civil law—from referring almost exclusively to passages from Roman law, commentaries on them in the standard gloss (*glossa ordinaria*), and the writings of civil lawyers. From his perspective, any legal problem posed by medieval society, which was characterized by a finely interwoven network of territorial and normative structures, could be resolved by legal insights provided by the tools of learned law and, more specifically, civil law. Neither did Bartolus's status as a civil law professor prevent Bishop Alexander from seeking his advice on the present case rather than that of a canonist. For Bishop Alexander, it seemed to be more important to engage a preeminent lawyer from the nearby University of Perugia who had some knowledge of the Umbrian area and personal experience on another provincial court of the Papal States, namely, that of the Mark of Ancona. From a university professor he also hoped for additional general directions on how to behave in similar cases in order to prevent future inquisitions of cities that were accused of having failed to prosecute crime effectively.

Whether a canonist would have advised Bishop Alexander differently on the case in question must remain in the realm of speculation. A canonist might have argued against the strict liability of an entire city and tried instead to limit the public responsibility to prosecute crime to the city's officials. On the other, it might have appeared inadvisable to attack directly constitutions that were, after all, founded on the papal authority delegated to his legates. Perhaps Bishop Alexander and Bartolus discussed the case before Bartolus rendered his consilium and agreed that it would be simpler to restrict the scope of Nocera's public responsibility to matters of proof alone.

As to the question of how and when there developed a category and a field of a public criminal law in the Middle Ages, Bartolus's *consilium* demonstrates that in Italy as early as the mid-fourteenth century a public *responsibility* to prosecute crime had developed as a counterpart to the perhaps earlier public *claim* of the authority to prosecute crime. Whereas earlier rulers had a theologically based duty to prosecute crime,[80] in the

---

[80] Frenz, 'Frieden, Gemeinwohl und Gerechtigkeit,' pp. 139–142.

late Middle Ages a legal mechanism that turned the ethical *obligation* into a legally enforceable *responsibility* developed. Not surprisingly, this public responsibility was established as a binding legal norm in the Papal States. The Church had long entertained the notion that public authorities were obliged to prosecute crime, which had led to the inquisitorial process that gave the judge greater powers and responsibility with respect to the punishment of crimes.[81] This concept was then transferred to the canon law construction of delictal responsibilities of communities. As such, it was posited at least as early as the Egidian Constitutions of 1357 and was part of the overall claim of the Avignonese papacy that it was working to restore peace and the rule of law in the ecclesiastical state. But to be effective, the concept had to be supported by the establishment of a new territorial court with jurisdiction over entire cities, in our case that of the provincial court of the duchy of Spoleto over the city of Nocera.

Perhaps another motivation of Bishop Alexander's rather general inquiry to Bartolus was the fear of losing exclusive jurisdiction in criminal matters—and thus an important part of the 'sovereignty' of a medieval city—to a higher instance already being conceived by the popes as competent for a larger territorial unit. As such, Bishop Alexander, combating the territorial ducal court with the legal help of Bartolus, can be seen as a worthy successor to an earlier bishop of Nocera who had been quite rebellious against papal officials earlier in the fourteenth century.[82] Thus, the phenomenon of collective subjects bearing public or collective responsibility, in our case the responsibility for prosecuting crime, combined with the new, extraordinary legal mechanisms, both institutional and procedural, mentioned above, is not a typical result of the modern world's problems or of a specific modern theory of agency.[83] Instead, it

---

[81] A common topic was 'ne crimina remaneant impunita.' Cf. the development of inquisitorial procedure and this legal topos: Schmoeckel, *Humanität und Staatsraison*, pp. 189–202.

[82] An example from 1319, in which the bishop of Nocera shows himself quite contemptuous in response to the ducal treasurer's questions regarding how many tithes his diocese had paid in the years before, is related by Reydellet-Guttinger, *L'Administration Pontificale*, p. 74. Who this bishop was could not be discerned, because in Gams *Series episcoporum ecclesie Catholicae* and Eubel *Hierarchia catholica Medii Aevi* there is a gap between Bishop John II (until 1315) and Bishop Guido II (installed 1327). Nocera had in 1305 also been part of a league of cities comprising Perugia, Spoleto, and Foligno that was opposing two papal messengers (*nuntii*) of Clement V (Waley, 'Il ducato di Spoleto dagli Svevi all'Albornoz,' p. 199).

[83] According to Krawietz, 'Fragmentierung der modernen Rechtsgesellschaft und Neue Unübersichtlichkeit,' pp. 524–527, legal responsibilities should no longer be exclusively derived from individual persons, but be focused more on legal entities

was used in the late Middle Ages by the Avignonese popes in their effort to establish a higher, territorial order and peace around the legitimizing potential of an effective public criminal law.[84] It might also remind us of modern- day efforts to establish a higher, international court of criminal justice to prosecute war crimes that otherwise would not be prosecuted by national states, and of the inherent injustice of imposing on entire populations responsibility for harboring—that is not prosecuting—terrorism.

Max-Planck-Institut für europäische Rechtsgeschichte
Frankfurt am Main, Germany

Works Cited

Ascheri, M. 'Le fonti e la flessibilità del diritto comune: Il paradosso del *consilium sapientis*,' pp. 11–53 in *Legal Consulting in the Civil Law Tradition*, ed. M. Ascheri, I. Baumgärtner, and J. Kirshner. Berkeley: Robbins Collection, 1999.

Calasso, F. 'Bartolo da Sassoferrato,' in *Dizionario biografico degli italiani*, vol. 6, pp. 640–669. Rome: Società Grafica Romana, 1964.

Chiodi, G. '"Delinquere ut universi": scienza giuridica e responsabilità penale delle *universitates* tra XII e XIII secolo' pp. 91–199 in *Studi di storia del diritto*. Pubblicazioni dell'Istituto di Storia del Diritto Italiano, Università degli Studi di Milano, Facoltà di giurisprudenza di Milano, vol. 3. Milan: A. Giuffrè, 2001.

Clarke, P. 'A Question of Collective Guilt: Popes, Canonists and the Interdict c. 1140–1250' *Zeitschrift der Savignystiftung für Rechtsgeschichte Kanonistische Abteilung* 85 (1999): 104–146.

Cohen, E. 'Inquiring Once More after the Inquisitorial Process,' pp. 41–65 in *Die Entstehung des öffentlichen Strafrechts*, ed. D. Willoweit. Konflikt, Verbrechen und Sanktion in der Gesellschaft Alteuropas, ed. K. Lüderssen et al., Symposien und Synthesen, vol. 1. Cologne, Weimar, and Vienna: Böhlau, 1999.

---

acting, for example, as anonymous subjects. The question, though, is whether in a concrete case in which collective responsibilities were to be enforced by a legal mechanism, even a 'modern' legal theory would have to develop standards of liability and negligence as Bartolus had done in the present inquiry. The relevance of the problems discussed in this article for contemporary European legal doctrine, especially the question of administrative criminal law, is illuminated by d'Urso, 'Persona giuridica e responsabilità penale,' pp. 513–517.

[84]On the institutional reform efforts of the Avignonese popes, mainly focused on the financing system, see Vasina, 'Il papato avignonese e il governo dello Stato della Chiesa.'

Colli, V. 'Consilia dei giuristi medievali e produzione libraria,' pp. 173–225 in *Legal Consulting in the Civil Law Tradition*, ed. M. Ascheri, I. Baumgärtner, and J. Kirshner. Berkeley: Robbins Collection, 1999.

Colliva, P. 'Angelo degli Ubaldi e le "Constitutiones Aegidianae",' pp. 219–236 in P. Colliva, *Scritti minori*, ed. G. Morelli and N. Sarti. Milan: Giuffrè, 1996.

Dahm, G. *Das Strafrecht Italiens im ausgehenden Mittelalter: Untersuchungen über die Beziehungen zwischen Theorie und Praxis im Strafrecht des Spätmittelalters, namentlich im XIV. Jahrhundert*. Beiträge zur Geschichte der deutschen Strafrechtspflege, vol. 3. Berlin, Leipzig: W. de Gruyter, 1931.

Deviziani, A. *Fonti delle costituzioni Egidiane: Le costituzioni di Bertrand de Deuc del 1336 per la Marca di Ancona e per il Ducato di Spoleto*. Savona: Ricci, 1923.

Engelmann, W. *Die Wiedergeburt der Rechtskultur in Italien durch die wissenschaftliche Lehre: Eine Darlegung der Entfaltung des gemeinen italienischen Rechts und seiner Justizkultur im Mittelalter unter dem Einfluß der herrschenden Lehre der Gutachtenpraxis der Rechtsgelehrten und der Verantwortung der Richter im Sindikatsprozeß*. Leipzig: K. F. Köhlers Antiquarium, 1938.

Eubel, G. *Hierarchia catholica Medii Aevi sive summorum pontificum, S.R.E. Cardinalium, Ecclesiarum antistium ...*, 2d ed. Münster: Regensbergiana, 1913.

Fatteschi, G. *Memorie istorico-diplomatiche riguardanti la serie de' Duchi e la topografia de' tempi di mezzo del Ducato di Spoleto*. Camerino, 1801.

Frenz, B. 'Frieden, Gemeinwohl und Gerechtigkeit durch Stadtherr, Rat und Bürger. Strafrechtshistorische Aspekte in deutschen Stadtrechtstexten des 12. und 13. Jahrhunderts,' pp. 111–145 in *Neue Wege strafrechtsgeschichtlicher Forschung*, ed. H. Schlosser and D. Willoweit. Konflikt, Verbrechen und Sanktion in der Gesellschaft Alteuropas, ed. K. Lüderssen et al., Symposien und Synthesen, vol. 2. Cologne, Weimar and Vienna: Böhlau, 1999.

Gams, P. B. *Series episcoporum ecclesie Catholicae*, 2d ed. Regensburg, 1886; reprint, Graz: Akademische Verlagsanstalt, 1957.

Gauvard, Cl. *'De grace especial': Crime, Etat et Société à la fin du Moyen Age*, vol. 2. Paris: Sorbonne, 1991.

Gauvard, Cl. 'De la difficulté d'appliquer les principes théoriques du droit pénal en France à la fin du Moyen Age,' pp. 91–120 in *Die Entstehung des öffentlichen Strafrechts*, ed. D. Willoweit. Konflikt, Verbrechen und Sanktion in der Gesellschaft Alteuropas, ed. K. Lüderssen et al., Symposien und Synthesen, vol. 1. Cologne, Weimar, and Vienna: Böhlau, 1999.

Gierke, O. *Das deutsche Genossenschaftsrecht*, vol. 3: *Die Staats-und Korporationslehre des Altertums und des Mittelalters und ihre Aufnahme in Deutschland*. Berlin, 1913; reprint, Graz: Akademische Druck- und Verlagsanstalt, 1954.

Gillet, P. *La personnalité juridique en droit ecclesiastique, spécialement chez les Décretistes et les Décrétalistes et dans le Code de droit canonique*. Malines: W. Godenne, 1927.

Gouron, A. 'L'apport des juristes français à l'essor du droit pénal savant,' pp. 337–371 in *Die Entstehung des öffentlichen Strafrechts*, ed. D. Willoweit. Konflikt, Verbrechen und Sanktion in der Gesellschaft Alteuropas, ed. K. Lüderssen et al., Symposien und Synthesen, vol. 1. Cologne, Weimar, and Vienna: Böhlau, 1999.

Groot, R. 'Proto-juries and Public Criminal Law in England,' pp. 23–39 in *Die Entstehung des öffentlichen Strafrechts*, ed. D. Willoweit. Konflikt, Verbrechen und Sanktion in der Gesellschaft Alteuropas, ed. K. Lüderssen et al., Symposien und Synthesen, vol. 1. Cologne, Weimar, and Vienna: Böhlau, 1999.

Heumann, H. and E. Seckel, *Handlexikon zu den Quellen des römischen Rechts*, 10th ed. Jena: Fischer, 1926; reprint, Graz: Akademische Druck- und Verlagsanstalt, 1958.

Kannowski, B. *Bürgerkämpfe und Friedebriefe: Rechtliche Streitbeilegung in spätmittelalterlichen Städten*. Forschungen zur deutschen Rechtsgeschichte, vol. 19. Cologne, Weimar, and Vienna: Böhlau, 2001.

Kirshner, J. '*Consilia* as Authority in Late Medieval Italy: The Case of Florence,' pp. 107–140 in *Legal Consulting in the Civil Law Tradition*, ed. M. Ascheri, I. Baumgärtner, and J. Kirshner. Berkeley: Robbins Collection, 1999.

Klerman, D. 'Settlement and the Decline of Private Prosecution in Thirteenth-Century England,' *Law and History Review* 19 (2001): 1–66.

Krawietz, W. 'Fragmentierung der modernen Rechtsgesellschaft und Neue Unübersichtlichkeit:? Individualismus versus rechtliche Kollektivsubjekte?' *Rechtstheorie [Sonderheft Estland]* 31 (1999): 521–534.

Kuehn, T. '*Consilia* as Juristic Literature in Private Law' pp. 229–253 in *Legal Consulting in the Civil Law Tradition*, ed. M. Ascheri, I. Baumgärtner, and J. Kirshner. Berkeley: Robbins Collection, 1999.

Lepsius, S. *Der Richter und die Zeugen. Eine Studie zum 'Tractatus testimoniorum' des Bartolus von Sassoferrato mit Edition*. Studien zur europäischen Rechtsgeschichte 158. Frankfurt am Main: Klostermann, 2003.

Lepsius, S. *Von Zweifeln zur Überzeugung: Der Zeugenbeweis im gelehrten Recht, ausgehend von der Abhandlung des Bartolus von Sassoferrato*. Studien zur europäischen Rechtsgeschichte vol. 160. Frankfurt am Main: Klostermann, 2003.

Marchetti, P. 'I limiti della giurisdizione penale: Crimini, competenza e territorio nel pensiero giuridico tardo-medievale,' pp. 85–99 in *Criminalità e giustizia in Germania e in Italia: Pratiche giudiziarie e linguaggi giuridici tra tardo medioevo ed età moderno/Kriminalität und Justiz in Deutschland und Italien: Rechtspraktiken und gerichtliche Diskurse in Spätmittelalter und Früher Neuzeit*, ed. M. Bellabarba, G. Schwerhoff, and A. Zorzi. Bologna: Il Mulino / Berlin: Duncker & Humblot, 2001.

Martinus de Fano, *Ordo Iudiciorum*, ed. L. Wahrmund. Quellen zur Geschichte des römisch- kanonischen Prozesses im Mittelalter, vol. 7. Innsbruck, 1906; reprint, Aalen: Scientia, 1962.

Michaud-Quantin, P. *Universitas: Expressions du mouvement communautaire dans le Moyen- Age latin*. L'Eglise et l'Etat au moyen âge, no. 13. Paris: J. Vrin, 1970.

Oxford Latin Dictionary. Oxford: Clarendon Press, 1968.

Quaglioni, D. '"Universi consentire non possunt": La punibilità dei corpi nella dottrina del diritto comune' pp. 409–425 in *Suppliche e 'gravamina'. Politica, amministrazione, giustizia in Europa (secoli XIV–XVIII)*, ed. C. Nubola, A. Würgler. Annali dell'Istituto storico italo- germanico, Quaderni no. 59. Bologna: Il Mulino, 2002.

Reydellet-Guttinger, Ch. *L'Administration pontificale dans le Duché de Spolète*. Studi dell'Accademia Spoletina. Florence: Leo S. Olschki, 1975.

Rousseaux, X. 'From Case to Crime: Homicide Regulation in Medieval and Modern Europe,' pp. 143–175 in *Die Entstehung des öffentlichen Strafrechts*, ed. D. Willoweit. Konflikt, Verbrechen und Sanktion in der Gesellschaft Alteuropas, ed. K. Lüderssen et al., Symposien und Synthesen, vol. 1. Cologne, Weimar, and Vienna: Böhlau, 1999.

Rousseaux, X. 'Construction et stratégies: Le crime et la justice entre production politique et ressources communautaires: Quelques réflexions sur l'histoire du crime et de la justice en Europe médiévale e moderne,' pp. 327–343 in *Criminalità e giustizia in Germania e in Italia: Pratiche giudiziarie e linguaggi giuridici tra tardo medioevo ed età moderno/Kriminalität und Justiz in Deutschland und Italien: Rechtspraktiken und gerichtliche Diskurse in Spätmittelalter und Früher Neuzeit*, ed. M. Bellabarba, G. Schwerhoff, and A. Zorzi. Bologna: Il Mulino / Berlin: Duncker & Humblot, 2001.

Sbriccoli, M. 'Giustizia negoziata, giustizia egemonica: Riflessioni su una nuova fase degli studi di storia della giustizia criminale,' pp. 345–364 in *Criminalità e giustizia in Germania e in Italia: Pratiche giudiziarie e linguaggi giuridici tra tardo medioevo ed età moderno/Kriminalität und Justiz in Deutschland und Italien: Rechtspraktiken und gerichtliche Diskurse in Spätmittelalter und Früher Neuzeit*, ed. M. Bellabarba, G. Schwerhoff, and A. Zorzi. Bologna: Il Mulino / Berlin: Duncker & Humblot, 2001.

Sbriccoli, M. '"Vidi communiter observari": L'Emersione di un'ordine penale pubblico nelle città italiane del secolo XIII' *Quaderni fiorentini per la storia del pensiero giuridico moderno* 27 (1998): 231–268.

Schmidt, T., ed. *Constitutiones Spoletani Ducatus a Petro de Castaneto edite (a. 1333)*. Fonti per la storia d'Italia 113. Rome: Istituto storico italiano per il medio evo, 1990.

Schmidt, T. 'La recente scoperta degli Statuti del ducato di Spoleto del 1333' pp. 977–982 in *Il ducato di Spoleto: Atti del 9° Congresso internazionale di studi sull'alto Medio Evo*, vol. 2. Spoleto: Centro Studi, 1983.

Schmoeckel, M. *Humanität und Staatsraison: Die Abschaffung der Folter und die Entwicklung des gemeinen Strafprozeß- und Beweisrechts seit dem hohen Mittelalter*. Cologne, Weimar, and Vienna: Böhlau, 2000.

Sella, P., ed. *Costituzioni Egidiane dell'anno MCCCLVII*. Rome: E. Loescher & Co., 1912.

Sella, P. 'Costituzioni dello Stato della Chiesa anteriori alla riforma Albornoziana' *Archivio storico italiano* 85 (1927): 3–36.

Sharpe, J. 'Criminal Law as an Instrument of Conflict Control in Late Medieval and Early Modern England: Towards a Long Term Context,' pp. 121–141 in *Die Entstehung des öffentlichen Strafrechts*, ed. D. Willoweit. Konflikt,

Verbrechen und Sanktion in der Gesellschaft Alteuropas, ed. K. Lüderssen et al., Symposien und Synthesen, vol. 1. Cologne, Weimar, and Vienna: Böhlau, 1999.

Stübinger, S. *Schuld, Strafrecht und Geschichte*. Konflikt, Verbrechen, Sanktion: Reihe Symposien und Synthesen, vol. 4. Cologne, Weimar, and Vienna: Böhlau, 2000.

Tabacco, G. 'Vescovi e comuni in Italia,' pp. 253–282 in *I poteri temporali dei Vescovi in Italia e in Germania nel Medioevo*, ed. C. G. Mor and H. Schneidinger. Annali dell'Istituto storico italo-germanico, vol. 3. Bologna: Il Mulino, 1979.

Tancred, 'Ordo iudiciarii', in *Pillius, Tancredus, Gratia, Libri de iudiciorum ordine*, ed. F. Chr. Bergmann. Göttingen: 1841; reprint, Aalen: Scientia, 1965.

Theiner, A., ed. *Codex diplomaticus dominii temporalis S. Sedis I. (756–1334)*. Rome: Imprimerie du Vatican, 1861.

Ullmann, W. 'The Delictal Responsibility of Medieval Corporations' *Law Quarterly Review* 64 (1948): 77–96.

d'Urso, F. 'Persona giuridica e responsabilità penale: Note storico-giuridiche a proposito di recenti riforme' *Quaderni fiorentini per la storia del pensiero giuridico moderno* 29 (2000): 511–550.

Vasina, A. 'Il papato avignonese e il governo dello Stato della Chiesa,' pp. 135–150 in *Aux Origines de l'État moderne: Le fonctionnement administratif de la Papauté d'Avignon*. Collection de l'École française de Rome, vol. 138. Rome: École française de Rome, 1990.

Waley, D. 'Il ducato di Spoleto dagli Svevi all'Albornoz' pp. 189–203 in *Il ducato di Spoleto: Atti del 9° Congresso internazionale di studi sull'alto Medio Evo*, vol. 1. Spoleto: Centro Studi, 1983.

Weber, W. *Die Constitutiones Sanctae Matris Ecclesiae des Kardinals Aegidius Albornoz von 1357 unter besonderer Berücksichtigung der Strafrechtsnormen*. Untersuchungen zur deutschen Staats- und Rechtsgeschichte N.F., vol. 24. Aalen: Scientia, 1982.

Willoweit, D.'Zum Begriff des Öffentlichen im späten Mittelalter: Ein erweiterter Diskussionsbericht' pp. 335–340 in *Neue Wege strafrechtsgeschichtlicher Forschung*, ed. H. Schlosser and D. Willoweit. Konflikt, Verbrechen und Sanktion in der Gesellschaft Alteuropas, ed. K. Lüderssen et al., Symposien und Synthesen, vol. 2. Cologne, Weimar and Vienna: Böhlau, 1999.

Willoweit, D. 'Die Entstehung des öffentlichen Strafrechts: Bestandsaufnahme eines europäischen Forschungsproblems,' pp. 1–12 in *Die Entstehung des öffentlichen Strafrechts*, ed. D. Willoweit. Konflikt, Verbrechen und Sanktion in der Gesellschaft Alteuropas, ed. K. Lüderssen et al., Symposien und Synthesen, vol. 1. Cologne, Weimar, and Vienna: Böhlau, 1999.

Willoweit, D. 'Gewalt und Verbrechen, Strafe und Sühne im alten Würzburg: Offene Probleme der deutschen strafrechtsgeschichtlichen Forschung,' pp. 215–238 in *Die Entstehung des öffentlichen Strafrechts*, ed. D. Willoweit. Konflikt, Verbrechen und Sanktion in der Gesellschaft Alteuropas, ed. K. Lüderssen et al., Symposien und Synthesen, vol. 1. Cologne, Weimar, and Vienna: Böhlau, 1999.

Zorzi, A. 'Negoziazione penale, legittimazione giuridica e poteri urbani nell'Italia comunale,' pp. 13–34 in *Criminalità e giustizia in Germania e in Italia: Pratiche giudiziarie e linguaggi giuridici tra tardo medioevo ed età moderno/Kriminalität und Justiz in Deutschland und Italien: Rechtspraktiken und gerichtliche Diskurse in Spätmittelalter und Früher Neuzeit*, ed. M. Bellabarba, G. Schwerhoff, and A. Zorzi. Bologna: Il Mulino / Berlin: Duncker & Humblot, 2001.

Appendix
Bartolus, «Isti nostri Nucerini»
Edited by Susanne Lepsius

Bartolus de Sassoferrato: Cons. I. 102[1]

Charissime domine: Isti nostri Nucerini sunt inquisiti a domino[2] rectore ducatus et eius curia,[3] quia ipsi fuerunt negligentes et remissi in capiendo quosdam homicidas, ex quo crimine certa pena[4] imposita[5] est civitati secundum formam constitutionum[6] provincialium.[a] Super qua inquisicione
5 quidam[7] testes examinati dicunt[8] commune et homines[9] civitatis fuisse negligentes, ut in[10] inquisicione continetur, nec reddunt causam sui dicti nec de causa[11] fuerunt interrogati.[12] An ex eorum dictis sit probata inquisicio et si non est probata: quid debuisset fieri ad eam probandam,[13] et quid commune[14] habeat facere[15] ad suam defensionem probandam?
10 Quia ista cottidiana sunt tam pro presenti quam pro futuro,[16] rogamus quod[17] plenius[18] rescribere[19] placeat. Alexander episcopus Nucerinus.[20]

Reverende mi[21] pater et[22] domine:[23] Ea de quibus queretis longam premeditacionem[24] requirerent.[25] Requirerent[26] eciam[27] hominem aliis cogitacionibus[28] non occupatum.[29] Ego vero[30] sum modo[31] in principio[32]
15 studii[33] multis lectionibus occupatus. Unde[34] ex eo, quod videre potui in illo modico[35] tempore, quod ad illam[36] investigacionem[37] adhibui,[38] rescribo que sencio.

Et primo antequam ad presentem investigacionem[39] accedam,[40] [1] videamus[41] in genere, si volo probare aliquem negligentem, quid probare
20 habeam.[42] Et certe quandoque[43] quis est obligatus[44] ad factum certum et limitatum tempore[45] et loco et[46] tunc eo ipso quod illo[47] non facit[48] est probata eius negligentia, nisi ille[49] ostendit[50] de impedimento, *ut l. iii § Si ad diem, ff. de re. mili.* (Dig. 49.16.3.7)[b] *et l. Qui comeatus* (Dig. 49.16.14)[c] *et ff.*[51] *si quis caut. l. ii § [Sed*[52] *et] si quis* (Dig. 2.11.2.1) *cum sy*. Quandoque
25 quis tenetur ad aliquid[53] faciendum in genere ut in casu proposito:[54] tenetur enim[55] commune ad capiendum[56] malefactores.[57] Et tunc ad ostendendam[58] negligenciam communis oportet[59] probari[60] primo, quod[61] commune sciverit[62] illud malefactum[63] esse[64] commissum illo tempore et loco, *ut ff. de admini.*[65] *l. Quidam decedens § fi.* (Dig. 26.7.6.7) *cum l. se*
30 (Dig. 26.7.7). Quod ut[66] puto probabitur probando[67] quod sic[68] erat publice notum,[69] *ut notatur*[70] *expresse C. de peric. tut. l. i*[71] *princ.*[72] *(Cod.*

---

[a] *Constitutiones Egidiane*, ed. P. Sella. Rome 1912, l. 4 c. 49, p. 189s; *Constitutiones Spoletani Ducatus a Petro de Castaneto edite (a. 1333)*, ed. T. Schmidt. Rome 1990, c. 25, p. 122f.

[b] Bartolo da Sassoferrato, *Commentaria*. Turin (apud Nicolaum Bevilaquam) 1573ss, in Dig. 49.16.3.7 *§ Si ad diem*, f. 229ra.

[c] Bartolo da Sassoferrato, *Commentaria* ad Dig. 49.16.14, *l. Commeatus*, f. 229rb.

162   A Renaissance of Conflicts

5.38.1 pr.), etiam ff.[73] *de iuris et fact. ignorancia l. Regula*[74] *§ Sed facti (Dig. 22.6.9.2) et l. Nec supina (Dig. 22.6.6) cum sy.*

Item[75] habet probare, quod locus,[76] in quo[77] maleficium fuit commissum, erat ita prope[78] civitatem,[79] villam vel habitaciones,[80] quod si homines sollicite traxissent[81] et rumorem[82] fecissent et alia, que circa hoc requiruntur secundum facti accidenciam, quod dictos[83] malefactores capere potuissent. Hoc[84] probatur per infrascripta[85] similia. Si enim volo[86] probare tutorem fuisse negligentem[87] in mutuando pecuniam,[88] debeo probare vere vel presumptive, quod in civitate erant homines quibus potuisset dicta pecunia mutuari,[89] aliter non probaretur negligencia, *ut ff. de admini. tu. l. Tutor*[90] *secundum dignitatem § i (Dig. 26.7.14.1).*[a] Item si volo probare tutorem fuisse negligentem[91] in emendiis prediis, debeo probare, quod predia utilia reperiebantur, que emere poterat,[92] *ut in aut. ut hii qui ob. se perhi.*[93] *ha. res. mi. § penultima,*[94] *coll. vi a (Aut. 6.2.7 'Si vero plus sunt').*[95,96]

Item si volo probare quem fuisse negligentem in eo, quod potuit per alium gerere,[97] debeo probare quod facile erat sibi[98] alteri comictere, *ut l. Idemque, ff. pro socio (Dig. 17.2.16)* ubi[99] hoc videtur expressum[b] et est expressum[100] in terminis nostre questionis [f. 37v] *ff. ad Sill.l. i § Si quis in villa (Dig. 29.5.1.30) et § sequenti (Dig. 29.5.1.31) et § Eodem autem tecto (Dig. 29.5.1.27) et C. ad sill.*[101] *l. fi. (Cod. 6.35.12).*

Et hoc probato, nisi ex alia parte probetur[102] diligencia,[103] negligencia est[104] probata. Si tamen possent reperiri[105] testes, qui dicerent ipsos[106] obmisisse trahere[107] et persequi[108] contra malefactores et facere[109] predicta que facere poterant et reddant[110] racionem, quia erat[111] presens[112] in loco, in quo non potuisset id fieri, quin ipse vidisset[113] secundum formam notatam *in aut. de her. et fal. § Si vero absunt (Aut. 1.1.2.1= Nov. 1.2.1),* tunc esset probacio clarior.

[2)] Super eo vero[114] quid in presenti[115] questione[116] queritur, an illi testes qui dicunt[117] commune et homines fuisse[118] negligentes, etiam[119] nihil aliud dicunt:[c] an[120] probent inquisicionem[121] vel[122] non?[123] Dico inquisicionem non[124] esse probatam, quid[124] probo primo,[126] quia dicere aliquem esse[127] negligentem est quid[128] mere negativum seu privativum, quia[129] negligencia nihil aliud est quam privacio diligencie; et privacio et negacio idem sunt, *ut ff. de ver. obl. l. Inter stipulantem*[130] *in principio (Dig. 45.1.83pr),* ubi[131] ista[132] verba dolum malum abesse dicuntur[133] negativa,[134] *ut infra*[135] *notatur in glossa super verbo canutivum*[d136] *et quod notatur per glossam,*[137] *ff. de doli exci. l. fi. 'in factum',*[138] *(Dig. 44.4.17)*[e] in ultima glossa facta,[139] *de itinere*

---

[a]Bartolo da Sassoferrato, *Commentaria* in Dig. 26.7.14, *l. Tutor secundum,* f. 57vb no. 3.

[b]Cf. Bartolo da Sassoferrato, Commentaria in Dig. 17.2.16, l. Idemque, f.115vb no.2.

[c]An testes deponentes aliquem fuisse negligentem et non interrogati de ratione dicti eorum probent negligenciam. *add. in marg.* **C**.

[d]glo. 'abnutivum' ad Dig. 45.1.83pr Venice 1569, p. 661a.

[e]glo. 'in factum' ad Dig. 44.4.1., p. 576a.

actu que[140] priva.[141] l. i.[142] § i (Dig. 43.18.1.1) et quod ibi notatur. Sed[143]
70 testes qui deponunt super[144] negativa,[145] nisi habeat[146] cohartacionem[147] tanti[148] loci vel temporis quod possit[149] sensu percipi, non probant, *ut extra de causa posses. et proprietat. c. Cum ecclesia Sutrina*[150] *facit (X 2.12.3), C. de probat. l. Actor et quod ibi notatur per doc. (Cod. 4.19.23).*[a] [3)] Preterea negligencia non est aliquid formatum, quod sensu percipiatur nec enim[151]
75 percipitur[152] visu vel auditu vel alio sensu,[153] sed alii[154] actus supradicti percipiuntur visu. Ex quibus actibus colligimus[155] negligenciam[156] per intellectum. Sed quando testis deponit, debet deponere super eo, quod sensu percipitur,[157] *ut C. de testi. l. Testium (Cod. 4.20.18) et in dicto § Si vero absunt et*[158] *nota. per Innoc. extra de testi. c. Cum causam (X 2.20.37)*[b] quod hic[159]
80 non fecerint,[160] ergo et supra.[161] Preterea[162] illi, qui dicunt de[163] negligencia tantum nec reddunt[164] rationem per aliquem sensum corporis, magis iudicant[165] per[166] intellectum quam testificentur de facto ad quod adhibiti sunt: et sic non debet[167] valere, *ut C. de execut.*[168] *rei iudic. l. Si ut proponis (Cod. 7.53.6) et hoc notatur expresse per Innoc. in d. c. Cum causam, extra de testi.*[c]
85 [4)] Preterea testis, qui vult probare negativam,[169] debet probare[170] illum actum se vidisse, ex[171] quo illa negativa[172] resultet,[173] *ut docet*[174] *Imperator in*[175] *dicto § Si vero absunt, in aut. de her. et falc.*[176]

Ad ultimum vero quid[177] queritis, quid habeat probare[d] [f. 38r] commune ad sui[178] defensionem, dico quod multa possunt occurrere secundum diversas
90 facti accidencias.[179] Pono[180] aliquas: primo,[181] quod maleficium fuit commissum in aliquo[182] loco absconso[183] et secreto,[184] *ff. quod vi aut clam. l. Semper § Hoc interdictum,*[185] *ver. sed et*[186] *si is (Dig. 43.24.15.5).* Nec[187] enim communi potest imputari, si ignoravit[188] et occisores reperiri non potuerunt,[189] *l. Si ideo,*[190] *C. de his qui. ut indig. (Cod. 6.35.7) facit,*[e] *de calump. l. Annus*[191]
95 *(Dig. 3.6.6).*[f] Item quod maleficium fuit factum in loco propinquo flumini vel[192] confinibus comitatus,[193] ita quod antequam homines possent[194] trahere,[195] poterat[196] flumen vel confinia[197] transisse,[198] ita quod postea capi[199] non poterat,[200] *ff. de noxa.*[201] *l. In delictis circa principio (Dig. 9.4.4pr.),*[g] *de edi. edic. l. Quid*[202] *sit fugitivus § Item*[203] *Cei*[204] *(Dig. 21.1.17.13).* Item quod
100 poterant[205] de facili in aliquid nemus vel aliquam[206] silvam fugere, ita quod

---

[a] Albericus de Rosate, *Commentarii in primam partem Codicis*, Venice 1586 reprint Bologna 1979, ad Cod. 4.19.23, f. 197va no. 2; Cinus Pistoriensis, *Lectura super Codice*. Frankfurt a.M. 1578, reprint Rom 1998, f. 215va no. 2, f. 216ra no. 6; Glossa Ordinaria ad Cod. 4.19.23 s.v. '*cum per eum naturam*', Venice 1578, p. 499.

[b] Innocentius IV., *Apparatus in V libros Decretalium*. Frankfurt 1570, ad X 2.20.37, f. 262va no. 1.

[c] Innocentius, *Apparatus in V libros Decretalium*, ibid., f. 262vb no. 3.

[d] Vero quod habet hoc probare universitas ad sui defensionem si non cepit malefactorem *add. in marg.* **C**.

[e] Bartolo da Sassoferrato, *Commentaria* in Cod. 6.35.7, l. *Si ideo*, f. 37rb.

[f] Bartolo da Sassoferrato, *Commentaria* in Dig. 3.6.6, *l. Annus*, f. 123va.

[g] Bartolo da Sassoferrato, *Commentaria* in Dig. 9.4.4, l. *In delictis*, f. 194ra.

difficilis vel quasi impossibilis[207] erat eius[208] persecutio *l. Naturalem*[209] *in princ.,*[210] *ff. de acquir. re. do. (Dig. 41.1.5), de acquir. pos. l.iii § Nerva (Dig. 41.2.3.13)*. Item quod istud[211] maleficium fuit factum clam sine rumore[212] et sine clamationibus,[213] ita quod non potuit praesentire,[214] *ff. ad Sill. l. i § Occisorum (Dig. 29.5.1.17)*[a] *et § se (Dig. 29.5.1.18)*. Item quod fuit factum in loco remoto ab habitacionibus,[215] ita quod inde[216] non poterant exaudiri[217] voces clamancium,[218] *ut dicta l. i § Eodem autem tecto et § Si quis in villa et Cod. ad Sill. l. fi*. Item quod commune et homines tunc erant occupati circa[219] aliud necessarium[220] magnum[221] vel eque necessarium[222], *arg. ff. ad Sill. l. i § Si cum omnis,*[223] *(Dig. 29.5.1.23?), ff. de re. iudi. l. Contumacia § i*[224] *(Dig. 42.1.53.1), l. Contra pupillum*[225] *(Dig. 42.1.54) et § Qui*[226] *ad maius*[227] *(Dig. 42.1.54.1)*.

Item quod dictum[228] maleficium[229] fuit commissum tali[230] tempore quo erant clause ianue civitatis vel erat suspicio in civitate, ita quod homines exire non poterant[231] ad eos capiendos,[232] *l. Si quis in gravi § Subvenitur*[233] *(Dig. 29.5.3.6)*[234] *et § se, ad Sill. (Dig. 29.5.3.7).*[b] Item[235] tanta erat multitudo malefactorum seu potencia,[236] quod capi non poterant[237] sine magno bello, *Cod. de epis. aud. l. Addictos*[238] *(Cod. 1.4.6) et de rap. virg. l. Raptores*[239] *§ Sine autem post*[240] *commissum (Cod. 9.13.1.1c) et de epi. et cle. l. Raptores (Cod. 1.3.53(54)),*[241] *Cod. de his qui latro l. fi. (Cod. 9.39.2)*. Item[242] illi malefactores statim se reduxerunt[243] in aliquam arcem seu[244] roccham vel munitionem[245] ita fortem,[246] quod non poterant[247] capi vel expugnari, *ff. ad legem Jul. maiest. l. iii. (Dig. 48.4.3)*. Si tamen illi, qui[248] locum illum tenent,[249] sunt[250] de[251] eorum iurisdictione,[252] scilicet communis, consilium est quod eis faciat[253] preceptum, quod restituant malefactores[254] secundum formam[255] *dicte*[256] *l. ultima,*[257] *Cod. de his qui latro*. Item quod[258] illi malefactores statim intraverunt ecclesiam seu monasterium vel locum religiosorum,[259] *ut ex. de immunitate eccle. c. Inter alia (X 3.49.6) [f. 38v] et C. de biis qui ad ec. confu. per totum (Cod. 1.12)*. Et omnia ista[260] si bene advertantur, sunt[261] ad probandum,[262] quod communi non potest[263] imputari negligencia.

[5] Potest etiam commune probare suam diligenciam multis modis. Primo[264] quod totum civile[265] officium, hoc[266] est officiales civitatis, exierunt,[267] ut illos[268] malefactores[269] possent comprehendere, *ut dicta l. fi.,*[270] *Cod. de biis qui latro. et de rap. virgi. l. i*[271] *§ Sin. aut. post commissum (Cod. 9.13.1.12)*. Item quod posuerunt custodes ad limites et loca confinia[272] unde verisimiliter poterant latrones[273] effugere,[274] *ut C. de offi. prefec. pret. affr.*[275] *l. In nomine domini iii*[276] *secunda*[277] *columna (Cod. 1.30.2)*. Item quod rumor fuit concitatus[278] et factus[279] in civitate seu[280] castro, ut omnes traherent ad comprehendendum[282] malefactores,[283] *ut ff. de vi. bo. rap. l. Pretor § Si quis*

---

[a] Bartolo da Sassoferrato, *Commentaria* in Dig. 29.5.1.17 § *Occisorum*, f. 179rb no. 2.

[b] Cf. Bartolo da Sassoferrato, *Commentaria* in Dig. 29.5.3.6 § *Subvenitur*, f. 180ra.

Public Responsibility for Failure to Prosecute Crime? 165

adventu (Dig. 47.8.4.6)[284] *et ad Sill. l. i § Tulisse*[285] *(Dig. 29.5.1.35)*[286] vel campana sonata,[a] *ut not. in l. Sed*[287] *et si ex dolo § i,*[288] *ff. de dolo (Dig. 4.3.16.1) et l. Aliud*[289] *§ Refertur, ff. de reg. iur. (Dig. 50.17.160.1).* Item quod diligenter fuit perquisitum per omnia loca, ubi verisimiliter poterant esse dicti malefac-
145 tores, *ut dicta l. iii §*[290] *Nerva,*[291] *ff.*[292] *de acquiri. pos. (Dig. 41.2.3.13).* Item[293] factum fuit preconium per civitatem quod quicumque assignaret[294] talem malefactorem,[295] haberet[296] tantum de auro[297] communis[298] et qui scirent[299] et non indicarent,[300] punientur,[301] *ut C.*[302] *de hiis qui pa.*[303] *li. occi. l. i (Cod. 9.17.1)*[304] *et ff. de iustit. iuris*[305] *l. i §*[306] *Bonos*[307] *non solum*[308] *metu penarum*
150 *(Dig. 1.1.1.1) etc. et ff.*[309] *ad sill. l. Lege*[310] *Cor.*[311] *(Dig. 29.5.25) cum simil.* Multa etiam alia possent[312] occurrere ad diligenciam ostendendam. Sed[313] unum tamen est advertendum, quod ista debent[314] fieri vere[315] non ficte ut quandoque fit:[316] si enim[317] de hac[318] fictione[319] posset constare, nichil[320] prodesset, *ut ff. ad sill.*[321] *l. i § Excusantur*[322] *(Dig. 29.5.1.34).* Ista[323] breviter
155 modo[324] comprehendi.[325] Bartholus.[326]

Notes

1. Transcribed according to the manuscript *Bernkastell–Cues 288, f. 36vb–38vb*= **C**; other manuscripts used: **E** = Eichstätt Universitätsbibliothek 7, f. 22ra–23ra; **B** = Bologna, Collegio di Spagna 83, f. 87v–88v; **V** = Biblioteca Apostolica Vaticana lat. 10726, f. 228r–229r; **D** = printed edition, Venice (apud Tortis) 1530, f. 32vb–33rb; **P** = printed edition, Basel (Froben) 1562, p. 327a–328b. Note: Changes in the word order comprising less than three words are not indicated. I chose C as a basis for the edition because it contains several better readings, in particular as far as legal allegations are concerned. V on the other hand, has quite a few misreadings and resembles closely the prints, in particular D. None of the manuscripts used is dated or bears any indications of being an original, e.g. there are no seals or original colophons to be found. The numbering of chapters is found in the printed editions, but not in the manuscripts. For sake of easier reference I have kept them and added some more paragraphs.
2. domino *om.* **V**.
3. et eius curia *om.* **E**.
4. certa pecunia **E**.
5. posita **E**.
6. constituentis **E**.
7. quidem **E**, *om.* **D, P**.
8. dictum *add.* **E**; dicte *add.* **D**.
9. dicte *add.* **E, B, V, D, P**.
10. dicta *add.* **D, P**.
11. de causa *om.* **E, B, V, D, P**.
12. queritur *add.* **E**.
13. eam probandam | dicta probanda **E**.
14. commune | ratione **E**.
15. facere | probare **E**.

---

[a] Bartolo da Sassoferrato, *Commentaria* in Dig. 29.5.1.34 *§ Excusantur,* f. 179va.

166   A Renaissance of Conflicts

16. et *add.* **E**; tam pro presenti quam pro futuro *om.* **B**.
17. quod | ut **D, P**.
18. plenius | plurime **E**; plene **V**.
19. scribere **E, V, D, P**.
20. Nucerinus *om.* **E**.
21. mi *om.* **E, B**.
22. pater et *om.* **B**.
23. dubitam *add.* **E**; illic probetur in aliquo foro utrum negligentem *add. in marg.* **C**.
24. longam premeditacionem | per longam meditacionem **E**.
25. requirerent | et querent **E** ; requirunt **V, D, P**.
26. requirerent *om.* **E, V, D, P**.
27. etiam | et **V**.
28. cogitacionibus | occupationibus **V** ; *om.* **D, P**..
29. non obest etiam cum hoc *add.* **D, P** (cum | hoc **P**).
30. vero *om.* **V**; vero | quidem **D, P**.
31. modo | nunc **D, P**.
32. principo **E**.
33. studii | Gymnasii **D, P**.
34. inde **E**.
35. modico | medio **V**.
36. illam *om.* **E**; hoc **D, P**.
37. investigandam **E, V, D, P**.
38. adhibuitur **B**.
39. inquisicionem **E, V**.
40. accedam | veniamus **D**; deveniamus **V**; *om.* **P**; aliter *add.* **B**.
41. videbimus **E**; videamus **P**.
42. habeam | debeam **B, V, D, P**.
43. quando **V**.
44. est obligatus | in obligatione tenetur **D, P**.
45. tempus **D**.
46. et *om.* **E**.
47. ille **E**; illud **D, P**.
48. fecit **E, B**.
49. ipse **E**; illi **P**.
50. ostendat **B, V, D**.
51. ff. *om* **V**.
52. sed *add.* **E, V**; *om.* **C**.
53. aliquid | aliquod factum **E**.
54. proposito | nostro **B**.
55. enim | quia **E**; *om.* **V, D, P**.
56. ad capiendum | capere **E**.
57. malefactorem **E**.
58. ostendendum **D, P**.
59. oportet | debet **E, D, P**.
60. probare **D, P**.
61. quod *om.* **D, P**.
62. scivisse **D, P**.
63. malefactum | maleficium **D, P**.
64. esse *om.* **E**.
65. tu. *add.* **E, V**.
66. quod ut | quid **D**; prout **V**.
67. probando *om.* **V**.
68. probando quod sic | si **D, P**.
69. notorium **E**.
70. notatur | probatur **E, D**; notatur expresse *om.* **P**.
71. i | Si tutor **E**.
72. princ. | *om.* **E, V**; probatur **D, P**.
73. ff. *om.* **V**.
74. l. Regula | l. ii **D, P**.
75. hoc *add.* **V**.
76. ille *add.* **B**.
77. in quo | ille ubi **V, D, P**.
78. castrum *add.* **E**.
79. quod *add.* **C**; vel *add.* **V**; *om.* **E, B, D, P**.
80. vel habitationes | habitantes **E**; *om.* **V** ; habitationem **D, P**.
81. transissent **E, B, V; D, P** (*et add.:* sollicite).
82. rumores **D, P**.
83. in *add.* **E**.
84. hoc *om.* **E**.
85. infrascripta | ista **E**; *om.* **D, P**.
86. volo | velit **E**.
87. negligentem *om.* **B**.
88. an *add.* **E**.
89. dicta pecunia mutuari | dictam pecuniam mutuare **V**.
90. tutor | emptor **V**.
91. in mutuando...- negligentem *om.* **E** (homoioteleuton).
92. poterat | potuisset **E, B, V, D, P**.
93. perhi. | prohi. **E**; *om.* **V**.
94. penultima | ultima **E**.
95. aut. ut hii...- coll. vi | aut. de consang. & uter. frat. qui haer. § i col. vi. (A. 6.12.1) **P;** aut de uter. infra qui here. § i col. vi **D**.
96. In a changed order of sentences, **E** has now the passage that was

lacking, s.o. no. 91: Item si volo tutorem probare fuisse negligentem in mensurando pecuniam, an debeo probare vere vel presumptive quod in civitate erant homines, quibus potuisset dicta pecunia mutuari, alias non probaretur negligentia, ff. de admi. tu. l. Tutor secundum dignitatem § 1 (Dig. 26.7.13.1).
97. si volo probare...–gerere *om.* **V** (homoioteleuton).
98. eam *add.* **B**; factum *add.* **E**.
99. ubi | et per hoc **E, B** ; pro **V, D, P**.
100. et est expressum *om.* **V, D, P**.
101. ad Sill. | eo ti. **B**.
102. probetur | probaretur **E, D, P**.
103. censetur *add.* **D, P**.
104. est *om.* **D, P**.
105. reperi **E;** reperire **D**.
106. ipsos | eos **D, P**.
107. obmississe inquirere | vidisse trahere **E;** trahere | contrahere **D;** inquirere **P**.
108. persequi | prosequi **B, V, D, P**.
109. fecisse **E**.
110. reddentur **E**.
111. essent **E;** erant **V, D, P**.
112. presentes **E, D, P**.
113. vidissent **E** ; testis *add.* **D**.
114. vero *om.* **D, P**.
115. presenti | precedenti **D, P**.
116. questione | actu **V**; *om.* **E**.
117. circa *add.* **B;** quod *add.* **V**.
118. fuisse | fuerunt **V**.
119. etiam | vel **E**; *om.* **B**.
120. dicunt an | probent **V**.
121. inquisicionem | inquisiciones **E;** inquisiti **V**; *om.* **D, P**..
122. nil aliud dicunt probant inquisiciones vel non *add. in tex.* **E**.
123. dicunt... – non *om.* **B** (homoioteleuton).
124. non *add.* **E, D, C (C** *inter lineas*); *om.* **V**; hanc *add.* **P**.
125. quod **E**.
126. primo *om.* **D, P**.
127. esse *om.* **E**.
128. quid | *om.* **E**; quodammodo **D, P**.
129. quia | nil **E**; *om.* **B, V, D, P**.
130. stipulantem | stipulationibus **V**.
131. ubi | et **V**; nota quod *add.* **D, P**.
132. ista | illa **E;** sic **V**.
133. dicantur **D, P**.
134. negativa | negligentia **P**.
135. infra | ibi **E, V**.
136. in verbo ob mutuum **E;** super verbo commitivum **B;** super verbo coniunctivum **V;** super verbo ad mortuum **D, P**.
137. per glo. *om.* **B**.
138. in factum | in fine **V**; *om.* **E**.
139. In factum...-facta *om.* **D, P** (homoioteleuton).
140. quod | quia **E;** actuque **D**.
141. priva. | predato **D**.
142. ii **D, P**.
143. sed *om.* **B**.
144. super | simpliciter **D, P**.
145. negativam **D**.
146. habeat | probent E; habeant **V, D**.
147. habeat cohartacionem | probent cohartacioni **E;** et limitationem *add.* **D, P**.
148. tanti | certi **E, V**.
149. possit *om.* **D**.
150. Sutriana **C**.
151. enim | eius essentia **D, P**.
152. nec enim percipitur *om.* **E**.
153. percipiatur nec... –alio sensu *om.* **E;** corporea *add.* **D, P**.
154. alii *om.* **E**.
155. colligitur **E**.
156. negligencia **E**.
157. percipit **D**.
158. et *om.* **E**.
159. hic | isti **E**.
160. fecerunt **V, D, P**.
161. ergo et supra *om*.**E**.
162. praetera | puta **E**.
163. de | quod est **E**.
164. reddunt | respondent **E**.
165. iudicant | inducant **E**.
166. pro **E**.
167. debet | videtur **D, P**.
168. execut. | excep. **B, D, P**; *om.* **E**

169. negativam l negligenciam **E, B, V**.
170. probare l affirmare **E, B, V, D, P**.
171. ex l a **E**.
172. illa negativa *om.* **B**.
173. resultat **E**.
174. nos *add.* **D**.
175. ut docet Imperator in *om.* **P**.
176. Conclude ergo dictos testes non probare *add.* **E, B**; concluditur ergo testes non probare *add.* **V, D, P**.
177. vero quid l quo **E**.
178. sui l suam **V**.
179. diversas... accidentias l evidencias **E**; diversa accidentia **D, P**.
180. pono l ponam **D, P** *et add.*: vobis
181. pono *add.* **E**.
182. aliquo *om.* **E, V, D, P**.
183. abscondito **E, B**.
184. secreto **P**; seneto **E**.
185. interdicto **B, V**.
186. et *om.* **B, D**.
187. nec l hoc **V**; non **E, B, P**.
188. ignoravit l ignorant **E, B, P**.
189. et occisores reperiri non potuerunt *om.* **E**.
190. l. Si ideo l ut in si Co. **B**; l. Si omne **E**; l. Si ratio **V, D, P**.
191. annis **D, P**.
192. in *add.* **V, D**.
193. comitatus l civitatis **B, D, P**; civitatis vel comitatus **V**.
194. possent l potuissent **V**.
195. poterant *add.* **D, P**.
196. poterat *om.* **E**; poterant **V, D**.
197. confinia l conflumina **D**.
198. transisse l transire **B, V, D**; transierat **E**; **P**.
199. capi l capere **B**.
200. poterant **E, B, D, P**.
201. nora l nox **P**.
202. quid l quis **E, P**.
203. idem l inde **B, D, P**.
204. Cecilius l Cecilia **E**.
205. poterant l poterat **E**; capi non poterat... –item quod poterant *om.* **V** (homoioteleuton).
206. aliquam l aliqua **E**; *om.* **D, P**.
207. quasi impossibilis l impossibiliter **E**.
208. eius l eorum **D, P**.
209. naturale l valere **B**.
210. l. Naturale in prin. l l. Naturaliter **D, P**.
211. istud l illud **B**; dictum **E**; tale **D, P**.
212. rumoribus **V, D, P**.
213. et sine clamationibus l acclamationibus B; clamoribus **V**; *om.* **D, P**.
214. praesentire l persentiri **V**; praesciri **D**; praesentari alias praesciri **P**.
215. habitacionibus l habitantibus **V**.
216. inde l exinde **D, P**.
217. exaudiri l audiri **E**.
218. clamancium l acclamancium **V**.
219. circa l in **E**.
220. aliud necessarium l necessarium *om.* **E**.
221. aliud necessarium magnum l alia necessaria magna **V**.
222. circa aliud magnum necessarium vel eque necessarium l circa alia necessaria magna vel eque necessaria **D, P**.
223. omnis l eius **E**; omnes **D, P**.
224. § i *om.* **D, P**.
225. l. Contra pupillum l compupillum **B**; pupillum *om.* **E**; l. Contractus **V**; § Contractus **D, P**.
226. qui l quid **E, D, P**.
227. maius l manus **D, P**.
228. dictum l illud **E**.
229. maleficium l delictum vel homicidium **D, P**.
230. tali l eo **E, V, B, D**.
231. poterant l potuerunt **D**.
232. ad eos capiendos l capi vel expugnari **D**; in B there follows at the bottom of f. 88r a long gloss that could not be read from the Microfilm version accessible to me in the Max-Planck-Institut.
233. subvenitur l subventum **D, P**.

234. subventur| subventum **P**.
235. quod *add*. **B, V, D, P**.
236. seu potentia *om*. **V, D, P**.
237. ad eos capiendos... -capi non poterant *om*. **C** (homoioteleuton).
238. de epis. et cle. l. Imperator *add*. **B, D, P**.
239. l. Raptores| l. Imperator **E**.
240. post | propter **V**.
241. § Sine... – l. Raptores *om*. **B, E, D, P** (homoioteleuton).
242. quod *add*. **E**; quia *add*. **D, P**.
243. eduxerunt **P**.
244. arcem seu *om*. **E**.
245. vel munitionem| *om*. **B**; alio loco **E, B**.
246. fortem| forti **E**; foret **P**.
247. poterant| potuerunt **D, P**.
248. qui *om*. **E**.
249. tenerent **B**.
250. sunt| scilicet **B, E** (**E** *add*.: quia est de).
251. de *om*. **P**.
252. iurisditionis **D, P**.
253. faciat| faciant **E**.
254. malefactores| dictum locum **E**.
255. dicte *add*. **B**.
256. dicte *om*. **E**.
257. ultima| fi. **E, B, V, D, P**.
258. quod *om*. **V, D**.
259. religiosum **E, V**.
260. ista| illa E
261. sunt| faciunt **D, P**.
262. ad probandum *om*. **D, P**.
263. potest| posset **B**.
264. multis modis. Primo *om*. **V**.
265. civile| curie **E**.
266. hoc| id **D, P**.
267. exierunt| transeunt **E**; transierunt **P**; traxerunt **B, D**; transerunt **V**.
268. illos | eos **V**.
269. malefactores *om*. **E, B, V, D, P**.
270. fi. | ultima **V**.
271. i| i **E, P**; ii **C**.
272. confinium **B**.
273. latrones *om*. **E**; dicti latrones **D, P**; inde *add*.**B**.
274. effugere| insurgere **D, P**.
275. affr. *om*. **E**.
276. iii| circa **B**, in **V**.
277. secunda| in ii **E**; § ii **P**; in secundum locum **D**.
278. concitatus| contitutus **E**.
279. et factus *om*. **B, D, P**.
280. seu| vel **E**.
281. traherent| trahentur **E**.
282. comprehendendum| capiendum **V, D, P**.
283. malefactores *om*. **E, B, V**.
284. adventu *om*. **E**; § Si quis adventu|§ Si quis tantum **P**; § Frequens tantum **D**.
285. tulisse| subtulisse **E**.
286. tulisse| subtulisse **E**.
287. sed *om*. **E**.
288. l. Sed si ex dolo § i| l. fi. de dolo **D, P**; § 1 *om*. **V**.
289. § aliud *add*. **D**.
290. iii § *om*. **E**; iii| i **P**.
291. Nerva| vera **E**.
292. ff. | § **E**.
293. quod *add*. **E**.
294. assignaret| assignaverit **E**.
295. malefactorem *om*. **E, B, V, D, P**.
296. haberet| habebit **E**.
297. auro **E, D, P**; adune **C**; anere **B**; auere **V**.
298. communi **E**.
299. scirent| sciverit **E**; sciret **B**.
300. indicaverit **E**; indicaret **B**.
301. punitur **E**; punirentur **V, D**; puniretur **B**.
302. ut **C**.| arg. **E, D, P**.
303. pa.| proprie **C**; pro premio **B**; premio **V**; pa. **E**; in priorum **D, P**.
304. occi. li.| proprie acci. li. **C**; li. occe. **E**; li. acceperit **B**; credi. loco **D, P**; succedunt *add*. **D**.
305. et dicitur recte add. **E**.
306. §| ubi **E**; ibi **B, V**.
307. bonos *om*. **D, P**.
308. ubi *add*. **D, P**.
309. ff. | **C**. **V**; *om*. **E**.
310. Lege | Lex **V**.
311. et... – cor. *om*. **B**.
312. possunt **D, P**.

313. sed | ad **E, B;** circa hoc **D, P.**
314. debent | dicitur **E.**
315. et *add.* **E, B.**
316. fit | fiunt **V;** sine auctoritate iudicis *add.* **D, P**.
317. enim | autem **V**.
318. si enim hac | et si de hoc **E**; *om.* **D, P**.
319. hac fictione | hoc victio **E.**
320. tamen *add.* **D, P**.
321. alias ad trebel. *add.* **D, P**.
322. excusantur | excussi sunt **V**; accusatur **D, P**.
323. ista | et ita **E, P.**
324. breviter modo | ad presens **B**; modo *om.* **V**.
325. comprehendi | potui comprehendere **E, B, V, D, P.**
326. de Saxoferrato legum doctor cuius anima etc. In nomine domini nostri Yhsu Xristi *add.* **B**.

Part II

Usury

Plate 4: 'Porta citatione,' p. 68 in Annibale Carracci. *Diverse Figure*. Rome: Lodouico Grignani, 1646. (University of Chicago Library, Special Collections Research Center.)

*Usury, Conscience and Public Debt: Angelo Corbinelli's Testament of 1419**

Lawrin Armstrong

On 27 April 1419, the Florentine wool merchant Angelo di Tommaso Corbinelli summoned the notary Francesco di Piero Giacomini da Castelfiorentino († ca. 1433) and seven witnesses from the Augustinian convent of Santo Spirito in order to make a will. The event in itself was unremarkable: both custom and law required heads of households to make timely provision for the disposition of their property; indeed, Florentine synodal law went so far as to threaten intestates with denial of burial.[1] A conscientious *paterfamilias*, Corbinelli had dictated a testament to the same notary in 1417. The earlier will was annulled by this new and, in the event, final testament, since Corbinelli died soon

---

*I wish to record my gratitude to Julius Kirshner of the University of Chicago, who drew my attention to Corbinelli's testament. I return it to him as an *antidoron* on the occasion of his retirement and by way of thanks for the generous help and advice he has given me since I began studying the Florentine debt controversy. I am also grateful to the Archivio di Stato di Firenze for permission to consult the protocol of Corbinelli's testament edited below and to Luca Boschetto, Margaret Haines, Alessandra Malquori, John Munro, Christiane Klapisch-Zuber, Allen Grieco, Dick de Boer, Johanna Will-Armstrong and Jamie Smith for valuable comments and references. Research was funded by grants from the President's Research Grant and the Social Sciences and Humanities Research Council Small Grant programmes of Simon Fraser University and by a fellowship at the Villa I Tatti Harvard University Center for Italian Renaissance Studies, whose support is acknowledged with thanks. The following abbreviations will be used: ASF (Archivio di Stato di Firenze); Notarile (Notarile antecosimiano); OSMN (Ospedale di Santa Maria Nuova); BNF (Biblioteca Nazionale Centrale di Firenze); and *DBI* (*Dizionario biografico degli Italiani*). The Florentine year began 25 March; I have converted all dates to the modern style. Translations are my own unless otherwise noted.

[1] Trexler, 'Death and Testament,' 47.

afterwards in Pisa, where he was serving on the commission charged with administering the recently annexed city.[2]

Nor were Corbinelli's extensive bequests and legacies exceptional in the light of his status and contemporary Florentine practice.[3] A rich man, Corbinelli established dowries for fourteen poor girls (12)[4] and left generous sums to the cathedral works commission (*Opera di Santa Maria del Fiore*; 5, 6), four monastic foundations (7–11) and two hospitals (13, 14). As might be expected, most of Corbinelli's instructions related to domestic arrangements: he bequeathed small sums to his siblings (26–29), repaid his wife's dowry and arranged for her maintenance (16–21), dowered two legitimate and one illegitimate daughter (22–25), manumitted and dowered his domestic slave (35, 36) and nominated guardians for the three sons who would jointly inherit his house and the bulk of his estate (30, 37–39).[5]

The feature of Corbinelli's will that distinguishes it from published examples of contemporary Florentine testaments and renders it significant for the history of economic mentalities is the testator's confession of his doubts about the morality of profiting from credits in the various *monti*, the public debt funds of the Florentine republic, on the grounds that such profit represented usury.[6] The legal and theological controversy over

---

[2]Corbinelli's testament of 5 July 1417 is recorded at ASF, Notarile 9042, fols. 55v–58v. Corbinelli was drawn for the Ten of Pisa (*Dieci di Pisa*) in 1419 and died in office soon after 1 May 1419, when he added a codicil to his testament of 27 April 1419; see ASF, Notarile 9042, fol. 76r–v; and *DBI* 28, s.v. 'Corbinelli, Angelo' by Molho. The *tratte*, the records of citizens drawn for political office, reveal that Corbinelli's name was drawn for the advisory council of the Twelve (*Dodici Buonuomini*) on 12 June 1419 but that he was not seated because he had already died; see Herlihy et al., eds., *Online Tratte of Officeholders*; accessed online 25 July 2002.

[3]On the typology of pious bequests in late-*Trecento* Florence, see Bonanno et al., 'I legati "pro anima."' For observations on Tuscan testaments in general, see English, 'La prassi testamentaria.' Cohn, *The Cult of Remembrance*, reviews changes in testamentary strategies between the late twelfth and early fifteenth centuries in six Tuscan and Umbrian cities. See also Cohn, *Death and Property in Siena*, for a study of testamentary practices in Siena over six centuries.

[4]References are to the numbered paragraphs of the edition in appendix 1.

[5]According to the *catasto* declaration that Corbinelli's heirs Bernardo and Tommaso filed in 1427, Corbinello, the third son mentioned in the testament, had died, but Angelo, born in 1419 after his father's death, survived (ASF, Catasto 17, fol. 236r; ASF, Catasto 65, fol. 91r).

[6]Other examples of Florentine testaments include Mazzei, *Lettere di un notaro*, 2: 273–310 (testament and codicils of Francesco di Marco Datini, † 1410; trans. Byrne, *The Wills and Codicils of Marco and Francesco di Marco Datini*; accessed online 25 July 2002); Sanesi, 'Il testamento di Marchionne di Coppo Stefani,' 321–326; Molho, 'The Brancacci Chapel,' 86–93 (four testaments of Felice Bran-

usury and public debt in Florence and other Italian city-states is well-known from the studies of John Noonan, Julius Kirshner and others.[7] The objective of this essay is to answer a question implicit in the literature: did the judgments of lawyers and theologians—especially their negative judgments—affect the behavior of government creditors? A consideration of Corbinelli's scruples in the light of the controversy, a review of the structure of his bequests and an examination of parallel evidence from other testaments suggest that they did. The paper therefore also contests the assumption of many historians influenced by neo-classical economics that the usury prohibition—in this view a limit on the pursuit of rational self-interest—did not influence the economic decisions of medieval Europeans.[8]

However, before turning to the testamentary evidence it will be useful to outline briefly how government debt was organized in Florence and why many theorists thought that it violated the usury prohibition.

The Public Debt

From the late thirteenth century, Florence, following the example of Venice and Genoa, increasingly resorted to voluntary and compulsory loans—the latter were called *prestanze*—from its citizens to meet expenses, usually military expenses, that exceeded ordinary revenues.[9]

---

cacci, 1422–1432); and Pandimoglio, 'Giovanni di Pagolo Morelli,' 163–181 (three testaments of Giovanni Morelli, 1415–1430). For contemporary humanist testaments, see Giustiniani, 'Il testamento di Leonardo Bruni'; and Celenza, 'The Will of Cardinal Giordano Orsini.'

[7] The only comprehensive study of the controversy in Florence and other Italian city-states is Kirshner, 'From Usury to Public Finance.' The core of this research was published in Kirshner, 'Reading Bernardino's Sermon' but see also Kirshner, 'The Moral Theology of Public Finance'; Kirshner, 'Conscience and Public Finance'; Kirshner; 'The Moral Problem of Discounting Genoese *Paghe*'; Kirshner, *Pursuing Honor While Avoiding Sin*; Kirshner, 'Storm over the *Monte Comune*'; Kirshner, '"*Ubi est ille?*"'; and Kirshner, 'Encumbering Private Claims to Public Debt.' For additional discussions, see Noonan, *The Scholastic Analysis of Usury*, 121–128, 294–310; and Trusen, 'Die Anfänge öffentliche Banken.' On the Florentine controversy in particular, see de Roover, 'Il trattato di fra Santi Rucellai' (texts critically edited in Fumagalli, 'I trattati di fra Santi Rucellai,' 289–332); Bernardino, *Sermo* XLI in *Opera omnia*, 4: 307–346; Spicciani, *Capitale e interesse*, 97–111; Santarelli, '"*Maxima fuit Florentiae altercatio*"'; Armstrong, 'The Politics of Usury'; and Armstrong, *Usury and Public Debt*.

[8] On the limitations of rational choice theory in the study of economic history, see the pertinent observations of Hobsbawm, 'Historians and Economists: II.'

[9] On the Florentine public debt prior to 1345, the fundamental study remains Barbadoro, *Le finanze della Repubblica fiorentina*. For the early history of the

Prestanze were imposed in periodic surveys of wealth called *estimi*, and all loans, compulsory and voluntary, were secured by liens on anticipated gabelles (consumption taxes) and levies on subject territories. When the term came due, loans were usually repaid in full with interest of eight to fifteen percent.[10] Between 1343 and 1345, however, costly wars with Pisa and Verona and the failure of several merchant banks forced the government to consolidate outstanding debts of some 600,000 florins into a central account, the *monte comune*.[11] No date was set for the redemption of the principal, and the interest rate was reduced to five percent, liabilities that were only partly offset by the establishment of a government-sponsored market where *prestanziati* (compulsory lenders) could sell their credits to other Florentines.[12] Fears that the government would default on the loans or suspend interest payments meant that credits rarely fetched more than a quarter of their nominal value between 1345 and 1470.[13]

---

monte, see Becker, *Florence in Transition* 2: 151–200; Trexler, 'Florence, by the grace of the Lord Pope'; Barducci, 'Politica e speculazione'; Barducci, 'Le riforme finanziarie'; Barducci, '"*Cum parva difficultate*"'; and Molho, 'Créanciers de Florence en 1347.' For the later fourteenth and fifteenth centuries, see Marks, 'The Financial Oligarchy'; Molho, *Florentine Public Finances*; Molho, 'L'amministrazione del debito pubblico'; Molho, 'Fisco ed economia a Firenze'; Molho, 'Debiti pubblici/interessi privati'; Molho, 'The State and Public Finance'; Palmieri, *Ricordi fiscali*; Conti, *L'imposta diretta a Firenze*; Ciappelli, 'Il cittadino fiorentino e il fisco'; and Ninci, 'La politica finanziaria della Repubblica fiorentina.' On the Venetian debt, see Luzzato, *Il debito pubblico della Repubblica di Venezia*; Lane, 'The Funded Public Debt of the Venetian Republic'; and Mueller, *Money and banking in medieval and Renaissance Venice*, 2: 453–557. For Genoa, the basic study remains Sieveking, *Studio sulle finanze genovesi*. For comparisons between Florence, Venice and Genoa, see Molho, 'Tre città-stato e i loro debiti pubblici.' For a comparative study of the earliest period of public debt-making in Tuscany, see Ginatempo, *Prima del debito*. On the Lucchese public debt, see Meek, 'Il debito pubblico nella storia finanziaria di Lucca'; and Meek, *Lucca 1369–1400*, 48–76, esp. 54–57, 63–76. For Siena, see Bowsky, *The Finance of the Commune of Siena*, 166–224; and Caferro, *Mercenary Companies and the Decline of Siena*, 103–171.

[10]On loans and rates prior to 1345, see Barbadoro, *Le finanze della Repubblica fiorentina*, 515–628. On gabelle revenues and assignments, see De La Roncière, 'Indirect Taxes or "Gabelles" at Florence.'

[11]Barbadoro, *Le finanze della Repubblica fiorentina*, 622–631. Cipolla, *The Monetary Policy of Fourteenth-Century Florence*, 1–12, provides a good brief sketch of the wider crisis. For a reassessment of the role of merchant bank failures in the crisis, see Hunt, *The medieval super-companies*.

[12]Barbadoro, *Le finanze della Repubblica fiorentina*, 632–654; and Barducci, 'Politica e speculazione.'

[13]Kirshner, 'From Usury to Public Finance,' 24–26. Market prices are provided at ibid., 25, table 2. For the period 1425–1475, see Conti, *L'imposta diretta*, 34, table 1. Prices peaked in 1418–1423, on the eve of the war with Filippo Maria Visconti, at sixty-one percent of face value (ibid., 32).

Despite these disadvantages, the Florentine elite considered public debt preferable to the alternative of direct taxes on private property, which they had successfully resisted since 1315.[14] If held, *monte* credits paid a modest but respectable return comparable to investments in land and ordinary business ventures. For those prepared to assume the risk, shares bought on the market at a discount yielded real interest rates of fifteen to twenty percent.[15]

The 1345 consolidation provided the model for subsequent debt funds. By 1419, after several expansionist campaigns in Tuscany and wars with the pope (1375–1378), Milan (1390–1406), Genoa (1410–1413) and Naples (1409–1414), the government owed around three million florins distributed among several accounts.[16] The *monte comune*, in which the bulk of the debt was inscribed, continued to pay an annual interest rate of five percent; the *monte dei prestanzoni* (literally, 'big *prestanze* fund'), which represented extraordinary levies during the latter phases of the war with Milan, paid eight percent; and the *monte di Pisa*, created in 1406 to finance the conquest of Pisa, ten percent. The interest on all three funds was, however, subject to a twenty-five percent stoppage (*ritenzione del quarto*) that reduced the real rates to 3.75, six and 7.5 percent respectively.[17]

---

[14] Barbadoro, *Le finanze della Repubblica fiorentina*, 124–131; de La Roncière, 'Indirect Taxes or "Gabelles" at Florence,' 142; and Molho, *Florentine Public Finances*, 63–64. Direct taxes were revived during two brief periods of signorial rule: in 1326 by the duke of Calabria, Charles of Anjou († 1328); and in 1342 by Walter of Brienne, titular duke of Athens († 1356). Both taxes proved unacceptable to the elite and were abolished on the restoration of communal government; see Barbadoro, *Le finanze della Repubblica fiorentina*, 161–197, 206–212; and Becker, *Florence in Transition*, 1: 80–88, 149–164.

[15] For comparisons between returns on *monte* shares and other investments, see Kirshner, 'From Usury to Public Finance,' 27. On profits from speculation, see Brucker, *Florentine Politics and Society*, 19; Brucker, 'Un documento fiorentino'; Kirshner, 'Storm over the *Monte Comune*,' 223; and Barducci, 'Politica e speculazione,' 202–217.

[16] Ninci's figures for 1 November 1407 indicate that the *monte comune* then represented 2.7 million florins of debt, the *monte di Pisa* 265,000 and the *monte dei prestanzoni* 340,000, for a total of 3,305,000 ('La politica finanziaria della Repubblica fiorentina,' 167). Molho estimates the size of the total debt in 1415 as 3.1 million florins; between 1414 and 1423 this sum was reduced by only 175,000 florins (Molho, *Florentine Public Finances*, 71–73). On the various conflicts, see Brucker, *Florentine Politics and Society*, 297–335; and Brucker, *The Civic World of Early Renaissance Florence*, 102–186, 203–208, 241–352.

[17] On these funds, see Molho, *Florentine Public Finances*, 102–103; and Conti, *L'imposta diretta*, 31–32, 142. Originally earmarked for the liquidation of the debt, deferred interest payments were periodically reimbursed up to 1439 (Conti, *L'imposta diretta*, 32).

Stoppages were treated as deferred interest payments (*paghe sostenute*) and entered into assessment declarations as a sort of *monte* credit.

The *Monte* Controversy

Despite the blessing of the Florentine political and economic elite, deficit financing was highly controversial. The creation of the *monte comune* was associated with challenges to the traditional distribution of power in the commune and the debt remained a central factor in political and class struggles for well over a century, not least because it siphoned wealth via consumption taxes and rural imposts from the poorest to the richest strata of Florentine society.[18] The establishment of public debts in Florence and elsewhere also raised legal and moral issues that became the focus of growing dispute in the course of the fourteenth and fifteenth centuries.[19] Theologians and lawyers rarely questioned the reliance of governments on debt, but many considered the payment of interest to public creditors a violation of the ban on usury, which theology and law defined as a charge for a loan.[20] It must be emphasized that in our period 'usury' denoted any rate of interest, not simply an excessive or illegal one. The ban applied to loans of money and other things whose use involved their consumption, such as wine, oil and grain.[21] Ordinary commercial profits,

---

[18] The abolition of the *monte* and the reinstatement of wealth taxes were central demands of the Ciompi insurrectionaries in 1378. On the fiscal programme of the Ciompi, see Rodolico, *I Ciompi*, 184–197; Barducci, 'Le riforme finanziarie,' 100–101; and Stella, *La révolte des Ciompi*, 17–32. For early fifteenth-century peasant insurgencies provoked by oppressive tax burdens, see Cohn, *Creating the Florentine State*. On the impoverishment of the rural economy through transfers that went largely to servicing the debt, see Epstein, 'Cities, Regions and the Late Medieval Crisis.' For discussions of the political context in which the *monte* was created, see Becker, *Florence in Transition*, 2: 151–168; Kirshner, 'Storm over the *Monte Comune*,' 222–239; Barducci, 'Politica e speculazione'; Armstrong, 'The Politics of Usury,' 17–21; and Armstrong, *Usury and Public Debt*, 28–33, 51–52, 72–78. For observations on the role of the public debt in subsequent political conflicts, see Martines, 'Forced Loans'; Molho, 'The State and Public Finance,' 104–127; Ninci, 'La politica finanziaria della Repubblica fiorentina'; and Armstrong, *Usury and Public Debt*, 41–52, 100–111.

[19] For the literature, see above, n. 7.

[20] The only comprehensive study of the Christian usury prohibition remains Noonan, *The Scholastic Analysis of Usury*. On the canonical doctrine in particular, see McLaughlin, 'The Teaching of the Canonists on Usury.' For a brief review of the prohibition, see Gilchrist, *The Church and Economic Activity*, 62–76; and documents in translation, ibid., 155–225. Important recent studies include Spicciani, *Capitale e interesse*; Langholm, *The Aristotelian Analysis of Usury*; and Langholm, *Economics in the Medieval Schools*.

[21] On the fundamental definition of usury and its restriction to 'fungibles,' see

rents and penalties for overdue loans did not come within the scope of the prohibition.

In Florence, the usurious dimensions of the public debt became the subject of controversy within a decade of the original consolidation. In public disputations in 1353–1354, the Franciscan master Francesco da Empoli († 1370) and the Dominican Piero degli Strozzi († 1362) agreed that *prestanziati* were immune from a charge of usury because their loans were coerced, but they divided over the status of the market.[22] According to Strozzi, speculators, who voluntarily acquired credits on the market with a view to profit, were morally indistinguishable from moneylenders because they sought the same benefit they could have obtained by a direct loan to the government. Francesco, by contrast, interpreted market transactions as purchase-sale agreements in which buyers obtained the sellers' rights to principal and interest; since usury occurred only in loan contracts, the usury prohibition was not applicable.

The distinction between *prestanziati* and speculators would run through the entire debate, but the initial consensus over compulsory lenders soon dissolved. In an influential *quaestio disputata* written in 1357 or 1358, the theologian and prior-general of the Augustinian friars Gregory of Rimini († 1358) severely circumscribed the conditions under which compulsory creditors of the Venetian *monte* might licitly accept interest.[23] In the early 1370s, two Augustinians of Santo Spirito, John Klenkock († 1374) and Guido da Bellosguardo († 1377), censured the entire Florentine public debt system, including compensation for *prestanziati*.[24] A similar

---

Noonan, *The Scholastic Analysis of Usury*, 38–51; and McLaughlin, 'The Teaching of the Canonists on Usury,' 1: 98–102.

[22] The dispute was reported by Villani, *Cronica*, bk. 3, ch. 106, vol. 1, pp. 459–462. For the text of Strozzi's *quaestio,* see Kirshner, 'Storm over the Monte Comune,' 258–276; the arguments are analyzed at ibid., 247–251. For an edition of Francesco da Empoli, see Armstrong, 'The Politics of Usury,' 28–44. For analyses, see *DBI* 49, s.v. 'Francesco da Empoli' by Kirshner; and Armstrong, 'The Politics of Usury,' 7–14. The coercion consisted in the fact that the failure to pay assessed loans resulted in the loss of political privileges.

[23] Gregory of Rimini, *Tractatus de imprestantiis Venetorum et de usura.* On the dating of this text and for an analysis of the argument, see Kirshner, 'From Usury to Public Finance,' 117–121; and Armstrong, *Usury and Public Debt*, 68–70. Although it was concerned with the Venetian debt, Gregory's *quaestio* strongly influenced debate in Florence: the canonists Lapo da Castiglionchio († 1381) and Lorenzo Ridolfi († 1443) framed their respective defences of the Florentine *monte* largely as responses to Gregory; see Armstrong, *Usury and Public Debt*, 81–82, 89–90, 93–94.

[24] Guido probably delivered his *consilium* at the chapter-general of the Augustinians held in Florence in May 1371, at which he was elected prior-general; see Kirshner, '"Ubi est ille?",' 567, n. 41. Klenkock's *consilium* likely dates from the

position was maintained more than a century later by Savonarola († 1498), who condemned citizens who refused to lend to the commune unless they were guaranteed a profit.[25]

Speculation remained intensely controversial. Some time in the mid-1360s or early 1370s, the Dominican master Domenico Pantaleoni († 1376) composed a detailed refutation of Francesco da Empoli's defence of the debt market.[26] Modelling his tract on that of his mentor Strozzi, Pantaleoni argued that the interest enjoyed by *prestanziati* was inalienable because it represented compensation for damages lenders individually sustained through their obligations to the government. To describe market transactions as sales of rights was therefore to mystify the real character of the agreement, which was nothing other than the usurious purchase of debt. Echoing the Council of Vienne (1311–1312), Pantaleoni condemned as a quasi-heretic anyone who maintained that the market in public debt was not usurious.[27] The same line was subsequently taken by several influential commentators, among them the Franciscans Guglielmo Centureri († 1402) and Bernardino of Siena († 1444), whose analyses of the debt market explicitly rejected the apologetics of their confrère Francesco da Empoli.[28]

---

same time. Both texts were reported and glossed by Lorenzo Ridolfi in his *Tractatus de usuris* (*Treatise on usury*) (1404), the only form in which they appear to survive; see the autograph, BNF, Fondo principale II, III, 366, fols. 98r–101v; and Ridolfi, *Tractatus de usuris* in *Tractatus universi iuris*, vol. 7, fols. 48va–50ra. For discussions, see Kirshner, 'From Usury to Public Finance,' 121–122; Kirshner, '"*Ubi est ille?*",' 567; and Armstrong, *Usury and Public Debt*, 67–68, 79–80. Villani reported that in the Florentine dispute of 1353–1354 the Augustinians sided with Piero degli Strozzi in condemning the *monte*, but he did not name the relevant masters; see *Cronica*, 3.106, 1: 461.

[25] Savonarola, *Predica* 26 (28 October 1496) in *Prediche sopra Ruth e Michea*, 2: 324–325. Savonarola's position was unusually harsh in the context of contemporary theological opinion; see de Roover, 'Il trattato di fra Santi Rucellai,' 22–23. In his own writings on the debt, fra Santi (Pandolfo di Giovanni) Rucellai († 1497), Savonarola's confrère at San Marco, portrayed *prestanziati* as victims of irregular interest payments and arbitrary stoppages and justified market discounts on the grounds of risk. For a discussion, see ibid., 18–19; and Kirshner, 'The Moral Problem of Discounting Genoese *Paghe*,' 139–41. For the text, see Fumagalli, 'I trattati di fra Santi Rucellai,' 324–328.

[26] Pantaleoni's tract is preserved in BNF, Conventi soppressi J.X.51, fols. 190r–200r; additional manuscripts are noted by Kaeppel, *Scriptores Ordinis Praedicatorum*, 332. The tract was often attributed to the Sienese canonist Federicus Petruccius (fl. 1322–1343); for the correct attribution, see Kirshner, 'A Note on the Authorship of Domenico Pantaleoni's Tract.' For an analysis of Pantaleoni's argument, see Kirshner, 'Storm over the *Monte Comune*,' 252–256.

[27] Kirshner, 'Storm over the *Monte Comune*,' 256. The decree *Ex gravi* (Clem. 5.5.1) is translated in Boyer and Kirshner, eds., *University of Chicago Readings*, 4: 317.

By contrast, canon lawyers, who in this period were often laymen of patrician origin, generally endorsed the market in public debt. Peter of Ancharano († 1416), Lapo da Castiglionchio, Bartolomeo Bosco († ca. 1437) and Lorenzo Ridolfi all interpreted the market in terms of the licit purchase of rights or income.[29] Peter of Ancharano and Bosco reinforced their analyses with the observation that the operations of the Venetian, Genoese and Florentine public debts had never been subject to formal papal or ecclesiastical censure.[30]

Modern discussions of the usury prohibition often focus on whether it really influenced behavior. Pioneers in the field of economic history such as Henri Pirenne, Roberto Lopez and Gino Luzzatto doubted that usury was ever more than a theoretical problem for medieval Europeans.[31] The

---

[28] For the text of Centueri's censure of the market, see Kirshner, 'Reading Bernardino's Sermon,' 593–609; for a discussion, see ibid., 573–587. Bernardino's *Sermo* XLI contains an attack on the market (*Opera omnia*, 4: 328–346). It was written some time between 1430 and 1444 (Kirshner, 'Reading Bernardino's Sermon,' 549). For a discussion of the text, demonstrating its dependence on Centueri, see ibid., 573–589. Positions on the market did not reflect the monastic affiliation of masters: the Dominicans Nicholas de Anglia (fl. 1402) and Antonino (Antonio di ser Niccolò Pierozzi), Archbishop of Florence († 1459), for example, implicitly rejected the critique advanced by Strozzi and Pantaleoni; see Kirshner, 'Storm over the *Monte Comune*,' 228–231; Kirshner, 'The Moral Theology of Public Finance,' 57–61; Noonan, *The Scholastic Analysis of Usury*, 166–169; and de Roover, *San Bernardino of Siena and Sant'Antonino of Florence*, 39. See, however, Todeschini, 'Oeconomica Franciscana,' 'Oeconomica Franciscana II,' and *Un trattato di economia politica*, 1–47, who argues more generally for a distinctive Franciscan discourse that was amenable to economic innovation.

[29] Peter of Ancharano's *Quaestio disputata de Monte Venetorum vel Florentinorum* is preserved in BNF, Magliabechiano xxix, 179, fols. 278v–288r. Delivered in Bologna in 1398, the *quaestio* was sometimes attributed to the civilian jurist Bartolo of Sassoferrato († 1357); for the correct attribution and additional manuscripts, see Kirshner, 'A *Quaestio de usuris* Falsely Attributed to Bartolus.' For the argument of the text, see Kirshner, 'Reading Bernardino's Sermon,' 565–572. For Lapo da Castiglionchio's *repetitio* on the Florentine *monte*, written between 1369 and 1381, see *Allegationes*, allegatio 137, n. 15, fols. 162va–164vb. The text is discussed by Kirshner, 'From Usury to Public Finance,' 191–194; and Armstrong, *Usury and Public Debt*, 81–82, 93–94, 98–99. On Bartolomeo Bosco, see Kirshner, 'Reading Bernardino's Sermon,' 572; and Kirshner, 'The Moral Problem of Discounting Genoese *Paghe*,' 116–119. The portions of Ridolfi's *Tractatus de usuris* dealing with the market in *monte* shares are edited in Armstrong, *Usury and Public Debt*, 236–260. For an analysis of the argument, see ibid., 93–99.

[30] Kirshner, 'Reading Bernardino's Sermon,' 566–568, 572.

[31] On the historiography, see Kirshner, 'Raymond de Roover on Scholastic Economic Thought,' 17–18. Pirenne sums up this perspective best with his remark that 'altogether the legislation against usury does not seem to have prevented it in practice very much more than the Volsted Act in America prevented the consump-

fact that between 1000 and 1300 Europe experienced a commercial revolution that would have been impossible without credit markets was proof that real economic agents in practice ignored the prohibition as an irrational constraint on the pursuit of their self-interest. This view persists in the more recent literature, where it is often suggested that the usury ban applied only to high-interest consumption or distress loans and that it was eroded by the progressive commercialization of the medieval economy.[32]

Historical reality, however, was more complex. The growth of the commercial economy was matched by an intensification of the prohibition, climaxing in the decree *Ex gravi*, which condemned the legitimation of usury as quasi-heretical and forbade the public licencing of usurers.[33] Those most immediately affected by anti-usury measures were moneylenders and pawnbrokers, who openly advanced credit on little or no security at rates as high as forty-three percent a year.[34] Such 'notorious' or 'manifest' usurers were deprived of the sacraments and Christian burial unless they furnished guarantees (*cautiones*) of full restitution in their wills.[35] In a

---

tion of alcohol' (Pirenne, *Economic and Social History of Medieval Europe*, 140). By contrast, Werner Sombart, *The Quintessence of Capitalism*, 246–250, argued that the prohibition *stimulated* economic activity by directing capital into investment rather than loans, a view echoed by Noonan, *The Scholastic Analysis of Usury*, 407.

[32]See, for example, Gilchrist, *The Church and Economic Activity*, 63–65. Ekelund et al., *Sacred Trust*, 113–130, argue that the prohibition was applied selectively with a view to advancing ecclesiastical economic interests. I am grateful to John Munro for the latter reference. For a change from the traditional view, see the recent synthesis by Hunt and Murray, *A History of Business in Medieval Europe*, 70–73, 215–216, which acknowledges that the usury prohibition did not distinguish between consumption and investment loans and therefore presented an impediment to medieval businessmen. I am indebted to Dick de Boer for this reference.

[33]A review of this process with extensive reference to local legislation is provided by Schnapper, 'La répression de l'usure,' 47–75. On penalties and jurisdiction, see McLaughlin, 'The Teaching of the Canonists on Usury,' 2: 1–22 For the decree of the Council of Vienne, see above, n. 27. The impact of Vienne on moneylending in Marseilles is discussed by Shatzmiller, *Shylock Reconsidered*, 119–121.

[34]Helmholz, 'Usury and the Medieval English Church Courts,' presents evidence for the prosecution of manifest usurers. On the market in consumer credit, see de Roover, *Money, Banking and Credit in Mediaeval Bruges*, 99–167; rates of interest are noted at ibid., 127.

[35]The third Lateran council (1179) excommunicated usurers and denied them burial. The second council of Lyons (1274) voided the testaments of usurers who failed to make provision for full restitution; the decree was incorporated into the *Liber sextus*, the collection of papal law promulgated by Boniface VIII in 1298 (VI 5.5.2). A good example of *cautio* occurs in the testament of Agostino di ser Migliorello, 13 June 1395: 'Item dixit et declaravit dictus testator quod ipse certo

study of local banking in fifteenth-century Florence, Richard Goldthwaite argues convincingly that the absence of consolidated ledgers and cash accounts among the surviving records of small bankers reflected their determination to avoid, or at least postpone, such penalties by concealing interest on the loans that made up the bulk of their trade.[36]

Studies of testamentary evidence by Benjamin Nelson, Armando Sapori and Florence Edler suggest, however, that not only moneylenders but even merchants as reputable as the Medici, whose credit transactions were limited to the realms of high finance and government and were therefore 'occult' rather than manifest, were acutely sensitive to the moral implications of their commerce.[37] Indeed, in the contemporary imagination there

---

tempore usuras exercuit in civitate Florentie et a pluribus et variis personis recepit pro interesse et usura ultra sortem plures et diversas pecunie quantitates et summas et quod postea idem testator prestita cautione usuras predictas restituit et incerta persolvit prout in prestita hodie per ipsam cautionem manu mei notarii latius continetur et quod post dictam restitutionem ipse testator non putat suo iudice aliquid per pravitate usurarum vel alio modo illicito percepisse. Et nichilominus ad plenam exonerationem anime sue, sicut etiam in dicta cautione promisit, voluit, disposuit, legavit et mandavit presenti suo testamento quod omnibus et singulis predicto modo vel alio quocumque ab ipso testatore aliquid habere debentibus, de suis bonis integre satisfiat prout infrascriptis suis fideicommissariis et heredibus visum fuerit' (ASF, OSMN 68, fol. 45v). For other examples, see ASF, Notarile 205 (*cautio* of Francesco di Zanobi Albizzelli, 6 June 1363); OSMN 67, fols. 377r–378v (testament of Giovanni di Buonaccorso Alberti, 28 August 1392); OSMN 68, fol. 45v (testament of Antonio di ser Chello, notary, 13 June 1395); OSMN 70, fol. 113r (testament of Michaele di Zanobi Benozzi da Prato, 31 August 1417).

[36] Goldthwaite, 'Local Banking in Renaissance Florence,' esp. 14–17, 28–37. This absence was all the more striking given the prevalence of double-entry bookkeeping in other fifteenth-century Florentine enterprises; see de Roover, 'The Development of Accounting prior to Luca Pacioli,' esp. 144–161.

[37] For a review of the literature on the religious psychology of the Florentine merchant that emphasizes the point made in this and the following paragraph, see de La Roncière, 'La foi du marchand.' Nelson, 'The Usurer and the Merchant Prince,' is still the best synthetic review of the problem of merchant restitution. Sapori, 'L'interesse del denaro a Firenze,' examines the execution of the testament of a merchant turned usurer, Bartolomeo Cocchi-Compagni († 1389), by the *monte* officials, who were responsible for executing the wills of manifest usurers. On this function of the officials, see Becker, 'Three Cases Concerning the Restitution of Usury.' Edler, 'Restitution in Renaissance Florence,' discusses the restitution of interest on commercial loans in the testament of Giuliano di Giovenco de' Medici († 1498), a member of a collateral branch of the better-known Medici. Ernst Gombrich attributed much of Cosimo de' Medici's († 1464) artistic patronage to conscientious scruples about usury; see 'The Early Medici as Patrons of Art,' esp. 36–40. Gombrich's inspiration was Vespasiano da Bisticci (1421–1498), who remarked of Cosimo that he suffered qualms of conscience because 'it seemed to him that his money was not altogether honestly acquired' ('allui pareva avere danari

was little to distinguish the moneylender from the merchant banker: two of the three usurers Dante encountered in the seventh circle of Hell were patrician Florentines.[38] Similar judgments expressed in contemporary sermons and *exempla* collections have led Jacques Le Goff to conclude that the purgatory doctrine itself can be ascribed in large measure to the impact of the usury prohibition on the merchant conscience.[39]

It is now difficult to sustain the view that the usury prohibition did not command popular assent, whatever practical contradictions this created for medieval businessmen. Even Raymond de Roover, who found the persistence of the ban an embarrassment to his project of identifying medieval precedents for modern business techniques, concluded that it had the practical effect of diverting banking from straightforward credit transactions into exchange.[40] Francesco Galassi goes further, arguing in a recent study based on Genoese testaments that the usury prohibition retarded the development of capital markets by channeling wealth into pious bequests rather than into productive investment.[41] Indeed, the moral risks associated with usury were such that, as Eric Hobsbawm has observed, 'in the fourteenth century the choice of leaving one's fortune to a monastery for the good of one's soul would, to many a merchant, have seemed as good a rational choice as leaving it to one's sons.'[42]

We know less about popular reactions to the accusation that government debt involved usury and for this reason Corbinelli's testament is of particular interest.

---

di non molto buono aquisito'). According to Vespasiano, Cosimo consulted Pope Eugenius IV († 1447), then resident in Florence, who advised him to endow the Observant Dominican convent of San Marco by way of expiation (Vespasiano, *Le vite*, 2: 177–178).

[38]Dante, *Inferno* 17.43–78. On the purses slung round the necks of the usurers, Dante recognized the arms of the Ubbriachi and the Gianfigliazzi. Luiso, 'Su le tracce di un usuraio fiorentino,' maintains that the latter was Catello di Rosso Gianfigliazzi († ca. 1283), who accumulated a fortune as a banker and moneychanger in Avignon and was made a knight on returning to Florence.

[39]Le Goff, 'The Usurer and Purgatory'; and Le Goff, *Your Money or Your Life*.

[40]De Roover, *The Rise and Decline of the Medici Bank*, 10–14; de Roover, *La pensée économique des scolastiques*, 76–93; de Roover, 'Cambium ad Venetias'; and de Roover, 'The Scholastic Attitude Towards Trade and Entrepreneurship.' For a review of de Roover's account of the usury prohibition, see Kirshner, 'Raymond de Roover on Scholastic Economic Thought,' 26–33.

[41]Galassi, 'Buying a Passport to Heaven.'

[42]Hobsbawm, 'Historians and Economists: II,' 115.

Corbinelli and His Scruples

The Corbinelli could trace their history back to the foundation of the guild republic, when, in June 1286, the civil lawyer messer Albizzo Corbinelli was drawn for the priorate. Corbinelli thereafter routinely appeared in the republic's highest offices and by the early fifteenth century they numbered among the most powerful families in Santo Spirito quarter.[43] The family's political influence had a solid material basis: wool merchants, merchant bankers and landowners, they were assessed the third richest household in Santo Spirito until the patrimony of Tommaso Corbinelli († 1376–1377) was divided around 1400 among his five sons, Bartolomeo († 1427–1430), Giovanni († 1438), Angelo, Parigi († 1429–1430) and Antonio († 1425).[44] It is a measure of the family's wealth that even after the division four of the brothers, among them Angelo, ranked among the top three percent of *prestanziati* in Santo Spirito.[45]

Born in 1373, Angelo went into the family business, investing in a wool *bottega* (workshop) and serving three terms as a consul of the Lana guild.[46] Not as politically conspicuous as his older brothers, Corbinelli was nevertheless active in public affairs: he was successfully drawn for the May–June priorate in 1412; served in 1413–1414 on the university board of governors (*ufficiali dello studio*), in 1417 as an *operaio* (commissioner) of the *Opera di Santa Maria del Fiore* and in 1418 on the commission for internal security (*otto di balìa*).[47] In 1404, he married Filippa di Lorenzo Bardi-

---

[43] On the family's history and status, see Martines, 'Addenda to the Life of Antonio Corbinelli,' 4–5; and Martines, *The Social World of the Florentine Humanists*, 319–320. For the complete record of Corbinelli among major officeholders, see Herlihy et al., eds., *Online Tratte of Officeholders*.

[44] Martines, 'Addenda to the Life of Antonio Corbinelli,' 4. On Bartolomeo and Antonio di Tommaso, see also *DBI* 28, s.v. 'Corbinelli, Bartolomeo' by Molho; and ibid., s.v. 'Corbinelli, Antonio' by Molho. Giovanni, Angelo, Parigi and Antonio were the sons of Tommaso by his second wife, Bartolomea di Piero Pasini. Giovanni was successfully drawn consul of the Lana (wool manufacturers') guild 15 April 1438 and was dead by 20 September 1438, when he was drawn for the *Mercanzia*; Parigi was successfully drawn for the *Dodici Buonuomini* 12 December 1429 and was dead on 15 December 1430, when he was drawn consul of the Lana guild (Herlihy et al., eds., *Online Tratte of Officeholders*).

[45] Martines, 'Addenda to the Life of Antonio Corbinelli,' 5–6; *DBI* 28, s.v. 'Corbinelli, Antonio' by Molho. The *prestanze* assessments of 1403, after the division of the patrimony, are supplied by Martines, *The Social World of the Florentine Humanists*, 362–364, appendix 2, table 4.

[46] Corbinelli was successfully drawn for Lana consulships in 1414, 1417 and 1418 (Herlihy et al., eds., *Online Tratte of Officeholders*).

[47] For these and minor offices held by Corbinelli, see *DBI* 28, s.v. 'Corbinelli, Angelo' by Molho. For Corbinelli's service on the university board, see also Davies, *Florence and its University*, 145. Corbinelli was elected *operaio* of the cathedral

Gualterotti (b. 1390–1391), a member of another powerful Santo Spirito merchant clan,[48] by whom he had six children: Bernardo (b. 1409–1410), Tommaso (b. 1412–1413), Corbinello († 1419–1423), Giulia († 1419–1423), Bartolomea (b. 1414–1415) and Angelo (b. 1419).[49]

Angelo di Tommaso and his younger brother Antonio, to whom he was particularly attached, are best known because of their connections with civic humanism. Both were disciples of the chancellor Coluccio Salutati († 1406) and both attended the public courses in Greek literature offered by Emmanuel Chrysoloras († 1415) and Guarino da Verona († 1460).[50] Guarino dedicated his translation of Plutarch's treatise on education (1411) to Angelo, and the two maintained a correspondence after Guarino left Florence in 1414.[51] Antonio assembled an important collection of classical texts which he bequeathed to the Badia monastery.[52] Angelo's humanist interests attracted the hostility of the Camaldolese monk Giovanni da San Miniato, who, in 1405, addressed to him a letter

---

works commission for the term 1 January–30 April 1417; see Haines, *Gli Anni della Cupola*, doc. o0201070.001va; accessed online 25 July 2002. Additional information on Corbinelli's service as commissioner is contained in the following: docs. o0201070.003ve, –.005e, –.008vb, –.009vc, –.010a, –.014ve, –.015e, –.015vb. Prominent in the Lana guild, which was responsible for the cathedral works, the Corbinelli frequently served on the board of commissioners. Angelo's brother Giovanni, for example, was a commissioner from 1 July–31 October 1418 (ibid., doc. o.0201074.002a).

[48]Angelo and his three full brothers, Giovanni, Parigi and Antonio, acknowledged receipt of a dowry of five hundred florins from Lorenzo di Totto Bardi-Gualterotti on 13 January 1404, and the marriage was solemnized the following day (ASF, Notarile 9035, fol. 49r–v). In her *catasto* declaration of July 1427, Filippa gave her age as thirty-six (ASF, Catasto 18, fol. 1288r; Catasto 65, fol. 49r–v).

[49]*DBI* 28, s.v. 'Corbinelli, Angelo' by Molho. The ages of Bernardo, Tommaso, Bartolomea and Angelo di Angelo were supplied in the *catasto* declaration filed by Corbinelli's heirs in July 1427 as eighteen, fifteen, twelve and eight respectively (ASF, Catasto 17, fol. 236r; Catasto 65, fol. 91r). Giulia and Corbinello appear to have died by 1423, since Filippa makes no reference to them in her testament of 9 December 1423 (ASF, Notarile 9042, fol. 120r–v).

[50]On Corbinelli's membership of Salutati's circle, see Martines, *The Social World of the Florentine Humanists*, 318. On the government's appointment of Chrysoloras to a public lectureship in 1396, see Davies, *Florence and its University*, 15, nn. 45 and 46; on Guarino, who taught privately in Florence from 1410–1414, see ibid., 82. Guarino lodged with Antonio during part of his Florentine sojourn and was an intimate of the Corbinelli family (Martines, *The Social World of the Florentine Humanists*, 319).

[51]Guarino da Verona, *Epistolario di Guarino Veronese*, 1: 15–16. Three other letters of Guarino to Angelo, dated 1417 and 1418, are edited at ibid., 168–169, 182–183, 192.

[52]On the library, see Blum, *La biblioteca della Badia fiorentina*.

attacking pagan poetry, which in turn provoked a famous exchange on the new learning, first between Salutati and Giovanni and subsequently between the humanist and the influential Dominican preacher Giovanni Dominici († 1419).[53]

Nothing in Corbinelli's published biography explains his reservations about the public debt. The relevant passage of the testament (33) reads as follows:

> The testator stated and declared that he never bought credits in any of the *monti* of the commune of Florence, although he is indeed described as a creditor in the books of the *monti* of the said commune for several sums of money and gold florins on account of *prestanze* and obligations he himself paid as well as those paid by his family and brothers. And because the testator himself often witnessed many masters, bachelors and other theologians dispute whether it was licit to accept payments on the aforesaid sums, and because he both saw and heard it said that highly judicious masters and theologians hold contrary opinions on this question, he was unable to be certain in his conscience. Wishing therefore as much as possible to unburden his conscience, he willed, prescribed and directed that if at any time a decision or declaration shall be made by the Roman church or a council or a commission of doctors appointed by the Roman church or its pastors to make a decision or declaration on whether the aforesaid payments, gifts and compensation, which citizens universally receive from the commune on account of their fiscal obligations, are licit or not, then his heirs should act in every respect in conformity with the decree, decision, determination or conclusion of the Roman church or its council or the commission of doctors to whom the resolution of the said question has been entrusted, with the exception of the legacies and bequests noted above and below.

Corbinelli began by distancing himself from the debt market, declaring that he never bought or sold credits by way of speculation or investment; and a sampling of the records of 1404, 1411 and 1418 suggests that this was true.[54] As was noted earlier, the market was the most controversial aspect of the *monte* system, condemned by critics as a thinly disguised form of voluntary lending. But the market also had weighty defenders. In the opinion of Lorenzo Ridolfi, a prominent jurist, university lecturer and member of the ruling elite, sellers and buyers of debt, and even brokers who paid the assessments of distressed *prestanziati* in return for

---

[53]See Ullman, 'A Letter of Giovanni da San Miniato to Angelo Corbinelli'; and Salutati, *Epistolario di Coluccio Salutati*, 4: 170–205. Salutati's response to the critique of pagan learning advanced by Giovanni Dominici in his *Lucula noctis* (1405), is at ibid., 205–240. For an account of the controversy, see Witt, *Hercules at the Crossroads*, 403–413, esp. 408.

[54]I reviewed ASF, Monte comune o delle graticole 3059 (3 January 1404–30 June 1404); 3101 (4 July 1411–29 December 1411); and 3137 (1 July 1418–30 June 1419).

title to the principal and future interest, were engaged in a licit traffic in rights and claims rather than a usurious trade in debt. Ridolfi delivered his judgment in an influential *Treatise on Usury* completed in 1404, a text almost certainly known to Corbinelli, as was its author, who was Corbinelli's neighbor in Santo Spirito and fellow amateur humanist.[55] Despite his endorsement of the market, Ridolfi felt obliged to conclude his analysis with a reservation that expressed the discomfort with which patricians such as Corbinelli—and apparently Ridolfi himself—viewed the market:

> Nevertheless in doubtful cases the safer way should always be chosen, and therefore I recommend that those who can do so should abstain [from the market] . . . as indeed I myself have always done.[56]

Since he did not play the market, Corbinelli's reservations related solely to credits he held because of loans he or his relatives had been obliged to make to the government. His uncertainty was inspired by his own observation that there was no consensus among theologians on the moral status of *prestanziati*. Nor, as he accurately observed, had the ecclesiastical authorities delivered a definitive judgment on the matter. Unfortunately, I have not been able to identify the theologians Corbinelli might have heard dispute the problem. Giovanni Dominici does not appear to have preached on the subject, and Bernardino of Siena would not compose his Lenten sermon on usury and public debt until the mid-1430s, some fifteen years after Corbinelli's death.[57] As was noted above, two Augustinians of Santo Spirito, a convent with which Corbinelli had close ties and where he was to be buried in the family chapel (3), had condemned the compensation of compulsory lenders in the 1370s, but whether this remained the position of the Florentine Augustinians in 1419 is unclear.

Anecdotal evidence nevertheless suggests that laymen were keenly aware of the issues at stake in the controversy. Matteo Villani, for example,

---

[55] On Ridolfi's biography and connections to civic humanism, see Armstrong, *Usury and Public Debt*, 7–27, 104–108. Ridolfi's analysis of the market is at ibid., 236–257. For a discussion of these passages, see ibid., 93–97, 110.

[56] 'Quia tamen in dubio uia tutior est eligenda, consulo quod abstineant qui aliud facere possunt . . . ut et ego hucusque feci' (ed. Armstrong, *Usury and Public Debt*, 249).

[57] I consulted the collection of Dominici's vernacular sermons in the Biblioteca Riccardiana, cod. 1301. For an analysis of this collection from the perspective of civic politics, see Debby, 'Political Views in the Preaching of Giovanni Dominici.' On Bernardino, see above, p. 181, n. 28. It should be noted, however, that in his extant writings Bernardino did not question the right of compulsory lenders to receive compensation; see Bernardino, *Sermo* XLI in *Opera omnia*, 4: 309–316.

attests that the original dispute of 1353–1354 provoked widespread public interest, remarking that because of disagreements among the various masters

> many people remained in doubt about these contracts; and many were in evident agreement with the arguments of master Francesco [da Empoli] and thus without pangs of conscience they sold and bought [credits], trading with one another as they would merchandise.[58]

In 1381, the poet and *novelliere* Franco Sacchetti († 1400) recorded in *Sposizione* 35 of his *Sposizioni di Vangeli*, a private collection of meditations on the liturgical readings for Lent, his own (rather eccentric) interpretation of the contradictory moral advice on the public debt he heard from the pulpit.[59] The most vivid impression of the controversy's impact is provided by Vespasiano da Bisticci's account of an encounter between Bernardino of Siena and the humanist and statesman Giannozzo Manetti († 1459) some time in the 1430s:

> [San Bernardino] condemned without exception every vice, but especially the damnable abyss of usury, the vice that consumes whole cities, lineages and provinces. Having preached one morning at Santa Maria del Fiore on contracts and restitution, and especially on the *monte* and the dowry fund, he went that evening, as was his custom, to the bookseller, where by chance he ran into messer Giannozzo Manetti. Manetti said to San Bernardino, 'You've consigned us all to damnation!' But he replied, 'I damn nobody; it's the sins and weakness of men that damn them.' Then Manetti asked San Bernardino about the dowry contract in which the capital is guaranteed. San Bernardino proved with strong reasoning that the contract was highly illicit. He added that the contract for girls' dowries in which the capital is guaranteed was more wicked than that of a Jew who lent behind the red curtain [i.e. at usury]. And so by powerful arguments and with great humanity he resolved all the objections that Manetti raised so that messer Giannozzo and all those who were with him were left completely satisfied.[60]

---

[58] Villani, *Cronica*, 3.106, 1: 462; trans. Kirshner, "'*Ubi est ille?*'," 559.
[59] On the context of this text and for an analysis, see Kirshner, "'*Ubi est ille?*'"
[60] Vespasiano, *Le vite*, 1: 250. The sermon, which does not appear among Bernardino's published works, was preached between 1425 and 1441, but probably after 1433 (Kirshner, *Pursuing Honor While Avoiding Sin*, 31, n. 97). Created in 1425, the dowry fund (*monte delle doti*) was a sort of insurance scheme. A father deposited a sum in the name of an unmarried daughter: if she was married at term, her husband was guaranteed a cash dowry representing principal and compound interest; meanwhile the government devoted the deposit to amortizing the *monte comune*. Rights in the fund were non-transferable and the deposit reverted to the government if the girl died or remained a spinster. The interest rate varied depending on the term and was periodically raised; by 1433 a five-year term earned 18.47 percent (ibid., 16–20). On the objectives and administration of the fund, see

Vespasiano unfortunately failed to record Bernardino's 'strong reasoning,' but the exchange between the preacher and the lay intellectual testifies to the seriousness with which those most implicated in the operation of the *monte* treated the arguments of the controversialists.

Corbinelli's references to a general council and commission of theological experts probably reflected discussions at the Council of Constance, which had adjourned in 1417. In 1416 the abbot of the Cologne Charterhouse appealed to the council on behalf of his order for a ruling on the licitness of annuities (*rentes* or *census*), which several Carthusian houses had purchased from municipal governments seeking to raise capital. The council itself refrained from making a judgment, but the committee of seven jurists and four theologians to whom the problem was referred declared annuities licit provided sellers could redeem them at face value.[61] Several theorists assimilated *monte* credits to *census*, interpreting the purchase of credits on the market as the purchase of rights over future communal income.[62] The fact, however, that credits

---

also Kirshner and Molho, 'The Dowry Fund and the Marriage Market'; and Molho, *Marriage Alliance in Late Medieval Florence*, 27–178. Florentine statutes required that the entrances to Jewish pawnshops be marked by a red curtain (Kirshner, *Pursuing Honor While Avoiding Sin*, 34, n. 105). On Bernardino's anti-Semitism, see most recently Mormando, *The Preacher's Demons*, 164–218; on Jewish moneylenders in particular, ibid., 182–191. On Christian attitudes to Jewish moneylending more generally, see Shatzmiller, *Shylock Reconsidered*, 43–103. On the regulation of Jewish moneylending in Florence and its territories, see Molho, 'A Note on Jewish Moneylenders in Tuscany'; and Gow and Griffiths, 'Pope Eugenius IV and Jewish Money-Lending in Florence.' For a profile of Manetti, see Martines, *April Blood*, 54–61.

[61] Schnapper, 'Les rentes chez les théologiens et les canonistes,' 976. Among the theological commissioners were such luminaries as Jean Gerson († 1429) and Pierre d'Ailly († 1420); the sole dissenter was the Cardinal of Florence, the eminent canonist Franciscus de Zabarellis († 1417; not Fredericus, as Schnapper reports; see Eubel, *Hierarchia Catholica Medii Aevi*, 251). See also Schnapper, *Les rentes au XVIe siècle*, 65–78. *Rentes* were subsequently endorsed by bulls of Martin V (1425), Nicholas V (1452) and Callistus III (1455), who specified that the annuities must be based on the real property of the seller, should pay no more than ten percent a year and be redeemable at their nominal value. For discussions of these decrees and the early history of *rentes*, see also Noonan, *The Scholastic Analysis of Usury*, 154–170, 160–161; van der Wee, 'Monetary, Credit and Banking Systems,' 303–304; Tracy, *A Financial Revolution in the Hapsburg Netherlands*, 7–70; and Munro, 'The Late-Medieval Origins of the Modern Financial Revolution.' I am grateful to John Munro for these references and for providing me with a draft version of his paper.

[62] Nicholas de Anglia analyzed *monte* credits as *census*; see Kirshner, 'The Moral Theology of Public Finance,' 60–61, 70. Peter of Ancharano took a similar position; see Kirshner, 'Reading Bernardino's Sermon,' 565–572. Lapo da Castiglionchio

were discountable and in practice non-redeemable led others to reject the analogy: Lorenzo Ridolfi, Giovanni Capistrano († 1456) and James of Erfurt († 1465) considered government annuities open to fraud except under very strict conditions.[63] Like most of the Florentine social and political elite, Corbinelli was almost certainly a conciliarist, and his deference to any future ruling on the *monte* probably reflected contemporary expectations that the councils, which had resolved the Great Schism, would prove to be agents of moral reform in the secular sphere as well.[64]

It may be significant that Corbinelli did not include a similar declaration in his testament of 1417. The imminence of death often inspires self-examination, but in Corbinelli's case an additional explanation is suggested by his recent service on the *Mercanzia*, the Florentine merchant tribunal.[65] In 1414 the *Mercanzia* created a special 'commission on illicit contracts' (*offitiales super illicitis contractibus*) to review potentially usurious agreements, and Corbinelli served at least two terms in 1417 and 1418 as a commissioner representing the Lana guild.[66] Although the operations of

---

considered government annuities questionable, but approved them nevertheless; see *Allegationes*, allegatio 137, fol. 164rb–vb. For a discussion, see Armstrong, *Usury and Public Debt*, 98.

[63] See Armstrong, *Usury and Public Debt*, 98–99, 257–260; and Schnapper, 'Les rentes chez les théologiens et les canonistes,' 979–980. On Giovanni Capistrano and James of Erfurt, see ibid., 980–981.

[64] On conciliarist sentiments among the Florentine elite, see Martines, *Lawyers and Statecraft*, 286–298; and Brucker, *The Civic World of Early Renaissance Florence*, 295–300, 417. The council had a strongly reformist agenda, declaring in the decree *Sacrosancta* (29 May 1415) that its mandate included not only the papal schism but heresy and the reform of the church in head and members (Alberigo et al., eds., *Conciliorum oecumenicorum decreta*, 392–393). The decree *Frequens* (9 October 1417) provided for the convention of a council after five, seven and thereafter every ten years (ibid., 414–415). The next council was convened in 1423 at Pavia (later transferred to Siena), and a third at Basel in 1431; neither addressed the issue of public debt.

[65] I am grateful to Luca Boschetto for this suggestion and for referring me to the relevant documents. Boschetto is currently preparing a study of the fifteenth-century *Mercanzia* that will deal with the tribunal's role in regulating usury. On the fourteenth-century *Mercanzia*, see Najemy, 'Guild Republicanism in Trecento Florence,' 62–63; Najemy, 'The Dialogue of Power in Florentine Politics,' 269–288; and Astorri, *La Mercanzia a Firenze*.

[66] For the communal provision establishing the *offitiales super illicitis contractibus*, see ASF, Provvisioni, Registri 103, fols. 50v–51v; and the register of the commission itself, ASF, Mercanzia 19, fols. 1r–4v. The last entry in the register is dated 13 June 1420 (ibid., fol. 12r). Corbinelli's election on 16 February 1418 is recorded at ASF, Mercanzia 261, fol. 29v; his presence on commissions rendering judgments at ASF, Mercanzia 19, fol. 6r (18 March 1417) and fol. 7v (10 May 1418).

the *monte comune* did not come within the commission's terms of reference, which were exclusively concerned with commercial contracts concealing usurious loans, it is possible that Corbinelli was exposed to debates over the debt while seeking advice from theological experts on other agreements.

In the light of Corbinelli's humanist associations, it is worth noting that his declaration shows no traces of the well-known humanist apologetic for wealth. In studies of the first generation of civic humanists, Hans Baron and Eugenio Garin emphasized how the humanists' exaltation of the active life and republican virtue involved a rejection of Franciscan and Stoic, that is, medieval, ideals of poverty in favour of an affirmation of wealth and material acquisition that certainly embraced institutions such as the *monte comune*.[67] Corbinelli's reservations about the public debt therefore reflected a traditional ethic that was in conflict with his intellectual inclinations.

If the precise inspiration of Corbinelli's scruples is unclear, his instructions to his heirs were not: they should conform to any judgment delivered by the Roman church, a general council or a theological commission appointed by church or council for the purpose of deciding whether profit on *monte* shares was licit. In the event of a censure, this would represent an extraordinary sacrifice, since a significant proportion of Corbinelli's capital was tied up in government debt. According to two post mortem inventories of assets compiled by Corbinelli's executors and the information his heirs supplied in 1427 to the *catasto* officials, the estate included *monte* credits and *paghe sostenute* with a nominal value of at least four thousand florins (see table 1).

Corbinelli's instruction applied only to the residuum of the estate: he explicitly exempted legacies to individuals and to religious and charitable foundations. Several of these were to be paid in cash: a florin to each of the witnesses (4); ten florins to the cathedral works commission (5–6)[68];

---

[67]See Baron, 'Franciscan Poverty and Civic Wealth as Factors in the Rise of Humanistic Thought,' revised as 'Franciscan Poverty and Civic Wealth in the Shaping of Trecento Humanistic Thought' and 'Civic Wealth and the New Values of the Renaissance.' See also Garin, *Italian humanism*, 43–46. For a discussion of the issue, see Jurdjevic, 'Virtue, Commerce, and the Enduring Florentine Republican Moment.' On the affinities between civic humanism and Lorenzo Ridolfi's apologetic for the *monte*, see Armstrong, *Usury and Public Debt*, 107–111.

[68]A provision of 6 December 1296 required every testator in the city and *contado* to bequeath at least twenty *soldi* to the *Opera di Santa Maria del Fiore* for the construction of the new cathedral. The provision is edited in Guasti, *Santa Maria del Fiore*, 458. It was renewed in 1392; see Haines, 'Firenze e il finanziamento della cattedrale e del campanile,' 74–76. Corbinelli's bequest was unusually generous. I am grateful to Margaret Haines for these references and for the last observation.

a hundred florins to endow poor girls (12)[69]; ten florins to Santo Spirito to underwrite an annual liturgical commemoration and meal (*pietanza*) (15)[70]; and twenty-five florins to his sister and to each of his full brothers (26–29). Similarly, Corbinelli allocated cash dowries of a thousand florins to each of his legitimate daughters (22), two hundred florins to place his illegitimate daughter Alessandra in a convent or third order (25)[71] and eighty to a hundred florins to endow his manumitted slave Margherita (36).[72]

The remaining bequests, which are listed in table 2, were payable either in cash or in *monte* credits, although the four whose execution can be confirmed were paid in the form of credits. In accordance with his moral preoccupations, Corbinelli imposed restrictions on such legacies.[73] Credits left to religious foundations and hospitals could not be sold or otherwise alienated but were to be held in perpetuity as interest-bearing endowments (7–11, 13–14). Credits bequeathed to individuals were also inalienable but with the further condition that they died with the legatees, after which the debt was extinguished and the government forgiven its obligations. The only exception was the reimbursement of Filippa's dowry of five hundred florins in the form of *monte* credits, on which Corbinelli placed no restriction since this sum by law reverted to his wife's control on his death (16).[74] But the supplement of 620 florins in *monte di Pisa*

A provision of 28 March 1298 required every testator to bequeath an unspecified sum to the commune for the construction and maintenance of the city's defensive walls; the heirs of those who failed to do so were fined a hundred *soldi* (Davidsohn, *Forschungen*, 4: 449).

[69]A popular act of piety designed to preserve the honor of girls who otherwise would be unable to contract a respectable marriage. For a discussion, see Kirshner, *Pursuing Honor While Avoiding Sin*, 3–15. On such legacies in late fourteenth-century Florentine testaments, see Bonanno et al., 'I legati "pro anima,"' 194–195, and the data on frequency and value at 192–193, table 1, and 200–201, table 3. For the twelfth to the fifteenth century, see Cohn, *The Cult of Remembrance*, 65–67; and the data at 68–69, table 4.

[70]On *pietanze*, see Strocchia, 'Burials in Renaissance Florence,' 330–358; and Henderson, *Piety and Charity*, 166–168.

[71]On illegitimates, now see Kuehn, *Illegitimacy in Renaissance Florence*.

[72]On slavery in late medieval Tuscany, see Boni and Delort, 'Des esclaves toscans'; Delort, 'Du servage et de l'esclavage'; and Delort, 'Note sur le vocabulaire de la servitude et de l'esclavage en Toscane.' I am grateful to Christiane Klapisch-Zuber and Allen Grieco for these references. For examples of manumission, see Origo, 'The Domestic Enemy,' 345, 351–353.

[73]For examples of restrictions on legacies in Florence, Pisa, Siena, Arezzo, Perugia and Assisi, see Cohn, 'Last Wills: Family, Women, and the Black Death in Central Italy.'

[74]On 7 September 1423, Filippa, with the consent of her guardian (*mundualdus*) Bartolomeo di Tommaso Corbinelli, directed the *monte* officials to transfer to her

and *monte dei prestanzoni* credits Corbinelli left to his widow in addition to her dowry represented only a life interest or usufruct (*ususfructus*) (17–19).[75] He attached identical conditions to the sums he bequeathed to his daughters (additional to their dowries), his confessor and his physician (24–25, 34).[76]

The structure of Corbinelli's legacies illustrates a more general social process and throws into relief the dilemma faced by Corbinelli and others who shared his scruples. As many historians have observed, by the early fifteenth century *monte* credits had come to represent a big and growing share of the wealth of the Florentine possessing classes.[77] The final assessment of Corbinelli's heirs in the 1427 *catasto* survey provides an impression of the ratio of debt credits to other assets in the estate. Out of net assets of 11,358 florins, 4472 represented liquid wealth, 3294 real estate and 3592— just under a third—public debt.[78] Moreover, because

---

account credits to the value of five hundred florins in settlement of the dowry (ASF, Notarile 9040, fols. 116v, 117r). The legal guardianship of Florentine women is discussed by Kuehn, '"Cum consensu mundualdi."' On the dowry rights of widows and for bibliography, see Kuehn, 'Figli, madri, mogli e vedove.' On Florence, see also Klapisch-Zuber, 'The "Cruel Mother."'

[75] In her 1427 *catasto* declaration, Filippa reported fl. 284 in the *monte di Pisa* and fl. 313 in the *monte dei prestanzoni* bequeathed to her by Angelo, noting that they would revert to the commune on her death (Catasto 18, fol. 1288r; and Catasto 65, fol. 91r).

[76] Corbinelli directed that ownership of the supplementary legacies to his two legitimate daughters not pass to their future husbands. On non-dotal assets, which, unlike the dowry, remained in the possession and under the control of the woman, see Kirshner, 'Materials for a Gilded Cage.' For a legal dispute regarding such property, see Kirshner and Pluss, 'Two fourteenth-century opinions on dowries, paraphernalia and non-dotal goods.'

[77] See Herlihy and Klapisch-Zuber, *Tuscans and Their Families*, 101–103, and the data presented at 102, figure 4.2. The increasing pressure on private assets is a central theme of Molho, *Florentine Public Finances*, 84–192; Molho, 'The State and Public Finance'; Conti, *L'imposta diretta*, 1–90; and Palmieri, *Ricordi fiscali*. See also the comments of Kirshner, 'Reading Bernardino's Sermon,' 558; and Martines, 'Forced Loans,' 300–310.

[78] The figures are from Herlihy and Klapisch-Zuber, eds., *Census and Property Survey of Florentine Domains in the Province of Tuscany*, accessed online 15 August 2002. Significant assets were, however, exempt from assessment, notably the family domicile and moveables. Liquid assets included cash, debts payable, working and fixed capital minus outstanding obligations. It should also be noted that the figures represent *assessed* values: in the case of real estate this resulted in a figure somewhat below market value; debt credits, on the other hand, were assessed on a scale that considerably inflated their market value. On the calculation of assets, see Herlihy and Klapisch-Zuber, *Tuscans and Their Families*, 13–17; and Conti, *L'imposta diretta*, 138–149. For the scales used by the *catasto* officials to assess

of their transferable character, credits had come to function as a kind of surrogate money in an extraordinary range of transactions. As Corbinelli's testament itself bears witness, credits endowed religious and charitable foundations and furnished dependents with income. In other contexts they could be used to pay fines and taxes, to provide collateral for loans, to settle debts and even to pay *prestanze* assessments.[79] Whatever moral reservations Corbinelli and other citizens might have entertained about the *monte comune*, the 'dull compulsion of economic relations' ensured that they had little choice but to put the value tied up in their credits to work in various ways.[80]

Other Examples

How typical was Angelo Corbinelli? At the present stage of our knowledge of Florentine testaments, it is difficult to generalize, but the existing scholarship and my own research suggest that even if Corbinelli was not typical, he was at least not unique in his scruples.

A review of the remaining testaments in Giacomini's register yields no example of a declaration similar to that of Corbinelli or, indeed, of the restrictions he placed on his legacies of *monte* credits.[81] Nor do Corbinelli's brothers and widow appear to have shared his reservations.[82]

---

debt shares and agricultural products in 1427, see Palmieri, *Ricordi fiscali*, 16–17. The *nominal* value of *monte* credits held by Corbinelli's heirs was fl. 6096 s. 19 d. 3 (ASF, Catasto 65, fol. 90r).

[79] On the use of credits to secure loans, see Goldthwaite, 'Local Banking in Renaissance Florence,' 25–31. For examples of the payment of *prestanze* with credits, see Kirshner, '"*Ubi est ille?*",' 564–565; and Palmieri, *Ricordi fiscali*, 217–252, passim. A good example of the use of *monte* credits to settle a debt occurs in the codicil of Nanna di Gasparo degli Alberti, widow of Lando di Lando, 7 March 1427 (ASF, Notarile 9042, fol. 152v). For additional observations on the secondary uses of credits, see Kirshner, 'Reading Bernardino's Sermon,' 548–549; and Kirshner, 'Encumbering Private Claims to Public Debt,' 20. For the late fifteenth century, see Kirshner and Klerman, 'The Seven Percent Fund of Renaissance Florence.'

[80] Marx, *Das Kapital*, vol. 1, ch. 24.3, p. 765.

[81] ASF, Notarile 9042 contains an additional 132 testaments and codicils redacted by Giacomini between 1411 and 1431. Although most of the estates must have included *monte* credits, only thirty-five referred explicitly to their disposition. Nine of the thirty-five created life usufructs, but on the death of the usufructuaries, credits reverted to the patrimony or, in three cases, passed to religious foundations. In all cases, credits were treated as sources of perpetual income. One testament, that of Briada di Niccolò Soderini, widow of Giovanni di Sandro Portinari, 3 July 1417, left *paghe sostenute* of 1415–1419 to the commune (fol. 52r).

[82] See the successive versions of Parigi di Tommaso's testament at ASF, Notarile 14663, fols. 189r–192r (19 June 1421), fols. 221r–224v (1 August 1423) and fols.

Two published cases, however, indicate that conscientious scruples were not unknown. In a testament contested by his heirs in 1375, the Franciscan fra Francesco di Tommaso de' Bardi left the commune seventy florins 'wrongly received and held by him as gift, damages or interest on his credit in the "old *monte*" of the said commune.'[83] Four years later, on the eve of his execution for treason, Giannozzo Sacchetti, Franco Sacchetti's brother, repaid the commune three hundred florins in interest he had received on his credits, declaring to the *monte* officials that he was worried about his salvation.[84]

The records of bequests to the hospital of Santa Maria Nuova between 1340 and 1450 allow us to supplement these scattered indications with additional examples, six of which are edited below in appendix 2.[85] The closest parallel to Corbinelli's declaration and instruction occurs in the testament dictated on 30 June 1383 by the notary ser Domenico Allegri († 1383–1387):[86]

> Considering that he had been and still was described as a creditor of the commune of Florence in the books or registers of the *monte* of the said commune on account of certain *prestanze* for certain quantities and sums of money on which he had received payments, as had other creditors of the aforesaid *monti*, and although the said testator believed that he was not obligated in any way with respect to the aforesaid payments, nevertheless,

---

319r–321v (17 April 1428), which contain extensive bequests of *monte* credits in the form of life usufructs and perpetual endowments of religious foundations. Antonio di Tommaso bequeathed the residue of his credits in the *monte comune* after the deduction of other legacies to Santa Maria Nuova on the condition that the hospital support his servant Andrea and a group of paupers nominated by three trustees; after the death of the trustees the credit was at the disposition of the hospital (ASF, OSMN 70, fol. 112v). Corbinelli's widow Filippa made no reference to her *monte* credits in her testament; see ASF, Notarile 9042, fol. 120r–v.

[83]'Communi Florentie reliquit et legavit LXX florenos de auro per eum, ut dixit, habitos et receptos indebite pro dono, dampnis, seu interesse sui crediti montis veteris communis predicti' (ed. Trexler, 'Florence, by the grace of the Lord Pope,' 150, n. 118). As the context makes clear, the date of 1357 in Trexler's note is a misprint for 1375. The 'old *monte*' was a term applied to the original consolidation of 1343–1345 to distinguish it from new funds created in the 1350s and 1360s.

[84]Kirshner, '"*Ubi est ille?*",' 580.

[85]I am grateful to Julius Kirshner for directing me to this source and providing several of the references. The following registers were reviewed for this paper: ASF, OSMN 60 (1340–1379); OSMN 65 (1363–1368); OSMN 67 (1377–1393); OSMN 68 (1389–1420); and OSMN 70 (1419–1488). The series contains copies of or extracts from testaments in which Santa Maria Nuova was named as heir, legatee or executor.

[86]The approximate date of Allegri's death is derived from data in Herlihy et al., eds., *Online Tratte of Officeholders*.

in order to lay to rest any doubt or scruple, if the said testator was obligated to make restitution of all or any of the payments and/or sums of money that he had received or would receive from the said commune, he left and bequeathed to the said commune of Florence every credit and every quantity of money which according to the books or registers of whatsoever *monte* or *prestanza* of the said commune the testator should receive or have from the aforesaid commune of Florence at the time of the said testator's death by reason of, in consequence of or on the occasion of any *prestanza* or *estimo* imposed on the said testator by the commune of Florence (appendix 2, no. 1).

A procedure for determining such moral liability is suggested by the testament of Lorenzo dei Benci, who restored interest paid to him by the government since 1360

> up to the amount that ser Giovanni di Cristoforo, priest and rector of the church of San Simone in Florence, shall decide or conclude in accordance with his own conscience that the testator should restore to the aforesaid commune (appendix 2, no. 2).

Corbinelli included a similar provision in his own will with regard to his commercial profits, granting Bartolomeo Corbinelli and his confessor master Agostino da Roma full authority (*balìa*) to review his account books and to make restitution from his estate within one year of 'anything that the said Angelo unjustly received or owned . . . in accordance with their own consciences and for the unburdening of the said testator's conscience' (31–32).

Few testators were as articulate as Domenico Allegri and Angelo Corbinelli: cancellations of all or part of the government's debt with no explanatory comment were not uncommon. They were often prefixed by formulas such as 'for the love of God and for the relief of his conscience,' which suggest that the motives were moral rather than simply patriotic.[87] For example, a testament dictated by the shoemaker Francesco di Lapo in August 1383 included the following direction:

> Since the aforesaid testator must depart this present world, for the relief of his soul and conscience he left and bequeathed to the commune of Florence

---

[87]See ASF, OSMN 60, fol. 130r (testament of Niccolò di Bartolo Montagliari, 21 July 1363); ASF, OSMN 65, fol. 41v (testament of Tuccio Falconieri, 14 December 1365); ASF, OSMN 67, fol. 88r (testament of Giovanni di Ricovero, 24 September 1382); fol. 121v (testament of Lapaccia di Alesso Martelli, widow of Giovanni di Nuto, 4 March 1378); fol. 178r (testament of Francesco di Donato, vintner, 16 March 1384); ASF, OSMN 68, fol. 149v (testament of Gregorio di ser Francesco, 4 February 1383); fol. 213r (testament of Niccolosa di Bartolo Chelli, widow of Bardo di Francesco Ammirati, 3 January 1409); ASF, OSMN 70, fol. 156v (testament of ser Jacopo di Domenico da Vinci, notary, 5 October 1435).

fifty gold florins out of the monies credited to his account and under his name in the books and registers of the *monte* of the commune of Florence, for which sums he is creditor of the commune of Florence and which sums the said commune owes him. And he gave his permission and consent to the scribes and notaries of the *monte* of the commune of Florence and to me, Domenico, the undersigned notary, as a public person acting on their behalf, to absolve and liberate the commune up to the said amount of fifty gold florins and to remove from the account of the said Francesco and from the books and registers of the *monte* the said amount of fifty gold florins and to transfer them to the authority of the commune of Florence and to inscribe them under its name (appendix 2, no. 3).

It would, of course, be a mistake to read too much into such pious formulas, which were often prompted by the redacting notary and often used to introduce non-pious legacies to relatives and acquaintances.[88] In other cases, however, we can be more confident that the testator was acting from motives of conscience. In her testament of 27 January 1380, Nora di ser Lippo Nerini, the widow of Francesco Buonaccorsi, bequeathed a third of her total debt holdings of 630 florins to the government so that, as she put it, 'the gift or interest that the said commune gives to creditors may not form part of the present legacy and bequest,' a provision that probably reflected doubts about the legitimacy of such interest payments (appendix 2, no. 4).

Other testaments attest to reservations about the market in public debt. Bernardo di Giovanni Portinari († 1455–1456)[89] confessed in a will of July 1436 to speculating in *monte di Pisa* credits:

The said testator said that he had long acquired from many and various people large sums of money and credits in the *monte di Pisa* of the commune of Florence and that afterwards he had exacted [settlement of] these sums and credits [from the commune]; and he said that these sums can be ascertained from the testator's account books. And because the testator was worried that his conscience might be burdened on account of the aforesaid, he directed and willed for the relief of his conscience that whatever was owed by right to any persons from whom he had bought or acquired money and credits in the *monte di Pisa* should be refunded, repaid and restored in full (appendix 2, no. 5).

---

[88] See, for example, the formula edited in Scalfati, *Un formulario notarile fiorentino*, 94. See also the remarks of English, 'La prassi testamentaria,' 463–465; de La Roncière, 'La foi du Marchand,' 246; and Cohn, *The Cult of Remembrance*, 15–17.

[89] The approximate date of Portinari's death is derived from data in Herlihy et al., eds., *Online Tratte of Officeholders*.

Similarly, in his will of 23 October 1417, Giovanni di Niccolò Soderini († 1419–1422) recalled how he went into partnership with Niccolò Ricci to buy discounted *accattoni*—compulsory but redeemable short-term loans at eight to ten percent—for some eight hundred florins (appendix 2, no. 6).[90] Although Ricci supplied half of the capital, the entire sum was credited to Soderini, who proceeded to exact payment from the commune at term and then to pay Ricci his share of the profits. For the relief of his conscience, Soderini instructed his heirs to seek a joint opinion (*consilium*) from a theologian and a canonist ('quidam sacre pagine professor et quidam decretorum doctor') on whether he was obliged to make restitution to the commune or to the original creditors. The heirs should act in accordance with the experts' decision, deducting the necessary sums from Soderini's thousand-florin legacy to Santa Maria Nuova.

Conclusion

Angelo Corbinelli's testament of 1419 represents the clearest documentary evidence to date that the legal and theological controversy over the usurious aspects of public debt influenced the behavior of government creditors. Corbinelli explicitly declared that his scruples were inspired by the debate, and both his directions to his heirs and the conditions he imposed on individual legacies of *monte* credits reflected his moral agitation. Moreover, a preliminary sampling of collateral sources indicates that Corbinelli was not an isolated eccentric but that his reservations were shared by a significant number of his co-citizens. Indeed, Giovanni Soderini's solicitation of a legal-theological judgment on his speculative activities on the debt market returns us to the very theologians and jurists who were the authors of the controversy in the first place.

Perhaps Corbinelli's scruples were ultimately misplaced. Neither church nor council ever passed judgment on funded public debts: for the next century, the debate remained in the domain of legal and theological experts, and among these the trend of opinion, with the exception of rigorists such as Savonarola, was towards the approval of public debts and their various operations. Indeed, if example was any guide, government creditors could soon point to the most distinguished of ecclesiastical authorities, Pope Eugenius IV, who made himself one of the principal creditors of the Florentine government in 1432 by investing in *monte* credits with a nominal value of a hundred thousand florins.[91]

---

[90]On the approximate date of Soderini's death, see Herlihy et al., eds., *Online Tratte of Officeholders*. For the definition of *accattone* and *accatto*, see Conti et al., *Le 'Consulte' e 'Pratiche' della Repubblica fiorentina*, 332, glossary; and Armstrong, *Usury and Public Debt*, 92.

Max Weber once remarked of the medieval usury prohibition that

> the wide chasm separating the inevitabilities of economic life from the Christian ideal was still frequently felt deeply. In any case this ethical separation kept the most devout groups and all those with the most consistently developed ethics far from the life of trade. Above all, time and again it tended to attach an ethical stigma to the business spirit, and to impede its growth.[92]

It is unnecessary to accept Weber's account of the origins of the capitalist spirit to concede the accuracy of this observation, made more than eighty years ago. On the basis of Corbinelli's testament and the other evidence adduced in this paper it seems to be equally applicable to the controversy over usury and public debt, which was anything but an abstraction for many late-medieval and early-Renaissance Italians.

University of Toronto
Toronto, Ontario

---

[91] On this incident, see Kirshner, 'Papa Eugenio IV e il monte comune.' Around the same time, Bernardino of Siena, on the authority of Guglielmo Centueri, denounced as absurd the suggestion that the popes had ever tacitly or explicitly countenanced the operations of the public debt; see Kirshner, 'Reading Bernardino's Sermon,' 575, 580–584. Non-Florentines were not usually permitted to invest in the *monte*; exceptions were made in the case of distinguished foreigners such as the pope and Italian princes (ibid., 575).

[92] Weber, *Economy and Society*, 2: 287. I am grateful to Johanna Will-Armstrong for this reference. For a discussion of Weber's religious sociology and his account of the potential of religion to promote or impede rational patterns of conduct, see Kaelber, *Schools of Asceticism*, 12–57.

Table 1: Angelo Corbinelli's *monte* credits in 1419 (nominal values).

monte comune * **	fl. 1781	s. 7	d. 9
monte di Pisa *	fl. 284	s. 10	d. 9
monte dei prestanzoni *	fl. 330	s. 0	d. 0
monte di Livorno *	fl. 403	s. 9	d. 8
monte dei cinque per cento colla ritenzione del quarto **	fl. 1101	s. 14	d. 6
paghe sostenute di monte comune dal 1415 al 1416 **	fl. 18	s. 12	d. 0
paghe sostenute dal 1415 al 1419 **	fl. 172	s. 9	d. 10
paghe sostenute di monte di Pisa al 1416 **	fl. 33	s. 0	d. 0
paghe sostenute di monte dei prestanzoni al 1419 **	fl. 25	s. 0	d. 9
paghe sostenute di monte dei prestanzoni dal 1390 al 1408 **	fl. 22	s. 19	d. 0
paghe sostenute di monte di Pisa al 1414 **	fl. 28	s. 8	d. 0
Total	fl. 4201	s. 12	d. 3

Sources: ASF, Notarile 9040, fol. 108r–v (7 September 1423); ibid., fols. 189v–190r (18 April 1425); ASF, Catasto 65, fol. 90r (1427). The table combines data from the inventories (marked *) with information in the 1427 *catasto* return (marked **), omitting levies imposed between 1419 and 1427. This procedure provides only a rough approximation, since it does not reflect credits that might have been alienated in the period 1419–1427 and additional levies in certain categories, particularly that of the *monte dei cinque per cento colla ritenzione del quarto*, during the same period. I have not found another reference to the *monte di Livorno*, but presumably it represented imposts during the war with Genoa (1410–1413).

Table 2: Angelo Corbinelli's legacies of *monte* credits,
27 April and 1 May 1419

Legatee	Amount	Form	Paid in
Santa Maria degli Angeli (Camaldolese monastery)	fl. 100	cash or *monte comune* credits	n/i
San Benedetto fuori della porta a' Pinti (Camaldolese monastery)	fl. 100	cash or *monte comune* credits	n/i
Santo Spirito (Augustinian convent)	fl. 100	cash or *monte comune* credits	n/i
Santa Croce (Franciscan convent)	fl. 100	cash or *monte comune* credits	n/i
Santa Maria Nuova (acute care hospital)	fl. 100	cash or *monte comune* credits	credits
Santa Maria della Scala (foundling hospital)	fl. 225	cash or *monte comune* credits	n/i
Filippa di Lorenzo Bardi-Gualterotti (widow)	fl. 290	*monte di Pisa* credits	credits
Filippa di Lorenzo Bardi-Gualterotti (widow)	fl. 330	*monte dei prestanzoni* credits	credits
Bartolomea di Angelo Corbinelli (daughter)	fl. 300	cash or *monte comune* credits	n/i
Giulia di Angelo Corbinelli (daughter)	fl. 300	cash or *monte comune* credits	n/i
Alessandra (illegitimate daughter)	fl. 200	cash or *monte comune* credits	n/i
Agostino di Niccolò da Roma (Augustinian friar)	fl. 50	cash or *monte comune* credits	n/i
Jacopo di Martino da Spoleto (physician)	fl. 100	cash or *monte comune* credits	credits
Total	fl. 2295		

Sources: ASF, Notarile 9042, fols. 68v–74r; ASF, Notarile 9040, fol. 116r–v; ASF, Catasto 18, fol. 1288r; ASF, Catasto 65, fol. 91r; ASF, OSMN 68, fol. 309v. The legacy to Jacopo di Martino da Spoleto was added in a codicil of 1 May 1419 (ASF, Notarile 9042, fol. 76v) and reported by the legatee in his *catasto* return of 1427 (Park, *Doctors and Medicine*, 186 and 251).

Works Cited

Manuscript Sources

Florence, Archivio di Stato (ASF)
    Catasto 17, 18, 65
    Mercanzia 19, 261
    Monte comune o delle graticole 3059, 3101, 3137
    Notarile antecosimiano 205, 9035, 9039, 9040, 9042, 14663
    Ospedale di Santa Maria Nuova (OSMN) 60, 65, 67, 68, 70
    Provvisioni, Registri 103
Florence. Biblioteca Nazionale Centrale di Firenze (BNF)
    Conventi soppressi J.X.51
    Fondo principale II, III, 366
    Magliabechiano xxix, 179
Florence. Biblioteca Riccardiana
    cod. 1301

Published Sources

Alberigo, J., P. P. Joannu, C. Leonardi and P. Prodi, eds. *Conciliorum oecumenicorum decreta*. Basel: Herder, 1962.

Armstrong, Lawrin. 'The Politics of Usury in Trecento Florence: The *Questio de monte* of Francesco da Empoli.' *Mediaeval Studies* 61 (1999): 1–44.

Armstrong, Lawrin. *Usury and Public Debt in Early Renaissance Florence: Lorenzo Ridolfi on the 'Monte Comune.'* Texts and Studies, 144. Toronto: Pontifical Institute of Mediaeval Studies, 2003.

Astorri, Antonella. *La Mercanzia a Firenze nella prima metà del Trecento. Il potere dei grandi mercanti*. Biblioteca storica toscana, 34. Florence: Olschki, 1998.

Bacchi, Giuseppe. 'S. Benedetto fuori della porta a' Pinti di Firenze.' *Rivista camaldolese* 2 (1927–1928): 449–456.

Barbadoro, Bernardino. *Le finanze della Repubblica fiorentina. Imposta diretta e debito pubblico fino all'istituzione del Monte*. Biblioteca storica toscana, 5. Florence: Olschki, 1929.

Barducci, Roberto. 'Politica e speculazione finanziaria a Firenze dopo la crisi del primo Trecento (1343–1358).' *Archivio storico italiano* 137 (1979): 177–219.

Barducci, Roberto. 'Le riforme finanziarie nel tumulto dei Ciompi' pp. 95–102 in *Il tumulto dei Ciompi. Un momento di storia fiorentina ed europea*. Florence: Olschki, 1981.

Barducci, Roberto. '. . . *Cum parva difficultate civium predictorum* . . .: Spunti introduttivi per un regesto della legislazione finanziaria fiorentina del Trecento (1345–1358)' in *Renaissance Studies in Honor of Craig Hugh Smyth*, ed. Andrew Morrogh, Fiorella Superbi Gioffredi, Piero Morselli and Eve Borsook, 2 vols., vol. 1, pp. 3–15. Florence: Giunta Barbèra, 1985.

Baron, Hans. 'Franciscan Poverty and Civic Wealth as Factors in the Rise of Humanistic Thought.' *Speculum* 13 (1938): 1–37.

Baron, Hans. 'Franciscan Poverty and Civic Wealth in the Shaping of Trecento Humanistic Thought: The Role of Petrarch' in *In Search of Florentine Civic Humanism: Essays on the Transition from Medieval to Modern Thought*, 2 vols., vol. 1, pp. 158–190. Princeton: Princeton University Press, 1988.

Baron, Hans. 'Civic Wealth and the New Values of the Renaissance: The Spirit of the Quattrocento' in *In Search of Florentine Civic Humanism: Essays on the Transition from Medieval to Modern Thought*, 2 vols., vol. 1, pp. 191–225. Princeton: Princeton University Press, 1988.

Becker, Marvin B. 'Three Cases Concerning the Restitution of Usury in Mediaeval Florence.' *Journal of Economic History* 17 (1957): 445–450.

Becker, Marvin B. *Florence in Transition*. 2 vols. Baltimore: Johns Hopkins Press, 1967–1968.

Bernardino of Siena. *Opera omnia*, vol. 4, *Quadragesimale de evangelio aeterno, sermones XXVII–LIII*. Quaracchi-Florence: Typographia Collegii S. Bonaventurae, 1956.

Bernocchi, Mario. *Le monete della Repubblica fiorentina*. 5 vols. Florence: Olschki, 1974–1985.

'Biglia, Andrea' in *Dizionario biografico degli Italiani*, vol. 10. Rome: Istituto della Enciclopedia italiana, 1968.

Blum, Rudolf. *La biblioteca della Badia fiorentina e i codici di Antonio Corbinelli*. Studi e testi, 155. Vatican City: Biblioteca Apostolica Vaticana, 1951.

Bonanno, Claudio, Metello Bonanno and Luciana Pellegrini. 'I legati "pro anima" ed il problema della salvezza nei testamenti fiorentini della seconda metà del Trecento.' *Ricerche storiche* 6 (1976): 183–220.

Boni, Monica and Robert Delort. 'Des esclaves toscans, du milieu du XIVe siècle au milieu du XVe siècle.' *Mélanges de l'École française de Rome, Moyen Âge-Temps Modernes* 112, 2 (2000): 1057–1077.

Bowsky, William M. *The Finance of the Commune of Siena, 1287–1355*. Oxford: Oxford University Press, 1970.

Boyer, John W. and Julius Kirshner, eds. *University of Chicago Readings in Western Civilization*, vol. 4, *Medieval Europe*, ed. and trans. Julius Kirshner and Karl F. Morrison. Chicago and London: University of Chicago Press, 1986.

Brucker, Gene A. 'Un documento fiorentino sulla guerra, sulla finanza e sulla amministrazione pubblica (1375).' *Archivio storico italiano* 115 (1957): 165–176.

Brucker, Gene A. *Florentine Politics and Society, 1343–1378*. Princeton: Princeton University Press, 1962.

Brucker, Gene A. *The Civic World of Early Renaissance Florence*. Princeton: Princeton University Press, 1977.

Byne, Joseph P., trans. *The Wills and Codicils of Marco (1348) and Francesco di Marco (1410) Datini*. Available at http://www.belmont.edu/honorsprogram/datwill.html/

Caferro, William. *Mercenary Companies and the Decline of Siena*. Baltimore and London: Johns Hopkins University Press, 1998.

Celenza, Christopher S. 'The Will of Cardinal Giordano Orsini (ob. 1438).' *Traditio* 51 (1996): 257–286.

Ciappelli, Giovanni. 'Il cittadino fiorentino e il fisco alla fine del Trecento e nel corso del Quattrocento: uno studio di due casi.' *Società e storia* 11 (1989): 823–872.

Cipolla, Carlo M. *The Monetary Policy of Fourteenth-Century Florence*. Berkeley, Los Angeles and London: University of California Press, 1982.

Cohn, Samuel K., Jr. *Death and Property in Siena, 1205–1800: Strategies for the Afterlife*. Baltimore and London: Johns Hopkins University Press, 1988.

Cohn, Samuel K., Jr. *The Cult of Remembrance and the Black Death: Six Renaissance Cities in Central Italy*. Baltimore and London: Johns Hopkins University Press, 1992.

Cohn, Samuel K., Jr. 'Last Wills: Family, Women, and the Black Death in Central Italy' pp. 39–56 in *Women in the Streets: Essays on Sex and Power in Renaissance Italy*. Baltimore and London: Johns Hopkins University Press, 1996.

Cohn, Samuel K., Jr. *Creating the Florentine State: Peasants and Rebellion, 1348–1434*. Cambridge: Cambridge University Press, 1999.

Conti, Elio. *L'imposta diretta a Firenze nel Quattrocento (1427– 1494)*. Studi storici, fasc. 136–139. Rome: Istituto storico italiano per il Medio Evo, 1984.

Conti, Elio, Maria Cristina Frassineti, Daniela de Rosa, Magda Cavaciocchi and Renzo Ninci, eds. *Le 'Consulte' e 'Pratiche' della Repubblica fiorentina nel Quattrocento*, vol. 1 *1401: Cancellierato di Coluccio Salutati*. Florence: Università di Firenze, 1981.

Dante Alighieri. *The Divine Comedy*, trans. and annotated by Charles S. Singleton. 6 vols. Bollingen Series, 80. Princeton: Princeton University Press, 1970–1975.

Davidsohn, Robert. *Forschungen zur Geschichte von Florenz*, part 4, *13. und 14. Jahrhundert*. Berlin: Mittler, 1908.

Davidsohn, Robert. *Geschichte von Florenz*, vol. 4, *Die Frühzeit der florentiner Kultur*, part 3, *Kirchliches und geistiges Leben, Kunst, öffentliches und häusliches Dasein*. Berlin: Mittler, 1927.

Davies, Jonathan. *Florence and its University During the Early Renaissance*. Education and Society in the Middle Ages and Renaissance, 8. Leiden, Boston and Cologne: Brill. 1998.

Debby, Nirit Ben-Aryeh. 'Political Views in the Preaching of Giovanni Dominici in Renaissance Florence, 1400–1406.' *Renaissance Quarterly* 55 (2002): 19–48.

De La Roncière, Charles-M. 'Indirect Taxes or 'Gabelles' at Florence in the Fourteenth Century: The Evolution of Tariffs and Problems of Collection,' trans. Janet Sondheimer, pp. 140–192 in *Florentine Studies: Politics and Society in Renaissance Florence*, ed. Nicolai Rubinstein. London: Faber and Faber, 1968.

De La Roncière, Charles-M. 'La foi du marchand: Florence XIVe– milieu XVe siècles' pp. 237–250 in *Le marchand au Moyen Age: Société des historiens médiévistes de l'enseignement supérieur public français, XIX Congrès*. Rheims: S.H.M.E.S., 1992. Reprinted in *Religion paysanne et religion urbaine en Toscane (c. 1250–c. 1450)*. Aldershot: Variorum, 1994.

Delort, Robert. 'Du servage et de l'esclavage: notes sur la société toscane des XIIIe et XIVe siècles' pp. 107–115 in *Les sociétés méridionales à l'âge féodal: Hommage à Pierre Bonnassie*, ed. Hélène Débax. Toulouse: C.N.R.S., Université de Toulouse-Le Mirail, 1999.

Delort, Robert. 'Note sur le vocabulaire de la servitude et de l'esclavage en Toscane à la fin du Moyen Âge.' *Mélanges de l'École française de Rome, Moyen Âge-Temps Modernes* 112, 2 (2000): 1079–1085.

De Roover, Raymond. *Money, Banking and Credit in Mediaeval Bruges: Italian Merchant-Bankers, Lombards and Money-Changers, A Study in the Origins of Banking*. Cambridge, MA: Mediaeval Academy of America, 1948.

De Roover, Raymond. 'Il trattato di Fra Santi Rucellai sul cambio, il monte comune e il monte delle doti.' *Archivio storico italiano* 111 (1953): 3–41.

De Roover, Raymond. *The Rise and Decline of the Medici Bank, 1397–1494*. Cambridge, MA: Harvard University Press, 1963.

De Roover, Raymond. *San Bernardino of Siena and Sant'Antonino of Florence: The Two Great Economic Thinkers of the Middle Ages*. Boston, MA: Baker Library, Harvard Graduate School of Business Administration, 1967.

De Roover, Raymond. *La pensée économique des scolastiques: doctrines et méthodes*. Montreal and Paris: Institut d'Études Médiévales and Librairie J. Vrin, 1971.

De Roover, Raymond. 'The Development of Accounting prior to Luca Pacioli according to the Account Books of Medieval Merchants' pp. 119–180 in *Business, Banking and Economic Thought in Late Medieval and Early Modern Europe: Selected Studies of Raymond de Roover*, ed. Julius Kirshner. Chicago and London: University of Chicago Press, 1974.

De Roover, Raymond. 'Cambium ad Venetias: Contribution to the History of Foreign Exchange' pp. 239–259 in *Business, Banking and Economic Thought in Late Medieval and Early Modern Europe: Selected Studies of Raymond de Roover*, ed. Julius Kirshner. Chicago and London: University of Chicago Press, 1974.

De Roover, Raymond. 'The Scholastic Attitude Towards Trade and Entrepreneurship' pp. 336–345 in *Business, Banking and Economic Thought in Late Medieval and Early Modern Europe: Selected Studies of Raymond de Roover*, ed. Julius Kirshner. Chicago and London: University of Chicago Press, 1974.

Edler, Florence. 'Restitution in Renaissance Florence' pp. 773–780 in *Studi in onore di Armando Sapori*. Milan: Istituto editoriale cisalpino, 1957.

Ekelund, Robert B., Robert F. Hébert, Robert D. Tollison, Gary M. Anderson and Audret B. Davidson. *Sacred Trust: The Medieval Church as an Economic Firm*. New York and Oxford: Oxford University Press, 1996.

English, Edward D. 'La prassi testamentaria delle famiglie nobili a Siena e nella Toscana del Tre-Quattrocento' pp. 463–472 in *I ceti dirigenti nella Toscana del Quattrocento*. Florence: Francesco Papafava, 1987.

Epstein, Stephan R. 'Cities, Regions and the Late Medieval Crisis: Sicily and Tuscany Compared.' *Past and Present* 130 (1991): 3–50.

Eubel, Conrad. *Hierarchia Catholica Medii Aevi*. 2nd ed. Vol. 1. Munich: Sumptibus et typis librariae Regensbergianae, 1913.

Fumagalli, Edoardo. 'I trattati di Fra Santi Rucellai.' *Aevum* 51 (1977): 289–332.

Galassi, Francesco. 'Buying a Passport to Heaven: Usury, Restitution, and the Merchants of Medieval Genoa.' *Religion* 22 (1992): 313–326.
Garin, Eugenio. *Italian Humanism: Philosophy and Civic Life in the Renaissance*, trans. Peter Munz. New York: Harper and Row, 1965.
Gilchrist, John. *The Church and Economic Activity in the Middle Ages*. London, Melbourne and Toronto: Macmillan, 1969.
Ginatempo, Maria. *Prima del debito: Finanziamento della spesa pubblica e gestione del deficit nelle grandi città toscane (1200–1350 ca.)*. Biblioteca storica toscana, 38. Florence: Olschki, 2000.
Ginori-Lisci, Leonardo. *I palazzi di Firenze nella storia e nell'arte*. 2 vols. Florence: Cassa di Risparmio di Firenze, 1972.
Giustiniani, Vito R. 'Il testamento di Leonardo Bruni.' *Rinascimento*, 2nd series, 4 (1964): 259–264.
Goldthwaite, Richard A. 'Local Banking in Renaissance Florence.' *Journal of European Economic History* 14 (1985): 5–55. Reprinted in *Banks, Palaces and Entrepreneurs in Renaissance Florence*. Aldershot: Variorum, 1995.
Gombrich, E. H. 'The Early Medici as Patrons of Art' pp. 35–57 in *Norm and Form: Studies in the Art of the Renaissance*. London: Phaidon, 1966.
Gow, Andrew and Gordon Griffiths. 'Pope Eugenius IV and Jewish Money-Lending in Florence: The Case of Salomone di Bonaventura during the Chancellorship of Leonardo Bruni.' *Renaissance Quarterly* 47 (1994): 282–329.
Gregory of Rimini. *Tractatus de imprestantiis Venetorum et de usura*. Reggio Emilia: Ludovicus de Mazalis, 1508.
Guarino da Verona. *Epistolario di Guarino Veronese*, ed. Remigio Sabbadini. 3 vols. Venice: [no publisher], 1915–1919.
Guasti, Cesare. *Santa Maria del Fiore: La costruzione della chiesa e del campanile secondo i documenti tratti dall'archivio dell'opera secolare e da quello di stato*. Florence: M. Ricci, 1887.
Haines, Margaret. 'Firenze e il finanziamento della cattedrale e del campanile' pp. 71–83 in *Alla riscoperta di Piazza del Duomo in Firenze*, vol. 3, *Il campanile di Giotto*, ed. Timothy Verdon. Florence: Centro Di, 1994.
Haines, Margaret. *Gli anni della cupola: archivio digitale delle fonti dell'Opera di Santa Maria del Fiore, 1417–1436*, available from http://www.operaduomo.firenze.it/cupola. Florence: Opera di Santa Maria del Fiore, 2002.
Helmholz, R. H. 'Usury and the Medieval English Church Courts.' *Speculum* 61 (1986): 364–380.
Henderson, John. 'The Hospitals of Late-Medieval and Renaissance Florence: A Preliminary Survey' pp. 63–92 in *The Hospital in History*, ed. Lindsay Granshaw and Roy Porter. London and New York: Routledge, 1989.
Henderson, John. *Piety and Charity in Late Medieval Florence*. Chicago and London: University of Chicago Press, 1997.
Herlihy, David and Christiane Klapisch-Zuber. *Tuscans and Their Families: A Study of the Florentine Catasto of 1427*. New Haven and London: Yale University Press, 1985.
Herlihy, David and Christiane Klapisch-Zuber, eds. *Census and Property Survey of Florentine Domains in the Province of Tuscany, 1427–1480*,

machine readable data file *Online Catasto of 1427 Version 1.1*, available at http://www.stg.brown.edu/projects/catasto. Providence, RI: Brown University, 1996.

Herlihy, David, R. Burr Litchfield, Anthony Molho and Roberto Barducci, eds. *Online Tratte of Office Holders, 1282–1532*, machine readable data file, available at http://www.stg.brown.edu/projects/tratte. Providence, RI: Brown University, 2000.

Hobsbawm, Eric. 'Historians and Economists: II' pp. 109–123 in *On History*. London: Weidenfeld and Nicolson, 1997.

Hoshino, Hidetoshi. *L'Arte della Lana in Firenze nel basso medioevo: Il commercio della lana e il mercato dei panni fiorentini nei secoli XIII–XV*. Biblioteca storica toscana, 31. Florence: Olschki, 1980.

Hunt, Edwin S. *The Medieval Super-Companies: A Study of the Peruzzi Company of Florence*. Cambridge and New York: Cambridge University Press, 1994.

Hunt, Edwin S. and James M. Murray. *A History of Business in Medieval Europe, 1200–1550*. Cambridge: Cambridge University Press, 1999.

Jurdjevic, Mark. 'Virtue, Commerce, and the Enduring Florentine Republican Moment: Reintegrating Italy into the Atlantic Republican Debate.' *Journal of the History of Ideas* 62 (2001): 721–743.

Kaelber, Lutz. *Schools of Asceticism: Ideology and Organization in Medieval Religious Communities*. University Park, PA: Pennsylvania State University Press, 1998.

Kaeppel, Thomas. *Scriptores Ordinis Praedicatorum Medii Aevi*. Vol. 1. Rome: Ad S. Sabinae, 1970.

Kent, Francis W. *Household and Lineage in Renaissance Florence: The Family Life of the Capponi, Ginori, and Rucellai*. Princeton: Princeton University Press, 1977.

Kirshner, Julius. 'Papa Eugenio IV e il monte comune: documenti su investimento e speculazione nel debito pubblico di Firenze.' *Archivio storico italiano* 127 (1969): 339–382.

Kirshner, Julius. 'A *Quaestio de usuris* Falsely Attributed to Bartolus of Sassoferrato.' *Renaissance Quarterly* 22 (1969): 256–261.

Kirshner, Julius. 'From Usury to Public Finance: The Ecclesiastical Controversy over the Public Debts of Florence, Genoa and Venice (1300–1500).' PhD dissertation, Columbia University, 1970.

Kirshner, Julius. 'The Moral Theology of Public Finance: A Study and Edition of Nicholas de Anglia's *Quaestio disputata* on the Public Debt of Venice.' *Archivum Fratrum Praedicatorum* 40 (1970): 47–72.

Kirshner, Julius. 'A Note on the Authorship of Domenico Pantaleoni's Tract on the *Monte Comune* of Florence.' *Archivum Fratrum Praedicatorum* 43 (1973): 73–81.

Kirshner, Julius. 'Raymond de Roover on Scholastic Economic Thought' pp. 15–36 in *Business, Banking and Economic Thought in Late Medieval and Early Modern Europe: Selected Studies of Raymond de Roover*, ed. Julius Kirshner. Chicago and London: University of Chicago Press, 1974.

Kirshner, Julius. 'Conscience and Public Finance: A *Questio disputata* of John of Legnano on the Public Debt of Genoa' pp. 434–453 in *Philosophy and*

Humanism: Renaissance Essays in Honor of Paul Oskar Kristeller, ed. Edward P. Mahoney. Leiden: Brill, 1976.

Kirshner, Julius. 'The Moral Problem of Discounting Genoese *Paghe*, 1450–1550.' *Archivum Fratrum Praedicatorum* 47 (1977): 109–167.

Kirshner, Julius. *Pursuing Honor While Avoiding Sin: The 'Monte delle doti' of Florence*. Quaderni di Studi senesi, 41. Milan: Giuffrè, 1978.

Kirshner, Julius. 'Reading Bernardino's Sermon on the Public Debt' pp. 547–622 in *Atti del simposio internazionale cateriniano-bernardiniano: Siena, 17–20 aprile 1980*, ed. Domenico Maffei and Paolo Nardi. Siena: Accademia senese degli Intronati, 1982.

Kirshner, Julius. 'Storm over the *Monte Comune*: Genesis of the Moral Controversy over the Public Debt of Florence.' *Archivum Fratrum Praedicatorum* 53 (1983): 219–276.

Kirshner, Julius. '"*Ubi est ille?*": Franco Sacchetti on the *monte comune* of Florence.' *Speculum* 59 (1984): 556–584.

Kirshner, Julius. 'Materials for a Gilded Cage: Non-Dotal Assets in Florence, 1300–1500' pp. 184–207 in *The Family in Italy from Antiquity to the Present*, ed. David I. Kertzer and Richard P. Saller. New Haven and London: Yale University Press, 1991.

Kirshner, Julius. 'Encumbering Private Claims to Public Debt in Renaissance Florence' pp. 19–75 in *The Growth of the Bank as Institution and the Development of Money-Business Law*, ed. Vito Piergiovanni. Berlin: Duncker und Humblot, 1993.

Kirshner, Julius. 'Francesco da Empoli' in *Dizionario biografico degli Italiani*, vol. 49. Rome: Istituto della Enciclopedia italiana, 1997.

Kirshner, Julius and Jacob Klerman. 'The Seven Percent Fund of Renaissance Florence' pp. 367–398 in *Banchi pubblici, banchi privati e monti di pietà nell'Europa preindustriale: Amministrazione, tecniche operative e ruoli economici*. Atti della società ligure di storia patria, n.s. 31, fasc. 1. Genoa: Società ligure di storia patria, 1991.

Kirshner, Julius and Anthony Molho. 'The Dowry Fund and the Marriage Market in Early Quattrocento Florence.' *Journal of Modern History* 50 (1978): 403–438.

Kirshner, Julius and Jacques Pluss. 'Two fourteenth-century opinions on dowries, paraphernalia and non-dotal goods.' *Bulletin of Medieval Canon Law* 9 (1979): 65–77.

Klapisch-Zuber, Christiane. 'The "Cruel Mother": Maternity, Widowhood, and Dowry in Florence in the Fourteenth and Fifteenth Centuries' pp. 117–131 in *Women, Family, and Ritual in Renaissance Italy*, trans. Lydia G. Cochrane. Chicago and London: University of Chicago Press, 1985.

Kuehn, Thomas. '"*Cum consensu mundualdi*": Legal Guardianship of Women in Quattrocento Florence' pp. 212–237 in *Law, Family, and Women: Toward a Legal Anthropology of Renaissance Italy*. Chicago and London: University of Chicago Press, 1991.

Kuehn, Thomas. 'Figli, madri, mogli e vedove: Donne come persone giuridiche,' trans. Silvana Seidl Menchi, pp. 449–457 in *Tempi e spazi di vita femminile tra medioevo ed età moderna*, ed. Silvana Seidl Menchi, Anne

Jacobson Schutte and Thomas Kuehn. Annali dell'Istituto storico italo-germanico in Trento, 51. Bologna: Il Mulino, 1999.

Kuehn, Thomas. *Illegitimacy in Renaissance Florence*. Ann Arbor: University of Michigan Press, 2002.

Lane, Frederic C. 'The Funded Public Debt of the Venetian Republic' pp. 87–108 in *Venice and History: The Collected Papers*. Baltimore: Johns Hopkins Press, 1966.

Langholm, Odd. *The Aristotelian Analysis of Usury*. Bergen, Oslo, Stavanger and Tromsø: Universitetsforlaget, 1984.

Langholm, Odd. *Economics in the Medieval Schools: Wealth, Exchange, Value, Money and Usury According to the Paris Theological Tradition, 1200–1350*. Studien und Texte zur Geistesgeschichte des Mittelalters, 29. Leiden, New York and Cologne: Brill, 1992.

Lapo da Castiglionchio. *Allegationes*. Venice: Johannes Variscus, 1571.

Le Goff, Jacques. 'The Usurer and Purgatory' pp. 25–52 in *The Dawn of Modern Banking*. New Haven and London: Yale University Press, 1979.

Le Goff, Jacques. *Your Money or Your Life: Economy and Religion in the Middle Ages*, trans. Patricia Ranum. New York: Zone Books, 1988.

Luiso, F. P. 'Su le tracce di un usuraio fiorentino del secolo XIII.' *Archivio storico italiano*, 5th series, 42 (1908): 1–44.

Luzzatto, Gino. *Il debito pubblico della Repubblica di Venezia dagli ultimi decenni del XII secolo alla fine del XV*. Milan: Istituto editoriale cisalpino, 1963.

Marks, L. F. 'The Financial Oligarchy in Florence under Lorenzo' pp. 123–147 in *Italian Renaissance Studies: A Tribute to Cecilia M. Ady*, ed. E. F. Jacob. London: Faber and Faber, 1960.

Martines, Lauro. 'Addenda to the Life of Antonio Corbinelli.' *Rinascimento* 8 (1957): 4–5.

Martines, Lauro. *The Social World of the Florentine Humanists, 1390–1460*. London: Routledge and Kegan Paul, 1963.

Martines, Lauro. *Lawyers and Statecraft in Renaissance Florence*. Princeton: Princeton University Press, 1968.

Martines, Lauro. 'Forced Loans: Political and Social Strain in *Quattrocento* Florence.' *Journal of Modern History* 60 (1988): 300–311.

Martines, Lauro. *April Blood: Florence and the Plot Against the Medici*. Oxford: Oxford University Press, 2003.

Marx, Karl. *Das Kapital: Kritik der politischen Ökonomie*. Vol. 1. Berlin: Dietz, 1974.

Mazzei, Lapo. *Lettere di un notaro ad un mercante del secolo XIV*, ed. Cesare Guasti. 2 vols. Florence: Le Monnier, 1880.

McLaughlin, T. P. 'The Teaching of the Canonists on Usury (XII, XIII and XIV Centuries).' *Mediaeval Studies* 1 (1939): 81–147; 2 (1940): 1–22.

Meek, Christine. 'Il debito pubblico nella storia finanziaria di Lucca nel XIV secolo.' *Actum Luce* 3 (1974): 7–46.

Meek, Christine. *Lucca 1369–1400: Politics and Society in an Early Renaissance City-State*. Oxford: Oxford University Press, 1978.

Molho, Anthony. *Florentine Public Finances in the Early Renaissance, 1400–1433*. Cambridge, MA: Harvard University Press, 1971.

Molho, Anthony. 'A Note on Jewish Moneylenders in Tuscany in the Late Trecento and Early Quattrocento' pp. 99–117 in *Renaissance Studies in Honor of Hans Baron*, ed. Anthony Molho and John A. Tedeschi. Dekalb: Northern Illinois University Press, 1971.
Molho, Anthony. 'The Brancacci Chapel: Studies in its Iconography and History.' *Journal of the Warburg and Courtauld Institutes* 40 (1977): 50–98.
Molho, Anthony. 'Corbinelli, Angelo' in *Dizionario biografico degli Italiani*, vol. 28. Rome: Istituto della Enciclopedia italiana, 1983.
Molho, Anthony. 'Corbinelli, Antonio' in *Dizionario biografico degli Italiani*, vol. 28. Rome: Istituto della Enciclopedia italiana, 1983.
Molho, Anthony. 'Corbinelli, Bartolomeo' in *Dizionario biografico degli Italiani*, vol. 28. Rome: Istituto della Enciclopedia italiana, 1983.
Molho, Anthony. 'L'amministrazione del debito pubblico a Firenze nel quindicesimo secolo' pp. 191–207 in *I ceti dirigenti nella Toscana del Quattrocento*. Florence: Francesco Papafava, 1987.
Molho, Anthony. 'Fisco ed economia a Firenze alla vigilia del Concilio.' *Archivio storico italiano* 148 (1990): 807–843.
Molho, Anthony. 'Debiti pubblici/interessi privati nella Firenze tardomedievale' in *La Toscana al tempo di Lorenzo il Magnifico: Politica, economia, cultura, arte*, 3 vols., vol. 3, pp. 825–855. Pisa: Pacini, 1992.
Molho, Anthony. 'Tre città-stato e i loro debiti pubblici: Quesiti e ipotesi sulla storia di Firenze, Genova e Venezia' pp. 185–215 in *Italia 1350–1450: Tra crisi, trasformazione, sviluppo*. Pistoia: Centro italiano di studi di storia e d'arte, 1993.
Molho, Anthony. *Marriage Alliance in Late Medieval Florence*. Cambridge, MA, and London: Harvard University Press, 1994.
Molho, Anthony. 'The State and Public Finance: A Hypothesis Based on the History of Late Medieval Florence' pp. 97–135 in *The Origins of the State in Italy, 1300–1600*, ed. Julius Kirshner. Chicago and London: University of Chicago Press, 1995.
Molho, Anthony. 'Créanciers de Florence en 1347: Un aperçu statistique du quartier de Santo Spirito' pp. 77–93 in *La Toscane et les Toscans autour de la Renaissance: Cadres de vie, société, croyances: Mélanges offerts à Charles-M. de La Roncière*. Aix-en-Provence: Université de Provence, 1999.
Mormando, Franco. *The Preacher's Demons: Bernardino of Siena and the Social Underworld of Early Renaissance Italy*. Chicago and London: University of Chicago Press, 1999.
Mueller, Reinhold. *Money and banking in medieval and Renaissance Venice*, vol. 2, *The Venetian money market, banks, panics, and the public debt, 1200–1500*. Baltimore and London: Johns Hopkins University Press, 1997.
Munro, John H. 'The Late-Medieval Origins of the Modern Financial Revolution: Overcoming Impediments from Church and State.' *International History Review* 25 (2003): 505–562.
Najemy, John. 'Guild Republicanism in Trecento Florence: The Successes and Ultimate Failure of Corporate Politics.' *American Historical Review* 84 (1979): 62–63.
Najemy, John. 'The Dialogue of Power in Florentine Politics' pp. 269–288 in *City States in Classical Antiquity and Medieval Italy: Athens and Rome,*

Florence and Venice, ed. Anthony Molho, Kurt Raaflaub and Julia Emlen. Stuttgart: Franz Steiner, 1991.

Nelson, Benjamin. 'The Usurer and the Merchant Prince: Italian Businessmen and the Ecclesiastical Law of Restitution, 1100–1550.' *Journal of Economic History*, supplement 7 (1947): 104–122.

Ninci, Renzo. 'La politica finanziaria della Repubblica fiorentina dopo il Tumulto dei Ciompi (1380–1425): Un tentativo di "Programmazione"?' pp. 151–167 in *La società fiorentina nel Basso Medioevo: Per Elio Conti*, ed. Renzo Ninci. Nuovi studi storici, 29. Rome: Istituto storico italiano per il Medio Evo, 1995.

Noonan, John T., Jr. *The Scholastic Analysis of Usury*. Cambridge, MA: Harvard University Press, 1957.

Origo, Iris. 'The Domestic Enemy: The Eastern Slaves in Tuscany in the Fourteenth and Fifteenth Centuries.' *Speculum* 30 (1955): 321–366.

Paatz, Walter and Elizabeth Paatz. *Die Kirchen von Florenz: Ein kunstgeschichtliches Handbuch*. 6 vols. Frankfurt am Main: V. Klostermann, 1955.

Palmieri, Matteo. *Ricordi fiscali (1427–1474)*, ed. Elio Conti. Studi storici, fasc. 132–135. Rome: Istituto storico italiano per il Medio Evo, 1983.

Pandimoglio, Leonida. 'Giovanni di Pagolo Morelli e la continuità familiare.' *Studi medievali*, 3rd series, 22 (1981): 129–181.

Park, Katharine. *Doctors and Medicine in Early Renaissance Florence*. Princeton: Princeton University Press, 1985.

Park, Katharine. 'Healing the Poor: Hospitals and Medical Assistance in Renaissance Florence' pp. 26–45 in *Medicine and Charity Before the Welfare State*, ed. Jonathan Barry and Colin Jones, 26–45. London and New York: Routledge, 1991.

Pirenne, Henri. *Economic and Social History of Medieval Europe*. London: Routledge and Kegan Paul, 1936.

Ridolfi, Lorenzo. *Tractatus de usuris* in *Tractatus universi iuris duce et auspice Gregorio XIII . . . in unum congesti*, vol. 7, fols. 48va–50ra. Venice: Franciscus Zilettus, 1584.

Rodolico, Niccolò. *I Ciompi: Una pagina di storia del proletariato operaio*. 3rd ed. Florence: Sansoni, 1980.

Salutati, Coluccio. *Epistolario di Coluccio Salutati*, ed. Francesco Novati. 4 vols. Rome: Istituto storico italiano, 1891–1911.

Sanesi, Ireneo. 'Il testamento di Marchionne di Coppo Stefani.' *Archivio storico italiano*, 5th Series, 9 (1892): 318–326.

Santarelli, Umberto. '"*Maxima fuit Florentiae altercatio*": l'usura e i *montes*' pp. 81–94, 98 in *Banchi pubblici, banchi privati e monti di pietà nell'Europa preindustriale: Amministrazione, tecniche operative e ruoli economici*. Atti della società ligure di storia patria, n.s. 31, fasc. 1. Genoa: Società ligure di storia patria, 1991.

Sapori, Armando. 'L'interesse del denaro a Firenze nel Trecento (dal un testamento di un usuraio)' in *Studi di storia economica (secoli XIII, XIV, XV)*, 3rd ed., 3 vols., vol. 1, pp. 223–243. Florence: Sansoni, 1955–1967.

Savonarola, Girolamo. *Prediche sopra Ruth e Michea*, ed. Vincenzo Romano. 2 vols. Rome: Angelo Belardetti, 1962.

Scalfati, Silio P. P., ed. *Un formulario notarile fiorentino della metà del Dugento*. Archivio di Stato di Firenze, Scuola di Archivistica, Paleografia e Diplomatica, 5. Florence: Edifir, 1997.

Schnapper, Bernard. *Les rentes au XVIe siècle: histoire d'un instrument de crédit*. École pratique des hautes études-vi^e section, Centre de Recherches Historiques, Affaires et gens d'affaires, 12. Paris: S.E.V.P.E.N., 1957.

Schnapper, Bernard. 'Les rentes chez les théologiens et les canonistes du XIIIe au XVIe siècles' in *Études d'histoire du droit canonique dédiées à Gabriel le Bras*, 2 vols., vol. 2, pp. 965–995. Paris: Sirey, 1965.

Schnapper, Bernard. 'La répression de l'usure et l'évolution économique (XIIe–XVIe siècles).' *Tijdschrift voor Rechtsgeschiedenis* 37 (1969): 47–75.

Shatzmiller, Joseph. *Shylock Reconsidered: Jews, Moneylending, and Medieval Society*. Berkeley, Los Angeles and London: University of California Press, 1990.

Sieveking, Heinrich. *Studio sulle finanze genovesi nel medioevo e in particolare sulla Casa di San Giorgio*. Atti della Società ligure di storia patria 35, fasc. 1 and 2. Genoa: Società ligure di storia patria, 1905–1906.

Sombart, Werner. *The Quintessence of Capitalism: A Study of the History and Psychology of the Modern Business Man*, trans. and ed. M. Epstein. New York: H. Fertig, 1967.

Spicciani, Amleto. *Capitale e interesse tra mercatura e povertà nei teologi e canonisti dei secoli XIII–XV*. Rome: Jouvence, 1990.

Stella, Alessandro. *La révolte des Ciompi: les hommes, les lieux, le travail*. Paris: École des hautes études en sciences sociales, 1993.

Strocchia, Sharon. 'Burials in Renaissance Florence, 1350–1500.' PhD dissertation, University of California, Berkeley, 1981.

Todeschini, Giacomo. 'Oeconomica franciscana: Proposte di una nuova lettura delle fonti dell'etica economica medievale.' *Rivista di storia e letteratura religiosa* 12 (1976): 15–77.

Todeschini, Giacomo. 'Oeconomica Franciscana II: Pietro di Giovanni Olivi come fonte per la storia dell'etica economica medievale.' *Rivista di storia e letteratura religiosa* 13 (1977): 461–494.

Todeschini, Giacomo. *Un trattato di economia politica francescana: il 'De emptionibus et venditionibus, de usuris, de restitutionibus' di Pietro di Giovanni Olivi*. Studi storici, fasc. 125–126. Rome: Istituto storico italiano per il Medio Evo, 1980.

Tracy, James D. *A Financial Revolution in the Hapsburg Netherlands: Renten and Renteniers in the County of Holland, 1515–1565*. Berkeley and London: University of California Press, 1985.

Trexler, Richard C. 'Death and Testament in the Episcopal Constitutions of Florence (1327)' pp. 29–74 in *Renaissance Studies in Honor of Hans Baron*, ed. Anthony Molho and John A. Tedeschi. Dekalb: Northern Illinois University Press, 1971.

Trexler, Richard C. 'Florence, by the grace of the Lord Pope . . .' *Studies in Medieval and Renaissance History* 9 (1972): 117–215.

Trusen, Winfried. 'Die Anfänge öffentlicher Banken und das Zinsproblem: Kontroversen im Spätmittelalter' pp. 113–131 in *Recht und Wirtschaft in Geschichte und Gegenwart: Festschrift für Johannes Bärmann zum 70.*

Geburtstag, ed. Marcus Lutter, Helmut Kollhosser and Winfried Trusen. Munich: C. H. Beck'sche, 1975.
Ullman, B. L. 'A Letter of Giovanni da San Miniato to Angelo Corbinelli' pp. 249–255 in *Studies in the Italian Renaissance*. Rome: Edizioni di storia e letteratura, 1955.
Van der Wee, Herman. 'Monetary, Credit and Banking Systems,' in *Cambridge Economic History of Europe*, vol. 5, *The Economic Organization of Early Modern Europe*, ed. E. E. Rich and C. H. Wilson, pp. 310–335. Cambridge: Cambridge University Press, 1977.
Vespasiano da Bisticci. *Le vite*, ed. Aulo Greco. 2 vols. Florence: Istituto nazionale di studi sul Rinascimento, 1970–1976.
Villani, Matteo. *Cronica con la continuazione di Filippo Villani*, ed. Giovanni Porta. 2 vols. Parma: Fondazione Pietro Bembo/Ugo Guanda, 1995.
Weber, Max. *Economy and Society: An Outline of Interpretative Sociology*, ed. Guenther Roth and Claus Wittich. 2 vols. New York: Bedminster Press, 1968.
Witt, Ronald G. *Hercules at the Crossroads: The Life, Works, and Thought of Coluccio Salutati*. Durham, NC: Duke University Press, 1983.

Appendix 1
Angelo Corbinelli
Testament

Notes on the Edition

Description. ASF, Notarile 9042: (1) Paper 295 mm. x 221 mm. (2) viii + 180 leaves, foliated 1–175. (3) Written space ruled with a plummet 223 mm. x 118 mm. exclusive of marginalia. (4) *Littera cursiva*, s. xv.[1] Hand of Francesco di Piero Giacomini da Castelfiorentino, notary and judge ordinary. (5) Contents: 116 testaments, seventeen codicils and thirteen miscellaneous other acts registered between 26 June 1411 and 7 April 1431.

Orthography and editorial conventions. With the exception of *u* and *v*, whose use I have modernized, I have preserved the notary's orthography: *e* for dipthongs *ae* and *oe*, *actritus* for the classical Latin *attritus*, *apoteca* (*apotheca*), *assummere* (*assumere*), *autoritas* (*auctoritas*), *centinarius* (*centenarius*), *exhonerare* (*exonerare*), *honera* (*onera*), *iusta* (*iuxta*), *nichil* or *nicchil* (*nihil*), *nichilominus* or *nicchilominus* (*nihilominus*), *nucupativus* (*nuncupativus*), *occaxio* (*occasio*), *oppinio* (*opinio*), *proibitio* (*prohibitio*), *proibuit* (*prohibuit*), *quactuor* (*quattuor*), *redditus* (*reditus*), *sotietas* (*societas*), *teologus* (*theologus*) and *vigesimus* (*vicesimus*). In accordance with Giacomini's practice elsewhere in the register I have expanded the abbreviations *coe* and *cos* as *comune* and *comunis* rather than as *commune* and *communis*. I have emended the text only in the few cases of obvious error, which are duly indicated. Material in angle brackets (< >) is editorial; material that should be deleted is indicated by square brackets ([ ]). The apparatus notes Giacomini's marginal memoranda, corrections, interlineations and marginal interpolations, although in the interests of brevity I have omitted corrections of a single letter. Capitalization, punctuation and paragraph divisions are editorial.

Vocabulary. Certain terms and usages merit an explanatory note; reference is to line numbers. *Prestantia* (It. *prestanza*; 467) was the Florentine word for a compulsory, non-repayable loan periodically levied on citizens in accordance with assessments determined by committees in each quarter. *Prestantiae* were inscribed in one or other of the debts funds, or *montes* (It. *monti*; 41 and *passim*), of which there were several by the early fifteenth century.[1] Payments were not described as usury, but as *interesse*, *dona* and *page* (42 and *passim*). The noun *interesse* was coined by the civilian jurist Azo († 1220) to denote legitimate compensation for a debtor's default. A creditor was permitted to accept a gift (*donum*) of gratitude from his debtor provided it did not represent his principal motive for lending. *Paghe* (sing. *paga*; 'payment') was the vernacular word for interest payments on debt credits, here Latinized as *page* (sing. *paga*). Credits could be bought and sold but because no certificates were issued these were book transactions recorded by the *monte* officials and consequently transfer of

---

[1] See above, pp. 177–178.

ownership was described as *transcriptio* ('transcription': 106 and *passim*). The *scribani montis* (566) were notaries and scribes employed by the debt officials to record such transactions. The expression *salvo iure calculi* (220, 226) means 'without prejudice to the reckoning' of the precise sums of credits to the testator's account, of which he gave only round estimates in the will.

The expression *in una partita* (It.; 47, 104) means 'collectively.' *Parabola* (565–566) here means 'permission' or 'licence,' and *balia* (458, 559) was a vernacular word denoting the legal 'power' or 'authority' to do something. A female *factor* or agent was a *factrix* (229). When a sum of money was described as *ponderis et conii florentini* ('of Florentine weight and issue': 210) this referred to its value in terms of the *fiorino d'oro*, a virtually pure gold coin worth in April 1419, s. 80 d. 1.22 in terms of the petty silver (but in fact largely copper) money used in daily transactions.[2] *Masseritia* (270, 271, 274) was a synonym of the classical Latin *supellex* (259), household goods or movables. *Redita* (258, 297) here refers to the right of a widowed daughter to return to her father's household or the right of a widow to remain in the household of her deceased husband.[3]

A *consorteria* (380, 389, 410), from *consors* (377 and *passim*), was 'a group of kinsmen tracing descent in the male line from a common ancestor.'[4] In law, *stirps* referred to a direct line of male descendents and an inheritance was said to be divided *in stirpem* when each son of the same father received an equal portion. If the father was predeceased by his son, the latter's share of the inheritance was divided equally among his own heirs *in capita*. Corbinelli directed (361–362) that if his heirs died before coming of age or without heirs of their own, half of his estate should be divided among his four brothers and their issue 'in stirpem et non in capita' so that the resulting four portions might remain intact and not be dissipated through further subdivision. *Monachare* (321–322) means 'to admit to a monastic order' and *pinzocherare* (322) 'to make a member of a lay third order' of one of the mendicant orders, Franciscan, Dominican or Carmelite. An *annuale* (204, 206) was an annual mass or office on behalf of the testator celebrated in conjunction with a *pietanza* (It.; spelled *piatanza* in the manuscript, 204), a commemorative meal sponsored by the testator.[5] The combination *et seu* (39 and *passim*) occurs frequently in Florentine public and private documents of the period and means simply 'and/or.' *Angelus* (It. *Angelo*; 6 and *passim*) and *Angnolus* (It. *Agnolo*; 1) are alternative forms of the same name.

---

[2]Bernocchi, *Le monete della Repubblica fiorentina*, 4: 195.
[3]On the right of return, see Klapisch-Zuber, 'The "Cruel Mother,"' 120–124.
[4]Kent, *Household and Lineage*, 6.
[5]See above, p. 193.

Angelo Corbinelli
Testament

ASF, Notarile antecosimiano 9042, fols. 68v–74r. Protocol of the testament of Angelo di Tommaso Corbinelli redacted by Francesco di Piero Giacomini da Castelfiorentino, notary and judge ordinary, 27 April 1419.

<68v> <Testamentum> Angnoli Corbinelli
<1> In Dei nomine amen. Anno domini ab eius salutifera incarnatione millesimo quadringentesimo decimonono, inditione duodecima et die vigesimaseptima mensis aprilis. Actum Florentie in populo Sancte Felicitatis de Florentia in domo infrascripti Angeli testatoris,[6] presentibus magistro Augustino Niccholai de Roma, sacre theologie doctore eximio, et fratre Niccholuccio Vannucci de Cascina, baccalario, et fratre Andrea Petri de Mediolano[7] et fratre Iohanne Antonii de Amatrice et fratre Arnoldo Iohannis de Alamania, fratre Iacopo Arrigi de Alamania et fratre Bartolomeo Iohannis de Florentia omnibus fratribus heremitanis ordinis Sancti Augustini et de conventu Sancti Spiritus de Florentia[8] testibus ab infrascripto Angelo testatore ad infrascripta proprio hore dicti testatoris vocatis, habitis et rogatis.

<2> Quum nichil certius morte nicchilque incertius ipsius hora et quamvis incerta et dubia sit mortis hora, tamen semper in prudentis animo debeat esse suspecta et imminente langore ipsius magis formidatur eventus, et ideo dispositioni substantie temporalis ne contingat patrem familias intestatum decedere tunc est precipue insistendum. Quapropter sapiens ac prudens vir Angelus quondam Tommasi de Corbinellis[9] per Christi gratiam mente, sensu ac intellectu sanus licet corpore languens, quia usque ad extremum vite ambulatoria est voluntas, suarum rerum et bonorum omnium dispositionem per presens nucupativum testamentum sine scriptis in hunc modum facere procuravit et fecit:

---

[6]Corbinelli's house stood on the site of the present *palazzo* Michelozzi, via Maggio 11, where the boundaries of the *popolo* (parish) of Santa Felicità overlapped those of the Nicchio *gonfalon* (ward) of Santo Spirito quarter. On the history of the buildings on the site, see Ginori-Lisci, *I palazzi di Firenze*, 2: 717–718.

[7]Andrea di Pietro Biglia, ca. 1395–1435, Augustinian friar, theologian and humanist; see *DBI* 10, s.v. 'Biglia, Andrea.'

[8]Santo Spirito, Augustinian convent that gave its name to the Oltrarno quarter of Santo Spirito, fd. 1250. On its history, see Davidsohn, *Geschichte von Florenz*, 4.3: 42; Davidsohn, *Forschungen*, 4: 406, 491–492; and Paatz, *Die Kirchen von Florenz*, 5: 117–208.

[9]Tommaso Corbinelli, † 1376–1377 (Martines, 'Addenda to the Life of Antonio Corbinelli,' 7, n. 8).

<3> Imprimis quidem animam suam omnipotenti Deo atque beate Marie virgini et toti celesti curie paradisi devotissime recommendavit. Corporis vero sui sepulturam, cum de hac vita eum mori contingerit, elegit et esse voluit apud ecclesiam Sancti Spiritus de Florentia[10] in sepultura patris ipsius testatoris.

<4> Item amore Dei legavit et reliquit cuilibet suprascriptorum testium florenum unum auri.

<5> Item legavit et reliquit operi murorum et operi Sancte Reparate de Florentia libras quinque florenorum parvorum.

<6> Item legavit nove sacrestie dicte opere Sancte Reparate libras quinque florenorum parvorum.[11]

<7> Item legavit et reliquit amore Dei et pro anima dicti testatoris capitulo et conventui fratrum Sancte Marie de Angelis de Florentia[12] ordinis camaldulensis in perpetuum et sine temporis prefinitione usumfructum, redditum et proventum florenorum centum auri et seu crediti florenorum centum auri ex illis de quibus dictus testator descriptus est creditor comunis Florentie in libris montium dicti comunis et de quibus dictum comune Florentie quolibet anno pro dono, pagis et interesse respondet et solvit creditori ad rationem quinque pro centinario.[13] Et pro executione predictorum voluit, iussit et mandavit dictus testator quod ex creditis et pecunia de quibus dictus testator descriptus est creditor comunis Florentie in libris dictorum montium heredes dicti testatoris separatim et in una partita de per se describantur creditores comunis Florentie in libris dictorum montium et quod iuxta dictam descriptionem et seu permutationem dictorum florenorum centum auri apponatur et describatur conditio, modus et seu forma quod omnes et

---

[10] The second Augustinian church, erected 1269–1308, destroyed by fire 1471 and demolished 1481–1489 (Paatz, *Die Kirchen von Florenz*, 5: 123–124, 152).

[11] On the mandatory testamentary payment to the *Opera di Santa Maria del Fiore* and the levy for the walls, see above, p. 192, n. 68. The cathedral is here referred to by its ancient name of Santa Reparata. Work on the north choir complex, including the new or north sacristy, began in 1401 (Paatz, *Die Kirchen von Florenz*, 4: 332). Corbinelli's heirs paid the total legacy of ten *lire* on 5 March 1420 (ASF, Notarile 21424, fol. 114v).

[12] Santa Maria degli Angeli, Camaldolese monastery in the present via degli Alfani, fd. 1295. For its history, see Davidsohn, *Forschungen*, 4: 495; and Paatz, *Die Kirchen von Florenz*, 3: 107–147.

[13] In an inventory of 7 September 1423, Corbinelli's executors reported a total of fl. 403 s. 9 d. 8 under his name in the *monte di Livorno* (ASF, Notarile 9040, fol. 108r–v). For additional credits recorded in this inventory, see below, nn. 19 and 20. A supplementary inventory of 18 April 1425 reported fl. 1781 s. 7 d. 9 of *monte comune* credits under Corbinelli's name and fl. 280 s. 17 d. 9 of *monte comune* credits in the names of his sons (ibid., fols. 189v–190r).

singule page, dona vel interesse dicte quantitatis in infinitum et in perpetuum dari et solvi debeant dicto capitulo et conventui fratrum Sancte Marie de Angelis de Florentia vel eorum legitimo sindico vel procuratori. Quod capitulum et conventum et quemcumque sindicum per dictum capitulum et conventum constituendum ad predicta dictus testator ex nunc suum et suorum heredum | <69r> et hereditatis procuratorem, actorem, factorem et certum nuntium specialem fecit et creavit specialiter et nominatim ad petendum, exigendum et recipiendum et seu se habuisse et recepisse confitendum pro dicto capitulo et conventu dictas pagas, dona et interesse pro dicta quantitate per comune Florentie solvenda in perpetuum, ut prefertur, et de hiis que receperit seu habuisse et recepisse confessus fuerit finiendum, liberandum et absolvendum dictum comune Florentie secundum stilum in talibus usitatum, et generaliter ad omnia et singula in predictis et circa predicta necessaria et opportuna faciendum, etiam si talia forent que mandatum exigerent speciale, dans et concedens huiusmodi sindico et procuratori, ut prefertur, constituendo in predictis et circa predicta plenum, liberum et generale mandatum cum plena, libera et generali administratione duraturum post mortem dicti testatoris et adita vel non adita vel iacente eius hereditate.

<8> Item simili modo et forma legavit et reliquit amore Dei fratribus, capitulo et conventui Sancti Benedicti ordinis camaldulensis extra et prope civitatem Florentie et prope ianuam que dicitur 'di pinti'[14] in perpetuum et sine temporis prefinitione usumfructum, redditum et proventum florenorum centum auri et seu crediti florenorum centum auri ex illis de quibus dictus testator descriptus est creditor comunis Florentie in libris montium dicti comunis et de quibus dictum comune Florentie quolibet anno pro dono, pagis et interesse respondet et solvit creditori ad rationem quinque pro centinario. Et pro predictorum executione et cetera, voluit et cetera, et procuratorem constituit et cetera, in omnibus et per omnia ut in precedenti capitulo et cetera; et extende ut ibi.

<9> Item amore Dei et pro anima dicti testatoris legavit et reliquit fratribus et capitulo et conventui fratrum Sancti Spiritus de Florentia usumfructum, redditum et proventum florenorum centum auri et seu crediti florenorum centum auri ex illis de quibus dictus testator descriptus est creditor comunis Florentie in libris montium dicti comunis et de quibus dictum comune quolibet anno pro dono, pagis et interesse respondet et solvit creditori ad rationem quinque pro centinario. Et pro executione predictorum voluit et cetera, permutari et cetera, et poni

---

[14]San Benedetto fuori della porta a' Pinti, Camaldolese monastery and dependency of Santa Maria degli Angeli, fd. 1395; see Bacchi, 'S. Benedetto fuori della porta a' Pinti di Firenze.' I am grateful to Alessandra Malquori for this reference and for guidance on the ecclesiastical topography of fifteenth-century Florence.

90   conditio et cetera, et fecit procuratorem et cetera ut supra in antecedenti capitulo et cetera extenditur ut ibi.

<10> Item amore Dei et pro anima dicti testatoris et simili modo et forma legavit et reliquit capitulo et conventui fratrum minorum Sancte Crucis de Florentia[15] in perpetuum usumfructum, redditum et proven-
95   tum florenorum centum auri et seu crediti florenorum centum auri ex illis de quibus dictus testator descriptus est creditor comunis Florentie in libris montium dicti comunis et pro quibus et de quibus dictum comune Florentie annuatim pro dono, pagis et interesse respondet et solvit creditori ad rationem quinque pro centinario. Et pro predictorum
100 executione et ad hoc ut predicta in perpetuum et in infinitum exequantur, voluit, iussit et mandavit dictus testator quod ex creditis et pecunia de quibus dictus testator descriptus est creditor comunis Florentie in libris dictorum montium heredes et seu hereditas dicti testatoris separatim et in una partita de per se describantur creditores comunis
105 Florentie in libris dictorum montium et quod apud et iusta huiusmodi talem descriptionem, permutationem seu transcriptionem dicti crediti apponatur et describatur conditio, modus et forma quod omnes et singule page, dona et interesse dicte quantitatis et seu crediti florenorum centum auri in infinitum et in perpetuum dari et solvi possint et debeant
110 dictis fratribus et capitulo et conventui fratrum Sancte Crucis vel cuicumque sindico pro dictis fratribus, capitulo et conventu constituendo pro comuni vel per comune Florentie.[16] | <69v> Quos sindicos in perpetuum, ut prefertur, constituendos et quemlibet eorum in solidum dictus testator suos et sue hereditatis ex nunc ad cautelam fecit et
115 ordinavit suos procuratores, actores et certos nuntios speciales ad petendum, exigendum et recipiendum et se habuisse et recepisse confitendum dictas pagas, dona et interesse dicte quantitatis dictorum florenorum centum et de his que receperit vel habuisse confessus fuerit finiendum dictum comune Florentie secundum stilum in talibus usi-
120 tatum, et generaliter ad omnia et singula in predictis et circa predicta faciendum necessaria et opportuna, etiam si talia forent que mandatum exigerent speciale, dans eis et cuilibet eorum in predictis et circa predicta plenum, liberum et generale mandatum cum plena, libera et generali administratione duraturum post mortem dicti constituentis,
125 etiam ipsius hereditate adita vel non et seu iacente eius hereditate.

---

[15]Santa Croce, Franciscan convent, fd. ca. 1211–1212. On its foundation and history, see Davidsohn, *Geschichte von Florenz*, 4.3: 26–36; Davidsohn, *Forschungen*, 4: 482–488; and Paatz, *Die Kirchen von Florenz*, 1: 497–701.

[16]Property bequeathed to the Franciscans of Santa Croce was not handled by the convent directly but administered on its behalf by sindics nominated jointly by the convent and the commune; see Davidsohn, *Geschichte von Florenz*, 4.3: 273.

<11> Et insuper ad hoc ut predicta quactuor legata suprascriptis conventibus Sancte Marie de Angelis et Sancti Benedicti et Sancti Spiritus et Sancte Crucis, ut prefertur, de usufructu dictorum florenorum centum de monte pro quolibet eorum facta in perpetuum vires habeant et exequantur, proibuit expresse dictus testator permutationem, transcriptionem, alienationem vel obligationem dictarum quantitatum et dictarum pagarum et seu ususfructus predicti, ut prefertur, legatorum dictis quactuor conventibus et cuilibet eorum. Et si et in quantum aliquis vel aliquod ex dictis capitulis vel conventibus Sancti Benedicti et Sancte Marie et Sancti Spiritus et Sancte Crucis consentire[n]t alicui permutationi, transcriptioni, alienationi, venditioni vel obligationi que fieret de dictis suprascriptis quantitatibus ad usumfructum, ut prefertur, legatis, tunc et in dicto casu dictum capitulum et conventum ex predictis qui dicte alienationi, permutationi vel obligationi seu transcriptioni vel venditioni quomodolibet tacite vel expresse consentiret per se vel alium quoquo modo privavit suprascripto legato dicti ususfructus florenorum centum, ut prefertur, tali capitulo vel conventui consentienti facto et dictum legatum in dicto casu pervenire et pertinere voluit ad alios ex dictis conventibus et capitulis qui dicte alienationi vel obligationi non consentirent et seu consensissent.

<12> Item amore Dei et pro anima sua legavit et reliquit florenos centum auri quos dari, distribui et erogari voluit pauperibus puellis nubendis amore Dei in subsidium dotium ipsarum pauperum puellarum eligendis per infrascriptos eius executores, dummodo eligant tales que sint nupte et viro desponsate et non tamen viro tradite, et cum hac limitatione quod uni eidem puelle ex dicta vel de dicta quantitate non possint dare ultra florenos decem auri.[17]

<13> Item amore Dei et pro anima sua legavit et reliquit hospitali Sancte Marie Nove de Florentia[18] cum honere et modo infrascripto

---

[17]Corbinelli's executors fulfilled this legacy between 29 January and 20 April 1420 by awarding fourteen girls with dowries of five to ten florins each (ASF, Notarile 9039, fol. 246r).

[18]Hospital of Santa Maria Nuova, founded by Folco Portinari in 1286. For its history, see Davidsohn, *Geschichte von Florenz*, 4.3: 53–54; Davidsohn, *Forschungen*, 4: 394–395; and Paatz, *Die Kirchen von Florenz*, 4: 1–64. Originally a poor house, by the later fourteenth century it was the biggest medical and acute care hospital in Florence with some 230 beds in 1427; see Henderson, 'The hospitals of late-medieval and Renaissance Florence,' 70–71; Henderson, *Piety and Charity*, 271, 347, 375; and Park, 'Healing the Poor.' Corbinelli's legacy is recorded at ASF, OSMN 68, fol. 309v. The bequest conformed to trends for the later fourteenth century observed by Bonnano et al., who note that Santa Maria Nuova reaped more than two-thirds of hospital bequests ('I legati "pro anima"', 198–199; 192–193, table 1; and 200–201, table 3).

222   A Renaissance of Conflicts

155   florenos centum auri et seu creditum florenorum centum auri ex illis de
       quibus ipse testator descriptus est creditor comunis Florentie in libris
       montium dicti comunis et de quibus dictum comune pro dono, pagis et
       interesse respondet dicto testatori ad rationem quinque pro centinario.
       Et voluit et mandavit quod pro predictorum executione ex pecunia et
160   quantitatibus de quibus dictus testator descriptus est creditor in dicto
       monte permutentur et transcribantur ad computum et nomen et sub
       nomine et computo dicti hospitalis dicti floreni centum auri cum hac
       conditione, modo et gravamine et seu honere quod dicta quantitas
       florenorum centum et seu dictum creditum florenorum centum in
165   perpetuum non possit finiri, vendi, alienari, permutari vel obligari, sed
       in perpetuum redditus dictorum florenorum centum pertineat ad dictum
       hospitale et pauperes dicti hospitalis Sancte Marie Nove. Et si et in
       quantum dictum hospitale vel eius hospitalarius vel quicumque eius
       rector, | <70r> administrator vel gubernator dictam quantitatem vel
170   creditum, ut predicitur, legatum alienaret, permutaret vel obligaret, tunc
       et in dicto casu dictum hospitale privavit dicto legato et relicto et ipsum
       legatum et relictum pervenire voluit ad hospitale Sancte Marie della
       Scala de Florentia. Et cum dicta conditione, modo, forma et gravamine
       dictam permutationem et transcriptionem fieri voluit de dictis florenis
175   centum in dictum hospitale.
         <14> Item amore Dei legavit et reliquit hospitali Sancte Marie della
       Scala de Florentia[19] florenos ducentos vigintiquinque auri et seu credi-
       tum florenorum ducentorum vigintiquinque auri ex illis et de illis de
       quibus dictus testator descriptus est vel descriptus reperiretur creditor
180   comunis Florentie in libris montium dicti comunis et de quibus dictum
       comune Florentie annuatim solvit creditori ad rationem quinque pro
       centinario. Et voluit et mandavit quod ex dictis creditis et pecunia de
       quibus dictus testator descriptus est creditor dicti comunis permutentur
       et transcribantur dicti floreni ducenti vigintiquinque auri sub nomine et
185   computo et ad rationem et computum dicti hospitalis Sancte Marie della
       Scala cum hiis honere, conditione, modo et gravamine quod dicta
       quantitas et seu creditum florenorum ducentorum vigintiquinque non
       possit in perpetuum vendi, alienari, permutari, obligari vel in alium
       transcribi sed perpetuo sit dicti hospitalis, et fructus et redditus et

---

[19]Hospital of Santa Maria della Scala, a dependency of the Sienese hospital of the same name, in the via della Scala, founded in 1316 by Cione di Lapo Pollini, now called San Martino della Scala. For its history see Davidsohn, *Geschichte von Florenz*, 4.3: 54–55; Davidsohn, *Forschungen*, 4: 400–401; and Paatz, *Die Kirchen von Florenz*, 4: 133–147. Under the patronage of the silk guild (Por Santa Maria), the hospital's principal function was the care of abandoned children, of which it housed 151 in 1427; see Henderson, 'The hospitals of late-medieval and Renaissance Florence,' 73; and Henderson, *Piety and Charity*, 348–349, 376.

190 donum et interesse dicte quantitatis perpetuo sit dicti hospitalis et pauperum ipsius. Et si et in quantum dictum hospitale vel aliquis rector vel gubernator eiusdem presens vel futurus dictam quantitatem et creditum predictum venderet, alienaret vel permutaret vel vendere, alienare vel permutare vellet, tunc in dicto casu dictum hospitale della
195 Scala privavit dicto legato et relicto dictorum florenorum .ccxxv. et in dicto casu dictum legatum devenire voluit ad hospitale Sancte Marie Nove de Florentia. Et cum dictis conditionibus, modis et formis voluit dictam permutationem et transcriptionem fieri in dictum hospitale della Scala in omnibus et per omnia ut supra dispositum et scriptum est.
200 <15> Item amore Dei voluit et reliquit et mandavit dictus testator quod per tempus et terminum viginti annorum proxime futurorum a morte dicti testatoris annuatim in die festivitatis Sancti Michaelis de mense septembri[20] cuiuslibet anni fiat et fieri debeat in ecclesia Sancti Spiritus de Florentia una 'piatanza' et seu unum offitium et a<n>nuale in quo
205 expendi voluit et iussit quolibet anno pro cera, luminibus et carnibus et pane et vino et aliis ad hoc necessariis pro dicto annuali florenos decem auri pro quolibet anno.[21]

<16> Item legavit et reliquit domine Filippe, alias vocate Pippe, eius uxori[22] dotes suas per dictum Angelum confessatas, que fuerunt et fuisse
210 dixit florenos quingentos auri ponderis et conii florentini.[23]

<17> Item ultra dictas dotes legavit et reliquit dicte domine Filippe sive Pippe eius uxori ut honorabilius secundo nubere possit, et in quocumque casu sive vidua steterit sive non, et sive [su-] | <70v> susceperit tutelam infrascriptorum eius filiorum sive non, toto tempore
215 vite dicte domine Filippe usumfructum, redditum et proventum omnium et singularum quantitatum pecunie et florenorum in quibus et de quibus dictus testator descriptus est vel descriptus reperiretur creditor comunis Florentie in libris montium dicti comunis, qui vulgariter dicitur 'monte

---

[20] Feast of St. Michael and All Angels, 29 September.

[21] In a codicil of 1 May 1419, Corbinelli reduced this sum to five florins a year (ASF, Notarile 9042, fol. 76r).

[22] Filippa di Lorenzo di Totto Bardi-Gualterotti, b. 1390–1391; see her *catasto* declaration of 12 July 1427, where she gave her age as thirty–six (ASF, Catasto 18, fol. 1288r; Catasto 65, fol. 91r).

[23] On the delivery of the dowry and the marriage, see above, p. 186, n. 48. On 7 September 1423, Filippa directed the *monte* officials to transfer to her account credits in the *monte comune*, the *monte di Pisa* and the *monte dei prestanzoni* with a total face value of five hundred florins in settlement of the dowry, nominating Ludovico di Silvestro Cessini her procurator for this purpose (ASF, Notarile 9040, fols. 116v and 117r). On 18 April 1425, Filippa and the other trustees appointed Giovanni di Tommaso Corbinelli procurator with the authority to seek interest on Angelo di Tommaso's outstanding *monte* credits (ibid., fol. 190r).

di Pisa,' quos, ut ipse testator recordabatur, dixit et asseruit fuisse et esse florenos ducentos nonaginta auri vel circa, salvo iure calculi.²⁴

<18> Item usumfructum, redditum et proventum omnium et singularum quantitatum pecunie et florenorum auri in quibus vel de quibus dictus testator descriptus est creditor comunis Florentie in libris montium dicti comunis, qui vulgariter dicitur 'monte di prestanzoni,' quos esse dixit et asseruit, si bene recordabatur, florenos trecentos tredecim vel circa, salvo iure calculi.²⁵

<19> Et ex nunc dictus testator ad cautelam fecit, constituit et ordinavit dictam dominam Filippam eius et sue hereditatis procuratricem, actricem, factricem et certam nuntiam specialem duraturam post mortem dicti testatoris et constituentis predicti et ipsius hereditate adita vel non, specialiter et nominatim ad petendum, exigendum et recipiendum et se habuisse et recepisse confitendum et recognoscendum in totum, particulariter et divisim, semel et pluries et quoties dictas pagas, dona et interesse dictarum quantitatum et dictum usumfructum, ut prefertur, sibi legatum, et de hiis que predictorum occaxione receperit finiendum, liberandum et absolvendum dictum comune secundum stilum in talibus usitatum; et ad substituendum in predictis et quolibet predictorum procuratorem, unum vel plures, semel et pluries et quoties; et substitutos revocandum et alium et alios de novo substituendum, presenti mandato nichilominus in suo robore permanente; et generaliter ad omnia et singula faciendum, procurandum et exercendum que iuris ordo et facti qualitas predictorum postulunt et requirunt, etiam si talia forent que mandatum exigerent speciale, dans et concedens dicte domine Pippe in predictis et circa predicta plenum, liberum et generale mandatum cum plena, libera et generali administratione duraturum, ut dictum est, post mortem dicti testatoris et eius hereditate adita vel iacente. Et post mortem dicte domine Filippe, dicta credita et proprietatem dictorum creditorum quorum ususfructus relictus est dicte domine Filippe legavit et reliquit dicto comuni Florentie et ex nunc secuta morte dicte domine Filippe et non ante, firmo tamen stante dicto usufructu supra legato dicte domine Filippe, dictus testator finivit, liberavit et absolvit dictum comune Florentie et me notarium infrascriptum pro dicto comuni recipientem de dictis creditis florenorum ducentorum nonaginta et florenorum trecentorum tredecim vel circa de quibus supra fit mentio.²⁶

---

²⁴The inventory of assets of 7 September 1423 identified credits worth fl. 284 s. 10 d. 9 in the *monte di Pisa* belonging to Corbinelli (ASF, Notarile 9040, fol. 116r–v).

²⁵The inventory of 7 September 1423 also noted fl. 330 under Corbinelli's name in the *monte dei prestanzoni* (ASF, Notarile 9040, fol. 116r–v).

²⁶In the 1427 *catasto* declaration filed by Corbinelli's heirs Filippa is described as the widow of Angelo di Tommaso resident in his house in the via Maggio (ASF, Catasto 17, fol. 229r; Catasto 65, fol. 88r). Because she possessed property in her

255 <20> Item in casu et si et in quantum dicta domina Filippa vidua steterit et habitare et stare voluerit cum filiis dicti testatoris et dotem et legatum suprascriptum non petierit, legavit et reliquit dicte domine Pippe reditam et habitationem et victum et vestitum condecentem et honorabilem in domo et supellectibus dicti testatoris. Et si et in quantum
260 dicta domina Filippa nollet vel non posset vel sibi non placeret stare vel morari cum dictis eius filiis in domo dicti testatoris vel alibi et dictum legatum ususfructus et dotem predictam peteret et seu petere vellet et vitam vidualem nicchilominus observaret, tunc et in dictis casibus dictam dominam Filippam privavit dicto legato alimentorum et victus et vestitus
265 et redditus in domo dicti testatoris de quo supra proxime fit mentio et in dicto casu, scilicet quo vitam vidualem servaret ubicumque et dictum legatum ususfructus dictarum quantitatum et dotes suas peteret vel petere vel exigere vellet, legavit et reliquit dicte domine | <71r> Filippe toto tempore quo vidua steterit et vidualem et honestam vitam servaverit
270 usum et usumfructum tot masseritiarum et rerum mobilium et ex tot masseritiis et rebus mobilibus dicti testatoris ad electionem dicte domine Pippe que sint valoris et comunis extimationis florenorum centum auri, cum hoc in predictis salvo, expresso ac disposito et ordinato quod dicta domina Pippa non teneatur finito dicto usufructu dictas masseritias et
275 res mobiles restituere in eo statu, valore vel extimatione quibus erunt tempore quo sibi tradentur vel earum extimationem vel earum deteriorationem sed possit eas restituere actritas vel consumptas et in eo statu quo erunt tempore quo finietur dictus usus absque eo quod aliquid pro deterioratione earum det vel solvat heredibus dicti testatoris.[27]
280 <21> Item quod in casu et quandocumque dicta domina Pippa vellet sibi satisfieri de dotibus suis et contentaretur et vellet quod sibi assignarentur super monte comunis Florentie, voluit dictus testator quod eidem Pippe eius uxori assignentur et in eam describantur libere et sine aliqua contradictione in satisfactione dicte dotis tot ex denariis et
285 pecunia et seu creditis de quibus dictus testator vel eius heredes essent descripti creditores comunis Florentie in libris montium dicti comunis,

---

own right, for purposes of the *catasto* she counted as an independent household (on this practice, see Herlihy and Klapisch-Zuber, *Tuscans and Their Families*, 13). In her own declaration, Filippa acknowledged in addition to eight hundred florins on her own account and forty florins in *paghe sostenute* the fl. 284 in the *monte di Pisa* and fl. 313 in the *monte dei prestanzoni* bequeathed to her by Angelo, noting that the latter two credits would revert to the commune on her death (Catasto 18, fol. 1288r; and Catasto 65, fol. 91r).

[27] On 30 July 1423, Filippa acknowledged receipt of household goods to the value of a hundred florins; the acknowledgement and inventory are recorded at ASF, Notarile 9040, fol. 108r–v.

qui sint valoris et comunis extimationis dictorum florenorum quingentorum auri.

<22> Item iure institutionis legavit et reliquit Iulie et Bartolomee filiabus legitimis et naturalibus dicti testatoris natis ex eo et dicta domina Filippa eius uxore predicta pro eis nubendis et dotandis et quando nubent florenos mille auri pro qualibet earum, et interim donec nuptui tradentur reliquit eisdem victum et vestitum et alimenta decentia in domo dicti testatoris.[28]

<23> Item eisdem Iulie et Bartolomee eius filiabus et cuilibet earum in casu viduitatis et donec et quousque vidue stabunt legavit et reliquit reditam et usum et habitationem in domum habitationis dicti testatoris et in qua dictus testator ad presens habitat et infra contenta et confinata.

<24> Item dicto iure instituit, legavit et reliquit dictis Iulie et Bartolomee et cuilibet earum postquam nupte et viro tradite fuerint toto tempore earum et cuiuslibet earum vite usumfructum, redditum et proventum florenorum trecentorum auri et seu crediti florenorum trecentorum auri pro qualibet earum ex illis et de illis de quibus dictus testator descriptus est creditor comunis Florentie in libris montium dicti comunis et de quibus comune providet ad rationem quinque pro centinario cum hoc salvo, expresso, declarato et ordinato quod dictus ususfructus sit proprium ipsarum eius filiarum et de eo possint dicte eius filie facere voluntatem suam et nicchil ex dictis fructibus dictarum quantitatum ad usumfructum, ut prefertur, eis relictarum queratur vel queri possit alicui viro vel marito dictarum Iulie et Bartolomee vel alicuius earum sed sit proprium dictarum eius filiarum. Et post mortem dictarum Iulie et Bartolomee et cuiuslibet earum dicte quantitates pecunie montium quarum ususfructus legatus est dictis filiabus dicti testatoris et proprietas dictorum florenorum sit comunis Florentie et ad ipsum pertineat et dicto comuni post mortem dictarum Iulie et Bartolomee firmo stante dicto usufructu legavit et reliquit et ex nunc secuta morte dictarum Iulie et Bartolomee et finito dicto usufructu et non ante dictum comune de dictis creditis et quantitatibus finivit, absolvit et liberavit.

<25> Item iure institutionis legavit et reliquit Alexandre filie naturali | <71v> dicti Angeli, nate ex dicto Angelo tempore quo solutus erat et ex quadam muliere etiam tunc soluta, pro ipsam Alexandram monachando vel pinzocherando et quando monacabitur florenos ducentos

---

[28]Bartolomea di Angelo Corbinelli, b. 1414–1415 (ASF, Catasto 17, fol. 236r), was betrothed to Daniele di Luigi dei Canigiani 22 August 1428 (ASF, Notarile 9040, fol. 360r–v). The marriage followed on 23 November 1428 (ibid., fol. 378r). On 5 January 1429, Daniele acknowledged receipt from Bernardo di Angelo Corbinelli of a dowry of a thousand florins plus a hundred-florin dotal legacy left to Bartolomea by her uncle Antonio di Tommaso (ibid., fol. 383v). Giulia appears to have died by 1423 (see above, p. 186, n. 49).

auri et interim alimenta decentia. Et ultra predicta eidem Alexandre postquam monacata fuerit legavit et reliquit toto tempore vite dicte Alexandre usumfructum, redditum vel proventum florenorum ducentorum auri et seu crediti florenorum ducentorum auri ex illis de quibus dictus testator descriptus est creditor comunis Florentie in libris montium dicti comunis, qui vulgariter dicitur 'monte comune' et de quibus dictum comune respondet creditori pro donis et interesse ad rationem quinque pro centinario. Et post mortem dicte Alexandre et finito dicto usufructu, dictum creditum et proprietas dictorum florenorum ducentorum auri sit comunis Florentie et ad ipsum comune pertineat et ex nunc finito dicto usufructu dictum comune de dicto credito florenorum ducentorum auri finivit et liberavit, firmo tamen manente dicto usufructu.

<26> Item legavit et reliquit Iohanni fratri carnali dicti testatoris et filio dicti olim Tommasi de Corbinellis[29] florenos vigintiquinque auri.

<27> Item legavit et reliquit Parisio eius fratri carnali et filio dicti olim Tom<m>asi[30] florenos vigintiquinque auri.

<28> Item legavit et reliquit Antonio fratri carnali dicti testatoris[31] florenos vigintiquinque auri.

<29> Item legavit et reliquit Tommase sorori carnali dicti testatoris florenos vigintiquinque auri.

<30> In omnibus autem aliis suis bonis presentibus et futuris sibi heredes universales instituit, fecit et esse voluit Bernardum, Tommasum et Corbinellum filios suos legitimos et naturales natos ex dicto testatore et dicta domina Filippa eius uxore predicta equis portionibus et eos ad invicem substituit vulgariter, pupillariter et per fideicommissum si et quandocumque aliquis eorum decesseri[n]t in pupillari etate vel postea quandocumque ante completum vigesimumquintum annum etatis talis decedentis.[32] Et si omnes dicti eius filii et heredes predicti decesserint in pupillari etate vel postquam quandocumque ante etatem vigintiquinque annorum sine filiis legitimis et naturalibus ex legitimo matrimonio procreatis, tunc et in dicto casu dictis eius filiis pupillariter, vulgariter et per fideicommissum substituit et seu sibi testatori heredes instituit et esse voluit hospitale Sancte Marie Nove de Florentia pro una quarta parte ex quactuor partibus hereditatis predicte et pro alia quarta parte hospi-

---

[29] Giovanni di Tommaso Corbinelli, † 1438; see above, p. 185, n. 44.

[30] Parigi di Tommaso Corbinelli, † 1429–1430; see above, p. 185, n. 44.

[31] Antonio di Tommaso Corbinelli, b. 1376–1377, † 1425; see above, p. 185, n. 44.

[32] According to their *catasto* declaration of July 1427, Bernardo and Tommaso di Angelo Corbinelli were eighteen and fifteen respectively; Corbinello had died, but Angelo, who had not been born when Angelo di Tommaso made his will, survived (ASF, Catasto 17, fol. 236r; Catasto 65, fol. 91r). They declared total assets of fl. 11,358 of which 3592 represented credits in various *monti* and *paghe sostenute* (ASF, Catasto 65, fol. 90r). See above, p. 194, n. 78.

tale Sancte Marie della Scala de Florentia, et pro reliquis duabus partibus ex quactuor partibus dicte sue hereditatis Bartolomeum,[33] Iohannem, Parisium et Antonium fratres carnales dicti testatoris et filios dicti olim Tommasi de Corbinellis equis portionibus et premortuorum ex eis filios et descendentos masculos legitimos et naturales in stirpem et non in capita. In qua medietate dicte sue hereditatis dictis fratribus dicti testatoris et premortuorum ex eis filiis relicta et in qua eos substituit, ut prefertur, computetur et designetur et assignari debeat et dictis eius fratribus heredibus substitutis predictis et premortuorum ex eis filiis legitimis et naturalibus et eisdem eius fratribus et eorum filiis in casu predicto reliquit et in eorum portione dicte hereditatis designari voluit et | <72r> mandavit domum habitationis dicti testatoris et in qua dictus testator ad presens habitat cum quactuor apotecis[34] positis et existentibus sub dicta domo, que domus sita et posita est in civitate Florentie et in populo Sancte Felicitatis in via que dicitur 'via Maggio,' quibus omnibus a primo dicta via, a secundo bona monialium monasterii Sancti Iohannis Ierosolimitani, a tertio Francisci Filippi Neri Cambi, a quarto via que dicitur 'chiasso Boldronai' infra predictas confines vel alias si qui forent plures aut veriores.[35] Que domus et apotece in perpetuum donec esset et seu viveret aliquis masculus legitimus et naturalis de consortibus et agnatis dicti testatoris et de dicta domo de Corbinellis natus vel nasciturus non possint in totum vel in partem vendi, alienari, permutari, donari, obligari vel in alium transferri vel ad non modicum tempus lucrari extra consortes et de domo, consorteria et progenie de dictis Corbinellis sed perpetuo sint dictorum eius fratrum et eorum descendentium masculorum predictorum seu aliorum consortium dicti testatoris ad quos iusto titulo pervenirent.

Et expresse ob causam et causas predictas prohibuit in perpetuum alienationem, venditionem, pignorationem et ad magnum tempus locationem et quamcumque translationem fieri de dicta domo et apotecis in aliquem extra domum et familiam de Corbinellis predictis donec erit vel vivet aliquis masculus legitimus et naturalis de dicta domo et familia

---

[33] Bartolomeo di Tommaso Corbinelli, ca. 1349–ca. 1430, Angelo di Tommaso's half-brother; see above, p. 185, n. 44.

[34] In their *catasto* declaration, Corbinelli's heirs reported the four shops on the ground floor of Corbinelli's *palazzo* but note that only one was rented in 1427 (ASF, Catasto 17, fol. 229r).

[35] On Corbinelli's house, see above, p. 217, n. 6. In 1427 a house on the corner of Chiasso dei Velluti (formerly Chiasso di Boldronai or Boldriani) belonged to Francesco di Filippo Cambi (Ginori-Lisci, *I palazzi di Firenze*, 2: 718, n. 1). Founded in 1362 as a hospital of the Knights of Malta, San Giovanni Gerosolimitano (now San Giovanni Battista della Calza) was refounded as a convent of Maltese nuns in 1362; see Paatz, *Die Kirchen von Florenz*, 2: 272–284.

et seu consorteria de Corbinellis, ut supra dictum est. Et si dicta domus et apotece in totum vel in partem quomodolibet alienarentur contra prohibitionem predictam, talis alienatio, venditio, donatio, obligatio, locatio vel translatio sit ipso iure nulla et nullius valoris, efficacie vel effectus. Et illico ille talis ex dictis eius fratribus vel consortibus, ad quos dicta domus in totum vel in partem perveniret vel pertineret, qui extra familiam alienaret contra prohibitionem et formam predictas sit ipso iure et ipso facto privatus et ex nunc dictus testator eum privavit omni iure et portione quam et quod talis alienans haberet in dicta domo et seu parte domus et bonorum que alienarentur, et illico dicta talis pars alienata vel in alium contra dictam prohibitionem tra<n>slata perveniat ad alios fratres et heredes dicti testatoris et premortuorum ex eis filios vel descendentes masculos predictos, si extarent. Et si dicti eius fratres vel eorum filii non extarent, vel extarent et tali alienationi contra formam predictam fiende tacite vel expresse consentirent vel ab aliquo contra dictam prohibitionem emente vel quomodolibet acquirente non vendicarent vel vendicare cessarent et seu nollent, tunc et in dicto casu et seu casibus dicta domus et apotece vel earum pars, que contra dictam prohibitionem alienaretur, perveniat ad alios proximiores agnates et consortes dicti testatoris successive de gradu in gradum qui tali alienationi non consentirent et talia bona contra dictam proibitionem alienata vendicare vellent donec erit aliquis de dicta consorteria cum eisdem honeribus et gravaminibus, conditionibus et proibitionibus quibus supra dictum est. Et si omnes dicti eius fratres et consortes predicti essent concordes in vendendo et alienando dictam domum et apotecas vel earum partem aliquam extra eorum consortes vel | <72v> tali huiusmodi alienationi contra dictam prohibitionem fiende consentirent tacite vel expresse vel tacerent vel vendicare cessarent vel differrent et seu nollent, tunc et in dicto casu dicta domus cum apotecis vel eorum pars, que contra dictam formam et prohibitionem alienaretur, perveniat ad hospitale Sancte Marie Nove de Florentia et eidem hospitali in casu et conditione predictis et pauperibus dicti hospitalis legavit et reliquit. Et si dictum hospitale Sancte Marie Nove vel quicumque hospitalarius dicti hospitalis qui pro tempore fuerit tali permutationi vel alienationi contra dictam prohibitionem de dictis bonis vel eorum parte, ut prefertur, fiende tacite vel expresse quomodolibet consentiret vel negligens esset vel cessaret vel differret vendicare et in vendicando et recuperando dictam domum et apotecas in casu et conditione predictis, tunc et in dicto casu dictus testator privavit dictum hospitale et pauperes predictos dicto legato et relicto dicte domus et voluit et mandavit dictam domum et apotecas vel eorum partem que, ut predicitur, contra dictam prohibitionem alienarentur, pervenire ad hospitale Sancte Marie della Scala de Florentia et in dicto casu eidem hospitali legavit et reliquit. Et similiter si dictum hospitale Sancte Marie della Scala vel aliquis eius hospitalarius vel rector qui tunc prefuerit dicto hospitali della Scala tali alienationi, venditioni

vel permutationi contra dictam prohibitionem de dicta domo et bonis
fiende consentiret tacite vel expresse vel tacere[n]t vel vendicare et
petere dictam domum et apotecas differret vel cessaret vel vendicare
nollet, tunc et in dicto casu dictum hospitale della Scala privavit dicto
legato et relicto et voluit dictam domum cum apotecis in dicto casu
pertinere et pervenire ad artem et universitatem artis Lane civitatis
Florentie[36] pleno iure et eidem arti in dicto casu dictam domum cum
apotecis legavit et reliquit.

<31> Item ad declarationem veritatis et exonerationem conscientie
dicti testatoris et declarationem creditorum et debitorum dicti testatoris,
dixit et declaravit dictus testator quod ipse habet libros et codices
rationum suarum in quibus continentur et creditores et debitores, et
quicquid in eis scriptum reperitur verum est et sine aliqua malitia
conceptum et scriptum, et ipsis libris in omnibus fidem adheri voluit,
iussit et mandavit prout in eis contentum et scriptum est.

<32> Item voluit, disposuit et mandavit dictus testator quod si dicto
Bartolomeo, eius fratri, et supradicto magistro Augustino de Roma
ambobus in concordia hinc ad per totum unum annum proxime futurum
post mortem dicti testatoris videretur vel appareret ipsum Angelum
aliquid indebite accepisse vel ipsum Angelum alicui teneri vel obligatum
esse quod ipsi Bartolomeus et magister Augustinus possint illud totum
declarare et de bonis dicti testatoris satisfacere et seu solvi et satisfieri
facere prout eorum conscientie et exhonerationi conscientie dicti testatoris viderint convenire, et eos ad predicta in presenti capitulo contenta
executores fecit eo quia de eis plene confidit, dans eis plenam baliam
duraturam per annum a morte testatoris predicta omnia in presenti
capitulo contenta exequendi et executionem mandandi et pro executione ipsorum omnia providendi, vendendi et alienandi et alia quecumque
faciendi que de ipsorum magistri Augustini et Bartolomei | <73r> amborum
in concordia libera processerit voluntate.

<33> Item dixit et declaravit dictus testator quod ipse numquam emit
aliquod creditum super montibus comunis Florentie sed revera quod
ipse testator est descriptus creditor in libris montium dicti comunis pro
prestantiis et honeribus dicti testatoris et tam per ipsum testatorem quam
eius parentes et fratres solutis comuni Florentie in quam pluribus
quantitatibus pecunie et florenorum auri. Et quia ipse testator multotiens
per multos magistros et baccalarios et alios teologos disputari vidit an
sit licitum pagas ex predictis quantitatibus assumere, et vidit et audivit
inter prudentissimos magistros et teologos oppiniones contrarias super
predictis teneri et reportari, propter que ipse testator in conscientia sua
certitudinem habere non potuit, et volens omnino, quantum in eo

---

[36] The *Arte della Lana*, the guild of wool manufacturers and merchant drapers.
On the guild in this period, see Hoshino, *L'Arte della Lana in Firenze*.

possibile sit, conscientiam suam exhonerare, voluit, iussit et mandavit quod si ullo unquam tempore per ecclesiam Romanam vel concilium vel per aliquod collegium doctorum cui per ecclesiam Romanam vel eius pastores commissa fuerit decisio et declaratio super predictis pagis, donis et interesse, que universaliter recipiuntur per cives a comuni de denariis pro eorum honeribus dicto comuni solutis, an licite sint vel non fieret aliqua declaratio vel decisio super predictis, quod tunc et in dicto casu, salvis legatis et relictis supra et infra factis, per heredes dicti testatoris fiat et observetur in totum et in omnibus et per omnia prout per dictam ecclesiam Romanam vel eius concilium vel collegium doctorum cui predicta decidenda commissa fuerint, ut prefertur, fuerit dictum, decisum, terminatum seu conclusum, et sic in omnibus et per omnia observari et fieri voluit.

<34> Item dictus testator amore Dei et pro remedio sue anime legavit et reliquit venerabili viro magistro Augustino Nicholai de Roma suprascripto toto tempore vite dicti magistri Augustini usumfructum, redditum et proventum florenorum quinquaginta auri descriptorum super monte comunis Florentie, scilicet ex illis de quibus dictus testator descriptus est creditor in libris montium dicti comunis et de quibus comune Florentie pro pagis, donis et interesse solvit creditori ad rationem quinque pro centinario pro quolibet anno. Et post mortem dicti magistri Augustini, dictam quantitatem florenorum quinquaginta et proprietatem dicti crediti florenorum quinquaginta legavit comuni Florentie et ex nunc finito dicto usufructu et sequuta morte dicti magistri Augustini et non ante dictum comune Florentie finivit, absolvit et liberavit de dicto credito dictorum florenorum quinquaginta auri. Et voluit, disposuit et mandavit dictus testator de dictis florenis quinquaginta auri ex quantitatibus de quibus dictus testator, ut prefertur, descriptus est creditor dicti comunis fieri unam descriptionem de per se cum conditionibus et modis et formis predictis ut dictus magister Augustinus sine alia solempnitate vel forma servanda dictas pagas, dona et interesse dictorum florenorum .l. toto tempore sue vite habeat et recipere et consequi possit, omni obstaculo et exceptione remotis.[37]

<35> Item amore Dei legavit et reliquit Margherite eius serve, si et in quantum servierit filiis et filiabus et heredibus dicti testatoris per sex annos proxime futuros post mortem dicti testatoris prout ad presens servit et serviebat familie dicti testatoris et sibi testatori, libertatem puram secundum usum et consuetudinem civitatis romane et eam finitis dictis sex annis et factis et observatis predictis et in casu et conditione predictis

---

[37] In his codicil of 1 May 1419, Corbinelli added a similar bequest of a hundred florins to his physician Jacopo di Martino da Spoleto (ASF, Notarile 9042, fol. 76v), who reported the legacy in his 1427 *catasto* declaration (Park, *Doctors and Medicine*, 186 and 251).

a sua et suorum heredum et filiorum predictorum manu, dominio et potestate penitus exemit et dimisit et | <73v> liberam, francam et absolutam esse voluit.

<36> Item, finitis et servitis dictis sex annis, ut prefertur, si et in casu et in quantum dicta Margherita nubere vellet, legavit et reliquit eidem Margherite pro eam dotando et in subsidium sue dotis et quando nubet libras octuaginta florenorum parvorum; et ultra dictas libras octuaginta usque ad libras centum florenorum parvorum illud quod videbitur infrascriptis eius executoribus vel maiori parti eorum et superviventium ex eis.

<37> Tutores vero et debito tempore curatores dictorum eius filiorum et filiarum necnon presentis testamenti et ultime voluntatis executores fecit, reliquit et esse voluit dictam dominam Filippam, dictam Pippam, uxorem dicti testatoris et Bartolomeum, Iohannem, Parisium et Antonium fratres carnales dicti testatoris et filios dicti olim Tommasi de Corbinellis et Tommasum nepotem dicti testatoris et filium dicti Bartolomei et quoscumque tres ex eis in concordia, in quorum numero semper sit et esse debeat dicta domina Filippa eius uxor dum vixerit et vidualem vitam servaverit, et nichil sine ea vel eius consensu fieri possit per alios tutores et curatores et executores predictos. Et cum hoc etiam expresso et declarato quod si aliqui ex dictis tutoribus et curatoribus decederent et remanerent solum quactuor vel pauciores ex dictis tutoribus, quod tunc et in dicto casu maior pars dictorum tutorum et curatorum superviventium dictam tutelam et curam et offitium executorie facere et administrare possint dum tamen semper in dicto maiori numero interesse debeat dicta domina Filippa et nichil sine ea vel eius consensu fieri possit.

<38> Item voluit et declaravit quod si quactuor ex dictis tutoribus et curatoribus decesserint vel se excusaverint vel remoti fuerint a cura et tutela predicta ita quod solum duo ex dictis tutoribus superessent, voluit dictus testator quod tunc et in dicto casu illi duo possint et valeant sine aliquo adiuncto tutelam et curam predictam administrare ac gerere.[38]

Ac etiam quod tunc et in dicto casu quando duo soli ex dictis tutoribus et curatoribus et non plures remanerent et essent in offitio dicte tutele

---

[38]Corbinelli granted the executors full powers of administration in a procuration dictated on the same day and before the same witnesses; see ASF, Notarile 9042, fols. 74r–76r. On several occasions the executors delegated their authority to procurators. For example, on 11 May 1422, Bartolomeo, Giovanni and Parisio di Tommaso and Tommaso di Bartolomeo Corbinelli appointed Pazzino di Taddeo Pazzini their procurator with respect to Angelo di Tommaso's estate (ASF, Notarile 9040, fol. 10v). Pazzini was reappointed as procurator 7 September 1423 (ibid., fols. 116v–117r). On 18 April 1425, Corbinelli's widow Filippa and the other trustees empowered Giovanni di Tommaso Corbinelli to act as their joint procurator with regard to the estate (ibid., fol. 189r–v).

et cure, voluit et disposuit dictus testator quod dicti duo super extantes et superviventes tutores seu curatores, si eis videbitur vel placuerit, possint renuntiare et se abstinere et excusare a dicta cura et tutela dictorum eius filiorum absque aliqua solempnitate in predictis observanda, et tunc et in dicto casu quo dicti duo renunciarent vel se excusarent vel abstinerent seu abstinere vellent a dicta tutela et cura, voluit tutelam et curam dictorum eius filiorum devolvi et devolutam esse in casu predicto ad offitiales pupillorum et adultorum comunis Florentie qui pro tempore fuerint, quos offitiales in dicto casu et conditione eveniente tutores et curatores dictorum eius filiorum reliquit, fecit et esse voluit, dans et concedens dictus testator dictis eius executoribus in numero et modis et formis suprascriptis plenam licentiam et liberam potestatem, autoritatem et baliam pro executione predictorum et contentorum in presenti testamento de bonis et rebus dicti testatoris vendendi et alienandi et legata suprascripta solvendi ac etiam pro executione dictorum suprascriptorum legatorum factorum de pecunia et creditis montium quascumque permutationes et transcriptiones dictorum creditorum faciendi et fieri faciendi in legatorios predictos | <74r> cum conditionibus, modis et formis superius annotatis et licentiam et parabolam dandi notario et scribanis montium dicti comunis dictas permutationes et transcriptiones faciendi secundum stilum in talibus usitatum et etiam prout et sicut dictis executoribus et tutoribus et curatoribus et tribus ex eis in concordia, ut supra dictum est, videbitur et placebit et de ipsorum libera processerit voluntate, et generaliter omnia et singula alia faciendi que pro predictorum omnium executione et effectu fuerint necessaria et opportuna et sine quibus predicta explicari non possent, etiam si talia forent que mandatum exigerent speciale, dans eis et maiori parti eorum et seu tali ex eis, ut supra dictum est, in predictis et circa predicta plenum, liberum et generale mandatum cum plena, libera et generali administratione duraturum etiam post mortem dicti constituentis et ipsius hereditate iacente vel non et seu adita vel non.

<39> Item voluit ac disposuit dictus testator quod si dictis eius tutoribus vel maiori parti eorum et superviventium ex eis videretur utile esse dictis pupillis vel alicui eorum quod pro ipsis filiis dicti testatoris vel aliquo eorum vel eorum nomine fieret ars Lane seu pannorum, finium vel grossorum in civitate Florentie una cum ipsis tutoribus vel aliquo eorum vel cum alia quacumque persona vel personis vel in aliqua sotietate in apoteca vel traffico artis Lane predicte vel quod pro ipsis pupillis vel aliquo eorum de per se fieret dicta ars et seu apoteca dicte artis Lane quod ipsi tutores et maior pars superviventium ex eis sine eorum preiuditio vel gravamine possint pro dictis pupillis et quolibet vel aliquo eorum dictam artem facere et seu fieri facere eo modo et forma et prout dictis tutoribus vel maiori parti eorum, ut dictum est, videbitur et placebit, non obstantibus quacumque lege vel ordine in contrarium disponente.

<40> Et hanc suam ultimam voluntatem asseruit esse velle, quam valere voluit iure testamenti et si iure testamenti non valeret, valeat saltim iure codicillorum et cuiuslibet alterius ultime voluntatis[39] quo vel quibus magis et melius valere potest et tenere, capsans, irritans et annullans omne et quodcumque aliud testamentum et ultimam voluntatem hactenus per dictum testatorem factam manu mei Francisci notarii insfrascripti vel alterius cuiuscumque notarii, non obstantibus quibuscumque verbis derogatoriis vel precisis in eis appositis, de quibus omnibus dixit se penitere et hic pro expressis haberi voluit. Et hoc testamentum et ultimam voluntatem pre ceteris predictis valere et exequi voluit et mandavit in omnibus et per omnia ut superius contentum et scriptum est, mandans per me Franciscum notarium infrascriptum de predictis omnibus publicum confici instrumentum.

Textual Apparatus

1 Angnoli Corbinelli *marg.*
1 Dicitur decessisse die . . . maii .1419. *not. marg.*
1 Rogatum *not. marg.*
1 Publicata et restituta domine Filippe tutrici institutio heredum usque 'et si omnes dicti' et cetera et postea 'tutores' usque in fine. Solvit grossos florenos .15. <heredita *post* tutrici *del.*> *not. marg. Vid. infra lin.* 208 *et lin.* 508.
6 doctore *scripsi*: MS doctori
14 ipsius *interlin.*
17 eventus *interlin.*
26 paradisi *interlin.*
29 dicti *post* patris *del.*
32 amore Dei *post* Item *interlin. et del.*
34 amore Dei *post* legavit *interlin. et del.*
38 usumfructum *post* camaldulensis *del.*
38 et sine temporis prefinitione *marg.*
40 ex illis de quibus *post* auri *del.*
44 pro executione predictorum *marg.*
47 de per se *marg.*
54 dictus *post* conventum *del.*
57 actorem *marg.*
61 et de hiis que recepit s– *post* solvenda *del.*
72 de *post* Benedicti *del.*
88 ad rationem *post* solvit *del.*
93 minorum *interlin.*
94 in perpetuum *interlin.*

---

[39]Francesco Giacomini recorded an earlier testament of Corbinelli on 5 July 1417; see ASF, Notarile 9042, fols. 55v–58v.

95 .c. et cetera de monte comuni et cetera et voluit et cetera et procuratorem *post* florenorum[1] *del.*
98 annuatim *corr. ex* annuatis
108 dictorum *post* crediti *del.*
110 sin– *post* vel *del.*
111 conventu *corr. ex* conventui
113 in solidum *marg.*
114 constit– *post* suos *del.*
136 transcriptioni *marg.*
136 obligationi *post* alienationi *del.*
139–140 seu transcriptioni vel venditioni *marg.*
142 facto *post* conventui *del.*
148 pau– *post* dotium *del. et expunc.*
154 cum honere et modo infrascripto *marg.*
156 creditor *post* quibus *del.*
156 ipse testator *interlin.*
159 pro predictorum executione *marg.*
177 florenos centum auri et seu creditum florenorum centum auri ex illis de quibus dictus testator descriptus est vel *post* Florentia *del.*
178 ducentorum *marg.*
187 florenorum decentorum *post* quantitas *del.*
194 quod *post* vellet *canc.*
194 dictum hospitale *post* casu *del.*
202–203 de mense septembri *marg.*
204 de Florentia *interlin.*
205 in *post* anno *del.*
208 Publicata et restituta comuni Florentie pro parte ad dictum comune pertinente. Item restituta dicte domine Pippe *not. marg.*
214 reliquit et legavit *post* non *del.*
214–215 toto tempore . . . domine Filippe *marg.*
220 salvo iure calculi *marg.*
224 Pisa *post* di *del.*
224 prestanzoni *marg.*
226 salvo iure calculi *marg.*
230 testatoris et *marg.*
248 de quibus *post* creditorum *del.*
249 et[2] *interlin.*
250 et non ante *marg.*
250 tamen *interlin.*
255 eius uxor predicta *post* Filippa *del.*
257–258 legavit et . . . domine Pippe *marg.*
259 et supellectibus *interlin.*
261–262 et dictum . . . petere vellet et *marg.*
265 de quo . . . fit mentio *interlin.*
267 et do– *post* legatum *canc.*

268 usum et usumfructum dicte domine Pippe usum et usumfructum *post* reliquit *del.*
271 que sint valoris *post* testatoris *del.*
274 de *post* teneatur *del.*
284 tot *post* contradictione *del.*
285 de qui *post* pecunia *del.*
295 et cuilibet earum *interlin.*
301 singula singulis referendo *post* vite *del.*
303–305 ex illis . . . pro centinario *marg.*
312 et cuiuslibet earum *marg.*
317 et non ante dictum comune *post* Bartolomee *del.*
339 eius *post* Antonio *del.*
339 florenos *post* carnali *del.*
343 Pone hic omnia scripta et notata infra in sequenti carta sub hoc signo % usque ad dationem tutorum *post* auri *not. marg. Vid. infra lin.* 442–516.
350 decesserint *interlin.*
353–354 pupillariter . . . fideicommissum *marg.*
356 sic *post* partibus *del. et expunc.*
359 carnales *marg.*
361 legitimos et naturales *interlin.*
362 dictis fratribus dicti testa– *post* medietate *del.*
363 et premortuorum ex eis filiis *marg.*
363–364 ut prefertur *interlin.*
364 heredibus substitutis pred– *post* dictis *del.*
365 et *post* fratribus *canc.*
366 et eorum filiis *interlin.*
380 de[1] *interlin.*
382 vel *post* predictorum *del.*
393–394 ad quos . . . vel pertineret *marg.*
396 eos *post* testator *del.*
400 si extar– *post* testatoris *del.*
408–410 qui tali . . . vendicare vellent *marg.*
420 legavit *post* predictis *del.*
420 dictam domum *post* hospitalis *del.*
422 alienationi *post* tali *del.*
424 consentiret *post* expresse *del.*
442 Omnia ista legata usque ad versiculum 'Tutores' et cetera positum infra in sequenti carta causa pulcrioris ordinis ponantur supra sub simili signo ante institutionem heredis *post* reliquit *not. marg. Vid. supra lin.* 343.
451 vider– *post* concordia *del.*
457 dans ambobus *post* convenire *del.*
461 faciendi *post* providendi *del.*
467 per *post* prestantiis *del.*
483 prout *scripsi*: MS *propterut*
508 Restituta et publicata dicte Margherite *not. marg.*

512 lib– *post* eam *del.*
515 et *post* et[1] *del.*
524 exec– *post* testamenti *del.*
525 eius *post* Pippam *canc.*
535 adminis– *post* tutorum *del.*
536–537 et offitium executorie facere et *marg.*
538 debeat *corr. ex* debeant
542 quactuor ex dict– *post* solum *del.*
548 seu curatores *marg.*
548 renunciare dicte *post* placuerit *del.*
553 devo– *post* et[2] *del.*
555 pro *post* qui *del.*
578–591 Item voluit . . . contrarium disponente *marg.*
581 pannorum *post* Lane *del. et expunc.*
584 quod *interlin.*
588 seu *interlin.*
594 quibus quo vel quibus *post* voluntatis *del.*
595 magis et *marg.*

Appendix 2
Extracts from Florentine Testaments

1. ASF, OSMN 67, fol. 140v. Extract from the testament of Domenico Allegri, notary, 30 June 1383.

Item dictus testator considerans se fuisse et hodie esse descriptum creditorem comunis Florentie in libris seu registris montis dicti comunis pro quibusdam prestantiis in quibusdam pecuniarum quantitatibus et summis, et se exinde recepisse pagas prout alii creditores montium predictorum, et licet ipse testator credat se de vel super predictis in aliquo non teneri, nichilominus ad omne dubium et scrupulum evitandum, si dictus testator in aliquo teneretur in recompensationem omnium et singularum pagarum et seu pecuniarum quantitatem per dictum testatorem quomodolibet receptarum et seu recipiendarum a dicto comuni, legavit et reliquid dicto comuni Florentie omne creditum et omnem pecunie quantitatem quod et seu quam ipse testator a predicto comuni Florentie deberet recipere vel habere tempore mortis dicti testatoris per libros seu registra cuiuscumque montis dicti comunis et seu cuiuscumque prestantie comunis eiusdem ratione, pretextu vel occasione cuiuscumque prestantie sive extimi sibi testatori impositi vel indicti per comune Florentie.

2. ASF, OSMN 60, fol. 161v. Extract from the testament of Lorenzo dei Benci, 5 October 1366.

Comuni Florentie reliquid quod restituatur totum id quod idem testator habuit et recepit ab ipso comuni et camerariis officii existentis dicti comunis solventibus pro ipso comuni ab anno domini .mccclx. de mense aprili citra si et in quantum deliberabitur seu declarabitur per ser Iohannem Christofori presbiterum et rectorem ecclesie sancti Simonis de Florentia secundum eiusdem ser Iohannis conscientiam ipsum testatorem teneri ad restituendum comuni predicto.

3. ASF, OSMN 67, fol. 369r. Extract from the testament of Francesco di Lapo, shoemaker, 25 August 1383.

Item testator predictus ad exonerationem anime et conscientie sue in quantum de presenti seculo ipsum migrari contigerit reliquid et legavit comuni Florentie de suis denariis scriptis in libris et registris montis comunis Florentie ad rationem ipsius et sub eius nomine in quibus est creditor comunis Florentie et quos recipere debet a dicto comuni florenos quinquaginta auri. Et dedit et prestitit licentiam et consensum scribanis et notariis montis comunis Florentie et mihi Dominico notario infrascripto ut persone publice pro eis recipiendi, finiendi et liberandi ipsum comune usque in dictam quantitatem florenorum quinquaginta auri et elevandi a et de ratione ipsius Francisci de dictis libris et registris montis dictam quantitatem florenorum quinquaginta auri et ponendi et scribendi ad ius et nomen comunis Florentie.

4. ASF, OSMN 67, fol. 39r. Extract from the testament of Nora di ser Lippo Nerini, widow of Francesco Buonaccorsi, 27 January 1380.

Comuni Florentie dicta testatrix reliquid et legavit tertiam partem omnium denariorum florenorum auri et pecunie quantitatum in quibus ipsa testatrix est seu reperiretur creditrix dicti comunis in quocunque monte et seu in libris vel per libros cuiuscunque montis dicti comunis, ita tamen quod in presenti relicto et legato non veniat donum vel interesse quod datur creditoribus dicti comunis.

5. ASF, OSMN 70, fol. 186r. Extract from the testament of Bernardo di Giovanni di Sandro Portinari, 29 July 1436.

Item dixit dictus testator se ipsum diu acquisivisse super monte Pisarum comunis Florentie a quam pluribus et diversis personis quam plura et multas quantitates pecunie et credita, quas quantitates et credita postea exegit; de quibus quantitatibus et creditis dixit constare per libros ipsius testatoris. Et quia ipse testator dubitat ne conscientia sua pro predictis sit gravata eapropter pro exhoneratione conscientie sue iuxit et voluit huiusmodi personis a quibus aliquid emisset vel acquisivisset pro denariis et creditis acquisitis super dicto monte di Pisa reddi et solvi et restitui omne id quod de iure restitui deberet et in quo conscientia sua est gravata prout gravata esset.

6. ASF, OSMN 70, fols. 31v–32r. Extract from the testament of Giovanni di Niccolò Soderini, 23 October 1417.

Item dixit et asseruit dictus testator quod olim ipse et Nicholaus Ardinghi de Ricciis emerunt nonnullos accattones et quantitates denariorum solutorum comuni Florentie pro accattonibus a pluribus et diversis personis, in emptione quorum denariorum ipsi testator et Nicholaus expendiderunt florenos octingentos vel circa, quorum ipse testator expendidit medietatem, quamquam omnes dixerint et scripti fuerint in ipsum testatorem; et quod medietatem dictorum denariorum sic emptorum in processu temporis postea ipse restituit dicto Nicholao prout in concordia remanserunt ad invicem hoc modo videlicet quod portionem dictorum denariorum emptorum contingentem dicto Nicholao vendidit et pretium ipsorum dicto Nicholao exhibuit; et quod eos denarios sic emptos, videlicet portionem suam, ipse testator exegit a comuni Florentie integraliter, si bene recordatur, de emptione quorum patet, ut dixit, in libro suo signato 'A' a carta .2. et a carta .9. et a carta .10., et etiam, ut credit, patet etiam alibi de huiusmodi emptione. Cuius emptionis et seu exactionis ipse testator, volens ipsius conscientiam exhonerare, disposuit et mandavit quod infrascripti eius executores et fideicommissarii, reperto fundamento et veritate dicte emptionis et exactionis secundum quod per librum suum predictum vel alios quoscunque suos libros ubi de predictis fieret aliqua mentio, consulant quendam sacre pagine professorem et quendam decretorum doctorem, qui simul congregati eisdem executoribus consulant utrum ad exonerationem sue conscientie pro predictis ipse teneatur in aliquo comuni Florentie et seu aliquibus singularibus personis occaxione dicte emptionis et exactionis et ad quid specificate teneatur; et recepto consilio predicto, distribuant et erogent illam quantitatem denariorum et ubi quam dicent et declarabunt et seu consulent dicti sacre pagine professor et decretorum doctor, conscientias dictorum infrascriptorum suorum executorum et fideicommiss<ari>orum onerans in predictis, hoc tamen addito, videlicet quod si vigore dicte declarationis et seu consilii fiende et seu reddende per dictum sacre pagine professorem et decretorum doctorem aliqua quantitas denariorum solvetur alicui persone, loco, comuni, collegio et seu universitati, tantumdem detrahatur et detrahi voluit, iussit et mandavit de dicta quantitate florenorum mille auri et seu de dicto legato florenorum mille auri supra facto dicto hospitali sancte Marie nove, ita quod in viginti annis proxime futuris a die mortis dicti testatoris dictum hospitale habeat et recipiat ab infrascriptis suis heredibus | id quod recipere debebit detracta de dicta quantitate florenorum mille auri id quod declaratum fuerit modo predicto, videlicet quolibet anno vegisimam partem eius quod recipere debebit.

Law, Religion, and Economics: Jewish Moneylenders in Christian Cortona[1]

Daniel Bornstein

The vicissitudes of Cortona's Jews follow a pattern made familiar by Ariel Toaff's studies of the Jewish communities in the nearby towns of Assisi, Perugia, Gubbio, and Città di Castello.[2] Throughout the region, the first Jews appeared soon after 1300 as tiny groups of immigrants from the ancient and populous Jewish community of Rome. They quickly established themselves as useful components of local credit markets, and by the fifteenth century Jewish bankers had become a constant, if always precarious, presence: usually just a household or two, licensed to loan money at interest against the pawn of some object of value, an occupation as despised as it was necessary.[3] Sensitive to the animosities aroused by their economic role and religious identity, they sought to protect themselves against violence by signing formal agreements stipulating the terms under which they would operate and guaranteeing their rights as residents of the town. They also spread the risks inherent in their trade by forming

---

[1] Research for this essay was supported in part by grants from Texas A&M University, under the Program to Enhance Scholarly and Creative Activities. My thanks go as well to Dott. Bruno Gialluca, for facilitating my research in innumerable ways.

[2] Toaff, *The Jews in Medieval Assisi*; Toaff, *Gli ebrei a Perugia*; Toaff, 'Gli ebrei a Città di Castello'; and Toaff, 'Gli ebrei a Gubbio.'

[3] On settlement patterns and economic roles, see Luzzati, 'Banchi e insediamenti ebraici'; Toaff, '"Banchieri" cristiani e "prestatori" ebrei?'; and Todeschini, 'Usura ebraica e identità economica cristiana.' On the Jewish contribution to regional credit markets in central Italy, see Botticini, 'A Tale of "Benevolent" Government.' For the territory of Arezzo in particular, see the chapters by Roberto G. Salvadori, 'Banchi di pegno ebraici nell'Arentino fra il XIV e il XV secolo' and 'Il prestito ebraico e i monti di pietà,' in Salvadori and Sacchetti, *Presenze ebraiche nell'Aretino*, 19–51. On the economic activities of the Jewish community in another nearby town, see Scharf, 'Fra economia urbana e circuiti monetari intercittadini.'

associations with Jewish bankers in other nearby towns, formalizing a web of reciprocal support.[4] People as well as capital circulated through the region; and when one of these licensed bankers left a town, he would pass his position and his lending privileges to another. They maintained their relatively stable position until the middle of the fifteenth century, when a vigorous preaching campaign by Observant Franciscan (and, to a lesser extent, Dominican) friars stirred anti-Jewish sentiment and promoted new credit institutions designed to take the place of Jewish pawnshops.

The case of Cortona does nothing to alter the main outlines of this familiar story, and there would be little point to confirming yet again a pattern that by now needs no further demonstration. Rather, the significance of the Cortonese documentation lies in what it reveals about the sustained pressure needed to break a system of providing credit that had functioned for over a century, and about the confluence of political, ecclesiastical, and economic interests that persuaded the Cortonese patriciate that it was worth making the requisite effort. It also points up some of the limits of recourse to the law and reliance on legal protections. At two key moments, half a century apart, fierce anti-Jewish preaching in the region and then in Cortona itself coincided with legal efforts to define the proprieties of lending at interest, in theory and in practice. The outcome of these legal cases threw into high relief incongruities between what the statutes declared to be legal and what the community felt to be just. Though the courts sided with Jewish and against Christian litigants on both occasions, Cortona's Jews discovered that winning a legal battle could sometimes mean losing the war for social acceptance.

* * *

Jews are first documented in Cortona in 1310–1311, when a cluster of notarial acts record the credit operations of three Jews from Rome – Melo del fu Salomone, Melo's son Vitale, and Abraham del fu Daniele – who were lending money and selling on credit.[5] On 8 February 1311, Melo constituted Abraham his agent, to receive on his behalf the right to reside in Cortona, appoint agents, hold suitable property, and pay taxes; and by 26 February 1311, Abraham had effectively taken up legal residence there.[6] He also owned property in the countryside near Cortona, since on 27 January 1316, this 'Abraham *ebreus* from Rome but presently residing in Cortona' sold a piece of land in Fratticciola.[7]

---

[4] Botticini, 'New Evidence.'
[5] Botticini, 'New Evidence,' 80.
[6] Archivio di Stato, Firenze, *Notarile Antecosimiano*, Ranieri di Guido, 17590, ff. 86v and 92r (quoted in Botticini, 'New Evidence,' 80).
[7] Biblioteca del comune di Cortona e dell'Accademia Etrusca [henceforth BCAE],

By the end of the fourteenth century, Cortona was fully enmeshed in the loose and flexible net of Jewish bankers that covered Tuscany and Umbria. Though Jews were forbidden to lend money in the commercial and financial metropolis of Florence, they provided the smaller towns of the region – ravaged by plague, drained of human and economic resources, and crushed by fiscal burdens – with a desperately needed infusion of capital.[8] Jewish bankers formed partnerships linking towns throughout Tuscany and Umbria, partnerships that dissolved and re-formed with the dismaying frequency of postwar Italian governments.[9] And like those Christian Democrat governments, which might change every eight months but always included Giulio Andreotti, the constantly shifting associations of Jewish bankers incorporated, in variable arrangements, the same small pool of individuals. Thus, when Gaio del fu maestro Angelo of Siena obtained a license to lend money in Arezzo in April of 1399, he did so as head of a partnership that also included Consiglio di Dattero di Consiglio of Siena, Sabato di Dattero di Consiglio of Pisa and his son Musetto, Manuello di Abramo di Dattero of Perugia and his brother Bonaventura, Deodato di Abramo di Deodato of Perugia (who, like the brothers Manuello and Bonaventura, resided in Città di Castello), Genatano del maestro Angelo of Perugia, and Salomone di Vitale of Montepulciano and his brother Sabatino.[10] Two of these associates, Deodato and Genatano, had previously operated a pawnshop in Perugia between 1385 and 1392; two others, Sabato di Dattilo and his son Musetto, opened a similar bank in Pistoia in the summer of 1399, just a few months after joining the partnership in Arezzo; and in 1404, Deodato di Abramo added to his other operations a pawnshop in Cortona.[11]

Deodato had established a presence in Cortona even before he obtained this license to lend money at interest there. When the town prepared a new survey of land holdings in 1402, Deodatus *ebreus* appeared as the owner of two pieces of property: a bit of farmland with

---

ms. 413: Imbreviaturae Francisci filii quondam Thomascini, 1315–1318, f. 13r–v.

[8]On the impact of Florentine taxation, see Molho, *Florentine Public Finances*, 22–59.

[9]A summary list of those partnerships in Arezzo and its territory, including Cortona, can be found in Salvadori and Sacchetti, *Presenze ebraiche nell'Aretino*, 33–35.

[10]The text of their agreement with the city of Arezzo is published in Molho, 'A Note on Jewish Moneylenders,' 111–117. As this list of partners suggests, Italian Jews in this period tended to employ a very limited number of given names, complicating the task of identifying individuals, tracking their movements and sorting out their affiliations.

[11]Toaff, *Gli ebrei a Perugia*, 27–31; Zdekauer, 'L'interno di un banco di pegno,' 91–94; Toaff, 'Gli ebrei a Città di Castello,' 4.

some vines, valued at £30; and a rather larger and much more desirable tract of vineyard and fruit trees just outside the city, valued at £521.5.[12] This second plot of land is noteworthy not only for its value, but for the way in which it is described. *Catasto* entries normally mention the former owner of a piece of property when that property is added to someone's declaration, or when someone's entire declaration is added to the register, but not when the item (like this one) forms part of the original declaration of someone included in the *catasto* at the moment of its redaction. Since this particular piece of land is described as having belonged to the *laudesi* fraternity of Santa Maria, its transfer from the Christian devotional association to the Jew Deodato must have been fresh in the tax assessors' minds when the *catasto* was redacted in 1402.

Deodato did not remain in Cortona for long. Just a year after he secured permission to operate a pawnshop there, Deodato's place in Cortona was taken by two of his erstwhile associates in the Arezzo partnership headed by Gaio, the brothers Manuello and Bonaventura, who opened up shop in Cortona in 1405 under a license, valid for 25 years, allowing them to loan money at a rate of six *denari* per *lira* per month, an annual rate of 30%.[13] A few years later, in 1409, Deodato transferred the less valuable of his two pieces of property – the vineyard worth £30 – to the people who had taken his place as suppliers of credit.[14] Manuello and Bonaventura never added to their holdings, and their possession of this single small plot of land might suggest that their status was modest and their roots in the community shallow. That impression, however, would be seriously misleading: these were persons of considerable financial resources, who received significant honors and managed to maintain their position in Cortona for an exceptionally long time.

As bankers, Manuello and Bonaventura conducted operations on a regional scale, and over the long term. Their father, Abramo di Dattero (or, to use the diminutive form, ambiguously affectionate or scornful, often applied to him in the sources, Abramuccio di Dattaluccio), was a prominent banker in Città di Castello; and they inherited his position there, signing contracts to loan money in Città di Castello, on the same terms as in Cortona, in 1390, 1396, 1402, 1404, 1411, 1413, and 1416.[15] In

---

[12] Archivio storico del comune di Cortona [henceforth ACC], C.6: Catasto del 1402, terziere di San Vincenzo de intus, f. 74v. The first plot of land had an extension of one *staioro*; the second was not just larger, at 6.52 *staiora*, but more prized, at an estimated value of £80 per *staioro*.

[13] Mancini, *Cortona nel Medioevo*, 314; Salvadori and Sacchetti, *Presenze ebraiche nell'Aretino*, 27.

[14] ACC, C.6, ff. 74v (Deodatus) and 166v (Manovellus et Bonaventura). The more valuable property went to a Christian, Guidonus Nucii.

[15] Salvadori and Sacchetti, *Presenze ebraiche nell'Aretino*, 21, n. 7. Perhaps as

1416 they also agreed to lend money in Arezzo, in association with Salomone di Leuccio and his brother Guglielmo.[16] From one angle, this might seem a revival of an earlier arrangement, since Salomone had taken the place vacated by the brothers' old partner in the Arezzo bank, Gaio, obtaining – just a few months after Gaio was expelled from Arezzo in 1406 by order of the Florentine government – a license to operate a pawnshop under the same terms and with the same privileges as those enjoyed by his predecessor.[17] From another point of view, it might be considered an expansion of the range of operations of an existing partnership, since Manuello and Bonaventura had already, in 1411, involved Salomone and Guglielmo di Leuccio in their business in Cortona (along with Dattero di Manuello of Montalcino and Dattero di Angelo of Corneto).[18] This association was to endure for decades, and span a generation: in 1421, Salomone and Guglielmo di Leuccio and Bonaventura di Abramo renewed their license to loan money in Cortona (though without the other partners to the 1411 contract); and in 1431 and again in 1436, Salomone di Leuccio and Bonaventura's son Salomone secured licenses to resume their credit operations.[19]

Given the duration of their banking relationship with the commune and community of Cortona, it is no surprise to find that Manuello and Bonaventura held onto their one bit of land for better than four decades, from 5 March 1409, when their acquisition of the vineyard from Deodato was recorded in the *catasto* register, to 10 June 1450, when the vineyard was cancelled from their declaration and entered on that of Antonio di Renzo di Antonio da Pacciano.[20] Their brief *catasto* declaration does, however, have two noteworthy features: an omission and an ascription. It makes no mention of their occupation as moneylenders, though they had plied that trade in Cortona for years – since 1405, when they signed a formal agreement allowing them to loan money at interest for the next 25 years. And it describes Manuello and Bonaventura as *cives Cortone*, citizens of Cortona.[21] The presence of the one identifier and the absence of the other are probably linked: citizens were not supposed to practice infamous trades, such as prostitution and usury, so it would have been

---

part of the *quid pro quo* for taking over Deodato's position and property in Cortona, Manuello and Bonaventura used their connections in Città di Castello to secure for Deodato the honor of citizenship in that city.

[16]Salvadori and Sacchetti, *Presenze ebraiche nell'Aretino*, 28.
[17]Molho, 'A Note on Jewish Moneylenders,' 105–106.
[18]Salvadori and Sacchetti, *Presenze ebraiche nell'Aretino*, 28 and 33.
[19]Salvadori and Sacchetti, *Presenze ebraiche nell'Aretino*, 28 and 33–34.
[20]ACC, C.6, f. 166v; ACC, C.2: Catasto del 1402, terziere di Santa Maria de intus, f. 34r.
[21]ACC, C.6, f. 166v.

prudent to maintain a discreet silence about the profession of these particular citizens.

Though they were the only Jews to be identified as citizens in the tax records of Cortona, Manuello and Bonaventura's citizenship status was not atypical for the region. In fact, the negotiated pacts or *condotte* under which Jews agreed to provide loans in a particular town often included a clause stipulating that they would be treated like citizens of that town in civil and criminal matters.[22] What is more, participating as they did in multiple partnerships, with operations in various localities, Jews like Manuello and Bonaventura could come to hold citizenship in several cities. Thus, in Arezzo in 1399, Gaio and his associates (including our Manuello and Bonaventura) were to be treated '*come cittadini*' of Arezzo, and in Florence in 1437, Abraham di Dattilo and his associates '*tractentur et reputentur . . . tanquam cives civitatis Florentie.*'[23] While it is not altogether clear that enjoying the contractual right to be treated like a citizen was quite the same as actually being one, the annotation in the Cortona *catasto* leaves no doubt: Manuello and Bonaventura were citizens of Cortona.

* * *

Given their status in Cortona, one might suspect that Manuello and Bonaventura involved other partners in their Cortona bank not only to increase its capital and spread the risks, but to serve as front men, distancing these Jewish citizens of Cortona from the daily operations of their business and the opprobrium of public usury. That certainly proved to be a useful shield in 1428, when Manuello and Bonaventura's 25-year contract was about to expire. The termination or renegotiation of a contract always risked heightening tensions, as the operators of a pawnshop pressed their customers to repay their loans and redeem pawned items or, spurred by the looming expiration of their authority to do so, issued new loans in great haste and dubious propriety. In 1461, for instance, Vitale da Montalcino incurred the enormous fine of 22,000 florins when he made 22 loans within a day of the expiration of his contract to loan money in Florence.[24] Perhaps it was with an eye to avoiding such troubles that Cortona and its Jews entered into an arbitration agreement in 1428. The parties to the arbitration were Dattero and Salomone, Manuello and Bonaventura's partners since 1411, and the case

---

[22] Gow and Griffiths, 'Pope Eugenius IV and Jewish Money-Lending,' 290–292.

[23] Molho, 'A Note on Jewish Moneylenders,' 112; Gow and Griffiths, 'Pope Eugenius IV and Jewish Money-Lending,' 290.

[24] Gow and Griffiths, 'Pope Eugenius IV and Jewish Money-Lending,' 318.

was submitted to the *collegium doctorum*, or association of lawyers, in Florence.[26]

The *collegium* took under consideration fourteen questions, including whether Jews could accept real estate in pawn, fold interest into the principal, and so on. Their decision, issued on 15 May 1428, went beyond simply clarifying doubts on these points. It granted the Jews the right to loan in Cortona for six years, fixing the rate at five *denari* per *lira* per month for the first three years and six *denari* for the next three, and ordered them to pay Cortona 350 florins; in return, Cortona was to guarantee them immunity from lawsuits and legal judgments. Although this decision effectively (albeit temporarily) lowered the permissible interest rate from the 30% a year allowed under the 1405 agreement to 25% and gave the city an immediate infusion of cash, Cortona protested that the *collegium* had exceeded its mandate and that Cortona's syndic did not have the authority to put to arbitration matters beyond those included in the original submission.

The dossier presented in support of Cortona's protest included legal opinions solicited from fourteen jurists, including Lodovico Pontano, Angelo Ubaldi, and Paolo da Castro.[27] Only the first of these *consilia*, attributed to Pontano, addresses the authority of the arbitrators; it upholds Cortona's position that under the terms of the arbitration agreement, the *collegium* had no authority to extend the Jews' contract to lend money in Cortona or determine what fee they should pay. The others in effect reopen the disputed points originally submitted for arbitration, considering whether the Jews could loan money against real property, written pledges, and personal obligations or only against pawns of movable goods, what happens to the proceeds of the sale of a pawned object, whether interest could be converted into principal, and so on. Every single one of this arsenal of judicial big guns held that the Jews could only loan against pawns of movable goods, and several tended to restrict still further the scope of their business and profits: for instance, proceeds from the sale of a pawn must be counted against the principal of the loan, not interest on it, and anything beyond the amount owed had to be returned to the debtor. To set the proper moral tone and establish the need to be restrictive in interpretation, several of the *consilia* open with surveys of the divine,

---

[26]Girolamo Mancini assembled the documents regarding this case in BCAE, ms. 520: Vertenze fra il Comune di Cortona e gli Ebrei assuntori privilegiati di prestiti nella città e nel contado Cortonese, 1428. The case is discussed briefly in Mancini, *Cortona nel Medioevo*, 315–316, and Salvadori and Sacchetti, *Presenze ebraiche nell'Aretino*, 28–30.

[27]I am deeply grateful to Thomas Kuehn for his expert assistance in deciphering and interpreting these *consilia*.

natural, civil, and canon law and denounce usury in general terms, responding to Cortona's lament that the Jews were abusing their position, gouging their clients, and exacting usurious rates of interest.

These complaints and the storm of legal rhetoric they elicited targeted Dattero di Angelo of Corneto, Salomone di Leuccio, and associates: that is, Manuello and Bonaventura's partners in the 1411 contract with the city, rather than Manuello and Bonaventura, suggesting that the brothers' effort to insulate themselves from just this sort of hatred had not been entirely fruitless. But neither had they been completely successful. Jews continued to lend money in Cortona, but under terms that were ever more restrictive and in circumstances growing ever more insecure. Their legal position and social standing in that city (as that of the Jews in other cities throughout northern and central Italy) was being eroded by the avalanche of vituperation spilling from the mouths of the leading preachers of the day.[28] Between 1424 and 1427, Bernardino da Siena delivered several spectacular series of sermons throughout the region: in Florence (1424 and 1425), Siena (1425 and 1427), Assisi (1425), Perugia (1425 and 1427), and so on. Bernardino da Siena may not have addressed the Jewish question systematically, nor with the ferocious intensity of other, slightly later Franciscan preachers such as Giovanni da Capistrano, Giacomo della Marca, Alberto da Sarteano, or Bernardino da Feltre; but his barbed observations on Jews and usury hooked his listeners and produced demonstrable results: anti-Jewish legislation, the abrogation of agreements permitting Jews to lend at interest, the expulsion of Jews from certain cities.[29] Perhaps Cortona's decision to initiate legal action against its Jews in 1428 owed something to Bernardino's calls for intolerance a year earlier.[30]

Like the other measures taken in response to Bernardino's appeals, this legal assault failed – in the short term. Jews continued to provide credit in Cortona, though Manuello and Bonaventura maintained an even lower profile after the court case of 1428 and distanced themselves even more assiduously from open involvement in usury: it was Bonaventura's son Salomone, not Manuello and Bonaventura, who contracted with the city of Cortona to lend money in partnership with Salomone di Leuccio in 1431 and again in 1436.[31] No longer trusting to formal pacts, which were continually revoked and renewed, the Jews tried to forge ties with powerful patrons. When Salamone di Abramo *ebreus di Frulivio* entered the *catasto* in 1455, he did so as joint owner of a mill for pressing oil,

---

[28] Hughes, 'Earrings for Circumcision'; Hughes, 'Distinguishing Signs.'

[29] Mormando, *The Preacher's Demons*, 164–218; the effects of Bernardino's preaching are detailed on pp. 200–208.

[30] One example can be found in Bernardino da Siena, *Prediche volgari sul Campo di Siena*, 1033–1035 (Predica XXXV, 178–190).

[31] Salvadori and Sacchetti, *Presenze ebraiche nell'Aretino*, 34.

held *pro indiviso* with a member of the richest family of Cortona.[32] Whereas his half of the mill (valued £100) constituted Salamone's total landed wealth, the declaration of his partner, Tommaso di ser Francesco di ser Ranieri di Guido Boscie, covers eleven folios, recto and verso; the mill appears on the twentieth page of his declaration, as just part of a piece of property with three houses, the mill, and land with vines, trees, olives, and woods.[33] The Jews who appear in the tax registers are no longer identified as citizens of Cortona, like Manuello and Bonaventura. They are labeled *feneratori*, an epithet spared Manuello and Bonaventura. They are specified as being from someplace else, like Salamone di Abramo from the Friuli in 1455 and Datolino di Salomone from Camerino in 1491, and they are registered in the section of the *catasto* devoted to *forestieri*.[34] And perhaps with a wary eye to the ban on loaning money against real estate and a corresponding concern to avoid any suspicion that their property holdings derived from foreclosed loans, they declare minimal possessions of land, which moreover remain in the register for no more than a few years at a time: Salamone di Abramo appears in 1455, is registered again in 1461, and cancelled in 1462; his heirs are entered in the *catasto* in 1466 and cancelled in 1472; Datolino di Salomone is added to the rolls on 27 January 1491 and cancelled from them on 31 August 1493.[35]

* * *

The final blow came with the establishment of a *Monte di pietà*. According to the definition offered by the Dominican friar Giovanni di Nanni of Viterbo and quoted in the measures creating Cortona's *Monte*, 'the *Monte di Pietà* or apostolic deposit is a certain quantity of money piously collected from the patricians and leading citizens of the city, and given by them to the association of the poor citizens, and ordained to be used for the perpetual assistance of the needy among them, in order that they might have someplace to turn to meet their needs, regulated by certain clauses and statutes to the public benefit of the poor and for the maintenance of the said money.'[36] These pious pawnshops appeared

---

[32] ACC, C.4: Catasto del 1402, terziere di San Marco de intus, section *forestieri*.

[33] ACC, C.4, ff. 197r–207v; the item in question appears on f. 206v.

[34] ACC, C.4, section *forestieri*; ACC, C.10: Catasto del 1461, terziere di San Marco de intus, section *forestieri*. The same distinction in legal status can be noted in Florentine tax records. Abraham di Dattilo appeared among the *forestieri* in the Florentine *catasto* of 1427, a decade before his 1437 contract to lend money in that city entitled him to be treated 'tanquam cives civitatis Florentie.' Gow and Griffiths, 'Pope Eugenius IV and Jewish Money-Lending,' 287 and 290.

[35] ACC, C.4, section *forestieri*; ACC, C.10, section *forestieri*.

[36] ACC, I'.3: Capitoli del Monte Pio del 1494, f. 2v: 'Monte di pietà o vero deposito

throughout northern and central Italy in the second half of the fifteenth century, promoted by mendicant friars – Dominicans such as our Giovanni di Nanni of Viterbo, but especially Observant Franciscans such as Fortunato Coppoli, Bernardino of Feltre, and Angelo of Chiavasso, whose name is also invoked in statutes of the Cortonese *Monte di pietà* – as an alternative to Jewish moneylending; and the establishment of the *Monti di pietà* was typically preceded by savage anti-Jewish preaching and followed by the expulsion of the now superfluous Jews. This is precisely what happened in Cortona, though the course of events in Cortona suggests that it was far from easy to rally support for expelling the Jews and muster the resources needed to replace them.[37]

The first attempt to found a *Monte di pietà* in Cortona occurred in 1472, when a group of citizens proposed to rescue the poor people of Cortona from 'the bottomless pit of usury and the deceit, fraud, and plundering from which the perfidious Jews, devourers of the property of the faithful Christian people, never cease. . . . Invoking the kind favor and assistance of our magnificent Florentine lords (who have never denied just requests), on 14 February 1472 they decided to remove from their backs the moth and leech of the foul usury of the Jews, and create in Cortona a town loan-office.'[38] The twelve citizens delegated to this task drafted a set of ordinances to govern the *Monte dei poveri di Cristo*. In this instance, however, Florence seems not to have honored Cortona's request, belying the propaedeutic rhetoric of the petition; and the draft ordinances remained merely a draft, a paper project left unenacted for the moment.

Still, both Jews and Christians could see which way the wind was blowing. Subjected to increasing pressure from their Christian hosts and neighbors, those Jews who chose to operate in Cortona made no attempt to put down roots there; they rarely acquired property, and never held it

---

apostolico è una certa quantità de pecunia dali patritij e optimati cittadini della città piatosamente ricolta e da quelli ala compagnia dei poveri cittadini donata e ordinata in uso di perpetua subventione de epsi bisognosi, acioché alle necessità loro habbino dove ricorrere, intervenendoce capituli e statuti a publico benefitio d'epsi poveri per mantenimento de decte pecunie.'

[37] More than thirty *Monti di pietà* were established between 1462 and 1472; but however rapidly it spread, this new credit institution did encounter stiff resistance in a number of cities. On the protracted efforts to create a *Monti di pietà* in Florence, see Menning, *Charity and State in Late Renaissance Italy*, 11–35.

[38] ACC, I'.1: Capitoli del Monte Pio del 1472, f. 1r: 'dala voragine dele usure e dali inganni, fraude e robbanti dal quali mai desistano el perfidi ebrei, devoratori dele substantie del fedeli populi christiani. . . . Impetrato el benigno favore e auxilio de nostri magnifici signori fiorentini, che mai dinegorono le giuste adimande, fece deliberatione sotto dì xiiii del mese di febraio MCCCCLXXII in tucto de levarse d'adosso la tignola e la sanguesugha dela pessima usura delli ebrei, et che in Cortona se faccia uno presto per lo comune.'

for long. In the wake of the abortive attempt to establish a *Monte di pietà*, the current holders of the license to lend money in Cortona evidently decided it would be wisest to hold their wealth in liquid form. On 17 July 1472, the *heredes Salamonis Habrae feneratores ad presens in civitatis Cortona* sold the substantial piece of rural real estate they owned in Rio Loreto, the valley just west of the city: a *palatius* with courtyard, vines, olives, and woods worth £470.[39] They did not, however, pull up stakes and leave town right away. On the contrary, in 1473 Abraam di Salomone entered a new agreement to operate in Cortona[40] – only to run almost immediately into trouble with one of his clients. In May of that same year, a certain Ugolino di Giovanni tried to defraud Abraam and his brother Samuele of the money he owed them.[41] Ugolino stopped by the brothers' house when Abraam was out and created such a stir that the befuddled Samuele let him walk off with his I.O.U. for £11 s. 10. (It may not be a simple coincidence that Abraam signed the *condotta* alone, without his brother: Samuele seems to have been altogether too gullible, or too easily confused, to be a reliable partner.) Ugolino gave the purloined document to his mother to hide and then, adding evil to evil, altered the entry in his own account book to show that he owed Abraam only £4 s. 10. Perhaps Ugolino thought that local sentiment against the Jewish moneylenders was sufficiently strong that he could get away with such flagrant fraud; but if so, he was quickly disabused of any such notion. Abraam and Samuele took him to court, where the Florentine magistrate, finding their allegations fully justified and Ugolino's actions reprehensible, sentenced him to pay a £20 fine. This legal victory notwithstanding, the brothers found their social position increasingly difficult, and by the end of the decade they had disappeared from Cortona, as they had earlier disappeared from its tax rolls.

Their place was taken by a family of Jews headed by Emanuele di Bonassisi di Salomone from Camerino, in the Marche, who in 1481 set up operations in both Cortona and San Giovanni Valdarno.[42] Like Abraam and Samuele before him, Emanuele hesitated to purchase real estate in a town where he felt insecure. Indeed, he never acquired land in Cortona, and it was only after nearly ten years of operating there that one of his colleagues (and probably a relative as well) took that step. On 26 January 1490 (or perhaps 1491), *Datolinus Salomonis de Camerino ad presens fenerator Cortone* had himself added to the tax rolls as the owner of some land with

---

[39] ACC, C.10, section *forestieri*. The transfer of this property to a certain Donato di Biagio di Donato was approved by Abraam, son and heir of the said Salamone.
[40] Salvadori and Sacchetti, *Presenze ebraiche nell'Aretino*, 34.
[41] ACC, A.1, pezzo 1: Atti criminali di Federigo Federighi, capitano 1473, ff. 7r–9v (inquest conducted on 12 May 1473) and 49r–52v (sentence issued 15 May 1473).
[42] Salvadori and Sacchetti, *Presenze ebraiche nell'Aretino*, 34.

vines and olives worth a mere £35.⁴³ Datolino did not remain a Cortonese property owner and taxpayer for long. Just a couple of years after he bought it, on 31 August 1493, Datolino sold his vineyard and olive grove and decamped. Emanuele da Camerino likewise vanished from Cortona, despite having taken a chance and renewed his *condotta* in 1491.⁴⁴

The anti-Jewish sentiment that pushed them to this decision can easily be imagined, for once again criticism of Jewish usury was sharpening and calls for an alternative growing louder. When the Observant Franciscan friar Bartolomeo di Nibia da Novara preached in Cortona during Advent of 1494, his attacks on 'the most cruel and voracious rabies of usury' found a ready audience.⁴⁵ The account book of the flagellant confraternity of Saints Antonio and Onofrio recalls how 'in his sermons he constantly pleaded and urged everyone in general to find some order, manner, and way to create the holy *Monte di pietà* so that those poor persons who need to borrow money will not be left undone (as in the past) by the usury of the Jewish dogs.'⁴⁶ 'Fired and inflamed by those most holy sermons,' the good citizens of Cortona took action. They founded, finally, a *Monte di pietà* – and this time its statutes were approved and adopted and drawn up in a fair copy on parchment, full of fine language lamenting the devastation wrought by usury and denouncing its perpetrators, those enemies of the Christian people, those most avaricious Jews. 'These,' proclaimed the preamble to the statutes, 'are those truly rabid and thirsty dogs who have sucked and still suck our blood and take, destroy, and steal the wealth and possessions of our people, to its great misfortune, handing those goods to foreigners and enriching themselves.'⁴⁷ Clearly, something had to be done to protect the ample patrimonies in their little homeland from being exhausted and entirely absorbed by the most wicked usury of the Jews –

---

⁴³ACC, C.10, section *forestieri*. Florence started the new year on the feast of the Incarnation, March 25, which would make this 26 January 1491 modern style — if the *catasto* officials were using the Florentine system of dating. But it is hard to be certain: Cortona was slow to adopt the calendar used by its Florentine masters, as it was slow to accept the Florentine *lira* in lieu of the Cortonese currency.

⁴⁴Salvadori and Sacchetti, *Presenze ebraiche nell'Aretino*, 35.

⁴⁵ACC, I'.3, f. 3r: 'la crudelissima e voracissima rabbia delle usure.'

⁴⁶ACC, Z.3, pezzo 12: Compagnia dei battitti di Sant'Antonio e Sant'Onofrio, entrata, 1457–1508, f. 172r: 'nelle suoi preddiche sempre pregando e confortando gieneralmente honni persona che si desse hordine modo e vija che si faciessi el monte [inserted above line: santo] de la pietà perchè le povere persone che anno bisogno de achattare denari non remanessero deffatti chomme per lo passato per l'uxura del chane giudeo.'

⁴⁷ACC, I'.3, f. 3r: 'Questi sonno quelli veri rabbiosi e setibundi cani che el nostro sangue hanno succhiato e succhiano e le substantie e ricchecçe del nostro populo tolgano, guastano e rapiscano, e con gravissima iactura di quello mandano ali alieni e loro si venghono a ricchire.'

who by now were irrevocably identified as foreigners, having long lost the privileged identity as citizens enjoyed by Manuello and Bonaventura early in the century.

Six citizens helped the priors to draft these statutes, and six others were chosen to help the priors implement them by instituting the *Monte di pietà* and organizing its treasury. To fill that treasury, they appealed to pious institutions such as the flagellant fraternity of Saints Antonio and Onofrio. On 6 January 1495 the fraternity assembled 'as many men of the fraternity as we could,' not in their usual meeting place, but 'in the palace of the priors, in the council chamber.' There they debated whether to contribute some of the fraternity's revenues to help establish the *Monte*, and put the matter to a vote: 'Whoever wished to express an opinion should place a black bean to indicate yes or a white one to indicate no. Iacomo del Buono, the person currently in charge of the fraternity's hospital, gathered the votes; and there were in all fifteen black beans in favor and one white bean opposed.'[48]

So when Cortona's *Monte di pietà* was finally founded in 1494, it was the culmination of more than twenty years of public pressure, catalyzed by the preaching of a Franciscan friar, confirmed and enacted by the priors, and financed by lay confraternities.[49] But how distinct were these various bodies that joined to create the *Monte di pietà*? Two of the six persons who drew up the statutes in 1494 figured among the group who had prepared the earlier draft proposal in 1472, and a third was the son of a member of that group. Yet another had a brother among the six citizens enlisted to help the priors get the *Monte* up and running. One of the priors belonged to the fraternity that helped fill the *Monte*'s coffers; another member of that fraternity, Francesco di Niccolò di Tomaso

---

[48]ACC, Z.3, pezzo 12, f. 172r: 'El sopradetto frate Bartolomeo mandò per noi e molto cie confortò et exortò che de le entrate de detta nostra compagnia dovessimo fare helemosina al sopradetto monte de quella quantita che a noi era possibile, et pertanto a noi parendo l'uopera laudabile e buona, el sopradetto dì 6 de gienaio raunammo in el palazzo dei priori in la sala del chonselglio quanti homini podemmo avere de la detta nostra compagnia, e' quali nominaremo de sotto per nome; e denanzi ale loro reverenzie e spetibilità propose le parole sopradette, che se a loro pareva se desse per l'amore de Dio al sopradetto monte de le dette entrate quanto si poteva, non pattendo dessdasio la compagnia. E sopra questo se miese el partito che a chi pareva e piacieva rendesse la fava nera per lo sì e a chi no la biancha. Recholse el detto partito Iachomo del Buono al presente spedalliere de detta compagnia, e fuorono in tutto per lo sì fave quindicie nere e fave una biancha per lo no in contrario.'

[49]In Borgo Sansepolcro, too, lay confraternities and hospitals were asked to contribute specified sums to the working capital of the *Monte*. Czortek, 'La fondazione del Monte di Pietà di Sansepolcro,' 7–25; the sums asked of the sponsoring fraternities are found on p. 9.

Pontelli, had had a hand in drafting both the statutes proposed in 1472 and those approved in 1494. It is easy to imagine him watching with satisfaction as his confraternal brethren voted overwhelmingly to help fund the project he had promoted for nearly a quarter of a century – and wondering, as I do, which one had had the temerity to cast that lone white bean in opposition. And who was the *depositorio del Monte della pietà* to whom the fraternity consigned £225 in cash and 150 *staiora* of grain?[50] None other than messer Marco Antonio di Piero di messer Nicolò Laparelli, *doctore in utroque iure* – and the very first name in the set of priors who approved the creation of the *Monte*.

Pontelli, Laparelli, and the rest were all, of course, wealthy and powerful representatives of the leading patrician families of Cortona, who made themselves even more wealthy and powerful by manipulating anti-Jewish sentiment. Drawing on their web of social connections and applying their political influence, they arranged to have pious fraternities place money into the *Monte di pietà*, which they would then control. They would assist the deserving people of Cortona (that is, those they deemed to be deserving) by loaning them money, and the money did not even have to come from their own well-lined pockets. And they could thereby secure the gratitude of those who received these loans, all the while basking in the glory of having rid the Christian city of Cortona of the foul usury of the bloodsucking Jews.

Texas A&M University
College Station, TX

Works Cited

Manuscript Sources

Cortona, Archivio storico del comune di Cortona,
    A.1, pezzo 1: Atti criminali di Federigo Federighi, capitano 1473
    C.2: Catasto del 1402, terziere di Santa Maria de intus
    C.4: Catasto del 1402, terziere di San Marco de intus
    C.6: Catasto del 1402, terziere di San Vincenzo de intus
    C.10: Catasto del 1461, terziere di San Marco de intus
    I'.1: Capitoli del Monte Pio del 1472
    I'.3: Capitoli del Monte Pio del 1494
    Z.3, pezzo 12: Compagnia dei battitti di Sant'Antonio e Sant'Onofrio, entrata, 1457–1508

---

[50]These contributions to the *Monte* were made on 1 April, 25 December, and 29 December 1495: ACC, Z.3, pezzo 12, f. 172r.

Cortona, Biblioteca del comune di Cortona e dell'Accademia Etrusca,
  ms. 413: Imbreviaturae Francisci filii quondam Thomascini, 1315–1318
  ms. 520: Vertenze fra il Comune di Cortona e gli Ebrei assuntori privilegiati di prestiti nella città e nel contado Cortonese, 1428
Firenze, Archivio di Stato,
  Notarile Antecosimiano, Ranieri di Guido, 17590

Published Sources

Bernardino da Siena. *Prediche volgari sul Campo di Siena, 1427*, ed. Carlo Delcorno. Milan: Rusconi, 1989.

Botticini, Maristella. 'New Evidence on Jews in Tuscany, ca. 1310–1435: The 'Friends and Family' Connection Again.' *Zakhor: Rivista di Storia degli Ebrei d'Italia* 1 (1997): 77–93.

Botticini, Maristella. 'A Tale of "Benevolent" Government: Private Credit Markets, Public Finance, and the Role of Jewish Lenders in Medieval and Renaissance Italy.' *Journal of Economic History* 60 (2000): 164–189.

Czortek, Andrea. 'La fondazione del Monte di Pietà di Sansepolcro e lo statuto del 1466.' *Proposte e ricerche: Economia e società nella storia dell'Italia centrale* 38 (1997): 7–25.

Gow, Andrew, and Gordon Griffiths. 'Pope Eugenius IV and Jewish Money-Lending in Florence: The Case of Salomone di Bonaventura during the Chancellorship of Leonardo Bruni.' *Renaissance Quarterly* 47 (1994): 282–329.

Hughes, Diane Owen. 'Earrings for Circumcision: Distinction and Purification in the Italian Renaissance City' pp. 155–182 in *Persons in Groups: Social Behavior as Identity Formation in Medieval and Renaissance Europe*, ed. Richard C. Trexler. Binghamton, NY: Medieval and Renaissance Texts and Studies, 1985.

Hughes, Diane Owen. 'Distinguishing Signs: Ear-Rings, Jews and Franciscan Rhetoric in the Italian Renaissance City.' *Past and Present* 112 (August 1986): 3–59.

Luzzati, Michele. 'Banchi e insediamenti ebraici nell'Italia centro-settentrionale fra tardo Medioevo e inizi dell'Età moderna' pp. 173–235 in *Storia d'Italia, Annali 11: Gli ebrei in Italia*, ed. Corrado Vivanti. Turin: Einaudi, 1996.

Mancini, Girolamo. *Cortona nel Medioevo*. Florence, 1897; reprint Cortona: Editrice Grafica l'Etruria, 1992.

Menning, Carol Bresnahan. *Charity and State in Late Renaissance Italy: The Monte di pietà of Florence*. Ithaca: Cornell University Press, 1993.

Molho, Anthony. 'A Note on Jewish Moneylenders in Tuscany in the Late Trecento and Early Quattrocento' pp. 103–117 in *Renaissance: Studies in Honor of Hans Baron*, ed. Anthony Molho and John A. Tedeschi. Dekalb, IL: Northern Illinois University Press, 1971.

Molho, Anthony. *Florentine Public Finances in the Early Renaissance, 1400–1433*. Cambridge: Harvard University Press, 1971.

Mormando, Franco. *The Preacher's Demons: Bernardino of Siena and the Social Underworld of Early Renaissance Italy*. Chicago: University of Chicago Press.

Salvadori, Roberto G., and Giorgio Sacchetti. *Presenze ebraiche nell'Aretino dal XIV al XX secolo.* Florence: Olschki, 1990.

Scharf, Gian Paolo G. 'Fra economia urbana e circuiti monetari intercittadini: il ruolo degli ebrei a Borgo San Sepolcro a metà del Quattrocento.' *Archivio Storico Italiano* 156 (1998): 447–477.

Toaff, Ariel. 'Gli ebrei a Città di Castello dal XIV al XV secolo.' *Bollettino della Deputazione di storia patria per l'Umbria*, vol. 72, no. 2 (1975): 1–105.

Toaff, Ariel. *Gli ebrei a Perugia.* Perugia: Arti Grafiche, 1975.

Toaff, Ariel. *The Jews in Medieval Assisi (1305–1487): A Social and Economic History of a Small Jewish Community in Italy.* Florence: Olschki, 1979.

Toaff, Ariel. 'Gli ebrei a Gubbio nel Trecento.' *Bollettino della Deputazione di storia patria per l'Umbria* 78 (1981): 153–192.

Toaff, Ariel. '"Banchieri" cristiani e "prestatori" ebrei?' pp. 265–287 in *Storia d'Italia, Annali 11: Gli ebrei in Italia*, ed. Corrado Vivanti. Turin: Einaudi, 1996.

Todeschini, Giacomo. 'Usura ebraica e identità economica cristiana: la discussione medievale' pp. 289–318 in *Storia d'Italia, Annali 11: Gli ebrei in Italia*, ed. Corrado Vivanti. Turin: Einaudi, 1996.

Vivanti , Corrado, ed. *Storia d'Italia, Annali 11: Gli ebrei in Italia.* Turin: Einaudi, 1996.

Zdekauer, Lodovico . 'L'interno di un banco di pegno nel 1417, con documenti inediti.' *Archivio Storico Italiano*, ser. 5, 18 (1896): 63–105.

Part III

Citizenship and Inheritance

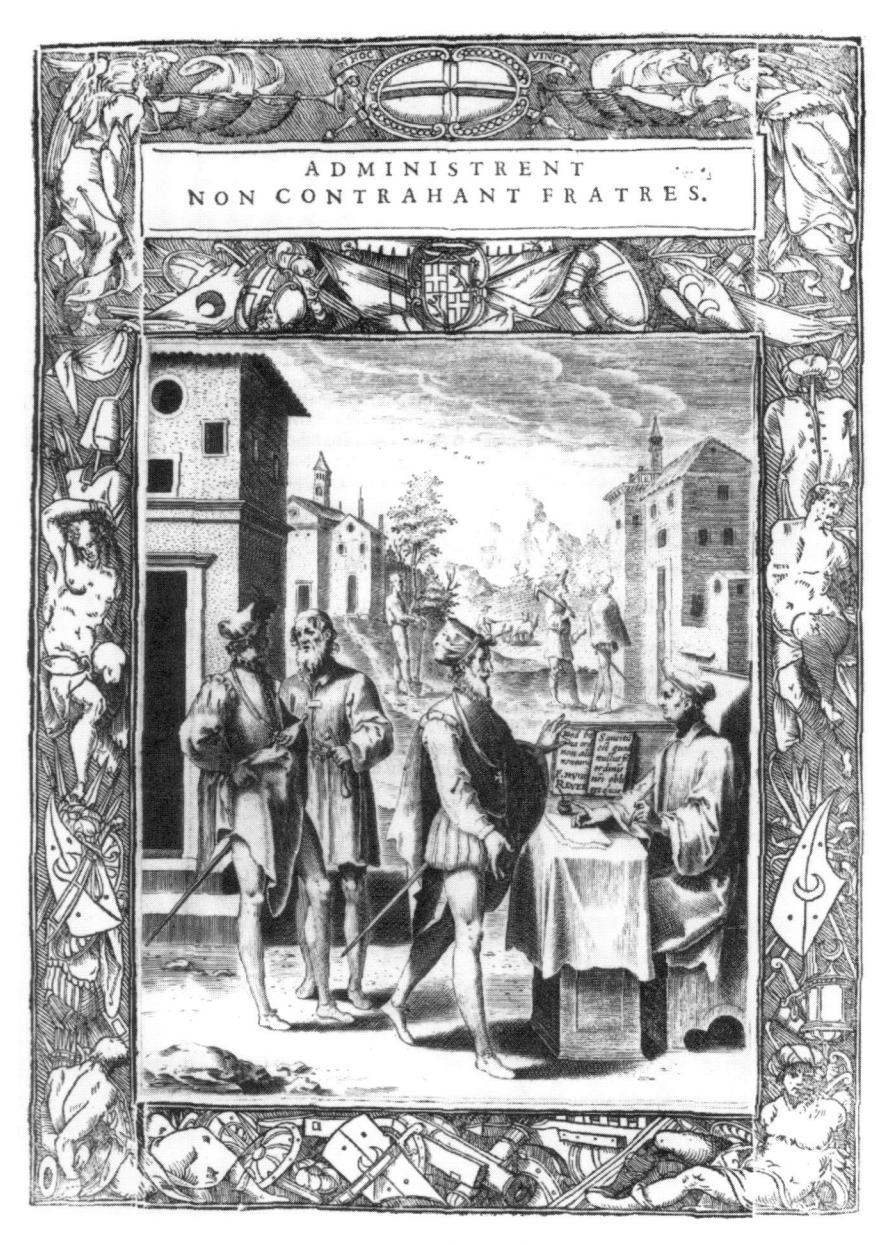

Plate 5: 'Administrent non contrahant fratres,' in *Statuta Hospitalis Hierusalem.* Rome: n.p., 1586. (Newberry Library, Chicago, Illinois.)

Piero Amadi Acts Like His Betters

James S. Grubb

Comment on Venice, long ago or recent, has consistently described its order of *cittadini originari* or 'original citizens' in purely functionalist terms. First and foremost, these elite and privileged commoners held exclusive right to the top managerial positions in the Republic's administration, particularly the offices of grand chancellor and secretaries to major magistracies. Inside the ducal palace, they drafted legislation and correspondence, oversaw voting, handled cryptography, maintained the archives, and served as experts on precedence and procedure; abroad, *cittadini* secretaries also served as occasional emissaries to foreign powers – the first three wars with the Turks were settled through negotiations by *cittadino* envoys, for example – and as resident representatives at lesser courts.

Second, and scarcely less important for the mythic self-image of the godly commonwealth, the *cittadini originari* were invested with a monopoly on leadership of the five *scuole grandi* or major confraternities that provided most of the city's social services, served as trust institutions, and commissioned numerous works of art for the glory of God and the city. While contemporaries predictably cloaked their descriptions of *cittadini* in flowery rhetoric of civic-mindedness ('willing to sacrifice not only their fortunes, but their very lives, for the common good'), they equally and more candidly acknowledged the more pragmatic effect of social pacification: delineation of a privileged subset of commoners co-opted the more energetic and talented members of a permanently excluded underclass, not only reinforcing the state's human resources but also buying off potential opposition.[1]

Historiography has traditionally concentrated on the *cittadini* as functionaries, strictly in terms of the services that they provided for state and society. This is understandable: that is why patricians had called the order into existence in the first place, to provide technical expertise, continuity

---

[1] E.g., Contarini, *De magistratibus et republica venetorum*, esp. pp. 322–325. For basic bibliography see Casini, 'La cittadinanza originaria a Venezia'; Bellavitis, *Identité, mariage, mobilité sociale*; Zannini, *Burocrazia e burocrati a Venezia*.

and management skills to a government and people grown vastly more complex and demanding. But the *cittadini* had lives outside of council-chambers and *scuola* meeting-rooms, as well. Increasingly clearly defined as a distinct corporate body, they sought and acquired a distinct identity; and increasingly conscious of their separation from the great mass of the truly common, they sought to position themselves as close as possible to the nobility. This paper takes a preliminary and largely anecdotal look at some of their behavioral norms and acts of self-presentation, which in turn speaks to how they identified themselves within their society through deeds and works. The gap in historiography, which has been predominantly institutional and structural, is that we know who they were and how they worked, but not what they were like – what they wanted, and how they went about getting it.

* * *

The inquiry might begin with the single sustained statement of *cittadino* values, the domestic treatise composed by the aged Benedetto Arborsani in 1543. It is the first such work in the vernacular in Renaissance Venice, and so should be of considerable interest. Alas, for the most part the content is entirely pedestrian: there is nothing that cannot be found in comparable treatises and commonplace-books from earlier centuries and from different places. At most, Arborsani demonstrated that he had embraced the same bourgeois values as a host of predecessors. He warned against usury and speculative or risky business ventures, and advised never to squander capital; he cautioned his progeny to live virtuously and avoid the company of drunkards and spendthrifts; he urged caution in contracting marriage, and strict supervision of a wife thereafter; he wanted his family to avoid pompous luxuries, but to eat and dress in accordance with their social standing, and so forth; he recommended a virtuous, sober lifestyle, and a firm upbringing of children to ensure that those values were perpetuated.[2] He offers, in short, little that is distinctive to the world of Venetian *cittadini*.

More revealing are the two pieces of evidence relating to the otherwise obscure Piero Amadi. The shorter and more attractive of the two is found in the family memoir, dated 1459, when Piero joined with his cousin and a small band of fellow-*cittadini* to establish a youth fraternity.[3] This was

---

[2]The bulk of the treatise, which serves as introduction to the family memoir, is ASV, Scuola Grande di S. Maria della Valverde (Misericordia), busta 50, fascicle 2, ff. 1r–13v (henceforth Arborsani memoir). An opening folio has been detached and is found in ivi, busta 47, loose folio.

[3]Venice, Biblioteca del museo civico Correr (henceforth Correr), ms. Gradenigo 56 (henceforth Amadi memoir), p. 86. For another commoner *compagnia*, see Bellavitis, *Identité, mariage, mobilité sociale*, pp. 337–353; Venice, Biblioteca

one of the scores of the so-called 'companies of the hose' that sponsored banquets and entertainments and occasional Masses, greeted visiting dignitaries, and generally vented youthful energies in (it was hoped) wholesome rituals of sociability and civic engagement. The *compagnie delle calze* have traditionally been thought of as exclusively patrician preserves, and certainly the overwhelming majority consisted strictly of nobles, but Piero and his companions demonstrate that elite commoners too might take part in the movement. Theirs, however, was an exclusively *cittadino* company, equal but separate.

Three years later, demonstrating a somewhat less acceptable venting of energies, Piero was summoned before the patriarchal tribunal of Venice. His accuser, the humbly-born Laura Triulzi, claimed that she and Piero had gone through a ceremony involving the exchange of words of present consent, before a priest and several friends, in the little church of San Vio. That act, declared Laura, creating a binding marriage, and she added that the union had been further ratified by regular sexual relations. She now demanded that Piero assume the marital duties of cohabitation and sustenance. Piero defended himself vigorously, claiming that no such ritual had occurred and that Laura was in any case a lying whore who was already married, but he could do little to discredit a string of witnesses who vouched for the event and for her character. He lost an initial judgment and appealed, and there the trail goes cold.[4]

The trial dossier is long, lurid, and tawdry. It is also, after a generation of studies of such episodes, familiar and dreary: a well-born youth arranges what he deems a fictive marriage ceremony, in order to seduce a lower-class young woman; she considers the ceremony valid and sues. Authors at the time perceived widespread upper-class sexual predation, and authors of crime and microhistory since have brought many instances to light. Piero's case is unusual only in that he seems to have been extraordinarily careless in executing his scheme, inept in defending himself, and unlucky in finding a judge that preferred his opponent. Still, there is one twist that gives the story some significance: Piero was not at all upper class. The Amadi were commoners, and despite some pretenses at nobility were destined to remain that way. Piero, that is, was assuming the distinctive behavioral codes of a social sector to which he did not and never would belong. However we regard his immediate motives of fraternity in the one anecdote and sexual gratification in the other, he was clearly engaging in behavior characteristic of another body of the population.

Marciana, 549 (henceforth Ziliol memoir), p. 334.
    [4]Venice, Archivio storico del patriarcato di Venezia (henceforth Patriarcale), Liber actorum 1461, s.d. January 7.

In both episodes, it would seem at first glance that Piero was merely engaging in the familiar practice of *imitatio*, itself wrapped in ancient notions of self-fashioning, *habitus* and performance. The archives offer plenty of evidence for explicit emulation of superiors, seen for example – to take one episode out of myriad – in one *cittadino* father's request that his daughter be dowered 'in the noble style.'[5] But there may be something more at play here, because there is only a very fine line between simple imitation of superiors' ways and trespassing onto their special territory. In many areas, Venice's elite commoners did not just ape their betters, but rather appropriated class-specific attributes of the patriciate, including the very notion of nobility itself. They seized not so much generalized patterns of behavior as they did the precise markers of aristocracy. Equally significant, Venetian nobles in turn yielded to many encroachments of *cittadini* onto their own terrain, and thus accepted partial derogation of their status exclusivity.

The memoir of the *cittadino originario* Freschi family, for example, contains several extended descriptions of lavish marriage rituals replete with jugglers, mimes, acrobats, trumpeters, pipers and singers, cakes adorned with sculptures made of sugar and pine nuts, and so forth. The significance of these elaborate sequences of events is not just that the Freschi indulged in the same vast expenditure and sumptuous display as nobles habitually did. Instead, rather than mere conspicuous consumption, the choreography of Freschi weddings repeated patrician prototypes, indeed took precisely those elements that had long been characteristic of patrician ceremonials. In the days prior to the ceremony itself, for example, betrothed Freschi women went in grand procession to visit their female kin in convents, as noble women had done for generations. In the string of opulent banquets that spread out over many days, Freschi males and their male kin often wore purple, a color that in court dress at least was traditionally reserved to the highest nobility. Some wore a black superhumeral 'as the greatest citizens of the city are accustomed to do.' Freschi women were adorned in dazzling outfits of silks, velvets, pearls, gems, gold jewelry and so forth, thus openly flouting sumptuary laws; in doing so, they demonstrated a characteristically aristocratic disdain for restrictions on pomp. The Freschi then compounded that defiance of norms by having full-length portraits of the married couples, dressed in the highest degree of forbidden luxury, painted into the memoir. At the time of Elisabetta Freschi's wedding in 1513, elaborate ceremonies were forbidden because of the war that threatened Venice, but the family still hosted a 'full and highly praised banquet' with the usual acrobats and actors, asking only that the singers keep their voices down. They hosted

---

[5]Romano, *Patricians and Popolani*, pp. 55–56.

sixty for lunch the next day, 'omitting no sort of rich food,' contravening sumptuary laws passed the year before. At Maria Freschi's wedding six years later, the memoir notes, 'nothing was lacking by way of copiousness, adornment and elegance.' Clearly, conspicuous consumption was no longer the exclusive province of the aristocracy. But not only did nobles not object to this singular display by commoners, they took part *en masse* and so ratified this appropriation of their ritual vocabulary: guests included a doge's son, ducal councilors, and members of the Council of Ten.[6]

To take another example of *cittadino* seizure of distinctly noble habits: the public display of coats of arms was originally, in Venice, associated with nobility. As a witness testified in another ecclesiastical courtroom,

> It is common knowledge that it's the usage and custom of the nobles of this city to keep coats of arms of all types fixed on the porticoes and in the rooms of their houses.[7]

The Freschi agreed, three times referring in the memoir to coats of arms as 'genteel insignia.' In doing so they referred to the local (and not so local) equation of gentility with nobility, and associated that rank with the display of family emblems.[8] But it was their own coat of arms that the memoir referred to, the arms carved into the family tomb or painted on wedding decorations; and as the Freschi regarded such heraldry as connoting aristocracy, they were equally making a claim for their own gentility. The Amadi too appropriated this badge of nobility, displaying their arms (still extant) over the doorway leading into their courtyard and in three other places in the city.[9] The *cittadino* family of the Arborsani displayed their arms publicly in two places, in a tomb in the Servite church and over the portico of the church of San Polo.[10] The Ziliol did them one better, with arms posted on two sets of houses and two tombs.[11] Grand chancellor Niccolò Aurelio's arms are placed prominently in the forefront of Titian's *Sacred and Profane Love*, which he commissioned; the arms of the three *cittadino* heads of the Silk Guild were sculpted over the door of the guild hall.[12] In a parallel vein, patricians had long worn a distinctive

---

[6]Venice, Biblioteca marciana, Ital. VII, 165 (8867) (henceforth Freschi memoir), ff. 3r–8r (portraits), 33v, 35r, 38r, 42v–44v, 46v–47v, 49v–50r (weddings). For sumptuary law, see Gilbert, 'Venice in the Crisis of the League of Cambrai,' pp. 279–280.

[7]Patriarcale, Liber actorum 1461, s.d. January 7.

[8]Freschi memoir, ff. 37r ('cum insigni gentilitio insculpto'), 43v ('gentiliciis insignibus'), 61v ('[s]culptum suis propriis gentilitium insignibus').

[9]Amadi memoir, p. 14; ASV, Storia Veneta 9 (Tassini, *Cittadini veneti*), f. 74r.

[10]Arborsani memoir, f. 4v.

[11]Ziliol memoir, pp. 337–338.

costume consisting of a long black robe with wide sleeves, a black beret and a black stole; by the 1490s, at least, *cittadini* were doing the same, to the point where 'gentlemen can't be distinguished from citizens because everyone goes about dressed in about the same way.'[13] The grand chancellor, chief among the commoners, was given the same state funeral as the doge, with chief magistrates (doge and Signoria) attending in mourning.[14]

As criteria for membership in the ranks of the *cittadini originari* were gradually clarified and standardized – the process occupied all of the fifteenth century, and was not completed until legislation of 1569 – and the privileges of original citizens were expanded and formalized, these elite commoners grew in self-confidence and began to reach still further, appropriating the very principle of nobility itself. Once again, they did so without any challenge from the patriciate. Many original citizens boasted titles of nobility. Initially, some may have done so for externally derived reasons such as an imperial or papal grant or (perhaps) a doctorate conferred by a mainland university: thus the Amadi could cite a privilege by the emperor Charles IV in 1363, and thus original citizens Giacomo Turloni in 1436 and Benedetto Franceschi in 1449, both graduates of Padua, were defined as *nobilis vir*.[15] Luca Arborsani had himself styled 'nobilis vir' in 1461; the Venetian governor of Padua signed the document, so Arborsani's claim must have been unobjectionable.[16]

Not long thereafter, this practice moved to Venice proper. About 1480, the Amadi styled themselves 'magnifici signori' — *magnifico* was previously associated with patricians alone.[17] Antonio Vinciguerra's tomb styled him 'clarissimus,' likewise a descriptive formerly applied only to the aristocracy.[18] By 1517 Anteo Amadi was referred to as 'nobel homo,' and in the same register several commoners were given the characteristic noble titles of 'magnifico' and 'generoso.'[19] This usage could hardly have been deemed offensive by the true hereditary aristocracy, as the register was compiled for the Avogadori di Comun, the magistracy charged with

---

[12]ASV, Arte della Seta, b. 650, fasc. 1, ff. 1r–3v.
[13]Sanudo, *De origine*, p. 22.
[14]Sansovino, *Delle cose notabili che sono in Venetia*, f. 10r.
[15]Zonta and Brotta, *Acta graduum academicorum* I, ## 1141, 2318.
[16]ASV, Scuola Grande S.M. Valverde, 46, bundle marked 'Misericordia,' s.d. 23 September 1461.
[17]Amadi memoir, p. 6. 'Magnificentia,' at least, was a distinctly patrician appellation: Sanudo, *De origine*, p. 23.
[18]Sansovino, *Venezia città nobilissima et singolare* p. 217.
[19]ASV, Avogaria di Comun 141, ff. 148v–149r (Amadi); other titles on ff. 36v, 39r–v, 243r, 243v, 138r–v; a commoner 'nobel madonna' in ivi, reg. 111, s.d. 22 October 1551; a commoner 'nobel misser' in ivi, reg. 142, ff. 363v–364r.

safeguarding the purity of noble blood. Nor was it a passing error: two decades later an Avogadori document referred to Girolamo Grifalconi as 'nobile et prudente,' and thirteen years after that the Avogadori styled Graziosa Martini as 'pudica et nobel.'[20] By the mid-sixteenth century, application of 'magnificus/a' to commoners was routine;[21] earlier, in the 1520s, it was regularly applied to the commoner leaders (*vardiani*) of the *scuole grandi*.[22] One notary of the *scuola* of S. Marco, either over-enthusiastic or making a serious point, spoke of a *vardian* as 'nobilissimo.'[23]

Prior to the covering law of 1569 there were several sorts of cittadini originari, with criteria for membership varying with the use to which the state put them. In the second quarter of the sixteenth century, well before that patrician legislation, original citizens took the initiative in coalescing and formalizing their ranks . They did so by appropriating the genre of the collective chronicle by which the patriciate had long listed its constituent families. These compilations, sometimes titled 'Caxade de Viniegia' and hence known as the *caxade* chronicles, provided thumbnail sketches of the geographic origins, personality traits, famous ancestors, feats of ecclesiastical patronage and coats of arms of those deemed noble. In 1536, and again in 1540, *cittadini originari* did precisely the same for their own ranks.[24] The texts are not identical, as membership criteria were still far from standardized and much rested upon perception rather than formal definition and approbation, but the most important of the original citizens are found in both: henceforth interested parties could gain a pretty clear vision of who counted as an elite commoner and who, by omission, did not. At the very least, the prosopographical *cittadini* chronicles mark the first step towards closing ranks, though legislation in 1569 was required to complete the process; and they did so by using precisely the vehicle by which the patriciate had proclaimed its *serrata* for generations previous.

But the 1540 chronicle aspired to something more. If its 1536 antecedent promised to list 'the ancient families of Venetian citizens,' that of 1540 proclaimed the intention of describing 'all the ancient and noble families of Venetian citizens who are not of the Great Council.' These families, that is, did not claim political enfranchisement via seats on the council – that would have been foolhardy and futile – but they did claim

---

[20]ASV, Avogaria di Comun 111, s.d. 22 October 1551; ASV, Avogaria di Comun 146, 153r–154r.

[21]ASV, Avogaria di Comun 147, ff. 18v–19r, 22r–89r–91r, 106v, 130r–v.

[22]E.g., recurrently in ASV, Scuola Grande San Giovanni Evangelista 73.

[23]ASV, Scuola Grande di S. Marco, b. 17, f. 111r.

[24]The 1536 text is Correr, Gradenigo 192, pp. 3–33; the 1540 text is Correr, Cicogna 2156, pp. 170–189 (another copy is Marciana, Ital. VII, 28 [7761]).

some sort of nobility. If it was a cadet nobility, it was still nobility, certainly not enough to establish parity with the patriciate but sufficient to provide an indelible status marker of separation from the truly common. Additionally, in making that claim, the 1540 chronicle expanded the noble pretensions of the *cittadini* in quantitative as well as qualitative terms, broadening its application from what had been scattered references to individuals – Anteo Amadi and a handful of colleagues in the Avogaria registers, for example – to some 150 families. Further, the 1540 chronicle marks the beginning of a sustained campaign to assert the collective nobility of original citizens. In the next century, writers termed the *cittadini originari* 'gentlemen of the second order of nobles,' or more poetically one of the 'two crowns' of the Venetian Republic.[25] As the author of that latter phrase looked back in his memoirs, 'at that time [the later fifteenth century] there was no difference except the ballot between those of the Council and the other citizens who were born and lived nobly.'[26] He said that, as did the author of the 1540 chronicle, without rebuttal.

Such recurrent appropriation of the central features of patrician privilege constituted trespass onto distinctly noble territory. That *cittadini originari* were allowed to do so with impunity, indeed with the tacit and sometimes explicit assent of patricians, must be regarded in the light of a considerable and persuasive historiography that sees precisely this period as erecting ever-rigid barriers between nobility and commoners.[27] Systematic registration of noble births and marriages, rigorous examination of candidates for admission to the Great Council, and exclusion not only of illegitimates but the offspring of noblemen and 'vile women' from the Council, indeed served to seal off what had been (or what was feared to be) occasional permeability. And yet the patricians that so vigorously kept most commoners at arm's length also embraced at least the *cittadini originari* among them. They allowed a few commoners to call themselves noble, and they made no objection when the prosopographical chronicle of 1540 conferred secondary nobility upon scores of families. They made no effort to enforce the sumptuary laws at Freschi weddings, and did not demur when the better sort of commoners affixed arms to palaces and tombs.

On the contrary: patricians regularly established strong bonds of kinship and sociability with *cittadini originari*. To be sure, the issue of

---

[25] Ziliol, *Le due corone della nobiltà veneziana*, Marciana, Ital. VII, 549 (7942); Correr, Cicogna 2156, pp. 127–138.
[26] Ziliol memoir, p. 343.
[27] Most recently Chojnacki, 'Identity and Ideology,' pp. 263–294; Victor Crescenzi, *'Esse de maiori consilio'*.

the frequency of intermarriage between the two groups is far from settled. My earlier calculations, taken from two lists of patrician marriages, indicated that somewhere around 14% of patrician men married non-patricians – the latter including women from noble families on the Venetian mainland as well as the *stato di mar*, in addition to women of original citizen families of Venice proper. Stanley Chojnacki's figures, derived from different samples, indicate only half that rate, with the incidence of cross-class marriage in decline from the fifteenth to the sixteenth centuries. Two further trace indicators support the higher figure, and indeed suggest that the lists significantly undercounted patrician exogamy, perhaps by a factor of half. First, the early *vadimoni* registers, recording widows' petitions to have their dowries restored, list twice as many patrician men marrying commoners as appear in the lists, thirteen vs. six. Second, while the later and more complete of those lists makes mention of eight marriages of Arborsani women to patrician males, the family's memoir lists sixteen; here too the lists significantly understate the true incidence of intermarriage. If that reckoning held true across the board, something on the order of one-fifth to one-quarter of patrician men married outside their class. But these samples are not generous, and the issue should remain open.[28] Judicial records offer yet another hint of undercounting. When one finds a *nobilis mulier* married to a nobleman, for example, it is instinctive to assume them both as patricians; but records of inheritance often reveal that such a woman was actually born a commoner, and had only become a *nobilis mulier* by virtue of her marriage.[29]

Whatever the incidence of intermarriage, the *meaning* of intermarriage merits some comment. It is usually assumed that patrician men married commoner women primarily for their abundant dowries, to restore noble

---

[28] *Vadimoni* registers are ASV, Giudice del Proprio, regs. 4–14. The lists are ASV, Avogaria di Comun 106 (sixteenth century) and ASV, Indice 86ter (19th century). See also Grubb, 'Elite Citizens,' pp. 351–352.

[29] Thus *nobilis mulier* Tomasina, widow of noble Marino d'Avanzago, was actually born to the *cittadino* Zuane de Francesco; similarly *nobilis mulier* Caterina, widow of the noble Tommaso Contarini but born to the commoner Corbelli family, and *nobilis mulier* Pellegrina, widow of noble Nicolò Barbo but born to the *cittadini* Franceschi family: ASV, Giudici di Proprio, Vadimoni 5, ff. 4v–5r, 6r, 11v–12r; similarly ivi, reg. 8, f. 13r (*nobilis dona* Lena, widow of noble Daniel Badoer, born to the *cittadino* Soligo family); similarly Barbarella, born to the commoner Greci family but made *nobilis et egregia mulier* by virtue of marriage to noble Bartolomeo Magna (ivi, Divisioni 1, ff. 98v–102r). See also the case of the 'noble woman' Fiordelisia Coppo, wife of the noble Marco Coppo, who had twice been married to commoners and was almost certainly herself common: ASV, Giudici di Petizion, Sentenze a giustizia 165, ff. 110r–115v, 174v–178v.

patrimonies reduced by economic downturns or lavish expenditure. There is certainly some anecdotal evidence to support this position. Thirteen Arborsani brides brought dowries averaging 2800 ducats to their patrician husbands over the course of the fifteenth century, for example, and eight Quartari brides were said to have brought dowries averaging 3100 ducats – at a time when the legal limit was only 1600 ducats. Since there were many more commoner women married to patrician men than the other way around, the net flow into aristocratic ranks would have been substantial. Granted, the dowry might revert to a *cittadina* woman's natal family at her death; but it just as commonly passed to her noble children.

But there is equal anecdotal evidence in the other direction, indicating that economic motives were not the driving force in bonding many patrician and *cittadino* families. In the *vadimoni* registers, for example, the dowries of commoner women who married noble men were seldom much larger than those of noble brides of noble men. Sometime they were rather less, as in the 454 ducats that commoner Cecilia Limonini brought to her marriage with the noble Nicolò Giustiniani — about a third of the going rate in noble unions – or the 500 ducats that noble Leonardo Marcello received in marriage to Graziosa dal Cortivo.[30] Sometimes, too, the money flowing out from patricians to commoners, when a noble woman married a *cittadino originario*, was substantial, as in the 3000 ducats that the 'nobel madonna' Felicita Foscarini brought to her marriage with Vettor Spiera and noble Elena Malipiero brought to Zuan Antonio Dario, or the 2700 ducats that noble Franceschina (we do not know her last name) brought to Martino Martini.[31]

Expressly non-economic forces governed at least one noble family's choice of a *cittadino* bride. The noble Caterina Vettori, recalling 'the great love and friendship' between her late husband Zuan and the commoner Andrea Fasuol, and now 'wanting to close and seal a mutual benevolence between one house and the other with the bond of matrimony' as her husband had always wanted, concluded a marriage between her son and Fasuol's daughter. The Fasuol in turn provided a dowry of only 500 ducats, so financial advantage was certainly not at play in Caterina's decision.[32]

That incident bespeaks close bonds of affection. Elsewhere there is evidence for significant social interaction, seen – in one example out of

---

[30] ASV, Giudice del Proprio, Vadimoni, reg. 9, f. 8r; ivi, Vadimoni, reg. 5, ff. 13r–v.
[31] ASV, Avogaria di Comun 111, s.d. 7 September 1526; ivi, Avogaria di Comun 146, ff. 1r–v; ASV, Giudici del Proprio, Vadimoni, reg. 5, ff. 7r–v.
[32] ASV, Avogaria di Comun 146, f. 261r.

myriad – in the visit of noble Contarina Michiel to view the wedding goods of the *cittadina* and new bride Fioruccia Basilio.[33] Equally common is evidence for patronage and mutual obligation: *cittadini* and patricians constantly set up trading companies with each other, named each other executors of estates, and established each other as godparents. As the *vardian grando* Vettor Ziliol set forth the imperative of utilitarian friendship in one of a long string of maxims, 'He who does not have charity has nothing … and he who doesn't serve acquires enemies.'[34]

But it should not be assumed that, amidst generalized social asymmetry, nobles were invariably the patrons and *cittadini* were invariably the clients. Social dynamics often worked in a direction opposite to that which might have been anticipated. *Cittadini originari* successful in public service, especially the chancery secretaries, were intimate with the mechanisms, personalities and issues of everyday politics; they were indeed insiders, with expertise and considerable behind-the-scenes influence. Patricians, on the other hand, were often poor, sometimes miserably so; and with increasingly fierce competition for state positions among fifteen hundred nobles or more, it was likely that many would remain on the margins without special help. In such circumstances a well-placed commoner might well be in a position to provide favors for less fortunate nobles, who in turn might regard a marriage alliance as a fair price to pay.

In the case of Caterina Vettori's decision to marry her noble son to a *cittadina* Fasuol, she was well aware that an earlier Fasuol had been grand chancellor, in charge of the day-to-day workings of government, and that the family remained well connected both in chancery and *scuola grande* circles. The above-mentioned noble Elena Malipiero was marrying the son of a ducal secretary and the grandson of a grand chancellor; she might well have brought such a rich dowry because her husband's family – albeit common – was better situated than hers. This sort of tradeoff certainly seems to have been the case for the noble Vincenzo Barbaro. His bride was not only common but illegitimate, and she brought him a mediocre dowry of a thousand ducats – but she was the daughter of the great Zuan Dario, 'one of the republic's most capable statesmen,' many times Venice's envoy to and peace negotiator with the Turks. Theoretical notions of class aside, the common Dario had a great deal more prestige than many branches of the noble Barbaro, and on a practical level had a good deal more to deliver.[35]

---

[33] ASV, Giudici di Proprio, Parentelle 1, ff. 93v–94r.
[34] ASV, Scuola Grande S. Marco 17, f. 59r.
[35] Babinger, *Mehmed the Conqueror and His Time*, pp. 368 (quote), 370.

To take another example: about two-thirds of the godparents chosen by the Freschi (the only family for which such information is extant) for their children were patricians. The resulting advantages to the Freschi – establishing spiritual kinship with noble coparents – seem obvious enough. But there were advantages in the other direction as well. Patriarch Zaccaria Freschi was a long-time secretary to the Council of Ten, and other members of the family served in magistracies nearly as prestigious. The Freschi knew the system, they had access to the records, and they knew the people who mattered: they could be very useful to nobles wanting to get ahead in government. Additionally, the Freschi – like the Fasuol – were active in the leadership of the *scuole grandi*, which had enormous spiritual and financial resources at their disposal. One suspects that patricians accepted with alacrity the invitation to serve as spiritual sponsors to Freschi newborns. Or, perhaps, friendship need not be instrumental at all. If Petrarch is any guide, the doge Andrea Dandolo and the grand chancellor Benintendi de' Ravagnani – both chroniclers — were extremely close during their parallel careers in the mid-fourteenth century. They possessed, said the poet, 'one heart beating in two breasts,' and on his deathbed Dandolo commended his wife and children to the grand chancellor.[36]

A final aspect of patronage is starkly material. Surrounded as we are by the architectonic and artistic testimony to vast patrician wealth, it is not hard to forget that, in fact, many patricians enjoyed (or endured) decidedly mediocre or even marginal standards of living. Apart from their right to participate in councils, many would have been indistinguishable from the commoners with whom they lived. While this phenomenon cannot be measured systematically, it constantly asserts itself in vignettes such as that of the noble Francesco Premarin, whose marriage with the daughter of a soapmaker was so regarded.[37] Under such circumstances, it is not surprising to find episodes in which nobles were objects of charity, in particular from commoners who were a good deal better off than they were. So, for example, the common but well-educated and apparently very wealthy physician Pietro Tommasi left fifty ducats to the *magnifica* but poor Susanna Fontana to assist with her dowry.[38] Even more striking, not to mention poignant, are the bundles of small parchments from the archive of the *scuola* of Santa Maria Valverde. Most are receipts, acknowledging the *scuola*'s distribution of testamentary bequests, payments for services, and alms. Among the latter are many from nobles, obliged to

---

[36]Bellomo, 'La vita e i tempi di Benintendi de' Ravagnani cancelliere grande della Veneta Republica', pp. 263–264.
[37]ASV, Giudici del Proprio, Parentelle 1, f. 17r.
[38]ASV, Procuratorie di S. Marco, Citra, Commissarie 120, s.d. 10 November 1456.

take charity from the *cittadino* officers of the *scuola* as marriage subventions. In 1431, for example, the young Maria – daughter of noble Pietro Gradenigo, wife of noble Alvise Tron – accepted forty ducats from the commoner *vardian* Pietro Zon as a marriage subsidy. She was fortunate: Bartolomeo Benedetti, born into the nobility, received only thirty ducats, while the *nobilis dona* Agnola Donà received only five.[39]

As was the case with Piero Amadi, the area of sociability has its negative as well as positive side. More dubious but no less intimate associations across class boundaries emerge constantly in the judicial records. An almost routine entry in the *Raspe* registers, for example, tells the tale of the noble Zuan Donà out on the town with the *cittadino originario* Alvise Tedaldini one night in 1460. After a visit to prostitutes, Tedaldini pulled a knife on a passing nobleman, Donà ran the captain of the night guard through the body with a lance, and both yelled insults ('They're all bung-holes!'). Their crimes were commensurate, and they received identical sentences.[40] Or there is the case of another pair of sidekicks, who 'in contempt of holy religion and led by a diabolical spirit' rowed out from the city to a convent in 1465. In a neat twist of symmetry, the *cittadino originario* Alvise Cavazza had sex with a noble nun, while the noble Marco Trevisan had sex with a commoner nun.[41] Here too the sentences were equal. Clearly, if some *cittadini* felt that they could borrow aristocratic disdain for social legislation such as the sumptuary laws, others assumed an equally aristocratic disregard for criminal norms. Patricians, for their part, felt no hesitation in choosing commoner companions for their nocturnal escapades.

If it is somewhat of a surprise to find patricians so accommodating to *cittadini originari*, even to the extent of tacit ratification of their secondary nobility in the midst of an era devoted to rigidifying aristocratic exclusivity, it is equally a surprise to find those *cittadini* showing occasional flashes of ambivalence toward the aristocracy. For all that the *cittadini* seized noble mores whenever possible, they were not infinitely deferential. On the contrary, they possessed a strong sense of what E. P. Thompson long ago termed a moral economy, a strong sense that all corporate bodies were subject to 'social norms and obligations' and that a refusal by superiors to abide by conventions of appropriate treatment in some measure legitimated resistance by inferiors.[42] The *cittadini* hardly qualified as an oppositional body, indeed were almost invariably polite,

---

[39] ASV, Scuola Grande S. Maria Valverde (Misericordia), Pergamene 7.
[40] ASV, Avogaria di Comun 3651, part 1, ff. 81r–v.
[41] ASV, Avogaria di Comun 3652, ff. 35r–v.
[42] Thompson,'The Moral Economy of the English Crowd in the Eighteenth Century', p. 79.

but they were not supine. They had their limits, and on the level of individual response were prepared to strike back against perceived patrician slights. This is particularly evident in the judicial archives, where testimony is often extraordinarily vivid. Commoner Pietro Ciera, for example, charged that his noble adversary Francesco Girardo, 'fearing neither God nor his honor, and rabid for my money, sought to do me harm' before various magistracies; the noble Marco da Lezze, claimed *cittadino* Zuan Mariani 'came to my house using words that, to preserve decorum, I wouldn't want to relate here.' According to Vettor Ziliol, his *scuola* stood toe to toe with the aristocratic monastery of SS. Giovanni e Paolo in a 'great fight, indeed rabid,' in the 1520s. The case had been heard before many tribunals, and the *scuola* always won, but the friars resisted and used 'injurious words, and what is worse threatened to harm even our lives, with certain displays of arms.' In the end the well-born friars capitulated.[43]

Several *cittadini originari* recorded their grudges for posterity. The patriarch of the Arian family, expelled from the nobility for fraudulent debt, sternly forbad his offspring to marry patricians, under penalty of disinheritance. For Lunardo Masser, citizen guard at the doors of the council chamber of the Collegio, familiarity with patricians bred only contempt: 'he was a very arrogant man, and thought little of gentlemen.' Benedetto Arborsani wanted his progeny to remember that a noble grandfather and uncles, from the mighty Corner family, had looted the patrimony of his own fatherless family: 'They didn't care that my father had died from plague; they stripped everything from the house, and laid their hands on all our assets.' His subsequent life experiences made him openly skeptical of service to the state, and his treatise is one of very few that belies the nascent myth of Venetian civic mindedness: 'he who serves the common good serves no one.' His very first piece of advice to descendants was not to seek government employment: 'keep yourself from going crazy over public office.'[44]

A more extended story of resistance revolves around the street-corner image of the Madonna and saints that had been commissioned by the Amadi family early in the fifteenth century. From August 1480 onwards many who prayed before it were miraculously cured of afflictions and

---

[43]ASV, Giudici di Petizion, Sentenze a giustizia 161, 178v–180v; ivi, b. 162, f. 137r–139r; ASV, Scuola Grande S. Marco 17, f. 102r–103v.

[44]Arian from Mueller, 'Espressioni di status sociale a Venezia dopo la "serrata" del Maggior Consiglio' p. 55; Molmenti, *Venice*, p. 169; Masser from Trebbi, 'La società veneziana', p. 177 n. 204; Arborsani from ASV, Scuola Grande S. Maria Valverde, b. 47, loose folio (detached first folio of Arborsani memoir) and Arborsani memoir, f. 1r.

travails, and the icon became the center of a considerable cult of pilgrims. For safekeeping, and better to organize worship, the Amadi removed it from the busy (and narrow) street to the courtyard of their own house. This act was hotly contested by the noble Barozzi family, on the wall of whose palace the image had originally been fixed. Barozzi influence secured a temporary patriarchal injunction against daily masses, while the family attempted to have the image removed to their own favored church of San Moise. The Amadi fought the issue in civil and ecclesiastical tribunals, eventually securing a judgment against the Barozzi. When it was decided to construct a church to house the image — the wondrous jewel box of Santa Maria dei Miracoli — two of the Amadi served on the board of commissioners that raised money and organized the works. On the day of dedication, the Amadi celebrated their victory over patrician neighbors in grand style: when an 'infinite number' of knights and doctors, 'a large part of the government,' the patriarch and all the *scuole grandi* gathered to accompany the picture to its final resting-place, Alvise Amadi and Angelo Amadi actually carried the miraculous icon, processing in quasi-regal fashion under an umbrella lofted by other members of the Amadi clan — and every Venetian knew that only the doge himself habitually processed under an umbrella, a privilege long ago granted by the Holy Roman Emperor.[45] Every bit as important as the Amadi's resolve in contesting the Barozzi is the fact that they never lacked patrician allies in doing so: noble judges gave them decisions, and other patricians served with them on the construction committee. Nobles were not inclined to close ranks against *cittadini*, especially when their own were behaving badly.

Again the edifying anecdote may be paired with one less uplifting but no less indicative. The noble Girolamo Giustiniani, we read in the criminal files, was accustomed to swaggering about the city with a stick or club in hand ('facendo largum cum uno bastono prout moris est'). One day in 1458 he became annoyed with one Michele Veruzzi and struck him on the hand. Now, Veruzzi may have been a commoner, but he also ranked in the top levels of the *cittadini originari* — the family was rich from the silk trade and active in *scuole grandi* leadership — and he had too much pride to put up with the affront. 'Burning with anger,' he hired thugs to kill Giustiniani, but 'by the grace of God the attempt was unsuccessful.' Obviously Veruzzi had to be prosecuted, and he was – in the Senate, no less — but his patrician judges made two gestures that hint at a certain amount of sympathy for his actions. First, a full quarter of the court abstained from passing judgment, a very high percentage indicating that

---

[45] Amadi memoir, pp. 1–2, 4–7, 10–12 (quotes on p. 10). The episode is discussed in Crouzet-Pavan, '*Sopra le acque salse*', pp. 617–641.

the senators were not fully hostile to Veruzzi's defence of his honor. Second, the eventual sentence shows a considerable degree of respect: if Veruzzi were found (he had fled) he was to be beheaded between the two columns of the Piazzetta, just outside the ducal palace, a type of execution (common criminals were hanged) and place of execution reserved for the eminent.[46]

If such acts of assertion by *cittadini originari* were by definition episodic, another form was recurrent. One of the special missions of the *scuole grandi* was to process around the city with precious relics on holy days. These parades were both sacred and splendid, attracting the notice of foreign visitors and writers of guidebooks alike. It is not often remarked, though, how aggressive they were. For example, in the famous Gentile Bellini painting of the *scuola* of San Giovanni Evangelista, carrying its piece of the True Cross under a fabulous canopy around the Piazza San Marco, the *cittadini* brethren of the *scuola* have invaded the city's main gathering space — usually the domain of patrician processions to glorify the patrician Republic — and in some sense have made it their own. They have extended their file around the entire vast perimeter of the piazza, pushing onlookers – including the patricians who frequented the ducal palace and the government buildings around the piazza – to the fringes. They may have glorified God and brought honor to the city, but equally they have obliged all present to do them reverence as well.

The same *scuola* once made the decision to parade its relic from its headquarters to the church of San Martino. In spatial terms, this dictated a procession from the southwest of the city to the northeast. First the brethren would have filed up the narrow street linking the major *campi* of the Frari, San Polo and San Aponal; then they would have marched through the commercial center of the Rialto, across the Rialto bridge (then the only pedestrian passage across the Grand Canal) and through the retail center of the Merceria before arriving at the political center of San Marco, then heading through less crowded neighborhoods before arriving at their destination. A piece of the Cross demanded veneration: life in these central zones of the Republic would have temporarily shut down as the reliquary passed by, and business and political negotiations would have turned to prayers. By organizing their route in this fashion, the brethren of San Giovanni demanded both full attention and deep respect. The *scuola*'s members were undoubtedly pious, but they were not retiring in their practice of piety; and all the city knew, as the uniformed brethren stopped traffic to march by behind their distinctive banner, that the *scuola* was the special province of the *cittadini originari*.[47]

---

[46] ASV, Avogaria di Comun 3651, part 1, f. 27r.
[47] ASV, Scuola Grande San Giovanni Evangelista 8, ff. 31v–32r.

No less assertive were their meeting centers. Four of the five *scuole* were either built or rebuilt in the decades surrounding the year 1500 (that of Santa Maria Valverde was reconstructed under the leadership of yet another of the Amadi family). They were sited in such a way that they could not be ignored, indeed had to be constantly acknowledged: that of San Marco flanked the great Dominican church of SS. Giovanni and Paolo, one of Venice's three main devotional centers; that of the Carità had to be seen by anyone traveling down the Grand Canal; anyone walking near San Giovanni had to walk under the *scuola*'s ornamental doorway and through its courtyard; Santa Maria Valverde would have been seen by all passing to the populous northern neighborhood of Cannareggio; San Rocco was right off the apse of the great Franciscan church of the Frari. The new buildings were constructed on the grand scale, with marble facing and architectural elements in the latest Renaissance motifs; and the paintings and decorations inside are well known among the glories of Venetian art. They gave glory to God, and they testified to the sanctity and charity of the city — but equally they gave witness to the particular vocation of the *cittadini originari* who alone held office in the *scuole*. It is insufficiently appreciated, I think, that a preponderant share of Renaissance art and architecture in Venice came into being not at the behest of patricians but at the prompting of that service class that lay just beneath; but people of the time would not have missed the association.

There is one further piece of class-assertive architecture, this one personal rather than corporate. The only 'signed' Venetian palace of the early Renaissance, with twenty-inch letters identifying the builder, comes not from the patriciate but from the *cittadino ordinario* Zuan Dario, high chancery official and sometime diplomat. Located at the fashionable lower end of the Grand Canal, where no passerby could possibly miss it, Dario's grand edifice certainly honors Venice – the classical inscription is dedicated to the genius of the city – but his own name comes first. It was an act of self-promotion never replicated by even the proudest of nobles, indeed ran hostile to an ideology – most forcefully articulated by an original citizen — that viewed ostentatious architecture in a dim light. The closest anyone else came was the *cittadino* Alvise Dardani, who placed his portrait bust prominently on the façade of his own palace.[48]

Coming full circle, I would return to the Amadi family, particularly to their role in the foundation of Santa Maria dei Miracoli. Their stewardship of the wondrous image secured, Anzolo Amadi moved to establish at least symbolic patronage over the church that was to house it. As the first foundation was laid, he placed in one corner a medallion inscribed with

---

[48]Dardani from de Peppo, '"Memorie di veneti cittadini." Alvise Dardani, cancellier grande', p. 442; anti-architectural comments in King, 'Personal Domestic and Republic Values in the Moral Philosophy of Giovanni Caldiera', p. 552.

his image, his name and the family's coat of arms; he returned at weekly intervals to lay similar medallions as the remaining corners were established.[49] That is, he marked the boundaries of the sacred with his own and his lineage's presence, in some measure perpetuating family's *juspatronatus* of the cult even as its physical core was transformed from simple street-corner image to magnificent convent.

* * *

It is not the intent of this paper to celebrate the Venetian patriciate. No doubt patricians were as arrogant and imperialistic as most of contemporary Europe thought when it combined against Venice in the League of Cambrai of 1508; no doubt they were just as venal and self-serving as the late Donald Queller claimed, and no doubt they were just as casually criminal and predatory as Guido Ruggiero has demonstrated. But the story of the *cittadini originari* shows them to have been politically astute and flexible as well, surprisingly so given the standard image of their ruthlessly aristocratic vocation. They gave up a good deal to these subaltern *cittadini* that they had brought into existence, and they tolerated a good deal of *cittadino* behavior that might seem to derogate or at least infringe upon their titles and their prestige. They yielded command of critical institutions and at least tacitly authorized the *cittadini* to claim a kind of social parity. Their own nobility was in no way compromised, of course, and perhaps their concessions were more symbolic than vital – but, even so, history offers precious few examples of a closed and jealous caste sharing its trappings in this way. And it worked: patricians gained in return a body of subordinates that proved unfailingly loyal (albeit prickly and sometimes fractious) managers of the state, possessed of just enough honors and dignities not to press for more. The functionalist image, it would seem, will not disappear anytime soon. What may change, though, is that image's portrayal of a gray, anonymous body of servitors. With further research, they are beginning to show personalities, and even signs of an identity.

University of Maryland, Baltimore County
Baltimore, MD

---

[49] Amadi memoir, pp. 13–14.

Works Cited

Manuscript Sources

Venice, Archivio di Stato (ASV),
    Arte della Seta, b. 650, fasc. 1
    Avogaria di Comun 106, 111, 141, 142, 147, 147, 3651 pt 1, 3652
    Giudice del Proprio, regs. 4–14.
    Giudici di Petizion, Sentenze a giustizia 161, 162, 165
    Giudici del Proprio,   Divisioni 1
                           Parentelle 1
                           Vadimoni, reg. 5, 9
    Indice 86ter
    Procuratorie di S. Marco, Citra, Commissarie 120
    Scuola Grande San Giovanni Evangelista 8, 73
    Scuola Grande S. Marco 17
    Scuola Grande di S. Marco, b. 17.
    Scuola Grande S.M. Valverde, 46 (bundle marked 'Misericordia')
    Storia Veneta 9 (Giuseppe Tassini, *Cittadini veneti*)

Venice, Archivio storico del patriarcato di Venezia, (Patriarcale)
    Liber actorum 1461.

Venice, Biblioteca del museo civico Correr
    Cicogna 2156
    ms. Gradenigo 56 (Amadi memoir), 192

Venice, Biblioteca nazionale marciana
    Ital. VII,   28 (7761)
    165 (8867) (Freschi memoir)
    549 (7942) (Ziliol, Alessandro. *Le due corone della nobiltà veneziana*)

Published Sources

Babinger, Franz. *Mehmed the Conqueror and His Time*. Princeton: Princeton University Press, 1978.

Bellavitis, Anna. *Identité, mariage, mobilité sociale: citoyennes et citoyens à Venise au XVIe siècle*. Rome: Ecole française de Rome, 2001.

Bellomo, Vincenzo. 'La vita e i tempi di Benintendi de' Ravagnani cancelliere grande della Veneta Republica,' *Nuovo Archivio Veneto*, n.s. 23 (1912): 263–264.

Casini, Matteo. 'La cittadinanza originaria a Venezia tra i secoli XV e XVI: una linea interpretativa,' pp. 133–150 in *Studi veneti offerti a Gaetano Cozzi*. Venice: Il Cardo, 1992.

Chojnacki, Stanley. 'Identity and Ideology in Renaissance Venice,' pp. 263–294 in *Venice Reconsidered. The History and Civilization of an Italian City-State, 1297–1797*, ed. John Martin and Dennis Romano. Baltimore and London: The Johns Hopkins University Press, 2000.

Contarini, Gaspare. *De magistratibus et republica venetorum* in *Opera*. Paris, 1571.

Crescenzi, Victor. *'Esse de maiori consilio': legittimità civile e legittimità politica nella Repubblica di Venezia (secc XIII–XVI)*. Rome: Istituto Storico Italiano per il Medio Evo, 1996.

Crouzet-Pavan, Elisabeth, *'Sopra le acque salse': Espaces, pouvoir et société à Venise à la fin du Moyen Age*. Rome: Ecole Française de Rome, 1992.

de Peppo, Paola, '"Memorie di veneti cittadini." Alvise Dardani, cancellier grande' *Studi veneziani*, n.s. 8 (1984): 442.

Gilbert, Felix. 'Venice in the Crisis of the League of Cambrai' pp. 274–292 in *Renaissance Venice*, ed. J. R. Hale. London: Faber & Faber, 1973.

Grubb, James S. 'Elite Citizens,' pp. 339–364 in *Venice Reconsidered: The History and Civilization of an Italian City-State, 1297–1797*, ed. John Martin and Dennis Romano. Baltimore: Johns Hopkins University Press, 2000.

King, Margaret. 'Personal, Domestic and Republican Virtues in the Moral Philosophy of Giovanni Caldiera' *Renaissance Quarterly* 28 (1975) 535–574.

Molmenti, Pompeo. *Venice: Its Individual Growth from the Earliest Beginnings to the Fall of the Republic*. Chicago: A.C. McClurg, 1906.

Mueller, Reinhold C. 'Espressioni di status sociale a Venezia dopo la "serrata" del Maggior Consiglio,' pp. 53–61 in *Studi veneti offerti a Gaetano Cozzi*. Venice: Il Cardo, 1992.

Romano, Dennis. *Patricians and Popolani: The Social Foundations of the Venetian Renaissance State*. Baltimore: The Johns Hopkins University Press, 1987.

Sansovino, Francesco. *Delle cose notabili che sono in Venetia libri due*. Venice, 1561.

Sansovino, Francesco. *Venezia città nobilissima et singolare*. Venice, 1663; reprint 1968.

Sanudo, Marin. *De origine, situ et magistratibus urbis venetae, ovvero La città di Venetia (1493–1530)*, ed. Angela Caracciolo Arico. Milan, Cisalpino-La Goliardica, 1980.

Thompson, E. P. 'The Moral Economy of the English Crowd in the Eighteenth Century' *Past & Present* 50 (1971): 76–136.

Trebbi, Giuseppe. 'La società veneziana,' pp. 129–213 in *Storia di Venezia*, vol. 6, ed. Rudolfo Pallucchini. Rome: Istituto della Enciclopedia Italiana, 1994.

Zannini, Andrea. *Burocrazia e burocrati a Venezia in età moderna: i cittadini originari (sec. XVI–XVIII)*. Venice: Istituto Veneto di Scienze, Lettere ed arti, 1993.

Zonta, Caspare and Brotta, Giovanni, eds. *Acta graduum academicorum gymnasii Patavini ab anno 1406 ad annum 1450*, 3 vols. Padua: Antenore, 1970.

Literature Meets Law: A Consilium of Antonio Strozzi for Lodovico Ariosto

Thomas Kuehn

On 11 July 1519 the poet Lodovico Ariosto in Ferrara penned a letter to a friend, the attorney Antonio Strozzi, in Florence. Just four days earlier, 7 July, Lodovico's cousin and the effective head of the Ariosto clan, Rinaldo di Francesco, had died. His death was the occasion for the letter; but Lodovico was not writing to inform Antonio Strozzi of Rinaldo's untimely demise. He was seeking legal advice about the estate, whose situation was so delicate that, as he informed Strozzi from the outset, he had 'changed the names because, as I am not acting on my own behalf and that I may not bring harm to myself when I publish it, I have not wanted to trust or confide in a doctor of Ferrara' ('mutati li nomi perché non facendo per me non m'havessi ancho a nocere quando io lo publicassi, non mi ho voluto fidare di conferirne cum doctore di Ferrara'). Ariosto assured Strozzi that he approached him not just because he was not Ferrarese but 'as you have always shown me goodwill I trust in that you will advise me most faithfully and keep the matter secret' ('quanto che per la benivolentia che mi ha sempre mostrato, mi confido in essa molto che mi habbia a consultare fidelissimamente et a tenere la cosa secreta').[1] So Strozzi set about his labors under the guise of dealing with the estate of someone named Manfredo, whose relationship to Ariosto was left vague. One has to wonder whether someone as close to Ariosto as Strozzi (as will be more apparent below) did not know soon or even from the start that the deceased was in fact Rinaldo Ariosto. In any case, at some point in October 1519, Strozzi composed a legal response, in Latin, in the form of an *allegatio*, or what could have served as part of an *allegatio* had Ariosto chosen to use it in litigation. Whatever one chooses to call the document (but the term *consilium* would seem only

---

[1] Quotation and references to both the letter and the legal text are from Masi, 'Le liti del Ariosto.'

280   A Renaissance of Conflicts

loosely to apply²), it conveyed Strozzi's professional reaction to the case put before him by Lodovico Ariosto, even if it did not carry the full authority of a formal *consilium*.³

We know of this exchange between the poet and the lawyer because the texts survive among Strozzi's abundant papers in the Archivio di Stato of Florence.⁴ In 1929 Gino Masi transcribed these texts in the second issue of the first volume of *Rivista storica degli archivi toscani*.⁵ Masi was undoubtedly and understandably attracted by the discovery of an autograph letter of Ariosto. All his attention was directed to Ariosto's links to the Strozzi (on which, more below) and the litigation over Rinaldo's estate. As for Strozzi's text, Masi did not go into the merit of the opinion because 'it would be out of harmony with the character of this journal and furthermore the dullness of the theme would bore the reader' ('perché stonerebbe con l'indole di questo periodico ed inoltre la pesantezza del tema annoierebbe il lettore').⁶ From my point of view, he jumped ship just when the voyage was getting interesting. Where Masi saw 'tanti meandri dialettici' (hardly the case in this brief text, in comparison to so many others I have seen), I see the unique opportunity to observe a sixteenth-century legal professional responding to a request for his expertise and how he and his 'client' (for such, I believe, we may term

---

²As the text makes no attempt at a pro-et-contra comprehensive review of the issues, it does not seem to fit the nature of a *consilium pro parte*. It is certainly not directed to a court, judge, or official. For a sense of what *consilia* were, see Ascheri, 'Le fonti e la flessibilità del diritto comune'; Luigi Lombardi, *Saggio sul diritto giurisprudenziale*. In addition to the Ascheri-Baumgärtner-Kirshner volume, there is Baumgärtner, ed., *Consilia im späten Mittelalter*, plus two programmatic pieces by her: 'Stadtgeschichte und Consilia im italienischen Spätmittelalter,' and 'Consilia—Quellen zur Familie in Krise und Kontinuität.'

³Cf. Kirshner, 'Consilia as Authority in Late Medieval Italy,' and Ascheri, *Tribunali, giuristi e istituzioni dal medioevo all'età moderna*, 185–209.

⁴Archivio di Stato, Firenze, Carte strozziane, 3rd ser., 41/6, fols. 80r–84r.

⁵See note 1.

⁶Masi, 'Le liti del Ariosto,' 84. Masi, in fact, was a careful archival scholar who had an interest in drawing attention to legal sources and to the importance of legal and institutional history. His 'Il sindacato delle magistrature comunali nel secolo xiv,' is still cited as a definitive study. He also provided a valuable edition of *Formularium florentinum artis notariae (1220–1242)*.

My rendering of the legal text differs from his in just a few particulars: *decederet* for Masi's *decederetur* (line 2 of text); *extra de renunciatione* [X. 1.9.10] for his *extranee de renunciationibus* (line 35); *morirentur* for *morerentur* (lin 69); *quia* for *quasi* (line 75); *substitutus* for *substitutio* (line 95); *quoniam* cancelled (line 98); *que* for *quos* (line 104); *quanta* for *quarta* (line 137). More importantly he inexplicably moved the final paragraph up before two others, confusing Strozzi's argument.

Ariosto even in the absence of evidence of any fee changing hands) constructed their stories.[7] Admittedly, this is also a peculiar opportunity. Ariosto had been to law school, so even though he notoriously hated and neglected his legal studies, on that score (beyond his fame as a poet) he was hardly a typical client. He could frame the facts of the case and his questions carefully. And as we will see, there was a disjunction between what Ariosto asked for and what Strozzi gave him, as well as a disjunction between the substance of their exchange and that around which Ariosto's later lawsuit gravitated.

It must be stated at the outset that we know what Ariosto asked (if not the exact meaning of it all), because we have his signed and sealed original letter as received by Strozzi. But we do not know precisely Strozzi's response, as we have only his working draft (replete with deletions, cancellations, emendations, and marginalia), into the middle of which was inserted Ariosto's letter. No formal copy apparently survives among Ariosto's papers nor in the documents from the lawsuit (which may indicate that Strozzi's opinion was never submitted in litigation because, as we will see, it suited other purposes). We have to trust that a fair and accurate copy was made from the draft. We also face the insoluble problem that months passed between Ariosto's letter of July and Strozzi's response of October. Ariosto's letter may have been delayed arriving. It may have been that Strozzi was absent from Florence and otherwise occupied on business, as he was an exception to the rule that Florentine lawyers had only parochial reputations.[8] He was a busy man. Finally, Ariosto's letter says he was sending Strozzi a copy of a codicil (presumably from Rinaldo's father's testament) with the names changed. It does not survive in Strozzi's papers, although it does in the litigation records in Ferrara.

Why Lodovico Ariosto approached Antonio Strozzi seems an easy question to answer, but why he posed to him the questions he did is less simple. Still, it may make sense to handle both at once, for there is an interesting paradox here, if not more than one.

The realities of Ariosto's situation were that his cousin Rinaldo had died possessed of his paternal inheritance but also of an extensive fief called 'le Arioste' near Bagnolo held from the Este (originally granted to his father Francesco in 1478). There was also another nice estate, 'el Boatin,' rented from Cardinal Ippolito d'Este, and various other holdings. However, Rinaldo's estate was also charged with some considerable debts and obligations (not least from the excessive spending of Rinaldo's third wife), but especially for several dowries, prompting Ariosto's biographer,

---

[7]Cf. Wickham, Conclusion, 241.
[8]On him, see Martines, *Lawyers and Statecraft in Renaissance Florence*, 302 n. 143, 486–487.

Michele Catalano, to label the entire estate 'considerable, but also very disordered and burdened with liabilities.'[9] This estate passed to Lodovico and his brothers in intestacy, as Rinaldo had left no will and, more importantly, no legitimate son. His three daughters, all married and dowered, were excluded from the inheritance by Ferrarese law.[10] These girls were entitled only to their mothers' dowries. But that was another complication to the estate: Rinaldo had been married three times so his property was obligated for the restitution of three dowries, including that of the wife who survived him. Then there was the dowry obligation for Rinaldo's sister and for his mother, who was still alive.

Nonetheless, the main complication lay in the rights to the fief that Alfonso d'Este could pretend to and the rights to the tithes and back rent owed Cardinal Ippolito d'Este. Ariosto seems to have been well aware of all these potential problems, for he moved immediately the day Rinaldo died to accept the inheritance (the legal act of *aditio*, here with benefit of inventory, which left obligations, but only to the value [*vires*] of the estate),[11] and delegated his brother-in-law to take physical possession of 'le Arioste.'[12] However, the Cardinal's and the Duke's officials quickly seized both properties, 'le Arioste' and 'el Boatin.'[13] Ariosto was in a legal fight to keep them, especially the first, which had been in Ariosto hands almost all his life, as he outlined in a letter to Mario Equicola in October, about the time Strozzi was writing his opinion.[14] Yet the duke was merely reclaiming a lucrative fief to which he had legal claims and for which there was no shortage of hopeful aspirants.[15]

Very surprisingly, Ariosto posed none of this to Antonio Strozzi.[16] He did not ask him to grapple with the discrete law of fiefs (as yet not something much found around Florence) or tithes. What his letter communicated to Strozzi was that he (Lodovico) was intestate heir to 'Manfredo' and had made *aditio*, 'because this estate is very indebted,

---

[9]Catalano, *Vita di Ludovico Ariosto*, 1: 507.

[10]By statute in Ferrara, as in so many other Italian communities, male paternal first cousins excluded dowered daughters: Niccolai, *La formazione del diritto successorio negli statuti comunali del territorio lombardo-tosco*, 65–100. See Kuehn, *Law, Family, and Women*, chap. 10, and 'Person and Gender in the Laws,' 87–106.

[11]On *aditio* and *repudiatio* see Kuehn, 'Law, Death, and Heirs in the Renaissance.'

[12]Catalano, *Vita di Ariosto*, 1: 507.

[13]The second would be returned on rental to Ariosto by Ippolito's successor in 1520 (cf. ibid., 508). Also on these events, though with less detail and accuracy, see Gardner, *The King of Court Poets*, 144–145.

[14]Catalano, *Vita di Ariosto*, 1: 507–508; Ariosto, *Satire e lettere*, 99.

[15]Catalano, *Vita di Ariosto*, 1: 509.

[16]Which is not necessarily apparent in Catalano's treatment (*Vita di Ariosto*, 510).

especially for the dowries of three wives that he had, and of three daughters to whom he had promised two thousand ducats each, and also he has badly managed many possessions' ('perché tal heredità è molto debitrice maxime a doti de tre mogli che ha hauto, et de tre figliole alle quali ha promesso dua mila ducati per una, et ancho ha mal messe molte possessioni'). The first thing he wanted to know from Strozzi was whether he could improve the value of his assets by denying restitution of these dowries 'because the resources are not sufficient to pay them without selling the possessions' ('perché le facultà non bastano a pagarle senza vendere le possessioni').[17] Also, as 'Manfredo's' mother Agnese (in reality, Francesca Fontana, who would die in 1523) was still alive and, by virtue of her husband's codicil, *usufructuaria* on the estate, Ariosto wanted to clarify that he was also heir to her 'tanquam proximior agnatus.'

Why did Ariosto not reveal the problem of the fief to Strozzi? It is hard to say. He may well have known that the case would be hard to make, as the Este were effectively their own judge in such matters. Dealing with the Este was a delicate matter for anyone, leave alone a dependent poet. Certainly Ariosto's first step was to try persuasion through others, like the Florentine Medici pope Leo X.[18] Such indirection, however, did not work; the matter ultimately went to court. And the subsequent lawsuit was long and futile (as will be seen below). Ariosto's estimation of the lack of trustworthiness of Ferrarese attorneys and jurists (the ostensible reason for his writing Strozzi in the first place) thus may have been justified.[19] We know from other sources that Ariosto was involved in casting aspersions on the character and conduct of a Ferrarese judge who held a commission to oversee all criminal cases and that that judge was eventually removed from office.[20]

There was another bit of reality Ariosto was willing to disclose to Strozzi and about whose legal ramifications he sought help. Rinaldo had left an illegitimate son, named Ercole. In fact, as a young and dashing noble Rinaldo had enjoyed quite a parade of females, beyond his three wives, resulting (it seems) in a case of syphilis that may have caused the kidney failure that killed him.[21] Among his amorous exploits were those with a mistress (a relationship of some duration). Lodovico's letter to Strozzi revealed that this liaison had produced two illegitimates, one born when Rinaldo was still married and the other born after his wife's death.

---

[17] Masi, 'Le liti del Ariosto,' 86.
[18] Catalano, *Vita di Ariosto*, 1: 509–510.
[19] On justice in the Este state and the use of jurists by the dukes, see Chambers and Dean, *Clean Hands and Rough Justice*; Santini, *Lo stato estense tra riforme e rivoluzione*; Cavina, *Carlo Ruini*.
[20] Cf. Chambers and Dean, *Clean Hands and Rough Justice*, 223.
[21] Chambers and Dean, *Clean Hands and Rough Justice*, 504–506.

There was an irony here. Ariosto hoped for a legal opinion inserting himself (and his brothers) into the inheritance instead of these bastards. But Ariosto himself was father to two illegitimate children. More immediately, and the reason in part that he knew Antonio Strozzi so well, he was openly involved in 1519 with Alessandra Benucci, widow of Tito di Leonardo Strozzi, with whom he had carried on an affair even prior to her husband's death. Ariosto had met her and became infatuated with her when in Florence a few years earlier.[22] She inspired his poetry and ultimately even his vow of marriage (to give her legal advantage after his death). She was not, however, mother of either of his sons.

Still, she was Ariosto's link to the Strozzi, a distinguished Florentine lineage, some of whose branches had been dispersed by political exile to other Italian cities. The branch descended from Palla di Nofri Strozzi had established itself in Padua following Palla's ouster at the time of the triumphant return of the Medici in 1434.[23] Even earlier Nanni di Carlo Strozzi had settled in Ferrara, where he was in Este service by 1394; and Tommaso di Marco's sons moved from exile in Ferrara to Mantua by 1385. These Ferrarese and Mantuan branches of the Strozzi kept alive memories of Florence (even if, in the poetry of Tito di Vespasiano, they seem more sentimental than real). Letters, often requesting favors, moved among the Strozzi households in the various cities. Kin in distant cities and their friends, patrons, and benefactors could all be called upon.[24] Thus a renowned court poet like Ariosto, romantically involved with a Strozzi widow, could approach Antonio di Vanni Strozzi for legal advice.

Although Ariosto rather notoriously had deserted the study of law and loathed institutions like marriage,[25] he gave Strozzi a carefully contrived legal description of the situation of Rinaldo's bastards. There were important distinctions in law among different types of illegitimates, categorized by the circumstances of their parents at the point of conception (the sexual act). Some might be conceived in incest, in adultery, or by parents bound by religious vows. Some might be conceived in casual encounters or brief relationships, free or coerced. But the main distinction was that all of these and others who could be grouped under the term *spurii* (and to whom the term *bastardus* also indiscriminately applied) were different from the *filius naturalis*, whose parents were both mar-

---

[22]On Ariosto's relationship with Benucci, see Catalano, *Vita di Ariosto*, 1: 401–415, and Gardner, *King of Court Poets*, 111–117.
[23]Cf. Lillie, 'Memory of Place,' 195–214.
[24]Cf. Kent, '"Più superba di quella de Lorenzo"'; Fabbri, 'The Memory of Exiled Families'; Fabbri, 'Da Firenze a Ferrara: Gli Strozzi tra Casa d'Este e antichi legami di sangue,' 91–108.
[25]On this theme, Ross, *The Custom of the Castle*, 60–63.

riageable (to each other), if not in fact married.[27] A *naturalis* enjoyed a higher status in law than any type of *spurius*. Ariosto knew enough to describe one of Rinaldo's sons as clearly adulterine, so *spurius* and thus disqualified from inheritance. But if the other were *naturalis*, even if not legitimated, he might claim inheritance in the absence of legitimate sons and thus exclude uncle Lodovico and his brothers or at least share with them.[28]

So on this score Ariosto fabricated a distinction for Strozzi that also interestingly mirrored Ariosto's own behavior with regard to his two illegitimate sons. By examining it we can learn something about how *cinquecento* elites saw illegitimates and how bastards learned how to be bastards. We can see how the story told in society (if not in literature) became a story in law.

Ariosto's story was that these boys were not treated as and did not act like sons. His tale deserves (translated) retelling:

> But he ['Manfredo'] never showed that he held these boys as his sons; rather, whenever people reprimanded him for letting them go about in rags and not sending them to school, nor giving them any sign of love nor of holding them as sons, he would respond that he did not think they were his sons, because their mother was a silly schemer [*gaglioffa*] and had dealings with all the servants he had in his house. It is true that the first was kept in his house as a servant boy [*ragazzo*], and he used to lead his mule and did the usual household services like the other servants, and sometime ago he ran away and settled with someone near here and now that 'Manfredo' is dead he has been placed in service with others. Not a single witness can be found who can say 'Manfredo' called him son nor that he called 'Manfredo' father. All that can be found in his favor is that 'Manfredo' sometimes said, 'if he makes himself a good man [*huomo da bene*] I will make him a house steward [*fattore di casa*],' and this suffices as to the first of the two children. The other, being raised by a wet-nurse when very little, 'Manfredo' had him in the house only a short time and gave him to a servant who had a wife who took him home and when he was about seven years old he placed him as a friar in San Francesco dei Conventuali, where he is found at present; but he had not yet made his profession because he is not yet ten years of age. And of this one again 'Manfredo' always took little account and has always said he is not his son, as also about the other.[29]

---

[27] On these distinctions, see above all Kuehn, *Illegitimacy in Renaissance Florence*, 36–37, 40–46 and the references therein; also *Law, Family, and Women*, chap. 7; 'A Late Medieval Conflict of Laws,' 243–273.

[28] In Ferrara, even legitimated sons were disqualified by legitimate, unless the legitimation (as Virginio's by Lodovico Ariosto) carried express paternal consent (Kuehn, 'A Late Medieval Conflict of Laws,' 257).

[29] Masi, 'Le liti del Ariosto,' 86–87.

The images here are striking—children going about in rags, unschooled, acting like servants (including walking before the mule, an animal which, by virtue of being an infertile hybrid itself, was a common symbol and synonym for bastards), callously raised elsewhere.[30] There is also the unflattering image of the readily and perhaps communally available mother (presumably mother to both children, although connection to the second is not explicit). Finally, there is the lack of verbal signification—not called sons, not calling 'Manfredo' father. Taken all together, these statements denied that there was any attitude, treatment, behavior, or symbolic identity that could serve to designate either of these boys as 'natural,' leave alone legitimate.

Ariosto's treatment of his own sons—prior to 1519—bore a striking consistency to the presumptions he laid out, although in his case he treated his sons very differently from each other. His sons could both be loosely termed *naturalis*, as their father was not married, nor were their mothers. Ariosto's oldest, Giambattista, was born in 1503; his mother (Maria) was a domestic servant. This son was little loved, although paternity was acknowledged. He was not legitimated. He was ignored in Lodovico's first testament of 1522. Only in a second will of 1533 was Giambattista left some right to support and a monthly allowance, even substituted for his brother as heir if he died childless. His legitimation would come only after his father's death, in 1539, when two uncles were at odds with the other son and boosted Giambattista's claims.[31]

Contrast his treatment to that of the second son, Virginio (born 1509), whose mother, Orsolina Catinelli, from a modest Modenese artisan family, was Ariosto's mistress for several years (1508–1513). Ariosto married her off soon after he began his involvement with Alessandra Benucci, giving her a dowry of 600 *lire* and a peasant husband who had obligations to him.[32] Lodovico's paternal recognition and treatment of Virginio was evident early on. On 23 January 1520 he legitimated Virginio (then only ten years old) with a complete but also formulaic assertion of the lad's virtuous behavior, in contrast to the paternal weakness that had led to his procreation.[33] Two years later Lodovico drew up a testament naming the

---

[30]On the connection between mules and bastards, see Kuehn, *Illegitimacy*, 140.
[31]Catalano, *Vita di Ariosto*, 1: 175–176, 2: 349. Gardner, *King of Court Poets*, 46, describes Giambattista as from a 'discreditable intrigue with a woman named Maria—practically one of his own servants.' Catalano surmises from the treatment that Lodovico may have doubted his paternity.
[32]Catalano, *Vita di Ariosto*, 1: 390–392.
[33]Catalano, *Vita di Ariosto*, 2: 213–214: 'Nos, considerantes, ut fide digno testimonio percepimus, dictum Virginium, quantum per aetatem licuit talia de se praestitisse et praestare majora in dies bonae indolis et virtutum signa, ut spes sit, virum evadere virtuosum et paternae incontinentiae non fieri imitatorem.' On

legitimated Virginio his heir (and permitting him to have his legitimation confirmed or repeated, thus clarifying paternal consent in that regard), substituting him for his four uncles, Lodovico's brothers (Gabriele, Carlo, Galasso, and Alessandro). There was no mention of Giambattista.[34] The cycle was later repeated with a legitimation of Virginio (then age 21) on 4 April 1530—this time with the assertion that Lodovico had no other children, 'nec legitimos, nec naturales'—and a lengthier testament in 1533.[35] It is apparent that Lodovico had much more paternal affection for Virginio, whose mother was of higher social status than Giambattista's, and who went on to become a cathedral canon in Ferrara and father his own illegitimate son.[36] That this meant that Lodovico showered him with the sorts of treatment that, he claimed, Rinaldo withheld from his sons, would seem evident. We are reminded how, at least with bastard children, paternity, in expression and behavior, was optional.

It was also variable. Lodovico had admitted in his letter to Strozzi that 'Manfredo' posed that he would treat his one son better if the son's character emerged as worthy. It was the worthiness of Virginio's character that was asserted in the 1520 legitimation, coming just a few months after Strozzi's response to his letter. His treatment of both his sons was evidently changed by the time of his 1533 testament, which also made provisions for Alessandra Benucci (not surprisingly) and for Virginio's mother (leaving her widowhood rights of lodging and support with her son). Then he recognized Giambattista and left him an annuity (and he was 30 years old by then).[37] Still, in contrast, he left to Virginio 200 scudi and all copies of *Orlando Furioso*, in addition to the bulk of his property. In this testament he allowed that, if Virginio died without legitimate issue, male or female, then he could be succeeded by bastards, natural or spurious, as long as Virginio legitimated them. Failing any issue from Virginio, Lodovico then permitted inheritance by Giambattista (with license to have himself legitimated and with similar allowance for legitimated bastards should he die without legitimate children).[38] In fact these sons were Lodovico's heirs and would be found in 1542 agreeing

---

legitimation, see my *Illegitimacy*, chap. 6, and *Law, Family, and Women*, chap. 7.

[34]Catalano, *Vita di Ariosto*, 2: 240–241.

[35]Catalano, *Vita di Ariosto*, 2: 307, 328–336.

[36]Gardner, *King of Court Poets*, 245.

[37]Two scudi a month if he lived with Virginio; four scudi if he chose to live elsewhere, which it seems he did.

[38]Catalano, *Vita di Ariosto*, 2: 333–335. Legitimation thus worked in this social situation, if not so in law, in a manner analogous to bridewealth in African societies that also treat marriage as a process rather than as an event or contract: cf. Jeater, '"Their Idea of Justice Is So Peculiar,"' 178–195; and Comaroff and Roberts, *Rules and Processes*.

to a division of assets of a paternal estate described as 'weak and burdened with many debts ('debilem et multis debitis gravatam').[39] This final testament revealed Lodovico's willingness to be succeeded by legitimated bastards and to see them, in turn, also succeeded by *legitimati*.

Ariosto was hardly unusual for a man of his class (or even of his lineage) in fathering bastards nor in his treatment of them, which varied in proportion to the emotional and domestic commitment he seems to have had with their mothers. He was not necessarily a 'bad' father in sixteenth-century terms. The inheritance case even seems to have contributed to some intensifying of his paternal concerns and energies after 1519. What, if anything, may the inheritance of Rinaldo and Antonio Strozzi's legal opinion have contributed to Lodovico's later appreciation of his sons? How much of his treatment, especially of Virginio, may simply have been an expression of noble disdain for pedestrian sexual morality?[40] Was this part of the attitude that allowed Ariosto comfortably to populate the pages of his masterpiece with a variety of bastards? Or that allowed the Este to make bastards heirs to the family's titles, fortune, and power?[41] These questions direct us to what Gino Masi largely ignored, Strozzi's text.

Ariosto's letter asked Strozzi first to look at the problem of multiple dowry restitutions incumbent on the estate and secondly at the possible inheritance by bastard sons. Strozzi went at the questions in reverse order, noting first that the codicil of 'Manfredo's' father's will allowed inheritance by *naturales* if there were no legitimate heirs. The legal issue was whether these sons were *naturales*. From the texts he cited Strozzi quickly demonstrated that *naturales* resulted from relations with a concubine kept in one's home 'indubitato affectu.' He admitted that there was a broad construction of *naturales* ('propter generalem consuetudinem loquendi') that considered children *naturales* even where the parents did not cohabit, as long as they were not married or prohibited from marrying each other and maintained their sexual relationship over some length of time. The difference between *naturales* and *spurii*, he simply put, is that the former had rights to support and even to intestate inheritance.[42]

As a good jurist Strozzi had to approach the issue through the authoritative texts of learned law. To this point Strozzi had let his eye roam over the *Corpus iuris civilis*, canon law, glosses, the doctrinal texts of Bartolo da Sassoferrato (1314–1357), Giovanni d'Andrea (d. 1348), and Baldo degli Ubaldi (1323–1400). The pivotal text in this portion of his opinion, however, was located in Alberico da Rosciate's (d. 1360)

---

[39]Catalano, *Vita di Ariosto*, 350–351.
[40]Cf. Martines, *Power and Imagination*, 233–234, 239–240.
[41]Bestor, 'Bastardy and Legitimacy,' 557.
[42]Masi, 'Le liti del Ariosto,' 88.

commentary on the *Codex*, in which he had considered the rights of *naturales* to inherit.

> And Alberico says in the rubric of the *Codex* On natural children, that otherwise there was a question of fact, that a noble had a son by one of his ignoble familiars and he treated her like a servant in food, drink, clothing and other respects, and it was determined that he could not leave anything to such a son as a *naturalis* according to said Authentica *Licet*, because it is necessary that the mother share the attributes of a concubine.[43]

Being treated like a servant in this case disqualified the woman from the category of concubine. From the treatment of the mother in Alberico's example, Strozzi slid easily to the sons in Ariosto's. He briefly dismissed the one son as obviously adulterine and thus *spurius*; 'as for the other son who was born at the time the marriage had ended, there remains a difficulty, yet in this instance too it is to be said that he cannot be called *filius naturalis* in view of what is presupposed in the facts, because he did not keep her as a concubine but as a servant.'[44] There was cohabitation with a servant, but there was no sign of the 'marital affection' that marked a woman as *concubina* and her child as *naturalis*.

In legal terms it was the relationship between the parents, not the treatment of the sons, that made them *naturales*. In a case only a few years earlier (1515) Strozzi had claimed that benevolent paternal treatment and calling a boy 'son' led only to a 'quasi possessio filiationis.' In another case he found that treating a bastard in the same manner as one's legitimate children (including schooling and apprenticeship) constituted *benemerita* to a legitimated child, because such treatment stood in contrast to treatment as a servant or slave usually accorded a bastard. But in both instances, in opposition to Ariosto's presumptions, Strozzi shied away from any attribution of status (as *spurius*, *naturalis*, or *legitimus*) on the basis of such treatment.[45] Nothing in Ariosto's description of paternal deportment spoke to conditions of conception directly. *Naturales* could be treated shabbily; *spurii* could be treated in princely fashion. But Strozzi's distinctions did speak to Ariosto's own circumstances (reflected in the differential treatment of his two sons), for one son was born of a concubine and the other of a servant.[46] But by that enlarged sense of *naturalis* as conceived of marriageable parents (even in the absence of cohabitation and other evidence of concubinary affection) even the servant's son might qualify. Perhaps then Lodovico's legitimation of Virginio within a matter of months was intended

---

[43] Masi, 'Le liti del Ariosto,' 88.
[44] Masi, 'Le liti del Ariosto,' 89.
[45] ASF, Carte Strozziane, 3rd ser., 41/9, fols. 306r–307v, and 41/3, fols. 410r–418r.
[46] The one significance of Strozzi's opinion in Masi's eyes is its drawing attention to the nature of concubinage ('Le liti del Ariosto,' 84–85).

to insert an undoubted legal space between him and his half-brother. Perhaps Ariosto learned something of the law from Strozzi and used it. At any rate, soon thereafter and in contrast to Rinaldo, he chose to avoid the pitfalls of intestacy and wrote up a will.

The second half of Strozzi's opinion concerned the codicil's substitution of 'Manfredo's' mother if these were *naturales* who died without children. In fact, of course, 'Manfredo's' father had had an heir, namely 'Manfredo,' so there was no substitution to the mother, as set forth in the codicil, according to Strozzi. The codicil's substitution to other agnates remained in effect, for, if the testator had wanted them to inherit along with *naturales*, then he certainly wanted them to inherit when there were no *naturales*. Here *consilia* of Strozzi's teachers, Alessandro Tartagni da Imola (1424–1477) and Pierfilippo da Corgna (1420–1492) were cited in support. In effect, Strozzi thus opened up a basis on which Lodovico and his brothers could share in the inheritance if they did not succeed in excluding both the illegitimate sons. Ever the lawyer, Strozzi then went on to other issues in the case—not raised and probably unwanted by Ariosto. But, as the father's wife was still alive, Strozzi was compelled to point out that the agnates could not proceed to take title to the inheritance (though Ariosto had done that immediately). She was heir as long as she lived.[47] Further, though the law on the matter was difficult, Strozzi declared that in this case the agnates were not direct heirs but only heirs *per fideicommissum*. That meant that the wife could subtract the Trebellianic quarter from the estate in the form of *fructus*; but in this case 'Manfredo' was bound by the *fideicommissum* and enjoyed the right to the Trebellianic quarter.[48]

In communicating with a client by letter and over some distance, Strozzi did not have or try to make opportunity to check the facts given him or elicit more information. We know only that he received Ariosto's letter and wrote a brief legal response. It was not a brilliant piece of work, but it was up to professional standards of a man with a flourishing legal practice. In the end he furnished his client with some compelling arguments against the claims of the illegitimate nephew, but he also demonstrated a weakness in the client's case in the rights of the mother. This lawyerly complication about *aditio* and maternal succession may have kept Ariosto from employing Strozzi's text in the ensuing litigation. He had a solid argument against the bastards, and so far as the records reveal, they had little role in the case. But he did not need the complication of possible maternal inheritance rights, even if the mother seems never to have pressed them and was, in any case, dead within a couple of years. On the other hand, Strozzi also totally ignored the request for an argument to dispense with the dowry obligations. Ariosto faced considerable troubles about those dowries

---

[47] Masi, 'Le liti del Ariosto,' 89–90.
[48] On the Trebellianic quarter, see Kaser, *Roman Private Law*, 326–327.

almost immediately and for more than a decade thereafter.[49] His biographer could not restrain himself from remarking on the *povero* 'educated to hate the laws, constrained by numerous lawsuits to stand always with the code at hand and to deal with lawyers, notaries, judges, attorneys, and other people who live off the hide of the disgraced litigants,' but fighting back with satire and humor.[50] The dowry obligations were legally solid if financially unpleasant. They were not subject to litigation. They were arbitrated to determine (or speed up) the timing and amounts in settlement.

Ariosto's immersion in the people and devices of law was largely his own doing. He and his brothers initiated and pursued for years, in several stages, their quest to retrieve 'le Arioste' from the hands of the Este. They had the gall to fight the palace—or to trust the law and their sense of right. At one point, in 1531 the Ducal Camera opposed Ariosto's claims with the argument that Rinaldo's natural son was the heir.[51] Proceedings were forced to deal with the status of the (then deceased) son and the concubine mother.[52] The bastard Ercole never himself advanced a claim to the paternal estate or 'le Arioste.' As the Duke's officials had taken possession of the estate, simple delay through procedural gimmicks and obfuscation suited them. Even after Lodovico's death his three surviving brothers and his son Virginio were still involved in the effort to reclaim 'le Arioste.'

On matters of dowry and inheritance above all, no matter what Ariosto thought about the law, he could not dispense with it. Here were areas for constant conflict of ambiguous and overlapping rules and competing interests. There was plenty for judges, lawyers, and notaries to do.[53] There was little outlet for the sorts of courtly, chivalric, and romantic acts that filled his literary fantasies. There were texts and there were facts, and a learned jurist like Strozzi had to interpret the relation between the two.[54] Ariosto did not present him with a terribly complex case (in comparison to so many others), and Strozzi was not obliged to exhaust the pros and cons of the issues before him.[55] He could handle them simply and

---

[49]Catalano, *Vita di Ariosto*, 1: 516–520.

[50]Catalano, *Vita di Ariosto*, 520.

[51]For these events, Catalano, *Vita di Ariosto*, 510–515.

[52]Catalano, *Vita di Ariosto*, 512–513.

[53]In addition to works of Baumgärtner cited above, see Kuehn, '*Consilia* as Juristic Literature in Private Law'; Romano, 'Letteratura consiliare e formazione dei diritti privati europei,' and his 'Diritto di famiglia e letteratura consiliare.'

[54]Cf. Grossi, *L'ordine giuridico medievale*, 227.

[55]He also was not paid; and, although his was not a formal *consilium*, it seems to give the lie to assertions that these texts always came with a high price tag and were a sign of power and prestige attached to the law. See Bellomo, *The Common Legal Past of Europe, 1000–1800*, 213–214, but in contrast, see Cavallar, 'Lo "stare fermo a bottega" del Guicciardini,' 113–144, and his *Francesco Guicciardini giurista: I 'Ricordi degli onorari'*.

straightforwardly. But he told a different story than Ariosto did, in his letter or his poetry. We have seen his letter. Let us consider his *Orlando*. Aldiger of Clairmont appears in Canto 25 described as bastard son of Buovo. There it is said 'the claim that he was legitimate son to Gerard is foolhardy and unfounded.'[56] He is also described as robust, prudent, generous, chivalrous, kind, including to his two legitimate brothers whom he helps rescue. Lucretia Bentivoglio was not labeled a bastard, though she was. Instead her excellence is praised and it is noted 'that the Duke of Ferrara was pleased and happy to be her father.'[57] Two bastard sons of Calabrun, King of Aragon, are despatched in combat with Zerbin.[58] Another pagan bastard of Marsilius is soon captured in the same battle.[59] Pagan bastards do not seem to have as much going for them as noble Christian ones do. But for all of them, their treatment by others and their deeds lift them above their legal and moral birth status as bastards.

Such a literary tale could not carry the same weight in law, where the deeds and words that mattered to jurists and judges were different. Nor did Ariosto use his story to criticize or question prevailing social mores as some of his contemporaries (albeit in other literary contexts) did.[60] Strozzi's tale, resting on the mother rather than the child, gave more reality to the authority of the law while giving enough attention to fact and form (versus rules and substance) as to make it seem familiar and believable.[61] Those sons were bastards whose mothers did not leave them much option, no matter how their fathers treated them. Only in the context of a legitimation (as Virginio's) could a narrative on the order of Ariosto's about moral character have legal effect—something that was later to be richly exploited in Latin America.[62] The legitimation showed that the bastard had emerged as a good social being, not submerged in the guise of a servant or a forgotten monk. Then the bastard became a person with a social and legal identity.[63]

There is here, of course, a third story—the one I have been telling—and it is more than time to bring it to a close. We have seen a 'client' approach

---

[56] I have used the Waldman translation, *Orlando Furioso*, 304.
[57] *Orlando Furioso*, 507.
[58] *Orlando Furioso*, 173.
[59] *Orlando Furioso*, 139, 174.
[60] Cf. Grendler, *Critics of the Italian World*, esp. 30–31.
[61] On these aspects of legal and judicial storytelling, see the contributions by Paul Gewirtz, Robert A. Ferguson, and Reva B. Siegel in *Law's Stories: Narrative and Rhetoric in the Law*.
[62] Cf. Twinam, *Public Lives, Private Secrets*; and Bouysse-Cassagne, 'In Praise of Bastards.'
[63] Cf. Goodrich, *Oedipus Lex*, 130–143. Making the point that identity is defined in the law, but also individuated in processes over which law claims no control are Collier, Maurer, and Suárez-Navaz, 'Sanctioned Identities,' 1–27.

a lawyer,[64] and we have seen the advice given in response. There was not a tight fit between the two—neither in timing nor in content. But there was, arguably, some effect. And there certainly were ironies. The one issue that engaged both men—that Lodovico Ariosto raised and Antonio Strozzi handled—was the possibility of inheritance by the bastard. Ariosto described the treatment of the son; Strozzi looked at the treatment of the mother; and as the long litigation played out the matter arose only briefly, years later, and as a result of Ducal officials. The issue Ariosto raised and Strozzi ignored, the dowries, in fact became a continuing problem for Ariosto. Perhaps his notable reluctance to marry was due to a concern with dotal entanglements; it certainly was not due to a fear of sexual entanglements or fatherhood. An issue that Strozzi raised and Ariosto did not—the mother—emerged as a nonissue. Strozzi's lawyerly precaution never became a subject of actual litigation. Finally, the issue Ariosto did not bring up and Strozzi could not, therefore, have handled, the title to the fief, became the heart of a long and bitter lawsuit—one carried on even by Ariosto's illegitimate son. Maybe Strozzi could not have helped him there, but perhaps also Ariosto believed that the act of *aditio* and sending his brother-in-law to take possession had solved any problems at the time he wrote Strozzi. If so, he was wrong. He made a political and a legal miscalculation. Ariosto was emboldened to legitimate his younger son and he later (November 1520) initiated a lawsuit against the duke. He may have had little choice, having too much to lose if he and his brothers just let the lands at 'le Arioste' slip away.

The master narrative, as posed by Masi, would be that Ariosto is far and away the more famous, illustrious, and creative of the two men. Historical attention would always be directed first and foremost to his literary production and to the events of his life that might serve to illuminate it. But in the crucible of his exchange with Antonio Strozzi, my story, I cannot neglect the attorney's insightful analysis of the material handed to him. He gave his client legal ammunition to fight the bastard's claims while not conceding anything to the legally ludicrous desire to avoid the dowry obligations. Ariosto the great courtier poet gave his patrons and others fascinating stories; in this instance he gave an inadequate story to his Florentine lawyer. He was a much better poet, even a better lover and father, than he was a client.

Clemson University, Clemson, SC

---

[64]Using this term with all the caution urged by Kirshner, '*Consilia* as Authority,' 118–119.

Works Cited

Manuscript Sources

Florence, Archivio di Stato,
    Carte strozziane, 3rd ser., 41/6
    Carte strozziane, 3rd ser., 41/9

Published Sources

Ariosto, Ludovico. *Orlando Furioso*, trans. Guido Waldman. Oxford and London: Oxford University Press, 1974.

Ariosto, Ludovico. *Satire e lettere*, ed. Cesare Segre. Milan: Ricciardi, 1954; reprint ed., Turin: Einaudi, 1976.

Ascheri, Mario. 'Le fonti e la flessibilità del diritto comune: il paradosso del *consilium sapientis*' pp. 11–53 in *Legal Consulting in the Civil Law Tradition*, ed. Mario Ascheri, Ingrid Baumgärtner, Julius Kirshner. Berkeley: The Robbins Collection, 1999.

Ascheri, Mario. *Tribunali, giuristi e istituzioni dal medioevo all'età moderna*. Bologna: Il Mulino, 1989.

Baumgärtner, Ingrid, ed. *Consilia im späten Mittelalter: Zum historischen Aussagewert einer Quellengattung*. Sigmaringen: Thorbecke, 1995.

Baumgärtner, Ingrid. 'Stadtgeschichte und Consilia im italienischen Spätmittelalter: Eine Quellengattung und ihre Möglichkeiten.' *Zeitschrift für Historische Forschung* 9 (1990): 129–154.

Baumgärtner, Ingrid. 'Consilia—Quellen zur Familie in Krise und Kontinuität' pp. 43–66 in *Die Familie als sozialer und historischer Verband*, ed. Peter-Johannes Schuler. Sigmaringen: Thorbecke, 1987.

Bellomo, Manlio. *The Common Legal Past of Europe, 1000–1800*. trans. Lydia G. Cochrane. Washington, DC: Catholic University of America Press, 1995.

Bestor, Jane Fair. 'Bastardy and Legitimacy in the Formation of a Regional State in Italy: The Estense Succession.' *Comparative Studies in Society and History* 38 (1996): 549–585.

Bouysse-Cassagne, Thérèse. 'In Praise of Bastards: The Uncertainties of *Mestizo* Identity in the Sixteenth-and Seventeenth-Century Andes' pp. 98–121 in *Inside and Outside the Law: Anthropological Studies of Authority and Ambiguity*, ed. Olivia Harris. London and New York: Routledge, 1996.

Brooke, Peter and Paul Gewirtz, eds. *Law's Stories: Narrative and Rhetoric in the Law*. New Haven and London: Yale University Press, 1996.

Catalano, Michele. *Vita di Ludovico Ariosto*. 2 vols. Geneva: Olschki, 1930–1931.

Cavallar, Osvaldo. *Francesco Guicciardini giurista: I 'Ricordi degli onorari.'* Milan: Giuffrè, 1991.

Cavallar, Osvaldo. 'Lo "stare fermo a bottega" del Guicciardini: giuristi, consulenti, procuratori e notai nel Rinascimento' pp. 113–144 in Baumgärtner, Ingrid, ed. *Consilia im späten Mittelalter: Zum historischen Aussagewert einer Quellengattung*, ed. Ingrid Baumgärtner. Sigmaringen: Thorbecke, 1995.

Cavina, Marco. *Carlo Ruini: Una 'autorità' del diritto comune fra Reggio Emilia e Bologna, fra xv e xvi secolo.* Milan: Giuffrè, 1998.
Chambers, D. S. and Trevor Dean. *Clean Hands and Rough Justice: An Investigating Magistrate in Renaissance Italy.* Ann Arbor: University of Michigan Press, 1997.
Collier, Jane F., Bill Maurer, and Liliana Suárez-Navaz. 'Sanctioned Identities: Legal Constructions of Modern Personhood.' *Identities* 2 (1995): 1–27.
Comaroff, John L. and Simon Roberts. *Rules and Processes: The Cultural Logic of Dispute in an African Context.* Chicago: University of Chicago Press, 1981.
Fabbri, Lorenzo. 'Da Firenze a Ferrara: Gli Strozzi tra Casa d'Este e antichi legami di sangue' pp. 91–108 in *Alla Corte degli Estensi: Filosofia, arte e cultura a Ferrara nei secoli xv e xvi*x, ed. Michele Bertozzi. Ferrara: Università degli Studi, 1994.
Fabbri, Lorenzo. 'The Memory of Exiled Families: The Case of the Strozzi' pp. 253–261 in *Art, Memory, and Family in Renaissance Florence*, ed. Giovanni Ciappelli and Patricia Lee Rubin. Cambridge and London: Cambridge University Press, 2000.
Gardner, Edmund G. *The King of Court Poets: A Study of the Work, Life, and Times of Lodovico Ariosto.* New York: Archibald Constable, 1906; reprint ed., New York: Greenwood, 1968.
Goodrich, Peter. *Oedipus Lex: Psychoanalysis, History, Law.* Berkeley and Los Angeles: University of California Press, 1995.
Grendler, Paul. *Critics of the Italian World (1530–1560): Anton Francesco Doni, Nicolò Franco and Ortensio Lando.* Madison: University of Wisconsin Press, 1969.
Grossi, Paolo. *L'ordine giuridico medievale.* Bari: Laterza, 1995.
Jeater, Diana. '"Their Idea of Justice Is So Peculiar": Southern Rhodesia 1890–1910' pp. 178–195 in *The Moral World of the Law*, ed. Peter Coss. Cambridge: Cambridge University Press, 2000.
Kaser, Max. *Roman Private Law,* 2nd ed., trans. Rolf Dannenbring. Durban: Butterworths, 1968.
Kent, F. W. '"Più superba di quella de Lorenzo": Courtly and Family Interest in the Building of Filippo Strozzi's Palace' *Renaissance Quarterly* 30 (1977): 311–323.
Kirshner, Julius. 'Consilia as Authority in Late Medieval Italy: The Case of Florence' pp. 107–140 in *Legal Consulting in the Civil Law Tradition*, ed. Mario Ascheri, Ingrid Baumgärtner, Julius Kirshner. Berkeley: The Robbins Collection, 1999.
Kuehn, Thomas. '*Consilia* as Juristic Literature in Private Law' pp. 229–253 in *Legal Consulting in the Civil Law Tradition*, ed. Mario Ascheri, Ingrid Baumgärtner, Julius Kirshner. Berkeley: The Robbins Collection, 1999.
Kuehn, Thomas. *Illegitimacy in Renaissance Florence.* Ann Arbor: University of Michigan Press, 2002.
Kuehn, Thomas. 'A Late Medieval Conflict of Laws: Inheritance by Illegitimates in *Ius Commune* and *Ius Proprium*,' *Law and History Review* 15 (1997): 243–273.

Kuehn, Thomas. 'Person and Gender in the Laws' pp. 87–106 in *Gender and Society in Renaissance Italy*, ed. Judith A. Brown and Robert C. Davis. London and New York: Longman, 1998.

Kuehn, Thomas. 'Law, Death, and Heirs in the Renaissance: Repudiation of Inheritance in Florence.' *Renaissance Quarterly* 45 (1992): 484–516.

Kuehn, Thomas. *Law, Family, and Women: Toward a Legal Anthropology of Renaissance Italy*. Chicago: University of Chicago Press, 1991.

Lillie, Amanda. 'Memory of Place: *Luogo* and Lineage in the Fifteenth-Century Florentine Countryside' pp. 195–214 in *Art, Memory, and Family in Renaissance Florence*, ed. Giovanni Ciappelli and Patricia Lee Rubin. Cambridge and London: Cambridge University Press, 2000.

Lombardi, Luigi. *Saggio sul diritto giurisprudenziale*. Milan: Giuffrè, 1967.

Martines, Lauro. *Lawyers and Statecraft in Renaissance Florence*. Princeton: Princeton University Press, 1968.

Martines, Lauro. *Power and Imagination: City-States in Renaissance Italy*. New York: Knopf, 1979; reprint ed., Baltimore: Johns Hopkins University Press, 1988.

Masi, Gino. 'Le liti del Ariosto in una lettera del poeta e un parere di Antonio Strozzi' *Rivista storica degli archivi toscani* 1 (1929): 79–90.

Masi, Gino. 'Il sindacato delle magistrature comunali nel secolo xiv (con speciale riferimento a Firenze)' *Rivista italiana per le scienze giuridiche*, n.s. 5 (1930): 43–115, 331–411.

Masi. Gino. *Formularium florentinum artis notariae (1220–1242)*. Milan: Giuffrè, 1943.

Romano, Andrea. 'Diritto di famiglia e letteratura consiliare: note sul *Regnum Siciliae* fra medioevo ed età moderna' pp. 177–188 in *Consilia im späten Mittelalter: Zum historischen Aussagewert einer Quellengattung*, ed. Ingrid Baumgärtner. Sigmaringen: Thorbecke, 1995.

Romano, Andrea. 'Letteratura consiliare e formazione dei diritti privati europei: l'esperienza del diritto di famiglia siciliano tardomedievale' pp. 255–291 in *Legal Consulting in the Civil Law Tradition*, ed. Mario Ascheri, Ingrid Baumgärtner, Julius Kirshner. Berkeley: The Robbins Collection, 1999.

Ross, Charles. *The Custom of the Castle: From Malory to Macbeth*. Berkeley: University of California Press, 1997.

Santini, Giovanni. *Lo stato estense tra riforme e rivoluzione: Lezioni di storia del diritto italiano*. Milan: Giuffrè, 1987.

Twinam, Ann. *Public Lives, Private Secrets: Gender, Honor, Sexuality, and Illegitimacy in Colonial Spanish America*. Stanford: Stanford University Press, 1999.

Wickham, Chris. Conclusion, pp. 240–249 in *The Moral World of the Law*, ed. Peter Coss. Cambridge: Cambridge University Press, 2000.

Part IV

Religion and Society

Plate 6: 'Vende quadri,' p. 19 in Annibale Carracci.
Diverse Figure. Rome: Lodouico Grignani, 1646. (University
of Chicago. Library, Special Collections Research Center.)

How to Harass an Inquisitor-General: The Polyphonic Law of Friar Francisco Ortíz

Lu Ann Homza

On 6 April 1529, Francisco Ortíz, OFM, climbed into the pulpit of San Juan de los Reyes in Toledo and delivered so inflammatory a sermon that fellow Franciscans pulled him off the podium and Spanish inquisitors threw him into jail. Ortíz's inquisition trial lasted from 1529–1532. Its findings forced him to retract sixty-three statements that involved disobedience, aid to heretics, and heresy; its sentence ordered him suspended for five years from preaching and hearing confessions, and enclosed for two in a Franciscan monastery in Torrelaguna. Ortíz remained at Torrelaguna after completing his penance, and died around 1545. His inquisition trial was infamous in the sixteenth century and remains well-known in the twentieth: its outline is so dramatic that it has invited moral interpretations of its actors and processes.[1]

Before he gave that sermon, Ortíz was a success. At thirty-two, he had already studied at Spain's best universities and become a preacher for the Franciscan order; he was a favorite homilist in the most prestigious venues, and even had been solicited for a position at the royal court. On April 6, though, he decided to risk everything by denouncing the public sin of Inquisitor-General Alonso de Manrique, who was the archbishop of Sevilla as well as the head of the Spanish Inquisition. In Ortíz's opinion, Manrique's sin came down to one specific act: his authorization to arrest Francisca Hernández on March 31.[2]

---

[1] Ortíz's trial was conducted by the inquisition tribunal at Toledo. The 399-folio manuscript was removed from Spain, probably in the nineteenth century; and now resides in Special Collections [*Sondersammlungen*], Martin-Luther-Universität in Halle, Germany. *Proceso contra Fray Francisco Ortíz, de la orden del San Francisco.* Sign. Yc 2º 20 (2). References to the trial manuscript will be cited as *Proceso*.

[2] In her authoritative study, Angela Selke argued that Francisca Hernández's arrest was planned in December 1528 by the inquisitors at Toledo, in collaboration

Francisca Hernández was one of many *beatas* in sixteenth-century Spain: the term designated women who took certain monastic vows, such as poverty and chastity, but who lived in the world, outside a formal religious order.[3] In Francisca's case, she enjoyed a substantial reputation as a religious figure, particularly among friars: by all reports, she could explain the secret of the Trinity, interpret scripture without reading Latin, and cure physical complaints, including masturbation, with the help of belts and handkerchiefs.[4] These abilities, along with a remarkable physical beauty, made her very popular: in Salamanca, the master of the Franciscan novices 'sent as many novitiates to her as he could,' and it looks as if she held a teaching authority or *magisterium* over her followers.[5] Not surprisingly, her power made her highly suspect to some. When rumors arose in 1519 that she was carnally involved with her fundamentally male entourage, the Inquisition tribunal of Valladolid interviewed her, but released her without any finding of heresy. In the late 1520s, the Franciscan guardian at Valladolid tried to restrict his monks' contact with her, and complained about her to the Franciscan authorities.[6]

These events were widely known, but they had no discernible effect on Fray Francisco Ortíz, who continued to cherish Francisca Hernández. By 1529, their acquaintance was of some standing: Ortíz had sought the beata's acquaintance in 1523, in the hope that she could cure his sin of masturbation. Once Francisca had consented to see him in Valladolid, they had conversed for five hours, and at the end of that encounter, she had handed him the belt that had remedied his particular vice.[7] After that meeting, they saw each other very infrequently, for Ortíz was in increasing demand as a preacher: when he could travel to Valladolid, he had to negotiate with the monastery's guardian for permission to visit the woman who for all intents and purposes had become his spiritual director.

---

with the guardian of Toledo's Franciscan monastery: Selke, *El Santo Oficio*, 33–34. She did not cite any specific testimony, though, to substantiate this assertion.

[3]For recent studies of Spanish beatas, see Bilinkoff, 'A Spanish Prophetess;' Muñoz Fernández, *Beatas y santas neocastellanas*; and Ahlgren, 'Francisca de los Apostoles.'

[4]Because Francisca Hernández's trial records do not survive, specifics about her life and teachings come from her followers' prosecutions. See, for instance, Selke, 'El caso del Bachiller Antonio de Medrano;' Selke, *El Santo Oficio*, passim, and especially 46–54; and the appendices in Llorca, *La inquisición española*. Mary E. Giles offers an English-language overview in 'Francisca Hernández.'

[5]On Francisca's following, see Selke, *El Santo Oficio*, 46. For that entourage within the context of the alumbrado movement, Homza, *Religious Authority*, 6–10.

[6]Selke, *El Santo Oficio*, 62. The Valladolid guardian, Padre Guinea, reiterated a connection between Francisca and monastic insubordination when he testified against Ortíz in 1531: *Proceso*, f. 72v.

[7]Selke, *El Santo Oficio*, 55–57.

Consequently, for the period 1523–1529, Ortíz and Francisca mainly communicated by letter: he presented her with spiritual petitions and begged for her intercession, while she used amanuenses to communicate with him and the rest of her widely-dispersed disciples, having never learned to write herself. Yet Francisca and Ortíz did manage to have a month-long visit in 1528, and that very encounter might have hardened his superiors' resolve to end his relationship with the beata. We know that the Valladolid guardian tried to prevent Ortíz from seeing Francisca when he came to that city. We also know that the same guardian complained to the vice-general of the order about the pair's intimacy. The vice-general subsequently wrote to Ortíz and ordered him to cease all contact with Francisca. Ortíz responded by threatening to become a Carthusian.[8]

No one would deny that Ortíz demonstrated his fidelity to Francisca in a particularly energetic way on April 6, 1529. On that day, his audience included prelates, monks from a variety of religious orders, and nobles from the royal court and the city itself. His homily was supposed to revolve around prayers for rain, since Toledo had been suffering from a protracted drought; as it had rained the day before, the service should have turned into one of thanksgiving. From an observer's point of view, there were other reasons for tranquility as well: Ortíz had lived in the monastery of San Juan de los Reyes for years, and preaching there should not have been unsettling; besides, he probably knew every spectator in the chapel.

But as Ortíz ascended the pulpit, his excitement was obvious to all, and the spectators' trepidation increased when he announced, '[I] am going to preach as if this were my last sermon, and as if [I] were to die after it.' Ortíz went on to connect natural disasters in the Old Testament, such as plague, to human sins. After reviewing possible reasons for temporal drought, he moved to the topic of 'spiritual' rain, and addressed possible obstructions of 'the spiritual rain of doctrine.' Ortíz told the crowd that God Himself might withhold Christian teaching as a test for the faithful, yet Christian precepts could also be undermined through the 'sins of the unjust who grind down the servants of God.' And then he revealed his surprise: God had commanded him to speak a particular truth, and so he would behave like the prophet Jeremias, whose temples were pierced with a stick because he did as God demanded. Like Jeremias, Ortíz was obliged to identify iniquity: he consequently had to report that the Inquisition, and especially its Inquisitor-General, Alonso de Manrique, had committed a notorious sin by arresting and imprisoning Francisca Hernández one week earlier.[9]

---

[8]Selke, *El Santo Oficio*, 62.
[9]*Proceso*, ff. 13r–19v, contains witnesses' statements about the sermon. See in particular ff. 15v–16r, and 19r–v.

Ortíz's audience was stunned; the shocks continued. He noted that the Gospel mandated the public disclosure of a public sin if two private admonitions failed to correct the offense. Ortíz then told the crowd that he and Manrique had twice spoken privately about Francisca's possible arrest. In their first conversation, the Inquisitor-General seemed sympathetic to Francisca's gifts and Ortíz's devotion, but by the second, he was determined to prosecute the beata. Finally, Ortíz told the crowd that the guardian of San Juan de los Reyes had poisoned the Inquisitor-General's mind and erased Ortíz's own influence.

At this point, Ortíz was yanked from the pulpit. He was subsequently deposited in a private house, where he became nearly catatonic and remained under a mendicant guard. That same night, Fray Barnabás – the guardian of San Juan de los Reyes, whom Ortíz had insulted – marched him to the inquisition tribunal of Toledo, where he became an inmate of the secret prison.

After Ortíz's arrest, the Inquisition went to work. Directed by inquisitors Alonso de Mexia, Juan Yáñes, and Juan de Vaguer, the tribunal's prosecutor or *fiscal*, Diego Ortíz de Angulo, deposed eyewitnesses to the incendiary sermon. He surveyed *alumbrado* trials from the mid-1520s in a quest to tie Ortíz to convicted heretics. And when he formally accused Ortíz on December 1, 1529, he introduced the charges by noting that the defendant was being indicted

> as a heretic and apostate against our holy Catholic faith, and as an abettor and defender of heretics, and as an impious defamer and injurer of the Holy Office of the Inquisition and of its ministers and officials. Being in name and position a Christian, and an esteemed person whose words the *pueblo* respects; not considering his habit and religious order and the prohibition of his prelates, and the place where he was, in offense of God and His Holy Church, and in deprecation of the Holy Office of the Inquisition, with great scandal and disturbance to the pueblo and the clergy of that city [of Toledo], Ortíz said many injurious words against the Holy Office and its ministers, and afterwards...defended his words with great obstinacy.[10]

---

[10] '... por herege apostata de nuestra santa fe catolica, y por fautor y defensor de hereges, y inpiador y infamador y injuriador del santo oficio de la inquisicion, y de sus ministros y oficiales; porque estando en nombre y posicion de cristiano, y en estima de persona a cuyas palabras el pueblo dava mucho credito, no aviendo consideracion a su abito y religion, y prohibicion de sus perlados, y lugar donde estava; en ofensa de dios nuestro señor, y de su sancta iglesia; y en menosprecio del santo oficio de la inquisicion, con gran escandalo y alteracion del pueblo y clero de la dicha ciudad, dixo muchas palabras injuriosas contra el santo oficio y sus ministros y despues ... defendiendo lo susodicho con mucha contumacia.' *Proceso*, f. 145r.

From the start, the prosecution stressed Ortíz's challenge to the Inquisition's authority, and that emphasis recurred throughout the accusation: fifty-two of the fifty-six charges highlighted his defiance in giving the sermon, defending the sermon, and believing in Francisca Hernández. Only the last four allegations had anything to do with the heresy of *alumbradismo*; there is no doubt that Ortíz's insolence drove the trial.[11]

Even after his arrest, Ortíz was not inclined to hold his tongue. He replied to the fiscal's accusation with a fifteen-folio, holograph statement. The fiscal responded with a nine-folio answer. Ortíz then handed the Toledo tribunal a disquisition of twenty-seven folios, which the fiscal answered in ten.[12] These fulsome interchanges took place from December 1529 to March 1530. Matters became rather more complicated in May 1531, when the inquisitors learned that certain prisoners had planned to kill the warden of the Inquisition's secret prison and escape, once they had burned every piece of paper they could find. Ortíz knew about this plot, and though he never intended to participate in it — and told the conspirators they were deranged for attempting it — the fiscal argued that he had committed a heresy by *not* telling the inquisitors what he knew.[13] Ortíz de Angulo added to the charges accordingly.

In July 1531, the inquisitors informed Ortíz that he would have to retract entirely sixty-three propositions that had been judged heretical. Ortíz then waffled for a solid month as to whether he would recant, and after August the case went nowhere. In December 1531, the General Council of the Inquisition, called the *Suprema*, demanded to know what was happening with the prosecution. In February 1532, Ortíz formally admitted that he had erred; on April 18, he recognized out loud, in front of the inquisitors, that he was mistaken about Francisca Hernández's gifts. He was sentenced on April 21 of that year in a private auto-de-fe.[14]

---

[11] For the fiscal's formal accusation, *Proceso*, ff. 145r–149v. The alumbrado-tinged charges involved the omission of oral prayer, the teaching of mental prayer, the rejection of external works, and the comment that 'Jesus was more perfectly in the soul of the just, than in the sacrament of the altar.' Significantly, the same fiscal pursued an identical, two-tier strategy in the prosecution of Juan de Vergara. For a short summary of the alumbrado heresy in Spain in the 1520s, and the difficulties historians face in studying it, see Homza, *Religious Authority*, 6–8.

[12] Ortíz's reply to the accusation, presented December 14, 1529, runs from ff. 151r–166r in the *Proceso*. The fiscal's response can be found on ff. 167r–176v. Ortíz's next salvo, which he wrote in February 1530, covers ff. 177r–204r; and the prosecutor's final exposition, dated March 1530, lies in ff. 257r–267r.

[13] For documentation on the prison scandal, *Proceso*, ff. 326r–340v.

[14] For the bickering over the retraction, July–August 1531, see *Proceso*, ff. 304r–325r. Ortíz's February recantation occurs on ff. 342v–343v; his April statement is on f. 346v.

The usual basics of inquisitorial law were in play during Ortíz's prosecution: the presumption of guilt, the excision of details from the evidence, and the possibility of recusing witnesses. His trial also had aspects in common with other high-profile trials from the same epoch, such as intervention by the Suprema as it attempted to monitor the case.[15] Finally, Ortíz's long-standing refusal to confess or recant was not unique: Juan de Vergara, and the noted beata María de Cazalla, did the same thing. But unlike other defendants — whether suspected judaizers, alumbrados, or even other subverters of inquisitorial authority — Ortíz's arrest was not caused by the depositions of neighbors, or the discovery of corruption among an inquisition staff. Instead, Ortíz literally dared the Toledo inquisitors to throw him into jail; he launched the sermon and hence the trial. From the start of his ordeal, he looks as much like a protagonist as a victim.

This impression of being an actor, rather than being acted upon, comes through repeatedly when we regard Ortíz-the-defendant, especially during the first months of the case. Between April 6–28, 1529, he wrote four holograph letters to Inquisitor-General Manrique from inside his jail cell, which charged Manrique with mortal sin for Francisca's arrest, and threatened him with Hell.[16] Ortíz directly and repeatedly claimed that even inquisitors were capable of error. And he insisted that his sermon deserved praise rather than censure, for God had commanded him to give it. The quantity of paper that Ortíz generated also creates the sense that he went on the offensive as soon as he was imprisoned. His letters to Manrique cover eighteen folios. A month later, in May 1529, he decided

---

[15] The relationship between the Suprema and the Inquisitor-General was never formally defined, even in the Inquisition's official *instrucciones*. Though the Suprema – constituting approximately six members in the early seventeenth century – and the Inquisitor-General most frequently peformed as a unit, the Suprema in particular could act independently. Such was potentially the case during the Ortíz prosecution, because Inquisitor-General Manrique was essentially banished to his estates in Sevilla in August 1529 for having offended the Empress Isabella. Accordingly, in July 1531, the Suprema notified the Toledo tribunal that disagreement among the inquisitors would result in the Ortíz case going to the Suprema itself for judgment. In December 1531, the Suprema wrote to Toledo to inquire about the progress and disposition of Ortíz's prosecution; and in March 1532, the Suprema pressured the Toledo tribunal again for a conclusion to the trial. The same kinds of communication occurred two years later, when the Suprema tried to intercede in the prosecution of Juan de Vergara. Taken together, such interventions may signal the Suprema's increasing interest in verdicts and penances, an interest that was eventually codified in the new instructions of Inquisitor-General Fernando de Valdés in 1561. For these details in the Ortíz case, see Selke, *El Santo Oficio*, 286, 294, 306.

[16] *Proceso*, ff. 34r–39v, 46r–49v, 64r–67v, 69r–72v.

to reproduce and amplify those letters' content: the result was a holograph text of forty-nine folios, which he called the *primer cuaderno*, or 'first notebook.' The amplitude of these texts makes it look as if Ortíz were trying to drown the tribunal in paper.[17]

The fact that Ortíz helped other prisoners with legal advice and refused to recant simply adds to his pro-active aura. Even the prosecution seems to have viewed him as a force, because one of the truly unusual aspects of the case is the fact that three different sets of 'prosecutors' – or individuals acting for the prosecution – tried to persuade him to retract. Luís Coronel, secretary to Inquisitor-General Manrique, came secretly to the tribunal to argue with Ortíz, probably in late April or early May of 1529. Next, a member of the Suprema, Fernando Niño, interrogated Ortíz on June 1, 2, 3, 5, and 7, 1529.[18] Neither Coronel nor Niño was attached to the Toledo tribunal; their actions were highly interventionistic. Meanwhile, Toledo's inquisitors and fiscal were soliciting genealogies and listening to depositions. No one would deny that Ortíz's ability to give the sermon, persist in a defense, and resist the prosecution illustrates a remarkable stamina under pressure.

It consequently is not surprising that the most authoritative scholarship on Ortíz's ordeal has fixed upon his sense of himself — and from there, his modernity — as the heart of the trial's meaning. When Angela Selke published her study of Ortíz in 1968, she was already well-known as a historian of the early Spanish alumbrados: her articles on Antonio de Medrano and Juan López de Celaín remain classics in the field.[19] She also was the first person since the nineteenth century to study the Ortíz *proceso* in its entirety, since the original trial documents lie in the Martin-Luther-Universität in Halle, Germany; with fragments in the Archivo Histórico Nacional in Madrid.

Selke's interpretation of Ortíz was clear. While she recognized that he had ties to the erasmian and alumbrado circles of 1520s Spain, she asserted that his real significance lay in his reliance on his own conscience.

> ... from the moment he entered the [inquisitorial] prison until his final surrender three years later, the rebellious attitude of the friar, the continual challenges he launched against the Inquisitor-General, the Inquisition, his prelates, and against all the 'unjust persecutors of the holy bride of God,'

---

[17] Ortíz's primer cuaderno runs from ff. 206r–255v. Between 1533–1534, Vergara would similarly attempt to suffuse the Toledo tribunal with his writings: Homza, *Religious Authority*, 30–31.

[18] *Proceso*, ff. 96r–122r.

[19] Selke, 'El caso del Bachiller Antonio de Medrano;' Selke, 'Vida y muerte de Juan López de Celain.' Selke's later important work was on the crypto-Jewish community of Majorca: *The Conversos of Majorca*.

Francisca Hernández; and, above all, his repeated assaults on the formalistic rigidity and traditions of the Church, give this trial a very distinct course and a much greater significance.... [this was] a battle between a tribunal and a defendant who...proclaims the absolute sovereignty of his conscience with the unbreakable conviction of one who speaks by divine command; and, completely inverting roles, treats his judges as if they were the accused.[20]

For Selke, Ortíz mattered because he was willing to act as an autonomous individual in the face of institutionalized repression: his challenges to the Inquisition were relentless; his independence spoke to a universal human value.[21] In contrast, the inquisitors who tried him were half-witted: in Selke's version of events, the officials of the Holy Office and Francisco Ortíz had nothing in common.[22]

Selke studied the Ortíz trial in the 1960s, and her conclusions were clearly indebted to that decade's politics. Given the relative inaccessibility of the manuscript — which was located in East Germany until reunification – and Selke's own professional reputation, her reading carried that much more weight. Still, because of the epoch in which she wrote, Selke could not take advantage of the post-1975 boom in Spanish inquisition studies, or our current awareness of how difficult past legal sources can be. As a result, her comments about the transparency of the documentation may strike current readers as naive.[23]

---

[20] '...la actitud rebelde del fraile, desde el momento de entrar a la carcel hasta su rendición final tres años después; los retos continuos que lanza contra el inquisidor general, el Santo Oficio, sus prelados y contra todos los "injustos perseguidores de la santa esposa de Dios," Francisca Hernández; y, sobre todo, sus reiterados asaltos contra la rigidez formalista y las tradiciones de la Iglesia, dan a este proceso un rumbo muy distinto y de mucha mayor envergadura... una batalla entre el tribunal y un reo, el cual...proclama, con la convicción inquebrantable del que habla por mandato divino, la soberanía absoluta de su conciencia; e, invirtiendo por completo los papeles, trata a sus jueces como si ellos fueron los acusados.' Selke, *El Santo Oficio*, 68. Selke was more open than her peers to a more fluid outlook on Spanish spirituality in the 1520s: she persuasively argued that Ortíz could not be classified as erasmian, Lutheran, or *alumbrado*, though he had strong connections to partisans of those three spiritual movements: Selke, *El Santo Oficio*, 24, 94–95. Selke used Bataillon's evidence to make the erasmian connection. For Bataillon's own interpretation of Ortíz, see *Erasmo y España*, first Spanish edition, 169, 187, 363.

[21] See, for instance, Selke, *El Santo Oficio*, 23, 177. Selke also contended that Ortíz's eventual retraction did not violate his sense of autonomy, because he framed his recantation as a denial of self, in honor of God: *El Santo Oficio*, 295–299

[22] Selke, *El Santo Oficio*, 200–201, 280–281.

[23] For example, Selke believed that Ortíz's trial 'scarcely need[ed] interpretation,' and that the inquisitorial notaries performed a 'merely mechanical' function. She also read emotion into the trial record, as when she described an inquisitor as

A more serious problem, though, lies in her argument that Ortíz possessed an utterly different intellect from his opponents. The friar's opinions, as well as his vocabulary, *were* remarkably consistent, and since one of his favorite nouns was *conciencia*, or 'conscience,' Selke did not come to her interpretation by accident. Nevertheless, the manuscript reveals that Ortíz did not inhabit a different mental or linguistic universe from the individuals who interrogated him, even though the trial's most obvious aspect was a heated contest between an inquisitor-general and a friar.

When I began to read the Ortíz trial, I thought his letters to Manrique would enhance my findings from the prosecution of Juan de Vergara (1533–1535). Vergara was a famous correspondent of Desiderius Erasmus's and a secretary to the archbishops of Toledo; he was as well-connected as he was learned. After the Inquisition arrested him, he turned his intellectual talents to writing folio after folio about right religious practice and the historical development of sacred languages, texts, and figures; he criticized the inquisitors themselves in a fulsome way. Notably, his arrest was also provoked by a challenge to the inquisitorial bureaucracy: he had suborned the Toledo inquisition staff between 1530–1533 with large, creative bribes, and it was the discovery of that graft that triggered his prosecution.

The similarities between Ortíz and Vergara seemed obvious. Their trials happened successively – 1529–1532, 1533–1535 – and engendered much public discussion.[24] Both men flourished within Spain's clerical hierarchy; both had noteworthy intellectual training, though Vergara's was more profound, and both had rebuked the Spanish Inquisition. Indeed, in the last respect Ortíz's temerity outstripped his peer's, since Vergara merely paid off notaries and a prison warden before his arrest, and publicly discussed his case afterwards by speaking to people in the street from the window of his jail cell.[25] The cases were positively analogous.

They finally proved to be complementary, but not in the way I expected. The first hint came from Ortíz's prose, which Selke herself described as baroque. Unlike Vergara, whose arguments were both straightforward and weighty, Ortíz wrote in a stream-of-consciousness style, in which three different subjects could be raised in three sequential

---

acting 'with visible irritation.' *El Santo Oficio*, pp. 23, 24, 131. Historians are now much more sensitive to the intermediary role of scribes, though not all agree about the appropriateness of ascribing feelings to actors in legal proceedings. For a recent study that attributes sensibilities to inquisitors and defendant alike, see Nalle, *Mad for God*.

[24] For a contemporary's vivid impression of the Ortíz case, see Bataillon, *Erasmo y España*, 434–435.

[25] Homza, *Religious Authority*, Chap. 1, evaluates Vergara's trial and describes his corruption of personnel at the Toledo tribunal.

lines, and tangents occurred everywhere, and lasted for folios. He tended to repeat the same sentiments over and over again, with more or less amplification, but absolutely no theory; in short, he preferred specificity to abstraction. For instance, he complained mightily about the guardian of San Juan de los Reyes and corruption within the Franciscan order but he would go no further than to lament that the guardian had 'poisoned' his reputation, and to decry the monks' fondness for wealth: in neither case did his disapproval move toward some larger 'end' about monasticism or money. Such examples could be multiplied: even when he attacked the Spanish Inquisition, it was on account of the Inquisitor-General, not the institution itself, a distinction that previous scholarship neglected to notice. Because Ortíz was so absorbed by details and reiterated the same ones so often, at first I was hard-pressed to do anything with his critiques except arrange them into lists of likes and dislikes: Francisca would be in the 'plus' column, the Inquisitor-General would not, and so forth. Thus in terms of intellectual criticism, it finally proved impossible to assess Ortíz vis-à-vis Juan de Vergara, because Vergara *did* extend his censure in a theoretical way.

Yet if the two prosecutions turned out to be incompatible in one respect, they agreed in another: surprisingly enough, their complementarity lay in matters of law. Vergara's responses to the Inquisition can be divided in two: either he argued on the basis of his intellect and status, or he appropriated the inquisitors' own legal formulas to attack their case. When he did the latter, he dismissed prosecution witnesses because they were unique, or licentious, or servants, or fundamental adversaries; he knew that such allusions to singularity, reputation, and capital enmity raised key concepts in inquisitorial law.[26] Throughout his trial, Vergara was capable of arguing like an inquisitor *with* inquisitors, and they took him seriously: some of his objections affected the verdict.

Significantly, although Ortíz has been presented as the antithesis of the inquisitors who tried him, as if he were offering a defense drawn solely from conscience and sacred commands, this impression is inaccurate. In fact, despite layers of divine revelation and scripture, and incessant allusions to God's mandates, Ortíz also adopted the Inquisition's vocabulary and concerns, and did so from the moment of his arrest. Like Vergara, he too demonstrates the way in which inquisitorial reasoning flowed beyond the inquisitors themselves. But unlike his counterpart, Ortíz simultaneously invoked inquisition edicts and divine mandates as he defended himself; he practiced a sort of 'polyphonic' law before the Inquisition.[27]

---

[26]Homza, *Religious Authority*, 34–36.

[27]Polyphony is a musical term for two or more independent melodic lines,

When it comes to the law that was argued before and by Spanish inquisitors, and on the ground rather than in theory, scholarship is practically bereft. Historians have studied inquisitorial practice through the tribunals, but their investigations have highlighted victimology, prosecution patterns, finance, and inquisitors as a professional class.[28] Others have attempted sociological typologies of inquisitors, or overviews of particularly important inquisitors-general, but their treatments have either involved too little evidence, or too much narrative and too little analysis.[29] In fact, there is no fully satisfactory study of a Spanish inquisitor and his career, and this scholarly gap may arise from our propensity to reify inquisitorial law, as if inquisitors-general's instructions traveled unscathed to inquisitors in the field, or inquisition procedure perfectly reflected inquisition manuals. Too often, studies of the Spanish Inquisition have been governed by 'an emphasis on normative structures and a disinterest in the law in practice.'[30]

Still, we know that inquisition tribunals were not ruled exclusively by theory, because inquisitors and their staff (and defendants and their entourages) toyed with the law all the time.[31] Inquisitors and jailors could manipulate processes out of lust, greed, or even concern for a defendant's sanity. Suspects could refuse to mount a defense, violate secrecy, or ignore orders; they also might challenge the collection of evidence and dispute the qualifications of their judges. When it comes to the legal maneuvers of defendants, scholars have not yet asked what such evidence implies for Spanish legal culture.[32] Yet Spanish inquisition trials often demonstrate the extent to which inquisitorial rules, procedures, and concepts reached a larger population. And sometimes, with the right defendant, a trial can reveal the law itself as a contested phenomenon. The Ortíz case offers both sorts of insights, because this friar spent much of the time talking to his interrogators in their own language, as well as

---

played or sung simultaneously.

[28] For instance, Contreras, *El Santo Oficio*; Dedieu, *L'Administration de la Foi*; Monter, *Frontiers of Heresy*; Haliczer, *Inquisition and Society*; Nalle, *God in La Mancha*; Prado Moura, *Inquisición y inquisidores*.

[29] Caro Baroja, *El señor inquisidor*, and González Novalin, *El Inquisidor-General Fernando de Valdés*.

[30] Kuehn, *Law, Family, and Women*, 8. Kuehn was describing the tendencies of Italian legal historians, but his remarks fit Spanish scholarship as well.

[31] Asensio, 'El Maestro Pedro de Orellana,' 793–794; Kagan, *Lucrecia's Dreams*, Chap. 6; Homza, *Religious Authority*, Chap. 1; Nalle, *Mad for God*, Introduction and Chap. 5.

[32] While historians have commented on the legal maneuvers of defendants, legal strategy has rarely been the point of their inquiry; for examples, see Kagan, *Lucrecia's Dreams*, and Nalle, *Mad for God*.

in a theological one. His case enhances our sense of the law in sixteenth-century Spain.

It has long been understood that inquisitors could elicit what they wanted to hear. When they asked defendants leading questions, they implicitly told them where they should go, linguistically and argumentatively; in the process, defendants could produce statements that fit the prosecution's preconceptions. Ortíz was cross-examined multiple times during his trial, whether in a narrow or broad sense of the term. Fernando Niño, member of the Suprema, questioned him for almost a week in June, 1529, and those sessions were transcribed by tribunal notaries. Six months later, the fiscal interrogated him through the formal accusation, which Ortíz was obliged to answer. Even Ortíz's earliest holograph writings – the four letters of April 1529, and the primer cuaderno of May of the same year – resulted from conversations with inquisitors. The April letters were as much Ortíz's thoughts on his direct interchanges with Manrique, as an explanation of his sermon. The cuaderno was composed after Ortíz had given his genealogy to inquisitors and, more importantly, spoken at length with secretary Luís Coronel: in it, Ortíz was speaking to Coronel, Manrique, the Toledo tribunal, and the Suprema, all at the same time.[33] Accordingly, we might infer that Ortíz expressed inquisitorial concepts only because he had been interviewed by legal experts, and decided to imitate their discourse. But that kind of passive process, in which inquisitors planted vocabulary and Ortíz reiterated it accordingly, is not what seems to have happened.

For one thing, Ortíz voiced the same legal arguments across all his large holograph statements between April 1529 and March 1530: that uniformity suggests that he entered prison with some basic concepts about inquisitorial procedure, though he also reacted to later interrogations by expanding his legal rationale. Secondly, as we shall see, Ortíz made mistakes when he argued with inquisitors, so it is unlikely that he was borrowing their discourse as they uttered it, especially since they called attention to his errors. Finally, and most importantly, Ortíz's initial holograph writings – the April letters and the May cuaderno – did not have to be composed. Ortíz had two conversations with the Inquisitor-General, but that official never instructed him to respond from prison, much less with eighteen folios' worth of letters. Ortíz gave an account of his family lineage to the inquisitors on May 14, but constructing a genealogy in an inquisition trial did not require further comments from a defendant. Finally, Ortíz talked for a long time with the Inquisitor-

---

[33] Ortíz wrote the primer cuaderno after he realized Manrique had never seen his letters; he wanted the notebook to go directly to the Suprema, but he wished Manrique to see it, too. *Proceso*, f. 209r.

General's secretary, but that conversation was so private that it wasn't even written down by notaries: our only version of it comes from the defendant himself, in his own handwriting, and again, he did not have to describe or explain that interchange to the Toledo tribunal. In sum, then, Ortíz's April letters and May cuaderno were not ordered by the Spanish Inquisition, but depended instead upon his own volition.[34] As a result, these earliest holograph texts are remarkably unsullied sources for Ortíz's reasoning, since they involve neither scribal mediation, nor inquisitorial mandates, nor lengthy exposure to inquisitorial questioning. Whether they divulge Ortíz's 'voice' is another matter, because it looks as if he had more than one: the evidence shows that he could assume a preaching voice, an exegetical voice, and an inquisitorial voice, and keep them in play at the same time.

There is no doubt that Ortíz's defense was especially complicated because it had so many objectives: his first concern was to champion the sanctity of Francisca Hernández, then to denounce her arrest, and finally to justify his own sermon.[35] Ortíz knew that Francisca was endowed with divine favors; therefore her capture offended God. Yet when it came to proving her gifts, Ortíz was not testifying about actions or verbal statements within a community, which multiple persons had observed. Instead, what he recognized to be true – her supernatural attributes – usually came from private conversations with her and private gifts from her, both of which were hidden from others. Thus he frequently argued on the basis of personal experience and divinely-inspired intuitions, and added scriptural examples as analogues. Because scriptural texts were the sources of legitimacy that Ortíz drew upon most often, they suggest that he was speaking a foreign language to the Spanish Inquisition. That impression is only strengthened by the fact that the fiscal demanded theological help when he had to respond to one of the friar's polemics.[36]

---

[34] It should be noted that Selke mixed up Ortíz's own terminology for the letters and the primer cuaderno, and treated the two sets of sources as interchangeable in content. This can lead to substantial confusion. *El Santo Oficio*, 72–76.

[35] Ortíz's writings from prison are packed with details about false sanctity, and it would be provocative to compare his specific defense of Francisca to other false sanctity cases in Spain and Italy. See Muñoz Fernández, *Beatas y santas neocastellanas*; Zarri, *Finzione e santità*; Schutte, *Autobiography of an Aspiring Saint*; Schutte, *Aspiring Saints.*.

[36] After Ortíz responded verbally to one of the fiscal's formal charges about alumbradismo, the fiscal told the inquisitors that 'since this material [Ortíz's response] is theological, and contains strange propositions, and I could easily err...I ask your lordships to provide me with a learned theologian, with whose advice and opinion I may respond [to Ortíz].' *Proceso*, f. 165v.

312   A Renaissance of Conflicts

The most obvious aspect of Ortíz's earliest writings is their divine messages and biblical imagery.[37] The honor of God was dearer to him than his own life. It was better to obey God's law than the laws of men [Acts 5:29], and God's justice would not allow the Inquisitor-General's dereliction to go unpunished.[38] In fact, Manrique was battling against God Himself in Francisca's prosecution, and he would not prevail in it.[39] Ortíz knew all this because of the graces he had received from Francisca: he had learned more from her in twenty days, than he would have in Paris, in twenty years.[40] More tellingly, Ortíz had received seven *maravillas* or 'wonders' from the beata in the course of their relationship: he had described them to the Inquisitor-General in a conversation outside of prison, he referred to them in his first letter inside prison, and he clarified them at length in the primer cuaderno. The first of the seven lay in Francisca's ability to expound scripture – such as the Psalms of David, the Sermon on the Mount, or the Apocalypse – with true wisdom, despite the fact that she did not know how to read or write, and had never learned grammar or theology. When Francisca glossed the Bible, she enlightened Ortíz's judgment, and he in turn preached the truths she taught him.[41] The second wonder occurred when she cured him of the sin of masturbation. The third was the way in which he became aware of his flaws through memories of her. Fourth, he had a vision of her with his bodily eyes when he was physically separated from her, and he knew of another friar who had a similar experience. Fifth, she once discerned the secret, carnal thoughts of one of her visitors while Ortíz watched; she was prone to this sort of insight. The sixth wonder lay in the fact that Ortíz had composed all of his Easter sermons in less than fifteen days, and the seventh was that he was managing to be happy in the Inquisition's prison.[42]

It was no accident that Ortíz attributed seven marvels to Francisca Hernández, given the sacredness of that number in Christian hermeneutics; he invoked similarly venerable traditions and texts throughout his writings. For example, in one description of his situation, he tacitly recalled Jesus' treatment at the hands of Pilate's guards: he noted that on

---

[37] Ortíz maintained the same biblical allusions and points from divine law in the four letters and the primer cuaderno, though he treated them more expansively in the latter. In the following description, I amass evidence from those five sources.

[38] *Proceso*, f. 34r, 49r. These remarks occur at the beginning of the first two letters to Manrique.

[39] 'Que en verdad, señor, contra dios peleais, y no prevalesceres en lo que avis empecado.' *Proceso.*, 64r. The quote comes from the third letter.

[40] *Proceso.*, f. 220v, in the primer cuaderno

[41] *Proceso*, f. 245r–v.

[42] *Proceso*, ff. 246v–253r.

the day of his sermon, he either could have displeased God by remaining silent about the truth, or he could have given the Holy Office a slap of the sort that it had not received for many years; indeed, after seeing Manrique's blow against God through Francisca, Ortíz had carried out a sort of ritualistic mourning on his own face, with many great slaps.[43] Elsewhere, he asserted that Francisca's enemies had called for her crucifixion, and relayed their demands to crucify her as 'crucifige eam,' a phrase that again called up Jesus as a model.[44]

The sacred comparisons that Ortíz liked best, though, involved Old Testament figures: he constantly compared himself to Jeremias and Daniel, and Francisca to Susanna. The opening lines of his first letter make this propensity clear:

> Holy Jeremias, whom the king...ordered unjustly imprisoned... says in Chapter 20 that the word of God was turned into an affront, and thus the prophet wanted to stop proclaiming it, because proclaiming it would cost him dearly; but having determined to be silent, he says a fire occurred within him that roasted him, and he swooned, not being able to endure it; and for this reason he decided to speak, even though he knew that all those who previously had been his peaceful friends would turn into his enemies. In the same way, this happened to me....that not being able to endure the fire that roasted within myheart, at seeing such a great offense against God, I decided to speak, even though it had to cost me dearly in the eyes of the blind.[45]

Vivid as this correlation was, Ortíz went on to find the story of the unjustly-maligned Susanna and the prophet David even more apt.

The biblical book of Susanna is apocryphal: it was added to the Old Testament book of Daniel when the latter was translated into Greek. Set during the Jews' exile in Babylon, it relays the story of Susanna, a 'very beautiful woman, and one who feared the Lord,' who was married to

---

[43] Ortíz wrote that he could either '...desagradar a dios si callava la verdad, o de dar tal bofetada a vuestro officio qual no se dio muchos años; ha mi rostro abofetre [sic] yo con muchas y grandes bofetadas, por ver que la bofetada que distes a dios en su sierva...' *Proceso*, f. 67v.

[44] *Proceso*, f. 46v. Ortíz also asserted that Jesus functioned as his book, f. 215r.

[45] 'El sancto jeremiah que el rey...mando injustamente encarcelar...dize en el capitulo xx que la palabra de dios se le torno en denuesto, y que por eso quiso cessar de hablalla [sic], porque le pareceria que le costava caro; mas determinando de callar, dize que se le hizo un fuego dentro de si que le abrasava y que desfallecia, no lo podiendo sufrir; y por eso determino de hablar, aunque sabia que se le avian de tornar enemigos todos los que antes le eran amigos pacificos. De esta manera me ha acontecido....que no podiendo sufrir el fuego que dentro del coracon me abrasava, de ver una tan gran offensa de dios, determine de hablar, aunque me avia de costar caro en los ojos de los ciegos.' *Proceso*, f. 34r.

Joakim, and who was lusted after by two tribal elders. These older men were 'overwhelmed by passion' for this woman; acting as a unit, they accosted her in her bath, and gave her a choice: either she could have sex with them, or they would accuse her of adultery with someone else. Susanna refused to do the former. The elders then brought charges of adultery before the people, Susanna cried out to God for justice, and God heard her pleas. A young man named Daniel confronted the crowd:

> And as she was being led away to death, God aroused the holy spirit of a young lad named Daniel; and he cried with a loud voice, 'I am innocent of the blood of this woman.' All the people turned to him, and said, 'What is this that you have said?' Taking his stand in the midst of them, he said, 'Are you such fools, you sons of Israel? Have you condemned a daughter of Israel without examination and without learning the facts? Return to the place of judgment. For these men have borne false witness against her.'[46]

Daniel then separated the two elders and questioned them separately; he quickly caught them in a contradiction. Afterwards, 'the assembly shouted loudly and blessed God, who saves those who hope in him. And they rose against the two elders, for out of their own mouths, Daniel had convicted them of bearing false witness.'[47]

Ortíz exhibited a great deal of wit in calling up the Susanna and Daniel story, because it seemed to perfectly match his defense. Before her arrest, Francisca *was* suspected of having sexual relationships with her overwhelmingly male retinue; for the first year of his trial, Ortíz relentlessly proclaimed her chastity, as well as his own. Moreover, he firmly believed that two of Francisca's former followers – Fray Gil López de Bejar, and Diego López de Husillos – had stirred up misgivings about her with the Franciscan superiors, and even with the Inquisitor-General.[48] In Ortíz's drama, then, the two 'elders' were Fray Gil and Diego López, Francisca was Susanna, and he was Daniel, who could confound the elders if only he could get at them.

> I say — confiding in Him who, through Daniel, liberated holy Susanna from the lying elders – bring to me all those accusers who assign indecency to this shining virgin, and I, with the grace of God and my all-being Jesus Christ crucified, will confound them, performing the work of holy Daniel, that is, 'not I, but the grace of God with me.' Thus it shall be known that

---

[46] *The New Oxford Annotated Bible*, expanded edition, revised standard edition. Susanna 1:44–49.

[47] Susanna 1:60–61.

[48] *Proceso*, ff. 66v–67r, 234r, 237r–v. In the last folio cited here, Ortíz enumerated Fray Gil's enmity toward *himself*, for they had competed for the same preaching position at the royal court.

this holy virgin [Francisca] has been another holy Susanna in our times; and this truth shall be much noted and recognized, because I offer to explain it, with the grace of God; because I know that the filth [against her] which filthy hearts have raised, won't float, given the purity that God has shown me and worked in me, through the means and intercession of his holy bride...[49]

Ortíz had a marked ability to relate his and Francisca's situation to scripture. He managed to put the Inquisitor-General in the Bible too, as Herod the Tetrarch.

From the moment he began to write inside his cell, Ortíz played John the Baptist to Manrique's Herod. The conflict between these scriptural figures is recounted in the Books of Matthew, Mark, and Luke, and though its scope differs in each, the basic elements remain the same.[50] Herod placed John the Baptist in prison because John had warned him that he could not lawfully possess Herodias, wife of his brother Philip. Herod was also afraid of John's reputation among the people as a prophet; he was looking for a way to execute him. Herodias and her daughter – called Salome by the Jewish historian Josephus – consequently plotted John's demise. Salome ended up dancing for Herod, Herod was pleased and promised her whatever she wished, and Salome promptly asked for John's head on a plate. Understandably enough, Ortíz focused on the beginning, not the end, of this scriptural episode: it mattered to him because it described a lower-ranking person rebuking a high-standing one.[51] As he remarked, John's reproach fulfilled the divine law of Leviticus 19:15, which reads, '...Respect not the person of the poor, nor honor the countenance of the mighty. But judge thy neighbor according to justice.'[52]

---

[49] '...que digo, confiando en aquel que por medio de Daniel libro a sancta susanna de los falsos viejos, que traigan a mi todos esos accusadores que ponen deshonestidad en este virgen esclarecido, i yo, con la gracia de mi dios y mi bientodo Jesu Cristo crucificado, los confundire, haziendo el officio del sancto Daniel, *non ego scilicet gratia dei mecum.* Para que asi se conozca que ha sido una nueva sancta susanna en nuestros tiempos esta virgen sancta, y esta verdad se note mucho y se ponga en effetto, porque me ofrezco con la gracia de dios a la aclarare, porque yo sé que no caben en un saco tales suiziedades que los suzios coracones han levantado, con la pureza que dios me ha mostrado y obrado en mi, por medio y intercession de su sancta esposa...' *Proceso,* f. 36v.

[50] Matthew 14:10, Mark 6:14–28; Luke 3:19–20, 23:7–11.

[51] The version recorded in Luke 3:19–20 reads, 'Herod the Tetrarch was reproved by [John] for Herodias, his brother's wife, and for all the evils which Herod had done...' Here Herod was reproved twice, which matched the number of times Ortíz had spoken with Manrique about Francisca's arrest. Ortíz first compared himself to John the Baptist and Manrique to Herod on f. 34r of the *Proceso,* which is the opening of his first letter. Clearly the example mattered to him.

[52] *Proceso,* f. 209v.

Significantly, many passages from the New Testament also addressed the private and then the public correction of a superior, and Ortíz could have justified his mandate through any of them. For instance, in Matthew 18:15, Jesus told his audience to correct an offending brother in private, and to do so twice, if necessary; if the offender continued to sin, he should be corrected in church. In Galatians 2:1–14, Paul publicly rebuked Peter's inconsistency when it came to circumcision; in 1 Timothy 5:20, Paul noted 'As for those who persist in sin, rebuke them in the presence of all, so that the rest may stand in fear.'[53] Moreover, Ortíz did not have to rely on the Bible alone for instruction, for he could have gone straight to Thomas Aquinas's *Summa theologica*, II.II., *quaestio* 33, articles 1–8, which treated 'on fraternal correction.' Aquinas broke down the subject into eight topics, among them whether fraternal correction were an act of charity and a precept, whether correction pertained exclusively to prelates, whether anyone were obliged to correct a prelate, and whether a known sinner could correct a delinquent. The quaestio also examined the ideal sequence between private admonition and open censure, and whether a public denunciation of sin had to be based on a witness's testimony.

Significantly, Aquinas argued that fraternal correction was a precept when the 'fruit' or benefit of the correction was clear. He also asserted that if correction were a charitable act, it could be anyone's office. Finally, he concluded,

> a secret admonition is fitting to precede the public denunciation of a wrongdoer, where the sins are hidden, and not against the common good; however, where the sins are public or secret, and are committed against the common good, it is not always necessary that a secret admonition come first, but in the event that the secret admonition is discarded, one should proceed to the [public] denunciation.[54]

Aquinas went on to remark that if a secret sin were likely to injure multiple, innocent persons, then it was appropriate to denounce the sin immediately, to prevent harm.[55]

---

[53] Ortíz referred to the incident between Peter and Paul, noting that the latter had dared to reprehend the former in public, though Peter 'was the true pope;' *Proceso*, f. 219v.

[54] 'Conclusio. Oportet secretam admonitionem, publicam praecedere delinquentis denuntiationem, ubi peccata occulta sunt, et non contra commune bonum: ubi vero publica peccata sunt, vel occulta contra bonum commune commissa, non est semper necesse praecedere secretam admonitionem, sed interdum secreta admonitione omissa, procedendum est ad denunciationem.' *Summa Theologica*, II.II., qu. 33, art. VII.

[55] 'Quaedam enim peccata occulta sunt, quae sunt in nocumentum proximorum vel corporale, vel spirituale....Et quia ille qui sic occulte peccat, non solum in se

Clearly Aquinas as well as the Bible could vindicate Ortíz's sermon. And so Ortíz thought he had the Inquisitor-General boxed into a corner: according to the Bible and the chief medieval theologian on morality, sin, especially public sin, could be corrected, first by two private admonitions, and then by public disclosure, and there were no restrictions on this action in terms of social position.[56] Moreover, when even secret sins could hurt more than just the offender, a public denunciation should occur. Ortíz had conversed twice with Manrique before Francisca's arrest, and tried to persuade him from prosecuting her; since Francisca possessed divine gifts, her arrest and imprisonment would injure many people. Ortíz justified his sermon with this reasoning from the moment of his imprisonment. In the opening folio of his first letter to Manrique, he wrote, 'I say that each and every time a public sin and scandal are committed, having been preceded by two secret warnings not to do it, that if there exists some preacher of truth who holds God's honor as dearer than his own life, then that preacher must and can oppose that sin publicly, without being blocked by any elevation of rank.'[57]

Ortíz also linked his sermon to charity, because one of his explicit goals was to save Manrique's soul. Throughout the letters to the Inquisitor-General, Ortíz sounded like the preacher he was: he worried about Manrique's repentance, reminded him of his mortal sin, and tried to terrify him with Hell.

> What I recommend to Your Reverend Lordship – so that you may reach eternal salvation, and pardon from this sin that you have committed, and so that you don't find yourself tricked at the hour of death, which is close, given your age – is that very quickly, without delay, postponing all other business and trials, you get involved in this case....and may worldly shame not prevent you from quickly undoing what you so rapidly did, for that shame is the snare of Hell.[58]

---

peccat, sed etiam in alios, oportet statim procedere ad denuntiationem.' *Summa theologica*, II.II, qu. 33, art. VII. Aquinas did caution that a public denunciation should take place *unless* someone believed that a private admonition would immediately correct the offender.

[56] Still, Aquinas explicitly noted that only prelates could pursue a public-denunciation-as-justice, when punishment was involved. *Summa theologica*, II.II., qu. 33, art. III, IV.

[57] 'digo que cada y quando que se comete un pecado publico y escandalo, se aviendo precedido dos amonestaciones secretas para que no se cometiesse, si ay algun predicador de la verdad que tenga en más la honrra de dios que su vida, deve y puede él tal arguir publicamente el tal pecado sin que lo estorve alguna alteza de dignidad.' *Proceso*, f. 34r. Ortíz repeated this sentiment verbatim in the primer cuaderno, f. 209v, but with greater precision: the private corrections were now 'fraternal,' the preacher an 'evangelical' one, and neither 'highness of rank or estate' could impede the public denunciation.

[58] 'Lo que yo consejo a vuestra Reverenda Señoria para que alcance salud eterna

Ortíz continued these warnings in subsequent epistles; he even began his second letter with the quote, 'cursed is he who does God's work carelessly,' [*maledictus qui opus dei facit negligenter* [sic] f. 46r.] He used all the rhetorical tricks he could muster to play on Manrique's nerves: the Inquisitor-General was not a young man, death could strike at any moment, and he should not want to die with the sin of Francisca's imprisonment on his conscience. The Inquisitor-General needed to repent, or else he risked condemnation from God; his only chance for salvation lay in admitting he had erred, and in being brave enough to correct his mistake. Ironically, by claiming Manrique's salvation as one of his objectives, Ortíz was competing with the inquisitors themselves, since their ultimate objective was to restore repentant heretics to the community of the faithful.

Our defendant revealed all the qualities we might expect in a Franciscan preacher arrested for heresy: he employed homiletic rhetoric, relied on biblical analogies, and owed a great deal to allegorical exegesis. Still, he can also offer surprises, because he occasionally injected his statements with a historical edge. For example, in the second conversation with Manrique – the one that ended so badly – the Inquisitor-General purportedly said that he was willing to believe every good thing about Francisca Hernández, if only she were a nun. Ortíz reacted vehemently: if Manrique would do some research, he would soon realize that men and women could reach a very high state of perfection without being monks or nuns; learned men agreed on this point, and it was even heretical to suggest otherwise. Ortíz did not intend to deprecate monastic life – after all, he had preached against Erasmus on this topic – but Manrique's critique of Francisca rested on a weak foundation, if proof of her sanctity simply came down to monastic vows.[59] Different times required different styles of sanctity, and at this very moment God could

---

y perdon deste pecado que a hecho, y no os halles burlado en la hora de la muerte — que segun la edad natural os es cercana — es que muy presto, sin dilacion, pospuestos todos otros negocios y procesos, entienda vuestra Señoria en esto....y no le venca a vuestra Señoria la verguenza del mundo en deshazer tan presto lo que tan acceleradamente hizo, que es esa verguenza lazo del infierno.' *Proceso*, f. 38v.

[59] '...que haga vuestra Señoria examinar entre letrados si se puede alcanzar muy alta pureza de perfeccion sin ser fraile o monja; para que perdiesse del el credito de la amada esposa de Jesus por no ser monja. No digo esto para perjudicar al estado de la religion, al qual dios por su misericordia me llamo, porque es publico quantas vezes he predicado contra Erasmo no ser de tener en poco; mas affirmo ser herejia ya en muchos concilios condenada affirmar que no puede ser alcanzado estado de perfeccion de charidad sino en estado de religion, porque vea vuestra Señoria quan flaco fundacion tomo para le quitar el credito.' *Proceso*, f. 36r.

be depositing other, even holier women in the corners of His churches, who were just waiting to be discovered.[60] As for the wonders that Francisca performed, which Manrique called diabolical illusions, Ortíz noted that the belt that cured his masturbation was not very different from the hem of Jesus' garment that cured the hemorrhaging woman [Matthew 9:20–23]. The Church believed in holy relics, so why couldn't his belt be one? Besides, if Manrique so fervently trusted the link between monasticism and holiness, then shouldn't all archbishops be friars?[61] Ortíz knew, of course, that Manrique had never taken monastic vows.

Ortíz's speeches about Christianity displayed both permanence and change: he moved easily between synchronic time (*figura*) and its diachronic counterpart (history). Scriptural examples could be eternally relevant: ergo, he and Francisca were Daniel and Susanna. Yet the features of wonders might alter, and thus a *beata* who had never taken monastic vows could still be the 'wife of God.'[62] What went along with this outlook was a certain respect for people as individuals, and a reluctance to treat them as representatives of a larger category. This attitude became apparent when Ortíz ridiculed the Inquisition's interest in tying his current predicament to his *converso* family, or when he slandered particular Franciscans but continue to praise the Franciscan order.[63] His perspective was a far cry from the Toledo inquisitors', which read a diatribe against the Inquisitor-General as slander against the institution itself.

---

[60] '...possible es tener Dios por los rincones de su iglesia otras muy mas santas.' *Proceso*, f. 241v. This line of reasoning occurred in the primer cuaderno, and substantially expanded what Ortíz had advanced in his four previous letters. Provocatively, Ortiz could also offer historical remarks about the development of Judaism, which were markedly similar to one of his teacher's comments on the same subject: Ortiz was instructed by Pedro Ciruelo. *Proceso* ff. 161v, 232v. See Homza, *Religious Authority*, Chap. 3.

[61] *Proceso*, ff. 233r, 235r.

[62] Ortíz called Francisca Hernández the 'wife of God' [*esposa de Dios*] at least fourteen times in the four letters, and twenty times in the primer cuaderno.

[63] After noting that he could not care less about flesh and blood on earth, Ortíz wrote, '...there's no reason that the inquisitors should think it fruitless to listen fully to what so touches souls, namely that in our souls we are all of God's lineage, as is written in Acts 17. And if something is fruitless, it should be the writing they have accomplished about sons and daughters, and fathers of daughters and mothers of sons, etc. [sic] I know not to take such things seriously, as shall be obvious through my reply...' *Proceso*, f. 207r. I agree with Selke that Ortíz's *converso* lineage played a significant part in his prosecution: certain remarks by witnesses and the fiscal were decidedly anti-Jewish. For example, on f. 176r, the fiscal told Ortíz that it was not wise for a *converso* to be so fond of the Old Testament. For other examples, Selke, *El Santo Oficio*, pp. 64–66, 276–277.

Ortíz's preoccupation with the individual – and his interest in specificity over abstraction – eventually culminated in a sense of exceptionalism. His divine revelations and Francisca's divine gifts should have been above suspicion, no matter what their backgrounds or histories might indicate to the inquisitorial bureaucracy. Ortíz was adamant that reciprocity and sympathy should affect the proceedings too: as a result, he often quoted the Golden Rule to his inquisitorial audience. Inquisitors in 1529 knew they were supposed to be merciful if conditions warranted it, and penance rather than execution was the sentence they usually exacted through most of the sixteenth century; the evidence suggests that they seriously entertained notions of expiation and forgiveness. At the same time, though, inquisitors were supposed to be judges of 'external, juridical law,' not of revelations or intuitions; and given his demands, Ortíz seemed to be asking the Inquisition for attitudes and standards that its officials could not supply.[64]

All these attributes suggest that Ortíz was arguing from a different sense of the law when he confronted the Inquisition between April and May, 1529. Scripture clearly was his guide; personal experience counted for much. His stubborn defense presupposed independence and bravery; his reliance on the Bible connoted a keen morality. The interpretation of earlier scholarship, which framed the Ortíz trial as a battle between individual conscience and institutional repression, is understandable. Still, it would be an overstatement to portray Ortíz as removed from all secular values and secular intellectual repertories, because he also worried about worldly matters such as rank. Manrique must have known about this tendency when he sent a message to him in prison, informing him that Toledo was shocked and saddened at his current status, given what his reputation had been before April 6.[65] In sending such a communiqué, Manrique undoubtedly intended to exert his influence. It would not be far wrong to think of him as the patron, and Ortíz as the client.

A large part of what drove Ortíz's rage was the fact that the Inquisitor-General had changed his good opinion of him so quickly and without warning. In their first private conversation, Manrique allegedly told Ortíz that he had always held him in high esteem and had always valued his sermons; indeed, he had said so publicly. By the second colloquy, though, Manrique told Ortíz he was deceived about Francisca Hernández, and when Ortíz asked him why, Manrique replied that several guardians of

---

[64] Eimeric, *El manual*, 132. Nevertheless, and contrary to Eimeric's counsel, the various interrogators of Ortíz — especially Fernando Niño and the fiscal – spent much if not most of their time trying to undermine his faith in divine gifts. See n. 73 below.

[65] *Proceso*, f. 50r.

the Franciscan order had opined that Ortíz was now 'lost' and preaching no telling what kind of doctrine, whereas before his acquaintance with the beata, he was an 'angel and a good religious.'[66]

Ortíz was offended that Manrique gave more credit to the guardians than to himself. As he said,

> It has been six years since I received such magnificent gifts from God, courtesy of the holy communication with Francisca; and your Lordship [Manrique] never knew me before I had communicated with her; and if I became 'lost' with her communication, then where did the reputation come from, in which Your Lordship held me, and the reason why I was praised? I want to know why you had to give more credit to the guardian, who came to rob me of my reputation with you...[67]

Such themes were repeated in the first three letters. The Inquisitor-General had invited Ortíz into high circles, and had displayed much affection for him before guardians unfairly undermined it. Ortíz was not a person whose reputation should be demolished so quickly, given the composure, obedience, and above all, the chastity of his life.[68] When Ortíz appealed to the respect Manrique had once shown him, and adduced proof of his own virtues, he demonstrated how valuable Manrique's friendship had been, and how much he would miss it.

He divulged an equal sensitivity to status when he contended that his professional life had been ruined by Francisca's arrest. Within two or three days of her seizure, 'when her imprisonment was already very notorious in the whole city,' Ortíz could barely leave the monastery: it seemed as if everyone were looking at him with new eyes and practically pointing their fingers at him, as if to say, 'Beware! there is the one who so praised Francisca Hernández to us.'[69] Ortíz found this loss of public credibility

---

66 *Proceso*, ff. 34v–35r.

67 'Que ya ha seis anos que recibi muy magnificas mercedes de dios con su comunicacion sancta, y nunca vuestra Señoria me conocio antes que yo la uviesse comunicado, y si con su comunicacion me perdi, de donde le venia a vuestra Señoria el credito que de mi persona tenia, y lo que me loava? Quiero yo saber porque avia de dar más credito al padre guardian, que venia a quitarme mi fama con vuestra persona.' *Proceso*, f. 35r.

68 *Proceso*, ff. 47r, 67v. Ortíz clearly connected chastity to his monastic vows, and then to an exemplary monastic life. His lengthy polemics about his own celibacy were attempts to bolster his own reputation, as well as to diminish misgivings about Francisca's. He rarely failed to mention his chastity in his holograph compositions.

69 'Dos o tres dias despues de la prision injusta de ésta...que ya que fue muy notorio su prision en toda la ciudad, tanto que yo no osava salir de casa....y porque me parecia que todos me mirarian con nuevos ojos, y me señalarian quasi con el dedo, como quien dize "catad alli él que nos alabava tanto a Francisca Hernández."'

especially pernicious because it cost him influence over the Christian pueblo. As a result, Manrique's arrest of Francisca was horrific not just through its offense to God, but

> it is also scandalous against everything I have worked for my whole life, that is, educating with such continual sermons. Everyone knows that I am such a child of [Francisca's] heart, that by imprisoning her with such dishonor, you have made all my teaching suspect, and you have robbed me of the authority to preach from this day forward.[70]

Ortíz's concern for the pueblo may have been pastoral, but this passage reveals that he also knew how much prestige he once enjoyed.

As for other signs of refined sensibilities, the defendant did not hesitate to write about his own honor, the authority of popes, and the Inquisition as a valuable and necessary institution.[71] It thus seems clear that Ortíz shared some values with the elite population of Toledo: indeed, when he described the April sermon, he said he knew 'his friends would turn into enemies' as a result of it. Before April 6, 1529, he was very well-connected. Afterwards, he lambasted his and Francisca's arrest for temporal as well as godly reasons.

The historiography on Ortíz has neglected to mention that he had a worldly temper as well as an independent streak. It has omitted other evidence too, the most provocative of which concerns his ability to debate like an inquisitor. When it came to the appropriateness of Francisca's seizure and imprisonment, and his own sermon, Ortíz did not simply argue from biblical analogues or divine favor: instead, he also called up legal norms that were supposed to have a clear place in inquisitorial procedure, which staff at the Toledo tribunal would instantly have recognized. Ortíz's ability to juggle all these angles all at once — for he argued from divine grace, scriptural authority, and secular law in nearly simultaneous fashion – illustrates how polyphonic the law could be for certain defendants in inquisitorial *audiencias*.[72] The fact that prosecutors took Ortíz seriously

---

Proceso, f. 213r. His fellow-monks looked at him in a new manner, too, f. 213r.

[70] 'Es tambien escandaloso contra todo lo que yo he trabajado toda mi vida en edificar con tan continuos sermones, que sabiendo todos que so[y] yo tan hijo de su coracon, prendiendola a ella con tanta deshonrra, toda mi dottrina tornastes sospechosa y toda la authoridad me quito vuestra Señoria para osar predicar de oy adelante.' *Proceso*, fol. 37v.

[71] For his attempts to defend Francisca with the historical memory of Pope Adrian VI, see below, and *Proceso*, f. 243r–v. Ortíz praised the Inquisition at the end of his letters: ff. 39v, 67v, as examples.

[72] No one would assert that Francisco Ortíz was a typical defendant. But at least one other suspect in the same epoch, María de Cazalla, mounted a similarly complex defense, since she too argued from intention, scriptural example, the

suggests that they too understood the prospect of multiple legalities, though they might not treat all of them as equally persuasive.[73]

In his letters, Ortíz was most concerned to justify his sermon, but since validating his homily finally depended upon proving the wickedness of Francisca's arrest, he addressed the legal shortcomings of her imprisonment as well as her divine gifts. Succinctly put, he blamed the Inquisitor-General for dereliction of duty and accused him of negligence [*negligencia*]. For Ortíz, 'negligence' had a wide reach: Manrique's carelessness had betrayed itself in their own conversations, and had affected the way witnesses were handled. For instance, in their talks before April 6, Ortíz had seen Manrique swing violently in his opinion of the beata, to the point of outright contradiction. He had also heard him make prejudicial remarks about Francisca because of her lack of monastic vows:

> ...in the second conversation, where your Lordship had already completely altered and refused to give me any credit; the thing that made the greatest impression on me was when you told me, 'if I were to see Francisca Hernández in a monastery, walking in obedience and following its choir and bell, I would believe everything that people say; I am very devoted to persons who are in monastic orders.'[74]

When Ortíz accused Manrique of bias, Manrique accused Francisca of being a lascivious woman.[75] Manrique then said that Fray Barnabás, the guardian of San Juan de los Reyes, was right to declare that he would see that virgin burned, and noted that Fray Barnabás's personal weight would suffice to get the burning carried out.[76]

---

credibility of witnesses, and rules about the ratification of witness testimony. See Cazalla, *Proceso de la inquisición*, 134–140, 183–185, 190–192.

[73] Besides their arguments about witnesses, evidence, and the importance of human investigation, Fernando Niño repeatedly warned Ortíz to think seriously about whether Francisca's 'gifts' were demonically inspired; as noted earlier, the fiscal would enlist a theologian's help to respond to Ortíz, and spend hours trying to persuade our defendant that he had been tricked by the Devil. The overall effect is to realize just how theological Spanish inquisitors could be, given the right circumstances.

[74] '...en esta segunda platica, donde estava vuestra Señoria ya todo mudado y ningun credito me quiso dar; la cosa en que más hincapie hizo conmigo, fue en que me dixo, "si yo viesse a Francisca Hernández en un monasterio, andar a obediencia y seguir su choro y campanilla, todo lo creeria quanto della me dizen, que yo soy muy devoto de los que estan en religion."' *Proceso*, f. 36r.

[75] 'Respondiome vuestra Señoria, "entonces sí, que bien conoscemos aqui a Francisca Hernández que es una muger lasciva."' *Proceso*, f. 36r.

[76] '...diziendome que tenia razon el padre guardian en dezir que él la haria quemar a esta virgin muy esclarecida de Jesus, y que él bastaria para ello.' *Proceso*, f. 47r.

For Ortíz, the more Manrique talked, the more his wrongdoing increased: not only was he overlooking his own inconsistency, but he was neglecting to notice others'. In fact, Fray Barnabás had also contradicted himself where the beata was concerned:

> In the chapter meeting that occurred a year ago, that took place in Escalona, my guardian [Barnabás] was talking with me about this business of the servant of God [Francisca], and about how wicked a certain Diego López [de Husillos] seemed, who, together with Fray Gil [López de Bejar], meant to sow discord with such rabid care. My guardian said these words to me, 'Who is paying that traitorous cleric to go through the court, speaking evil of Francisca Hernández?' And when I came from Castrillo, he asked me, 'have you seen that servant of God, that holy woman?' I replied yes, and he then asked me, 'are you happy?' and I replied, 'the happiest in the world.' Then he said to me, 'what is this letter that the commissioner-general wrote you in Castrillo, threatening you with the Inquisition?' I replied, 'father, I already wrote him to say it was in vain to threaten me with the persecutions that I love, and here in Toledo I shall await his reply.' Then he said, 'do you not see that he is now the Vice-General of the Order?' and I replied, 'I wouldn't care if he were pope.' Then my guardian embraced me with a laugh and we were very happy.[77]

With this anecdote, Ortíz attacked the legitimacy of Francisca's arrest on three grounds. The guardian, Fray Barnabás, had not always expressed negative thoughts about that *beata*: only one year earlier, he had called her a servant of God, criticized her enemies, and endorsed Ortíz's relationship with her. Thus when the same guardian complained to Manrique in 1529, he was reversing himself, and if Fray Gil and Diego López had deposed against Francisca, then they too were contradictory: once fervent admirers, they had turned into her enemies, which was why the guardian had called them treasonous. Ortíz had tried to relay all this

---

[77]'Y es que en el capitulo que agora ha un año, se tuvo por este tiempo en Escalona hablandome mi guardian en este negocio de la sierva de Cristo, y de quan mal le parecia un Diego López que junto con Frai Gil entendia en sembrar esta zizannia con tan ravioso cuidado. Me dixo él mi guardian, "Quien le paga a aquel clerigo traidor para que ande por la corte a dezir mal de Francisca Hernández?" Y quando yo vine de Castrillo ... me pregunto, "vistes a aquella sierva de dios, aquella santa muger?" I yo dixe que sí, y él me pregunto más, "venis alegre?" I yo respondi, "que lo más del mundo." Entonces me dixo, "pues que es aquella carta que os escrivio el commissario general a Castrillo, amenazando os con la inquisicion?" I yo respondi, "padre, ya le escrivi que era por demas amenazarme con las persecuciones que yo amava, y aqui en Toledo espero lo que me responder." Entonces él dixo, "no veis que es agora Vice-General?" i yo respondi, "aunque sea papa." Entonces él me abraco con risa y quedamos muy alegres.' *Proceso*, ff. 66v–67r.

to Manrique in their direct conversations: if Manrique had paid attention to him and properly supervised the case, Francisca's arrest would never have happened.[78] Instead, the Inquisitor-General had ignored what he did not wish to hear.[79] And Ortíz suspected that Manrique's dereliction of duty extended in the opposite direction as well, since he probably had looked for a way to justify Francisca's arrest: he might be using the Inquisition's 1519 investigation of her as a reason to imprison her *now*, when she had not even been imprisoned *then*.[80]

Throughout Ortíz's critique, his favorite charge was *negligencia*, or negligence; and every time he used that word, he implicitly called up the contrasting noun *diligencia*, or diligence, a term he would also employ explicitly.[81] Significantly, in this context, diligencia meant assiduity in legal proceedings, and in this time period, the word diligencia occurs in the Inquisition's instructions, in prosecutors' reports, among inquisitors themselves, and among consultants to the same. Thus in 1484, 1499, and 1561, inquisitors'-general's *instrucciones* told officials to act 'diligently' with their cases and with all witnesses.[82] In 1526, consultants told the Toledo tribunal to 'perform more diligencias to ascertain' whether witches flew bodily, and remarked that the Inquisition must 'perform diligencia' by looking for actual witnesses to witchcraft, instead of relying solely on witches' confessions.[83] Ortíz's charge of negligencia and injunctions about diligen-

---

[78] '...pudiesses convenir a vuestra Señoria en esta causa lo que se sigue...que si diligentissimamente la investigarades, no se uviera hecho tan gran offensa a dios, ni uvierades escondido la candela que dios encendio por luz de muchos; que no os dieron para eso el poder, sino para edificacion...mas lo que affirmo con entera verdad es que en este pleito los que la acusan y condenan y han encarcelado estan muy caidos con la culpa.' *Proceso*, f. 37r.

[79] '... la negligencia que vuestra Señoria ha tenido en escuchar lo que juzga ser necessario de oir.' *Proceso*, f. 69v. See below for the importance of *negligencia* in Ortíz's objections.

[80] *Proceso*, f. 34r.

[81] See Ortíz's prose in nn. 78 and 79 above.

[82] See, for example, Gaspar Isidro de Arguello, *Instrucciones del Santo Oficio*, ff. 6r, 12v.

[83] Examples of *diligencia* are italicized. 'El Licenciado Baldes, al primer question, dixo que parece que de los procesos vistos, en quanto no esta probado en manera que concluya que realmente, ni tampoco por fantasia, cometan actos delictos las personas que quien se trata, e que por esto se debe mandar a los inquisidores que hagan más *diligencias* para averiguar la verdad.... Doctor Arcilla...que se a de estar a sus confessiones fechas, segun orden de derecho, porque en algunas cosas particulares, y en ser llevados de un lugar a otro corporalmente, se pueden algunas vezes illudei, y en estas cosas *se debe hazer diligencia* y tomar testigos para que hagan entera probanca.' 1526 Inquisition consultation on the reality of witchcraft. Archivo Histórico Nacional, Sección de la Inquisición, Libro 1231, ff. 634v, 635v.

cia would have resonated with any inquisitor or prosecutor who read his writings.

His comments about witnesses and their character were also perspicacious. Ortíz knew that inquisition law gave the greatest weight to a confession, or two credible eyewitnesses to the same event; he also knew that charges of infamy were less persuasive when they were made by disreputable people. He was quite sure Francisca had not confessed; he consequently tried to manipulate the legal authority of pairs of deponents, and in the process he kept raising the negative meaning of inconsistent behavior. For example, the guardian had contradicted himself in his opinion of the beata, and so had Manrique: those discrepancies should make their negative opinion less authoritative, though they now held it in common. By the same token, since Fray Gil and Diego López had also changed from devotees to antagonists, their sworn statements should be thrown out too.[84] Finally, because the guardian had shared Ortíz's opinion of Fray Gil and Diego López, the guardian and Ortíz could become two eyewitnesses to that pair's duplicity. (In this instance, our defendant decided to forget his own slander about the guardian's character, and to concentrate instead on the power of two.)

Ortíz not only undermined potential multiple witnesses for the prosecution, but attempted to create pairs of them for the defense. In his third letter to Manrique, dated April 20, 1529, he tried to verify his stance through a colleague, a Franciscan friar named Muñoztello. Ortíz explained that Muñoztello had an irreproachable reputation, to the point that he was put in charge of novices and offered a guardianship of a convent in Villaselos; he too was an ardent supporter of Francisca Hernández. Ortíz heightened the doubling even further by noting that he and Muñoztello had both had received spiritual gifts from Francisca and suffered persecutions on her behalf. Eleven months earlier, in fact, they had been with her in Castrillo. During that visit,

> This servant of God [Muñoztello] then stirred and fortified me with his very holy words, that I 'not be discouraged, even if I had to fight with your very illustrious Lordship [Manrique];' and it seemed as if his very judicious spirit

---

[84]Like other defendants, Ortíz never would have learned the identities of prosecution witnesses, at least not officially, because of the Inquisition's rule of secrecy. Here, in a strategy seen everywhere, he was attempting to identify possible deponents whom he expected to be hostile; if he could prove their antagonism, they might be recused. Though he never explicitly raised the notion of *capital* enmity – which was an ill will deep enough to erase credibility – he alluded to it when he described Fray Gil and Diego López as evil rumormongers. When it came to witnesses' contradictions under oath, inquisitors certainly were expected to take them seriously; see, for instance, Kagan, *Lucrecia's Dreams*, p. 153.

felt or guessed what was to happen later. And I promised him with much cheer that even if the fight with your Lordship came, I would not be discouraged. And then this blessed father said to me, with his usual humility, 'oh, how much I want to be your deacon, in the sacrifice of your person that you have to offer'... And although that blessed father is not a preacher by profession, as I am, to say in the pulpit what I said, I know that wherever an opportunity presents itself, he will say the same as me, performing the same aggravation to your Holy Office that I did.[85]

Ortíz was interested in producing two witnesses' worth of credit: he and Muñoztello had unblemished characters, and were willing to preach in concert against the same enemy.

By highlighting the place of witnesses, inconsistency, and integrity, Ortíz's four letters to the Inquisitor-General revealed an awareness of some of the standard rules of inquisition trials. According to the crucial authority Nicolau Eimeric, who wrote the fourteenth-century *Directorium inquisitorum*, inquisitors should be aware of implausible accusations. They should investigate the relationships between the witnesses and the accused, and check for enmity; they should prefer unambiguous testimony.[86] If Ortíz's objections were correct, then Francisca's arrest and imprisonment might have been advanced on less-than-solid grounds — assuming, of course, that everyone involved shared the same perspective on contradictions and lies.

Ortíz never cited a secular legal source in his four letters, so it remains a matter of conjecture as to how he came to grasp the theoretical importance of multiplicity, consistency, and veracity to the Spanish Inquisition.[87] He had fraternized in the past with high ecclesiastics,

---

[85] 'Y este siervo de Jesu Cristo [Muñoztello] me desperto y fortifico entonces con sus muy sanctas palabras, ha que yo no desmayasse aunque uviesse de tener la contienda con vuestra muy illustre Señoria, que no parece sino que sentia o barruntava su muy discreto espiritu lo que despues ha succedido. I yo le prometi con mucho regozijo que aunque fuesse la contienda con vuestra Señoria no desmayaria y entonces me dixo este bendito padre, con su humildad, o quanto desseo ser diacono vuestro en el sacrificio que aves de ofrecer de vuestra persona....Y aunque aquel bendito padre no es predicador de palabras por officio, como yo; para dezir en el pulpito lo que yo dixe, sé yo que donde quiera que se hallare ofrecida opportunidad dira lo mesmo que yo dixe, haziendo el mesmo agravio a vuestro santo officio que yo hize.' *Proceso*, ff. 65v–66r.

[86] Eimeric, *El manual*, 135, 138, 140–141, 253. Eimeric's Latin original, *Directorium inquisitorum*, was printed in Barcelona in 1503, courtesy of Spanish Inquisitor-General Diego Deza.

[87] Provocatively, it is conceivable that the instructions of inquisitors-general reached more than an inquisitorial audience: though we lack a transmission history for such texts, internal evidence from the 1484, 1485, 1498–1499, 1500, and 1516 *instrucciones* suggests they were printed, and it is well-known that they were

including Manrique himself; it certainly is possible that an understanding of the Inquisition's mandates filtered down and out to a wider population, because other defendants exhibited a similar knowledge of the theoretical inquisitorial process.[88] What is clear is that Ortíz amplified his legal objections after he was interviewed by Luis Nuñez Coronel, Manrique's secretary.

Coronel had studied at the Sorbonne, where he became a doctor of theology in 1514; he became attached to the royal court of Charles V in 1520, as a preacher and confessor, and he also worked for the Inquisition in Brussels. A correspondent of Erasmus's, a delegate at the Valladolid conference of 1527, and a noted author on logic, Coronel was both famous and influential.[89] Soon after Ortíz's arrest, Manrique secretly sent Coronel to the Toledo tribunal: apparently his mission was to show Ortíz the flaws in his reasoning, and persuade him to retract his statements.

In Ortíz's version of their interchange — the only one we possess — he took much comfort in Coronel's arrival, because it meant that 'this business was passing into the hands of someone in whom was joined much learning and godly fear; hence the justice of my case might be more obvious.'[90] As Ortíz recounted what Coronel had said, he arranged the secretary's points into matters of greater and lesser importance; the arguments that provoked his greatest response were threefold. First, Coronel argued that Manrique would not have ordered Francisca's arrest without cause. Second, he noted that even if Ortíz thought the testimony against her was insufficient, Manrique had never said as much. Third, he pointed out that new and better witnesses could have appeared between the time Ortiz spoke with Manrique, and Francisca's arrest.

> the lord Doctor [Coronel] argued with me, saying 'let's assume it was true, that after your conversations with Reverend Manrique, no witnesses came forward against this servant of God [Francisca], who had some new

---

composed in Spanish. See Arguello, *Instrucciones del Santo Oficio*. Arguello compiled the early instructions listed above, as well as the crucial ones issued by Fernando de Valdés in 1561, which were also composed and printed in Spanish.

[88]Given the legal arguments of Juan de Vegara, Ortíz, María de Cazalla, and a servant named Diego de Aguilar, it looks as if an awareness of legal rules and mechanisms – even the Inquisition's – was not off-limits in sixteenth-century Spain. See n. 72 above, and Homza, *Religious Authority*, Chap. 1, and 228 n. 58, 229 n. 68, 230 n. 77.

[89]Coronel's *Tractatus syllogismorum* was published in 1508, and his *Physice perscrutationes* in 1511. Bataillon, *Erasmo y España*, 17, 137–138, 140–141, 443 n. 21.

[90]'...con cuya venida descanso mucho mi anima: porque passando este negocio por manos de persona en quien se junta con las muchas letras, el temor de dios; quedara mi justicia más manifiesta.' *Proceso*, f. 210r.

testimony that would be enough to have her placed in this public jail.' Still, [Coronel said] I was obliged to think that the Reverend Archbishop would not order such a thing without sufficient cause; and although I had a clear understanding that the reasons given to me in the last conversation with the Reverend Archbishop...were not enough for such imprisonment, a negative proposition was not made known to me, which was necessary to know if I were to have a decisive reason to make my reprehension [of Manrique] just.[91]

Coronel's training in logic was obvious. It also was no accident that he referred to Manrique as an *archbishop* throughout, since he wanted to stress the uprightness of his superior's actions.

In short, Coronel wanted Ortíz to think about credentials, intelligence, and obligation. It was the Inquisitor-General's station to review what was alleged and to pronounce what was proven. Ortíz might guess who the witnesses were, he might even think they had lied, but it was Manrique's business to judge their credibility, just as it was his responsibility to authorize testimony that might have appeared later. Moreover, before Ortíz's own arrest, no one had ever told him explicitly that the evidence to seize Francisca was insufficient, which was the 'negative proposition' that he needed to justify his sermon. Finally, Ortíz simply could not know whether additional deponents had come forward before March 31. He was ignorant of the facts, though Manrique was not; because he was ignorant and yet preached the sermon anyway, he was guilty of reckless judgment against a superior. He had added 'sin to sin' when he wasn't content to keep his bad opinion to himself, but voiced it in public.[92]

Ortíz replied with even more specific aspersions. If Fray Gil and Diego López had testified, they undoubtedly had lied, no matter when they

---

[91] 'Arguyo me este señor Doctor, diziendo que dado caso que asi era verdad, que despues de las platicas que yo tuve con el Reverendo Manrique, no avian venido testigos contra esta sierva de dios que tuviessen algun nuevo testimonio sufficiente para la mandar poner en esta carcel publica, pero que yo era obligado a pensar del reverendo arcobispo que no mandaria tal cosa sin causa sufficiente; y que aunque yo tenia claro conocimiento que las causas que me avia dado en la postrera platica que avia tenido antes con el reverendo señor arcobispo...no eran sufficientes para tal prision: pero no me constava a my [sic] una proposicion negativa que era neccessaria de saber para que yo tuviesse causa perentoria que hiziesse ser justa mi reprehension.' *Proceso*, f. 210r–v.

[92] Ortíz's rendition of Coronel's arguments was, 'que aunque yo supiesse ser ella verdadera sierva de Cristo, y aunque los testigos fuessen falsos; pues es justo que el juez juzgue segun lo allegado y provado; y entienda en pesquisar y inquirir lo que se alego. Y yo no sabia no aver venido tales testigos. Siguiesse que temerariamente juzgue y pense ser pecador en este hecho el Reverendo Señor Manrique; y que añadi pecado a pecado quando no contento de concebir este mal juizio dentro de mi, lo hable en publico.' *Proceso*, f. 210r–v.

deposed, and hence their evidence should be moot. Given the Inquisitor-General's negligence and bias, he probably ignored the falsity of these witnesses, or, if they never came forward at all, he simply kept the process in play until he had the necessary evidence to keep Francisca in prison.[93] It was perfectly plausible that Manrique had actively drummed up evidence against the beata, after the fact. And false, non-existent, or retroactive depositions were fraudulent grounds for an inquisition trial. Ortíz maintained, 'it was absolute heresy to imprison people without sufficient evidence, just as would occur in the reverse.'[94]

He didn't think hypothetical evidence was convincing, either. Ortíz had noticed Coronel's use of the conditional voice, and tackled him on it. He declared,

> ...After I spoke to the Reverend Lord Archbishop of Sevilla, until the last day of March [1529]...no new testimony arose that was sufficient to justly order her imprisonment. Everyone has been insisting on this testimony, not as if it were true in fact, but as if it were possible, affirming that this contingency alone – that other witnesses had come forward – is enough to convict me of having sinned....[If other witnesses had shown up], they would have told me, because evidence from acceptable witnesses would have been the clearest way for me to know that I had erred...[95]

Coronel said witnesses existed because the Inquisitor-General's character and inquisitorial procedure dictated it. In this instance, Ortíz denied that the Inquisition had functioned properly in the abstract, because the logic of his own experience made it implausible.

---

[93] *Proceso*, f. 211r. Ortíz also believed that one of his own, highly emotional letters to Francisca could have been used by Manrique as another excuse to imprison the *beata*: Ortiz had left the letter in his monastic cell, where it was discovered by Fray Barnabás, who consequently insisted on Francisca's arrest. For Ortíz, what mattered here was the fact that both Manrique and the guardian already possessed negative opinions of Francisca, and then treated the amatory letter as proof of their negative outlook. Neither actually possessed persuasive evidence against her. For the discovery of the letter, and Ortíz's fear that it could have provoked Francisca's arrest, ff. 213v–214r.

[94] *Proceso*, f. 212r.

[95] '...que despues que yo hable al Reverendo Señor Arcobispo de Sevilla, hasta el postrero dia de marco inclusive...no avia venido otro nuevo testimonio que fuesse sufficiente para justamente mandar la encarcelar: porque todos han hecho hincapie, no en lo que de derecho fue, sino en lo que fuera possible, affirmando que esta sola possibilidad que uvo para aver venido otros testigos, basta que no me pueda excusar de aver pecado en lo que predique....ya me lo uvieran dicho y authenticamente mostrado, porque la evidencia de estos testigos sufficientes, fuera la más evidente razon para que yo me conociera aver errado...' *Proceso*, ff. 210v–211r.

Throughout his conversations with Coronel, Ortíz maintained the same legal objections but magnified the details and the malediction. He stretched his defense strategy too, by producing another, even more powerful witness than Friar Muñoztello: he now adduced the support of Adrian of Utrecht, who was inquisitor-general in 1519, supervised Francisca's first inquisition investigation the same year, and became Pope Adrian VI in 1522.[96] The fact that Adrian had died in 1523 did not make him any less useful: not only did his stature trump Manrique's, but Adrian could compete with Manrique as an eyewitness, since each of these inquisitors-general had seen exactly one incident involving the beata.[97] It was Adrian's decision on Francisca's case that mattered most: Ortíz reported that in 1519, Francisca had abjured with only a slight penance, and noted that Adrian had only punished her because 'it seemed to him that such happy eyes and so much laughter were not appropriate for a servant of God;' if Adrian and the inquisitors had detected heresy, they never would have allowed her to remain free throughout the 1520s.[98] Ortíz finally insisted that he could prove these things were true, because he had yet one more witness to them, namely Adrian's secretary, who was still alive. With these comments, Ortíz produced a parallel model of inquisitorial authority — Adrian and his secretary — which might rival Manrique and *his* secretary. Ortíz clearly believed his pair could outweigh anyone or anything Manrique managed to produce.

The problem, though, was that Ortíz's inventiveness extended only so far, and he remained vulnerable to objections. For example, he had justified his public sermon of April 6 through the public nature of Manrique's sin, but Coronel turned that equation in an unexpected direction. He told Ortíz,

> You publicly said that a public sin was committed in the imprisonment of this person [Francisca], and from here, it follows that the inquisitors who ordered her imprisoned were public sinners, and thus their sin was public, and obvious to the pueblo. [But] this is clearly false, because though *you* knew the sin, *the community* did not, whereby it follows that you have unjustly deprived the inquisitors of their reputation...[99]

---

[96] Ortíz never actually listed Muñoztello or Adrian as defense witnesses, so their value to his case was minimal on a practical level. Like Juan de Vergara, Ortíz basically refused to mount a defense.

[97] Vergara too would summon Adrian VI against the inquisitors in Toledo: Homza, *Religious Authority*, 42–43.

[98] '...porque le parecio que tenía los ojos alegres y que tanta risa no convenia a sierva de dios.' *Proceso*, f. 243r.

[99] 'vos dixistes publicamente que se avia cometido un pecado publico en la prision de esta persona; y de aqui, se sigue que los que la mandaron prender fueron publicos pecadores, y por consiguiente, su pecado era publico y manifiesto

By fixing Ortíz's terms and extrapolating to their reasonable conclusion, Coronel put the friar in the position of having said that Toledan society viewed the Toledo inquisitors as public sinners. Our defendant responded, weakly, that 'public' could connote different things, that his phrase *pecado publico* had a different meaning from Coronel's *publico pecado*, and that he had a right to give his homily even if Manrique's sin were not well-known. One month later, Ortíz was told he had no first-hand knowledge of the testimony collected or the diligencias undertaken in 1519 or 1529, but was simply 'sticking his hand into someone else's wheat' when he objected to the Inquisition without legal training.[100] He replied that though it was true he knew none of the details, he was sure the inquisitors' diligencias were not up to God's standards.[101]

In both these instances, the interrogators were highly incisive about language and just as adamant about professional qualifications, and they forced Ortíz to back away from his assertions. He could have been undermined by theoretical guidelines, too. When it came to false witnesses, the Inquisition required all deponents to swear an oath that their testimony was true, and they could be charged with heresy if they testified falsely. But when it came to men who were not under oath when they lied, and who had told their falsehoods in the past, inquisitors could employ their testimony if they believed that they were currently acting for the benefit of religious orthodoxy: thus the depositions of Fray Gil and Diego López could be valid.[102] Finally, though two witnesses or a confession were the ultimate standards of proof, and witnesses should possess legal majority and decent characters, testimony from the infamous could be accepted, given the seriousness of heresy.[103] The fact that Ortíz was trying to recuse witnesses in someone else's trial did not help his efforts, either.

Yet however implausible Ortíz's arguments might have become, he still argued with the Inquisition according to concepts and vocabulary that came from inquisitorial law. He stressed the pivotal role of human inquiry. He fixed on the importance of multiple witnesses. He knew that public character — and publicly-known contradictions — ought to affect the persuasiveness of one's testimony. Of course, Spanish Inquisition trials routinely feature objections over singularity, enmity, and ratification where witnesses are concerned. But Ortíz's writings illustrate how much broader

---

al pueblo. Lo qual era manifiestamente falso, porque aunque vos conociades el pecado, no le sabian ellos, de lo qual se sigue que injustamente quitastes a los senores inquisidores quanto fue de vuestra parte la fama...' *Proceso*, f. 217r–v.

[100]This objection came from Fernando Niño, the Suprema member, in May 1529: *Proceso.*, f. 100r–v.

[101]*Proceso*, f. 100r.

[102]Eimeric, *El manuel de los inquisidores*, 250.

[103]Eimeric, *El manuel de los inquisidores*, 249–250.

and deeper exceptions could be at even this early stage of inquisition history, for he was willing to pursue his objections to their ultimate end. He did not just reject a specific deposition, but went on to tie that affidavit to the director of the entire inquisitorial system; in the process, he remembered damaging anecdotes about everyone. He was dangerous not only because he claimed to be inspired by God, but because he could cite details of legal malfeasance; the threat that he posed helps to explain why three different authorities cross-examined him in an effort to make him retract. His first interrogator, Coronel, tried to shake him with a sense of professionalism and a statement of the theoretical maxims: inquisitors-generals had certain obligations inherent in their office, while rules of secrecy blocked defendants from knowing who said what to whom. The friar understood those maxims and insisted they had not been in play: he grounded his objections in historical specificity, and spurned Coronel's attempt to make the inquisitorial system off-limits.

It is worth remembering, though, that Ortíz always flipped between legal and theological language. After he rebuked Manrique for not investigating lying witnesses, he immediately offered to act like Daniel and confound them himself; as frequently as he called himself a theologian, he just as often asserted that he was Francisca Hernández's lawyer. This ability to move between and even blend the theological and the legal is best demonstrated by one of Ortíz's most telling maneuvers: his attempt to tie his own salvation to the identification of prosecution witnesses. In the primer cuaderno, Ortíz declared that he was worried about his potential sin for having delivered the April sermon; he said he would think about retracting his statements if someone could convince him that he had erred. He then wrote that the *single best way* to persuade him would be to show him the depositions against Francisca Hernández, 'because evidence from these acceptable witnesses would [be] the clearest way' for him to see his mistake.[104]

There's no doubt that Ortíz could have worried about his sins vis-à-vis his homily; by raising his own potential damnation, he was also appealing to the inquisitors' primary objective to save souls. But if he had been granted access to the prosecution's testimony, and then been able to communicate the details to Francisca, she in turn could have identified and disqualified the witnesses against her. Notably, requests for depositions were not the only favors Ortíz asked of the tribunal: he also begged for a servant named Rios to be placed in Francisca's cell, and justified his petition with long, pathetic descriptions of Francisca's poor health.[105] Provocatively, in this period inquisition prisoners in Toledo were having their servants act as go-betweens among the cells, and carry letters and advice from one prisoner to another. Ortíz could have asked for Rios in

---

[104] *Proceso*, f. 211r.
[105] *Proceso*, ff. 38v, 47v, 67r, 71v–72r.

order to provide Francisca with additional eyes and ears inside the tribunal; Rios would have been trustworthy because she was the niece of Antonio de Medrano, one of Francisca's most ardent admirers.[106] What makes Ortíz's entreaties for prosecution testimony and a faithful servant that much more intriguing is the fact that he and Francisca were imprisoned in the Toledo tribunal at the same time, and allegedly visited each other's cells through holes in the walls, despite theoretical rules to the contrary.[107]

The inquisition ordeals of Francisca Hernández have been lost, and even if we possessed them, they probably would not tell us whether she coached the friar, or vice-versa. We know that at least one inquisitor, Alonso de Mexía, spoke extensively to Ortíz about Francisca's case; previous scholarship has contended that Ortíz only recanted in 1532 because he finally saw damaging depositions against her.[108] No matter what he learned or what he did with the information, though, his trial illustrates the difficulty of capturing a historical 'voice' in a univocal way, despite a consistent vocabulary, lengthy holograph writings, and a relative absence of custodial interference. Ortíz complicates the historian's task because he believed that he could act as a theologian and a lawyer all at once, and argue about the law in multiple ways, from various sources. The legal polyphony that he promoted sharpens our understanding of him, and should prompt us to ask new questions of inquisition sources, given what they may reveal about the fluidity of legal culture in early modern Spain.

College of William and Mary
Williamsburg, VA

---

[106]The extent of the prison scandal at Toledo can be deduced from the *interrogatorios* preserved in Cazalla, *Proceso de la inquisición*; for references to Francisca and Ortíz's alleged meetings, see 543, 548, 553–554. Also Homza, *Religious Authority*, Chap. 1.

[107]Selke contended that Francisca could not have influenced Ortíz because the two could not have met in prison until after June 1531. She did not cite any evidence to support her claim: *El Santo Oficio*, 305. In the period 1529–1534, Francisca was shuffled between the Toledo and the Valladolid tribunals of the Inquisition; prisoners' secret correspondence was circulating in the Toledo prison as of 1530.

[108]When Ortíz replied to the *fiscal*'s formal accusation, he said that Inquisitor Mexia had spoken to him about 'important testimony' against Francisca: *Proceso*, f. 151r. Selke argued that Mexia literally showed that testimony to the friar – *El Santo Oficio*, p. 299 – but produced no evidence to confirm it.

Works Cited

Manuscript Sources

Halle, Martin-Luther-Universität. *Sondersammlungen.* Sign. Yc 2° 20 (2). *Proceso contra Fray Francisco Ortíz, de la orden del San Francisco*, 1529–1532.

Madrid, Archivo Histórico Nacional. Sección de la Inquisición. Libro 1231, ff. 634–637. 'Dubiae quae in causa presenti videntur.' 1526 Inquisition consultation on the reality of witchcraft.

Published Sources

Ahlgren, Gillian T.W. 'Francisca de los Apostoles: a Visionary Voice for Reform in Sixteenth-Century Toledo' pp. 119–133 in *Women in the Inquisition*, ed. Mary E. Giles. Baltimore and London: Johns Hopkins University Press, 1998.

Arguello, Gaspar Isidro de. *Instrucciones del Santo Oficio de la Inquisicion.* Madrid: Imprenta Real, 1630.

Asensio, Eugenio. 'El Maestro Pedro de Orellana, minorita luterano: Versos y procesos' pp. 785–795 in *La Inquisición Española: Nueva visión, nuevos horizontes*, ed. Joaquin Pérez Villanueva. Madrid: Siglo Veintiuno Editores, 1978.

Bataillon, Marcel. *Erasmo y España.* Mexico City: Fondo de Cultura Económica, S.A. de C.V., 1950.

Bilinkoff, Jodi. 'A Spanish Prophetess and Her Patrons: the Case of María de Santo Domingo.' *Sixteenth Century Journal* 23 (1992): 21–35.

Caro Baroja, Julio. *El señor inquisidor y otras vidas por oficio.* Madrid: Alianza Editorial, 1968.

Cazalla, María de. *Proceso de la inquisición contra María de Cazalla*, ed. Milagros Ortega Costa. Madrid: Fundación Universitaria Española, 1978.

Contreras, Jaime. *El Santo Oficio de la Inquisición en Galicia, 1560–1700.* Madrid: Akal, 1982.

Dedieu, Jean-Pierre. *L'Administration de la Foi: l'Inquisition de Tolède XVI–XVIII siècle.* Bibliothèque de la Casa de Velázquez, vol. 7. Madrid: Casa de Velázquez, 1989.

Eimeric, Nicolau. *El manual de los inquisidores.* Trans. Francisco Martín, with commentary by Francisco Peña. Barcelona: Muchnik Editores, 1983.

Giles, Mary E. 'Francisca Hernández and the Sexuality of Religious Dissent' pp. 77–97 in *Women in the Inquisition*, ed. Mary E. Giles. Baltimore and London: Johns Hopkins University Press, 1998.

González Novalin, Jose Luis. *El Inquisidor-General Fernando de Valdes (1483–1568): su vida y obra.* 2 vols. Oviedo: Universidad de Oviedo, 1968 and 1971.

Haliczer, Stephen. *Inquisition and Society in the Kingdom of Valencia, 1478–1834.* Berkeley: University of California Press, 1990.

Homza, Lu Ann. *Religious Authority in the Spanish Renaissance.* Baltimore and London: Johns Hopkins University Press, 2000.

Kagan, Richard L. *Lucrecia's Dreams: Politics and Prophecy in Sixteenth-Century Spain.* Berkeley: University of California Press, 1995.

Kuehn, Thomas. *Law, Family, and Women: Toward a Legal Anthropology of Renaissance Italy*. Chicago: The University of Chicago Press, 1991.

Llorca, Bernardino, SJ. *La inquisición española y los alumbrados*. Bibliotheca Salmanticensis, no. 32. Salamanca: Universidad Pontificia de Salamanca, 1980.

Monter, E. William. *Frontiers of Heresy: the Spanish Inquisiton from the Basque Lands to Sicily*. Cambridge: Cambridge University Press, 1990.

Muñoz Fernández, Ángela. *Beatas y santas neocastellanas: ambivalencia de la religión, correctoras del poder (ss XIV–XVII)*. Madrid: Comunidad de Madrid, 1994.

Nalle, Sara T. *Mad for God: Bartolomé Sánchez, the Secret Messiah of Cardenete*. Charlottesville, VA: University Press of Virginia, 2001.

Nalle, Sara T. *God in La Mancha*. Baltimore and London: Johns Hopkins University Press, 1992.

Prado Moura, Angel de. *Inquisición y inquisidores en Castilla: el Tribunal de Valladolid durante la crisis del Antiguo Regimen*. Valladolid: Secretario de Publicaciones, Universidad de Valladolid, 1995.

Schutte, Anne Jacobson. *Aspiring Saints: Pretense of Holiness, Inquisition, and Gender in the Republic of Venice, 1618–1750*. Baltimore and London: Johns Hopkins University Press, 2001.

Schutte, Anne Jacobson. *Autobiography of an Aspiring Saint: Cecilia Ferrazzi*. Chicago: University of Chicago Press, 1996.

Selke, Angela. *The Conversos of Majorca: Life and Death in a Crypto-Jewish Community in XVII Century Spain*. Hispania Judaica, vol. 5. Jerusalem: Magnes Press, 1986.

Selke, Angela. *El Santo Oficio de la Inquisición: Proceso de Dr. Francisco Ortíz (1529–1532)*. Madrid: Ediciones Guadarrama, 1968.

Selke, Angela. 'Vida y muerte de Juan López de Celain.' *Bulletin Hispanique* 62 (1960): 136–162.

Selke, Angela. 'El caso del Bachiller Antonio de Medrano, iluminado epicúreo del siglo xvi.' *Bulletin Hispanique* 58 (1956): 393–420.

Zarri, Gabriella. *Finzione e santità tra medioevo ed età moderna*. Turin: Rosenberg & Sellier, 1991.

A Bridge between Renaissance and Counter-Reformation: Some Sources of Theatine Spirituality

William V. Hudon

The struggle to identify the similarities and differences between Renaissance and Reformation culture in early modern Italy, to say nothing of comprehending those differences and similarities, remains the subject of vigorous debate among historians. Those asserting an essential difference between the cultures settled early upon a characterization of the Reformation—or 'Counter-Reformation' when describing Italy—as repressive and retrograde, the very antithesis of the Renaissance. A host of scholars continue to rely on such a depiction of Italy after the sack of Rome. They quarrel with historians who have insisted that similarities in the two cultures existed in their common literary humanism and ardent religiosity. Despite pronouncements that this dichotomy and the quarrel, plus polemics over the reliability of related terms like 'Catholic Reform' and 'Tridentine Reformation' were all passé, the quarrels go on. Such pronouncements are now more than a decade old, but they never reflected contemporary historiographic realities, nor do they today. New ways of characterizing the sixteenth century, and not just in Italy, turn today on its alleged promotion of 'disciplining' and the efficacy of its presumably systematic 'social control.' To some, these terms may sound innovative. But when applied to Italy, they suggest little other than the same old repressive 'counter' reforming by yet another name.[1]

There is a subthesis within this overall assessment of early modern European culture that relates to religious women in that age. Historians treating religious women especially in Italy frequently describe their

---

[1] I have elsewhere laid out the tortured history of the quarrel over the problem of naming and accurately describing the early modern religious history of Italy. See Hudon, 'Religion and society,' and more recently, Hudon, 'The papacy.' An even better job was done by John W. O'Malley. See O'Malley, *Trent and all that*. For another overview of the problem, see Zardin, 'Controriforma.'

condition and status in fairly dismal terms. While there may have been a Renaissance for men that was shut down by expansive imperial and papal authority in the Counter-Reformation, there was no rebirth to speak of for women, only repression. Any influence they may have exercised over developing early modern religious thought and institutions was quickly snuffed out. It was an era, according to some historians, in which women entering convents were placed there against their will, and out of financial, not religious, motivation. This incarceration was then perpetuated by rapidly centralizing papal authority, through monastic rules on claustration rigidified by the male clerics who dictated the decrees of the Council of Trent. While being held powerless in such a condition, the religious ideas and attitudes of these women, with virtually no exceptions, many believe, were discounted and had virtually no influence upon men.[2] While there is no doubt that portions of this stereotype contain truth, neither is there any doubt that it is an oversimplification that cannot stand unqualified against careful analysis of sources written by and about women in this period. A number of historians have stepped forward to outline the important qualifications needed to move away from the stereotype to a more human portrait of the era. They have indicated that in certain contexts, women could and did act with creativity, strength and determination, subverting efforts to restrict their autonomy and power that are today too frequently seen as driven simply by gender. The examples of such women are not limited to the few blockbuster personalities we associate with early modern culture, either.[3]

The development of the Theatine order of clerics regular during the sixteenth century provides a perfect case study for testing the old dichotomies and standard images associated with early modern Italian society. At the foundation of this order stood not just the infamous Gian Pietro Carafa (1476–1559), the intransigent inquisitor and man responsible

---

[2] The essay that set the terms of this general position was written by Joan Kelly-Gadol. See Kelly-Gadol, 'Did Women Have a Renaissance?' Other examples can be found in both specialized and general historical works. For some examples, see Delumeau, *Le péché*; Brown, *Immodest acts*; Ruggiero, *Binding passions*; Klapisch-Zuber, *Women, family*; Firpo, 'Paola Antonia Negri'; and Jantzen, *Power, gender*.

[3] Among the best of these are the recent works of Anne Jacobson Schutte. See her edition of Ferrazzi, *Autobiography*, 3–18, and Schutte, *Aspiring saints*. For some others, see Blaisdell, 'Angela Merici'; Harline and Put, 'A bishop'; King, *Women*; and Zarri, *Le sante vive*. A recent work asserts that nuns developed techniques to protect their own interests even during the eleventh and twelfth centuries, when Roman leaders defined the clerical world as womanless and eliminated most of the direct influence women had previously maintained over churchmen and ecclesiastical institutions: McNamara, *Sisters in arms*.

for the reestablishment of the Roman ghetto. Also present was a rather different co-founder, Gaetano da Theine (c.1480–1547), and his spiritual advisor, a nun from Brescia named Laura Mignani (1480–1525). They exchanged letters between 1517 and 1521, just prior to the foundation of the Theatine order in 1524.[4] In the letters, Thiene revealed his reliance upon Mignani for guidance, advice and intercession in his efforts to build a stronger spiritual relationship with Christ. He idealized her relationship, which he described as spousal, with their common savior. At the other end of the sixteenth century, stood another Theatine inspired in part by late medieval feminine spirituality, Lorenzo Scupoli (1530–1610). He was perhaps the most important devotional writer in the history of the Theatine order. He extensively employed the ideas of Camilla Battista da Varano (1458–1524), a Franciscan nun and rough contemporary of Laura Mignani, in the composition of his own classic contribution to western devotional literature, *Il combattimento spirituale* (*The spiritual combat*). His revised and edited version of Varano's *I dolori mentali di Gesù nella sua passione* (*On the mental sufferings of Jesus during his passion*) even appeared in a nineteenth century edition of his own *Opere*.[5] Consideration of these texts can provide the opportunity to rethink not just stereotypes associated with the status of women and of Catholic action, or better, 'reaction,' in the early modern period. The texts also provide further, Italian, evidence of a phenomenon identified quite sometime ago by John Van Engen and others: that there was a decided connection between late medieval spirituality and devotional expressions more commonly associated with the literature of the 'Counter' Reformation.[6]

The reality of this connection is enjoying something of a revival. It was not at all uncommon to identify points of similarity in the devotional lives and literature of nuns and monks between the later Middle Ages and the Counter-Reformation about two scholarly generations ago. Old-fashioned survey works like Kenneth Scott Latourette's *History of Christianity* and the classic treatment of the spirituality of the Middle Ages by Jean Le Clercq and his colleagues, emphasized connections. They found an affective approach in the devotional works of both eras. When explaining

---

[4] For more on both of them, see Hudon, *Theatine spirituality*, 16–65. This volume also contains their surviving correspondence, in English translation.

[5] For additional information on both Scupoli and Varano, see Hudon, *Theatine spirituality*, 42–62. The edition of Scupoli's works that contains Varano's *I dolori mentali* is Scupoli, *Opere*, 301–326.

[6] Van Engen, *Devotio moderna*, 10–11. I am grateful to Christopher Bellitto for first bringing Van Engen's point to my attention. A similar assertion was made by Clarissa W. Atkinson in her work on Margery Kempe, a fourteenth century devotional writer that she felt resembled Counter-Reformation authors. See Atkinson, *Mystic and pilgrim*, 151–155.

the actions of women in spiritual life across the two eras they emphasized common reliance upon Franciscan spirituality and upon its meditation techniques that utilized the humanity—and especially the passion—of Christ.[7] Historians who wrote in the 1970's and 1980's and traced the experience of women religious, on the other hand, located a rather firm disconnection instead. For them, the earlier, late medieval, period witnessed the last flowering of a relatively independent female spirituality and devotional vitality that was snuffed out in the repressive, male, clerically dominated world of the later, Counter-Reformation period. Everything interesting, from apostolic initiatives, to homosexual eroticism, to mystical devotions, was squashed amid the post-Tridentine move to control religious women, essentially by claustration.[8] Recent investigations have illustrated that plans for claustration were implemented with only limited success in the first hundred years after Trent, and that where those aims succeeded, it was as often due to the interests of members of the laity as to the plans of clergy.[9] More recent studies have also acknowledged that many of the female voices in devotional literature from the Counter-Reformation—both the well-known and the not so well-known—operated, as Anne Jacobson Schutte explained it, in part as subjugated objects, but in part as active subjects, as well.[10] Some of the most scholarly recent studies, however, rely far more heavily on images

---

[7] For some examples, see Latourette, *History*, 2:697–702, 2:840–883; Le Clercq, et al., *Spirituality*, 298–300, 469–472; and Petry, *Late Medieval Mysticism*, 17–20, 263–69, 392–398. Most scholars looking at these topics are anxious to read what Bernard McGinn has to say about the early modern period in his forthcoming *Change and continuity in western mysticism*, the fourth installment in his massive, magisterial series entitled *The Presence of God*.

[8] For some examples, see Brown, *Immodest acts*, 3–20, 134–137; Firpo, 'Paolo Antonia Negri,' 58–59, 64–65, 71–80; Tomizza, *Heavenly supper*, 165–174; and Jantzen, *Power, gender*, xii–xvii, 242–277. Jean Delumeau, whose classic, *Le péché et la peur* is available in English translation, characterized the entire era, beginning to end, as one dominated by exaggerated pessimism and contempt for the world. He recognized that his history of guilt could not be reduced to a simple history of clerical power, admitted that fear can be either salutary or destructive, and insisted that historians should not pass judgment on the past, but he went ahead and did so anyway, finding the pessimism 'dangerous,' reflective of a 'seige mentality,' and 'oppressive.' See Delumeau, *Sin and fear*, 3–5, 9–33, 555–557.

[9] In a recent study of the Ursulines, an early modern order that endured perhaps most infamous example of post-Tridentine repressive claustration, Charmarie J. Blaisdell argued that the impetus to control the group must be located partly in the families, not just in the male, clerical authorities above these sisters. See Blaisdell, 'Angela Merici,' 106–116.

[10] Ferrazzi, *Autobiography*, 13.

of disconnection than do the authors of more popular recent explanations.[11]

The relationship between Laura Mignani and Gaetano da Thiene can illustrate just how misleading is the suggestion that late medieval and Counter-Reformation spiritualities were neatly, let alone purely, disconnected. The Brescian nun and the soon to be co-founder of the Theatine order bound themselves together in a relationship of spiritual direction between 1518 and 1522. Thiene revealed some of the outlines of that relationship in letters he wrote to Mignani over those same years. The other side of this correspondence, unfortunately, has been lost. These two individuals, inspired by their understanding of scripture and by the Christocentric, imitative devotional life most often associated with the so-called Northern, 'Christian' Renaissance, developed an intense mutual direction, encouraging and advising one another.

A great deal more is known about Thiene than about Mignani. He was born in Vicenza in 1480, and was a student of philosophy and law at Padua, where he received degrees in both civil and canon law in 1505. He aimed at a curial career, and purchased an office in good Renaissance tradition, during the administration of Julius II (1503–1513). He passed through the minor clerical orders in 1516 and 1517, and then was ordained a priest against the wishes of his mother. He experienced visions of the Nativity, of Christ's circumcision, and of the visit of Magi, and joined the Oratory of Divine Love in Rome. He engaged in hospital work and priestly ministry in Rome, Vicenza, Verona, Venice, and perhaps Brescia between 1518 and the foundation of the Theatine order in 1524. In Vicenza, he placed himself under the spiritual direction of Battista Carioni da Crema (c.1460–1534), a Dominican friar in a convent Thiene's mother had endowed. Thiene met Laura Mignani through a Brescian cleric named Bartolomeo Stella (1488–1554), who also, at Thiene's recommendation, joined the Oratory.[12] Laura was the daughter of Matteo Mignani, a member

---

[11] Compare, for instance, the balanced treatment in the brief (140 page) study in Ranft, *Women and the religious life*, with the series of essays in Scaraffia and Zarri, *Donne e fede*. The latter may sport excellent essays by Anne Jacobson Schutte, E. Ann Matter, and others, but in key sections—like those by Giulia Barone and Gabriella Zarri—the spirituality of the late medieval period is fully disconnected from that of the Counter-Reformation. Barone concluded her essay with the assertion that 'a whole era,' in devotional life 'came to an end.' Zarri illustrated the continuing scholarly popularity of identifying disconnection in her statements that the prophetic tension aiming at church reform 'exhausted itself' between 1530 and 1560 as a 'transformation' of formerly independent female monastic governance was accomplished through 'rigorous enclosure' with 'bars and bolts.' See Scaraffia and Zarri, *Women and faith*, 42–71, 96, 103.

[12] For more on Thiene and the Oratory of Divine Love, see Vezzosi, *I scrittori*,

of the Brescian nobility. She became an Augustinian nun at the convent of Santa Croce in Brescia in 1491, twenty years after its foundation. She apparently was renowned for her piety, austerity, and penitential practices, and many sought her advice. She corresponded on spiritual matters with the duchesses of both Ferrara, (Lucretia Borgia) and of Urbino, (Elisabetta Gonzaga). More important for her contribution to the development of Theatine spirituality were her contacts with far lesser-known male clerics like Thiene, Bartolomeo Scaini di Salò, and Stella. She was a spiritual director to all of them.

Mignani and Thiene engaged in a fascinating relationship that amounted to mutual spiritual direction. There can be no doubt that from Thiene's point of view, Mignani provided all the important direction. He constantly referred to her as his spiritual mother and praised her devotional prowess, suggesting that he hoped to gain strength in his own faith through their relationship. For him, she was the powerful one. 'The divine fire so lights up in you,' he explained, that even those distant from her, like himself, 'receive heat,' from the 'glowing blaze' Christ had promised to cast upon the earth.[13] Thiene sought her direction especially after the death of his own mother in 1520. Still, his letter to Mignani on that occasion reveals that he too gave her direction. Thiene acknowledged the importance of her direction at the beginning of the letter, relating that 'you make me thirst for Him, sweet mother.' He closed the letter with a postscript asking the other sisters living in Mignani's convent to 'compel' her 'to take me as her son, since the soul of my mother has departed.' In between these two passages is a remarkable paragraph where Thiene gave spiritual advice to her, urging her to imitate the saints and even Christ himself. 'Have in your heart St. Paul and St. Martin,' he recommended, 'in order to desire to remain here for the good of our neighbors.' He urged Mignani to remember that she 'must not seek more' for herself. 'Rather seek,' he told her, 'to forget yourself in everything for Jesus and Christ, and be only like Jesus, suffering for your neighbors.'[14] Only recovery of Mignani's side

---

2: 341–344; Paschini, *San Gaetano*, 7–27; Andreu, 'Introduzione,' xv–xxii; Jorgensen, 'Oratories,' 1–17, 143–298; Solfaroli Camillocci, *I devoti della carità*, 27–33, 78–104, 217–236; plus the biographical articles by Mas 'Gaétan de Thiene,' and by Andreu, 'Gaetano Thiene.' For an early biography, see Castaldo, *Vita*. There are no modern biographies. More on the relationships between Mignani, Thiene and Stella can be found in Cistellini, *Figure*, 56–103. Stella was a familiar (and *major domo*) of Cardinal Reginald Pole and a bit on their relationship can be found in the new biography of Pole: see Mayer, *Reginald Pole*, 72, 140.

[13]Gaetano Thiene to Laura Mignani, 18 January 1518, from Rome. For the text in English translation, see Hudon, *Theatine spirituality*, 72–74.

[14]Thiene to Mignani, 22 November 1520, from Vicenza, in Hudon, *Theatine spirituality*, 80–82.

of this correspondence, apparently lost, would allow complete understanding of the complexities in this mutual relationship.

If Thiene is representative, then the bulk of the advice sought and received from Mignani by her correspondents was spiritual, but on occasion, she also gave them practical advice. Mignani made a contribution, for example, to Thiene's developing notion of the importance of clerical reform, through consideration of financial matters. She had warned Bartolomeo Stella to abandon a plan to purchase a curial office in 1518, during the administration of Pope Leo X (1513–1521). Thiene indicated that he took the advice just as Stella did. Thiene was apparently considering such a purchase quite seriously, since he wrote to Mignani explaining his reasons. 'In order to marry my niece with a dowry,' he said, and to pay other undisclosed family 'debts,' there was in the curia 'only one affordable office.' The price was '2600 ducats, the money on which I live,' he added. He decided against making what might appear a perfectly reasonable investment, given his obvious responsibilities, but he did not. 'I know that your Charity advised Bartolomeo not to buy one, and so I have done the same,' he related. In asking for her prayers, he expressed hope for either the strength to endure poverty, or else the inspiration of God 'to sell all in order to have life.'[15] In his next surviving letter to Mignani, it seems that Thiene took the further step to negotiate sale of the office he had earlier purchased. On 8 June 1520 he wrote to her from Venice, unsure about 'what to think or do concerning the sale of my office.' In her earlier advice Thiene clearly perceived the voice of God, as he again suggested that he wanted to divest himself from attachments. He expressed hope, moreover, that 'Christ would purify my heart...so that I no longer may be a rebel to his holy will.'[16] Thiene here expressed concern over clerical possession of financial resources, specifically fixed income, that were later matters of contention when the new order was being established. When, in 1524, he finally gave up the office he described to Mignani in 1520, he was paid for it, of course. Gian Pietro Carafa, the co-founder of the order, had to give up several bishoprics in 1524 to participate in the founding, and he too received remuneration. The irony of the allegedly 'reform' inspired Theatine order coming into existence under these circumstances seems to have been lost on the participants. It is clear, however, that Mignani had something to do with Thiene's acceptance of the Gospel ideal of discipleship when reflecting upon his responsibilities as a priest.

---

[15]Thiene to Mignani, no date, but circa 1518–1520, from Vicenza, in Hudon, *Theatine spirituality*, 77–79. Cf. also Cistellini, *Figure*, 77–81.

[16]Theine to Mignani, 8 June 1520, from Vicenza, in Hudon, *Theatine spirituality*, 79–80.

Thiene looked for more than just advice from Mignani: he also sought her intercession. He asked Mignani for her advocacy on his behalf with the Virgin Mary. He even likened Mignani, on occasion, to Mary. In the midst of a long letter describing a visionary experience of the Nativity, Thiene asked Mignani to help him gain humility from Mary. 'I know,' he explained, 'that she wants the ministers of her sweet baby Jesus to be humble like her.' So, he reasoned, 'it is to hope I turn, so that my Patroness and Star will be begged by you for the gift, making a bond and assurance out of me.'[17] Thiene compared Mignani to Mary herself using a scriptural allusion and in an embarrassing circumstance: when Bartolomeo Stella had apparently contracted syphilis. Once he was healed physically, Thiene asked Mignani to intercede with Christ to return Stella's peace of mind. He likened Mignani to Mary at the wedding feast at Cana. He explained that Jesus did the favor Mary asked then, and might be willing to do the same this time 'for even if it is not the hour,' he wrote, 'if the Queen wishes it, Jesus will do it all.'[18] Thiene considered Mignani the mystical spouse of Christ and expressed confidence that her relationship with Christ could help him and many others. 'Pray that your Spouse may not disdain prayers from me,' he asked in 1517, 'but may answer me through you.' Some years later he went so far as to suggest that Mignani possessed some salvific powers herself. 'Desire,' he wrote, 'as I know you have, that all the world may be thrown upon you, so that they may be saved.' He urged her to note the anger of God over the misbehavior of contemporary Christians and to cry out, like Christ himself, with the words 'to me, to me you must convert yourselves.'[19] It is clear from this correspondence that Mignani and Thiene drew their inspiration from a scripturally based, Christocentric approach to the devotional life.

Thiene and Mignani exchanged letters that suggest their mutual commitment to a 'spiritual combat' image of the devotional life. This image is most often associated with the second generation Theatine Lorenzo Scupoli, and with Counter-Reformation spiritual militarism, rather than with early sixteenth century figures like Thiene and Mignani. Allusions to this concept recur in their correspondence. Thiene considered himself 'cold, lazy, and tied to the affections of this miserable life,' and described these three things as 'pestiferous enemies' against which he needed to conduct 'constant warfare,' in a 1518 letter to Mignani. In

---

[17] Thiene to Mignani, 28 January 1518, from Rome, in Hudon, *Theatine spirituality*, 72–73.

[18] Thiene to Mignani, no date, but circa 1518–1520, from Vicenza, in Hudon, *Theatine spirituality*, 78. Cf. Andreu, *Le lettere*, 24.

[19] Thiene to Mignani, 31 July 1517, from Rome, in Hudon, *Theatine spirituality*, 71, and Thiene to Mignani, 22 November 1520, from Vicenza, ibid., 81.

another letter from later that same year, Thiene described himself and his colleague Stella as devotional 'novices, devoid of spiritual arms,' struggling against an 'enemy [that] never rests,' but that he hoped could 'be put to flight.' In 1520, at the prospect of their journey to Rome, Thiene maintained that he and Stella needed 'to be armed from on high,' apparently because of the temptations he expected to find in that place to which Christ had 'commanded' them both.[20] When considered in light of the later writings of Scupoli, these passages suggest that the Theatine spirituality which developed in the later sixteenth, and in the seventeenth century, was at least as closely tied to the early sixteenth century origins of the order as it was to any dramatically new Counter-Reformation attitude.

It would be an oversimplification to suggest that Theatine spirituality underwent no change amid the shifting definitions of orthodoxy in the middle decades of the sixteenth century, however. Thiene himself provided evidence of some change in his correspondence with another nun, Maria Carafa, the sister of the co-founder of the Theatines. Thiene became the spiritual director of the Neapolitan convent in which she lived, and in which she became abbess. He wrote letters to her and the other sisters in the convent, known as the *Sapienza*, between 1533 and 1552. Thiene was much more directive in these letters than in his earlier ones to Mignani. He did not hesitate to correct her, or the sisters generally, when he believed they had made mistakes or if he considered them likely to diverge from the proper path. He did so on one instance when considering their practice of the divine office. He pithily rejected the 'choral' chant recitation that reportedly was in use there, and instructed Carafa to 'see that it is done in nothing other than a low chant.' He suggested that she ought to correct, and perhaps punish, the individual responsible for introducing the choral work.[21] Thiene also corrected Carafa on the employment, quite common in contemporary convents, of preferential treatment for particular sisters. He apparently considered it rather dangerous. 'See that you do not even think,' he told her, of assigning living quarters to a new sister, 'other than that described for all the other professed sisters.' To do so would 'snatch away glory from Christ,' he explained. It would also, he said, represent not just 'scandal,' but also a 'violation of your constitution.'[22] Still, there was another

---

[20]For these quotations, see the letters of Thiene to Mignani, 28 January 1518, from Rome, 7 August 1518 from Vicenza, and 22 November 1520 from Vicenza, in Hudon, *Theatine spirituality*, 72, 77, 81.

[21]Thiene to Carafa, no date, from Naples, in Hudon, *Theatine spirituality*, 106–107.

[22]Thiene to Carafa, no date, from Naples, in Hudon, *Theatine spirituality*, 105.

important side to the relationship between Thiene and Carafa. He viewed Carafa as a leader—a spiritual mother to be more precise—and he described this in words reminiscent of his correspondence with Mignani. 'The mother of children in the flesh,' he told Carafa, 'has pleasure in conceiving and experiences pain in giving birth.' He contrasted this with the experience of the spiritual mother who 'conceives with fear and sorrow but gives birth with joy.' He urged Carafa to be 'strong and composed' in her own spiritual mothering.[23] Thiene obviously viewed Carafa and her fellow sisters as embarked on the same journey as he: a journey toward spiritual perfection. He frequently related his own failings and recommended to them the same sort of humility he pursued himself.[24] Spiritual perfection was a state to which he hoped they would aspire. By implication, it was also a state he believed they could attain.

Other good reasons to reject the characterization of Renaissance and Counter-Reformation spiritualities as separate and disconnected can be found in the career of Camilla Battista da Varano, and in the history of the reception of her principal works, especially her text *I dolori mentali di Gesù*. A mystic and spiritual author, Camilla was born on 8 April 1458, the illegitimate daughter of Giulio Cesare da Varano, lord of Camerino. Despite her illegitimate birth, and perhaps in part because she was the first born of a man who was himself an orphan, she shared the life of her father's palace, not to mention the education typical of such fifteenth century northern Italian courts. She joined the Franciscan order in Urbino, in 1481. Later, she established a convent of Poor Clares in Camerino. According to her biographers, Varano led a life of great devotion and of intense desire for the reform of both monasticism and of the church at large. Her devotion and these desires surely were influenced by contemporary observant Franciscans, whose Christocentric popular preaching and rigorous pursuit of poverty were famous throughout the region.[25]

Varano wrote extensively, and her prose was the rather direct result of her maturing devotional life. After she heard the Lenten preaching of Francesco da Urbino in 1479, she initiated correspondence with him and composed a *Lauda della passione* in the very next year. After emerging from a period of psychological depression linked to familial opposition

---

[23]Thiene to Carafa, no date, from Naples, in Hudon, *Theatine spirituality*, 104–105.

[24]Ibid, letters #21, 22, 26, 36.

[25]For early biographies of Camilla, see Pascucci, *Vita*; V. da Porto S. Giorgio, *Vita della beata Battista*; and Marini, *Vita della beata Camilla*. There are also a number of twentieth century biographies of Camilla: Aringoli, *La beata*; Aringoli, et al., *Camilla*; Boccanera, *Biografia*; G. Papasogli, *Beata*; Cardarelli, *Camilla*; Giannini, *Storia*; and Luzi, *Camilla*. This last, most recent work seems to contain a considerable devotional agenda.

to her entrance into religious life, she wrote even more. She composed her *Ricordi di Gesù* in 1483, about a year after she completed her novitiate. After visions of the Virgin Mary and of Santa Chiara in the mid-1480's, she wrote in 1488 perhaps her most famous text, 'On the mental anguish of Jesus in his passion' (*I dolori mentali di Gesù*), at the insistence of her abbess, Pacifica da Urbino. In the text, Varano made a substantial, creative contribution to the development of western devotional literature. Varano's readers, both in her own day and across the one hundred years that separated her from the heart of the Counter-Reformation, recognized the importance of her contribution and creativity. Her writings, and the use made of them long after her death, are part of the information needed to humanize, rather than to falsely demonize or heroize, the history of women within the culture of the Counter-Reformation in early modern Italy.[26]

At first glance, this work by Varano seems perfectly conventional and completely predictable. She wrote this text as an extended treatment of the synoptic gospel story of agony of Jesus in the garden after the Last Supper.[27] In pursuing this theme, she remained solidly within the tradition of Franciscan spirituality developed since the thirteenth century, to consider the proper response to particular events—especially the sufferings and passion—in the life of Christ. Varano adhered to traditions and conventions when writing about herself, not just Jesus. She presented herself consistently in deferential, even self-deprecating terms that are representative of *topoi* in late medieval and early modern female devotional literature. To begin with, in a preface addressing the work to Pietro da Mogliano, her spiritual director, she insisted that she wrote only after being commanded to do so by her abbess, Sister Pacifica, who 'begged me again and again to write these things.' She then attributed all the ideas within the text to someone else, an unnamed sisted from the convent of Santa Chiara in Urbino. She stated this clearly in an introduction to the work, asserting that Christ, 'by his piety and grace,' made her 'worthy to communicate with a Franciscan sister from Santa Chiara,' who expressed these 'very devout things' to her. In her foreword to Mogliano, Varano indicated that she long desisted from writing, claiming that she would not do so 'until that sister was dead.' When pressed by Pacifica, Varano explained, she inserted attributive phrases referring to the other nun and

---

[26]There is a critical edition of her complete writings: Varano, *Le opere*. All quotations in this essay come from that edition, and the translations are my own. There is an English pamphlet edition of *I dolori mentali*: Varano, *The mental sorrows*. In the notes for my translations below, I have indicated the comparable passages in the earlier, somewhat defective, English translation.

[27]Matt. 26:36–46; Mk. 14:32–42; Lk. 22: 39–46.

wrote the introduction 'in order to validate the fiction, so that readers would not think that it was I.'[28] Varano reiterated this self-deprecation elsewhere in the text, and again quite conventionally, applied it to her religious colleagues and to all women generally. In a chapter otherwise devoted to assertions of the heroic sympathy and devotion of Mary Magdalen, Varano indicated that Christ told her that Magdalen was 'not as capable of those higher, profound things as John,' who experienced foreknowledge of the passion but never attempted to thwart its progress as she would have done.[29] In the dedication of the text to her confessor, Varano said that she wrote especially for women who look for comfort in the passion of Christ but who are intellectually incapable of doing so. She explained that 'not every intellect is fit to navigate in such a sea, especially us women who don't have much ability.'[30] She also utilized a theme identified as conventional among both male and female authors of works of piety in the late medieval period: the food to be derived from the passion of Christ. She attributed desire for such food to the sister whom she credited with the text, while admitting her own desire for the same food in her message to Mogliano. She also said that one desiring this food of the passion of Christ ought not to 'lick around the edges of the divine vessel of his humanity,' but rather enter and drink deeply.[31]

Varano may have utilized conventional, deferential language and assertions of humility, but she mixed that language and those assertions with decided spiritual self-confidence. Her self-deprecating statements, hence, have to be considered somewhat false, and not only because assertions of humility are—in any Christian context—claims to heroic, Christ-like behavior. She indicated that Christ is generous and gives special abilities to those who persevere. In the eighth chapter of his treatise, on the anguish Christ experienced in the garden due to the ingratitude of his creatures, she continued the 'fiction' that she was writing about another sister. While doing so, Varano alternated assertions of humility with references to graces she believed the sister had received, including a mystical marriage with Jesus. She explained that the unnamed sister's illumination came from 'Christ alone,' but that 'she felt such humility in her heart that she truly confessed to God and to all the celestial court that she had received more graces and blessings from God than Judas, [but] ...that she had betrayed [Jesus] worse [than he].' Still, according to Varano, this sister addressed Christ, saying, 'You...made me

---

[28]Varano, *Le opere*, 146, 154. Cf. Varano, *Mental sorrows*, 7.
[29]Varano, *Le opere*, 157. Cf. Varano, *Mental sorrows*, 18.
[30]Varano, *Le opere*, 172.
[31]Ibid. For the identification of the convention, see the numerous works of Caroline Walker Bynum, especially *Holy feast.*

your daughter and spouse, [and have made me capable of] more than a miracle: you have made me lead myself voluntarily to [this] place, [the convent], where I am.'[32] Once reading Varano's admission to Mogliano that the information in the treatise was based on what Christ had himself 'revealed' to her, and that the other, unnamed sister was a fiction, we are faced with a woman who apparently did not consider herself weak, powerless, or lacking in spiritual prowess at all. She thought herself capable of providing direction, and an example to others, albeit under the cover of an unnamed fellow Franciscan nun. She even expressed confidence in the ability of others to gain the same things that she had gained, telling Mogliano that 'God gives every person the ability that she seeks and desires.'[33]

Varano wrote her treatise on the agony in the garden with doctrinal creativity and bold imagery. While she made constant allusions to the Gospel in the treatise, she was selective in using Scripture, and creative in working with the text. She omitted, for example, any use of the image that is probably more automatically connected with the agony in garden than any other: the image of Jesus sweating drops of blood.[34] In addition to such selective use, she conflated Gospel stories to suit her literary purpose as well, inserting exposition on the Last Supper into her analysis of the agony. She related the story of the conversation between Jesus and his apostles at the moment when he washed their feet, and then composed a striking account of the unspoken thoughts of both Jesus and John at that moment. Christ revealed to her, she explained, that when he came to John's feet, John could not contain himself after what he had just witnessed: Jesus washing the feet of Judas. 'He threw both arms around my neck,' Christ told her, and 'held me,…pouring out most abundant tears.' 'Voicelessly he spoke to me,' Christ continued in Varano's retelling, 'and said, 'O dear master, brother, father, God and my Lord, how did your soul bear to wash—and then to kiss with your most holy mouth—those damned feet of that traitor dog?"[35] In the same chapter she played not only with Gospel narrative, but also with gender, describing Jesus with the physical characteristics—namely the long hair—of the woman who washed his feet when he ate dinner at the home of a Pharisee.[36] In addition, Varano explained unspoken thoughts in the mind of Jesus when washing the feet of Judas. She used a decidedly vulgar word, '*escorreti*,'

---

[32] Varano, *Le opere*, 165. Cf. Varano, *Mental sorrows*, 25.
[33] Varano, *Le opere*, 172.
[34] Lk. 22:44.
[35] Varano, *Le opere*, 162–163. Cf. Varano, *Mental sorrows*, 23.
[36] For the Gospel accounts, Lk. 7:36–50; Jn. 12, 1–8. Varano, *Le opere*, 162. Cf. Varano, *Mental sorrows*, 22.

to describe the odor emanating from the feet of Judas, and then related Jesus's thoughts: "O Judas, what have I done to you that you would so cruelly betray me? O son of perdition, why are you separating yourself from your father and master?' Varano put another question into the mouth of Jesus: 'If you wanted thirty pieces of silver, why didn't you go to our common mother, who would have sold herself in order to save you and me from such danger and death?" For Varano's female audience there was considerable shock value in the suggestion that Mary might have sold her soul—let alone her body—in order to save Judas from eternal damnation and Jesus from the pain of his redemptive action.[37]

Varano addressed a predominantly female, monastic audience, but her message was carefully read by, and profoundly influential upon, men much later. This fact violates the stereotypical image we have of Counter-Reformation rejection of female voices that were not somehow controlled by males. Perhaps the best example of a man who read and was influenced by Varano's work was, of course, the Theatine Lorenzo Scupoli. He has long been connected with Varano's treatise despite his fairly impeccable credentials as a Counter reformer. The Theatine order to which he belonged may have found its inspiration in the lay-dominated Oratory of Divine Love, but it turned, many believe, under the direction of the inquisitor-pope Paul IV, to become one of the principal forces behind the Catholic version of early modern repression and disciplining. Scupoli was also the author of that battle image laden classic of Counter-Reformation spirituality, *The spiritual combat*. But Varano's text was attributed to him for sometime, and for good reason. There are striking similarities between the approaches of the two authors to the sufferings of Christ in the passion, and these similarities make the attribution plausible. An 1831 edition of Scupoli's *Opere* included Varano's text among his works, but with a condescending note indicating that she was the original author and that he had merely edited and 'rendered it in a better style.'[38] Scupoli considered the work of this woman important enough to edit and revise some one hundred years after she wrote. The fact is curious given the context. Over those one hundred years, the Protestant Reformation had begun, and so, some historians would have us believe, had systematic, Counter-Reformation repression of non-clerical, and especially female, voices on all religious matters. More curious still is the fact that in his editorial work, Scupoli both removed and retained elements of Varano's doctrinal and literary originality.

Indeed, it could be argued that Scupoli was shaped by, as much as he himself reshaped, the imaginative nature of Varano's religious insights

---

[37] Varano, *Le opere*, 161–162. Cf. Varano, *Mental sorrows*, 22–23.
[38] Scupoli, *Opere*, 301.

and the unique voice she developed in her prose. Scupoli did some serious editing, no doubt. He removed much of the conversational tone of the text, and some of the vulgar images that Varano included. He eliminated entirely her *sfogo* ('outpouring' or 'ventilation' of soul) that provided not only the beautiful, pleading prose of a spiritual crisis she endured, but also a context for her work on the agony in the garden. He completely eliminated her creative, apparently vision-revealed, message on the thoughts of Jesus when washing the feet of the apostles. Still, he retained a great deal more. At times it could be said that he edited in the interest of making the text useful to a wider audience. On occasion he took, for example, her feminine pronouns on occasion and made them 'we,' or 'our.' Still, he removed few of her references to women, and none of her most developed descriptions of women, like those of the Virgin Mary and of Mary Magdalen.[39] He adjusted her description of the Virgin Mary, omitting Varano's assertion that she was 'one' with Jesus. He may have done so because it suggested that Mary possessed a semi-divine status, even though Varano appeared careful to insist that Mary lacked divinity. Still, he retained Varano's assertion that through imitation of Mary one could gain higher exaltation in heaven. When editing Varano's work, Scupoli even retained her insistence that Mary Magdalen was categorically different from the other apostles. If any of them had suffered more than Magdalen, according to Varano and Scupoli, Jesus would have appeared to them first after his resurrection. Scupoli even retained her more generally heroic portrayal of Magdalen. Varano indicated Christ's revelation that no one can understand the pain he suffered in seeing Magdalen afflicted during his passion, 'because all holy and spiritual loves that ever were or ever will be have their foundation and origin in her and in me.'[40] Scupoli related the words of Christ in this way: 'Neither you nor any other person can ever fully understand my perfection as loving master and her delight and goodness as loving disciple, [for] after Magdalen there was no such [disciple], nor will there ever be another except her alone.' He retained Varano's assertion that Magdalen was the 'apostle of apostles,' who evangelized the others. This represents a bold exception to the standard early-modern shift in depictions of Magdalen toward emphasis on her penitent, not evangelical, character.[41]

---

[39] In chapter 2, Varano used words like *separandose*, and *unirse*, to explain the words Jesus spoke in responding to the sister to whom Varano attributed the revelation, where Scupoli used forms like *separandoci*, *unirci*, and *disgiugendoci*.
[40] Varano, *Le opere*, 157. Cf. Varano, *Mental sorrows*, 17.
[41] For the text, Scupoli, *Opere*, 314, 317. Cf. Varano, *Mental sorrows*, 17–18. For more on Mary Magdalen and on the 'apostle of apostles' image typical in the patristic and early medieval periods that was rarely utilized in early modern portrayals of Magdalen, see Haskins, *Mary Magdalen*, 59–97, 229–296.

Perhaps the best indication of the impact Varano had upon Scupoli lies not in what he retained or deleted in his version of her devotional treatise, but in elements of her prose that he incorporated into his writings. Like her, he utilized graphic imagery. The two writers clearly hoped to shock their readers. Varano was at her gory best when likening the damned to dead limbs hacked away using a carpenter's adze and when describing the stripes of blood that marked the 'divine vase' that was Christ's body. Scupoli provided similarly imaginative prose in his *Il combattimento spirituale*, including point-by-point descriptions of the passion, from the scourging that left his body torn by the adding of 'blow upon blow to the same place,' to instructions that the reader attempt to smell the stench of decomposing bodies on Calvary.[42] He used all this, moreover, to reinforce the same general point Varano hoped to make: that the physical sufferings Jesus endured were small in comparison with his mental anguish. In *Il combattimento spirituale*, Scupoli argued that Christ's physical pain was nothing compared to the 'unequaled internal pain that tormented him' when persons who were part of his mystical body chose to separate themselves by sin. The separation, he said, was 'more painful than that of parts of the body when they are dislocated from their natural place.'[43] In this portion of his work, he not only incorporated the general point behind Varano's treatise, but even adopted the dislocation image she exploited in the first chapter of *I dolori*, when she explained that 'spiritual dislocation is so much more painful than corporal dislocation, just as the soul is more valuable than the body.'[44] Scupoli also used the form of rhetorical comparison that Varano employed here. Indeed, among the difficulties in rendering his prose into English is his constant use of this technique and the convoluted, subjunctive-laden sentences that he composed as a result. These same comparative subjunctive phrases were a trademark of her prose. The sources behind Scupoli's works have been difficult to define precisely, but it seems undeniable that Varano was among the more important ones, considering the language, imagery, and literary techniques common to both.

Soon after a protracted spiritual crisis that lasted from 1488 to 1490 Varano composed another important work, *La vita spirituale*. In this spiritual biography covering her life to age 33, she provided a further illustration of her intense spirituality. She also provided material that connects her not just with Scupoli, but also with the main lines of

---

[42]Scupoli, *Combattimento*, 114–116, 163–164. English translation in Hudon, *Theatine spirituality*, 147, 182.

[43]Scupoli, *Combattimento*, 168–172. English translation in Hudon, *Theatine spirituality*, 187–188.

[44]Varano, *Le opere*, 148–149. Cf. Varano, *Mental sorrows*, 9–10.

post-Tridentine female devotional literature, and hence, further reason to reject the neat, but false, separation often made between Renaissance and Counter-Reformation examples of such literature. Just as in her text on the mental sufferings of Jesus, in this one Varano composed prose that was complex and multifaceted when recounting her spiritual development. She wrote at times in pious commonplaces, and at other times with earthy language and allusions. She turned a critical eye not simply toward herself, but to her own religious community. This spiritual autobiography that she composed quickly in 1491 was a rich story. She told a tale laced with typical Christocentric theology and traditional personal vows. She also told a tale of uncommon discernment of spirits and of willful determination.[45]

Varano employed colorful imagery to evoke a response from her readers, just as Counter-Reformation spiritual writers frequently did. She commonly inserted herself into the scene she was contemplating. While listening to the Good Friday preaching of Domenico da Leonessa in either 1466 or 1468 (that is, at the age of 8 or 10), Varano heard him relate the interview of Jesus before Herod. She prayed that 'Jesus...would respond to him so that he would not be put to death.' She added disbelief at Jesus's silence, addressing him directly. 'You are condemned, why didn't you respond to him?' she asked, adding, 'It seems that you yourself wish to die.' 'Excuse me, my blessed Lord,' she continued, 'but I do not understand you.' She prefaced this whole dialogue with the comment that Domenico's preaching had 'gripped' her with 'compassion.'[46] Varano employed a similarly affective and colorful voice in another context. When relating a vision of Jesus she experienced after emerging from a period of dryness in prayer during 1479, she described him in close physical detail. 'He was dressed in the whitest of garments,' she said, adding that he 'was larger than all other great men,' bearing 'such beauty in his head that I was not worthy to see it.' She described his 'beautiful...blond and copious hair,' his 'well-proportioned shoulders,' and she concluded, 'He was something marvelous.'[47] She used evocative imagery also when tracing her struggle in deciding to enter the convent. The conflict, she said, made her sweat physically, due to her 'great agony.' When she finally

---

[45] The text appears in Varano, *Le opere*, 3–67. All quotations from the text in this essay come from that edition, and the translations are my own. There is an English pamphlet edition of *La vita spirituale*: Varano, *My spiritual life*. In the notes for my translations below, I have indicated the comparable passages in the earlier, somewhat defective, English translation.

[46] Varano, *Le opere*, 9–10. Cf. Varano, *My spiritual life*, 18.

[47] Varano, *Le opere*, 34–35. Cf. Varano, *My spiritual life*, 37–38.

resolved to take what she considered God's course of action—that is to enter the convent—she felt, 'completely refreshed,' and 'at peace.'[48]

Varano used imagery and expressions of affective piety reminiscent of some of the giants in female devotional literature, including near contemporaries like Caterina da Bologna (d. 1463), but also figures from the Counter-Reformation like Teresa of Avila (1515–1582), and Maria Maddalena de' Pazzi (1566–1607). In chapter eight of her spiritual autobiography, for example, she explained that her dryness in prayer was more than relieved after her decision to enter the convent. 'In just a few days, all the cataracts of heaven were opened above me,' she said, 'and the flood of the abyss of His ancient mercy engulfed all the sins of my soul.' She likened herself to the prodigal son, describing with delight God's 'fatherly embrace,' and the 'sweet kiss of His holy peace.' It came from His own mouth, and not just once, but 'again and again.' Her fear over past sins was gone, she maintained, 'and thus He flooded and submerged me completely in love.'[49] She also related visions of Christ as her spouse, when, as she said, she 'loosened the bridle on the love of my heart, …and …let it go impetuously and furiously.' Her spiritual marriage included, she explained, 'such a sweeter, subtler flavor that one cannot communicate it or explain it human terms.' That didn't stop Varano from trying, however, as she told of her 'divine conversation, in the loving arms of the Celestial Spouse.'[50] She explained that Jesus had her 'name written' upon his heart 'in golden letters.' 'How good those large and antique letters…I LOVE YOU CAMILLA,' looked, she said, and she told him, 'I was amazed that You loved me so.'[51] While these expressions might be reminiscent of the writings of her predecessors like Caterina da Bologna—one person Varano most assuredly admired—they also evoke the language of heavy spiritual rain and mystical marriage of later authors like Teresa of Avila. Toward the end of the tenth chapter in her spiritual autobiography, Varano also expressed her desire to see Christ in the context of a meditation on the transfiguration. She linked this hope to an intense desire to suffer because of her sins. She received, she explained, 'a burning desire to endure pain,' and was determined to 'drown' herself, if possible, in 'that bitterest sea of the…anguish of the heart of Jesus.' 'If he had wanted to give me paradise without suffering pain,' she continued, 'I would not have wanted it.' She asked to be clothed 'in that garment in

---

[48]Varano, *Le opere*, 23–24. Cf. Varano, *My spiritual life*, 29.

[49]Varano, *Le opere*, 24–25. Cf. Varano, *My spiritual life*, 30–31.

[50]Varano, *Le opere*, 26–29. Cf. Varano, *My spiritual life*, 31–33. There is an excellent recent overview of the theme of mystical marriage: see Matter, 'Mystical marriage.'

[51]Varano, *Le opere*, 38–39. Cf. Varano, *My spiritual life*, 41.

which his beloved Son was clothed,...the garment of suffering pain in this world.'[52] Her prose is similar to that composed by Maria Maddalena de' Pazzi, a Tuscan author of affective devotional literature, but, like Teresa, one solidly inside the period of Counter-Reformation. Maria expressed her desire to participate in the sufferings of Christ frequently, and one of her dialogues (#36) she narrated a vision in which she took part in the major scenes of the Passion, acting out the role of Christ himself.[53] Varano did not perform her meditative illuminations in quite the same way described by the most recent student of Maria Maddalena de' Pazzi, but the content of their devotions carries marked similarities.[54]

When calling for reformed devotional practice, Varano displayed a critical eye she was apparently unafraid to turn in any direction. At about the age of ten she had taken a vow that she would, every Friday, 'desire to cry at least one tear for love of the passion of Christ,' in response to the Lenten preaching of Fra Domenico, but in her autobiography she explained her difficulty in fulfilling it.[55] She felt 'ashamed,' she said, accusing herself of a 'lack of wisdom,' or 'sprightliness,' or of engaging in 'laughing and chattering' that got in the way. Varano indicated that she found some help in a written meditation on the passion by an author she did not name. Although the text helped, this didn't stop Varano from suggesting that it was probably 'written by some person who did not know how to think.' She, of course, later wrote a text of her own on the same topic. Still, Varano idealized this early period in her devotional life, the three years she lived, still at home, after taking the vow. She related a considerable regimen of fasting, prayer, midnight recitations of the rosary, and use of a scourge over those years. She contrasted this with her convent life while she was writing the autobiography. She indicted the whole institution, insisting that 'now that I am a nun I do not get up and I do nothing good.'[56] Varano also leveled criticism—albeit oblique—against members of the clergy who failed to mirror the character of the Franciscan preachers she admired. Francesco da Urbino was perhaps the one she admired most. She considered him inspired by God, even, as she

---

[52]Varano, *Le opere*, 30–31, 39–40. Cf. Varano, *My spiritual life*, 34–35, 41–42.

[53]Maria Maddalena de' Pazzi left texts collected in a 7 volume edition: Pazzi, *Tutte le opere*. There is a recent, English translation of selected portions of her writings: Pazzi, *Maria*. For more on her spirituality, see Armando Maggi's introduction to that volume (pp. 5–53). See also Zaninelli, 'Influssi culturali'; Mortari, *Santa Maria*; and Secondin, *Santa Maria*.

[54]On the performance quality of Maria Maddalena de' Pazzi's visions, see Maggi, 'Performing/annihilating the word.'

[55]Varano, *Le opere*, 10–11. Cf. Varano, *My spiritual life*, 19.

[56]Varano, *Le opere*, 14. Cf. Varano, *My spiritual life*, 21–22.

said, 'an angel of God, not a human creature.'[57] Varano contrasted him with the 'chief priests' he criticized in a Holy Saturday sermon for their acquiescence in illicit Eastertide reception of the Eucharist. She was likely alluding to the bishop and cathedral chapter members who ministered to familiars of the palace household whom Francesco—and apparently Varano— considered less than sincere in their determination to leave sin behind.[58]

Varano frequently asserted her independence, self-motivation, and determination in pursuing a closer relationship with God. She carefully described the opposition she faced when she desired to enter the convent. That opposition came from the palace court in which she lived, and especially from her father. She believed the court represented 'worldly Egyptian servitude,' and elaborated fully on the comparison, likening her father himself to 'the powerful Pharoah.' She insisted that her personal 'Red Sea' could be found in 'puffy worldly pomp and the signorial state.' The sea, she said, 'seems very beautiful,' but 'in reality it is not…because it is nothing other than smoke and the flame of [burning] straw, which doesn't last long.' She said that she 'saw Pharoah and all his soldiers' submerged in the sea along with 'the devil with all his snares, vices, and sins.' Passing through this trial, amid what she called its 'infirmity and…threats,' made her 'content,' and Varano left the world, as she said, for 'the desert of holy religion,' with great 'devotion and affection.'[59] Varano at times defied her religious superiors, too. When Pietro da Mogliano, the provincial vicar, came to visit her convent in 1484, she rejected his repeated request to hear her confession. Later, she said, realizing that 'I was a big ass' to refuse, 'I wrote to him begging pardon' and requesting that he return to hear her confession. Her desire to confess was 'increased so that I found no rest,' she said, and her 'spiritual peace' returned only when Mogliano did and she made a general confession.[60]

Although she boldly asserted herself and her own desires, Varano often drew inspiration from male clerics and at times leaned upon their guidance. It was, after all, the preaching of a Franciscan friar that Varano considered, long afterward, as the beginning of her spiritual life. Varano expressed her wishes for clerical help as a set of bookends to her autobiography. She alluded at the beginning to her desire for this assistance, as she struggled in spiritual anguish over whether to write at all. The 'fervent, hot, vehement inspiration' to write conflicted with a reticence derived from concern that 'the spirit of pride' was misleading her. After resorting to prayers and

---

[57]Varano, *Le opere*, 18. Cf. Varano, *My spiritual life*, 25.
[58]Varano, *Le opere*, 20–21. Cf. Varano, *My spiritual life*, 27.
[59]Varano, *Le opere*, 35–37. Cf. Varano, *My spiritual life*, 39.
[60]Varano, *Le opere*, 46–47. Cf. Varano, *My spiritual life*, 47.

finding help in God's grace, she wrote, but not before expressing her dismay over 'being destitute of all human aid and counsel.'[61] Varano indicated in the final chapters of the text that she had seen Mogliano, upon whom she had relied, only three times over the course of her two-year spiritual crisis, and by the time she felt the inspiration to write the autobiography, he had died. In the ambiguous final chapters of the work, she appears to have received scanty attention from yet another clerical confidant, and lamented the situation. 'O my father, where have you been?' she wrote. She considered herself in this context 'more cruelly afflicted and beaten than ever before.'[62] All of these allusions to the need for clerical assistance or guidance should be tempered against the realities of the text. Although she looked for help, the story she related was one of do-it-yourself discernment, with assistance at decidedly limited points. There is no question, however, that she idealized clerics like Leonessa and Mogliano because of their commitment to what she considered good devotion and true religiosity. She even seemed to be promoting Mogliano's cause for sainthood at the end of her text, when she described his assistance from beyond the grave. 'You immediately took all power from my enemies,' she said, 'and led me back to the way of truth.'[63]

Varano apparently had a deep knowledge of the Scriptures, and employed them creatively. She often used passages from both the Old and the New Testaments in her spiritual autobiography. A passage from *Lamentations* became a theme in her text. 'Is it nothing to you, all who pass along the path of divine love?' she asked, adding, 'look and see if there is any sorrow like my sorrow.'(*Lam.* 1:12)[64] She repeated the line again and again to give voice to her pain in spiritual distress, when she felt she had lost the grace and favors earlier enjoyed in conversations with Christ. Varano inserted the words 'of divine love' on her own, reiterating the centrality of her visions and spousal relationship with Jesus. She used Scripture most creatively in her description of escape from the court as a passage to religious life. 'Do not be surprised if I have usurped the symbol of that chosen people the Jews,' she concluded, in her reference to story of the parting of the Red Sea. 'I do not know among whom I could find a better symbol for the countless blessings I have received from God,' she added, 'or even more for my infinite obduracy and ingratitude.'[65]

---

[61] Varano, *Le opere*, 6. Cf. Varano, *My spiritual life*, 15–16.
[62] Varano, *Le opere*, 61–64. Cf. Varano, *My spiritual life*, 58–61.
[63] Ibid.
[64] Varano's use of this passage is almost continual, in every chapter of *La vita spirituale*, with her first use at the end of the very first chapter.
[65] Varano, *Le opere*, 37. Cf. Varano, *My spiritual life*, 39.

In short, in her writings, Varano described a personality and spirituality whose characteristics are far from unique. Instead, the connecting points between her life and prose on the one hand, and the rest of reform doctrine and devotional teachings on the other, are the intriguing matters. Varano expressed ideas and intentions that are not always associated with the late-medieval experience of religious women. The whole of her spiritual autobiography, really, is the story of a process of discernment carried out with considerable independence. She chose her vocation not due to the pressure of, but rather over the opposition of, her father and of the noble court that was her home, and she defended the choice. She relied upon God, and her mystical, spousal relationship with God, for direction. She acknowledged a need for clerical guidance, but only from those whom she considered good enough to provide it. Even then, at times, she asserted herself and won. She believed that she could attain union with God, and that she had done so. She believed it so strongly that she expressed dismay when the favors she received seemed to have been taken away, despite recognition of her own sinfulness. Varano wrote in a way that is reminiscent of some elements of more typically medieval spirituality. She had drunk deeply from the devotional tradition of the Franciscan order whose preachers she loved, the same reform-minded, itinerant crew whose successors would become suspect of heresy in the not-too-distant Counter-Reformation. Her emphasis on meditation concerning the events of the life of Christ, especially the passion, placed her in their tradition, as well as in the tradition of female, and male, devotional writers who both preceded and followed her chronologically. Varano, her spiritual life, and her writings, and their incorporation into classic 'Counter-Reformation' spiritual texts, like those of Scupoli, provide evidence of the devotional *longue durée* characteristic of medieval and early modern spirituality.

It is just this devotional *longue dureé* that remains essential for the full understanding of both the history of the Theatine order, and the history of the early modern period, especially in Italy. The Theatines have for too long been considered a typically repressive, Counter-Reformation order. They have for too long been connected almost exclusively with the process of implementation of the Council of Trent, and with the activities of the Roman Inquisition during the reigns of the two most vigorous inquisitor-popes, Paul IV and Pius V. Historical emphasis upon this connection is understakable given the large number of Theatines who gained episcopal appointments in the seventeenth century, the critical one for implementation of the Tridentine decrees, and because the original inquisitor-pope himself, Paul IV, was a co-founder of the order. But emphasis on these facets of the organization that excludes consideration of the long-run development of the Theatine approach to Christian life provides something less than half the story of the order.

A more comprehensive understanding of the sources of Theatine spirituality may point toward even broader conclusions, if they can be confirmed with still more early modern sources. Gaetano da Thiene demonstrated in his correspondence that there may well have been a bridge between late-medieval religiosity and the devotional themes and attitudes more commonly associated with the Counter-Reformation. He looked to a woman for spiritual guidance, but he was also insistently directive, even dictatorial, in his spiritual guidance of other religious women. He has become known as the co-founder of a reforming religious order, but even as he participated in the foundation he at least considered, and probably engaged in curial transactions 'reformers' typically viewed as simonious. A humanist approach to Scripture as the source of religious inspiration was behind both the Christocentric devotional theology Thiene expressed, and behind his identification of spiritual combat as one of the proper images for comprehending Christian life. Just like his co-founder, Gian Pietro Carafa, Theine was a man of contradictions. Lorenzo Scupoli drew inspiration, themes, and sometimes even words, for the construction of his Counter-Reformation devotional classics from a high Renaissance woman, Camilla Battista da Varano. That inspiration did not stop him, at times, from writing about women in a denigratory fashion, however, or to emphasize the need for female obedience to spiritual fathers. Of course, his use of Varano's ideas and language, not to mention the overall tone and message of *Il combattimento spirituale* suggests that he believed women capable of the highest forms of spiritual perfection.

Consideration of the historical complexities behind the first two generations of the Theatine order constitutes further reason to reject the firm disconnection between Renaissance and Counter-Reformation more generally. The devotional era from which Mignani and Varano came did not suddenly end in the mid-sixteenth century, as Giulia Barone and other commentators have either implied or asserted directly. It must surely be noted that there was a shift from male solicitation of spiritual advice from women to male direction of the spiritual lives of women in this era. But the traditional feminist historiography that asserts female influence over ecclesiastical institutions and their history was over when Christianity became the official religion of the Roman Empire—or if not then, certainly after the Gregorian reform in the eleventh century—just as surely represents an oversimplification begging for revision. The four individuals described in this essay demonstrate the oversimplification. The suggestion by Joan Kelly-Gadol that there was no Renaissance for women is just as glaringly overstated as was Jacob Burckhardt's nineteenth century characterization of Renaissance women as the equals of men.[66] No one has

---

[66] For Kelly-Gadol, 'Did women have a Renaissance?' 137. Cf. Burckhardt,

yet argued that women faced no repression at all during the Counter-Reformation, but to do so would be as incorrect as to argue that women were as a whole controlled or dominated by their male counterparts in the sixteenth and seventeenth centuries. Hunting for the specific qualifications needed to revise such oversimplifications will always be best done through investigation of individuals and through case studies. The hunt—which will allow scholars to adequately describe persons, not to mention whole eras, in the past—must be the target of all historical investigations, especially those in early modern European studies.

Bloomsburg University
Bloomsburg, PA

Works Cited

Andreu, Francesco. 'Introduzione' pp. xxiii–xxxiv in *Le lettere di San Gaetano da Thiene*, ed. Francesco Andreu. Vatican City: Biblioteca Apostolica Vaticana, 1954.

Andreu, Francesco. 'Gaetano Thiene.' In *Dizionario degli istituti di perfezione*. Rome: Edizioni Paoline, 1974—.

Aringoli, D. *La beata Battista Varano*. Fabriano, 1926.

Aringoli, D., G. Boccanera, and A. Sestili, *Camilla Battista da Varano nel centenario della beatificazione (1843–1943): la principessa, la scrittrice, la santa*. Camerino: Università degli studi di Camerino, 1943.

Atkinson, Clarissa W. *Mystic and Pilgrim: The Book and the World of Margery Kempe*. Ithaca: Cornell University Press, 1983.

Blaisdell, Charmarie J. 'Angela Merici and the Ursulines' pp. 99–136 in *Religious Orders of the Catholic Reformation*, ed. Richard De Molen. New York: Fordham University Press, 1994.

Boccanera, Giacomo. *Biografia e scritti della beata Camilla Battista da Varano, clarissa di Camerino, 1458–1524*. Rome: Editrice 'Miscellanea francescana', 1957.

Brown, Judith C. *Immodest Acts: The Life of a Lesbian Nun in Renaissance Italy*. New York: Oxford University Press, 1986.

Burckhardt, Jacob. *The Civilization of the Renaissance in Italy*, trans. by S. G. C. Middlemore. New York: Penguin 1990.

Bynum, Caroline Walker. *Holy Feast and Holy Fast: The Religious Significance of Food to Medieval Women*. Berkeley: University of California Press, 1987.

Cardarelli, L. *Camilla Battista da Varano*. Macerata, 1972.

Castaldo, G.B. *Vita del B. Gaetano da Thiene, fondatore della religione de chierici regolari*. Rome, 1612.

Cistellini, Antonio. *Figure della riforma pretridentina*. Brescia: Morcelliana, 1948.

Civilization, 250.

Delumeau, Jean. *Le péché et la peur: La culpabilisation en occident xiiie—xviiie siècles*. Paris: Librairie Artheme Fayard, 1983. (Also available in English translation: *Sin and fear: The Emergence of a Western Guilt Culture, 13th–18th Centuries*, trans. by Eric Nicholson. New York: St. Martin's Press, 1990).

Ferrazzi, Cecilia. *Autobiography of an Aspiring Saint*, ed. by A. J. Schutte. Chicago: University of Chicago Press, 1997.

Firpo, Massimo. 'Paola Antonia Negri, monaca Angelica,' pp. 35–82 in *Rinascimento al femminile*, ed. by Ottavia Niccoli. Rome-Bari: Laterza, 1991.

Giannini, B. *Storia d'una principessa: la giovinezza della beata C. B. Varano*. Assisi, 1988.

Harline, Craig and Eddy Put. 'A Bishop in the Cloisters: The Visitation of Mathias Hovius (Malines, 1596–1620).' *Sixteenth Century Journal* 22 (1991): 611–639.

Haskins, Susan. *Mary Magdalen: Myth and Metaphor*. New York: Harper Collins, 1993.

Hudon, William V. 'Religion and Society in Early Modern Italy—Old Questions, New Insights,' *American Historical Review* 101/3 (June, 1996): 783–804.

Hudon, William V. *Theatine Spirituality: Selected Writings*. New York: Paulist Press, 1996.

Hudon, William V. 'The Papacy in the Age of Reform, 1513–1644,' pp. 46–66 in *Essential Articles on Early Modern Catholicism*, ed. by Kathleen Comerford and Hilmar Pabel. Toronto: University of Toronto Press, 2001.

Jantzen, Grace M. *Power, Gender and Christian Mysticism*. Cambridge: Cambridge University Press, 1995.

Jorgensen, Kenneth J. 'The Oratories of Divine Love and the Theatines: Confraternal Piety and the Making of a Religious Community,' Ph. D. Diss., Columbia University, 1989.

Kelly-Gadol, Joan. 'Did Women Have a Renaissance?' pp. 134–164 in *Becoming Visible: Women in European History*, ed. by Renate Bridenthal and Claudia Koonz. Boston: Houghton Mifflin, 1977), 134–164.

King, Margaret L. *Women of the Renaissance*. Chicago: University of Chicago Press, 1991.

Klapisch-Zuber, Christiane. *Women, Family and Ritual in Renaissance Italy*, trans. by Lydia G. Cochrane. Chicago: University of Chicago Press, 1985.

Latourette, Kenneth Scott. *History of Christianity*. 2 Vols. New York: Harper Collins, 1953, 1975.

Le Clercq, Jean, François Vandenbroucke and Louis Bouyer, *The Spirituality of the Middle Ages*, A History of Christian Spirituality, vol. II. New York: Seabury, 1982.

Luzi, Pietro. *Camilla Battista da Varano, una spiritualità fra papa Borgia e Lutero*. Turin: P. Gribaudi, 1989.

Maggi, Armando. 'Performing/Annihilating the Word: Body as Erasure in the Visions of a Florentine Mystic,' *TDR. The Drama Review* 41 (Winter 1997): 110–127.

Marini, A. M. *Vita della beata Camilla Battista Varani*. Camerino, 1882.

Mas, Bartolomeo. 'Gaétan de Thiene.' In *Dictionnaire de spiritualité ascétique et mystique doctrine et histoire*. Paris: Beauchesne, 1937–1995.

Matter, E. Ann. 'Mystical marriage,' pp. 31–41 in *Women and Faith: Catholic Religious Life in Italy from Late Antiquity to the Present*, ed. by Lucetta Scaraffia and Gabriella Zarri. Cambridge: Harvard University Press, 1999.

Mayer, Thomas F. *Reginald Pole: Prince and Prophet*. Cambridge: Cambridge University Press, 2000.

McGinn, Bernard. *The Presence of God: A History of Western Christian Mysticism*. New York: Crossroad, 1991–.

McNamara, Jo Ann Kay. *Sisters in Arms: Catholic Nuns Through Two Millennia*. Cambridge: Harvard University Press, 1996.

Mortari, Luisa. *Santa Maria Maddalena de' Pazzi*. Rome: Istituto nazionale di studi romani, 1987.

O'Malley, John W. *Trent and all That: Renaming Catholicism in the Early Modern Era*. Cambridge: Harvard University Press, 2000.

Papasogli, Giorgio. *Beata Camilla Battista da Varano*. Assisi, 1959.

Paschini, Pio. *San Gaetano, Gian Pietro Carafa e le origini dei chierici regolari teatini*. Rome: Scuola tipografica Pio X, 1926.

Pascucci, M. *Vita della beata Battista Varani*. Macerata, 1680.

Pazzi, Maria Maddalena de'. *Tutte le opere di Santa Maria Maddalena de' Pazzi*. 7 vols. Fulvio Nardini, et al. eds. Florence: Centro internazionale del libro, 1960–1966.

Pazzi, Maria Maddalena de'. *Maria Maddalena de' Pazzi: Selected Revelations*, trans. by Armando Maggi. New York: Paulist Press, 2000.

Petry, Ray C. *Late Medieval Mysticism*. Philadelphia: Westminster Press, 1957.

Porto S. Giorgio, V. da. *Vita della beata Battista Varani*. Bologna, 1874.

Ranft, Patricia. *Women and the Religious Life in Premodern Europe*. New York: St. Martin's Press, 1996.

Ruggiero, Guido. *Binding Passions: Tales of Magic, Marriage and Power at the End of the Renaissance*. New York: Oxford University Press, 1993.

Scaraffia, Lucetta and Gabriella Zarri, *Donne e fede: Santità e vita religiosa in Italia*. Rome: Laterza, 1994. (Also available in English translation: *Women and Faith: Catholic Religious Life in Italy from Late Antiquity to the Present*. Cambridge: Harvard University Press, 1999.

Schutte, Anne Jacobson. *Aspiring Saints: Pretense of Holiness, Inquisition, and Gender in the Venetian Republic, 1618–1750*. Baltimore: Johns Hopkins University Press, 2001.

Scupoli, Lorenzo. *Combattimento spirituale*. Milan: Edizioni Paoline, 1992.

Scupoli, Lorenzo. *Opere*. Milan, 1831.

Secondin, Bruno. *Santa Maria Maddalena de' Pazzi: esperienza e dottrina*. Rome: Istitutum Carmelitanum, 1974.

Solfaroli Camillocci, Daniela. *I devoti della carità: le confraternite del Divino Amore nell'Italia del primo Cinquecento*. Naples: Edizioni La Città del Sole, 2002.

Thiene, Gaetano da. *Le lettere di San Gaetano da Thiene*, ed. Francesco Andreu.Vatican City: Biblioteca Apostolica Vaticana, 1954.

Tomizza, Fulvio. *Heavenly Supper: The Story of Maria Janis*, trans. by Anne Jacobson Schutte. Chicago: University of Chicago Press, 1991.

Van Engen, John. *Devotio Moderna: Basic Writings*. New York: Paulist Press, 1988.

Varano, Camilla Battista da. *Le opere spirituali*, ed. by Giacomo Boccanera. Iesi: Scuola tipografica Francescana, 1958.
Varano, Camilla Battista da. *The Mental Sorrows of Jesus in His Passion*, trans. by Joseph Berrigan. Toronto: Peregrina, 1986.
Varano, Camilla Battista da. *My Spiritual Life*, trans. by Joseph Berrigan. Toronto: Peregrina, 1989.
Vezzosi, Antonio. F. *I scrittori de' chierici regolari detti Teatini*. 2 vols. Rome: Sacra Congregazione di Propaganda Fide, 1780.
Zaninelli, Tiziana. 'Influssi culturali nell'esperienza di Santa Maria Maddalena de' Pazzi,' *Rivista di ascetica e mistica* 17 (1992): 46–74.
Zardin, Danilo. 'Controriforma, Riforma cattolica, cattolicesimo moderno: conflitti di interpretazione,' pp. 289–307 in *Identità italiana e cattolicesimo: una prospettiva storica*, ed. by Cesare Mozzarelli. Rome: Carocci, 2003.
Zarri, Gabriella. *Le sante vive: Cultura e religiosità femminile nella prima età moderna* Turin: Rosenberg and Sellier, 1990.

Part V

Politics, History, and Prophecy

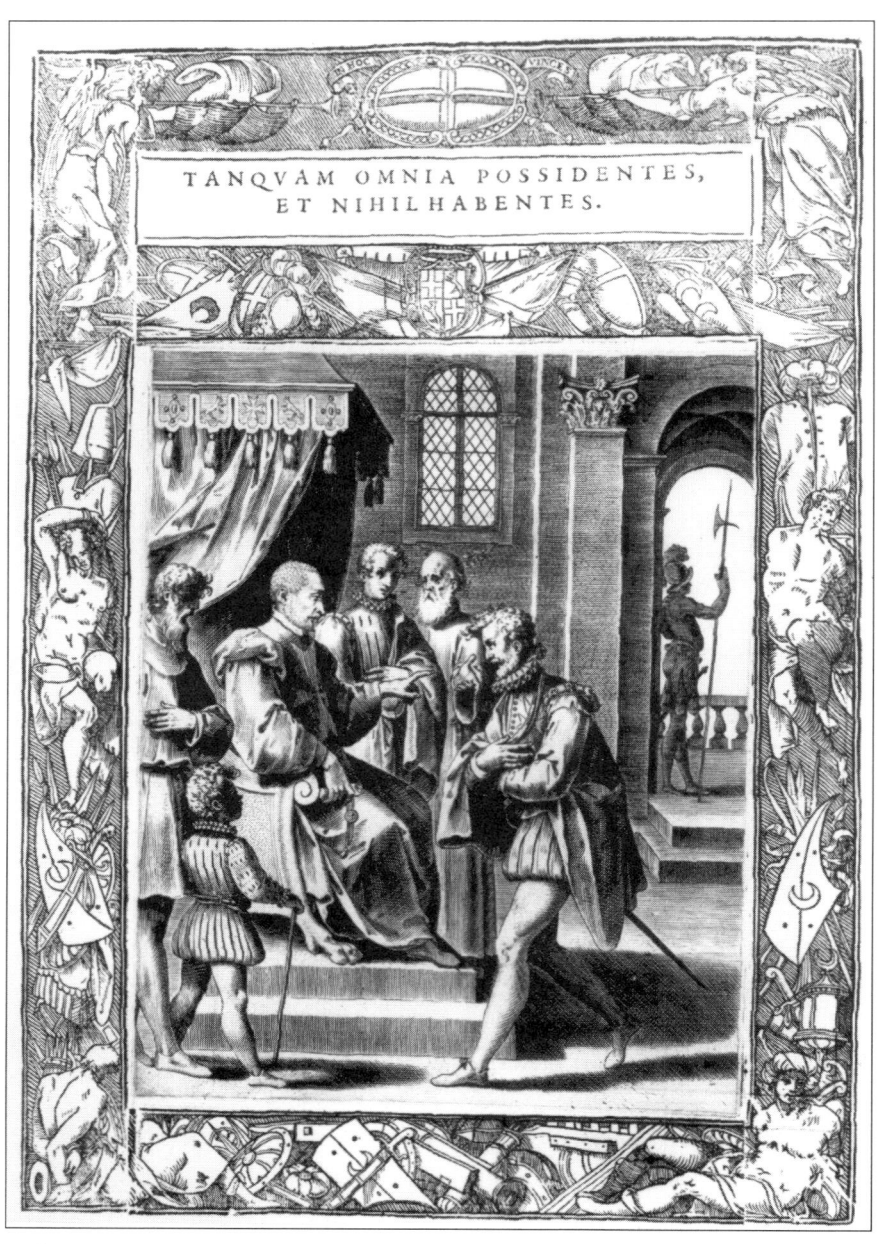

Plate 7: 'Tanquam omnia possidentes, et nihil habentes,' in *Statuta Hospitalis Hierusalem*. Rome: n.p., 1586. (Newberry Library, Chicago, Illinois.)

An Anti-Campanellan Vision on the Spanish Monarchy and the Crisis of 1595*

John A. Marino

Following the death of Sixtus V Peretti (1585–1590) on 23 August 1590 until the election of Clement VIII Aldobrandini (1592–1605) on 30 January 1592, three short pontificates of only two weeks, ten months, and two months, with four Vacant Sees of two and one-half weeks, two months, two weeks, and one month between papal elections, created opportunities for the jockeying of position in Rome's political factions among the great nations, their surrogate cardinals, and the local Roman population.[1] Philip II's power and influence in his declining years were not what they had been and Clement VIII was not the Spaniards' first choice in 1592. Cardinal Santori was their leading candidate; and, after his candidacy failed, further Spanish favor on Cardinals Madruzzo, Galli, Paleotto, and Colonna also faltered. Only the last of their compromise candidates, Ippolito Aldobrandini, was able to secure the thirty-five of fifty-two votes

---

*My thanks to Robert Westman and Luce Giard for their careful reading, criticism, and many suggestions. An earlier version was presented to the Sixteenth Century Studies Conference, Denver, CO (October 26, 2001), where Thomas F. Mayer made especially helpful suggestions.

[1] The three short-lived popes were Urban VII Castagna (15 September 1590–27 September 1590), Gregory XIV Sfondrati (5 December 1590–15 October 1591), and Innocent IX Facchinetti (29 October 1591–30 December 1591). Nussdorfer, 'The Vacant See: Ritual and Protest in Early Modern Rome,' which focuses on the Vacant See of 1644, summarizes the general ambiguity and uncertainty during the Vacant See, p. 174: 'There was no doubt about it; Romans, and foreign governments too, looked to the Vacant See as an opportunity to get even and as an occasion to get ahead. But, despite the contemporary rhetoric, the Vacant See was not merely, 'time out,' when anarchy reigned around the tomb of the apostles. It was also a chance to enact an alternative political regime in which all strata of Roman society played a part.' Ibid., p. 188 also cites the example of 'settling accounts' by an angry crowd's harassment of the banker and architect of Sixtus V in 1590.

needed for election after nineteen scrutinies.[2] Clement VIII's pontificate coincided, however, with the tenure of Gonzalo Fernández de Córdoba, duke of Sessa, the very effective Spanish ambassador in Rome (1592–1603), who had succeeded the count of Olivares at the end of December 1591 a few days before Innocent IX's death and who worked ceaselessly to further Spanish interests.

Five popes in less than a year and one-half, moreover, disrupted the continuity of papal policies and left much unfinished business. The papacy under Clement VIII faced four pressing problems: brigandage and famine at home, the French and the Turks abroad. Domestically, endemic banditry in the Roman Campania from the notorious Abruzzese bandit Marco Sciarra had increased after 1584 until Sciarra's assassination by his former lieutenant in 1593;[3] and, grain shortages from 1585 caused decade-long want, with severe famine 1590–1593 and plague in 1591.[4] Internationally, the problem of Protestantism and war in France remained unresolved with the 1589 accession of Henry of Navarre as Henry IV (1589–1610), while Henry's abjuration of Calvinism in 1593 led to his coronation in 1594 and attempts at absolution and reconciliation with the papacy. At the same time Ottoman threats to the Holy Roman Empire and Vienna, with Turkish capture of the last imperial fortress at Bihac on Croatia's Una River in June 1592, caused Clement to consider formation of an anti-Turkish league. With the invasion of Hungary in 1593, fears in the East began to overshadow and affect all other papal policies.[5]

In late sixteenth-century Rome, social and economic crises mixed with political exigencies in the popular religious mind and often found expression in prophetic visions or astrological prognostications. In 1586 Sixtus V had explicitly condemned astrology in the bull *Contra exercentes*, and Rosario Villari has argued that its repeated promulgation 'one Sunday each year during the Holy Mass' demonstrates that the papacy's concerns focused on pious superstitions and 'the link between prophecy and social

---

[2]Pastor, *The History of the Popes*, vol. XXIII, *Clement VIII (1592–1605)*, pp. 6–18, and 436 for the scrutinies.

[3]Villari, *The Revolt of Naples*, pp. 48–55. Clement had sent a strong army under Giovanni Francesco Aldobrandini and Flaminio Delfino to the borders of Spanish Naples against the bandits in March 1592. Sciarra and 500 of his men escaped by Venetian galleys to be stationed on an island in defense of pirates. Papal protests to the Venetians forced them to attack and dislodge the bandits. Sciarra escaped with four others, but his former lieutenant, Battistella, murdered him near Ascoli in March 1593 as Sciarra was returning to the Abruzzi. In exchange, Battistella and thirteen companions were granted a papal pardon.

[4]Burke, 'Southern Italy in the 1590s: Hard Times or Crisis?' pp. 177–190.

[5]Pastor, *The History of the Popes*, vol. XXIII, *Clement VIII (1592–1605)*, pp. 265–268.

and political unrest.'[6] The church maintained that prophetic rabble-rousers' attempts to explain society's ills were the work of the devil and might provide rationalization for popular protest. Tommaso Campanella's Calabrian conspiracy of 1599, consequently, would fall directly into the kind of rebellion that the Church feared. Campanella's end-of-the-century prophetic voice in his *Monarchia di Spagna*, however, was only one among many of the divergent interpretations for the sorry state of the world and the need for aggressive action that was widely diffused and deeply imbedded in the fabric of Spanish Italy in the 1590s. The question at issue was the relationship between Church and State—not simply what state best promoted religion; but also conversely, could religion explain political affairs.

On St. Anthony of Padua's day (13 June) 1595, Juan de Garnica, a Spanish doctor of law at Rome and formerly in Salamanca and Naples, 'started a *librito* for Your Excellency to use with' a book manuscript, *De Hispanorum Monarchia*, that had been completed the previous day.[7] The Excellency addressed in this preface was the duke of Sessa, Spanish ambassador in Rome, who may have aspired to become viceroy in Naples upon the departure of Juan de Zuñiga, count of Miranda (viceroy, 1586–1595), later in November 1595.[8] So as not to be 'left destitute and without resources,' Garnica petitioned Sessa for patronage and position with his learned *libro* and *librito*, because they demonstrated Garnica's 'vast experience of the world and of Spain, of sea and land, and of the kingdom of Naples in all its customs and uses.'[9] Naples had a special relationship to Rome since it was a papal fiefdom whose annual feudal dues of 7,000 ducats and a symbolic gift of a white Neapolitan horse (the *chinea*) were presented to the pope by the Spanish ambassador in Rome in a gala procession on the feast of St. Peter (29 June).[10] Unfortunately for Garnica, Enriquez de Guzmán, count of Olivares, who was the viceroy of Sicily (1592–1595) and had been Sessa's predecessor as head of mission in Rome (1582–1592) where his son the later Count-Duke 'favorite' of

---

[6] Villari, *The Revolt of Naples*, pp. 61.

[7] Garnica, University of Chicago Library, Special Collections, ms. 1120, 'Prophetic Treatise on the Turks and Christianity,' 1st num., p. 1. My thanks to Jorge Mariscal for reading and correcting my transcription of part 1 of the Spanish *librito*, and to Ana Varela Lago for translating the *librito* transcription and locating the Latin *libro* in Madrid.

[8] For short portraits of the Neapolitan viceroys, see Coniglio, *I Vicerè Spagnoli di Napoli*.

[9] Ibid., pp. 6, 121.

[10] Dandelet, *Spanish Rome, 1500–1700*, pp. 55–57, 78 describes the *chinea* procession under Philip II.

Philip IV was born, was appointed Neapolitan viceroy in July 1595 instead of Sessa, with formal entrance into Naples on 27 November.

Garnica's books became forgotten products of an unsuccessful office-seeker. Like other advice literature by clients demonstrating their expertise to prospective patrons—Machiavelli's *The Prince* being the most famous—Garnica's texts move between the immediate occasion and general principles. Having been 'dismissed and scorned…deprived of office and support at the end of [his] service and age' without cause, Garnica seeks 'temporal and spiritual justice.' He gives his 'compendium not in vain,' but in truth from his 'life at court, and in Naples, and its Kingdom.'[11] Garnica's observations, advice, and prognostications allow us to establish the wider world of political thought and action in Spanish Italy from an erudite, but otherwise ordinary and obscure man at the end of the sixteenth century.

Garnica's 744-page tome, *De Hispanorum Monarchia*, which is preserved in the Biblioteca Nacional, Madrid in the same hand as the *librito*, is dated St. Lawrence's Day (10 August) 1595 and dedicated to Philip III.[12] The dedication in the Madrid copy was clearly revised after Olivares rather than Sessa was appointed viceroy of Naples. Still three years before Philip II's death, the dedication to Philip III ('Ad Serenissimum Philippum tertium, Hispaniarum Principem maximum') is a peculiar anomaly, since the text itself recognizes in a very early chapter's title 'That Philip II, King of Spain, is today temporal Monarch, and not Emperor of the world' (Bk 1, Chap. 3). Juan Beneyto Pérez in his 1942 study of the idea of empire in Spanish political thought emphasizes two sections of the text: an 'Epistola ad hispanos' among the proems, and chapter three on Philip II.[13] For John Headley, whose interest in 'world empire or universal monarchy' in his study of Tommaso Campanella relies on Juan Beneyto for information about Garnica, what is of interest is Garnica's distinction between empire and universal monarchy.[14] Garnica exalts the Spanish monarchy's task as defender and advocate of the Church—whence it enjoyed the title of 'the Catholic Kings.' Consequently, Philip II was not

---

[11] Garnica, Biblioteca Nacional, Madrid (BNM), ms. 7382, 'De Hispanorum Monarchia,' pp. 119–122.

[12] Ibid., pp. i–vi.

[13] Beneyto Pérez, *España y el problema de Europa. Contribución a la historia de la idea de imperio*, pp. 327–328. For a summary of Juan Beneyto's career that moved from his formation and early research in legal history to sociology and pioneer in Spain in the new disciplines of communication and information science, see Benito, 'Introducción,' in *Comunicacion y sociedad. Homenaje a Juan Beneyto*, pp. 9–20.

[14] Headley, "Ehe Türckisch als Baptisch': Lutheran Reflections on the Problem of Empire, 1623–1628,' pp. 3–28 and idem., *Tommaso Campanella and the Transformation of the World*, pp. 197–201 follows Beneyto Pérez, *España y el problema de Europa*.

Emperor, but rather a universal, temporal monarch analogous to the universal, spiritual monarchy of the pope. Garnica claims that greed, violence, and sin gave birth to the empire as a tyranny and he presents the new argument, still according to Juan Beneyto, that anticipates Pufendorf and Peñaranda that the Imperial title was an empty one, 'a name only, a sounding trumpet, a title without an object.' As suggestive as these references to Garnica's originality may be, he not only remains a minor footnote in the larger projects of Juan Beneyto on empire and pluralistic society or Headley on Campanella and universal monarchy/universal theocracy, but the true import and importance of Garnica's thought is not examined. We shall see that such a minor figure has much to tell us about late Renaissance apocalyptic thought—Campanella and Bruno were not lone geniuses studying the stars, foretelling the future, and theorizing upon the relationship between politics and theology.[15]

The manuscript's title page announces that the work is divided into two parts. The first part concerns 'the present monarchy of Philip II, the universal prince, the monarchy of Adam, and successive monarchies up to the Romans, with the continuation of the Holy Faith in everything.'[16] The first two books, thus, define terms such as spiritual and temporal monarchy (I. 1–8) and the distinction between pope and emperor (II. 1–5), and the last three books delineate biblical history into three periods: first, Adam's monarchy and his sons Cain, Abel, and Seth (III, 1–7); next, the monarchies from the story of Noah up to the Tower of Babel and the division of languages, peoples, and the invention of idols (IV, 1–11), and finally, monarchies from Abraham and the Patriarchs through Moses and the Kings of Israel to the Assyrians, Chaldeans, Persians, Greeks, and Romans (V, 1–17). Garnica's tripartite division of 'historical' time into three parts owes a debt to Joachim of Fiore's trinitarian scheme of the apocalypse, even if the temporal divisions differ.

The Madrid text has some important lacunae. It ends on page 744, followed by an unpaginated 50-page alphabetical index, but without including an eighteenth chapter in Book Five listed in the table of contents, 'An exposition on Psalm 109, in which is declared what will fulfill the destruction [of the world].' The second part of the book indicated in the table of contents, likewise, is not contained in the manuscript. It is said to describe how Noah prophesized, after the flood and succession by Japhet, the preordained end and plan of the Hispanic Monarchy.[17]

---

[15] Grafton for the importance of astrology in Renaissance intellectual life.
[16] Garnica, BNM ms. 7382, title page, 'de praesenti Monarchia, et de universorum principiis, ac de Monarchia Adae, et caeteris usque ad Romanos, cum Fidei Sanctae continuatione in omnibus.'
[17] Ibid., unnumbered p. xiii in table of contents: 'Cap. 18. Expositio super Psalmo

Both of these millennial predictions—Psalm 109 and Noah's prophecy, no doubt, would have emphasized the Second Coming, the passing of God's powerful kingship to his faithful followers, and their victory over their enemies, as an interpretation of the psalm's declaration of the 'punishment of nations':

> The Lord said to my lord,
> 'You shall sit at my right hand
> when I make your enemies the footstool under your feet.'
> When the Lord from Zion hands you the scepter, the symbol of your power,
> March forth through the ranks of your enemies. (Psalms 109:1–2)

Similarly, the most famous verse of Psalm 109 would likely have received special emphasis: 'Thou art a priest forever after the order of Melchisidech' (Psalms 109:4), with this line's repetition as millennial fulfillment in the New Testament (Hebrews 7:17).

Whatever the significance of the missing exegesis of Psalm 109 and biblical prophecies, the length of Bk. II, chaps. 4–5 suggests their emphasis and importance for Garnica's thesis.[18] These two chapters argue that the world is made up of four sects of idolaters—Jews, Mohammedans, Heretics (Protestants), and the Anti-Christ or Idolaters of all kinds—who are ignorant of their purpose in God's plan and their fate. They correspond to the biblically prophesized four millennial beasts. All four groups are sects and not true religions; all the world's idolaters fall into these four sects, with Garnica's Catholicism the one and only true religion. This explication of Daniel's dream (Daniel 7:1–28) highlights the *libro*'s 'scriptural erudition,' noted by Beneyto Pérez and stylistically shared by the *librito*. Such copious scriptural citations are used to support theological glosses and eschatological reasoning.

How does the *librito* help us understand the argument of his major work on the Spanish monarchy? By linking biblical exegesis to the

---

centessimo nono, in qua declaratur, quid sit, implebit ruinas'; and title page, 'In secunda agitur de Hispanorum Monarchia, et de eius fine et proposito á Domino Deo praeordinatis, et aperiuntur multa de Fide Sancta: et quomodo de hac Monarchia prophetavit Sanctus Patriarcha Noë, post mundi renovatione in dilatatione Japhet.'

[18] Ibid., Bk. II, Chapters 4 ('Quod mundi sectistae ignorant principum et finem suum, et media per quae procedunt. Et generaliter sectae sunt quatuor') and 5 ('Quod omnes quatuor praedictae sunt sectae, et nulla earum religio: et omnes mundi sectae sub praedictis quatuor continentur: nostra autem unica et sola religio est') comprise 173 of the 744 pages, more than 23% of the text, and their argument is outlined in detail in an additional page and one-third from the bottom of the table of contents, in the same hand but smaller cursive.

immediate crisis of 1595, Garnica makes his theological analysis come alive, as he shows how the concerted forces of the four apocalyptic animals, namely the fleets and armies of Turkish Muslims and heretic French Protestants, threaten to invade Rome, which has been weakened by mixing the Roman Church's spiritual and temporal authority. This hermeneutic key explains the contemporary crisis of the time.

Garnica's 'small little book' contains a dedication and two short treatises, which Garnica presents as being unrelated.[19] The first treatise discusses the immediate occasion in terms of a Turkish prophecy, the imminent threat of a Turkish attack on Rome; the second text describes the office of viceroy and the ceremonial of the court of Naples.[20] Both parts are linked by the short dedication, which ingratiates the author for his learning and experience to the Spanish ambassador in Rome, but quickly makes its centerpiece a prophetic injunction in millennial images:

> My tongue will be an arrow taken from the quiver of a mighty hand, a fiery ax, which guides and illuminates those who follow it, and burns and consumes everything it finds.[21]

The arrow and the ax are military images of power and leadership aimed at followers, while discovery and destruction are destined for enemies. The prophecy, proclaimed by these shafts of light and darkness that are launched on the tongue's flight, targets the 'infidel' Turk and their 'corrupted envious,' 'heretical' companions (the French of Henry IV). Both the Turks and the French once again are vilified near the conclusion, when Garnica reinvokes the same images of the potent bow and arrow given by God and the fiery ax by the Holy Spirit.[22] The introduction continues with a long apocalyptic paraphrase from a source only identified as a book that Garnica read, which proclaims in astrological images the Anti-Christ and his minions. This unknown book to which he turned his eyes is reminiscent of the sealed book opened in the last days in Apocalypse 4.

---

[19] Garnica, University of Chicago ms. 1120, 1st num., p. 1: 'Tiene dos partecillas, si bien no concernientes en la materia. La segunda parte, que de la primera se divide con una hoja blanca: se continua al otro librito, que V. Excellencia se sirvio acceptar de mi mano, para las cosas tocantes al officio /2/ de Virrey de Napoles. La primera, es differente en materia: pero conveniente à todos los Principes Ecclesiasticos y seglares, que tienen officio y gobierno en el pueblo Christiano.'

[20] Cherchi, 'Juan de Garnica: un memoriale sul cerimoniale della corte napoletana,' pp. 213–224 transcribes the second treatise.

[21] Garnica, University of Chicago, ms. 1120, p. 2: 'Mi lengua sera saeta sacada del aljava de mano potente. Hacha de fuego encendida, que guia y alumbra à quien la sigue: y abrasa y consume donde halla materia.'

[22] Ibid., p. 118.

Seized from me while resting and turning my eyes, I read a book that said: My house is abandoned, and you toil each one for yours. The earth exhales with impetus and the sea evaporates continuous humors. They join in the cold region, where they condense into clouds and occupy the sun's view and light. The planets wander from their zodiac, and lose the influence of their signs. The moon darkens and becomes blood. The stars fall from the sky, and they are stepped on, and trampled. They look to the most but it becomes the least. They set their nest very high, wishing to free themselves from the preying hand. Stones from the walls will call out and the wood from the rooftops will reply with shouts. They leave their wives poor and widowed and their children abandoned and orphaned, and the pupils, searching for bread, exhale their souls. They wield the sword with the left hand, putting the right one behind their back. They convert their gold into dregs and God Our Lord takes their wheat and wine to His granary. He takes for himself their wool and flax and leaves their shame exposed. The sky becomes metal and it neither gives nor does it receive. The untilled land becomes hard as iron. 'Cursed be the man who puts confidence in the flesh; cursed be the man who falsifies the work of the Lord.' The hills are craggy and full of vanity. The loftiest truth has interposed a cloud. The truth will be revealed that the world has not known me.[23]

Garnica continues by presenting himself as a prophet unrecognized in his own time, until now:

The cause will be one among many, either because my sins have not called for it, because Satan has prevented me, as St. Paul says, or for the reason given by beautiful and grieved Sarah of her seven husbands. Or perhaps because my time has not yet come, until I finish my book, even though I was very expert, as the Holy Spirit says, or because God wanted to try me

---

[23]Ibid., pp. 2–4: 'Estando en mi requie, me la arrebataron: y bolviendo mis oios, lei en un libro que dezia, Mi casa es desamparada, y vosotros os afanais cada uno por la suya. La tierra exhala con impetu: y la mar evapora humores continuos. Juntanse en la region fria, donde se quaxan en nube, y occupan la vista y luz del sol. Los planetas van errando de su zodiaco, y pierden la influencia de sus signos. La luna se escurece y convierte en sangre: Las estellas caen del cielo, y las pisan, y huellan. Miran à lo mas, y se les convierte en menos. Ponen su nido muy alto, pensando librarse de la mano que haze presa: y daran vozes las piedras de las paredes: y los maderos de los techos responderan con alaridos. Dexan sus mugires pobres y vivdas, y los hijos desamparados y huerfanos: y los pupilos, buscando pan, exhalan sus animas. Juegan la es/4/pada con la mano hizquierda: y bueluen átras la derecha. Convierten su oro en escoria: y el Señor Dios toma su trigo y vino, y lo lleva à su cillero. Toma para si su lana y lino: y dexa los descubiertas sus verguenças. El cielo se haze de metal, y no da ni recibe: La tierra inculta, se endurece como hierro. Maledictus homo qui confidit in carne: et maledictus homo qui facit opus Domini fraudulenter. Los collados estan fragosos, y llenos de vanidad. La summa verdad ha interpuesto una nube. Ella manifestara que el mundo no me ha conocido.'

before it could get published, as wisdom says. And it could also be because his divine Majesty has wanted to guard me, until I was put under the shelter and protection of Your Excellency, like his temple was protected by Solomon, or Elijah by the woman of Zarephath in Sidon, or Naaman the Syrian by Elisha.[24]

This apocalyptic vision ends with Garnica's personal plea to his patron and the inevitable conclusion of fire next time:

> Your Excellency, remember that you are a Prince, a faithful Christian, that you have children, that you seek the kingdom of Heaven, that it is in God's hands to give and to take away, and in conclusion, everything will be burned, only the good and his goodness will remain, a true man is very hard to find, and this matters much to all Christendom.[25]

That good and true man, whose clear vision sees the truth and whose book exposes it for all to see, is none other than the author who signs his introduction as he whom 'God has put under the power and in the hands of Your Excellency who kisses Your feet and hands, Your humble servant, Juan de Garnica.'[26]

The text of part one of Garnica's *librito* turns from his own prophetic vision in the dedication to the concrete case at hand, imminent Turkish invasion and a Turkish prophecy. Chapter One identifies an immediate threat to the city of Rome in this present year 1595 from the 'Turk with a great Armada in confederation with Bandoma.' The threat is said to be contained in Turkish prophecy and is to be fulfilled within three years to 'oppress Spain and burn Italy.' For Garnica, the best path to follow is the preparation made by Joseph in Egypt, for God says that 'prudence is better than force.'[27]

---

[24] Ibid., pp. 4–5: 'La causa sera alguna de muchas: o por que mis peccados no han dado lugar: o por que satanas me ha impedido, come dize San Pablo: o por la /5/ razon que dixo la hermosa y affligida Sara de sus siete esposos. O por ventura que aun no ha sido tiempo, hasta acabar mi libro, y fuesse yo muy experto, como dize el Spiritu Santo: ò porque Dios me probasse antes ques me publicaze, como dize la sapiencia. Y tambien puede ser, porque su divina Magestad me ha querido guardar, hasta ponerme devaxo el abrigo y amparo de V. Excellentia como a su templo para solo Salomon: o como à Elías para la muger de sarepta en Sidonia: ò como Naaman Syro para solo Eliseo.'

[25] Ibid. pp. 5–6: 'Y V. Excellentia se acuerde que es Principe, y Fiel Christiano, y tiene hijos, y busca el reino del cielo, y esta en mano de Dios quitar y poner: y /6/ en conclusion, todo se ha de quemar, quedando solo el bueno y el bien con el: y un hombre raras vezes se halla: y ese importa mucho à toda la Christiandad.'

[26] Ibid., p. 6: 'y Dios me ha tenido à poder y manos de V. Excellentia cuyos pies y manos besa Su humile criado, Juan de Garnica'

[27] Ibid., pp. 7–11: 'el Tur[c]o viene con grande armada este año presente de 1595, confederado con Bandoma….en aprieto à España, y abrasaranlo de Italia…'Te

376   A Renaissance of Conflicts

The discussion of the Turkish prophecy of the imminent invasion reinforces the dedicatory introduction's eschatological vocabulary—Garnica's main interpretive tool—to see the future more clearly. The contending forces of good and evil have their leaders and their prophets as they fight one another for the good government or tyrannical rule of the earth. Garnica argues that the physical threat is bad enough, but because the Turks claim that it comes from their God Allah, it is unbearable.

> If the evil derived only from its tyrannical audacity it would be bearable, but alas! it takes wings, from he who pretends to give spirit and force to its inhuman body and tyrannical power.[28]

Garnica reports that he was told the prophecy 'by a Turk from his own mouth.'

> I asked the Turk who had made that prophecy? He was a bit surprised, and in the end he said, asking me, 'Don't you have prophecies in your law?' I answered, 'Yes.' The Turk replied, 'We too have prophecies in ours.' We left it at that, because I did not find either the occasion or the subject for more.[29]

Such Turkish prophecies circulated throughout the sixteenth century, with the 1545–1546 writings of Bartolomej Georgijevic (c. 1510–c. 1566), an escaped Turkish captive, for example, often reprinted as late as 1598 in Lyons. His allusion to the Turks plucking the 'red apple' was taken as a reference to the predicted Ottoman conquest of Rome.[30]

Just as Garnica's words will 'burn and consume everything it finds,' so too do 'the said pretensions and threats [of Bandoma and the tyrant] bring fear, cowardice, and terror' along with subjugation to Spain and fire to

---

hago saber que es major la prudencia que la fuerça."

[28]Ibid., pp. 7–8: 'Y si el mal naciesse de sola su audacia tyranna: seria supportable: pero guai que toma alas, de quien /8/ pretende que da espiritu y fuerça á su cuerpo inhumano y tyranna potencia.' There is no record of whom this Turkish prophet may have been. As a rhetorical device—whether from a real person or from tradition, it work well in juxtaposes Christian and Isalamic prophetic power.

[29]Ibid., p. 8: 'Dizen que tienen profecia dello: y á mi me lo dixo un Turco de su propria voca. Pregunté'yo al Turco, que quien havia hecho aquella profecia? Estubo un poco turbando: y al ultimo me dixo preguntando, Vosotros no teneis profecias en vuestra ley? Respondi yo, Si. Replico el Turco, Tambien nosotros tenemos profecias en la nuestra. Quedamonos en esto, porque no halle lugar, ni sugeto para mas.'

[30]Deny, 'Les pseudo-prophéties concernant les Turcs au XVIe siècle,' pp. 217–218 explicates Georgijevic's texts, *De Turcarum ritu et cerimoniis* (Paris, 1545), *Prognoma sive praesagium Mehemetanorum* (Antwerp, 1546), from a combined edition *De turcarum moribus epitome* (Lyons, 1553).

Italy. What is worse, the Turkish tyrant is confederated with the 'perfidious' Bandoma, who is none other than the French king Henry IV, called by his Bourbon title duke of Vendôme (Bandoma), no doubt, to denigrate his royal pretensions in Navarre as well as to deny his victory in the Wars of Religion and ascension to the French throne.[31]

After the Lepanto war of 1570–1574, in which the Holy League won one battle but lost the war that ceded Venetian Cyprus to the Turks, the separate treaties between the various Christian powers and the Turks established a kind of detente between the two hegemonic powers, a Spanish sphere in the Western Mediterranean and an Ottoman sphere in the Eastern Mediterranean.[32] Border clashes continued to threaten the peace on both land and sea, especially in Hungary between the Holy Roman Emperor and the Ottoman Sultan. By March 1593, news reached Rome that the Turks had declared war against the Emperor and that they were preparing a large expeditionary force against Vienna.[33] Despite the divisions and difficulties presented by Spain and Venice, Clement VIII worked with diligent crusading zeal to forge an alliance against the Turks, even providing the Emperor 30,000 florins a month beginning in June 1594. The danger seemed to subside in January 1595 with three news items: the alliance between the rulers of Transylvania and Wallachia/Moldavia had successfully defeated the Turks on the lower Danube, the Transylvanians had entered into an alliance with the Emperor, and Sultan Murad III had died in Constantinople. The result was that the Turkish assault would be delayed until the middle of the summer, which gave time for further war preparations in the West. On 16 May the pope's nephew, Gian Francesco Aldobrandini, returned to Rome to take command of the papal forces, and Clement outlined to a consistory on 22 May papal assistance offered the Emperor. On 4 June a solemn mass at Santa Maria Maggiore blessed Aldobrandini as he was formally invested as captain-general and

---

[31] The published BNM catalogue, *Inventario general de Manuscritos de la Biblioteca Nacional.*, gives four references to Bandoma between 1558–1561, docs. 76, 106, 111, and 784; the BNM 'catalogo de manuscritos' reports in its handwritten 'Indice de manuscritos' two references—one to the Chicago manuscript and the other to a 1572 papal dispensation for marriage to the king's sister Marguerite of Valois (Queen Margot), both apparently missing—that identify Bandoma as Henry IV. The former refer to Anthony of Bourbon, duke of Vendôme (Bandoma) (1518–1562); the latter to his son, Henry of Navarre (1553–1610), who succeeded to his father's title and after the death of his mother Jeanne d'Albret in 1572 to the Kingdom of Navarre. My thanks to Ana Varela Lago for these BNM references.

[32] Hanlon, *Early Modern Italy, 1550–1800*, p. 185 characterizes Lepanto as 'an indecisive if gigantic border conflict.'

[33] Pastor, *The History of the Popes*, vol. XXIII, *Clement VIII (1592–1605)*, pp. 265–288.

on 16 June he left Rome via the Marches and the Romagna to enlist more recruits. The papal army of about 7,600 infantry and 260 cavalry joined the imperial troops besieging Gran (modern Esztergom, Hungary) on the Danube northwest of Budapest on 22 August. Thus, Garnica began his short text on 13 June at the height of war fever as the papal troops departed for the Turkish war being fought in Hungary.

If the Turkish threat in the East had diminished by January 1595, war in the West had not, as Henry IV declared war on Philip II on 17 January. By the end of May, the French king had concentrated his forces around Troyes, halfway between Paris and Dijon. He defeated the Spanish and their League allies near Dijon at Fontaine-Française on 5 June 1595 and again at Gray on 12 July.[34] The composition of Garnica's *librito* on 13 June would have begun before news of the Spanish defeat could have been known in Rome, but fears and rumors of the impending battle in Burgundy would have swirled about the papal capital.

France's anti-Spanish policy had led it to develop trade and diplomatic relations with the Turks from the 1520s and the Ottomans had granted favored commercial privileges to the French over the Venetians in 1569 on the eve of the 1570–1574 Lepanto war.[35] After the war, France began to displace the Venetians; by the early seventeenth century, some 1,000 French ships in the Eastern Mediterranean accounted for half of France's total trade. In the 1590s, with Spanish and imperial forces fighting the French in the West and the Turks in the East, a two-front war and the unholy alliance between Christians and Muslims against the papacy and its temporal protector, the Spanish monarchy, constituted a real threat.

At the same time, intense lobbying and negotiations were under way in Clement VIII's court concerning the possible removal of the ban of excommunication on Henry IV.[36] Discussions concerning the reconciliation of Henry IV to Catholicism had tentatively begun in 1594 and by December the pope unrealistically hoped to bring Spain and France together in peace to help wage war against the Turks. One of Philip II's goals in the declaration of war against France in January 1595 was to prevent the pope from granting absolution to Henry and to maintain Spain's unchallenged hegemony in Italy; but Spanish defeats in France weighed heavily in the process. By chance, on the same day as the Spanish

---

[34] Martinez de Campos y Serrano, *España belica el siglo XVI. Secunda Parte*, p. 233.

[35] Inalcik, 'Imtiyazat,' 3: 1182–1185, and Inalcik, *The Ottoman Empire. The Classical Age 1300–1600*, p. 137.

[36] Pastor, *The History of the Popes*, vol. XXIII, *Clement VIII (1592–1605)*, pp. 73–142 discusses developing events in detail from Henry's investiture 25 July 1593 to the pope's bull of absolution 17 September 1595.

defeat at Gray, 12 July, Clement received the French envoy Bishop Du Perron in Rome and the process leading to the papal reconciliation was well in motion despite strong Spanish opposition orchestrated by Ambassador Sessa. By 29 July Bishop Du Perron and the papal envoy Cardinal Ossat submitted an official request for papal absolution, which was finally granted on 17 September 1595. Garnica's shrill condemnation of 'Bandoma' as a lying heretic unquestionably comes from a Spanish partisan trying to get the ear of Sessa, the key Spanish negotiator working to prevent Henry IV's reconciliation with the papacy, at the very moment that the diplomatic controversy was coming to a head.

The centerpiece of the *librito* is Chapter Two, once again as in the *libro*, a long meditation on the famous apocalyptic vision in the Book of Daniel, 7:1–28.[37] Garnica paraphrases and retells Daniel's dream with an update for the present moment. He reinterprets the four beasts—lion, bear, leopard, and the ten-horned beast. They are not four kingdoms or four ages per traditional exegesis, but four universal religious sects. The lioness stands for the Jews in their pride and arrogance. Their wealth is spent in lechery and debauchery practiced as a result of the vice and superstitious sins derived from the literal observance of the law. The bear is the Mohammedan sect, fierce, slow, and cruel. Its three rows of teeth are grown from its three schisms or sects— Moors, Arabs with the Sufi, and the Turks. The leopard, known for its agility, cunning, and treachery, is the universal sect of all heretics. Their dissimulation makes them like cats, like wolves in sheep's clothing, and like a stained, spotted body filled with infinite opinions and such confusion that they will never convert. The four wings of the heretics stand for four kinds of heretical beliefs: first, heresies denying the truth of eternity, the trinity, and unity; second, heresies against the person of Christ and his Mother Mary; third, heresies against the Church, pope, and seven sacraments; and fourth, heresies against free will, angels, demons, hell, purgatory, resurrection, and good works. The fourth beast is the Anti-Christ, a composite of the other three with 'Martin Luther the precursor of the Anti-Christ, Judaism its nourishment, and Mohammed its arm and power.'[38]

Interpretation of Daniel's dream had a deep resonance in the sixteenth century among Catholics and Protestants alike. Jean Bodin's *Method for the Easy Comprehension of History* (1566) provides an encyclopedic overview of the difficulties of the text:

> A long-established, but mistaken, idea about four empires, made famous by the prestige of great men, has sent its roots down so far that it seems difficult

---

[37] Garnica, University of Chicago ms. 1120, 1st num., pp. 11–40 takes up 25% of the *librito* text.
[38] Ibid., p. 40.

to eradicate. It has won over countless interpreters of the Bible; it includes among modern writers Martin Luther, Melanchthon, Sleidan, Lucidus, Funck, and Panvinio—men well read in ancient history and things divine. Sometimes, shaken, by their authority, I used to think that it ought not to be doubted. I was stirred also by the prophecy of Daniel, whose reliability it is a crime to disparage, whose authority it is wicked to question. Yet afterwards I understood that the obscure and ambiguous words of Daniel could be twisted into various meanings; and in interpreting the prophecies I preferred to take that formula of the courts, 'it doth not appear' (*Non liquet*), than recklessly to agree with anyone because of the opinions of others, which I did not understand.... I do not see how we are to relate the wild beasts and the image discussed by Daniel to those empires which flourish everywhere now-a-days and have flourished for so many centuries.[39]

Bodin's position, twenty years before Sixtus V's condemnation of astrological and 'natural' prophecy, rejects facile figural application of biblical prophecy to contemporary politics because, in order to understand Daniel's meaning, we must first clarify 'what is this thing which we call monarchy,' one of the main concerns of the *Methodus* and his later *Six Books of the Republic* (1576). Bodin argues against the German Protestant line of interpretation as anachronistic in its attempt to make the contemporary Germans, because they were now Holy Roman Emperors, equivalent to the ancient Romans in Daniel's original prophecy. Bodin argues that the Germans have confused 'empire' with 'monarchy,'[40] one of the main points of Garnica's long treatise on the Spanish monarchy. According to Bodin, the German's error derives from Flavius Josephus, who had first identified the four beasts as monarchies or ages under the Medes, Persians, Greeks, and Romans, even though Daniel made no reference to the Romans.

> But in that way spread the mistaken custom that each man should interpret the prophecies of Daniel according to his own judgment, not according to accurate history.[41]

Garnica's interpretation of identifying the four beasts and ages as religions instead of monarchies is in this line of ahistorical reasoning, but within the tradition of figural exegesis.

In Chapter Three, Garnica examines 'the infallibility of all the Holy Roman Church,' not to prove what he considers to be an established fact, but to distinguish between the spiritual and the material Church. The Roman Church's spiritual infallibility rests upon the rock of St. Peter. Here

---

[39] Bodin, *Method for the Easy Comprehension of History*, p. 291 and all of chap. 7, 'Refutation of the Four Monarchies,' pp. 291–302.
[40] Ibid., p. 292.
[41] Ibid., p. 296.

Garnica's scriptural references are piled up and most of the argument focuses on definitions. 'Jordan' means river of judgment; 'the waters of the Jordan' mean all peoples, nations, and languages; 'testament in Scripture' means the covenant between God and man. That covenant 'is called testament because the covenant was made to make us heirs of the Kingdom of God.' The Son of God's Incarnation fulfilled the covenant, but in order for his heirs to inherit, the testator had to die. Thus, Christ suffered and died, broke the old law, and made a new covenant for 'us eternal heirs of his Father's Kingdom.' The Church faithful are the true inheritors and the superior waters of the Jordan; whereas 'the inferior waters are all the heretics with all the sects or beasts of this world.' Peter and Paul, who 'live as friends and companions in Rome with their sacred bodies,' still look over Rome and its Church. False tongues preach that the Church will pass to the Indies, a common theme often argued as compensation for the loss of the Protestant heretics. Garnica insists, however, that there is no scriptural evidence for such a claim and the Roman Church will not pass from the earth.[42]

'The place of the Church' is discussed in Chapter Four, where Garnica argues that the trials and persecutions of the Roman Church came as a result of 'mixing the things of God with matters of State.' The ministers of the Church are at fault, for it is well-known from every pulpit that 'God never gave a state to St. Peter, not even a sack so that he could keep

---

[42] Garnica, University of Chicago ms. 1120, 1st num., pp. 40–56: 'De la infallibilidad de la Iglesia Sancta Romana...Jordan, quiere dezirrio del juicio...Las agues del rio Jordan, significan todas las gentes, naciones, pueblos y lenguas del mundo...Testamento en la Scriptura, quiere dezir, confederacion entre Dios y el hombre. Llamase testamento por que la confederacion se hizo para hazernos herederos del reino de Dios. Heredero no puede ser sin muerte del testador. Y por que en la ley vieja no hubo muerte del testador, por que aun no era hombre encarnado: no pudo haver herencia, ni se pudo abrir el cielo por la ley....y por eso murio, y nos hizo herederos sempiternos del reino de su Padre....Esta es el Arca que estubo en el Jordan, que es el Sanctissimo Sacramento de la Eucharistia. Dividieronse con su presencia las agues superiors de las inferiors. Y assi se dividen todos los infieles y hereges del mundo, de la Iglesia, y pueble de Dios, que somos nosotros. Las agues superiors somos esta Iglesia, que con la presencia del Santo Sacramento, nos congregamos en una fe, y humillandonos por ella, nos levantamos en un espirtu de puridad hasta llegar al cielo. Las agues inferiors son todos los hereges con todas las sectas, ò bestias del mundo, que huyendo desta verdad, se van a precipitar al mar muerto del infierno....San Perdro y San Pablo viven, como amigos y compañeros en Roma, con sus sagrados cuerpos: han la con sagrado con su sangre y muerte: han la fundado sobre si: son fundamento de toda la Iglesia, y pueblo de Dios...Cessen las lenguas que predican, que la Iglesia se passara à las Indias. Hombres sin fundamento de Scriptura, ni de verdad. Adonde lo hallaran escrito, ò con que espiritu lo publican?'

things from one day to the next.' For Garnica, God's intent was clear, 'God did not want that in paying attention to the temporal, the spiritual would be forgotten.' God gave temporal things in the old law, and 'under that shadow and figure he promised spiritual things.' The reason that the Levites did not receive 'any estate from God, not an inch of land' was twofold: temporal things or acquisitions did not belong to the priests, they were to concentrate on the divine cult alone; and the priesthood sustained the people with the spiritual, while the people sustained them with the temporal. This mutuality created 'an indivisible charitable communion.' A long biblical exegesis from both Old and New Testaments culminate in prophetic words of God Himself, 'Good is the state for those who do not abandon Me for the state.' God's wrath awaits those who have broken his command and His irrevocable punishment will come to pass, but we know not when. 'Each one must wait in fear and await with faith.' When it does come, 'such great wrath and tempest will last' 1,260 days, that is, about 3-1/2 years later around 25 November 1598 at the beginning of the liturgical year 1598/99.[43]

One might have thought that his calculations would have predicted the end of the world for the oft-prophetic end of century in 1600, rather than the end of the year 1598. But 1,260 days invokes the mystical number of Joachim di Fiore's *annus mirabilis* for the beginning of the seventh and last age of the third *status* or stage of the spirit.[44] Two numerological

---

[43]Ibid., pp. 56–73: 'Del lugar de la Iglesia Romana veremos en el capitulo siguiente.' Cap. 4: '"De los travajos y persecuciones que han de venir à la Iglesia Romana, por que trata las cosas de Dios con material de estado...Si dixessemos que Dios nunca dio estado à San Pedro, ni aun çurron paraque guardasse de un dia para otro: no diriamos cosa ignota, sino muy sbida por todos los pulpitos. Todo esto fue por que no queria Dios, que con occasion de lo temporal, se olvidasse lo espiritual...Entremos mas à dentro con el myserio. En la ley vieja, todo lo que Dios daba eran cosas temporales: y devaxo de tal sombra y figura prometia las espirituales...Al summo Pontifice, y à los Sacerdotes, y todos los Levitas: no quiso dar Dios estado, ni un palmo de tierra...Todo esto fue para dar à entender dos cosas. La una, que el sacerdocio no se havia de occupar en cosas, ni acquisiciones temporales: sino solo en el culto divino, y que para eso se vastava tener lo necessario, y no estado ni pompa. La otra, que el sustento del Sacerdocio, es commu y obligatorio à todos los Christianos. Y assi se haze una communion caritativa indivisible: que ellos nos sustentan con lo espiritual, y nosotros à ellos con lo temporal...Dize el Señor Dios, Bueno es el estado para quien no me dexa por el estado...Señor mio, y Dios mio: quato durara tan grande ira y tempestad? Mil, y dozientos y sesenta dias.'

[44]For a summary of Joachim's thought, see McGinn, *The Calabrian Abbot: Joachim of Fiore in the History of Western Thought*, and for a short introduction with representative texts in the larger apocalyptic tradition, see McGinn, *Visions of the End: Apocalyptic Traditions in the Middle Ages*, pp. 126–141.

explanations for the number 1,260 suggest the complexity of the reasoning. It is made up of the factors 3, 5, 7, 12 in Joachim's scheme with 3 for the Trinity, 5 for the second *status*, 7 for the third *status*, and 12 the sum of the numbers for the second and third *status*; or again, the factors are 7, 12, 15 by multiplying the reign number of significant sultans or emperors (7 x 12 x 15 = 1,260).[45] Whatever Garnica's mode of mathematical mysticism, he is certainly thinking in the tradition of prophetic numerology of the kind that Bodin discusses in the *Methodus* on 'whether changes in empires can be calculated from the Pythagorean numbers.'[46] The chapter ends with a prayer for mercy and perseverance.

Garnica returns to 'the threats from the Turk and his vain prophecy' in Chapter Five.[47] Garnica argues that the true nature of Prophecy is to prophesize Christ. Turkish prophecies are those of false prophets and barbarian charlatans. We may feel fear, but should have no fear because we are among God's people upon whom He acts through miracles and providence. Above all, evidence of the secret providence of God in directing his people to victories in the Indies (East and West) can be found in the contemporary historical record. The purpose of the secular arm is to fight with weapons and wield the sword, that of the clerical arm to build. To conflate or confuse the two is to invoke the Anti-Christ instead of God.

Finally, the text comes full circle in Chapter Six, with the 'perfidious Bandoma,' Henry IV, and the imminent danger of an invasion of Rome. The need for the two sisters, Church and state, to unite and work for God's victory must be the overriding concern of all.

> The two sisters must not feel envy, because from them is born the fruit and good of the universe. They should embrace and kiss each other with tender love, as God will embrace them and bring them together with him in this

---

[45] McGinn, *Visions of the End: Apocalyptic Traditions in the Middle Ages*, p.128 explains Joachim's figures and patterns. Deny, 'Les pseudo-prophéties concernant les Turcs au XVIe siècle,' pp. 219–220 explains the importance of the numbers 7 and 12 in apocalyptic prognostications as related to the number of rulers (that is, the seventh and twelfth sultan) per Bartolomej Georgijevic, and Campanella follows Antonio Arquato in identifying that the end will come with the fifteenth Turkish emperor (Campanella, *La Monarchia di Spagna: Prima stesura giovanile*, Chap. iv, p. 25, fn. 19.).

[46] Bodin, *Method for the Easy Comprehension of History*, pp. 223–236, esp. 227–230. Bodin goes on to examine the 'seven days' of Daniel in a mumbo-jumbo of numbers and erudite references to find that 496 is the perfect number 'that coincides strangely with changes in government.'

[47] Garnica, University of Chicago ms. 1120, 1st num., p. 71: 'De las amenaças del Turco, y su vana profecia.'

world with triumph and victory and in the other one with eternal glory. Amen.[48]

Old Testament examples all again point the way to fulfillment of God's promise.

At the end of his argument, Garnica recapitulates the prophetic images of his opening—'this arrow and this bow so potent...the word, and this fiery ax'[49]—in a conclusion filled with special pleading, claims of expert knowledge, past unjust persecutions, and future fawning service. Garnica claims that the virtue and power of Holy Scripture shines through in his 'Monarchy of Spain' and 'illuminates the blindness and darkness of the world' because 'Our Lady and St. John the Evangelist, who opened the Apocalypses to me in Madrid,' taught it to him 'the same year that Your Excellency left for Rome with the embassy.'[50] Overall, the biblical quotations stick out for their frequency and erudition. This is a political text written in a prophetic idiom and supported by biblical example, such as the stories of Judas and Simon Maccabeus and Kings Ahab and Jehoshaphat, with practical political lessons drawn to the contemporary world of the 1590s. The story of the Maccabees according to Garnica, for example, reveals that there can be no peace with the infidel Turks. After Judas made peace with the Romans, with whom he 'was very pleased by [their] virtues of justice, nobility, loyalty, counsel, and prudence,' he was killed. And when Simon 'renewed the peace with the Romans, he was killed by treason.' The lesson follows:

> Note Your Excellency that the Holy Scripture tells the virtues of the Romans, who in matters of reason had no equals. Why does God tell us this? To teach us that if with men so virtuous God did not want his people to have peace and friendship because they were infidels, what would he not do with heretics and Turks, obvious demons, abominable in their customs, anathematized by the Church, more perfidious than infidels?[51]

---

[48] Ibid., p. 105: 'No se tengan embidia las dos hermanas: por que dellas nace el fruto y bien del universo. Abracense, y besense con amor tierno: por que Dios las abraçara, y agluntinara consigo en este mundo con triumfo y vitoria: y en el otro con sempiterna Gloria. Amen.'

[49] Ibid., p. 118: 'Esta saeta medio Dios: y este arco tan potente, medio el Verbo: y esta hacha en fuego ardiendo, medio el Spiritu Santo.'

[50] Ibid., pp. 121–122: 'De todo lo que digo en este compendio, mi doctrina da testimonio de la verdad. Y mi Monarchia de España, manifiesta el resplandor de la Sagrada Scriptura, y alumbra la ceguedad y tinieblas del mundo. Y à V. Excellencia la presento con la palabra que dize Dios: La Sapiencia escondida, y el thesoro que no se communica, son sin provecho en el mundo. Esta virtud y potencia me enseño nuestra Señora con San Juan Evangelista, que me a brio el Apocalypsi: en Madrid, el mismo año que V. Excellencia partio para Roma con la Embaxada.'

The exegesis of these examples ends with a rhetorical question: 'So I ask, which is best, God, the state, or the company of infidels?'[52]

The relationship between the two empires of Church and state, the fact that there is no compromise between biblical theology and expedient politics, is clearly the primary theoretical focus of the *librito*. Imminent danger and prophetic visions may be the proximate occasion, but imperial order and universal cooperation establishes God's justice and providence. Such prophetic warnings and intemperate prejudices might indeed 'alarm the world';[53] but, they are presented as reasoned theology in the apocalyptic tradition.[54]

The second short text in the *librito*, the ceremonial of the court in Naples, seems to have little to do with the current arguments advanced about coming dangers or about Church and state. Garnica presents a much more concrete and practical introduction to the way things work in Naples. First, he explores the question of justice in the public and secret law courts before the viceroy as well as in particular hearings, with sections on participants, rank, honors, languages spoken in court, and issues adjudicated. Next, Garnica outlines the Neapolitan councils of the Collateral and the whole bureaucracy with their attendant officials and concerns for the daily business of appointments, commissions, and finances. Third, Garnica draws attention to the public sermons preached before the viceroy on Sundays and feast days and the disorder in the courtyards of the palace from the number of coaches coming and going. Finally, the public rituals patronized by the Spanish in Naples on Good Friday and the prayers of supplication for Philip II, his son, and all the people of the world unite all the people of Naples, Italy, and Spain in the common bond of the universal Church and the Spanish imperium.

---

[51] Ibid., pp. 113–114: 'Judas Machabaeo, religioso, pio y en armas sin par en aquel mundo: se agrado mucho de las virtudes de iusticia, nobleza, lealtal, consejo y prudencia de los Romanos...Succediole Simon su hermano...luego fue muerto à traicion. Y note V. Excellentia que la Scriptura Sagrada, cuenta las virtudes de los Romanos, que en sola ley de razon, no tubieron iguales. A que fin las cuenta Dios? Para enseñarnos, que si con hombres de tantas virtudes, no quiso Dios que los suyos tubiessen paz ni amistad, por que eran infieles: con hereges y turcos, demonios descubiertos, puercos en las costumbres, anathematizados de la Iglesia, mas perfidos que los mas infieles, que hara?'

[52] Ibid., p. 117: 'Pregunto aora, qual es major, Dios, ò el estado, ò la compañia de los infieles.'

[53] Ibid., p. 122: 'Aquien supplico tenga por averiguado, que si hablasse turbaria el mundo.'

[54] On the apocalyptic tradition, see Barnes, *Prophecy and Gnosis: Apocalypticism in the Wake of the Lutheran Reformation*, and Reeves, *The Influence of Prophecy in the Later Middle Ages. A Study in Joachimism*.

Prognostications and prophecies about the Spanish monarchy made in Rome and Naples circa 1600 immediately bring to mind the two Neapolitan Dominicans, Giordano Bruno (burned at the stake by the Inquisition in Rome's Campo dei Fiori in February 1600) and Tommaso Campanella (arrested for conspiracy in September 1599 and imprisoned by the Inquisition in Naples and Rome for the next thirty years until 1629). In Spain a decade earlier, the four hundred fifteen dreams of Lucrecia de Len between 1587 and 1590 caught the attention of the Inquisition.[55] Philip II at the center of power in the Spanish Empire was the object of her dreams as she found fault with 'a corrupt church, oppressive taxes, lack of justice for the poor, and a weak national defense.'[56] Prophets and seers, both high and low, propagated their visions of problems, threats, failings, political programs, public policy, and crises, as well as their consequent remedies and responses throughout the Spanish world in the 1590s. This crisis of the 1590s,[57] a generalized European-wide demographic and economic slow-down that led to social disorder and severe stress in governments, had begun with sharp climatic variation and harvest failures in the mid-1580s. As famine and epidemic spread, high mortality increased, social unrest heightened, and prophetic fever rose. A clear divergence began to separate Northern from Southern Europe as the Mediterranean economy stalled, local markets gained at the expense of long-distance trade, and imperial centralization of power in both the Spanish and Ottoman world weakened.

Generalized prophetic mania, however, does not address the specificity of the confluence of Garnica's thought with that of Campanella's. The similarity in the ideas and references on monarchy, the date and place of composition, and the analysis of the political situation in the spring of 1595 point to some kind of contact and exchange between them.

Campanella's formative political thought was first written down between June 1593 and September 1595, that is, from the conversion of Henry IV to the removal of the papal ban of excommunication. Campanella's lost *De Monarchia Christianorum* and his early drafts of the *Monarchia di Spagna* introduce us to the debates about universal theocracy, universal monarchy, and apocalyptic prophecy at the heart of Garnica's manuscript. Most of the scholarly discussion on Campanella's political thought (theocratic and monarchic) is focused on the final published versions of his texts, their influence in later decades, and their unusual character. Examining the context of Spanish Italy and Naples in the 1590s, however, helps us to reconstruct Campanella's formative period

---

[55] Kagan, *Lucrecia's Dreams: Politics and Prophecy in Sixteenth-Century Spain.*
[56] Ibid., p. 2.
[57] Burke, 'Southern Italy in the 1590s: Hard Times or Crisis?' pp. 177–190.

and restore his thought to the mainstream of contemporary debates when apocalyptic prophecy flourished at the turn of the century.

The lost *De monarchia Christianorum* and the earliest draft of the *De regimine ecclesiae* date from Campanella's imprisonment by the Inquisition in Padua, September–December 1593. The lost 'On the Monarchy of Christians' presumably outlined the theoretical arguments for Church governance, as references in letters of 1607 and 1618 assert: 'no philosopher before has been able to depict the commonwealth as instituted by the apostles at Rome' or to demonstrate 'to the lord pope and all the nations regarding their jurisdictions and grades and their fraternity according to Scripture and nature; and the ruin of Christians is born from neglect of what this book contains.'[58] Garnica, as we have seen, however, unequivocally emphasizes that the Church's claims to temporal power and the protection of the city of Rome both go back to the apostolic foundation of the Christian community in Rome by Peter and Paul, whose 29 June feast day in Rome, we might remember, was celebrated with the procession in which papal suzerainty over its vassal Spanish monarch in Naples was affirmed. The more practical 'On Ecclesiastical Governance,' in its earliest redactions, appears to lay out Campanella's continuing commitment to the triple identity of the pope as prophet, priest, and king who unites in himself the spiritual kingdom, the papacy's secular realm, and the broad-based community of Christians gathered from all peoples, nations, and languages under the New Law. Garnica's completed and newly commenced texts of St. Anthony's day 13 June 1595 strongly diverges from Campanella's praise for a secular and spiritual papacy.

In the same way, arguments for the dating of Campanella's political treatise, the *Monarchia di Spagna*, find original composition would have taken place either in Padova, where Campanella was enrolled in the university from June 1593 and under investigation by the Inquisition, as we have already seen; at Venice, where he was arrested by the Inquisition in early 1594; or in Rome, where he had been transferred and record of his torture dates from July 1594.[59] Campanella remained in Rome under investigation where he abjured *de vehementi* on 16 May 1595, only a month before Garnica's composition on St. Anthony's Day. After abjuring, Campanella continued to be held in the Dominican convent of Santa Sabina on the Aventine in Rome for the next year and one-half until December 1596. John Headley concludes that Campanella's completed his original draft during his Roman imprisonment between the July 1594 torture and the end date of Henry IV's papal dispensation in September

---

[58]Headley, *Tommaso Campanella and the Transformation of the World*, pp. 261–264.
[59]Ibid., pp. 28–34.

1595.⁶⁰ There is about one year in Rome before and also after Garnica's dated texts for conversation and contact between them.

Campanella's original draft is without the later printed versions' lengthy interpolation from Giovanni Botero.⁶¹ What distinguished the early draft is its immediacy as a work of occasion—its 'scriptural, prophetic, and astrological evidence' that points to the fulfillment of prophecy in Spain's emergence as the fifth monarchy and its subordination in the secular world to the primacy of the spiritual monarchy of the papacy.⁶² For Campanella astral signs have already appeared. In Chapter iv ('On the Spanish Empire according to the first cause [that is, God's providential plan]'), 'we already see almost verified the prophecy of the end of the world, both in nature and in politics, because the fixed stars in Taurus and Scorpio have changed places, the Sun has fallen 10,000 miles toward the earth, and the transposed equinoxes cause so many eclipses.' While Plato interprets celestial phenomena as portents of 'great changes, flood, universal fire, or change of monarchies, the Evangelist [John] and Seneca see them as signs of the end of the world.' ⁶³ In Chapter vi ('If there can be among Christians a universal monarchy other than the Pope, and how one ought to have relations with him'), the tongue is mightier than the sword and is the chief weapon of the pope's rule.⁶⁴ Parallel to Garnica's prophetic tongue is Campanella's description of the tools of universal theocracy, 'wherein the tongue precedes the sword, which only confirms the conquest affected by the expansive, preached word.'⁶⁵ Prophecy speaks in tongues, employs a unique language, and is a weapon shot to the heart.

---

⁶⁰Ibid., p. 34.

⁶¹Campanella, *La Monarchia di Spagna: Prima stesura giovanile*. Since the 32 chapter titles remained the same, I have also consulted the expanded Campanella text in the Amsterdam, 1640 edition and the English Chilmead translation in the London, 1660 edition.

⁶²Headley, *Tommaso Campanella and the Transformation of the World*, p. 212. See also Dandelet, *Spanish Rome, 1500–1700*, pp. 98–101 for other examples of Spanish propaganda in Italy, such as Jerónimo Gracián, *Trattato del giubileo dell'anno santo* (Rome, 1599).

⁶³Campanella, *La Monarchia di Spagna: Prima stesura giovanile*, p. 23: 'Già si vede quasi verificata la profezia della fine del mondo, tanto nella natura, quanto nella politica, poiché le stele fisse di Tauro e Scorpione han mutato sito, e il Sole è calato a terra dieci mille miglia, e gli equinozi trasposti appareno tanti ecclissi, quale cose secondo Platone significano mutazioni grandi per tali esorbitanze celesti, o di deluvio, o d'incendio universale, o di mutazion di monarchie le più rare del mondo, ma secondo l'Evangelio e Seneca son segni della fine del mondo.'

⁶⁴Ibid., p. 28: 'Se ci può esser tra Cristiani monarchia universale altri che il Papa, e come si debba trattar con lui…il Papa è il vero monarca universale del mondo, e questo necessariamente per ragione della religione, che vince gli animi, no che I corpi soli, e ha per armi le lingue, che sono istromento di questo imperio.'

Campanella proclaims that 'the end of the monarchies is already come' and cites the Christian millennial tradition on 'what will be the end of the four monarchies and the death of the Anti-Christ, according to Lactantius, St. Irenaeus, Tertullian, Origen, Victorinus of Pettau, San Bernardino of Siena, Joachim di Fiore, and infinite other theologians, philosophers, and poets.'[66] He immediately turns to scripture, 'the statue of Daniel is completed [Daniel 2:32 ff], the three heads and twelve wings of the eagle in Esdras [4 Esdras 11:1 ff] came to an end in the Roman Empire.' The core of Campanella's thought on the four monarchies is derived from the Ferrarese doctor and astrologer, Antonio Arquato, who was associated with the Aragonese court in Naples after 1490 and whose century-old prophecy still commanded attention. Campanella follows Aquato that after the fall of the Roman Empire, monarchy was divided into three heads: on the right in the west were the Germans, on the left in the east were the Turks and Saracens, and in the middle were the Byzantines in Constantinople.[67] Campanella repeats Arquato's explanation that the Byzantine center was devoured by the Turks and that the German emperor would defeat the Turks in Hungary to become the lords of the world, the new fifth monarchy, and usher in the end of the world.[68] The afterlife of Arquato's prognostications continued into the 1590s with publication of Joannes Leunclavius's *Historiae Musulmanae Turcorum* (Frankfurt, 1591) substituting prognostications on the Turkish destruction in 1534, 1535, and 1536 for an updated 1593, 1594, and 1595.[69] Campanella and Garnica follow the main lines of this tradition.

---

[65] Headley, *Tommaso Campanella and the Transformation of the World*, p. 263 cites the later Campanella 1624–1631 *Discorsi universali del governo ecclesiastico per far una gregge e un pastor*, p. 469.

[66] Campanella, *La Monarchia di Spagna: Prima stesura giovanile*, p. 25: 'Dico dunque che il fine delle monarchie é già venuto, ed ogni cosa ha da resolversi nell'imperio felicissimo de Santi e della Chiesa, il che sarà finite le Quattro monarchie e morto l'Antecristo, secondo Lattanzio, santo Ireneo, Tertulliano, Origene, Vittorino, santo Bernardino, l'abbate gioachino e infiniti altri teologi, filosofi e poeti, come altrove dichiarai.'

[67] Ibid., chap. iv, p. 25: 'E già la statua di Daniele è finita, le Quattro bestie, le tre ebdomadi, e le dodici penne dell'aquila del IV libro d'Esdra son terminate nell'Imperio romano, il quale, secondo il medesimo, essendo babilonico, per successione fu diviso in tre capi. Primo nel destro, ch'è l'occidentale de Germani; secondo nel sinistro, ch'è l'orientale de Turchi e Saraceni, e terzo nel mezzo, ch'è il constantinopolitano, che così s'interpreta destro e sinistro secondo Mosè.' See also, p. 25, fn. 19 and chap. xxx, p. 70

[68] On Arquato's *De Eversione Europae* and how its prognostications relating to Mattia Corvino, king of Hungary, in 1480 continued to be reprinted through the sixteenth century, Thorndike, *A History of Magic and Experimental Science*, 4: 467–472; and Niccoli, *Prophecy and People in Renaissance Italy*, p. 136.

While Campanella, like Garnica, underlines the danger presented by the Turks and by alliance between France and the papacy per the rapprochement between Henry IV and Clement VIII, many other of Campanella's topics are not found in the Garnica text. Campanella sees the opportunity for Spanish success or new religious advances in Germany, the Holy Roman Empire now ruled by the Spanish kings' Habsburg cousins. Further, Campanella envisions a Hispanization of the world through unification of the Spanish kingdoms, marriage and eugenics, and universal imperial citizenship. In Chapters xxxi and xxxii he praises the spread of Christianity to the New World, and Campanella is likely one of those unnamed apologists whom Garnica railed against for prophesizing the transfer of Christian leadership to the Americas and presenting the conversion of the Indies as compensation for failures in the Old World. But above all, again without direct reference, Garnica writes in opposition to Campanella's insistence that the universal theocracy of the pope is the only true monarchy.[70]

Would it be too presumptuous to suggest that Garnica was pointing to Campanella's unnamed writings when he refers in the *librito*'s introduction to a book that he had read?[71] Garnica could well have read some of Campanella's early work on secular or spiritual government and even have had occasion to meet and converse with him at Santa Sabina. The coincidence of images, conclusions, and analysis all worked out between 1594–1595 in Rome does not appear to be by chance. This cross-fertilization of ideas, if not inspiration and imitation, certainly appears to be argumentation and refutation between Garnica and Campanella. In the intellectual climate of Spanish Rome, it should not be surprising to find high officials in the Spanish administration, such as Garnica's prospective

---

[69]Deny, 'Les pseudo-prophéties concernant les Turcs au XVIe siècle,' pp. 211–212 cites Johannes Leunclavius (1533?–1593), *Historiae Musulmanae Turcorum, de monumentis ipsorum exscriptae, libri XVIII. Opus Jo. Leunclavii ... quod gentis originem, progressus, familias & principatus diuersos, res Osmaneas a Suleimane Schacho, ad Suleimanem II memoriae nostrae, cum aliis maxime raris, & hactenus ignotis, continet. Accessere commentarii duo, Libitinarius index Osmanidarum, quo fides historiae gentiliciis e thecis, ac titulis eorum funebribus, adstruitur; & Apologeticus alter ...* (Frankfort: Apud heredes Andreae Wecheli, Claudium Marnium & Ioann. Aubrium, 1591).

[70]McGinn, *Visions of the End*, pp. 147–148 explains that Joachim 'had no place for a Messiah-like Last World Emperor, but had rather exalted a future Holy Pope along with the 'spiritual men.'' Reeves, *The Influence of Prophecy in the Later Middle Ages. A Study in Joachimism* is the standard source on the tradition.

[71]I do not think that Garnica's unnamed 'book that he had read' (see above, fn. 23) could have been John's Apocalypse, from which he received inspiration in Spain in 1592 before coming to Italy (above, fn. 50), because there would have been no reason not to name it, since he had done so earlier.

patron, the duke of Sessa, ambassador in Rome, and Campanella's inquisitorial interlocutor or ecclesiastical protector, who may have commissioned his treatise, take part in this exchange of ideas.

Ideas and favors flowed up and down the Spanish patron-client network in sixteenth and seventeenth-century Italy. The instructions issued by the king to newly appointed viceroys of Naples reflect how the system assimilated and addressed these same topics and concerns found in the works of outsiders such as Campanella and Garnica. Two exemplary instructions of Philip III to the Viceroy Count of Lemos in April 1599 and to the Viceroy Count of Benavente in September 1602 follow a similar pattern in the exact same words.[72] Both begin with dutiful submission to the spiritual arm of the pope and emphasize the secular arm's role in defense of the faith from heretics and the Turk. Likewise the viceroy is to provide protection of the royal patrimony and fisc, as well as the equitable administration of justice to vassals and subjects. By the end of the sixteenth century, these investiture instructions had become formulaic, while instructions on military affairs and strategic issues were delivered secretly, specific to the moment and occasion. The nominee to the office of viceroy had become more a symbolic deputy in the bureaucratic chain of command than an actual power.[73]

Strangely, then, what at first might have seemed wild prophetic ravings from the pen of Campanella or Garnica were, in fact, the standard bureaucratic complement to the assumption of high office in Spanish Italy—Milan, Naples, and Sicily—and not millennial paranoia circa 1600. Universal monarchy, the two sisters of Church and state, the omnipresent Turkish threat, and French Bourbon resurgence reduced to formulaic discourse should make us return to Campanella's text. The 'mad' Calabrian genius Campanella was no less mad and no less prescient than many others who shared the wide vision, practical experience, and deep anxiety of a common world-view and tradition of spiritual and statist thought constantly under siege.

University of California, San Diego
La Jolla, CA

---

[72]Coniglio, *Declino del viceregno di Napoli (1599–1689)*, 'Istruzioni di Filippo III al vicerè conte di Lemos,' (20 April 1599), pp. 71–143; and 'Istruzioni di Filippo III al vicerè di Napoli conte di Benavente,' (17 September 1602), pp. 174–241.

[73]Rivero Rodríguez, 'Doctrina y práctica política en la monarquía hispana; Las instrucciones dadas a los virreyes y gobernadores de Italia en los siglos XVI y XII,' pp. 197–213.

Works Cited

Manuscript Sources

Garnica, Juan de. University of Chicago Library, Special Collections, ms. 1120, 'Prophetic Treatise on the Turks and Christianity.' 1st num. recto only, dedication, 1–6; text, 7–122. 'On Ceremonies in Naples.' 2nd num. recto and verso, 9–60. Rome, 13 June 1595.

Garnica, Juan de. Biblioteca Nacional, Madrid (BNM), ms. 7382, 'De Hispanorum Monarchia.' 10 August 1595.

Published Sources

Barnes, Robin. *Prophecy and Gnosis: Apocalypticism in the Wake of the Lutheran Reformation.* Stanford, CA: Stanford University Press, 1988.

Beneyto Pérez, Juan. *España y el problema de Europa. Contribución a la historia de la idea de imperio.* Madrid: Editoria Nacional, 1942.

Benito, Angel. 'Introducción.' In *Comunicacion y sociedad. Homenaje a Juan Beneyto*, ed. Angel Benito, 9–20. Madrid: Universidad Complutense, 1983.

Bodin, Jean. *Method for the Easy Comprehension of History.* Trans. Beatrice Reynolds. Orig. 1566. New York: W. W. Norton, 1945.

Burke, Peter. 'Southern Italy in the 1590s: Hard Times or Crisis?' pp. 177–190 in *The European Crisis of the 1590s*, ed. Peter Clark. London: George Allen & Unwin, 1985.

Campanella, Tommaso. *La Monarchia di Spagna: Prima stesura giovanile*, ed. Germana Ernst. Naples: Istituto Italiano per gli Studi Filosofici, 1989.

Cherchi, Paolo. 'Juan de Garnica: un memoriale sul cerimoniale della corte napoletana.' *Archivio storico per le provincie napoletane* 92 (1975): 213–224.

Coniglio, Giuseppe. *I Vicerè Spagnoli di Napoli.* Naples: Fausto Fiorentino, 1967.

Congilio, Giuseppe. *Declino del viceregno di Napoli (1599–1689).* Naples: Giannini, 1990.

Dandelet, Thomas James. *Spanish Rome, 1500–1700.* New Haven and London: Yale University Press, 2001.

Deny, Jean. 'Les pseudo-prophéties concernant les Turcs au XVIe siècle.' *Revue des etudes islamiques* 10 (1936): 201–220.

Grafton, Anthony. *Cardano's Cosmos: the Worlds and Works of a Renaissance Astrologer.* Cambridge, MA: Harvard University Press, 1999.

Inventario general de Manuscritos de la Biblioteca Nacional. Madrid: Ministerio de Educacion Nacional, Dirección General de Archivos y Bibliotecas, Servicio de Publicaciones, 1956.

Hanlon, Gregory. *Early Modern Italy, 1550–1800.* New York: St. Martin's Press, 2000.

Headley, John M. ''Ehe Türckisch als Baptisch: Lutheran Reflections on the Problem of Empire, 1623–1628' pp. 3–28 in *Church, Empire and World. The Quest for Universal Order, 1520–1640*, ed. John M. Headley. Aldershot/Brookfield: Ashgate, 1997.

Headley, John M. *Tommaso Campanella and the Transformation of the World*. Princeton, NJ: Princeton University Press, 1997.
Inalcik, Halil. 'Imtiyazat.' In *The Encyclopaedia of Islam*. New ed., 3: 1182–1185. Leiden and London, 1960–.
Inalcik, Halil. *The Ottoman Empire. The Classical Age 1300–1600*, trans. Norman Itzkowitz and Colin Imber. London: Weidenfeld and Nicolson, 1973.
Kagan, Richard L. *Lucrecia's Dreams: Politics and Prophecy in Sixteenth-Century Spain*. Berkeley and Los Angeles: University of California Press, 1995.
Martinez de Campos y Serrano, Carlos. *España belica el siglo XVI. Secunda Parte*. Madrid: Aguilar, 1965.
McGinn, Bernard. *The Calabrian Abbot: Joachim of Fiore in the History of Western Thought*. New York: Macmillan, 1985.
McGinn, Bernard. *Visions of the End: Apocalyptic Traditions in the Middle Ages*. New York: Columbia University Press, 1979.
Niccoli, Ottavia. *Prophecy and People in Renaissance Italy*, trans. Lydia G. Cochrane. Princeton, NJ: Princeton University Press, 1990.
Nussdorfer, Laurie. 'The Vacant See: Ritual and Protest in Early Modern Rome.' *Sixteenth Century Journal* 18,2 (1987): 173–189.
Pastor, Ludwig von. *The History of the Popes*, ed. Ralph Francis Kerr, vol. XXIII, *Clement VIII (1592–1605)*. London: Routledge & Kegan Paul, 1952.
Reeves, Marjorie. *The Influence of Prophecy in the Later Middle Ages. A Study in Joachimism*. Oxford: Clarendon Press, 1969.
Rivero Rodríguez, Manuel. 'Doctrina y práctica política en la monarquía hispana; Las instrucciones dadas a los virreyes y gobernadores de Italia en los siglos XVI y XII.' *Investigaciones Históricas* 9 (1989): 197–213.
Thorndike, Lynn. *A History of Magic and Experimental Science*. New York: Columbia University Press, 1934.
Villari, Rosario. *The Revolt of Naples*, trans. James Newell with the assistance of John A. Marino. Cambridge: Polity Pres, 1993.

Astrology and the End of Science in Early Modern Italy

Brendan Dooley

It has become a truism of studies on early science that the Renaissance philosophy of nature, both in Italy and in Northern Europe, drew upon a powerful mix of seemingly contradictory elements: geometry and mysticism, scholasticism and vitalism. And to be convinced of the striking range of combinations, even in the case of Galileo Galilei, there is no need to pay any more than due attention to his dabbling in astrology and his affinity with Neoplatonism.[1] Among many thinkers, long-standing beliefs about the relation between the macrocosm of heavenly spheres and the microcosm of human affairs combined with humanist attitudes to ancient texts and new conceptions about the application of mathematical models to physical reality. What has not yet been examined in any great detail is the extent to which popular ideas may have influenced certain aspects of this culture that are better known in their erudite formulations.[2]

---

[1] Consider Ernst, 'Aspetti dell'astrologia e della profezia in Galileo e Campanella'; Hankins, 'Galileo, Ficino, and Renaissance Platonism.' For a mise à point of recent work defining natural philosophy, Christoph Lüthy, 'What to Do with Seventeenth-Century Natural Philosophy.' In addition, Copenhaver, 'The Occult Tradition and its Critics'; and his 'Natural Magic, Hermetism and Occultism in Early Modern Science.' Also note earlier articles such as those by Allen G. Debus, Leland L. Estes, and Karin Johannisson in Merkel and Debus, eds., *Hermeticism and the Renaissance*; and those in Vickers, ed., *Occult and Scientific Mentalities in the Renaissance*, strongly influenced by Frances Yates. In addition, Shumaker, *Natural Magic and Modern Science*; Webster, *From Paracelsus to Newton*. For a particularly critical reading of the relation between science and the occult, note Zambelli, *L'ambigua natura della magia*, especially chap. 1.

[2] An interesting volume aimed at focusing attention on this problem was related to the conference entitled 'Scienza, credenze occulte, livelli di cultura'. See also Ginzburg, *The Cheese and the Worms*, and Zambelli's response, 'Uno, due, tre, mille Menocchio.'

Recent work on the social history of science, meanwhile, has drawn the gaze of the researcher from the heights of intellectual creativity down to the level of the daily practice of many important protagonists. Daily practice compelled an interchange with individuals at many different social levels, put the protagonists in situations where the common language of natural knowledge was spoken in many different dialects—high and low.[3] From this perspective, Galileo's involvement with astrology, a set of concepts and activities as deeply inscribed within circuits of popular as of erudite knowledge, takes on new significance. His friendship with Orazio Morandi, tried for judicial astrology and other crimes in 1630, demands further investigation. And so do the astrological interests of Galileo's antagonist in the trial of 1633, Pope Urban VIII.

A preliminary reexamination of the evidence suggests that the ancient science of the stars, not the Ptolemaic tradition rediscovered by Renaissance natural philosophers, but the one passed down by word of mouth and developed to a considerable degree of sophistication by sixteenth and seventeenth-century practitioners, played a far more important role in the Galileo affair than has previously been supposed. This paper attempts to shed some new light on a major turning point in modern cultural history by broadening the context and reinterpreting some of the ideas involved.

To be sure, the attribution of astrological interests to Galileo may seem more far-fetched now than it could have seemed in his lifetime.[4] When he came to Rome to solicit support for the publication of his *Dialogue Concerning the Two Chief World Systems*, the Roman newsletter writers picked up the story. And according to one of them, Antonio Badelli, the new book by 'the astrologer' Galileo inveighed 'against the Jesuits'—not an entirely inept characterization. But 'the astrologer' had done much more. In fact, the real news, according to Badelli, was that he had predicted the death of Pope Urban VIII; and not satisfied with that prediction, had apparently added another one about the death of Taddeo Barberini, the pope's nephew, not to mention yet another one about the

---

[3] I have in mind, for instance, Smith, *The Business of Alchemy*; and the articles in Pumfrey, Rossi and Slawinski, eds., *Science, Culture, and Popular Belief in Renaissance Europe*.

[4] No attempt will be made here to take account of the vast bibliography implied here regarding Galileo's life and works. Apart from standard sources like Geymonat, *Galileo Galilei*; Koyré, *Études Galiléennes*; Drake, *Galileo at Work*, keeping in mind the review by Shea in *Annali dell'Istituto e Museo di Storia della Scienza, Firenze*; and articles in *Novità celesti e crisi del sapere*; and other works mentioned from time to time below, there are Redondi, *Galileo Heretic*, and Biagioli, *Galileo, Courtier*, about which more will be said later on.

birth of a male heir to Donna Anna Colonna, Taddeo's wife, and about the future peace of Italy.[5]

Nothing in the writings or activities of the real Galileo justifies any such attributions. However, regarding the veracity or falsehood of astrology as a science, quite apart from the foibles of the astrologers themselves, Galileo was more guarded in his affirmations than his reputation might lead us to believe. Disagreement with Ptolemaic notions about the organization of the cosmos did not prevent him from suggesting that the planets 'abounded in influences'—though he never specified of what sort.[6] Arguably, planetary influences were again one of those working hypotheses, or indeed, unprovable axioms (such as the primacy of mathematics), from which Galileo's science was no more exempt than was that of any of his contemporaries—or indeed, of our own. Most probably, the several horoscopes now extant, drawn up in Galileo's hand, especially for members of the Medici family, should be viewed in the wider context of the natural philosophy of the time.[7]

If, as it seems, Galileo as a natural philosopher was not a categorical opponent of the ideas that stood at the foundations of astrology, he was in good company. Few physicians of the sixteenth and seventeenth centuries denied planetary influences outright. Late antique ideas concerning the heating, drying, cooling and moistening action of each planet still combined with medieval notions about the four humors, yielding the four major personality types—melancholy, sanguine, bilious, phlegmatic. And the theory of Galen and Hippocrates concerning the planets' role in determining critical days and the patterns of ebb and flow of diseases still enjoyed the popularity gained for them by Agostino Nifo's widely read works on the subject.[8] No wonder medical faculties still staffed chairs of astrology, or else chairs of mathematics whose curriculum was expected to include astrology.

To be convinced that astrology was a serious matter among Galileo's philosophical contemporaries there is no need to take certain passages of Francis Bacon out of the closet where a Whiggish historiography once

---

[5] *Edizione nazionale delle opere di Galileo Galilei*, 14: 103, newsletter dated May 18, 1630.

[6] *Opere di Galileo*, 11: 108; letter to Piero Dini dated 21 May 1611. The entire letter concerns the problem of the significance, for the theory of planetary influences, of the newly discovered satellites of Jupiter, and Galileo's conjectures in this regard.

[7] For instance, Righini, 'L'oroscopo galileiano di Cosimo II de' Medici.'

[8] Nifo's work was *De diebus criticis*. On Girolamo Cardano's contributions concerning critical days, Siraisi, *The Clock and the Mirror*., chap. 6. Concerning astrology and humoral theory see Saxl, Klibansky and Panofsky, *Saturn and Melancholy*, part 2, chap. 1.

put them. The influential theorist of a new approach to nature called for undertaking a new compilation and sorting of data regarding astral influences: 'The astrologers may, if they please, draw from real history all greater accidents, as floods, plagues, wars, seditions, deaths of kings, etc., as also the motions of the celestial bodies . . . to . . . erect a probable rule of prediction.' Such information was of course to be carefully scrutinized. 'All traditions should be well-sifted, and those thrown out that manifestly clash with physical reasons, leaving such in their full force as comport well therewith.' He never questioned the planetary influences themselves, upon which astrology was based—i.e., 'the universal appetites and passions of matter' that constituted 'those physical reasons [that] are best suited to our inquiry,' along with 'the simple genuine motions of the heavenly bodies.' This, he avowed, 'we take for the surest guide to astrology.'[9]

Nor is there any need to resort to the conventional citations of Johannes Kepler, a notorious astrologer-astronomer. At one point Kepler claimed that the beneficent influence of Jupiter, Venus, and Mercury was due to the structurally stable triangular faces of the polygons that, according to his calculations, yield the planetary distances from the sun:

> Mars, however, agrees with Saturn in evil alone. I therefore take this into consideration with the instability of their angles, which I find common to both. An opposite argument would thus suggest good qualities, that is, considering the stability of the angles at the bases. This is why Jupiter, Venus and Mercury are beneficial.[10]

Later he claimed that the planetary aspects or angles between planets in the zodiac (i.e., opposition, trine, etc.) were not effective in themselves, but only in so far as they affected the world soul, which in turn influenced the operation of all things in the universe. In eclipses, this world soul was 'strongly disturbed by the loss of light.'[11] The configurations of the stars at birth reminded individual souls of their 'celestial character' and endowed them with the particular features that accompanied the subject through life.[12]

---

[9] All from *Advancement of Learning*, ed. Creighton, III: 4 (p. 90 in this edition). Not in the least Whiggish of course is Rossi, *Francesco Bacone: Dalla magia alla scienza*; and especially see Walker, 'Spirits in Francis Bacon.' In addition, Curry, *Prophecy and Power*; and compare Geneva, *Astrology and the Seventeenth-Century Mind*. Still fundamental are Böll, et al., *Sternglaube und Sterndeutung*.

[10] Modified from Kepler, *The Secret of the Universe*, pp. 115–116. In general, Simon, *Kepler: Astronome, Astrologue* and Hallyn, *Structure poétique du monde*, and Field, 'A Lutheran Astrologer: Johannes Kepler,' all to be compared with Stephenson, *Kepler's Physical Astronomy*.

[11] *De fundamentis astrologiae certioribus*, 4: 418.

[12] *Gesammelte Werke*, 6: 264–286. Cited in Thorndike, *A History of Magic and*

If the popular mind confused Galileo the astrologer with Galileo the astronomer, this was hardly surprising. Not only did well-regarded ancients like Ptolemy write on both subjects, even the most serious modern compilers of astronomical information, such as Erasmus Reinhold, author of the Prutenic Tables of planetary motions, larded their works with astrological information of various types. With astrological and astronomical texts standing side by side in major libraries all over Europe, even Kepler himself could not decide which was the other's 'silly little daughter'—astronomy or astrology; and in various writings he referred to each by one or the other characterization.[13]

More important than Galileo's own involvement with astrology was his involvement with astrologers—such as the Bolognese Franciscan friar Ilario Altobelli. Already in 1610, Altobelli tried to induce Galileo to send him the necessary lenses for making a telescope.[14] On the basis of a new and more accurate set of tables of celestial movements, he attempted to work out a more exact division of the twelve houses than had hitherto been possible. Irregularities, due to the obliquity of the ecliptic with respect to the celestial equator, caused different houses to have different lengths. In rejecting the equal house method and eight other methods currently in use, Altobelli claimed to 'confound the followers of Regiomontanus'—not to mention also those of Cardano.[15] Had his ideas not been stolen by Andrea Argoli, another correspondent of Galileo, and incorporated into the latter's latest *Ephemerides*, so he complained to Orazio Morandi, he would surely have won credit for having restored the reputation of Ptolemy, who, in his view, came closest to the truth.[16]

Another acquaintance of Galileo was Rafaello Gualterotti, a Florentine nobleman, poet and virtuoso with whom he occasionally shared horoscopes.[17] Like other astrologers of the time, Gualterotti attributed enor-

---

Experimental Science, 7: 22.

[13]Compare *Gesammelte Werke*, 10: 36 with 4: 161.

[14]*Opere di Galileo* 10: 317, letter dated 17 April 1610. See Stano and Balsinelli, 'Un illustre scienziato francescano'; and the article by Odoardi in *Dizionario biografico degli Italiani* 2 (1960): 567–568.

[15]The quote is in Rome, Archivio di Stato, Governatore, Processi sec. XVII, b. 251 [hereafter, *Morandi trial*], fol. 758r. Compare *Opere di Galileo*, 10: 116, 118, 132, 135, 317. See also Grafton, *Cardano's Cosmos*, chap. 3. Concerning the various methods of calculation of astrological charts, see North, *Horoscopes and History*.

[16]Altobelli's chief works were *Tabulae regiae divisionum dodecim partium coeli et syderum obviationum ad mentem Ptolomaei* and *Demonstratio ostendens artem dirigendi et domificandi Ioannis de Monteregio non concordare cum doctrinam Ptolomaei*.

[17]Galluzzi, 'Motivi paracelsiani in Toscana,' p. 55; Jacoli in *Bullettino di bibliografia e di storia delle scienze matematiche e fisiche di B. Buoncompagni* 7 (1874): 377–415; Casati, *Dizionario degli scrittori d'Italia*, vol. 3, p. 55. On the

mous importance to the nova of 1604, about which he conferred with Galileo. And the fact that the nova was accompanied by the great conjunction of the superior planets as well as a solar eclipse in the sign of Libra, so he wrote in his book on the subject, was all the more significant. The great conjunction began in Sagittarius, which ruled the frontiers of the Spanish Empire, the Tyrrhenian Sea, Buda and Jerusalem. And Libra, where the eclipse occurred, was the native territory of Rome and the rest of Italy, along with Syria and Persia. 'Many provinces,' he concluded, 'are threatened with evils, with war, and with death.'[18]

Perhaps the most interesting of Galileo's astrological associates was Orazio Morandi, best known for his ill-fated prophecy about the death of Urban VIII in 1630.[19] Laureate *in utraque* from the Sapienza university in Rome in 1590, Morandi had begun his ecclesiastical career at the headquarters, outside Florence, of the Vallombrosa order, a branch of the Benedictines. In Florence he became a fixture of the local cultural scene before finally attracting the attention of Don Giovanni de' Medici, the natural son of Cosimo I. In the company of Giovanni, he studied natural philosophy and practiced alchemy and astrology. His abilities as an astrologer helped cement his connections with the Medici family, to whom he, like Galileo, apparently gave astrological consultations. Eventually, Medici patronage gained for him a transfer to Rome as abbot of the monastery of Santa Prassede, and the generalship of his order.

The extent of the collaboration between Galileo and Morandi is unknown. For bringing the two men together, Galileo's legendary Vallombrosa connection (he was supposedly sent to school for a time at the order's Tuscan headquarters) was probably less decisive than Morandi's Medici connection.[20] There were opportunities to meet in Florence, where Galileo was tutor to the Medici princes while on the faculty at the University of Padua. In any case, the association between the two men must have begun before 1613, when Morandi sent his congratulations upon Galileo's appointment to the Accademia de Lincei.[21] We do not

---

sharing of horoscopes, *Opere di Galileo*, 10: 198, letter dated 29 March 1608.

[18] *Scherzi degli spiriti animali detati con l'occasione dell'oscurazione dell'anno 1605*, chap. 22.

[19] The bibliography on Morandi is not long: Ernst, 'Scienza, astrologia e politica nella Roma barocca'; in addition, Sala, *Dizionario storico-biografico di scrittori letterati ed artisti dell'ordine di Vallombrosa*, 76–77; Tarani, *L'Ordine Vallombrosano*, 127; Bertolotti, 'Giornalisti, astrologi e negromanti in Roma nel secolo XVII' pp 478–479; Fiorani, 'Astrologi, superstiziosi e devoti nella società romana del Seicento,' 97ff; not to mention Bracciolini, *Oratio . . . de laudibus . . . Horatii Morandi romani*. Now see my *Morandi's Last Prophecy*.

[20] Compare Favaro, *Galileo Galilei e lo Studio di Padova*, 1: 7–8.

[21] *Opere di Galileo*, 11: 530, letter dated 6 August 1613.

know how often in the following years Morandi sent books to his friend, acknowledging Galileo's gratitude in a mutilated correspondence of which the Galileo side has been entirely lost.[22] We also know that the monastery somehow acquired, along with a nearly-complete collection of Galileo publications, an authentic 'telescope of Galileo'—as it was described in the documents. The two men were on familiar enough terms in 1626 for Morandi to intercede for Galileo with the Congregation on Councils on behalf of a young monk who happened to be the cousin of a Galileo acquaintance.

When both men were in Rome, it is thus highly likely that Morandi was among the many philo-Florentines whom Galileo frequented. Just how many times they met at the monastery is yet another tantalizing blank spot in the record. The best known letter from Morandi to Galileo states: 'Next Sunday, the Day of the Most Holy Trinity I am expecting to be favored by Your Lordship to do penance up here at Santa Prassede where there will be the Father Consultor, Master Ludovico Corbusio, ex-Inquisitor of Florence, and Padre [Rafaello] Visconti, secretary to the Most Reverend Father, the Master of the Sacred Palace. There is no need for you to bother to reply; but simply get ready to come. I expect you without fail.'[23] Most likely, the worldly astrologer was not inviting his illustrious contemporary for a prayer meeting. Nor, in all likelihood is the word 'penance' to be taken to refer to some literal form of austerity. Quite the opposite. With the fine sense of irony typical of this elite environment, 'penance' might well have indicated a sumptuous repast—especially since the Sunday of the Holy Trinity was not a day of abstinence. Our host expected no hesitation from his guest, and probably got none. For a brief period several months later, the fortunes of the two men were fatefully intertwined when Galileo was rumored to be the author of the prophecy about Urban VIII that had actually been pronounced by Morandi.

Morandi worked his way to the height of Roman ecclesiastical society in part by the relatively unusual method of prodigious bookmanship. Almost as soon as he arrived in Rome, he began acquiring books and manuscripts for the monastery's modest library, especially in fields that interested him. To the existing collections he added numerous texts on mathematics, natural history, chemistry, astronomy, alchemy, natural magic, astrology.[24] And along with perfectly unexceptionable works of

---

[22]E.g., *Opere di Galileo*, 13: 319, letter dated 17 April 1626.
[23]E.g., *Opere di Galileo*, 14: 107, letter dated 24 May 1630.
[24]A census taken by the Roman authorities of books in the library around 1600 is recorded in Biblioteca Apostolica Vaticana, mss. Vat. lat. 11288, fols. 211r–215v. A list of books attributed personally to Morandi appears in duplicate in *Morandi trial*, at fols. 556r–562v.

theology, literature and rhetoric, he acquired some of the great prohibited classics of the time. Of course, the library catalogues must be accompanied by collateral evidence to distinguish between items accessioned by Morandi himself and those purchased by others, perhaps before he arrived. We may never know with any certainty whether Morandi or some enlightened predecessor purchased copies of dangerous works by Boccaccio, Machiavelli, Johannes Trithemius, and Johannes Sleidan. But there is no doubt that he alone was responsible for the presence of a manuscript copy of Tommaso Campanella's *Astrology*, dangerous because of the reputation of its writer, and bound copies of the contemporary clandestine newsletters known as 'avvisi,' full of secret political gossip and forbidden by law.

By opening up the monastery library to a select portion of the Roman community as a lending library, Morandi procured for himself protection and favors. Along with the priests and laymen, artists and patrons, writers and scribes, students and women whose needs for information Morandi satisfied, and whose names, along with the books they borrowed, appeared in the library lending list, he managed to attract some of the most important cardinals in the curia.[25] Indeed, library patrons such as Cardinals Capponi, Tiberio Muti, and Luigi Caetani, besides their exalted rank, also happened to be sitting on one of the most important committees in ecclesiastical government—namely, the Congregation on the Index. And just in case their authority was not enough to guarantee Morandi's safety, there was also Niccolo Ridolfi, the Master of the Sacred Palace, whose signature was required on every permit to publish a book in Rome.

At the same time, Morandi turned the monastery into an astrological Mecca for the fortunate and the less fortunate. And in the monks' astrological logbook, a record of consultations appended to the trial record, we find nativities not just of children but of an elderly neighbor known only as the 'Old Man of Arezzo'; and not only of a 'youth who made copies' but of a servant to the Florentine ambassador. We find that of a student (the son of one Giambattista Carpani) as well as that of a certain 'Lodovico who is in jail,' of the Duke of Rethel's heir, Leopold (the Archduke of Austria), and Vitellio Malespina (son of Count Giambattista).[26] And among highly placed ecclesiastical officials there were Francesco Usimbardi of the Camera Apostolica, and Francesco Maria Ghisleri, an auditor of the Sacra Romana Rota. There also came Francesco Maria Merlini, later bishop of Cervia, and Giovanni Pietro Savio, the bishop of Sebenico. No doubt they all, like the last client mentioned, awaited the results of their consultation 'as the Messiah.' Because 'my

---

[25] Morandi's lending list is in *Morandi trial*, fols. i–xviii.
[26] *Morandi trial*, fols. 1280r–1313v.

only consolation,' he added to Orazio Morandi, 'is the hope of future happiness.'[27]

The monastery, of course, was not the only place in Rome where astrological information could be had. 'All Rome is filled with these charlatans,' it was said, by one of the more detached observers.[28] And apart from 'various Spaniards,' a 'knife seller' in Monte Giordano, 'a certain Battelli,' as well as 'Jacobelli the physician,' a 'son of the hatmaker at S. Pellegrino,' and a 'friar in S. Francesco a Ripa,' there were many other practitioners whose absence from the criminal records makes them very hard to trace.[29] Nor was one witness exaggerating when he noted, 'astrology has become a recognized profession, and almost everyone has nativities drawn up. . . . [Indeed,] there is no cardinal or prelate or prince who does not have discourses drawn up telling his fortune based on his nativity. . . . Of course,' he was quick to add, 'only for secondary causes, because everything in the final analysis depends on God.'[30]

Nor did the astrological dilettantes shrink from predicting the highest honors to the most conspicuous personages—as did Francesco Lamponi, an associate of Santa Prassede, not only to Cardinal Desiderio Scaglia, but also to his nephew, the bishop of Melfi. 'There are no complimentary words or written thanks,' Melfi replied. 'Only acts of the most affectionate servitude that one soul may give to another to which it is bound in perpetual obligation, as mine is.'[31] In Melfi's opinion, Lamponi had 'managed my stars and seen the essence of my condition.' Not only did he draw ultimately flattering conclusions for the future on the basis of information Melfi had provided, he also made fortunate guesses concerning earlier episodes in the cardinal's life. 'Since you discovered the facts so accurately in these and other things,' Melfi stated in the same document, 'I can only conclude that all the future events will be verified as well'—include the promise of the papacy.

Morandi distinguished his operations from the crowd of his competitors by a conspicuous demonstration of quasi-scientific methodology. Interrupted at the planning stage by the court's investigations, the comprehensive astrological encyclopedia he undertook for in-house consultation

---

[27] *Morandi trial*, fol. 755, letter dated 29 July, 1627. The activities of the people in question are recorded in *Morandi trial*, fols. 467r and 572r (Ghisleri), fols. 130r, 192r, 398r (Scaglia), fols. 110r and 123r (Usimbardi).

[28] *Morandi trial*, fol. 183r, deposition of Marcantonio Conti, 6 August 1630. Concerning the astrological tradition in Rome, Troncarelli, ed., *La città dei segreti*.

[29] *Morandi trial*, fol. 436v, deposition of Francesco Modesti, 9 September 1630.

[30] All from *Morandi trial*, fol. 504r, deposition of Agostino Lamponi, 5 November 1630.

[31] All from *Morandi trial*, fol. 536r, letter dated 21 March 1628. Scaglia's nativity is in ibid., at fol. 1062r.

would have brought together the expertise and teamwork of the entire monastery.[32] And apart from chapters dedicated to such technical subjects as solstice points, the aspects, the theory of the houses according to Ptolemy and according to Regiomontanus, and the theory of directions according to both, he would compare a vast array of natal charts to the fortunes of their subjects—exactly what Francis Bacon had recommended. Monks were deputed to peruse the parish records when they could not get oral testimony. The results would be divided into subsections on good fortune by evading dangers, and (much longer), ill fortune resulting in a frightening catalogue of catastrophes.

If these investigations were intended to gain credit for astrology in a period of scientific change, while distinguished visitors shielded the monastery's activities from prosecution according to the various papal anti-astrology bulls, the strategy appears to have worked brilliantly. Authoritative presences flocked the monastery halls. Morandi was able to invite the greatest cardinals in Rome over for his monastery soirées. The company occasionally included Galileo; and the monks themselves provided entertainment, including music and theatrical presentations.[33]

But scientific astrology was not enough for Morandi; nor was he satisfied by the local notoriety he had already achieved. He needed to make an outstanding demonstration of his techniques. There were plenty of examples of virtuosity, in the fast-paced intellectual environment of the time. Natural philosophers like Galileo Galilei competed for the attention of powerful patrons by spectacular coups de scène.[34] Clearly, preeminence in astrology belonged to the successful bearer of an important prediction—a prediction about the future of an individual whose position in the firmament was of great interest not only to the usual satellites, but also to others of truly planetary importance. Finally the chance came, so Morandi thought, in 1630, and the object was none other than Urban VIII.

Predicting the death of a personage as eminent as Urban VIII, of course, was fraught with difficulties. For one thing, the prediction might fail. And only three years before, the pope's health seemed to be so sound that a previous Venetian ambassador saw no reason not to expect a 'long pontificate.'[35] However improbable a prediction of death might be, it was

---

[32]Here and below, *Morandi trial*, fols. 959r and ff.

[33]*Morandi trial*, fol. 572r.

[34]For the performance aspect of science in this period, apart from Biagioli, *Galileo Courtier*, chap. 2, see Findlen, 'Jokes of Nature and Jokes of Knowledge: The Playfulness of Scientific Discourse in Early Modern Europe'; Tribby, 'Cooking [with] Clio: Eloquence and Experiment in Seventeenth-Century Florence.'

[35]Barozzi and Berchet, *Relazioni degli stati europei lette al Senato dagli ambasciatori veneti*, vol. 1, p. 211, from the report of Pietro Contarini in 1627.

almost certain to encounter strong disapproval from the personage in question. Julius Firmicus Maternus was by no means the first astrologer in history to refuse to draw up nativities for the eminent because of their capacity for retaliation. Nor was Luca Gaurico the last to suffer for having done them. Half a century after Gaurico went to the torture chamber for having predicted Giovanni Bentivoglio's problems with Pope Julius II, the English astrologer Thomas Harriot was thrown in jail for having cast nativities of the king and crown prince on the eve of the Gunpowder Plot that narrowly missed destroying them both.[36]

Of all possible subjects for astrological prophecies, Urban VIII was perhaps among the most sensitive. Even those who knew him well admitted that the rumors about his singular dedication to this science were partly true. Two years before, when some of the Roman astrologers, including Francesco Lamponi, a member of the Santa Prassede circle, had foreseen an imminent threat due to a solar eclipse followed by a lunar eclipse, the Tuscan ambassador reported, 'the pope has begun to calculate his nativity more than ever.'[37] To counter the fatal astral influences, he called in none other than astrology expert Tommaso Campanella, who happened to be enjoying a rare period of relative freedom from the prisons of the Inquisition. With Campanella's help he had a room of Castel Gandolfo fitted out as a veritable magic chamber, decorated with dried reeds and white linen sheets, perfumed with burnt essences of laurel, rosemary, and cypress, and illuminated with burning torches in circles on the floor representing the spheres of the universe. Only Campanella's own later testimonies stand as proof that what went on in that room contained nothing to arouse suspicions of witchcraft or necromancy.[38] No pope could fail to wonder what the consequences might be of such behavior.

Morandi was presented with a nativity for Urban VIII drawn up for the 5th of April, 1568 at 1:29 PM, with the sun in Aries in the ninth house and Leo in the ascendant.[39] According to his analysis, the sun was the life-giving planet in this configuration, but its favorable effects were entirely vitiated by the presence of Mars and the Moon. Venus, though favorably situated, was no match for these evil planets, especially because

---

[36] Cases mentioned in this paragraph are documented in Bowden, *The Scientific Revolution in Astrology*, p. 110; Grafton, *Cardano's Cosmos*, chaps. 2, 6.

[37] Amabile, *Tommaso Campanella ne' castelli di Napoli, in Roma ed in Parigi*, 2: 153; 172ff.

[38] Described by Campanella in his *De siderali fato vitandi*, a pirated version, published in 1629 without his knowledge, as Book 7 of his *Astrologicorum*. See Ernst, *Religione, ragione e natura*, chap. 1.

[39] Several versions of Urban VIII's horoscope can be found in *Morandi trial*, with slight differences, at fols. 13r, 1050r, 1264r.

it in turn was blocked by the opposition of Saturn in the eighth house. Urban was very fortunate, said Morandi, to have lived beyond the age of seven. Things started looking better if these directions were progressed to the year 1630. The ascendant would be back, unaccompanied by any unfavorable planets, and Venus would be in its own house and in a good position to counteract Saturn. But none of these benefits were of much use if Urban was doomed to die in any case. That year, a solar eclipse would occur in June in the sign of Gemini, in the vicinity of Mars, the planetary ruler of late middle age, Urban's current stage of life. And concerning the influence of solar eclipses, Morandi paid less attention to Ptolemy's *Tetrabiblos* than to the Pseudo-Ptolemaic *Centiloquium* (which he erroneously attributed to Hermes Trismegistus).[40] On the basis of this reading, his conclusion was inescapable: Urban VIII was doomed. And the fact that Rome was under Taurus, a whole sign away from Gemini, where the eclipse would be occurring (although Italy was sometimes said to be under Libra), was not enough to save his life.

Among the circle of individuals connected with the monastery, a universal chorus of assent greeted Morandi's analysis. No one, it turned out, could convince Francesco Usimbardi and two academicians, namely, Vitellio Malespina and Bartolomeo Filicaia, that the prediction conveyed *viva voce* to them by Morandi might not be true.[41] Whereas the poet Francesco Bracciolini believed the prophecy because of the authority of its bearer, the astrologer Francesco Lamponi believed it because he had reached the same conclusions on his own—to the delight of his patron, Cardinal Desiderio Scaglia, whose papal aspirations suddenly seemed less fanciful than ever.[42]

Just in case news about the prophecy did not spread far enough spontaneously, Morandi himself communicated it by mail to Simon Carlo Rondinelli, former librarian of Giovanni de' Medici in Florence, and to many other correspondents whose identities he later refused to reveal to the court.[43] Soon the news found its way into the manuscript newsletter network; and just as inevitably, it went through a few transformations along the way. With mediocre comprehension, an anonymous newsletter writer on the payroll of the duke of Modena attributed the prophecy to Tommaso Campanella, much to the chagrin of the latter, who immediately rushed to defend his already precarious position at the papal court.[44]

---

[40]Pseudo-Ptolemy's *Centum Ptolomaei sententiae* also called *Centiloquium* was published by Aldus Manutius in Venice (1519) among others.
[41]*Morandi trial*, fol. 110r, Morandi deposition, 15 July 1630.
[42]*Morandi trial*, fol. 536r, letter dated 21 March 1628.
[43]*Morandi trial*, fol. 110r, Morandi deposition, 15 July 1630.
[44]Amabile, *Tommaso Campanella*, 2: 149, quoting a report in the files of the

Another newsletter, as we said, attributed the prophecy to Galileo. In many forms and in many cities, the prediction made the news, and Naples was by no means the only place besides Rome where it was widely reported as a proven fact.[45]

As the prediction about Urban VIII rapidly slid out of its author's control, it became part of the bitter factional struggle in Rome. Among those of the pro-Spanish faction who could hardly contain their joy at the prospect of an imminent conclusion to Urban's notorious French favoritism was Ludovico Ridolfi, brother of the outgoing Master of the Sacred Palace. He forthwith recruited Raffaele Visconti to help communicate his sentiments 'by day to the princes' (so Tommaso Campanella later recalled) and 'by night, to the Spanish.' With Urban's fate apparently decided, the question arose of who might be the next pope.[46] A flood of clandestine publications concerning the possible outcomes of the next conclave encouraged further speculation.[47]

Unfortunately, Morandi's careful calculations were in error, and Urban lived on for another fourteen years, to 1644. He did not die in 1630. Nor was he pleased about what he discovered going on around him. He was all the more incensed at having made the discovery not on his own, nor even by way of the many informants he had scattered around the city, but by way of a message from Cardinal Richelieu, in the course of negotiations between France and Spain concerning the War of Mantua—as Urban himself later related to Theodore Ameyden, who once frequented the Santa Prassede circle.[48] If Richelieu already knew about monastery activities, and knew others who knew, the French were better informed than the Pope himself. And if the international community was as saturated with the rumors as Richelieu claimed, there was no wonder the Spanish cardinals were already enroute to Rome to take part in conclave preparations that were secretly under way. Richelieu's very presence before him on that occasion, Urban must have suspected, was probably intended to gain favor for the French cause by portraying the Spanish as shameless intriguers. The conclusion, in any case, was inescapable: Morandi must be stopped and his punishment made an example to the others.

Este secretary of state, dated 4 May 1630.

[45]Campanella, *Lettere*, 288, letter to Urban VIII dated 9 April 1630.

[46]Campanella, *Lettere*, 287–288. Cited in Ernst, 'Scienza, astrologia e politica nella Roma barocca,' p. 221.

[47]Amabile, *Tommaso Campanella*, 2: 150, from a report in the files of the Este secretary of state, dated 18 May 1630.

[48]See Bastiaanse, *Teodoro Ameyden*, p. 56.

Rather than waiting for the clumsy Roman bureaucracy to run its course, Urban demanded immediate action. To Antonio Fido, lieutenant governor of Rome, 'We order you,' he wrote on July 13, 'to make the necessary incarcerations and investigations of the said abbot and any other person you may consider appropriate.'[49] No holy place was to be spared, regardless of the degree of ecclesiastical immunity it was supposed to enjoy——not even 'the monastery and the church of Santa Prassede' itself. To ensure 'the unity and perfect order of all the above mentioned proceedings already under way and still to begin,' Urban ordered the trial to take place in the governor's court and not be split between that court and the Inquisition. And the same evening just after sunset, under the terrified gaze of his fellow monks, Morandi was led off by two policemen to the prisons at the Tor di Nona, near the eastern end of the Ponte St. Angelo, and charged with 'exercising judicial astrology, composing political and malicious writings and keeping prohibited books.'

Soon afterwards Morandi was found dead in jail—according to the doctor's report, which is in the trial record, due to complications from a high fever and not, the doctor is quick to add, from poisoning. Perhaps the doctor protested too much. A quick dispatching of the suspect may well have been ordered to protect the reputations of the many illustrious persons in the curia, more and more of whose names were being dredged up during the course of the trial and copied down in the record. The following year Urban published the severest bull yet against the astrologers, emphasizing, with obvious reference to Morandi, the aggravation of the crime when the accused disseminated his astrological conclusions far and wide.

In vain, the astrologers protested that canceling astrology would cancel all astronomy because people mainly looked at the stars to see what they could get out of them. Said one, 'I think few people really care about Mars or Jupiter unless they can incorporate this knowledge into a prediction.'[50] Without this motive, the astrologer suggested, there would be no stargazing, no planetary calculation, and eventually no means even of determining the proper time for the Easter cycle (based on the vernal equinox and the phases of the moon)—with grave consequences for religion, for faith, and for the Holy Catholic Church. Kepler, echoing an argument Galileo made about astronomy, suggested that prohibiting astrology was tantamount to prohibiting all philosophy, inasmuch as the science of the stars was bound up with every other aspect of natural

---

[49] This and the following quotes, *Morandi trial*, fol. 3r.
[50] *Morandi trial*, fol. 753r.

knowledge. And Campanella reinterpreted the bull in such a fashion that astrologers should have been able to go on much the same as before.[51]

Urban VIII was not concerned about the consequences to astronomy if astrology was severely limited; and any possible utility that science might have for religion was far less important to him than his own survival. Never mind that he could always put to work the defense procedures suggested to him by Campanella. It was as unseemly for a pope to be reportedly engaging, to the full knowledge of the Roman public and the rest of Europe, in quasi-magical ceremonies proposed by a suspected heretic as it was for him to receive warnings of imminent death from one of his subjects. In the bull *Inscrutabilis,* he anathematized those who 'do not blush at publicizing prognostications and predictions by word of mouth and even by writing, to the deplorable perdition of their souls and the grave scandal of Christendom.'[52] But his real target was 'the dusky human intellect, constrained in the prison of the flesh,' which, 'with nefarious curiosity, arrogates itself to explore the arcana hidden in the divine mind.' But he was inclined to proscribe all stargazing whatsoever. And the Galileo case, involving dangerous public speculations regarding his own planet, the sun, only steeled his resolve. How to control it?

Now, we only have indirect evidence about Urban's thoughts upon receiving the news that Galileo had begun making dangerous public speculations about the main planet in the pope's horoscope—i.e., the sun. We may suppose that, from his standpoint, the less stargazing the better; and that the Galileo case, which came up two years after the publication of the anti-astrology bull, only confirmed this view. He was not disposed to permit any more meddling with the stars, in spite of his confidence in the methods of defense suggested by Campanella. The trial offered the opportunity to suppress all stargazing whatsoever—a prospect that could only have been of particular satisfaction to the Urban VIII we are coming to know.

To Galileo Galilei, the events of 1630–1631 could only have proven more conclusively what he had come to suspect: that for winning the curia over to the conclusions of the modern astronomers, time was running out. He too, like the rest of those who counted in Rome, had foresworn any further direct contact with Morandi as soon as the indictment was announced. However, we know he followed the trial 'about which Your Lordship wishes to be informed' (in the words of a correspondent), as the hopeful news of early August began to give way

---

[51] *Atheismus triumphatus*, special section entitled *Disputatio an bullae SS. Pontificum Sixti V et Urbani VIII . . . calumniam in aliquo patiantur,* 255–273.

[52] Here and below, *Bullarum, diplomatum et privilegiorum,* 14:211, dated 1 April 1631, and entitled *Inscrutabilis.*

to the more guarded prognostications of later on. By March 1631 he received news that Raffaele Visconti and Gherardo Gherardi, close members of the Santa Prassede circle and deeply compromised in the trial, had been exiled from Rome, 'more because of the hatred for judicial astrology than for any particular charges against them,' said another correspondent.[53] For matters concerning the curia, Galileo had relied upon Visconti, still the assistant to the Padre Maestro or Master of the Sacred Palace while the post passed from Niccolò Ridolfi to Niccolò Riccardi, derisively dubbed 'Padre Mostro' or 'Father Monster' by Campanella. After the Morandi affair, Visconti's pre-publication approval of the *Dialogue Concerning the Two Chief World Systems*, Galileo's latest plea for acceptance of his doctrines, was not likely to be of much help in steering the troublesome book amid the various clashing opinions in the ecclesiastical bureaucracy that the theories in it had begun to arouse. Perhaps the contrary.[54]

Nonetheless, Galileo persevered. Armed with the approval of Visconti and the signature of the Padre Mostro, he next obtained the consent of the Florentine Inquisitor. Using the recent death of his Roman friend Federico Cesi as a convenient excuse to get away from the increasingly impossible Roman environment, he had the book published in Florence instead of in Rome. In February, 1632, then, the *Dialogue* came out under the imprint of the local printer Giovanni Battista Landini. Galileo's troubles seemed to be over.

The book Galileo published, as we all know, was a far cry from what the Padre Mostro had anticipated.[55] Their conversation had led the Padre to expect a cautious account, offering conclusions hypothetically and not definitively, defending the propriety of the decree of 1616 that had condemned the writings of Copernicus on the grounds that the sun-centered universe was theologically incorrect. Galileo instead published the most powerful defense of the heliocentric theory of the universe ever compiled—far more persuasive even than that of Copernicus, because its arguments were drawn largely from everyday experience and not exclu-

---

[53] *Opere di Galileo* 14: 236, dated 29 March 1631.

[54] Here, and for what follows, the bibliography again is immense and cannot be summarized here. In addition to works mentioned above and below, still useful concerning the Florentine context Cochrane, *Florence in the Forgotten Centuries*, book 3. In addition, Rosino, 'Il *Dialogo* come occasione per il processo e la condanna di Galileo'; D'Addio, *Considerazioni sui processi a Galileo*; Garin, 'Gli scandali della nuova "filosofia"'; Simoncelli, 'Galileo e la curia: un problema.'

[55] Note *Opere di Galileo*, 19: 350, referral of Melchiorre Inchofer, 1632; and 19: 359, referral of Zacharia Pasqualigo, analyzed in Chapter 1 of my *Science and the Marketplace in Early Modern Italy*.

sively from geometry. Publishing the work in vernacular Italian rather than in Latin, he had obviously intended it for a broad audience.

As the cumbersome Roman bureaucracy rolled into action, many circumstances conspired to ensure Galileo's downfall. For one thing, any time or energy Urban VIII himself might have had left over for contemplating the long-term consequences of leaving the Galileo case to a small band of disgruntled theologians was entirely occupied in contemplating the short-term consequences of the French victory in the War of Mantua and the new opportunities now open to the papacy by the Italian episodes of the Thirty Years War.[56] Worse yet, Cosimo II de' Medici in Florence was no longer alive to protect Galileo from the fury of a foreign court. And even if the next grand duke had been remotely interested in natural science, the great plague of 1629 that had already annihilated a third of the population of the Tuscan capital, while threatening still more destruction in the provinces, captured all of Ferdinando II's attentions.[57]

But Galileo's real problem was not the absence of help from Florence. Nor was it the impact of the Thirty Years' War. Nor again was it Urban VIII's bureaucracy. Still less did it have to do with supposed suspicions about Galileo's attachment to the doctrines of atomism in some earlier works, as an influential study published some years ago suggested.[58] According to that study, Galileo published his *Assayer*, with its innovative theory of how the particles of matter produce sensation, just when Jesuits and other conservative apologists for the Roman Catholic Church were asserting the doctrine of the Eucharist as a bulwark against advancing heresy. And there is no doubt that atomism was regarded as incompatible with current views about the Eucharist that drew arguments and language from the traditions of medieval Scholasticism. How, it was thought, could Transubstantiation take place if not by a change of Substance, leaving Form intact? But an anonymous document of spurious origin, found among the Inquisition papers and condemning the particle theory in Galileo's *Assayer*, is not enough to prove that the stars were not the real issue in Galileo's trials from the start. Nor is a cryptic reading of some of Galileo's letters, offered in the same study.

In the case of the *Dialogue*, Galileo's disobedience of a supposed directive by Cardinal Roberto Bellarmino issued on the occasion of the 1616 condemnation of Copernicus may well have played a role. Galileo always believed that Bellarmino had simply warned him, as a friend, to

---

[56] Consider Parrott, 'The Mantuan Succession, 1627–1631.'

[57] On the situation in Florence also note Dooley, 'Introduzione,' to Baldinucci, *Quaderno: Guerra, peste e carestia nella Firenze del Seicento* .

[58] See the evaluation of the Redondi thesis in Ferrone and Firpo, 'Galileo tra inquisitori e microstorici.'

steer clear of dangerous topics, and that the condemnation did not regard him personally. Investigators at the trial insisted that Bellarmino instead had enjoined Galileo specifically, in light of the condemnation, to avoid speaking and teaching about heliocentrism. The more successfully he did this in the *Dialogue*, according to this view, the guiltier he was. Documents were produced at the trial to support both interpretations of the Bellarmino meeting, and no definitive answer has ever been given.[59]

What finally tipped the scales against Galileo was Urban VIII himself. When news of the publication of the *Dialogue* first came out, as the Florentine ambassador later recorded, 'His Holiness exploded into great anger, and suddenly he told me that even our Galilei had dared to enter where he should not have, into the most serious and dangerous subjects that could be stirred up now.'[60] Nothing the ambassador said could mollify the pope. It made no difference that Galileo had spent nearly two years trying to steer the book through the meandering paths of the Roman bureaucracy before finally getting the go-ahead from the Padre Mostro. Urban VIII cared nothing that the book had been approved both in Rome and Florence. Galileo, like Morandi two years before, must be stopped, the sooner the better. Why did Urban turn from a bemused admirer into a fierce enemy?

That Galileo proved to be a disappointing courtier, as other scholarship has suggested, may have had something to do with changing Urban's mind so decisively.[61] Courtiers were expected to be amusing and ironic, without actually being self-deprecatory. Galileo's constant insistence on the veracity of his views rather than their vivacity, on their truth rather than their wit, on their capacity to increase knowledge rather than their capacity to produce astonishment, may well have changed him from a good courtier to an annoying gadfly in the eyes of the patron, Urban VIII. Never mind that Galileo was never exactly a courtier of Urban VIII; and never mind that, as far as the environment around the pope was concerned, there were many versions of what might be acceptable behavior. And we can be sure that some actual courtiers, such as the antiquary Ferdinando Ughelli, were far more pedantic on their best days than Galileo could ever have been even at his worst.

Far more pertinent may well have been Galileo's alleged portrait of Urban VIII in the character of 'Simplicio' as one of the interlocutors in the *Dialogue*. Seeing himself depicted, reputedly, in the guise of the

---

[59] See, however, Bucciantini, *Contro Galileo*.
[60] *Opere di Galileo*, 14:383–384, Francesco Niccolini to Andrea Cioli, 5 September 1632.
[61] Concerning the Biagioli thesis, note Shank, 'Galileo's Day in Court'; Biagioli, 'Playing with the Evidence' ; and Shank, 'How Shall We Practice History?'

Astrology and the End of Science in Early Modern Italy 413

irreducible traditionalist who fails to be won over to Galileo's eminently logical arguments, placed in the mouth of the far more intelligent 'Sagredo,' must have been a hard blow to a pope who prided himself on his philosophical understanding. Yet nothing Galileo could have said came even close to matching the virulence of the infamous anonymous pasquinades pasted every morning on the statue of Pasquino in the square of the same name, spreading insinuations about the pope's artistic programs, his political policies, and even his libido.[62]

That the Morandi affair conditioned Urban's state of mind, galvanizing his opposition to Galileo's work, adding to whatever motivations may have come from the causes we have mentioned, seems to be the most likely explanation for what happened. To Urban, the two trials must have seemed very much alike. They both concerned the publication of dangerous views; they both concerned the stars. Indeed, in some sense they both concerned astrology—at least according to contemporary definitions of the term.

Although Urban VIII was a man of many parts, science was most assuredly not one of them. He was an art connoisseur of considerable acuity, an antiquarian with impeccable taste; and before becoming pope he wrote a poem celebrating the natural history accomplishments of Ulisse Aldrovandi.[63] He wrote another poem at the same time addressed to Galileo, paying tribute to the discoveries of sunspots and the moons of Jupiter ('found by your glass, O wise Galileo')—the very discoveries whose heliocentric implications had provoked the condemnation of Copernicus' *On the Revolutions of the Heavenly Spheres* during the previous papacy, in 1616. Galileo referred to Urban's pontificate as a 'remarkable conjunction,' likely to put Copernicus' work back into circulation.[64]

However, Urban's interest in the stars was limited to the good or evil they might do to him. Rather than that of the erudite scholars, his astrology was that of the popular oral tradition and visual symbolism.[65] With him in charge, the Barberini palace at the Quattro Fontane in Rome was decorated with motifs depicting astrological configurations, including the

---

[62] See my 'De bonne main.'

[63] Spini, *Galileo, Campanella e il 'divinus poeta'*, pp. 41–58.

[64] 'Io raggiro per la mente cose di qualche momento per la repubblica letteraria, le quali se non si effettuano in quest mirabile congiuntura, non occorre, almeno per quel che si aspetta per parte mia, sperare d'incontrarne mai una simile.' Letter to Federico Cesi, dated 9 October 1623, in Gabrieli, ed., 'Il carteggio linceo della vecchia Accademia di Federico Cesi,' p. 683.

[65] Concerning the astrological tradition in Rome, Ernst, 'Astrology, Religion and Politics in Counter Reformation Rome.' Compare Capp, *English Almanacs, 1500–1800*.

one that occurred on the day of his election to the papacy.[66] His birth planet was the sun, and this he was having plastered on everything in sight. For the Barcaccia fountain situated at the foot of what are now the Spanish Steps, he had Gian Lorenzo Bernini sculpt two fantastic spouts in the shape of suns at either end of a low-set ship. On the baldachin over the tomb of St. Peter in the basilica at the Vatican, hundreds of tiny suns alternate with the tiny bees drawn from the Barberini coat of arms.[67] Surely the Urban we are coming to know, in the city we are discovering, would not have had such elements sculpted into his projects for the sake of mere decoration; nor for the sake of simply representing the family's authority. Would he not also view them as talismans, such as those used in those ceremonies with Tommaso Campanella to counter the fatal astral influences?

Like many of his contemporaries, including the newsletter writer who called Galileo 'the great astrologer,' Urban may well have had difficulty distinguishing Galileo's practices from Morandi's. As a dedicated believer in astrology, he may have found some cause for dismay in Galileo's *Dialogue*, where the Ptolemaic basis for astrology seemed utterly destroyed and astrologers were treated with undisguised disdain.[68] Whether he also suspected that Galileo's new cosmos might call for yet another embarrassing afternoon in a magic chamber in the papal palace, such as the one designed for him in 1628 by Campanella, protecting himself from who knew what fatal new astral influences, we cannot say. In any case, the bull of 1631 was supposed to put an end to astrological meddling of every kind. And who was to define Galileo's world-shaking conclusions as anything else?

To ensure Galileo's destruction, all Urban had to do was to avoid diverting the new trial from its inevitable conclusion. Then Galileo's adversaries would be given free rein; and so would a disgruntled associate of the Santa Prassede astrological circle who was now on the Inquisition committee: Cardinal Desiderio Scaglia. For when Orazio Morandi had made his famous prediction about Urban VIII's death in 1630, to whom had the other astrologers in his orbit promised the vacant see? Now was the chance to cut down the most ambitious astrologer of them all.[69]

---

[66]Scott, *Images of Nepotism*.
[67]Rice, *The Altars and Altarpieces of New St. Peter's*. Concerning the fountain, Hibbard and Irma Jaffe, 'Bernini's Barcaccia'; and D'Onofrio, *Le fontane di Roma*, pp. 356–370.
[68]Day Two, speech by Salviati: 'E dove lasciate voi le predizioni de' genteliaci, che tanto chiaramente doppo l'esito si veggono nel tema o vogliam dire nella figura celeste?' *Dialogo sopra i due massimi sistemi del mondo tolemaico e copernicano*, p. 135.
[69]Concerning Scaglia there is Peroni, Biblioteca bresciana, 3: 222. Also, Tedeschi,

Little of what we know about popular astrological traditions has yet been integrated into our knowledge of their learned counterparts within the tradition of Renaissance natural philosophy. However, the battle between 'the astrologer' Galileo and his adversary, the star-crossed pope, was clearly a case of these two worlds colliding. Galileo was as pitiless against the tradition of popular astrology as Urban was credulous of it. And Urban's struggle against an adverse destiny written in the stars had powerful unintended consequences for the history of science.

In the heat of the conflict between the philosophers and their accusers, the various strands within Renaissance culture that had been bound together by a thread began to come undone.[70] Nor were there any signs of what might replace them. The campaign against astrology cast a shadow over the whole practice of natural philosophy that had been built on unified theories concerning the relation between the celestial and terrestrial worlds. If investigations of the future significance of occult forces in the universe could be proscribed, there was no telling what other investigations regarding the forces in the universe might be proscribed along with them.[71] At the same time, the campaign against heliocentrism and against Galileo cast a shadow over the culture of experience, of real data, of experimentation, that had in some way supplied a method and a program where grand theory had begun to wear thin. But the proposition that all questions were to be answered by reference to the Holy Scriptures, as interpreted by theologians with no expertise in the laws of natural causation, was no more acceptable now than it had been when Galileo had expressed his reservations about it in a celebrated *Letter to the Grand Duchess* of Tuscany in 1615. For the moment, science and astrology shared the same fate—but not for long.

International University Bremen
Bremen, Germany

'The Question of Magic and Witchcraft in Two Unpublished Inquisition Manuals of the Seventeenth Century.'

[70] Concerning this theme, see Headley, *Tommaso Campanella and the Transformation of the World*, 'Epilogue.'

[71] On this theme, Westfall, *Science and Religion in Seventeenth-Century England*; Osler and Farber, eds., *Religion, Science, and Worldview*; Feyerabend and Thomas, eds., *Wissenschaft und Tradition*. In addition, Feldhay, *Galileo and the Church*; Festa, *L'erreur de Galilée*; Poupard, ed., *Après Galilée: science et foi: nouveau dialogue*; Tassot, *La Bible au risque de la science: de Galilée au P. Lagrange*; Schirrmacher, *Galilei-Legenden*. The present interpretation is not meant as an alternative to, but as a concomitant to the so-called epistemological interpretation of the Galileo affair.

Works Cited

Manuscript Sources

Rome, Archivio di Stato,
   Governatore, Processi sec. XVII, b. 251
Vatican City, Biblioteca Apostolica Vaticana, mss.,
   Vat. lat. 11288

Published Sources

Altobelli, Ilario. *Demonstratio ostendens artem dirigendi et domificandi Ioannis de Monteregio non concordare cum doctrinam Ptolomaei*. Foligno: 1629.

Altobelli, Ilario. *Tabulae regiae divisionum dodecim partium coeli et syderum obviationum ad mentem Ptolomaei*. Macerata: Bonomi, 1628.

Amabile, Luigi. *Tommaso Campanella ne' castelli di Napoli, in Roma ed in Parigi*. 2 vols. Naples: Morano, 1887.

Bacon, Francis. *Advancement of Learning*. ed. Edward Creighton. New York: Colonial Press, 1900.

Barozzi, Nicolò and Guglielmo Berchet. *Relazioni degli stati europei lette al Senato dagli ambasciatori veneti*. ser. 3: *Italia: Relazioni di Roma*. vol. 1. Venice: Naratovich, 1877.

Bastiaanse, Alexandro. *Teodoro Ameyden (1586–1656). Un Neerlandese alla corte di Roma*. 'sGravenhage: Staatsdrukkerij, 1968.

Bertolotti, Antonio. 'Giornalisti, astrologi e negromanti in Roma nel secolo XVII' *Rivista europea* 5 (1878): pp. 466–514.

Biagioli, Mario. *Galileo, Courtier*. Chicago: University of Chicago Press, 1993.

Biagioli, Mario. 'Playing with the Evidence' *Early Science and Medicine* 1 (1996): 70–105.

Böll, Franz, et al., *Sternglaube und Sterndeutung. Die Geschichte und das Wesen der Astrologie*. Leipzig: Teubner, 1931.

Bowden, Mary Ellen. *The Scientific Revolution in Astrology: The English Reformers, 1558–1686*. PhD diss., Yale, 1974.

Bracciolini, B. Benigno. *Oratio . . de laudibus . . . Horatii Morandi romani*. Rome: Francesco Corbelletti, 1626.

Bucciantini, Massimo. *Contro Galileo: alle origini dell'"Affaire."* Florence: Olschki, 1995.

Campanella, Tommaso. *Atheismus triumphatus*. Paris: Dubray, 1636.

Campanella, Tommaso. *Lettere*. ed. Vincenzo Spampanato. Scrittori d'Italia 103. Bari: Laterza, 1927.

Campanella, Tommaso. *De siderali fato vitandi*. Leyden: Prost, 1629 [actually, Rome: Brogiotti, 1629].

Capp, Bernard. *English Almanacs, 1500–1800: Astrology and the Popular Press*. Ithaca: Cornell University Press, 1979.

Casati, Giovanni. *Dizionario degli scrittori d'Italia*, vol. 3. Milan: Ghirlanda, 1934.

Cochrane, Eric. *Florence in the Forgotten Centuries*. Chicago: University of Chicago Press, 1973.

Copenhaver, Brian P. 'Natural Magic, Hermetism and Occultism in Early Modern Science' pp. 261–303 in *Reappraisals of the Scientific Revolution*, ed. David C. Lindberg and Robert S. Westman. Cambridge: Cambridge University Press, 1990.

Copenhaver, Brian P. 'The Occultist Tradition and its Critics', pp. 454–513 in *Cambridge History of Seventeenth-Century Philosophy*, ed. Daniel Garber and Michael Ayers. Cambridge: Cambridge University Press, 1998.

Curry, Patrick. *Prophecy and Power: Astrology in Early Modern England*. Cambridge: Polity Press, 1989.

D'Addio, Mario. *Considerazioni sui processi a Galileo*. Rome: Herder, 1985.

Dooley, Brendan. 'De bonne main: la circulation des actualités à Rome au dix-septième siècle' *Annales: Histoire, Sciences Sociales* 6 (Nov–Déc 1999): 1317–1344.

Dooley, Brendan. 'Introduzione,' pp. vii–xlii in Giovanni Baldinucci, *Quaderno: Guerra, peste e carestia nella Firenze del Seicento*, ed. B. Dooley and Barbara Marti Dooley. Florence: Polistampa, 2001.

Dooley, Brendan. *Morandi's Last Prophecy and the End of Renaissance Politics*. Princeton: Princeton University Press, 2002.

Dooley, Brendan. *Science and the Marketplace in Early Modern Italy*. Lanham, Md.: Lexington Books, 2001.

D'Onofrio, Cesare. *Le fontane di Roma*. Rome: Società Editrice, 1986.

Drake, Stillman. *Galileo at Work*. Chicago: University of Chicago Press, 1978.

Ernst, Germana . 'Astrology, Religion and Politics in Counter Reformation Rome,' pp. 249–273 in *Science, Culture, and Popular Belief in Renaissance Europe*, ed. Stephen Pumfrey, Paolo L. Rossi and Maurice Slawinski. Manchester: Manchester University Press, 1991.

Ernst, Germana. 'Aspetti dell'astrologia e della profezia in Galileo e Campanella' pp. 255–266 in *Novità celesti e crisi del sapere. Atti del convegno internazionale di studi galileiani, 1982*, ed. Paolo Galluzzi. Florence: Giunti-Barbera, 1984.

Ernst, Germana. *Religione, ragione e natura. Ricerche su Tommaso Campanella e il tardo Rinascimento*. Milan: Angeli, 1991.

Ernst, Germana. 'Scienza, astrologia e politica nella Roma barocca,' pp. 217–252 in *Bibliothecae Selectae da Cusano a Leopardi*, ed. Eugenio Canone. Florence: Olschki, 1993.

Favaro, Antonio. *Galileo Galilei e lo Studio di Padova*. 2 vols. Florence: Le Monnier, 1883.

Feldhay, Rivka. *Galileo and the Church : Political Inquisition or Critical Dialogue?* Cambridge: Cambridge University Press, 1995.

Ferrone, Vincenzo and Massimo Firpo, 'Galileo tra inquisitori e microstorici' *Rivista storica italiana* 97 (1985): 177–238, trans. in *Journal of Modern History* 58 (1986): 485–524.

Festa, Egidio. *L'erreur de Galilée*. Paris: Editions Austral, 1995.

Feyerabend, Paul and Christian Thomas, eds. *Wissenschaft und Tradition*. Zurich: Verlag der Fachvereine, 1983.

Field, J. V. 'A Lutheran Astrologer: Johannes Kepler.' *Archive for the History of the Exact Sciences* 31 (1984): 189–272.

Findlen, Paula. 'Jokes of Nature and Jokes of Knowledge: The Playfulness of Scientific Discourse in Early Modern Europe' *Renaissance Quarterly* 13 (1990): 292–331.
Fiorani, Luigi. 'Astrologi, superstiziosi e devoti nella società romana del Seicento,' pp. 97–162 in *Ricerche per la storia religiosa di Roma*. 2. Rome: Edizioni di Storia e Letteratura, 1978.
Gabrieli, Giuseppe, ed. 'Il carteggio linceo della vecchia Accademia di Federico Cesi' *Memorie della R. Accademia Nazionale dei Lincei*, Cl. Sci. Mor. Stor e Fil., ser. 6, vol. 7 (1938–1942): 683.
Galilei, Galileo. *Dialogo sopra i due massimi sistemi del mondo tolemaico e copernicano*, ed. Libero Sosio. Turin: Einaudi, 1996.
Galilei, Galileo. *Edizione nazionale delle opere di Galileo Galilei*, 20 vols., ed. Antonio Favaro. Florence: G. Barbera, 1967^3.
Galluzzi, Paolo. 'Motivi paracelsiani in Toscana' pp. 31–62 in *Scienza, credenze occulte: livelli di cultura*. Florence: Olschki, 1982.
Garin, Eugenio. 'Gli scandali della nuova "filosofia"' *Nuncius* 8 (1993): 417–431.
Gaude, Francisco. *Bullarum, diplomatum et privilegiorum*. vol. 14. Turin: Dalmazzo, 1868.
Geneva, Ann. *Astrology and the Seventeenth-Century Mind: William Lilly and the Language of the Stars*. Manchester: Manchester University Press, 1995.
Geymonat, Ludovico. *Galileo Galilei*. Turin: Einaudi, 1957.
Ginzburg, Carlo. *The Cheese and the Worms*, tr. John and Anne Tedeschi. Baltimore: Johns Hopkins University Press, 1975.
Grafton, Anthony. *Cardano's Cosmos: The Worlds and Works of a Renaissance Astrologer*. Cambridge, Mass.: Harvard University Press, 2000.
Gualterotti, Raffaello. *Scherzi degli spiriti animali detati con l'occasione dell'oscurazione dell'anno 1605*. Florence: Giunti, 1605.
Hallyn, Fernand. *Structure poétique du monde: Copernic, Kepler*. Paris: Seuil, 1987.
Hankins, James. 'Galileo, Ficino and Renaissance Platonism' pp. 209–237 in *Humanism and Early Modern Philosophy*, ed. M.W.F. Stone and Jill Kraye. London: Routledge, 1999.
Headley, John M. *Tommaso Campanella and the Transformation of the World*. Princeton: Princeton University Press, 1997.
Hibbard, Howard and Irma Jaffe. 'Bernini's Barcaccia' *Burlington Magazine* 106 (1964): 159–170.
Jacoli, F. 'Intorno a due Scritti di Raffaele Gualterotti Fiorentino,' in *Bullettino di bibliografia e di storia delle scienze matematiche e fisiche di B. Buoncompagni* 7 (1874): 377–415.
Kepler, Johannes. *The Secret of the Universe*, tr. A. M. Duncan. New York: Abaris, 1981.
Koyré, Alexandre. *Études Galiléennes*. Paris: Hermann, 1966.
Lüthy, Christoph. 'What to Do with Seventeenth-Century Natural Philosophy' *Perspectives on Science* 8 (2000): 164–195.
Merkel, Ingrid and Allen G. Debus, eds. *Hermeticism and the Renaissance: Intellectual History and the Occult in Early Modern Europe*, Washington, D.C.: Folger Books, 1988.

Nifo, Agostino. *De diebus criticis.* Venice: Ponti, 1504.
North, John David. *Horoscopes and History.* Warburg Institute Surveys, vol. 13. London: Warburg Institute, 1986.
Odoardi, G. 'Altobelli, Ilario' pp. 567–568 in *Dizionario biografico degli Italiani* 2 (1960).
Osler, Margaret J. and Paul Lawrence Farber, eds.. *Religion, Science, and Worldview: Essays in Honor of Richard S. Westfall.* Cambridge: Cambridge University Press, 1985.
Parrott, David. 'The Mantuan Succession, 1627–1631: A Sovereignty Dispute in Early Modern Europe' *English Historical Review* 112 (1995): 20–65.
Peroni, Vincenzo. *Biblioteca bresciana* 3 vols. Brescia: 1818–1823.
Poupard, Paul ed. *Après Galilée: science et foi: nouveau dialogue.* Paris: Desclée de Brouwer, 1994.
Pumfrey, Stephen, Paolo L. Rossi and Maurice Slawinski, eds. *Science, Culture and Popular Belief in Renaissance Europe.* Manchester: Manchester University Press, 1991.
Redondi, Pietro. *Galileo Heretic.* Princeton: Princeton University Press, 1987, orig. Torino, Einaudi, 1983.
Rice, Louise. *The Altars and Altarpieces of New St. Peter's: Outfitting the Basilica, 1621–1666.* New York: Cambridge University Press in association with the American Academy in Rome, 1997.
Righini, G. 'L'oroscopo galileiano di Cosimo II de' Medici' *Annali dell'Istituto e Museo di Storia della Scienza di Firenze* 1 (1976): 29–36.
Rosino, Leonida. 'Il *Dialogo* come occasione per il processo e la condanna di Galileo' pp. 173–191 in *Giornate Lincee indette in occasione del 350° anniversario della pubblicazione del 'Dialogo sopra i massimi sistemi' di Galileo Galilei, Roma, 6–7 maggio 1982.* Rome: Accademia Nazionale dei Lincei, 1983.
Rossi, Paolo. *Francesco Bacone: Dalla magia alla scienza,* 2nd ed. Turin: Einaudi, 1974.
Sala, Torello. *Dizionario storico-biografico di scrittori letterati ed artisti dell'ordine di Vallombrosa.* 2 vols. Florence: Istituto Gualandi, 1929.
Saxl, Fritz, Raymond Klibansky and Erwin Panofsky. *Saturn and Melancholy.* London: Nelson, 1964.
Schirrmacher, Thomas. *Galilei-Legenden: und andere Beiträge zu Schöpfungsforschung. Evolutionskritik und Chronologie der Kulturgeschichte 1979–1994.* Bonn: Verlag für Kultur und Wissenschaft, 1995.
Scienza, credenze occulte, livelli di cultura. Florence: Olschki, 1982.
Scott, John Beldon. *Images of Nepotism: The Painted Ceilings of Palazzo Barberini.* Princeton: Princeton University Press, 1991.
Shank, Michael. 'Galileo's Day in Court' *Journal of the History of Astronomy* 25 (1994): 236–243.
Shank, Michael. 'How Shall We Practice History? The Case of Mario Biagioli's *Galileo Courtier*' *Early Science and Medicine* 1 (1996): 106–150.
Shea, William R. Review of Stillman Drake *Galileo at Work* in *Annali dell'Istituto e Museo di Storia della Scienza, Firenze* 5, (1980): 93–94.
Shumaker, Wayne. *Natural Magic and Modern Science: Four Treatises, 1590–1657.* Binghamton, NY: Medieval and Renaissance Texts and Studies, 1989.

Simon, Gérard. *Kepler: Astronome, Astrologue.* Paris: Gallimard, 1979.
Simoncelli, Paolo. 'Galileo e la curia: un problema' *Belfagor* 48 (1993): 29–42.
Siraisi, Nancy G. *The Clock and the Mirror: Girolamo Cardano and Renaissance Medicine.* Princeton: Princeton University Press, 1997.
Smith, Pamela. *The Business of Alchemy: Science and Culture under the Holy Roman Empire.* Princeton: Princeton University Press, 1994.
Spini, Giorgio. *Galileo, Campanella e il 'divinus poeta.'* Bologna: Mulino, 1996.
Stano G. and F. Balsinelli, 'Un illustre scienziato francescano' *Miscellanea francescana* 43 (1943): 81–149.
Stephenson, Bruce. *Kepler's Physical Astronomy.* New York: Springer Verlag, 1987.
Tarani, D. F. *L'Ordine Vallombrosano: Note storico-cronologiche.* Florence: Scuola Tipografica Calasanziana, 1920.
Tassot, Dominique. *La Bible au risque de la science: de Galilée au P. Lagrange.* Paris: de Guibert, 1997.
Tedeschi, John. 'The Question of Magic and Witchcraft in Two Unpublished Inquisition Manuals of the Seventeenth Century' *Proceedings of the American Philosophical Society* 131 (1987): 92–111.
Thorndike, Lynn. *A History of Magic and Experimental Science.* 8 vols. New York: Columbia University Press, 1923–1958.
Tribby, Jay. 'Cooking [with] Clio: Eloquence and Experiment in Seventeenth-Century Florence' *Journal of the History of Ideas* 52 (1991): 417–439.
Troncarelli, Fabio, ed. *La città dei segreti: magia, astrologia e cultura esoterica a Roma (secoli XV–XVIII).* Milan: F. Angeli, 1985.
Vickers, Brian, ed. *Occult and Scientific Mentalities in the Renaissance.* Cambridge: Cambridge University Press, 1984.
Walker, D.P. 'Spirits in Francis Bacon' pp. 315–327 in *Francis Bacon: Terminologia e fortuna nel secolo XVII.* Rome: Edizioni dell'Ateneo, 1984.
Webster, Charles. *From Paracelsus to Newton: Magic and the Making of Modern Science.* Cambridge: Cambridge University Press, 1983.
Westfall, Richard S. *Science and Religion in Seventeenth-Century England.* New Haven: Yale University Press, 1958.
Zambelli, Paola. *L'ambigua natura della magia.* Milan: Il Saggiatore, 1991.
Zambelli, Paola. 'Uno, due, tre, mille Menocchio' *Archivio storico italiano* 137 (1979): 51–90.

Epilogue

Contexts

Lauro Martines

The studies in this volume voice an underlying concern for the historical document as 'maker' of the past. Their large suggestion is that *in* the writing of history, any significant shift in interpretations – some kind of 'revisionism' – is likely to come from new readings of the documents already in play, not from new sources. So tersely summed up, this proposition, with its tacit acceptance of valid or stable 'new' readings, is beset by theoretical problems, despite the fact that the fresh reading of documents is customary procedure for historians. Indeed, in literary scholarship, all along the boundaries of historical study, the fresh reading of 'documents' is the defining activity. Then how can new readings generate theoretical problems?

During the past generation, one of the most fashionable strains in critical theory held that the main problem lay in the naïve assumption that the document – call it the 'text' – is an object 'out there' which we, in the act of reading, proceed to understand and to share with other readers. Seen thus, this act – it was argued – is lodged in a rich plurality of individual or cultural viewpoints, whereupon the document or text being read is converted into a quiddity so unstable and protean as to undo the presumption that it could ever have any certain status out there. After all, the document itself was the product of a changing mind, place, and time; and it is now also subject, in the minds and eyes of readers, to a storm of perceptions that render it all the more incommensurable and almost mysterious.

Such at least was the theoretical claim, and there was enough to it – it seemed logical enough – to batter the study of literature as an academic discipline. Although historians were less subject to the assault of theory, it is clear that during the years of their Chicago collaboration (1970–1985), Eric Cochrane and Julius Kirshner – moving from more traditional foundations – sought to impart the lessons of careful reading to their students, of reading in strict linguistic and historical contexts. In a well-known expression of their outlook, a co-authored and controversial review of Frederic C. Lane's *Venice: A Maritime Republic*, they confronted a book whose thesis seemed rooted not so much in strict historical contexts as in an ethnocentric 'model whose inspirational value is eternal' and a 'political ideology intended to remind us of our usable past.'[1]

In the face of a combative theory, however, no reading could ever be 'careful' enough, sufficiently so to deliver a document in an objective or steady state. Theory had put texts and the act of reading into a light that seemed to turn the study of documents into an epistemological nightmare. Nevertheless, the reading of historical and literary texts went on. In practice, some text was always being assumed to have a reality out there, especially when it was certified by an interested constituency of readers, such as in their study, say, of a work by Machiavelli, Rousseau, or William James. Out of this continuing and necessary practice came Cochrane's revisionist stance regarding Florentine history after 1530, and his idiosyncratic judgments on the Renaissance Italian historiographic tradition; so too came Kirshner's front-line readings of the work of famous jurists, who are seen to move against the realities of civic statutes and the conventions of notaries.

The common practice of actually reading documents is our fixed commission; there is no getting away from this, just as there are no easy logical solutions to the theoretical puzzle in which every reading so transforms a text that the theorist may go on asking, where is the text? What text?[2] Has it not been absorbed by the reader? In this phase of theory, when readers get at a document, at that moment too it turns into a springboard for its own effacement.

But critical theory also had its comical, posturing side. In the 1980s, when it rose to high fashion, and it became possible to take a Ph. D. in that 'area,' as I saw at the University of California, I noticed a two-class system which also spilled over into the department of history. Graduate students who worked in the field of theory went around employing a special language; they read theory chiefly, nearly always of the most recent sort; they separated themselves out from (and rather looked down on) the common mob of other graduate students who were busy reading non-theoretical texts; and of course they defined themselves by their easy use of a technical vocabulary. There were the high priests or votaries, male and female, of the kind of study that truly mattered; and then there were all the others, the unimaginative helots or cave-dwellers who spent their days scrutinizing shadows.

Yet the experiences of those years were also a tonic, because they nailed down the realization that it is impossible to teach *careful* reading, in the sense at least of training someone to do readings that are unassailable. There can never be any such thing, and we have always known this. What the craze for theory did, however, was to make us more suspicious and

---

[1] Cochrane and Kirshner, 'Deconstructing Lane's Venice,' pp. 321–334.
[2] See, most recently, Mowitt, 'What is a Text Today,' pp. 1217–1221.

sophisticated – if you like, less credulous about canonical or traditional readings. We now knew – the point was easily made – that traditions themselves were and are in flux, that change may be a fundamental datum, and that contrasting viewpoints have to be taken for granted, hence assumed to be impinging on the reading process. Even so, we remained with the professional obligation – the dilemma persists – to read carefully: that is, with all the fine care and nous that can be brought to bear on a text. But as for how we actually taught this ability, here we looked out to tricky ground again and all the difficulties came storming back. For once we find the reading skills that we expect in educated individuals, how exactly do we then get them to read, say, Guicciardini's *Considerations* on Machiavelli's *Discourses* in the Florentine and wider Italian context of the early sixteenth century, in the stricter context of the political language of Florence, and in the light of Guicciardini's own life, while also trying to get them to shed their ideological baggage, if, indeed, we even think this possible?

Any effort to teach careful reading must proceed through theory, in the need, namely, to convey general principles. Yet every significant text is bound to be a structure of particularities, so that suddenly, when engaging with such a text, we find that generalities offer little or no help to the way we actually read, because the many operations that garner sense from a document are specific. This is to say that every text presents new difficulties by calling for analytical moves that are indefeasibly detailed, above all when the effort is being made to contextualize it: to move back and forth between text and context in a labor of acceptable interpretation. Which is why careful reading cannot be taught. All we can do is to convey suspicion, caution, a sense of the polysemy of documents, and the need to grasp meanings in their linguistic and historical settings. But once any reading begins, the operational skills – the delicacy, knowledge, sparkle, insight, and ability to make connections – will all rest with the reader and belong to his or her capacities.

Working mainly with juridical and legal material, Cavallar, Lepsius, Armstrong, and Kuehn show a mastery of parts of the technical vocabulary, including usage, of late medieval Italian law, while also demonstrating a keen sense of the social and institutional worlds that surround their cases. In these essays – I cite them only as examples – the readings loop a good deal, not only in relating different texts, but also by moving back and forth between the texts in question and the historical world of action and event. As in John Marino's essay, they both grapple with texts as such and execute a learned choreography of movement between texts on one side and, on the other, affairs in the real world. More than the primary task of understanding words, sentences, and arguments, careful reading here has turned into a learned exercise of judgment, knowledge, and experience; and this may mean – in principle at all events – that the older student in the field is more likely to have the advantage.

We have seen that in practice – whatever about theory – the document does not shatter into as many monads as there are readers. Specific scholarly communities go on dealing with particular plays or sonnets by Shakespeare; historians go on talking about the same document when L. B. Alberti's *Momus* holds the center of discussion; and the process generates a common or shared discourse. The real shattering begins – that is, remarkable differences of interpretation come forth – in the quest for links with other texts or with non-textual activity in the surrounding historical world. It begins, in short, when the learned reader starts to move away from the text to a context, but only in order to return to the text in the effort to cast more light on it, or to extract its polyphony of meanings.

The question of contexts is crucial, because it is the question about all the matters lying outside the document, though in some significant relation to it – matters that may then be brought to bear on the reading. This question, too, is the one which elicits the voices of special interests in the scholar: feminism, 'psychobiography,' political concerns, the history of ideas, economic forces, the quest for popular culture, an eye for social structures, and so on. If we ask the generic question, what *is* a context, any serious answer breaks into a series of replies, depending first of all upon the document in question, and then on the compelling interests of the historian who proposes to do the reading. But the richer and more devious or complex a document, the more likely will it be to carry the signs or shadows of different contexts: of political strains, social structures, current ideas, local practices, or chronic community needs. In such a case, therefore, the varieties of analysis – feminist, political, economic, rhetorical – will each be doing a part, but only a part, of the job of glossing and interpreting the document. In theory, the job can never be completed, and theorists may insist on the conflictual aspect of readings. In practice, it is usually the case that new readings incorporate some of the earlier ones, and then proceed to introduce refinements or additions, with the result that the on-going discussion is likely to evolve in a gradual fashion, while also retaining a good deal of stability.

*　　*　　*

Let us call our subject – more pretentiously – the problem of contexts. Although seldom discussed by historians, it is fundamental. I met the problem almost daily when I set out to read poems and tales as historical texts, doing so merely by striving to take hold of them in their wider historical contexts.[3] My aim was not only to throw light on them, but also to draw on their light, and so convert them *tout court* into historical

---

[3] In two books: Martines, *Society and History in English Renaissance Verse* and *An Italian Renaissance Sextet: Six Tales in Historical Context.*

documents. That I was doing nothing queer is attested to by the fact that any complex or 'difficult' document is bound to require a discussion of its contextual setting, if it is to surrender its meanings; and the more 'literary' it is, such as Pascal's *Pensées* or Rousseau's *Confessions*, the more sustained and winding will be the operations needed to relate the text to the impinging phenomenal world of non-texts.

One general point seems clear at the outset: contexts may be as wide as the world and even wider, because they also include ideas and imaginary worlds, such as the contents of the Bible, or, on a different scale, the fear of communism and the writings of Sigmund Freud, all three of which serve as contexts, as outside input, for many a text. But the problem, luckily, is quickly narrowed and focused by the nature itself of the document in play. Thus a religious text will at once call in one range of interests and possible links, while legal *consilia* and family log books (*ricordanze*) will look out to other sorts of connections in the impinging world.

In late medieval and Renaissance Italy, the legal opinions of jurists (*consilia*) rank among the most interesting of documents, because their contexts are other legal texts *and* disputes in the real world (lawsuits). *Consilia* teem with references to other jurists and to the main parts of the Roman law, the *Digest* and the *Institutes*. But their aim is always to render an opinion in a real dispute between contending parties; and the range of arguments is likely to specify current social practice – e. g., the claims of widows, managing dowries, or the treatment of illegitimate children – in the light of local codes and the more general prescriptions of civil law. The result is that texts and social realities (*non*-texts) are continually yanked together in the tight arguments and rhetorical flourishes of *consilia*.

Last wills, family journals, chronicles, and business letters also trail their own contexts: their business looks out to connections with people and affairs in the phenomenal world. But already in these writings, as in the case of *consilia*, the interests or 'world views' (prejudgments?) of the writers insert accents which the modern reader may elect to explore with an eye to exposing submerged ideas or attitudes. In such a reading, the eye of the reader has moved out and away from the immediate text, in order to bring in elements which appear *prima facie* to have no place there. And it may be the eye of a feminist, of a student of ritual, a biographer, or an economic historian.

Religious and highly idealized writings, like many of the writings of the humanists, are texts that do not easily surrender their contexts. A fifteenth-century prayer may look back to the late thirteenth century and the *laude* of Jacopone da Todi (hence to other texts), and/or it may be anchored in the immediate world, such as in having references to a local plague, a confraternity, or a pressing political crisis. But prayers are more likely to float, so to speak, in being applicable to different situations. For their language, pleas and settings are designed to transcend circumstances by speaking mainly for and to the despair of the suppliant, rather than to the external causes of his despair. The context here, therefore, turns out to be a cargo of emotion; but since the emotion can be summed up by the sense of a generalized despair, the text has a strong note of something impersonal or universal, which is precisely why it is able to float across time and space in its applicability. For the right eighteenth-century person, a moving fourteenth-century prayer from Siena could carry a charge equal to its original force and intention.

At the outset of the 1970s, when talk about the writing of 'history from below' became fashionable, the whole conception of contexts – a matter that had been quietly taken for granted – was inadvertently revolutionised. From this time on, women, peasants, and the urban lower classes would be drawn forcefully on to the proscenium of history; but in addition, although more gradually, historians began to read all sorts of documents – even, occasionally, the documents of high culture – in the light of the men and women 'from below.' This extraordinary widening of the social focus, taking in people who had no practical or institutional political power, also meant a drifting away from politics and political history. It meant the introduction of new materials for long-term inquiry: the history of dress, marriage, childhood, 'the family,' sexuality, deviants, popular beliefs and practices, crime and punishment, ceremonies and ritual, and even the uses of urban space. No wonder, then, that historians began to look for method and narratives in anthropology, as they turned to the study of enduring structures, social roles, cyclical activity, rituals such as gift giving, and the mixing of magic with religion.

Texts are exploded by contexts: by the transfer of contexts into texts, or, more precisely, by the calling forth of the contexts that seem embedded in texts; and of course all this is transacted by 'careful' reading and exegesis. But once the field of study began to be radically opened up in the late 1960s, and an expanding agenda of new subjects and themes was put on the historical gaming table, historians had more materials to pick from and so could approach their documents, their texts, with a richer sense of the different voices that might be found there. Texts too, therefore, became more problematic: it was all one and the same process.

The ways in which we construct contexts around a document, or around an event for that matter, are likely to call forth our prejudices and specializations. So if, for example, in the analysis of a religious procession held in a time of famine, I elect to concentrate on rituals, on the participation of women, on the tradition of processions, and on the order of precedence enjoyed by certain confraternities or guilds, I have chosen to see 'reality' in a particular way, in a take that minimizes political and economic factors. My context has excluded these, and why not? After all, I was in search of something else. I may happen to be a specialist in ritual studies or in the field of religious practices, and so it was simply the case that my preparation as a specialist rightly imposed its priorities. Do the academic disciplines not worship at the altar of specialization?

The foregoing example is, I believe, paradigmatic. Although contexts in theory are as wide as the world, they are narrowed in practice by the event or text in play. But in addition, the limitations of specialization have a profound effect on the ways in which we construct contexts, and this kind of a blinker has no *a priori* validity, for all its respectable status. If in my analysis of the religious procession in a time of famine, I also bring in a consideration of politics and economic matters, then my adduced context will be richer, possibly more validly so. However, if there was also an opportunity to treat the impact of political ideas, because the event (or the descriptive document) lent itself to this, and I failed to do so, on account of my having failed to pick up the apposite clues, then my context will be that much the poorer, and my 'reading' will have been incomplete.

Specialization may serve to sharpen our vision of things, of the things selected, but it also blinds us to others. As the *maitre à penser* Kenneth Burke used to say, a way of seeing is also a way of not seeing.

It seems clear by now that the late twentieth-century quarrels about 'where the text is' had chiefly to do with contexts: with the world that the scholar brings to the text, or purports to elicit from it, in his quest for meaning. Sentence for sentence, paragraph for paragraph, texts are always there for us to read; and we may even all agree about the meaning of one sentence after another. The trouble is suddenly born, as we have seen, when the scholar begins to link one text with another, or to link texts and affairs in the world (non-texts). Now ideologies, specializations, and private quirks, filtering through the scholar, enter into the text and transform it. And this is why I would hold that the following claim is almost axiomatic: Tell me what a historian puts into his construction of contexts, and I will tell you about his politics and his vision of reality. Thus – collaterally – in the aftermath of the attack on the Twin Towers (9/11), many people felt that the 'terrorists' and their backers were little more than anti-American mad dogs who should be killed on sight. The whole question seemed to stop there. But there were also many others who insisted that the attack had sinuous political and economic causes, plus a complex global background, and hence deserved some sustained and rational analysis.

If there can be no texts without contexts, then this is a tandem which theory should have highlighted. For rightly or wrongly, the distinction between the two is constantly made. Indeed, it has to be made, because every text – grammatical emendations to one side – comes to us, as it were, without a gloss and in a kind of pure state. Its virgin status is only lost when the inquiring scholar goes to work on it.

Many years ago, as a graduate student at Harvard, I had a fellow graduate student say to me one day: 'I don't want to get into the kind of history and documents about which people are always asking, what does this *really* mean? What the hell, isn't it obvious in most cases?' Amazed, I decided that he wasn't very bright. His point, however, seemed to be that he longed to work with events and documents of the sort that can be flatly described and inventoried. There are, to be sure, infinities of factual and quantitative documents, and simple texts requiring uncomplicated levels of analysis and interpretation. But even these require fancy footwork, reflection, and imagination, when they are joined together to form larger pictures, as in demography or prosopography; and we end again with the constructive input of the historian.

If contexts are the curse of texts, can there be texts without contexts? Example: what can the context possibly be of an idealized love sonnet? Over a span of fourteen lines, (a) mistress and lover are entirely imagined; (b) the love argument is presented without a single reference to the external world, apart from imagery regarding animals or flowers; (c) the attitude of the poet-lover is adoring; and (d) the central theme is universal. Thus far, then, it would be silly for the historian to cast about for any kind of an immediate worldly context, although of course the literary scholar would have little trouble summoning up *literary* contexts for the poem, such as in the body of contemporary love poems, or in the amatory tradition as exemplified by verse forms, attitudes, metaphors, and standard locutions. Social historians, it would seem, could not get a foothold here, because the sonnet has been put into a seemingly pure literary context. All the contextual links are with other texts, and the historical world of society and politics, or of 'popular' and 'elite' ideals, is accorded no entry.

I have chosen the love sonnet as the best example of the kind of text that may be said to have no links with the world of non-texts. Yet when we look into the claim, even this exception falls away. For in expressing the attitudes that characterize the love poetry of the age – attitudes toward women, marriage, pleasure, hunting, hierarchies, and even authority – the sonnet speaks for a time and place; and the real world of the poet, ghosting through his attitudes, thus finds its way into his most fanciful lucubrations. Note, however, that the foregoing construction of a worldly context did not proceed by a direct movement of analysis from sonnet to world (non-text), but rather by steps that moved first from the original sonnet out to the body of contemporary love verse, for the purpose of identifying current attitudes. Only then do these attitudes become the context for the sonnet in question, providing the invisible links with the phenomenal world. Consequently, the reading of a single sonnet may be based upon the prior reading of hundreds or even thousands of other love poems and sonnets, provided that all come from the same period and region, place, or country.

The text of a prayer, as we have seen, may also seem to be without immediate connections in the surrounding world, unless we are satisfied with the emotional or moral needs of a single suppliant. But many late medieval and early-modern Italian prayers come down to us stamped with local signs of one sort or another, whether of confraternities, of the mystic traditions of Umbria and Siena, the popularity of certain saints, the more worldly stamp of Florence, intimations for merchants, or pleas showing that some prayers were intended for women rather than men. A prayer, in short, even while 'floating' in its universality, and appearing to transcend time and place, may also have more immediate roots in the surrounding world.

Some historians will ask: why should we seek out documents such as poems, prayers, or for that matter short fiction, when these are texts in which the play of contexts is bound to be problematic? Can we not work more easily with documents that belong readily and 'naturally' to historical reality: diaries, account books, letters, court records, manuals, minutes of political debates, treaties, diplomatic dispatches, and even philosophical works? This question implies that ease of analysis, or the relative simplicity of a document, should govern our choice of texts. And such a claim, if openly made, would ring as absurd. Or is the real objection here really another: namely, that poems and prayers have nothing of 'democratic' value to tell us about peoples, poverty, mental worlds, social life, politics, and so forth?

This is no place to make a plea for the use of 'forbidden' texts. The plea here is another, and it takes in a variety of pleas. That is, that once we take for granted the ability to read texts at the grammatical level, we find at once that the construction of contexts is the historian's cardinal task. It is what the writing of history *au fond* is all about. When we spurn the history of 'kings and battles,' we are spurning simple cause-and-effect relations; we are seeking richer social and cultural worlds, and these will instantly complicate the reading of any relevant document, however simple the text may seem at the outset. In practice, it is true that historians – I think shamefully so – tend to stay away from the full-scale study of 'literary' works; but even so, the 'new' history *has* made reading a more complex enterprise, one in which we dare not frankly declare, 'this document isn't for us, or, it is too complex.'

Everything is now grist to our mill, even if women, popular culture, neighborhood groups, sexuality, ethnicities, servitudes, 'the family,' off-beat interests, the laboring classes, and the like, hold the top of the current agenda. Is history, then, the history of just about everything? Not quite. That way lies chaos and a rejection of the whole idea of mainstreams.

One of the chief victims of the expansion of contexts and subject matter has been the study of politics and political history, for the new commitment to the 'story' of the multitudes (including women) who were politically powerless has necessarily worked a shift away from politics toward the routines and life cycles of the people 'from below.' And yet, paradoxically, to demote politics is to demote something essential: I mean the sufficient study of the elites, practices, and institutions that held the power of life and death over women and the large masses of people. The same demotion, moreover, brings a gradual loss of direction, of the sense of change or development in history, as historical inquiry drifts away from the vital centers. Structures and life cycles may move in given directions over the long term, but meanwhile what do we do about the shorter stretches, the course of change over several generations? This is where the shapes and vicissitudes of politics, in being more divisible and having sharper outlines, are likely to help orient us; but they must be kept in mind, and we should be well informed about them.

In reflecting on my own way of constructing contexts, I find that a concern with the basic lineaments of politics, economic life, and social structures is primary. They are the *sine qua non* for me. In the sustained discussion of a theme or problem, I may assign no remarkable emphasis to these lineaments, but I have certainly had them in my horizons all along the way. More importantly, I conceive of the three – material life, politics, and social groupings – as inseparable from a mental world consisting of attitudes, ideals, and feelings, including religious beliefs and practices: a configuration that will have been years in the making, one developed over a period of study, hence always subject to change. Of course the construct also comes with a stream of events and documents (texts); and when I engage with a new text or a new incident, it will be drawn into the whole. This operation is not mechanical. Texts are protean realities (because we are), not leaden weights; and they may be so significant as to alter something in the entire construct. There must always be the possibility of inter-play, of some dialectical relation between text and context, for the two are 'alive,' and although sonnets cannot (as it were) 'push' the context, they may contain material that enables me to see something about the impinging world for the first time. In this sense, by working through the historian, poems may indeed be able to change something about the envisaged society, the context.

To take an extreme but illustrative example, Picasso's *Guernica* can never in itself be a context for Europe in the late 1930s; but its startling proximity to political events was such that, in the reconstructions of historians now, it could figure as an important part of Europe's larger cultural context at the time; and in this prospect, it might even feature as a material part of the impinging world. On the other hand, a wonderful picture of flowers on a table, say by Matisse, painted at about the same time, could never be worked into Europe's political and social strains, unless it was somehow negotiated through the whole of Matisse's life and artistic evolution, where it might be seen to hold a special place – conceivably as a utopian moment – in the trajectory of his oeuvre.

In these reflections, we begin to see that the writing of history is (or should be) a self-conscious enterprise: skeptical, deeply pondered, and yet also piloted by a purposeful method. Seen in this fashion – and with so many experts looking on over our shoulders – it is not as rhetorical as some theorists have made it out to be. It is, however, very much a conceptualizing business, more so, curiously, than many historians realize.

Emeritus, *University of California*
Los Angeles, CA

Works Cited

Cochrane, Eric and Julius Kirshner. 'Deconstructing Lane's Venice.' *Journal of Modern History* 47,2 (1975): 321–334.
Martines, Lauro. *Society and History in English Renaissance Verse*. Oxford: Basil Blackwell, 1985.
Martines, Lauro. *An Italian Renaissance Sextet: Six Tales in Historical Context*. New York: Marsilio, 1994.
Mowitt, John. 'What is a Text Today.' *PMLA* 117 (October 2002): 1217–1221.

Index

Abraam di Salomone 251
Abraham di Daniele 242
Abraham di Dattilo 246
Abramo di Dattero 244
Accademia de' Lincei 400
Accursius (jurist) 37, 50
Adrian VI (pope) 331
Agostino da Roma 197
Aimo, Battista 36, 38
Alberico da Rosciate (jurist) 288-289
Alberti, Leon Battista 424
Alberto da Sarteano 248
Aldobrandini: Gian Francesco 377;
   Ippolito 367
Aldrovandi, Ulisse 413
Alessandra 193
Alessandri, Nicola 43, 46
Alexander of Nocera (bishop)
   136-140, 144-148, 153-154
Alfonso d' Este (duke) 282
Allegri, Domenico 196-197
Alonso de Mexa 302, 334
Altobelli, Ilario 399
Amadi: family 264, 272-273, 275;
   Alvise 273; Angelo 273; Anteo
   264, 266; Anzolo 275; Piero 20,
   260, 262, 271
Ameyden, Theodore 407
Ammirato, Scipione 4
Andreotti, Giulio 243
Angelo of Chiavasso (jurist) 250
Antonio de Medrano 305, 334
Antonio di Renzo di Antonio da
   Pacciano 245
Aptis, Franciscus de (jurist) 39
Aquinas, Thomas 316-317
Arborsani: family 263, 267-268;
   Benedetto 260, 272; Luca 264
Arezzo 243-246
Argoli, Andrea 399
Arian: family 272
Ariosto: Alessandro 287; Carlo 287;
   Ercole 283, 291 Gabriele 287;
   Galasso 287; Lodovico 20,
   279-293; Rinaldo di Francesco
   279, 281-285, 288, 290-291;
   Virginio di Lodovico 286-289,
   291-292
Armstrong, Lawrin 19, 423
Arquato, Antonio 389
Assisi 241, 248
Astuti, Guido 35
Aurelio, Niccol 263
Avogadori di Comun 264-265
Azo (jurist) 37, 50

Bacon, Francis 397, 404
Badelli, Antonio 396
Badia fiorentina 186
Bardi, Francesco di Tommaso 196
Baker, Keith 5-6
Barbaro: family 269; Vincenzo, 269
Barberini, Taddeo 396
Bardi-Gualterotti, Filippa di Lorenzo
   185-186
Barnabás, Fray 323-324
Baron, Hans 8
Barozzi: family 273
Bartolomeo di Nibia da Novara 252
Bartolomeo Scaini di Sal 342
Bartolomeo Stella 341-344
Bartolus of Sassoferrato (jurist) 1-2,
   18-19, 24, 31-34, 36-37, 39-57,
   59-73, 131, 135-137, 139-141,
   145-146, 148-154, 288; *De
   Guelphis et Gebellinis* 32, 45-48,
   52-54, 57, 72-73; *De Hispanorum
   Monarchia* 370; *De Monarchia
   Christianorum* 386-387; *On
   Insignia and Coats of Arms*
   34-35, 41, 43-44, 46, 52, 73;
   Tiberiadis 31, 33-36, 38, 40-41,
   44-54, 56-57, 60-62, 68, 70-73; *De
   Tryanno* 184; *On Witnesses* 52-53
Basilio, Fioruccia 269
Bassianus, Johannes (jurist) 135

Baxandall, Michael 36
Bellarmino, Robert (cardinal) 411-412
Bellini, Gentile 274
Belviso, Iacopo di 144
Benedetti, Bartolomeo 271
Benedict XI (pope) 144
Benci, Lorenzo 197
Benincasa, Cornelio 36
Benintendi de Ravagnani 270
Bentivoglio, Giovanni 405
Benucci, Alessandra 284, 286-287
Bernardino da Feltre 248, 250
Bernardino of Siena 180, 188-190, 248, 389
Bernardus de Parma (jurist) 39
Bernini, Gian Lorenzo 414
Bevagna (city) 144
Bihac 368
Bodin, Jean 379-380, 383
Bonaventura di Abramo 243-246, 248, 249, 253
Boniface VIII (pope) 144
Bornstein, Daniel 19
Borrel, Jean 38
Bosco, Bartolomeo 181
Bossi, Egidio 36
Botero, Giovanni 388
Bottrigari, Ercole 35, 40, 67
Boyer, John 6
Bracciolini, Francesco 406
Brescia 339, 341-342
Bruno, Giordano 21, 371, 385
Brussels 328
Budapest 378
Burckhardt, Jacob 359

Caetani, Luigi (cardinal) 402
California, University of 422
Camerino 249, 251, 346
Campanella, Tommaso 21, 369-371, 386, 388-389, 391, 402, 405-407, 409, 414
Canon law 56, 64, 133, 135, 145, 151, 248, 288, 341
Cantimori, Delio 3, 8

Carafa: Gian Pietro 338, 343, 359; Maria, 345-346
Carazzi, Carlo 37
Carpani, Giambattista 402
Castrillo 326
Catalano, Michele 282
Catasto 192, 194, 244, 248-249
Caterina da Bologna 354
Catinelli, Orsolina 286
Cavallar, Osvaldo 18, 423
Cavazza, Alvise 271
Celaín, Juan López de 305
Centureri, Guglielmo 180, 245
Cesi, Federico 410
Charles IV (emperor) 31, 264
Chicago: University of 1-6, 10-12, 21-22, 421; University Press 6-7
Chojnacki, Stanley 267
Chrysoloras, Emmanuel 186
Ciera, Pietro 272
Cipolla, Bartolomeo 36
Città di Castello 73, 241, 243-244
Clement VIII (pope) 367-368, 377-379, 390
Coccapani, Sigismondo 36
Cochrane, Eric 3-12, 21-23, 32, 421
Codex 52, 138, 289
collegium doctorum (Venice) 247
Colli, Vincenzo 39
Colonna, Donna Anna 397
Columbia University 7
compagnie delle calze 261
Consiglio di Dattero di Consiglio 243
consilia 20, 23, 52, 54, 62, 131, 135, 137-139, 144-145, 148, 152-153, 247, 279-280, 290, 425
Constantinople 377, 389
Copernicus, Nicolaus 410-411, 413
Coppoli, Fortunato 250
Corbinelli: Albizzo 185; Angelo d'Angleo 186; Angelo di Tommaso 19, 173-175, 185, 187-195, 197, 199; Antonio di Tommaso 185; Bartolomea d' Angelo 186; Bartolomeo di Tommaso 185, 197; Bernardo d'Angelo 186; Corbinello

d'Angelo 186; Giovanni di Tommaso 185; Giulia d'Angelo 186; Parigi di Tommaso 185; Tommaso 185; Tommaso d'Angelo 186
Corbusio, Ludovico 401
Córdoba, Gonzalo Fernández de, duke of Sessa 368, 370, 379, 391
Corner: family 272
Corneto 245
Coronel, Luís Nuñez 305, 310, 328-333
Corpus iuris civilis 36, 288
Cortona 19, 241-252, 254
Council of Constance 190
Council of Ten (Venice) 263, 270
Council of Trent 338, 340, 358
Council of Vienne 180
Count of Benavente (viceroy) 391
Count of Lemos (viceroy) 391
Counter-Reformation 3, 9, 21, 338-340, 344-347, 350, 353, 355, 358, 359
crime(s), criminality 132-134, 140, 142-143, 147, 149-153
Cynus de Pistoia (jurist) 63-64

Dandolo, Andrea 270
Dante, Alighieri 184
Dardani, Alvise 275
Dario, Zuan Antonio 268-269, 275
Datolino di Salomone 249, 252
Dattero di Angelo 246, 248
Dattero di Manuello 245-246
Davis, Natalie Zemon 3 de Roover, Raymond 184
Déaulx 141-142
Delumeau, Jean 8
Deodato di Abramo di Deodato 243-245
Diego López de Husillos 314, 324, 326, 329, 332
Diego Ortíz de Angulo 302-303
Digest 49, 52, 138, 140, 152, 425
Dijon 378
Diplovatazio, Tommaso 67
Domenico da Leonessa 353

Dominici, Giovanni 187-188
Donà: Agnola 271; Zuan 271
Du Perron, Bishop 379

Edler, Florence 183
Egidian Constitutions (Egidian) 140-142, 145-146, 150, 154
Eimeric, Nicolau 327
Emanuele da Camerino 252
Emanuele di Bonassisi di Salomone 251
Equicola, Mario 282
Erasmus, Desiderius 307, 318
Este: family 281, 283-284, 288, 291; Ippolito (cardinal) 281-282
Estimi 176
Euclidean geometry 35, 40, 50, 60, 62, 65-67, 71
Eugenius IV (pope) 199

Fano 141
Fasuol family: 269-270; Andrea 268
Febvre, Lucien 6
Ferdinando II (duke) 411
Ferrara 279, 281, 284
Fido, Antonio 408
Filicaia, Bartolomeo 406
Florence 3-4, 8-9, 19, 22, 73, 175, 178-179, 186, 243, 248, 250, 279, 284, 400-401, 411, 429
Fontana: Francesca 283; Susanna 270
Foscarini, Felicita 268
Franceschi, Benedetto 264
Francesco Buonaccorsi 198
Francesco da Empoli 179-180
Francesco di Lapo 197
Fratticciola 242
Freschi: family 262-263, 266, 270; Elisabetta 262; Maria 263; Zaccaria 270
Freud, Sigmund 425
Friuli 249

Gaio del fu maestro Angelo 243-246
Gaius (jurist) 58, 62, 68
Galassi, Francesco 184

Galilei, Galileo 21, 24, 395-397, 399-401, 404, 407-415; *Dialogue Concerning the Two Chief World Systems* 396, 410-412, 414
Garin, Eugenio 8, 192
Garnica, Juan de 369-376, 378-390
Gaurico, Luca 405
Genatano del maestro Angelo 243
Genoa 175, 177
Georgijevic, Bartolomej 376
Gherardi, Gherardo 410
Ghisleri, Francesco Maria 402
Giacomini, Francesco di Piero 173, 195
Giacomo della Marca 248
Giambattista 286-287
Gil López de Bejar (friar) 314, 324, 326, 329, 332
Giotto di Bondone (artist) 67
Giovanni d' Andrea (jurist) 288
Giovanni da Capistrano 191, 248
Giovanni da San Miniato 186-187
Giovanni di Cristoforo 197
Giovanni di Nanni 249-250
Girardo, Francesco 272
Giustiniani: Girolamo 273; Nicolò 268
Gobbi, Antonio 36
Goldthwaite, Richard 183
Gradenigo: Maria 271; Pietro 271
Grafton, Anthony 21
Gran (modern Esztergom, Hungary) 378
Gray, Hanna 5
Graziosa dal Cortivo 268
Great Council (Venice) 265-266
Gregory of Rimini 179
Grifalconi, Girolamo 265
Grossi, Paolo 61
Grubb, James 20
Gualterotti, Rafaello 399
Guarino da Verona 186
Gubbio 241
Guicciardini, Francesco 423
Guido da Bellosguardo 179
Guido da Suzaria (jurist) 39
Guido de Basio (jurist) 39
Guido de Perusio (jurist) 45, 69

Guzmán, Enriquez de, count of Olivares 369

Harriot, Thomas 405
Harris, Neil 5
Headley, John 370, 387
Henry IV (king) 368, 373, 377-378, 383, 387, 390
Henry VII (emperor) 52
Herde, Peter 8
Hernández, Francisca 299-303, 306, 308, 311-315, 317-329, 331, 333-334
Hobsbawm, Eric 184
Holy League 377
Homza, Lu Ann 20
Hudon, William 20-21
Huguccius (jurist) 43, 50

Illegitimate (children) 174, 193, 283-285, 286-289, 292-293, 346
Innocent IX (pope) 368
Inquisition 299, 302-303, 306, 309, 311, 319, 325, 327-328, 330, 332-334, 358, 386, 405; Spanish inquisition 20
Institutes 425
Isidore of Seville 43
Italy 7-9, 337, 347, 358, 369, 385, 395

Jacopone da Todi 425
James of Erfurt 191
James, William 422
Jerusalem 400
Joachim de Fiore 382, 389
Journal of Modern History 6, 10
Juan de Vaguer 302
Juan de Vergara 304, 307-308
Julius II (pope) 341, 405

Karafiol, Emile 5
Karl, Barry 5
Katz, Stanley 5
Kelly-Gadol, Joan 359
Kepler, Johannes 398-399, 408

Index 437

Kirshner, Julius 1-3, 5-12, 21-22, 175, 421-422
Klenkcock, John 179
Kristeller, Paul Oskar 7
Kuehn, Thomas 20, 423

Lamponi, Francesco 405-406
Landini, Giovanni Battista 410
Lane, Frederic C. 421
Laparelli, Marco Antonio di Piero di messer Nicolò 254
Lapo da Castiglionchio (jurist) 181
Latourette, Kenneth Scott 339
Le Clercq, Jean 339
Le Goff, Jacques 184
Leo X (pope) 283, 343
Leopold, the Archduke of Austria 402
Lepsius, Susanne 19, 52, 423
Leunclavius, Joannes 389
Limonini, Cecilia 268
Little, Lester 5
Lopez, Roberto 181
Lucrecia de Len 386
Luzzatto, Gino 181
Lyons 376

Machiavelli, Niccolò 10, 17, 370, 402, 422-423
Madrid 384
Malespina, Vitellio 402, 406
Malipiero, Elena 268-269
Manetti, Giannozzo 62, 189
Mann, Arthur 5
Manrique, Alonso de 299, 301-302, 304-305, 307, 310, 312-313, 317-326, 328-331
Mantua 284
Manuello 244-246, 248-249, 253
Manuello di Abramo di Dattero 243-244
Marcello, Leonardo 268
Marco de Lezze 272
Marco, Tommaso di 284
María de Cazalla 304
Mariani, Zuan 272
Marino, John 21, 423

Mark of Ancona 142, 145, 153
Marongiu, Antonio 54
Martines, Lauro 22
Martini, Graziosa 265
Martini, Martino 268
Masi, Gino 280, 288, 293
Masser, Lunardo 272
Maternus, Julius Firmicus 405
Matisse 430
McGrath, William 5
McNeill, William 4
Medici: family 397; Cosimo I (duke) 4, 400; Cosimo II (duke) 411; Giovanni 400, 406
Melo di Salomone 242
Merlini, Francesco Maria (later Bishop of Cervia) 402
Michiel, Contarina 269
Mignani, Laura 339, 341
Mignani, Matteo 341-345
Milan 73, 177, 391
Mirandola, Giovanni Pico della 62
Modena 406
Molho, Anthony 5
Momigliano, Arnaldo 8
Montalcino 245
monte (debt fund) 174, 176-179, 187, 189-199
Monte di pietà 249-254
Montefalco (city) 144, 150
Montepulciano 243
Morandi, Orazio 21, 396, 399-409, 412-414
Mostro (Padre) 410, 412
Mundy, John 7
Muñoztello 326-327, 331
Musetto 243
Muti, Tiberio (cardinal) 402

Naples 18, 177, 369, 373, 385, 387, 389, 391, 407
Nelson, Benjamin 183
Neoplatonism 395
Newberry Library 6
Nifo, Agostino 397
Niño, Fernando 305

438 Index

Nocera 131, 136-138, 144, 147-149, 154
Noonan, John 175
Nora di ser Lippo Nerini 198
Novick, Peter 5

Opera di Santa Maria del Fiore 174, 185
Oratory of Divine Love 341, 350
Ordinaria Glossa 50, 52, 69
Orlando Furioso 287, 292
Ortíz, Francisco (friar) 20, 299-334
Ossat, Cardinal 379
Ostia 51
Otto di balìa (Florence) 185

Padua (Padova): 264, 284, 341, 387; University of 400
Panofsky, Erwin 2
Pantaleoni, Domenico 180
Paolo da Castro (jurist) 247
Papal States 136, 140, 143, 145, 150, 153-154
Papias (jurist) 43, 50-51
Paris 378
Pascal, Blaise 425
Patrus de Assisio 63
Paul IV (pope) 350, 358
Paulus (jurist) 68
Pavia, University of 41-42
Pazzi, Maria Maddalena de 354-355
Pérez, Juan Beneyto 370-372
Perugia: 31, 33, 44-45, 51-52, 54, 60, 64, 73, 143, 241, 243, 248; University of 39, 45-46, 63-64, 137, 144, 153
Peter of Ancharano (jurist) 181
Petrarch 41, 270
Philip II (king) 367, 370, 378, 385-386
Philip III (king) 370, 391
Philip IV (king) 370
Philippus de Cassolis (jurist) 39
Picasso, Pablo 430
Pierfilippo da Corgna (jurist) 290
Pierre de Castanet 142
Pietro da Mogliano 347-349, 356-357

Pirenne, Henri 181
Pisa: 31, 34, 52, 59, 73, 174, 176-177, 243; University of 46
Pistoia 243
Pius V (pope) 358
Pontano, Lodovico (jurist) 247
Pontelli, Francesco di Niccolò di Tomasso 253-254
Portinari, Bernardo di Giovanni 198
Premarin, Francesco 270
Prestanze 175-177, 179-180, 185, 187-188, 195-197

Quaglioni, Diego 73
Quartari: family 268

Reformation 337, 350
Renaissance 337, 341, 346, 359, 395-396, 415
Riccardi, Niccolò 410
Ricci, Niccolò 199
Rice, Eugene 7
Richelieu, Cardinal 407
Ridolfi: Lorenzo 181, 187-188, 191; Ludovico 407; Niccolò 402, 410
Roffredus, Beneventanus (jurist) 50
Rome 18, 21, 31, 51, 54-55, 57, 73, 241-242, 337, 341, 345, 368-369, 375, 379, 383, 386-388, 390-391, 400-401, 406-408, 410
Rondinelli, Simon Carlo 406
Rousseau, Jean Jacques 422, 425
Ruggiero, Guido 276

Sabatino di Vitale 243
Sabato di Dattero di Consiglio 243
Sacchetti: Franco 189; Giannozzo 196
Salamanca 300, 369
Salamone di Abramo 248-249
Salomone di Leuccio 246, 248
Salomone di Vitale 243
Salutati, Coluccio 186-187
Samuele 251
San Fortunato 150
San Giovanni Valdarno 251
Santa Maria Nuova 196, 199
Santo Spirito 173, 188, 193

Sapori, Armando 183
Savio, Giovanni Pietro, (Bishop of Sebenico) 402
Savonarola, Girolamo 180, 199
Scaglia, Desiderio (cardinal) 403, 406, 414
Schutte, Anne Jacobson 340
Sciarra, Marco 368
scuole grandi 265, 269-270, 272-274
Scupoli, Lorenzo 21, 339, 344-345, 350-352, 359
Segoloni, Danilo 63, 73
Selke, Angela 305-307
Sevilla 299, 330
Sewell, William 5
Siena 243, 248, 426, 429
Sixtus V (pope) 367, 380
Sleidan, Johannes 402
Soderini, Giovanni di Niccolò 199
Spain, monarchy 369, 386-387
Spella (city) 144
Spiera, Vettor 268
Spini, Giorgio 8
Spoleto 136-137, 142-145, 151, 154
Stearns, Peter 5
Stone, Lawrence 11
Strozzi: Antonio 20, 279-285, 287-290, 293; Nanni di Carlo 284; Palla di Nofri 284; Piero 179-180; Tito di Leonardo 284; Tito di Vespasiano 284
Swerdlow, Noel, 5

Tancredus de Corneto (jurist) 39
Tartagani, Alessandro da Imola (jurist) 290
Tebalducci Claudio 38
Tedaldini, Alvise 271
Tedeschi, John 3
Teresa of Avila 354
Theatine Order 21, 338-339, 341, 345, 358
Theine, Gaetano da 339, 341-345, 359
Thompson, E.P. 271
Tiber 34, 49, 51, 54-55, 57, 59, 61, 73
Titian (Tiziano Vecelli) 263

Toaff, Ariel 241
Todi (city) 51, 54-55, 57, 73
Toledo 299, 301-305, 307, 310, 320, 322, 332
Tommasi, Pietro 270
Tommaso di ser Francesco di ser Ranieri di Guido Boscie 249
Torrelaguna 299
Trevisan, Marco 271
Trithemius, Johannes 402
Triulzi, Laura 261
Tron, Alvise 271
Troyes 378
Turloni, Giacomo 264

Ubaldi: Angelo (jurist) 247; Baldo degli (Baldus de Ubaldis) (jurist) 39, 288
Ufficiali dello studio (Florence) 185
Ughelli, Ferdinando 412
Ugolino di Giovanni 251
Urban VIII (pope) 21, 396, 400-401, 404-409, 411-415
Urbino 346-347
Urbino: Francesco da 346, 355; Pacifica da 347
Usimbardi, Francesco 402, 406
Usury 174-175, 178-182, 184, 188-189, 200, 245-246, 248, 252

Valla, Lorenzo 32, 41-44
Valladolid 300
Van Engen, John 339
Varano: Camilla Battista da 21, 339, 346-359; *Il combattimento spirituale* 339, 352, 359 *I dolori mentali di Ges* 346; *I dolori mentali di Ges nella sua passione* 339; *Ricordi di Ges,* 347; *La vita spirituale* 352; Giulio Cesare da, 346
Varro 43
Venice 18, 20, 73, 175, 259, 261-262, 264, 267, 275, 341, 377
Venturi, Franco 8
Verona 176, 341
Veruzzi, Michele 273-274

Vespasiano da Bisticci 189-190
Vettori, Caterina 268-269
Vicenza 341
Vienna 368, 377
Villani, Matteo 189
Villari, Rosario 368
Villaselos 326
Vinciguerra, Antonio 264
Visconti, Rafaello (Raffaele) 401, 407, 410
Vitale da Montalcino 242, 246
Viterbo 249-250

Walther, Helmut G. 50
Weber, Max 200
Weintraub, Karl 5

Yáñes, Juan 302

Zabarella, Francesco 64
Ziliol: 263; Vettor 269, 271
Zon, Pietro 271
Zuiga, Juan de, count of Miranda 369

Publications of the Centre for Reformation and Renaissance Studies

Renaissance and Reformation Texts in Translation

Du Bellay, Ronsard, Sébillet. *Poetry and Language in 16th-Century France*. Trans. and Intro. by Laura Willett (2004), pp. 116. ISBN 0-7727-2021-5

Girolamo Savonarola. *A Guide to Righteous Living and Other Works*. Trans. and Intro. by Konrad Eisenbichler (2003), pp. 243. ISBN 0-7727-2020-7

Godly Magistrates and Church Order: Johannes Brenz and the Establishment of the Lutheran Territorial Church in Germany, 1524-1559. Trans. & Ed. J.M. Estes (2001), pp. 219. ISBN 0-7727-2017-7

Giovanni Della Casa. *Galateo: A Renaissance Treatise on Manners*. Trans. & Ed. K. Eisenbichler and K.R. Bartlett. 3rd ed. (2001), pp. 98. ISBN 0-9697512-2-2

Romeo and Juliet Before Shakespeare: Four Stories of Star-Crossed Love. Trans. & Ed. N. Prunster (2000), pp. 127. ISBN 0-7727-2015-0

Jean Bodin. *On the Demon-Mania of Witches*. Abridged, trans. & ed. R.A. Scott and J.L. Pearl (1995), pp. 219. ISBN 0-9697512-5-7

Whether Secular Government Has the Right to Wield the Sword in Matters of Faith: A Controversy in Nürnberg in 1530. Five Documents trans. & Ed J.M. Estes (1994), pp. 118. ISBN 0-9697512-4-9

Lorenzo Valla. *'The Profession of the Religious' and Selections from 'The Falsely-Believed and Forged Donation of Constantine'*. Trans. & ed. O.Z. Pugliese. 2nd ed. (1994), pp. 114. ISBN 0-9697512-3-0

A. Karlstadt, H. Emser, J. Eck. *A Reformation Debate: Karlstadt, Emser and Eck on Sacred Images*. Trans. & Ed. B. Mangrum and G. Scavizzi. 2nd edition (1991), pp. 112. ISBN 0-9697512-7-3

Nicholas of Cusa. *The Layman on Wisdom and the Mind*. Trans. M.L. Führer (1989) pp. 112. ISBN 0-919473-56-3

Bernardino Ochino. *Seven Dialogues*. Trans. & Ed. R. Belladonna (1988), pp. xlviii, 96. ISBN 0-919473-63-6

Tudor and Stuart Texts

Early Stuart Pastoral: 'The Shepherd's Pipe' by William Browne and others, and *'The Shepherd's Hunting' by George Wither*. Ed. & Intro by J. Doelman (1999), pp. 196. ISBN 0-9697512-9-X

The Trial of Nicholas Throckmorton. A modernized edition. Ed. & Intro by A. Patterson. (1998), pp. 108. ISBN 0-9697512-8-1

James I. *The True Law of Free Monarchies* and *Basilikon Doron*. Ed. & Intro by D. Fischlin and M. Fortier (1996), pp. 181. ISBN 0-9697512-6-5

Essays and Studies

The Renaissance in the Nineteenth Century / Le XIXe siècle renaissant. Ed. Y. Portebois and N. Terpstra (2003), pp.302. ISBN 0-7727-2019-3

The Premodern Teenager: Youth in Society 1150-1650. Ed. K. Eisenbichler (2002), pp. 349. ISBN 0-7727-2018-5

Occasional Publications

Annotated Catalogue of Editions of Erasmus at the Centre for Reformation and Renaissance Studies, Toronto. Comp. J. Glomski and E. Rummel (1994), pp. 153. ISBN 0-9697512-1-4

Register of Sermons Preached at St. Paul's Cross (1534-1642). Comp. M. MacLure. Revised by P. Pauls and J.C. Boswell (1989), pp. 152. ISBN 0-919473-48-2

Language and Literature. Early Printed Books at the CRRS. Comp. W.R. Bowen and K. Eisenbichler (1986), pp. ix, 112. ISBN 0-7727-2009-6

Published Books (1499-1700) on Science, Medicine and Natural History at the CRRS. Comp. W.R. Bowen and K. Eisenbichler (1986), pp. ix, 35. ISBN 0-7727-2005-3

Bibles, Theological Treatises and Other Religious Literature, 1492-1700, at the CRRS. Comp. K. Eisenbichler et al. (1981), pp. 94. ISBN 0-7727-2002-9

Humanist Editions of Statutes and Histories at the CRRS. Comp. K. Eisenbichler et al. (1980), pp. xxi, 63. ISBN 0-7727-2001-0

Humanist Editions of the Classics at the CRRS. Comp. N.L. Anderson et al. (1979), pp. ix, 71. ISBN 0-7727-2020-7

To order books, and for additional information, contact:
CRRS Publications, Victoria University
71 Queen's Park, Toronto ON, M5S 1K7, CANADA
tel: (416) 585-4465 / fax: (416) 585-4430
e-mail: <crrs.publications@utoronto.ca> / web: www.crrs.ca